Lecture Notes in Artificial Intelligence 2416

Subseries of Lecture Notes in Computer Science
Edited by J. G. Carbonell and J. Siekmann

Lecture Notes in Computer Science
Edited by G. Goos, J. Hartmanis, and J. van Leeuwen

T0191636

Springer
Berlin
Heidelberg
New York
Barcelona
Hong Kong
London
Milan
Paris
Tokyo

Susan Craw   Alun Preece (Eds.)

Advances in
Case-Based Reasoning

6th European Conference, ECCBR 2002
Aberdeen, Scotland, UK, September 4-7, 2002
Proceedings

 Springer

Series Editors

Jaime G. Carbonell, Carnegie Mellon University, Pittsburgh, PA, USA
Jörg Siekmann, University of Saarland, Saarbrücken, Germany

Volume Editors

Susan Craw
The Robert Gordon University, School of Computing
St. Andrew Street, Aberdeen AB25 1HG, Scotland, UK
E-mail: S.Craw@scms.rgu.ac.uk

Alun Preece
University of Aberdeen, Computing Science Department
Aberdeen AB24 3UE, Scotland, UK
E-mail: apreece@csd.abdn.ac.uk

Cataloging-in-Publication Data applied for

Die Deutsche Bibliothek - CIP-Einheitsaufnahme

Advances in case based reasoning : 6th European conference ; proceedings /
ECCBR 2002, Aberdeen, Scotland, UK, September 4 - 7, 2002. Susan Craw ;
Alun Preece (ed.). - Berlin ; Heidelberg ; New York ; Barcelona ; Hong Kong ;
London ; Milan ; Paris ; Tokyo : Springer, 2002
  (Lecture notes in computer science ; Vol. 2416 : Lecture notes in
  artificial intelligence)
  ISBN 3-540-44109-3

CR Subject Classification (1998): I.2, J.4, J.1, F.4.1

ISSN 0302-9743
ISBN 3-540-44109-3 Springer-Verlag Berlin Heidelberg New York

Springer-Verlag Berlin Heidelberg New York,
a member of BertelsmannSpringer Science+Business Media GmbH

http://www.springer.de

© Springer-Verlag Berlin Heidelberg 2002
Printed in Germany

Typesetting: Camera-ready by author, data conversion by Steingräber Satztechnik GmbH, Heidelberg
Printed on acid-free paper   SPIN: 10873764   06/3142   5 4 3 2 1 0

Preface

The papers collected in this volume were presented at the 6th European Conference on Case-Based Reasoning (ECCBR 2002) held at The Robert Gordon University in Aberdeen, UK. This conference followed a series of very successful well-established biennial European workshops held in Trento, Italy (2000), Dublin, Ireland (1998), Lausanne, Switzerland (1996), and Paris, France (1994), after the initial workshop in Kaiserslautern, Germany (1993). These meetings have a history of attracting first-class European and international researchers and practitioners in the years interleaving with the biennial international counterpart ICCBR; the 4th ICCBR Conference was held in Vancouver, Canada in 2001. Proceedings of ECCBR and ICCBR conferences are traditionally published by Springer-Verlag in their LNAI series.

Case-Based Reasoning (CBR) is an AI problem-solving approach where problems are solved by retrieving and reusing solutions from similar, previously solved problems, and possibly revising the retrieved solution to reflect differences between the new and retrieved problems. Case knowledge stores the previously solved problems and is the main knowledge source of a CBR system. A main focus of CBR research is the representation, acquisition and maintenance of case knowledge. Recently other knowledge sources have been recognized as important: indexing, similarity and adaptation knowledge. Significant knowledge engineering effort may be needed for these, and so the representation, acquisition and maintenance of CBR knowledge more generally have become important. Applications have always been a theme of the European and International CBR conferences. Wide-ranging application areas are a feature of this proceedings, with a special emphasis on the customization and personalization for e-commerce and recommender systems. The papers are organized into three sections: two invited papers are followed by 31 research papers and 14 application papers.

The chairs would like to thank all those who contributed to the success of ECCBR 2002. Particular thanks goes to all the program committee and additional reviewers without whose time and effort this volume of selected papers would not exist. We are also appreciative of the work of the Industry Day Chair, the three Workshop Chairs and their various committee members for preparations for the Industry Day and Workshops. We also wish to thank the invited speakers, Haym Hirsh and Ian Watson, and all session chairs. A special thanks goes to Nirmalie Wiratunga for local arrangements and Jacek Jarmulak for assistance with the conference website. Finally, the Chairs wish to thank Springer-Verlag for their assistance in publishing this volume.

June 2002

Susan Craw
Alun Preece

Conference Chairs

Susan Craw   The Robert Gordon University, UK
Alun Preece   University of Aberdeen, UK

Industry Day Chair

Rob Milne   Sermatech Intelligent Applications

Local Arrangements

Nirmalie Wiratunga   The Robert Gordon University, UK

Program Commitee

Agnar Aamodt   Norwegian University of Science and Technology
David W. Aha   Naval Research Laboratory, USA
Robert Aarts   Nokia Group, Finland
Klaus-Dieter Althoff   Fraunhofer IESE, Germany
Ralph Bergmann   University of Hildesheim, Germany
Enrico Blanzieri   Universita' di Torino, Italy
Derek Bridge   University College Cork, Ireland
Pádraig Cunningham   Trinity College Dublin, Ireland
Boi Faltings   EPFL, Lausanne, Switzerland
Mehmet H. Göker   Kaidara Software Inc., USA
Pedro A. González-Calero   Univ. Complutense de Madrid, Spain
Jacek Jarmulak   Ingenuity Systems, USA
David Leake   Indiana University, USA
Brian Lees   University of Paisley, UK
Ramon Lopez de Mantaras   IIIA-CSIC, Spain
Michel Manago   Kaidara Software S.A., France
David McSherry   University of Ulster, UK
Bart Netten   TNO-TPD, The Netherlands
Petra Perner   IBaI Leipzig, Germany
Enric Plaza   IIIA-CSIC, Spain
Luigi Portinale   Universita del Piemonte Orientale, Italy
Michael M. Richter   Universty of Kaiserslautern, Germany
Rainer Schmidt   University of Rostock, Germany
Barry Smyth   University College Dublin, Ireland
Maarten van Someren   University of Amsterdam, The Netherlands
Jerzy Surma   Technical University of Wroclaw, Poland
Henry Tirri   University of Helsinki, Finland
Brigitte Trousse   INRIA Sophia Antipolis, France
Ian Watson   University of Auckland, New Zealand
Stephan Wess   Empolis Knowledge Management, Germany
David C. Wilson   University College Dublin, Ireland

Additional Reviewers

Josep-Lluís Arcos
Eva Armengol
Eric Auriol
Paolo Avesani
Robin Boswell
Keith Bradley
Patrick Clerkin
Chris Fairclough
Raimund L. Feldmann
Andreas Jedlitschka
Brian MacNamee
Ana Gabriela Maguitman
Paolo Massa
Kerstin Maximini

Rainer Maximini
Lorraine McGinty
Petri Myllymaki
Anna Perini
Emanuele Pianta
Jörg Rech
Andrea Sboner
Martin Schaaf
Sascha Schmitt
Raja Sooriamurthi
Marco Spinelli
Armin Stahl
Alexander Tartakovski
Torsten Willrich

Table of Contents

Invited Papers

Research Papers

Application Papers

Integrating Background Knowledge
into Nearest-Neighbor Text Classification

Sarah Zelikovitz and Haym Hirsh

Computer Science Department
Rutgers University
110 Frelinghuysen Road
Piscataway, NJ 08855
{zelikovi,hirsh}@cs.rutgers.edu

Abstract. This paper describes two different approaches for incorporating background knowledge into nearest-neighbor text classification. Our first approach uses background text to assess the similarity between training and test documents rather than assessing their similarity directly. The second method redescribes examples using Latent Semantic Indexing on the background knowledge, assessing document similarities in this redescribed space. Our experimental results show that both approaches can improve the performance of nearest-neighbor text classification. These methods are especially useful when labeling text is a labor-intensive job and when there is a large amount of information available about a specific problem on the World Wide Web.

1 Introduction

The abundance of digital information that is available has made the organization of that information into a complex and vitally important task. Automated categorization of text documents plays a crucial role in the ability of many applications to sort, direct, classify, and provide the proper documents in a timely and correct manner. With the growing use of digital devices and the fast growth of the number of pages on the World Wide Web, text categorization is a key component in managing information.

The machine learning community approaches text-categorization problems as "supervised" learning problems. In this case a human expert simply has to label a set of examples with appropriate classes. Once a corpus of correctly labeled documents is available, there are a variety of techniques that can be used to create a set of rules or a model of the data that will allow future documents to be classified correctly. The techniques can be optimized and studied independently of the domains and specific problems that they will be used to address. The problem with the supervised learning approach to text classification is that often very many labeled examples (or "training examples") must be used in order for the system to correctly classify new documents. These training examples must be hand-labeled, which might be quite a tedious and expensive process.

The question that we address is as follows: Given a text categorization task, can we possibly find some *other* data that can be incorporated into the learning process that will improve accuracy on test examples while limiting the number of labeled training examples needed? We believe that the answer is most often "yes". For example, suppose

S. Craw and A. Preece (Eds.): ECCBR 2002, LNAI 2416, pp. 1–5, 2002.

that we wish to classify the names of companies by the industry that it is part of. A company such as *Watson Pharmaceuticals Inc* would be classified with the label *drug*, and the company name *Walmart* would be classified as type *retail*. Although we many not have numerous training examples, and the training examples are very short, we can find other data that is related to this task. Such data could be articles from the business section of an on-line newspaper or information from company home pages. As a result of the explosion of the amount of digital data that is available, it is often the case that text, databases, or other sources of knowledge that are related to a text classification problem are easily accessible. We term this readily available information "background knowledge". Some of this background knowledge can be used in a supervised learning situation to improve accuracy rates, while keeping the hand-labeled number of training examples needed to a minimum.

One common approach to text classification is to use a k-nearest-neighbor classification method, wherein the k documents closest to a test document are found and their labels "vote" on the classification of the new example. The standard approach for representing text documents for use by such methods is to represent each document simply by the "bag" of words in the document. Each word is viewed as a dimension in a very high-dimension vector space, one dimension per word. Every document is then a vector in this space, with a zero in its vector for every word that does not appear in the document, and a non-zero value for every word that does appear in the document. The non-zero values are set by using weighting schemes whereby words that occur frequently in a document are given higher values, with values scaled down by the extent to which the word also occurs frequently throughout all documents. With each document now representable in this vector space, similarity between two documents is measured using the cosine of the (normalized) vectors representing the two documents.

This paper describes two approaches for integrating background knowledge into text classification. In the next section we describe an approach by which background knowledge is compared to both the training and test examples to determine which training examples are closest to the test example (Zelikovitz & Hirsh, 2000). Section 3 then describes our second approach, in which the background knowledge is used to reformulate both the training examples and test examples, so that document comparisons are performed in the new space (Zelikovitz & Hirsh 2001). In both cases we show that classification accuracy is generally improved by these two different approaches for incorporating background knowledge.

2   Using Background Knowledge to Assess Document Similarity

Instead of simply comparing a test example to the corpus of training examples, our first idea is to use the items of background knowledge as "bridges" to connect each new example with labeled training examples. A labeled training example is useful in classifying an unknown test instance if there exists some set of unlabeled background knowledge that is similar to both the test example and the training example. We call this a "second-order" approach to classification (Zelikovitz & Hirsh, 2000), in that data are no longer directly compared but rather, are compared one step removed, through an intermediary. To accomplish this goal we use WHIRL (Cohen, 1998) which is a conventional database system augmented with special operators for text comparison. It has been shown to yield an extremely effective nearest-neighbor text classification method (Cohen & Hirsh, 1998).

WHIRL makes it possible to pose SQL-like queries on databases with text-valued fields. Using WHIRL we can view the training examples as a table with the fields *instance* and *label*, and the test example as a table with the field *instance* and the background knowledge as a table with the single field, *value*. We can then create the following query for classification:

SELECT Test.instance, Train.label
  FROM Train AND Test AND Background
 WHERE Train.instance SIM Background.value
   AND Test.instance SIM Background.value

The SIM function computes distances between vectors using the cosine metric described earlier, which returns a score between 0 and 1 that represents the similarity between the documents. Here each of the two similarity comparisons in the query computes a score, one comparing the background item to the training example, and the second comparing the background item to the test example. WHIRL multiplies the two resulting scores to obtain a final score for each tuple in an intermediate-results table. The final voting is performed by projecting this intermediate table onto the *Test.instance* and *Train.label* fields (Cohen & Hirsh 1998). All examples among the k nearest neighbors having the same class label vote by combining their score using the "noisy or" operation. Whichever label has the highest score in the resulting projected table is returned as the label for the test instance.

We ran both the base approach for nearest neighbor classification and our method incorporating background knowledge on a range of problems from nine different text classification tasks. Details on the data sets can be found elsewhere (Zelikovitz 2002); each varied on the size of each example, the size of each piece of background knowledge, the number of examples and number of items of background knowledge, and the relationship of the background knowledge to the classification task. Results are graphed in Figure 1. The x axis corresponds to percent accuracy on the test set when using the base method and the y axis corresponds to percent accuracy on the test set when background knowledge is incorporated. Each plotted point represents a different set of data, and those above the line $y = x$ have higher accuracy with the inclusion of background knowledge. As can be seen, on some data sets performance was hurt slightly by using background knowledge, but in most cases performance was improved, in some cases by more than 50%.

3   Using Background Knowledge to Reformulate Examples

In our second approach the background knowledge is used to redescribe both the training and the test examples. These newly expressed documents therefore contain information based upon the set of background knowledge. The newly expressed training examples are then compared to the redescribed test example so that the nearest neighbors can be found.

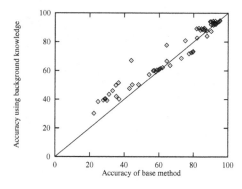

Fig. 1. Comparison of accuracy rates with and without background knowledge

A corpus of text documents represented as vectors can be looked at as a large, sparse term-by-document ($t \times d$) matrix. Latent Semantic Indexing (LSI) (Deerwester *et al*, 1990) is an automatic method that uses the $t \times d$ matrix to redescribe textual data in a new smaller semantic space using singular value decomposition. The original space is decomposed into linearly independent dimensions or "factors", and the terms and documents of the training and test examples are then represented in this new vector space. Documents can then be compared as described in the last section, only now comparisons are performed in this new space. Documents with high similarity no longer simply share words with each other, but instead are located near each other in the new semantic space.

LSI is traditionally used for text classification by performing the singular value decomposition using the training data. Our key idea is to use the background text in the creation of this new redescription of the data, rather than relying solely on the training data to do so. The background knowledge is added to the training examples to create a much larger $t \times d$ matrix (Zelikovitz & Hirsh 2001), where the terms now include all terms from the background knowledge, and the documents in the background knowledge are added as columns to the original matrix. LSI is then used to reduce this matrix so that the training examples are redescribed in a smaller semantic space that was created based upon the background knowledge. New test examples can be redescribed in this space as well, and a test example can then be directly compared to the training examples, with a cosine similarity score determining the distance between the test example and each training example. A test document is then classified with the label associated with the highest score.

Results for using LSI for classification without background knowledge versus with background knowledge is presented in Figure 2. As before, each point represents a data set, with the y-axis presenting the accuracy of the LSI method using background knowledge, and the x-axis presenting the accuracy of the base method. Here, too, the use of background knowledge most often improves the learner.

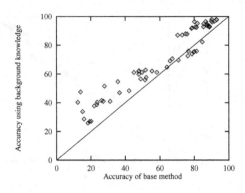

Fig. 2. Comparison of accuracy rates with and without background knowledge

4 Summary

Text classification is a process of extrapolating from the labels of given training data to assign labels to test data. Nearest neighbor methods perform this process by finding the training examples near each test example and having them vote for the label of the example. This paper has described two ways to modify nearest-neighbor text classification methods to incorporate background knowledge. Our first approach redefines the similarity metric by bridging each training and test example by one or more pieces of background knowledge. Our second approach redefines the space in which similarity is assessed, using Latent Semantic Indexing on the training data and background knowledge to create a new vector space in which the documents are placed. In both cases we were able to show consistent improvements in classification accuracy on a range of benchmark problems.

References

1. William Cohen. A web-based information system that reasons with structured collections of text. *Proceedings of Autonomous Agents*, 1998.
2. W. Cohen and H. Hirsh. Joins that generalize: Text categorization using WHIRL. *Proceedings of the Fourth International Conference on Knowledge Discovery and Data Mining*, pages 169–173, 1998.
3. S. Deerwester, S. Dumais, G. Furnas, and T. Landauer. Indexing by latent semantic analysis. *Journal for the American Society for Information Science*, 41(6):391–407, 1990.
4. S. Zelikovitz. *Using Background Knowledge to Improve Text Classification*. PhD thesis, Rutgers University, 2002.
5. S. Zelikovitz and H. Hirsh. Improving short text classification using unlabeled background knowledge to assess document similarity. *Proceedings of the Seventeenth International Conference on Machine Learning*, pages 1183–1190, 2000.
6. S. Zelikovitz and H. Hirsh. Using LSI for text classification in the presence of background text. *Proceedings of the Tenth Conference for Information and Knowledge Management*, 2001.

Applying Knowledge Management: Techniques for Building Organisational Memories

Ian Watson

AI-CBR
Department of Computer Science
University of Auckland
Auckland, New Zealand
Ian@ai-cbr.org

Abstract. Over the previous two years I have collected case-studies of successfully fielded commercial knowledge management systems that use case-based reasoning (CBR). These case-studies have been collated into a book to be published by Morgan Kaufmann in November 2002[1]. This paper summarises the findings of the book, showing that CBR is ideally suited to the creation of knowledge management systems. This is because of the close match between the activities of the CBR-cycle and the process requirements of a knowledge management system. The nature of knowledge within an organisation is briefly discussed and the paper illustrates the dynamic relationship between data, information and knowledge, showing how CBR can be used to help manage the acquisition and reuse of knowledge.

1 Introduction

The function of knowledge management (KM) is to allow an organisation to leverage the information resources it has and to support purposeful activity with positive definable outcomes [1]. Knowledge and consequently its management is currently being touted as the basis of future economic competitiveness, for example:

In the information age knowledge, rather than physical assets or resources is the key to competitiveness... What is new about attitudes to knowledge today is the recognition of the need to harness, manage and use it like any other asset, This raises issues not only of appropriate processes and systems, but also how to account for knowledge in the balance sheet [2].

Entrepreneurs are no longer seen as the owners of capital, but rather as individuals who express their tacit knowledge by "*knowing how to do things*" [3]. Boisot [4] sees information as the key organizing principle of the organization; "*information organizes matter.*"

The introduction of information technology on a wide scale in the last thirty years has made the capturing and distribution of knowledge widespread, and brought to the forefront the issue of the management of knowledge assets [5]. The "knowledge

---

[1] Watson, I. (Ed.) *Applying Knowledge Management: techniques for building organisational memories.* Morgan Kaufmann Publishers Inc., San Francisco, CA. November 2002.

S. Craw and A. Preece (Eds.): ECCBR 2002, LNAI 2416, pp. 6–12.

management" function is spreading throughout the organisation, from marketing, information management systems and human resources.

With knowledge now being viewed as a significant asset the creation and sharing of knowledge has become an important factor within and between organizations. Boisot [4] refers to the "paradox of value" when considering the nature of knowledge, in particular its intangibility and inappropriateness as an asset and the difficulty of assessing and protecting its value [6]. If, as this paper and the forthcoming book postulates, CBR is of significant value in KM we first need to consider the nature of knowledge.[2]

2   A Knowledge Framework

A common approach to considering knowledge often highlights its relationship to information in terms of difference. This perceived distinction between information and knowledge is not helpful and has led to the current confused preoccupation in the management literature with what is conceived of as a clear distinction between "knowledge management and information management. Indeed, it is common to see document management systems branded as KM systems.

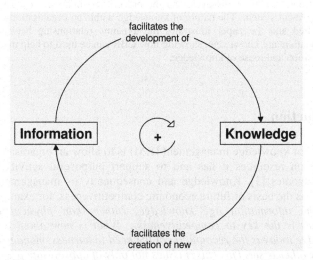

Fig. 1. The Dynamic Relationship between Information and Knowledge

Although the relationship between information and knowledge may be been seen as "closely associated," it should be more appropriately seen in terms of a "dynamic and interactive relationship." Information facilitates the development of knowledge, which creates more information that deepens knowledge, ad infinitum. For example, Nonaka and Takeuchi [7] stated:

---

[2] Since this paper is delivered to a CBR audience I am assuming familiarity with the basic processes of CBR. An introduction to CBR can be found in [10].

Information provides a new point of view for interpreting events or objects, which makes visible previously invisible meanings or sheds light on unexpected connections. Thus, information is a necessary medium or material for eliciting and constructing knowledge [7]

Whilst Polyani [8] and Choo [9] have viewed this dynamic interactive relationship as part of the process of knowing which facilitates the capacity to act in context. The dynamic nature of this relationship is illustrated below in Figure 1.

Similarly, to look at information purely in terms of the degree to which it has been processed, i.e., the data, information, knowledge hierarchy [5 & 11] oversimplifies the complex relationship between the three intangibles. Stewart [12] notes:

The idea that knowledge can be slotted into a data-wisdom hierarchy is bogus, for the simple reason that one man's knowledge is another man's data [12].

The categories defined by Boisot and their interactions may be seen in Figure 2. It is important to note the feedback element within this figure that illustrates the dynamic and interactive relationship of information and knowledge as a positive feedback loop.

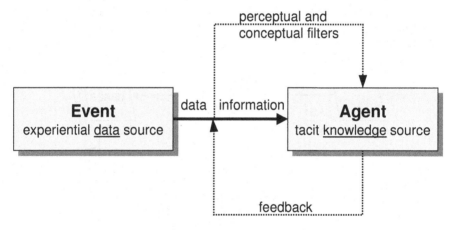

Fig. 2. Data, Information and Knowledge (after [4])

Data is discrimination between states - black, white, heavy, light, dark, etc. - that may or may not convey information to an agent. Whether it does or not depends on the agents prior stock of knowledge. For example, the states of nature indicated by red, amber and green traffic lights may not be seen as informative to a bushman of the Kalahari. Yet, they may perceive certain patterns in the soil as indicative of the presence of lions nearby.

Thus, whereas data can be characterised as a property of things, knowledge is a property of agents predisposing them to act in particular circumstances. Information is that subset of the data residing in things that activates an agent - it is filtered from the data by the agent's perceptual or conceptual apparatus [4]. This has a direct echo in Alan Newell's principle of rationality:

"If an agent has knowledge that one of its actions will lead to one of its goals, then the agent will select that action" [12]

3   CBR Is a Methodology for KM

What then are the requirements of a KM system? At a recent workshop held at Cambridge University a group of people active in KM and AI identified the main activities needed by a KM system [13]. These were mapped to AI methods or techniques. The main KM activities were identified as the: acquisition, analysis, preservation and use of knowledge. This section will show how CBR can meet each of these requirements.

I argued in 1999 that CBR is not an AI technology or technique like logic programming, rule-based reasoning or neural computing. Instead, CBR is a methodology for problem solving [14]. Checkland & Scholes [1] define a methodology as:

"…an organised set of principles which guide action in trying to "manage" (in the broad sense) real-world problem situations" [1]

Now consider the classic definition of CBR:

"*A case-based reasoner solves problems by using or adapting solutions to old problems.*" [15]

This definition tells us "what" a case-based reasoner does and not "how" it does what it does. It is in Checkland's sense an organised set of principles. The set of CBR principles are more fully defined as a cycle comprising six activities[3] called the CBR-cycle as shown in Figure 3.

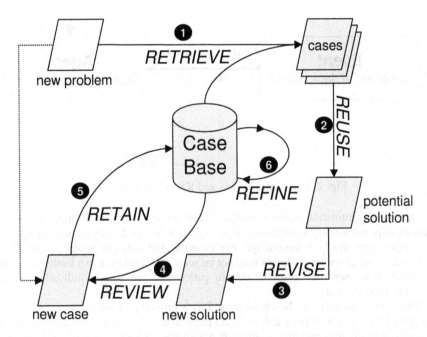

Fig. 3. The CBR-cycle

---

[3] Note that the original CBR-cycle of Aamodt & Plasa [16] comprised only four activities.

This cycle comprises six activities (the six-REs):

1. *Retrieve* similar cases to the problem description
2. *Reuse* a solution suggested by a similar case
3. *Revise* or adapt that solution to better fit the new problem if necessary
4. *Review* the new problem-solution pair to see if they are worth retaining as a new case
5. *Retain* the new solution as indicated by step 4.
6. *Refine* the case-base index and feature weights as necessary.

The six-REs of the CBR cycle can be mapped to the activities required by a knowledge management system. Let us revisit Figure 2 and superimpose the steps of the CBR-cycle upon it.

Now we can easily see that the event is the episodic data that comprises a case. The case is *retained* in a case-base but typically undergoes some pre-processing and filtering (indexing and feature weighting in CBR terminology). The agent or the reasoner *retrieves* the case to solve some problem and attempts to *reuse* it. This may result in some *revision* or adaptation of the case's solution resulting in a new episodic data and hence a new case being created. The new case is reviewed (involving comparing it against cases already retained in the case-base) and if it is judged useful *retained*. In addition, the use of the case (successfully or otherwise) may result in the case-base's indexing scheme being or the feature weights *refined*. This completes the knowledge management cycle indicated on Boisot's original diagram.

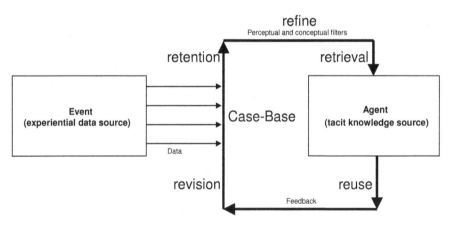

Fig. 4. The CBR-cycle supporting Knowledge Management

4   KM Case-Studies

Seven case studies in the book illustrate the relationship between CBR and KM. The case-studies are:

1. Managing Product Quality: Total Recall at National Semiconductor
2. Developing Expertise: Color Matching at General Electric Plastics
3. Improving Process Design: Knowledge Sharing in Aluminium Foundries
4. Benchmarking Best Practice: Internal Financial Control at Deloitte Touche

5. Information Retrieval: Intelligent Online Product Selection for Analog
6. Distributed Sales Support: Web-based Engineering at Western Air
7. Personalising Information Services: Intelligent Digital TV at
    ChangingWorlds

The case studies were selected for a variety of reasons; they span a range of organisational types, from large multinational companies to small engineering firms and new technology start-ups. The case-studies describe systems that are customer facing or are purely for internal use; moreover, they provide a variety of services including information retrieval, product selection and configuration, diagnostic trouble shooting and benchmarking. Some of the companies were already very familiar with CBR (e.g., General Electric and ChangingWorlds) and so implemented their own bespoke CBR systems, whilst others used external consultants and commercial CBR tools. Interestingly, only one case study (General Electric) performed automated case adaptation or revision, all the others revised cases manually or revision was considered not appropriate. Also of interest was that significant organisational change was only required in a minority of the case-studies. This may imply that the emphasis that the KM community places on management culture and organisational change is not always necessary.

5 Conclusion

CBR closely matches KM's requirements for the acquisition (revision and retention), analysis (refinement), preservation (retention) and use of knowledge (retrieval, reuse and revision). Dubitsky et al. [17] refer to this as KM/CBR synergy and it explains why CBR is used successfully in many KM systems [18]. However, it is not a one-sided relationship. KM has as much to offer the success of CBR and vice versa. In particular, KM researchers and practitioners recognise the importance of organisational issues in the success of a KM system and there is much that CBR practitioners can learn from the KM community about this issue.

KM systems are perhaps best viewed in a holistic system-thinking manner rather than the more restrictive technology view of a system [11]. As such, a KM system must support all activities that would encourage a knowledge sharing culture within a learning organisation. CBR only provides methodological support to some of those activities.

References

[1] Checkland, P. & Scholes, J. (1990). Soft Systems Methodology in Action. Wiley, UK.
[2] Moran, N. (1999). Becoming a Knowledge Based Organization, Financial Times Survey -
     Knowledge Management, 28th May 1999, London, UK.
[3] Casson, M. (1997). Information and Organization, A New Perspective on the Theory of
     the Firm, Clarendon Press, Oxford, UK.
[4] Boisot, M. (1998). Knowledge Assets, Securing Competitive Advantage in the
     Information Economy, Oxford University Press, Oxford, UK.
[5] Davenport, T. D. (1997). Information Ecology, Mastering the Information and knowledge
     Environment, Oxford University Press, Oxford, UK

[6] Priest, W. C. (1994), An Information Framework for the Planning and Design of 'Information Highways', Berkley Information Site.

[7] Nonaka, I. & Takeuchi, H. (1995). The Knowledge-Creating Company: How Japanese Companies Create the Dynamics of Innovation, Oxford University Press, Oxford, UK.

[8] Polyani, M. (1967). The Tacit Dimension, Routledge & Kegan Paul, London, UK

[9] Choo, C. W. (1998). The Knowing Organization, Oxford University Press, Oxford, UK.

[10] Watson, I. (1997). Applying Case-Based Reasoning: techniques for enterprise systems. Morgan Kaufmann, San Francisco, US.

[11] Checkland, P. & Howel, S. (1998). Information, Systems and Information Systems, Making Sense of the Field, John Wiley & Sons, UK.

[12] Newell, A. (1982). The Knowledge Level. AI Vol. 18 pp. 87-127.

[12] Stewart, T.. A. (1997). Intellectual Capital, Nicholas Brearly.

[13] Watson, I. (2000). Report on Expert Systems 99 Workshop: Using AI to Enable Knowledge Management. In, Expert Update Vol. 3 No. 2, pp. 36-38.

[14] Watson, I., (1999). CBR is a methodology not a technology. In, the Knowledge Based Systems Journal, Vol. 12. no.5-6, Oct. 1999, pp.303-8. Elsevier, UK.

[15] Riesbeck, C.K. & Schank, R. (1989). Inside Case-Based Reasoning. Erlbaum, Northvale, NJ, US.

[16] Aamodt, A. & Plaza, E. (1994). Case-Based Reasoning: Foundational Issues, Methodological Variations, and System Approaches. AI Communications, 7(i), pp. 39-59.

[17] Dubitzky, W., Büchner, A.G. & Azuaje, F. J. Viewing Knowledge Management as a Case-Based Reasoning Application. In Exploring Synergies of Knowledge Management and Case-Based Reasoning David Aha, Irma Becerra-Fernandez, Frank Maurer, and Hector Munoz-Avila, (Eds.) AAAI Workshop Technical Report WS-99-10, pp.23-27. AAAI Press, Menlo Park CA, US.

[18] Aha, D., Becerra-Fernandez, I., Maurer, F. & Munoz-Avila, H. (1999). Exploring Synergies of Knowledge Management and Case-Based Reasoning. AAAI Technical Report WS-99-10. ISBN 1-57735-094-4

On the Complexity
of Plan Adaptation by Derivational Analogy
in a Universal Classical Planning Framework

Tsz-Chiu Au[1], Héctor Muñoz-Avila[2], and Dana S. Nau[1]

[1] Department of Computer Science and Institute for System Research
University of Maryland, College Park, MD 20742, USA
{chiu, nau}@cs.umd.edu
[2] Department of Computer Science and Engineering
Lehigh University, Bethlehem, PA 18015, USA
munoz@cse.lehigh.edu

Abstract. In this paper we present an algorithm called DerUCP, which can be regarded as a general model for plan adaptation using Derivational Analogy. Using DerUCP, we show that previous results on the complexity of plan adaptation do not apply to Derivational Analogy. We also show that Derivational Analogy can potentially produce exponential reductions in the size of the search space generated by a planning system.

1 Introduction

As reported in several independent experiments, case-based planners using Derivational Analogy have consistently outperformed the base-level, first-principles planner on which these case-based planners were constructed [1,2,3]. On the other hand, formal studies on the complexity of adaptation versus the complexity of first-principles planning seem to suggest that in the worst case, adaptation can be harder than planning from scratch if certain conditions on the adaptation strategy are satisfied [4]. These complexity results raise questions about the effectiveness of adaptation and case-based planning in general and Derivational Analogy in particular. In this paper we intend to clarify this apparent contradiction.

We take advantage of an algorithm called Universal Classical Planning (UCP) [5] that can be regarded as a general model of STRIPS-Style planners [6]. In this paper we formulate a general algorithm for Derivational Analogy called DerUCP that can be regarded as a general model of Derivational Analogy built on top of STRIPS-Style planners.

We analyze the results of [4] and examine the assumption that led to that paper's main result about plan modification being harder than planning from scratch. We show that adaptation by Derivational Analogy does not fall under the assumption, and thus the worst case analysis in [4] does not apply to adaptation with Derivational Analogy.

S. Craw and A. Preece (Eds.): ECCBR 2002, LNAI 2416, pp. 13–27, 2002.
© Springer-Verlag Berlin Heidelberg 2002

Furthermore, we show that Derivational Analogy can never make planning harder, and can potentially make planning much easier. More specifically, we show that if s_1 is the search space that can potentially be explored by an instance of DerUCP and s_2 is the search space that can potentially be explored by the corresponding instance of UCP, then s_1 is never any larger than s_2, and s_1 can be exponentially smaller than s_2.

This paper is organised as follows. Section 2 reviews the definition of UCP. Section 3 describes the DerUCP algorithm. Section 4 presents the complexity results. Finally, Section 5 analyzes the efficiency of DerUCP.

2   Universal Classical Planning

UCP is a generalized algorithm for classical planning that encompasses traditional planning approaches into a single framework [5]. UCP can be instantiated into a variety of planners, such as STRIPS-Style planners, SNLP and PRODIGY [5].

UCP operates on a *partial plan* P that represents some set of candidate solution plans $\mathcal{P}$. Formally, P is a 5-tuple $\langle \mathcal{T}, \mathcal{O}, \mathcal{B}, \mathcal{ST}, \mathcal{L} \rangle$, where $\mathcal{T}$ is the set of steps in the plan, $\mathcal{ST}$ is the symbol table which maps step names to actions, $\mathcal{O}$ is the partial ordering relation over $\mathcal{T}$ (the corresponding relational operator is $\prec$), $\mathcal{B}$ is a set of codesignation and non-codesignation constraints on the variables in the preconditions and post-conditions of the operators, and $\mathcal{L}$ is a set of auxiliary constraints. There are three kinds of auxiliary constraints. (1) An interval preservation constraint (IPC) is denoted as $(t \overset{p}{-} t')$, which means the condition p must be preserved between the operators corresponding to steps t and t'. (2) A point truth constraint (PTC) is a 2-tuple $\langle p@t \rangle$, which ensures condition p must be true before step t. (3) A contiguity constraint $t_i * t_j$ does not allow any step between t_i and t_j. These constraints restrict the ground linearization of the steps in the set $\mathcal{P}$ of candidate solution plans represented by P.

UCP begins with a *null plan* $t_0 \prec t_\infty$, where t_0 is the initial step which has the initial state as its postcondition, and t_∞ is the final step which has the goal state as its precondition. UCP's objective is to find a *solution*, i.e, a partial plan that contains a ground linearization of steps which achieves the goal state from the initial state. UCP tries to find a solution by performing *refinements*, i.e., by adding new steps and constraints to the partial plan. A refinement may eliminate some of the candidate solution plans, in which case the refinement is *progressive*, or it may not eliminate any candidate solution plans, in which case the refinement is *nonprogressive*.

The *header* of P consists of the step t_0 plus all steps t_i such that $i > 0$ and $t_{i-1} * t_i$. The *head fringe* is the set of all steps that can come immediately after the header. The *trailer* and the *tail fringe* are defined analogously, but with respect to the final step of the plan rather than the initial step.

In UCP, the progressive refinements are classified into three types: *forward state-space (FSS) refinements* add constraints or new steps at the head fringe of the plan, *backward state-space (BSS) refinements* add constraints or new steps

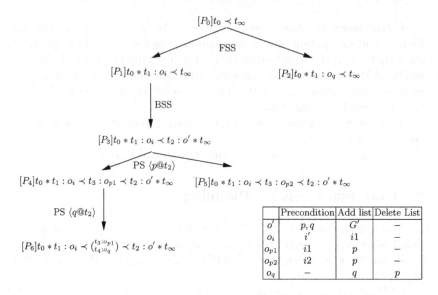

Fig. 1. An example of plan generation with UCP in [5]

at the tail fringe of the plan, and *plan-space (PS) refinements* add constraints or new steps somewhere between the head fringe and the tail fringe. The non-progressive refinements are also classified into three types: *refine-plan-pre-order* adds ordering constraints between steps, *refine-plan-pre-position* adds contiguous constraints between steps, and *refine-plan-pre-satisfy* resolves conflicts in the partial plan.

The following example, which is taken from page 19 of [5], shows how various refinements work in UCP. UCP begins with a null plan $t_0 \prec t_\infty$, where t_0 is the initial step which has the initial state $\{i'\}$ as its postcondition, and t_∞ is the final step which has the goal state $\{G'\}$ as its precondition. In the figure, each node represents a partial plan, the label below the node represents the particular refinement strategy that UCP is using at this node, and the set of branches emanating from the node represents the set of alternative refinements produced by the refinement strategy. UCP chooses among these refinements nondeterministically. In this particular example, the algorithm introduces an FSS refinement, a BSS refinement, and two PS refinements, and finally produces a partial plan which contains a ground linearization of steps achieving the goal. We will generate a derivational trace for this example in Section 3.1.

3   DerUCP: Derivational Analogy in UCP

Derivational Analogy is a widely used adaptation method that has been the subject of frequent studies [1,2,7,8,9,10,11,12]. In Derivational Analogy cases contain the *derivational trace*, the sequence of decisions made to obtain a plan, rather than the plan itself. Typically in a problem-solving session, part of a solution plan is obtained through case replay of the derivational traces stored in retrieved cases, and part through first-principles planning.

We will now formulate an algorithm that we will call DerUCP, for performing Derivational Analogy on top of UCP. DerUCP serves as a general model for Derivational Analogy in STRIPS style planning since its instantiations include derivational analogy case-based planners such as Prodigy/Analogy [1], CAPlan/CbC [13] and DerSNLP [11].

3.1   Derivational Trace

Suppose we run an instantiation of UCP on a planning problem, and we keep a record of the sequence of choices it made at each of the nondeterministic choice points. This record, which called a *derivational trace*, consists of a sequence of *decision records*, each of which tells the particular choice that was made at one of UCP's nondeterministic choice points. The decision record gives the refinement strategy (such as FSS or PS), the *refinement goal* i.e., what portion of the partial plan is relevant for applying the refinement strategy, and the *decision* i.e., which particular refinement was chosen from among the alternative refinements produced by the refinement strategy.

More specifically, here is the information that needs to go into the decision records for the different kinds of refinements that UCP can make:

1. Decision record for a forward state-space refinement:
   - Refinement goal: the head-state s at the time the refinement was applied.
   - Decision: what step t was chosen (out of the set of all steps whose preconditions are satisfied by s), and whether t was a new step or a previously existing step.

   If the decision record says that t was a new step, then this means that UCP added t to the partial plan, and added a contiguity constraint between the head step and t. If the decision record says that t was an existing step, then this means that UCP simply added a contiguity constraint between the head step and t.

2. Decision record for a backward state-space refinement:
   - Refinement goal: the tail-state s at the time the refinement was applied.
   - Decision: what step t was chosen (out of the set of all steps that do not delete any condition in s and achieve at least one condition in s), and whether it was a new step or a previously existing step.

   If the decision record says that t was a new step, then this means that UCP added t to the partial plan, and added a contiguity constraint between t and the tail step. If the decision record says that t was an existing step, then this means that UCP simply added a contiguity constraint between t and the tail step.

3. Decision record for a plan-space refinements
   - Refinement goal: a point truth constraint $\langle p@t' \rangle$.

- Decision: what step t was chosen (out of the set of all steps that can establish the point truth constraint $\langle p@t' \rangle$), whether it was a new or existing step, and whether an IPC was added to the plan.

If the decision record says t was a new step, it means that UCP added it to the plan, and in any case it means that UCP added constraints to require that $t \prec t'$ and to prevent any step from coming between t and t' and deleting p.

4. Decision record for a refine-plan-pre-order refinement:
   - Refinement goal: a pair of unordered steps t_1 and t_2.
   - Decision: Whichever of the following two plans was chosen: $P + (t_1 \prec t_2)$ or $P + (t_1 \nprec t_2)$.

5. Decision record for a refine-plan-pre-position refinement:
   - Refinement goal: a pair of non-contiguous steps t_1 and t_2.
   - Decision: Whichever of the following two plans was chosen: $P + (t_1 * t_2)$ or $P + (t_1 \not\ast t_2)$.

6. Decision record for a refine-plan-pre-satisfy refinement:
   - Refinement goal: an auxiliary constraint C and a step t_3 in conflict with C.
   - Decision: the way in which P was refined in order to make C hold in every possible ground linearization of P. For example, if C is an IPC $(t_1 \overset{p}{-} t_2)$, then the possible refinements of P may be any plans of the form $P + (t_3 \prec t_1) \vee (t_2 \prec t_3)$ or $P + \pi^p_{t_3}@t_3$, where t_3 is a step having an effect that unifies with $\neg p$, and $\pi^p_{t_3}$ is as described in [5].

These decision records take all search choice points in the UCP algorithm into account. As an example of these decision records, Table 1 shows a derivational trace for the example in Section 2.

Note that the set of choice points and decisions confronted by an execution of DerUCP depends on the particular instance of DerUCP. Therefore, a derivational trace recorded from an execution of instance of UCP cannot be used for a different instance of UCP. For example, if we construct a derivational trace for a partial-order planner, some of the decision records in the derivational trace would not make sense for a total-order planner; a total-order planner can only add new steps at the head fringe or at the tail fringe of the partial plan whereas a partial-order planner can add steps anywhere in the partial plan.

3.2 DerUCP Algorithm

The DerUCP algorithm extends the UCP planning algorithm by adding the *derivational replay* before the refinement steps. This section describes only the derivational replay mechanism, which relies on the replay step and the procedure **Replay**. For a precise description of other parts of the UCP algorithm, please refer to [5].

Figure 2 shows the pseudocode of the DerUCP algorithm. The DerUCP algorithm is a recursive search procedure in which partial plans are refined by

Table 1. A derivational trace for the example in Section 2.

Step: 1
Type: forward state-space refinement
Refinement goal: the head-state $\{i'\}$
Decision: a new step with operator o_i.
Step: 2
Type: backward state-space refinement
Refinement goal: the tail-state. $\{G'\}$
Decision: a new step with operator o'.
Step: 3
Type: plan-space refinement
Refinement goal: the point truth constraint $\langle p@t_2 \rangle$.
Decision: a new step with operator o_{p1}
Step: 4
Type: plan-space refinement
Refinement goal: the point truth constraint $\langle q@t_2 \rangle$.
Decision: a new step with operator o_q
Step: 5
Type: refine-plan-pre-satisfy
Refinement goal: IPC $(t_3 \overset{p}{-} t_2)$ and t_4
Decision: the plan $P + t_4 \prec t_3$.

additions of new steps and constraints in the refinement steps in each iteration until a solution is found. Instead of allowing nondeterministic choice in the algorithm description of UCP, DerUCP explicitly maintains a priority list which stores the pending partial plans. The priority list plays a role similar to the open list in the $A*$ search algorithm. At the beginning, the priority list containing an empty partial plan is provided, together with a case library. The DerUCP algorithm first picks up one of the partial plans from the priority list according to a choice function (Step 0), which depends on the particular UCP instance. If the partial plan contains a solution, the algorithm returns it and terminates (Step 1). Otherwise, the algorithm proceeds to the replay step, which selects a case achieving any refinement goal and replays it (Step 2). The details of Replay procedure are discussed below. After the replay step, the partial plan, P, is refined. This refined plan is used in the remaining steps. Note that the steps after the replay step, i.e., the progressive refinement, the non-progressive refinement, and consistency check, are optional, and therefore they can be skipped (Steps 3-5). Finally, all the partial plans generated by the refinement steps are inserted into the priority list and DerUCP is invoked recursively (Step 6).

In the replay step, the set of refinement goals of the current partial plan is computed (Figure 3). The possible refinement goals are the refinement goals of all six decision records described in Section 3.1. The replay of the current case continues only if the next goal in the case g_c matches the refinement goal g (Steps 2-3). Each decision record in the derivational trace guides the selection of appropriate refinements. The Replay procedure recursively iterates over the

procedure DerUCP(*PL, CL*)
    Inputs: *PL* - a priority list
             CL - a case library
begin
    0. Plan Selection
        Select one partial plan *P* from *PL* (by a choice function).
        Remove *P* from *PL*.
    1. Termination Check
        If *P* contains a ground operator sequence that solves
           the problem, returns it and terminates.
    2. Replay
        Construct a list of refinement goals *G* for *P*.
        Let $S \subseteq CL$ be the set of cases which achieve
           some refinement goals in *G*
        if *S* is not empty **then**
           Select one case *C* from *S* according to a metric
           $P := \texttt{Replay}(P, G, C, PL)$
           $PL := PL \cup \{P\}$
    3. (optional) Progressive Refinement
        Using `pick-refinement` strategy, select any one of
           1. `Refine-plan-forward-state-space`(*P*)
           2. `Refine-plan-backward-state-space`(*P*)
           3. `Refine-plan-plan-space`(*P*)
        Let L' be all of the returned plans. $PL := PL \cup L'$
    4. (optional) Non-progressive Refinement
        For each P' in L', select zero or more of:
           1. `Refine-plan-conflict-resolve`(P')
           2. `Refine-plan-pre-ordering`(P')
           3. `Refine-plan-pre-positioning`(P')
        Let L'' be all of the returned plans. $PL := PL \cup L''$
    5. (optional) Consistency Check
        For each P'' in L'', select zero or more of:
        If the partial plan P'' is inconsistent or
           non-minimal, remove P'' from L''.
    6. Recursive Invocation:
        Call **DerUCP**(*PL, CL*)
  end

Fig. 2. The DerUCP algorithm

decision records of the case, and in each iteration it checks if the refinement suggested by the decision of the current decision record is a valid refinement in the current partial plan (Steps 4-6). If so, the refinement is selected and the alternative refinements are put on the priority list for possible backtracking (Steps 7-10). After each iteration DerUCP makes a nondeterministic choice to continue with the next decision record or stop the replay process (Step 11).

Eager and Interleaved Replay. DerUCP supports the two variants of Derivational Replay: eager and interleaved replay. In *eager replay*, case replay is done

procedure Replay(P, G, C, PL)
begin
1.   **if** C is null **then** return P
2.   Let g_c be the refinement goal of $first(C)$
3.   **if** $\exists g \in G$ that match g_c **then**
4.   Let d_c be the decision for g_c in C
5.   Let cs be the set of applicable refinements for g
6.   **if** $\exists r \in cs$ that $matches(decision(r), d_c)$ **then**
7.   Apply the refinement r to P to obtain P'
8.   Apply the refinements in $cs - \{r\}$ to P to obtain
                 a set of partial plans PS
9.   Append PS to PL with a lower priority
10.   Construct a list of refinement goals G' for P'
                 (G' can be obtained by modifying G)
11.   Select one of the following:
                     return Replay$(P', G', next(C), PL)$, or
                     return P'
      else
12.   Select one of the following:
                 return Replay$(P, G, next(C), PL)$, or
                 return P'
end

Fig. 3. The Replay Procedure

first and then the partial plan obtained is completed by a first principles planner. It is called "eager" since each of the selected cases is replayed as long as possible. That is, in steps 11 and 12 of the Replay procedure, the recursive call is always made. An example of a system performing eager replay is DerSNLP [11]. In *Interleaved Replay*, case replay may be interleaved with first-principles planning and it is not eager. An example of a system implementing the interleaved approach is Prodigy/Analogy. Interleaving is covered in DerUCP in two places: first, in the recursive call of Step 6 of the DerUCP algorithm, interleaving between first-principles planning and case replay is secured. Second, the nondeterministic choices of steps 11 and 12 in the Replay procedure ensure that the cases need not be eagerly replayed. In Prodigy/Analogy heuristics are used to decide whether to continue replay of the current case or not.

4   Complexity Analysis of Plan Adaptation

We now analyze the main result in [4] that sometimes has been quoted as proof that plan adaptation is harder than planning from scratch. First the standard definitions of a planning problem, i.e., "planning from scratch", is given. [14]

Definition 1. *An instance of propositional STRIPS planning is denoted by a tuple $\langle P, O, I, G \rangle$, where:*

- *P is a finite set of ground atoms. Let L be the corresponding set of literals:*
  $L = P \cup \{\neg p : p \in P\}$.
- *O is a finite set of operators of the form Pre $\Rightarrow$ Post, where Pre $\subseteq$ L is the preconditions and Post $\subseteq$ L is the postconditions or effects. The positive postcondition is the add list, while the negative postcondition is the delete list.*
- *$I \subseteq P$ is the initial state.*
- *$G \subseteq L$ is the goal.*

A state *S is a subset of P, indicating that $p \in P$ is true in that state if $p \in S$, and false otherwise. A state S is a goal state if S satisfies G, i.e., if all positive literals in G are in S and none of the negative literals in G is in S.*

Definition 2. *PLAN-EXISTENCE (Π) Given an instance of the planning problem $\Pi = \langle P, O, I, G \rangle$, does there exist a plan Δ that solves Π?*

The following is the definition of plan adaptation used in [4]:

Definition 3. *MODSAT (Π_1, Δ, Π, k)*
Given the instance of the planning problem $\Pi_1 = \langle P, O, I_1, G_1 \rangle$, and a plan Δ that solves the instance $\Pi = \langle P, O, I, G \rangle$, does there exist a plan Δ_1 that solves Π_1 and contains a subplan of Δ of at least length k ?

This definition states what the authors of [4] call a *conservative* plan modification strategy in the sense that it is trying to reuse as much of the starting plan Δ to solve the new plan. The main conclusion from [4] is that in the worst case MODSAT is harder than PLAN-EXISTENCE. That is, plan adaptation is harder than planning from scratch with a conservative strategy plan modification strategy .

In [4], Priar [15] and SPA [16] are cited as examples of systems performing this conservative adaptation strategy. Interestingly, neither of these systems performs plan adaptation by Derivational Analogy; cases in these systems contains plans and provably correct plan transformation rules are used to perform adaptation.

So the question remains: does adaptation by derivational analogy perform a conservative plan modification strategy in the sense of the MODSAT definition or not? If it does, then the worst case analysis applies and thus the empirical results reported about case-based planners such as Prodigy/Analogy, DerSNLP and CAPlan/CbC outperforming their respective underlying first-principles planners would have been mere accidents. As it turns out, *adaptation by derivational analogy does not perform a conservative adaptation strategy in the sense of MODSAT.*

The key to our analysis lies in Step 11 of the **Replay** procedure. Clearly, if the algorithm stops replaying the derivational trace rather than executing the recursive call, the adaptation is not conservative as the remaining parts of the derivational trace are not taken into account. This typically happens in Interleaved Replay. But what would happen if the recursive call always occurs, as happens in Eager Replay? The answer to this question can be seen from step

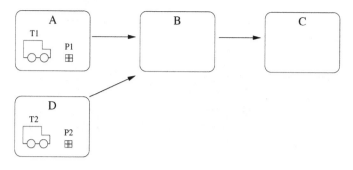

Fig. 4. A simple planning problem from the Logistics domain

6 of the `Replay` procedure. Step 6 stops the replay process of a derivational trace if the current decision record is not applicable. At this point all of the remaining decision records are ignored. This is not a conservative strategy; in this situation, a conservative strategy would try to fix the impasse, for example by adding a few plan steps or revising the previous decision record, and then continuing with the remaining decision records.

This can be easily illustrated with an example from the *logistics* domain [1], in which packages must be relocated using some transportation methods. There are some restrictions imposed on the transportation methods. For example, trucks can only deliver packages within a city. Figure 4 shows a possible configuration. There are four locations A, B, C and D. A truck T1 and a package P1 are in location A and another truck T2 and another package P2 are in location D. Suppose that our goal is to relocate both packages in location C. The arrows in Figure 4 show the paths followed by the trucks to achieve this problem. The first truck, T1, loads P1 and drives to B. Meanwhile, the second truck, T2, loads P2 and also drives to B. Once in B, P2 is unloaded from T2 and loaded into T1. T1 continues to C where both packages are dropped. Now, suppose that the derivational trace of this plan is stored in a case and that our particular instance of UCP performs only forward state-space refinement (i.e., steps can only be added to the head fringe of partial plan).

Let us suppose that a new problem is given which is almost identical to our previous example. The only difference is that T2 is not available. The corresponding instance of DerUCP will start replaying the first part of the plan in which P1 is loaded into T1 and T1 drives from A to B. At this point the replay fails since P2 is not in B (to be precise, the condition at Step 6 of the `Replay` procedure fails). DerUCP either continues by planning from scratch or by using a case that can continue solving this problem. This is not a conservative strategy in the sense of the MODSAT definition; a conservative strategy will drive T1 to D pick the second package, drive back to B and continue reusing the rest of the case. DerUCP never "continues" replay from a point at which a failure occurs because the replay step is always done from the beginning of the derivational trace. Thus, DerUCP would ignore the rest of the derivational trace even though most of it could have been used. One could constructs a similar example for partial order planning.

5   Efficiency of DerUCP

The analysis of the efficiency of DerUCP is divided into two parts. We first analyze the efficiency of the replay of one case, and then extend the analysis to the replay of multiple cases.

5.1   Replay of a Single Case

We consider the efficiency of DerUCP with exactly one case being replayed during the whole planning process. In other words, the `Replay` procedure is invoked once only. This analysis is an extension of a similar analysis for eager replay in Section 5 of [2].

Theorem 1. *Suppose exactly one case is replayed in DerUCP. Furthermore:*

- *Let the branching factor b be the average number of partial plans that can be generated from a given plan by the application of a single refinement.*
- *Let the depth of the solution d be the average length of the solution path from the initial (null) plan to a solution.*
- *Let l_s be the number of nodes before the replay begins.*
- *Let l_c be the number of nodes visited during the replay.*
- *Let l_b be the number of nodes on the replay path that are backtracked.*

Then the search space size is $O(b^{d-l_1})$, where $l_1 = l_c - l_b$.

Proof. When only one case is replayed in the whole planning process, we can divide the execution of DerUCP into four phases: planning from scratch before the call to `Replay` procedure, the replay of the case, backtracking over various decisions suggested by the case, and finally using first-principles planning to extend the resulting partial plan to produce the final solution.

Figure 5 shows a possible exploration of the search space by DerUCP. The solid arrows represent the paths traversed by means of first-principles planning. The dashed arrow refers to the path due to derivational replay. The major difference between the solid arrows and the dashed arrow is that the searching on the solid arrows is possibly over the whole search tree which has size exponential to the length of the path. The searching on the dashed arrows is a traversal of a single branch of the search tree, which is guided by the decisions encoded in the derivational trace of the retrieved case. Therefore, the dashed arrow can be seen as a shortcut that enables the searching process to jump from one point in the search space to the other. Only the regions of the search space bounded by the two bold triangles are explored by first principles. Thus, a total of $l_c - l_b$ node expansions of the search tree are skipped, and the total search space size is $O(b^{d-(l_c-l_b)})$. □

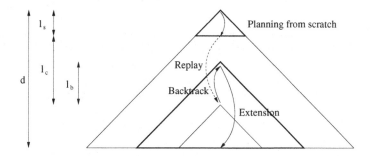

Fig. 5. The search-space size for DerUCP with one call to `Replay` is $O(b^{d-l_1})$, where b is the branching factor, d is the depth of the solution, l_s is the number of nodes before the replay begins, l_c is the number of nodes visited during the replay, l_b is the number of nodes on the replay path that are backtracked, and $l_1 = l_c - l_b$.

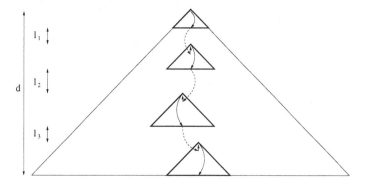

Fig. 6. The search-space size for DerUCP with multiple calls to `Replay` is $O(b^{d-\sum l_i})$, where each l_i is the number of refinements during the i'th replay that are retained for use in the final plan.

If the planning is done by merely planning from scratch without derivational replay, then the search space size is $O(b^d)$ (see [17]). In the worst case, this is exponentially larger than the $O(b^{d-(l_c-l_b)})$ search space size of DerUCP as stated in Theorem 1, since $l_c - l_b \geq 0$.

5.2 Replay of Multiple Cases

We now consider the situation in which more than one case is replayed. When multiple cases are replayed, the search process contains more than one path that is guided by the derivational trace of the cases. Since the paths may interleave with each other in a complicated way, it is hard to identify which part of the search space is skipped. To simplify the analysis, consider only replays in which some refinements are retained in the final plan, as these guided refinements replace the node expansion of the search tree—the effect is similar to pruning the search space. Figure 6 shows a typical search space for DerUCP. The bold triangles are the regions of the search spaces explored by first principles. Other regions are essentially skipped by replay. Therefore, the search space size is $O(b^{d-\sum l_i})$, where each l_i is the number of refinements that occur between the $(i-1)$'th and i'th bold triangles. By generalizing this argument, we get:

Theorem 2. *If two or more cases are replayed in DerUCP, then the search space size is $O(b^{d-\sum l_i})$, where each l_i is the number of refinements during the i'th replay that are retained for use in the final plan.*

Theorem 2 states that whenever some refinements suggested by any case are retained in the final plan, the search space size can be reduced.

These results show that Derivational Analogy can potentially make an exponential reduction in the size of the search space visited during adaptation. The reduction in the size of the exponent is proportional to the number of steps obtained during replay that remain when the solution plan is completed, i.e., it is proportional to the number of steps taken during replay that were not revised to obtain the solution plan. The worst-case scenario occurs when all decisions taken during replay need to be revised. In such a situation the size of the search space is $O(b^d)$ since $l_b = l_d$ in Theorem 1. This worst-case search-space size is the same as the search-space size generated by the underlying planner. This proves the following theorem:

Theorem 3. *In the worst case, the size of the search space potentially generated by DerUCP is $O(b^d)$, i.e., the same as the size of the search space potentially generated by UCP.*

6   Conclusion

This paper describes the DerUCP algorithm, which is a general model of plan adaptation using Derivational Analogy. DerUCP is an extension of the well known UCP algorithm [5], which is a general model for classical AI planning. DerUCP covers all existing forms of Derivational Analogy that we are aware of, including Interleaved and Eager Replay.

Our analysis of DerUCP resolves the difference between theoretical results [4] suggesting that plan adaptation is worse than planning from scratch and empirical results [1,2,3] suggesting that Derivational Analogy does better than planning from scratch. In particular, we have shown the following:

- The conservative plan adaptation strategy as defined in [4] does not hold for Derivational Analogy. Thus, the worst-case complexity result in [4] about plan adaptation being harder than planning from scratch does not apply to Derivational Analogy.
- If we compare the size of the search space for any instance of DerUCP with the size of the search space for the corresponding instance of UCP, the DerUCP search space is no larger—and can potentially be exponentially smaller—than the UCP search space.

The amount of reduction is directly proportional to the number of steps obtained through case replay that remain after the solution plan is completed. Thus, performance improvements depend on the retrieval method being able to select cases that require fewer revisions. This is precisely what instances of DerUCP such as Prodigy/Analogy, DerSNLP and CAPlan/CbC do; these systems implement sophisticated retrieval and indexing techniques to improve the accuracy of the retrieval and reduce backtracking on the replayed steps.

Acknowledgments

This work was supported in part by the following grants, contracts, and awards: Air Force Research Laboratory F306029910013 and F30602-00-2-0505, Army Research Laboratory DAAL0197K0135, and the Office of Research at Lehigh University. The opinions expressed in this paper are those of authors and do not necessarily reflect the opinions of the funders.

References

1. Veloso, M., Carbonell, J.: Derivational analogy in PRODIGY: Automating case acquisition, Storage and Utilization. Machine Learning (1993) 249–278
2. Ihrig, L., Kambhampati, S.: Plan-space vs. State-space planning in reuse and replay. Technical report, Arizona State University (1996)
3. Muñoz-Avila, H.: Case-Base Maintenance by Integrating Case Index Revision and Case Retention Policies in a Derivational Replay Framework. Computational Intelligence **17** (2001)
4. Nebel, B., Koehler, J.: Plan reuse versus plan generation: a theoretical and empirical analysis. Artificial Intelligence **76** (1995) 427–454
5. Kambhampati, S., Srivastava, B.: Unifying Classical Planning Approaches. Technical report, Arizona State University (1996)
6. Fikes, R., Hart, P., Nilsson, N.: Learning and executing generalized robot plans. Artificial Intelligence **3** (1972) 251–288
7. Carbonell, J.G.: Derivational analogy: A theory of reconstructive problem solving and expertise acquisition. Machine Learning (1986)
8. Bhansali, S., Harandi, M.T.: When (not) to Use Derivational Analogy: Lessons Learned Using APU. In Aha, D., ed.: Proceeding of AAAI-94 Workshop: Case-based Reasoning. (1994)
9. Blumenthal, B., Porter, B.: Analysis and Empirical Studies of Derivational Analogy. Artificial Intelligence **67** (1994) 287–328
10. Finn, D., Slattery, S., Cunningham, P.: Modelling of Engineering Thermal Problems - An implementation using CBR with Derivational Analogy. In: Proceedings of EWCBR'93, Springer-Verlag (1993)
11. Ihrig, L., Kambhampati, S.: Derivation Replay for Partial-Order Planning. AAAI-1994 (1994)
12. Muñoz-Avila, H., Weberskirch, F.: Planning for Manufacturing Workpieces by Storing, Indexing and Replaying Planning Decisions. Proc. 3rd Int. Conference on AI Planning Systems (AIPS-96) (1996)
13. Muñoz-Avila, H., Paulokat, J., Wess, S.: Controlling Nonlinear Hierarchical Planning by Case Replay. In: Proceedings the 2nd European Workshop on Case-Based Reasoning (EWCBR-94). (1994) 195–203

14. Bylander, T.: The Computational Complexity of Propositional STRIPS Planning. Artificial Intelligence **69** (1994) 165–204
15. Kambhampati, S.: Exploiting causal structure to control retrieval and refitting during plan reuse. Computational Intelligence **10** (1994) 213–244
16. Hanks, S., Weld, D.S.: A Domain-Independent Algorithm for Plan Adaptation. Journal of Artificial Intelligence Research **2** (1995) 319–360
17. Korf, R.: Planning as Search: A Quantitative Approach. Artificial Intelligence **33** (1987) 65–88

Inductive Learning for Case-Based Diagnosis
with Multiple Faults

Joachim Baumeister, Martin Atzmüller, and Frank Puppe

University of Würzburg, 97074 Würzburg, Germany
Department of Computer Science
Phone: +49 931 888-6740, Fax: +49 931 888-6732
{baumeister, atzmueller, puppe}@informatik.uni-wuerzburg.de

Abstract. We present adapted inductive methods for learning similarities, parameter weights and diagnostic profiles for case-based reasoning. All of these methods
can be refined incrementally by applying different types of background knowledge. Diagnostic profiles are used for extending the conventional CBR to solve
cases with multiple faults. The context of our work is to supplement a medical
documentation and consultation system by CBR techniques, and we present an
evaluation with a real-world case base.

1 Introduction

The main advantage of case-based reasoning (CBR) systems is its quite natural knowledge acquisition process, because cases often must be documented for various purposes
and can then be exploited for decision support. However, cases are not sufficient for CBR,
which needs four knowledge containers [1]: vocabulary, case base, similarity measure
and adaptation knowledge. In a structured documentation system high quality cases are
available with a predefined vocabulary. In this paper, we show how to extract the knowledge for the other two containers (similarity measure, adaptation knowledge) from the
cases (semi-)automatically, in order to augment a structured documentation system by
CBR. In particular, we discuss, which background knowledge is helpful in learning the
content for the two containers and measure its effects in tests. The main difficulty is how
to deal with multiple faults in cases, which makes it a rare event, that cases have exactly
the same solution. For solving this difficulty we learn diagnostic profiles, i.e. typical
observations for each diagnosis, infer set-covering knowledge from the profiles, and use
the capabilities of set-covering inference for multiple faults. The results are tested by
combining appropriate cases.

Our context is a structured documentation system in medicine, being used for doc-
umenting the results of specialized examinations. The cases are detailed descriptions
of symptoms and findings of the examination(s), together with the inferred diagnoses
(faults), i.e. a case consists of a list of attribute-value pairs (observations) together with a
list of solution elements. Both observations and diagnoses may be ordered hierarchically
due to the structured data gathering strategy, i.e. findings are usually first specified in
general terms and then further detailed with follow-up questions, and diagnoses have
a specialization hierarchy as well. This setting yields – in contrast to many other CBR

S. Craw and A. Preece (Eds.): ECCBR 2002, LNAI 2416, pp. 28–42, 2002.

projects – a high quality of the case base with detailed and usually correct case descriptions.

Our implementation and evaluation is based on the knowledge-based documentation and consultation system for sonography SONOCONSULT (an advanced and isolated part of HEPATOCONSULT [2]) being in routine use in the DRK-hospital in Berlin/Köpenick based on the diagnostic shell kit D3 [3]. In addition to an documentation system, SONO-CONSULT also infers diagnoses with heuristic expert knowledge, but this capability is not important for our approach. SONOCONSULT documents an average of 300 cases per month and generates a conventional physician's letter with a rule-based template from the structured input entered in hierarchical questionnaires. Included are the inferred diagnoses, which can be corrected manually, but are usually correct due to first evaluations of SONOCONSULT.

The goals for adding a CBR component to SONOCONSULT are to validate the solution for the current case and to provide additional information, e.g. explanations based on the presented similarity to former cases and the possibility to look up information in the corresponding patient records concerning therapy, complications, prognosis or the treating physician as contact person for special questions. In general, we envision a hybrid way of building intelligent documentation systems, by defining the data gathering, data abstraction and basic diagnostic inference knowledge in a rule-based representation and using case-based reasoning for fine-tuning and maintenance.

The rest of the paper is organized as follows: In Section 2 we define case-based diagnosis and diagnostic profiles. We introduce our basic concept of case-based reasoning with multiple faults. In Section 3 we describe methods for learning partial similarities, weights and diagnostic profiles from cases. These knowledge extensions are applied when retrieving a new case. In Section 4 we present the usage of the learned knowledge in a dynamic retrieve process, which is appropriate for handling multiple faults. An evaluation with a real-world case base is given in Section 5. We will conclude the paper in Section 6 with a discussion of the presented work and we show promising directions for future work.

2   Case-Based Diagnosis with Diagnostic Profiles

In this section we give the basic definitions needed for the learning methods presented in Section 3 and the reasoning task in Section 4. We introduce a similarity measure to compare cases and we define diagnostic profiles, which support the case-based reasoning process. Furthermore we present a concept for handling cases with (possibly) multiple faults in the retrieve step.

2.1   Basic Definitions

Let Ω_D be the set of all diagnoses and Ω_P the set of all parameters (attributes). To each parameter $p \in \Omega_P$ a range $dom(p)$ of values is assigned. Further we assume Ω_F to be the (universal) set of findings $(p = v)$, where $p \in \Omega_P$ is a parameter and $v \in dom(p)$ is a possible value. Let CB be the case base containing all available cases that have been solved previously. A case $c \in CB$ is defined as a tuple

$$c = (F_c, D_c, I_c) \tag{1}$$

where $F_c \subseteq \Omega_F$ is the set of findings observed in the case c. These findings are commonly called *problem description*. The set $D_c \subseteq \Omega_D$ is the set of diagnoses describing the *solution* for this case. We see, that the solution D_c for a case c can consist of multiple diagnoses (faults). The case can also contain additional information I_c like therapy advices or prognostic hints.

To compare the similarity of a new case c with another case c' we apply the commonly used weighted similarity measure given in Equation 2, which is an adaptation of the *Hamming distance* with weights and partial similarities between values of parameters p (e.g. see [4], page 183f.) :

$$sim(c, c') = \frac{\sum\limits_{p \in \Omega_P} w(p) \cdot sim_p\big(v_c(p), v_{c'}(p)\big)}{\sum\limits_{p \in \Omega_P} w(p)} \tag{2}$$

where $v_c(p)$ is a function, which returns the value of the parameter p in case c, and $w(p)$ is the weight of parameter p. If weights for parameters are not available, then we set $w(p) = 1$ for all $p \in \Omega_P$.

Now we will introduce diagnostic profiles, which describe a compact case representation for each diagnosis, since they contain the findings that occur most frequently with the diagnosis.

Definition 1 (Frequency Profile). *A frequency profile F_{P_d} for a diagnosis $d \in \Omega_D$ is defined as the set of tuples*

$$F_{P_d} = \big\{(f, freq_{f,d}) \,\big|\, f \in \Omega_F \wedge freq_{f,d} \in [0,1]\big\} \tag{3}$$

where f is a finding and $freq_{f,d} \in [0,1]$ represents the frequency the finding f occurs in conjunction with d, i.e.

$$freq_{f,d} = \frac{\big|\{c \in CB \,|\, f \in F_c \wedge d \in D_c\}\big|}{\big|\{c \in CB \,|\, d \in D_c\}\big|}. \tag{4}$$

Since we consider cases with multiple faults, it can be quite helpful to know the set of diagnoses a given diagnosis usually occurs with. For this reason we augment frequency profiles with this information in the next step.

Definition 2 (Diagnostic Profile). *A diagnostic profile P_d for a diagnosis $d \in \Omega_D$ is defined as the tuple*

$$P_d = (F_{P_d}, D_{P_d}^{corr}) \tag{5}$$

where F_{P_d} is a frequency profile for diagnosis d. The set

$$D_{P_d}^{corr} \in \big\{ (d', freq_{d',d}) \,\big|\, d' \in \Omega_D \wedge freq_{d',d} \in [0,1] \big\}$$

contains all diagnoses d' that appear together with d in the solution part of the cases in CB. The number $freq_{d',d}$ represents the frequency the diagnosis d' co-occurs with d.

2.2   Basic Concept for Handling Multiple Faults

We give a brief overview of the basic concept we developed for handling multiple faults (diagnoses) in case-based reasoning. In Sections 3 and 4 we focus on the methods in more detail.

To improve the quality of the case-based reasoner and to handle multiple diagnoses in an appropriate way, we apply the following steps:

1. Use the available cases for learning knowledge about partial similarities and weights for parameters.
2. Construct diagnostic profiles utilizing the learned knowledge and infer basic set-covering knowledge [5,6] from the profiles.
3. Apply learned knowledge for case-based reasoning as described in Equation 2.
4. If no case is sufficiently similar, then combine cases guided by the set-covering knowledge.

For the first two steps we provide the opportunity of a manual adaptation of the learned knowledge (similarities, weights, diagnostic profiles) for refinement. In the third step we apply the learned knowledge in the retrieve step of the case-based reasoner. For a new case we firstly try to find a sufficiently similar case in the case base. If a sufficiently similar case has been solved before, then we simply reuse the solution of this case. We say, that a case is *sufficiently similar* to another case, if the similarity between these two cases exceeds a given (and usually high) threshold. Since we consider a domain with cases containing multiple faults, such matches might be rare.

If no sufficiently similar case has been found, we apply an abductive reasoning step using the diagnostic profiles to find diagnoses, that can explain the current problem description. On the basis of this explanation we construct prototypical candidate cases containing cases of the case base. These candidates are presented to the user as possible solutions for the current case.

Related Work. The combination of case-based reasoning with other knowledge representations has already been investigated in many approaches. The systems CASEY [7] and ADAPtER [8] are prominent examples for approaches that use case-based reasoning in a first step for selecting solved cases, which match the current observation best. In a second step, abductive knowledge is applied to adapt the old cases with respect to the current observation and give a verbose explanation for the adaptation. In our work we use the reverse approach, when using abductive reasoning for guiding the search of how to combine cases.

Another aspect of the work presented here is the problem of learning abductive models from cases containing multiple faults. Work in this field has been done by Thompson and Mooney [9] with an inductive learning algorithm, that generates set-covering relations from cases containing multiple faults. For this, a simple hill-climbing strategy is applied which adds more specific set-covering rules until the classification accuracy decreases. In contrast to our approach no additional knowledge like partial similarities is used to increase the diagnostic quality. Wang et al. [10] presented a connectionist approach when learning fuzzy set-covering models from cases generated by a simulation environment. They use an adapted back-propagation method that learns fuzzy set-covering relations by adjusting connective weights. But, besides the fuzzy covering relations, no additional knowledge like feature weights is applied in this method. Schmidt et al. [11] considered a simple generation process of prototypes from cases with the ICONS project. This case-based system has been developed for selecting an appropriate antibiotics therapy for patients in ICU domains. For this purpose, prototypes are generated from previous cases to supply retrieval and adaptation of a newly entered case. The construction of the prototypes is quite simple, since they are formed out of cases containing equal findings and therapy advices. When a new case is entered, the system adapts the most similar prototypes with respect to contra-indications for the given therapy advices. Furthermore new prototypes are generated, if new cases do not fit in existing ones.

3 Inductive Learning of Similarities, Weights and Diagnostic Profiles

In this section we consider the problem of inductively learning partial similarities for parameter values and weights for parameters. We further show how to build diagnostic profiles for single diagnoses.

3.1 Preprocessing Heterogenous Data

The algorithms presented in the further subsections are designed to handle discrete value domains of parameters. Nevertheless the available case base also contains some continuous data as well. Therefore we will transform continuous parameters into parameters with discrete partitions in a preprocessing step. The discretization is only done for the learning task and will not change the case base in principle. A lot of work has been done on the discretization of continuous parameters and there exists a wide range of methods (cf. [12,13] for empirical comparisons).

Automatic Partitioning of Parameter Domains. The simplest method applicable to our problem is the *Equal Width Interval Binning*, which divides the domain $dom(p)$ of a parameter p into equal sized bins. A more promising approach seems to be the usage of clustering methods (cf. [14] for a survey), that groups partitions relative to the frequency the findings occur in the single partitions. Due to the limited space we will omit a more detailed description of appropriate clustering methods.

Predefined Partitions. For some continuous parameters the expert already defined reasonable partitions. In the case, that there are predefined partitions available, we use these instead of the automatic binning methods mentioned above.

3.2 Similarity Knowledge for Parameter Values

The use of similarities between finding values can improve learning methods and reasoning capabilities dramatically. For example, the construction of diagnostic profiles benefits from similarity knowledge, because similar values of a parameter can work together in a diagnostic profile, rather than to compete against each other. Thus we consider learning similarities before building diagnostic profiles.

In the following we will use the term *distance function*, but it is obvious, that a distance function d directly corresponds to a similarity function sim. For two findings $(p = x)$ and $(p = y)$ we define their similarity by

$$sim_p(x, y) = 1 - d_p(x, y) . \tag{6}$$

Common Distance Functions. One of the most commonly known distance function is the *City-Block* or *Manhattan* distance function, which is defined as follows:

$$d_p^m(x, y) = \frac{|x - y|}{\alpha} \tag{7}$$

where x and y are values for parameter p and $\alpha = x_{max} - x_{min}$. Obviously the Manhattan distance function is only appropriate for continuous or scaled parameters p.

For discrete parameters we implemented the *Value Difference Metric* (VDM) as proposed in [15] and improved in [16]. Given two findings $f_1 = (p = x)$ and $f_2 = (p = y)$ the VDM defines the distance between the two values x and y of parameter p:

$$vdm_p(x, y) = \frac{1}{|\Omega_D|} \cdot \sum_{d \in \Omega_D} \left| \frac{N(p = x \,|\, d)}{N(p = x)} - \frac{N(p = y \,|\, d)}{N(p = y)} \right| \tag{8}$$

where $N(p = x)$ is the number of cases in CB, for which parameter p is assigned to value x, i.e. $(p = x) \in F_c$. $N(p = x \,|\, d)$ is the number of cases c in CB with diagnosis $d \in D_c$, and parameter p is assigned to value x, i.e. $(p = x) \in F_c$.

With this measure, two values are considered to be more similar, if they have more similar correlations with the diagnoses they occur with. Thus we obtain the following distance function d for a parameter $p \in \Omega_P$ with values $x, y \in dom(p)$:

$$d_p(x, y) = \begin{cases} 1 & \text{if } x \text{ or } y \text{ is unknown,} \\ vdm_p(x, y) & \text{otherwise.} \end{cases} \tag{9}$$

Distance Metrics Using additional Knowledge. Since the underlying knowledge base is highly structured, we were able to utilize helpful information to augment the distances between parameter values.

Abnormalities. During the knowledge-acquisition process discrete and nominal values were marked to describe, whether they represent a normal or an abnormal state of their corresponding parameter (e.g. *pain=none* is normal, whereas *pain=high* is abnormal). Abnormal states can be sub-categorized into five degrees of abnormality (i.e. $A1$, $A2$, $A3$, $A4$, $A5$). We can utilize this information to divide the value range into an abnormal and a normal partition. To obtain the distance between a normal value y and an abnormal value x we use the following matrix

$d_p(x, y)$	abn(x)=A1	abn(x)=A2	abn(x)=A3	abn(x)=A4	abn(x)=A5
abn(y)=A0	0.6	0.7	0.8	0.9	1

where $abn(x)$ is a function returning the abnormality for the given value and $A0$ defines a normal value. So we get a maximum distance between a normal and a totally abnormal value, e.g., $d_p(x, y) = 1$ for $abn(x) = A5$ and $abn(y) = A0$.

After that, we compute the similarities for the remaining values by applying the VDM method (see Equation 8) for the values contained in the "normal values"–partition and for the values contained in the "abnormal values"–partition.

Scalability Knowledge. Beyond abnormalities the expert may mark some of the parameters as *scaled* to characterize, that values, that are closer to each other, are more similar. For example, $dom(pain) = \{none, little, medium, high\}$ is scaled, whereas $dom(color) = \{green, black, red\}$ is not scaled. We can utilize this flag, by applying the VDM method not for all distinct pairs of values within each partition, but only for adjacent values. Then, we interpolate the remaining distances by the following equation

$$d_p(v_i, v_{i+k}) = d_p(v_i, v_{i+k-1}) + d_p(v_{i+k-1}, v_{i+k}) \tag{10}$$

where $k > 2$. After interpolating the remaining distances we have to normalize the whole distance matrix for parameter p, so that for all values $v, v' \in dom(p)$ it holds that $0 \le d(v, v') \le 1$.

3.3   Learning Diagnostic Profiles from Cases

The available cases usually contain more than one diagnosis (multiple faults). This characteristics makes it difficult to generate exact profiles for each single diagnosis, because it is not obvious, which findings are caused by the single diagnoses. Since we had a sufficient number of cases containing each diagnosis but rare repetitions of combinations of the diagnoses, we applied a statistical method for learning the most frequent covered symptoms of a diagnosis.

In the following we present an algorithm for building diagnostic profiles describing single diagnoses. Each profile contains at least all relevant findings for the specified diagnosis. We divide the algorithm into two parts: In Algorithm LCP we learn coarse profiles from the cases given by the case base. In Algorithm BDP we build diagnostic profiles from the coarse profiles learned before.

Learning Coarse Profiles. In Algorithm LCP we will consider the cases contained in the training set CB. For each case $c \in CB$ we will update the diagnostic profiles of the diagnoses contained in the solution part of c. So, for each diagnosis $d \in D_c$ we will add the findings of the case to the corresponding diagnostic profile P_d, respectively increase their frequencies. Additionally we will update P_d by increasing the frequencies of the diagnoses d' co-occurring with d. Diagnoses $d' \in D_c \setminus \{d\}$ with a very high frequency, i.e. co-occurring very often with diagnosis d, tend to depend on d. Therefore the profiles for both diagnoses may have equal subsets of findings, which are only caused by one diagnosis. Thus, removing findings from the diagnostic profile, that are caused by the other diagnosis, will increase the quality of the profiles. Due to the limited space of this paper we will omit a detailed consideration of learning dependency between diagnoses (e.g. [17] introduces learning dependencies).

Build Diagnostic Profiles. The diagnostic profiles learned in Algorithm LCP will also contain rare findings. In a second step we will remove these unfrequent findings from the profile. Before that, we will consider similarities between findings in the profile. For example, if a coarse profile includes the finding *pain=high* (*p=h*) with frequency

---

Algorithm 1. Lcp: Learning Coarse Profiles

Require: Cases c contained in CB
1: **for all** cases $c \in CB$ **do**
2:     **for all** diagnoses $d \in D_c$ **do**
3:        /* *Update profile $P_d = (F_{P_d}, D_{P_d}^{corr})$* */
4:        **for all** findings $f \in F_c$ **do**
5:           Increment frequency of f in F_{P_d}
6:        **end for**
7:        **for all** diagnoses $d' \in D_c \setminus \{d\}$ **do**
8:           Increment frequency of d' in $D_{P_d}^{corr}$
9:        **end for**
10:    **end for**
11: **end for**
Ensure: Coarse Diagnostic Profile $P_d = (F_{P_d}, D_{P_d}^{corr})$ for each diagnosis d

---

0.4 and the finding *pain=very high* ($p=vh$) with frequency 0.4 then both findings might be too rare to remain in the profile (e.g. with a threshold $\mathcal{T}_{DP} = 0.5$). But, since both findings are very similar to each other, an adapted frequency may be sufficiently frequent to remain in the profile. For example, if $sim_p(h, vh) = 0.8$, then an adapted frequency $freq'_{x,d}$, concerning similar findings, will be

$$freq'_{p=h,d} = freq_{p=h,d} + \left(sim_p(h, vh) \cdot freq'_{p=vh,d} \right)$$
$$= 0.4 + (0.8 \cdot 0.4) = 0.72 .$$

We will adapt this idea, when we firstly compute a combined frequency $freq'_f$ for each finding $f \in F_{P_d}$, regarding similarities between values of the same parameter. After adapting the frequencies, we will remove all findings from the profile, which are still too unfrequent with respect to a given threshold $\mathcal{T}_{DP}$. We point out, that a diagnostic profile can contain more than one value of the same parameter, if their adapted frequencies exceed the threshold $\mathcal{T}_{DP}$.

It is worth mentioning, that the threshold $\mathcal{T}_{DP}$ directly corresponds to the resulting size of the diagnostic profiles. For a large threshold we will compute sparse profiles, which may be too special to cover all common findings for the diagnosis. Small thresholds will result in too general profiles, which will cover too many findings. This can yield a bad diagnostic quality.

The result of the algorithm is a set of a diagnostic profiles, where each diagnostic profile directly corresponds to a set-covering model [5,6] defining the frequently observed findings of the diagnosis. A set-covering model contains set-covering relations, which describe relations like: *"A diagnosis d predicts, that the finding f is observed in $freq_{f,d}$ percent of all known cases."* We denote set-covering relations by

$$r = d \rightarrow f \; [freq_{f,d}] . \tag{11}$$

Further, we define $cause(r) = d$ and $effect(r) = f$. A set-covering model SCM_d for a diagnosis d is defined as a set of covering relations

$$SCM_d = \{ r \in \mathcal{R} \mid cause(r) = d \} \tag{12}$$

where $\mathcal{R}$ is the set of covering relations included in the knowledge base. As shown in [5], set-covering models are able to process similarities, weights and frequencies.

To transform a given diagnostic profile $P_d = (F_{P_d}, D_{P_d}^{corr})$ into a set-covering model SCM_d, we simply have to perform the following step: For all findings $f \in F_{P_d}$, create a new covering relation $r = d \rightarrow f\ [freq_{f,d}]$ and add the relation to the set-covering knowledge base.

If we have a small count of cases for the learning task, then the resulting profiles can be poor. For this reason we provide an editor for visual presentation and adaptation of the learned diagnostic profiles. Thus, the expert is able to inspect the single profiles in order to justify the threshold parameter $\mathcal{T}_{DP}$ or to possibly refine the profile by manually inserting additional findings or deleting unimportant ones.

3.4 Learning Weights of Parameters from Cases

Weights for parameters are another common knowledge extension for case-based reasoning systems. After the construction of diagnostic profiles, we will now describe how to learn weights of parameters. In general, the weight $w(p)$ of a parameter p specifies the importance of the parameter.

Learning Weights without Additional Knowledge. Our approach is inspired by a procedure mentioned in [18], when using the VDM method to discriminate the importance of attributes. However, our interpretation also considers additional information like abnormalities and structural knowledge.

A parameter p is defined to be important, if p has a high *selectivity* over the solutions contained in the case base CB. The degree of selectivity directly corresponds to the importance (weight) of the parameter. So, if different values of a parameter p indicate different diagnoses, then the parameter is considered to be *selective* for the diagnostic process.

Algorithm 2. BDP: BUILD DIAGNOSTIC PROFILES

Require: Coarse profile P_d is available for each diagnosis d,
        defined threshold $\mathcal{T}_{DP}$ for pruning unfrequent findings
1: **for all** diagnostic profiles $P_d = (F_{P_d}, D_{P_d}^{corr})$ **do**
2:     Generate finding sets $F_{P_d}^m$ such that each finding contained
        in set $F_{P_d}^m$ is assigned to the same parameter m.
3:     **for all** finding sets $F_{P_d}^m$ **do**
4:         /* compute adapted frequencies of findings regarding their similarities */
5:         **for all** findings $f \in F_{P_d}^m$ **do**
6:             $freq'_{f,d} = freq_{f,d} + \sum_{f' \in F_{P_d}^m \setminus \{f\}} freq_{f',d} \cdot sim(f,f')$
7:         **end for**
8:     **end for**
9:     /* Remove findings with frequency less than threshold $\mathcal{T}_{DP}$ */
10:     $F_{P_d} = \{ f \in F_{P_d} \mid freq'_f \geq \mathcal{T}_{DP} \}$
11: **end for**
Ensure: Created diagnostic profile P_d for each diagnosis.

We define the *partial selectivity* of a parameter p combined with a diagnosis d by the following equation

$$sel(p, d) = \frac{\sum\limits_{x,y \in dom'(p)} \left| \frac{N(p=x \mid d)}{N(p=x)} - \frac{N(p=y \mid d)}{N(p=y)} \right|}{\binom{|dom'(p)|}{2}} \tag{13}$$

where $x \neq y$ and $dom'(p) \subseteq dom(p)$ contains only values, that occur in cases $c \in CB$. To compute the global *selectivity* of a parameter p, we average the partial selectivities $sel(p, d)$

$$sel(p) = \frac{\sum\limits_{d \in D^p_{rel}} sel(p, d)}{|D^p_{rel}|} \tag{14}$$

where $D^p_{rel} = \{ d \in \Omega_D \mid \exists p \in \Omega_P, x \in dom(p) : \frac{N(p=x|d)}{|CB|} > \mathcal{T}_w \}$. So we only investigate the selectivities between parameters and diagnoses, whose combined frequency is larger than a given threshold $\mathcal{T}_w$.

Since $sel(p, d) \in [0, 1]$ for all diagnoses $d \in D^p_{rel}$ and all parameters $p \in \Omega_P$, we see that $sel(p) \in [0, 1]$ for all parameters $p \in \Omega_P$. The lower bound 0 is obtained, if parameter p has no selectivity over the diagnoses contained in Ω_D; the upper bound 1 is obtained, if p has a perfect selectivity over the diagnoses contained in Ω_D, i.e. each value $x \in dom(p)$ occurs either always or never with the diagnosis.

After determining the selectivity of the parameter, we use the following logarithmic conversion table to transform the numerical selectivity into a symbolic weight.

sel(p)		w(p)	sel(p)		w(p)
0	⇁	G0	(0.08, 0.16]	⇁	G4
(0, 0.02]	⇁	G1	(0.16, 0.32]	⇁	G5
(0.02, 0.04]	⇁	G2	(0.32, 0.64]	⇁	G6
(0.04, 0.08]	⇁	G3	(0.64, 1.00]	⇁	G7

We accept the loss of information to facilitate a user-friendly adaptation of the learned weights by the expert in a later step. So, similar to the diagnostic profiles, the weights can be adapted manually by the expert to refine the learned knowledge.

Utilizing Abnormalities for Learning Weights. If there are abnormalities available for a given parameter p, then we can use this information to improve the learning algorithm. In this case we will adapt Equation 13 to consider only the selectivity between normal and abnormal parameter values.

$$sel(p, d) = \frac{\sum\limits_{x \in abnormal(p) \land y \in normal(p)} \left| \frac{N(p=x \mid d)}{N(p=x)} - \frac{N(p=y \mid d)}{N(p=y)} \right|}{|abnormal(p)| \cdot |normal(p)|} \tag{15}$$

where $abnormal(p) = \{ x \in dom(p) \mid abn(x) \neq A0 \}$ is the set of values $x \in dom(p)$ representing an abnormal state, and $normal(p) = dom(p) \setminus abnormal(p)$.

Optimizing Parameter Weights by Structural Knowledge. As mentioned in the introduction of this paper, we operate on a highly structured knowledge base, where parameters (questions) are arranged in sets called *examinations* (corresponding to the diagnostic tests during the clinical use).

Examinations contain an *examination weight* to mark their significance in the overall examination process. These weights help us to adjust the weights of the parameter contained in the examination. So parameters contained in dense examinations (i.e. containing many parameters) will receive a decreased weight, whereas parameters contained in sparse examinations with fewer parameters will obtain an increased weight. Thus, for a parameter p contained in examination E we will obtain an adjusted weight $w'(p)$ defined by Equation 16.

$$w'(p) = \frac{w(p)}{\sum\limits_{p' \in E} w(p')} \cdot w(E) \tag{16}$$

where $w(E)$ is the *examination weight* for examination E. The heuristic given in Equation 16 is motivated by the fact, that in the applied domain single phenomena are structured in single examinations. Thus, if the examination contains many parameters describing the phenomenon, then this examination is likely to contribute more weights than an examination with fewer parameters. Nevertheless, each examination only describes one phenomenon. It is worth mentioning, that this method is not reasonable in general, but can be used, when highly structured case bases are available.

3.5   Additional Knowledge Used by the Learning Task

Now we will shortly summarize the processing facilities of additional knowledge (e.g. abnormalities, scalability, examination structure) during the learning task. We remark, that similarities, profiles and weights depend on each other, since we apply similarity knowledge for learning diagnostic profiles and utilize diagnostic profiles, when determining weights of parameters.

	no knowledge	abnormalities	scalability * / examination structure **
similarities	We apply the VDM method to compute similarities between each distinct value pair $v, v' \in dom(p)$.	We partition the value range $dom(p)$ into abnormal and normal values, and use the VDM method only within the partitions.	* Use VDM method only for adjacent values, normalize interpolated distance matrix. If abnormalities given, divide the value range into 2 partitions before comp. distances.
profiles	Similarities are required	Improve similarities for computing the diagnostic profile	* Improve similarities for computing the diagnostic profile
weight	Use a modified VDM method, that determines the weight of a parameter by its selectivity between the given diagnoses.	Adapt the modified VDM method, so that we only consider selectivities between normal and abnormal parameter values.	** Normalize weight of parameters w.r.t. the weight of their corresponding examination.

The table give a brief overview of the adaptations we made to the presented learning methods in this section.

4   Dynamic Retrieval of Cases with Multiple Faults

In this section we describe an adapted retrieve process, following the notions of Aamodt and Plaza. In [19], they defined the case-based reasoning process as a cycle containing the following four sub-processes: *Retrieve, Reuse, Revise, Retain.* For handling multiple faults we need to adapt the *Retrieve* step in the following way:

Typically starting with a (partial) problem description of observed findings the retrieve process ends with a previously solved case best matching the given problem description.

In a first step we try to find a sufficient similar case, i.e. containing a sufficient similar problem description. We use a high threshold $\mathcal{T}_{CBR}$ of the required similarity to define *sufficient similarity*. If we have found a sufficient similar case, then we propose this case as a possible solution in the *Reuse*-step. If no sufficient similar case has been found, then we apply the following steps:

1. Use the transformed set-covering models to compute the k best hypotheses. A hypothesis is a set of diagnoses, that can explain the problem description of the new case, i.e. the observed findings.
2. Given the hypotheses we generate a set of *candidate cases*: A candidate case contains several cases, whose combined solutions yield the diagnoses of one of the hypotheses generated in the step above.
3. Compare each candidate with the new case c using Equation 2 and remove all candidates c' with $sim(c, c') < \mathcal{T}_{CBR}$.
4. Propose the three most similar cases as retrieved solution.

We combine single cases to a candidate case by 1) joining sets of the solutions contained in the single cases, and 2) joining problem descriptions of the cases. If the cases contain a parameter with different values, then we take the value with the highest abnormality. We motivate this approach with the following heuristic: If a patient has two (independent) diagnoses, then it seems to be reasonable, that the more severe finding will be observed. If there are no abnormalities defined, then we either try to take the value contained in the new case, if included in one problem description, or we take the value, which is most similar to the value listed in the new case.

5   Evaluation and Discussion

As mentioned in the introduction, we applied a real-world case base to our learning algorithms. The SONOCONSULT case base currently contains 744 cases, with a mean of diagnoses per case $M_d = 6.71 \pm 04.4$ and a mean of relevant findings $M_f = 48.93 \pm 17.9$ per case. For the evaluation of our experiments we adopted the *intersection accuracy* measure proposed in [9]. Let c be a new case and c' the retrieved case, that is most similar to c. Then the *intersection accuracy* $\mathcal{IA}$ is defined as follows

$$\mathcal{IA}(c, c') = \left(\frac{|D_c \cap D_{c'}|}{|D_c|} + \frac{|D_c \cap D_{c'}|}{|D_{c'}|} \right) / 2 \qquad (17)$$

where D_c is defined as the set of diagnoses contained in case c.

In the following table we present results of the experiments E0–E4. For each experiment we incrementally applied additional background knowledge: 1. Predefined abnormalities in the knowledge base (*Abn*), 2. Learned partial similarities (*PaSim*), 3. Learned weights (*Weight*), 4. For unsolved cases, dynamic candidate case generation based on learned diagnostic profiles (*CCG*). Additional knowledge enables us to decrease the case similarity threshold T_{CBR} without receiving a dramatically decreased intersection accuracy of the solved cases. Cases below this threshold were withdrawn and marked as "*not solvable*", because no sufficiently similar case was found. For the experiments we applied two versions of the case base. The first one (CB_{raw}) contains only the raw data, whereas the second one (CB_{abs}) additionally contains findings gained by data abstraction. The abstracted data is inferred with rules based on expert knowledge, which is not available in typical case-based applications. As expected, it shows a significant increase in the number of solved cases and accuracy, but still is clearly insufficient to deal with the multiple fault problem.

	used knowledge / method					CB_{raw}		CB_{abs}	
	Abn	*PaSim*	*Weight*	*CCG*	threshold T_{CBR}	solved cases	mean accuracy	solved cases	mean accuracy
E0	–	–	–	–	0.60	8	0.96	12	0.74
E1	+	–	–	–	0.55	14	0.81	19	0.77
E2	+	+	–	–	0.55	26	0.71	43	0.72
E3	+	+	+	–	0.50	29	0.75	74	0.71
E4	+	+	+	+	0.26	429	0.70	–	–

The small number of solved cases in the evaluations E0–E3 is justified by the special characteristic of our case base, which shows a high count of diagnosis combinations per case and rare repetitions of diagnosis combinations in the case base. The high variance of diagnosis combinations on the other hand causes a high variance of possible problem descriptions. The numbers in the table above show, that standard CBR-methods are performing poor for cases with multiple faults even when additional knowledge like similarities and weights is applied. This conclusion strongly motivates the usage of set-covering techniques in the case-based process, which was evaluated in E4. Here we can see, that a dynamic candidate case generation can present similar cases for 429 cases. Figure 1 clearly shows the trend, that additional knowledge increase the number of solved cases. In Figure 2 we can see the intersection accuracy for the 40 most similar

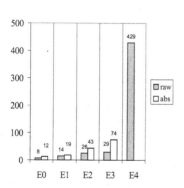

Fig. 1. Number of solved cases in experiments E0–E4

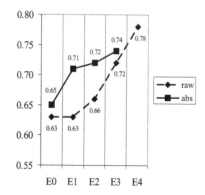

Fig. 2. Mean accuracy for the 40 most similar cases retrieved in E0–E4.

cases in E0–E4, which suggests the trend, that learned knowledge improves the quality of the solved cases.

The results presented above are quite promising. Nevertheless, we see enhancements for the number of solved cases and intersection accuracy, when applying a more detailed integration of diagnosis hierarchies into the data preprocessing step and when assessing the intersection accuracy. In general, a well-elaborated data preprocessing step will increase the quality of the learned similarities, profiles and weights.

6   Summary and Future Work

In this paper we presented a new approach for handling multiple faults in case-based reasoning, describing inductive methods for learning similarities, weights and diagnostic profiles. We found diagnostic profiles to be very useful for handling multiple faults, since they can be combined to explain a new problem description, that had not been emerged before. We integrated this idea in a dynamic retrieval process, that does not leave the paradigm of case-based reasoning, since it always explains its presented solutions in parts of cases. For the inductive learning methods we pointed out, that additional knowledge can improve the resulting quality of the learned similarities, weights and profiles. In this case, the knowledge can be applied incrementally depending on its availability. Experiments have shown, that the dynamic candidate generation method using diagnostic profiles significantly improved the number of solved cases.

In the future, we are planning to consider more detailed adaptations of the presented learning methods. For example, preprocessing heterogeneous data or learning parameter weights still needs improvements. Besides the diagnostic profile generation process, we are currently working on an enhanced approach taking advantage of causal independencies between groups of diagnoses. Furthermore the case base is still growing due to the routine usage of the system in a clinical environment. An evaluation of the presented methods with a larger number of cases should yield better results.

References

1. Michael Richter. The Knowledge contained in Similarity Measures. Invited talk at ICCBR-95, http://www.cbr-web.org/documents/Richtericcbr95remarks.html, 1995.
2. Hans-Peter Buscher, Ch. Engler, A. Führer, S. Kirschke, and F. Puppe. HepatoConsult: A Knowledge-Based Second Opinion and Documentation System. *Artificial Intelligence in Medicine*, 24(3):205–216, 2002.
3. Frank Puppe. Knowledge Reuse among Diagnostic Problem-Solving Methods in the Shell-Kit D3. *Int. J. Human-Computer Studies*, 49:627–649, 1998.
4. Christoph Beierle and Gabriele Kern-Isberner. *Methoden wissensbasierter Systeme. Grundlage, Algorithmen, Anwendungen*. Vieweg, 2000.
5. Joachim Baumeister, Dietmar Seipel, and Frank Puppe. Incremental Development of Diagnostic Set–Covering Models with Therapy Effects. In *Proc. of the KI-2001 Workshop on Uncertainty in Artificial Intelligence*, Vienna, Austria, 2001.
6. Joachim Baumeister and Dietmar Seipel. Diagnostic Reasoning with Multilevel Set–Covering Models. In *Proc. of the 13th International Workshop on Principles of Diagnosis (DX-02)*, Semmering, Austria, 2002.

7. Phyllis Koton. Reasoning about Evidence in Causal Explanations. In *Proc. of the Seventh National Conference on Artificial Intelligence*, pages 256–261, 1988.
8. Luigi Portinale and Pietro Torasso. ADAPtER: An Integrated Diagnostic System Combining Case-Based and Abductive Reasoning. In *Proc. of the ICCBR 1995*, pages 277–288, 1995.
9. Cynthia A. Thompson and Raymond J. Mooney. Inductive Learning for Abductive Diagnosis. In *Proc. of the AAAI-94, Vol. 1*, pages 664–669, 1994.
10. Xue Z. Wang, M.L. Lu, and C. McGreavy. Learning Dynamic Fault Models based on a Fuzzy Set Covering Method. *Computers in Chemical Engineering*, 21:621–630, 1997.
11. Rainer Schmidt and Bernhard Pollwein and Lothar Gierl. Case-Based Reasoning for Antibiotics Therapy Advice. In *Proc. of the ICCBR 1999*, pages 550–559, 1999.
12. James Dougherty, Ron Kohavi, and Mehran Sahami. Supervised and Unsupervised Discretization of Continuous Features. In *Proc. of the International Conference on Machine Learning*, pages 194–202, 1995.
13. Dan Ventura and Tony R. Martinez. An Empirical Comparison of Discretization Methods. In *Proc. of the 10th Int. Symp. on Computer and Information Sciences*, pages 443–450, 1995.
14. Jiawei Han and Micheline Kamber. *Data Mining: Concepts and Techniques*. Morgan Kaufmann Publishers, San Mateo, California, 2000.
15. Craig Stanfill and David Waltz. Toward Memory-Based Reasoning. *Communications of the ACM*, 29(12):1213–1228, 1986.
16. D. Randall Wilson and Tony R. Martinez. Improved Heterogeneous Distance Functions. *Journal of Artificial Intelligence Research*, 6:1–34, 1997.
17. Judea Pearl. *Probabilistic Reasoning in Intelligent Systems: Networks of Plausible Inference*. Morgan Kaufmann Publishers, San Mateo, California, 1988.
18. Dietrich Wettschereck and David W. Aha. Weighting Features. In Manuela Veloso and Agnar Aamodt, editors, *Case-Based Reasoning, Research and Development, First International Conference*, pages 347–358, Berlin, 1995. Springer Verlag.
19. Agnar Aamodt and Enric Plaza. Case-Based Reasoning: Foundational Issues, Methodological Variations, and System Approaches. *AI Communications*, 7(1), 1994.

Diverse Product Recommendations
Using an Expressive Language for Case Retrieval

Derek Bridge and Alex Ferguson

Department of Computer Science,
University College, Cork
d.bridge/a.ferguson@cs.ucc.ie

Abstract. We describe Order-Based Retrieval, which is an approach to
case retrieval based on the application of partial orders to the case base.
We argue that it is well-suited to product recommender applications because, as well as retrieving products that best match customer-specified
'ideal' attribute-values, it also: allows the customer to specify soft constraints; gives a natural semantics and implementation to tweaks; and
delivers an inherently diverse result set.

1 Introduction

When CBR has been applied to product recommender systems, similarity is
generally the sole retrieval criterion: products whose descriptions in a product
catalogue are similar to the customer's 'ideal' product are retrieved and recommended to the customer [10] [11]. But 'pure' similarity-based retrieval may not
suffice in this application. In [2], we introduced a new form of retrieval, Order-
Based Retrieval (OBR), which we revised and described in more detail in [3]. A
major motivation was to allow a query in a recommender system to capture *soft
constraints* (e.g. a desired maximum price), as well as 'ideal' values.

Diversity of retrieval may be an additional criterion, again with particular
application to product recommender systems [8]. In product recommendation,
similarity between the retrieved cases and the customer's 'ideal' values is desirable, but too much similarity *between the retrieved cases themselves* may be less
desirable. If the customer is not satisfied with the most similar case in the result
set, for example, the chances of him or her being satisfied with an alternative
case in the result set are increased if a diverse set is recommended. Diversity is
different in nature from similarity: similarity is a property of individual cases in
the result set (relative to the query); diversity is a property of the result set as
a whole.

There have been a number of attempts to increase retrieval diversity. For
example, Smyth & Cotter [8] use a hybrid system, in which similarity-based
recommendations are made more diverse by the inclusion of additional recommendations from a collaborative recommender. In other work, Smyth & his co-
authors [9] [1] apply an additional selection rule within retrieval to increase result
set diversity. We argue in this paper that our new approach, OBR, gives good

S. Craw and A. Preece (Eds.): ECCBR 2002, LNAI 2416, pp. 43–57, 2002.

result set diversity as a natural consequence of the query language semantics, without recourse to additional mechanisms.

In Section 2, we will summarise OBR's query language. Section 3 introduces some example data that will be used in subsequent sections of the paper. Section 4 illustrates the operation of OBR and argues that it is more expressive than pure similarity-based retrieval. Section 5 report the results of a comparison between OBR and the approach described in [9] & [1].

2 The Order-Based Retrieval Query Language

Order-Based Retrieval is founded on a key observation: the success of similarity-based retrieval rests on its ability to order the cases in the case base. If we call the customer's query q, then case $c_i \in CB$ is lower in the ordering than case $c_j \in CB$ iff $\mathrm{Sim}(c_i, q) < \mathrm{Sim}(c_j, q)$. The numbers that are used to denote the degrees of similarity are less important than the ordering induced on the cases.

Using the relative similarities of cases to a query of 'ideal' values is only one way of ordering a case base. The idea behind OBR is that we can construct orders in other ways too. In product recommendation, the customer will supply a variety of information ('ideal' values, maximum values and minimum values, for example) and we will construct an ordering relation from this information. We will apply this ordering to the case base, retrieve the maxima (or a suitable number of the products at the top of the ordering) and recommend them to the customer.

Accordingly, we have developed a new query language for constructing *partial orders*. Presently, the language comprises six operators. To save space, we present here only the five that we make use of in this paper. Furthermore, the fifth operator listed below (LSPO) is a special case of a more general operator (which we call Prioritisation Ordering, PO). We are only using LSPO in this paper so, again, to save space we do not show the more general definition. The definitions can be found in full in [3].

In the following definitions of the operators, x, y and v may be attribute-values or whole cases. In the way that we list the operators here, their usefulness may not be immediately apparent. But they are exemplified in subsequent sections of this paper. The reader may wish to skim this section on first reading, and then refer back to it as necessary when working through later sections.

Filter-Ordering (FO): Given a unary predicate, p, we can construct an ordering from p as follows:

$$x <_{\mathrm{FO}(p)} y \mathrel{\hat{=}} \neg p(x) \wedge p(y)$$

The definition says that x is lower than y iff y satisfies p but x does not.

Similarity-Ordering (SO): Given a similarity measure, Sim, and an 'ideal' value, v, then x is lower than y iff x's similarity to v is lower than y's similarity to v:

$$x <_{\mathrm{SO}(\mathrm{Sim},v)} y \mathrel{\hat{=}} \mathrm{Sim}(x,v) < \mathrm{Sim}(y,v)$$

About-Ordering (AO): Given a partial order, $<$, and an 'ideal' value v, then a new ordering can be defined by 'breaking the back' of the existing ordering at v [7]. Values to either side of v will be ordered by their distance from v in the original ordering:

$$x <_{AO(<,v)} y \,\hat{=}\, (x < y \leq v) \vee (x > y \geq v)$$

Cross-Product Ordering (CPO): This operator combines two partial orders, $<_1$ and $<_2$, into a single partial order:

$$x <_{CPO(<_1,<_2)} y \,\hat{=}\, x \leq_1 y \wedge x \leq_2 y \wedge \neg(x =_1 y \wedge x =_2 y)$$

This is simply the conjunction of the two orders: for x to be less than or equal to y, it must be less than or equal to y in both orders (and, to be strictly less than y, it must also not equal y).

Less Strict Prioritisation Ordering(LSPO): Here $<_1$ takes precedence over $<_2$:

$$x <_{LSPO(<_1,\,<_2)} y \,\hat{=}\, x <_1 y \vee (x \not<_1 y \wedge x \not>_1 y \wedge x <_2 y)$$

That is, when $<_1$ judges two values to be equal or incomparable, the 'tie' is broken using $<_2$.

This operator yields a partial order only when applied to certain first argument orders $<_1$. In this paper, we apply it only to orders that result from the application of FO. In [3] we prove that if $<_1$ results from an application of FO, then LSPO yields a partial order.

Many more operators could be given, but these form a good starting point for building OBR Recommender Systems.

3   Example Case Base

We will be using a case base of 794 properties that were available for rent in the London area in Summer 2001.[1] Each case in this case base has six descriptive attributes: the price, the number of bedrooms, the number of bathrooms, the location, whether the property is a flat or a house, and whether the property is furnished or not. (There are a further two attributes used only for case identification: a unique number and an address.) Figure 1 shows these attributes and their types (permissible values). In the case of numeric-valued attributes, the ranges of permissible values are based on values currently in the case base.

In places where we use pure similarity-based retrieval in this paper, we will need similarity measures for each of the six attributes. These attribute-specific similarity measures are given in Figure 2. For *location*, only a fragment of an invented similarity measure is shown.[2] *price*, *bdrms* and *bthrms* would use Sim_N with different values for the *range*: 8373 for *price*, 7 for *bdrms* and 6 for *bthrms*. Sim_{Eq} can be used as the similarity measure for *propType* and *furnished*.

---

[1] This case base is accessible at: http://www.cs.ucc.ie/~dgb/research/obr.html

[2] The similarity measure we use in our software is a bit simpler; it is based on London postal codes.

Attributes with ordered types	
Attribute	**Type**
price	127-8500
bdrms	0-7
bthrms	1-7

Attributes with unordered types	
Attribute	**Type**
location	{Clapham, Chelsea,...}
propType	{Flat, House}
furnished	{Yes, No}

Fig. 1. Attributes and their Types

$\mathrm{Sim}_{location}(Battersea, Battersea) = 1.0$
$\mathrm{Sim}_{location}(Battersea, Clapham) = 0.7$
$\mathrm{Sim}_{location}(Battersea, Chelsea) = 0.5$
$\mathrm{Sim}_{location}(Battersea, Hounslow) = 0.3$
$\mathrm{Sim}_{location}(Battersea, Richmond) = 0.0$

$$\mathrm{Sim}_N(x, y) \triangleq 1 - \frac{\mathrm{abs}(x-y)}{range}$$

$$\mathrm{Sim}_{Eq}(x, y) \triangleq \begin{cases} 1 \text{ if } x = y \\ 0 \text{ otherwise} \end{cases}$$

Fig. 2. Attribute-Specific Similarity Measures

We distinguish *ordered types* from *unordered types*. Attributes *price*, *bdrms* and *bthrms* have ordered types. Their permissible values have an obvious ordering defined on them (the usual numeric-less-than relation). (Although these examples are all numeric, non-numeric ordered types are also possible [3].) For these attributes, OBR does not require similarity measures.

Attributes *location*, *propType* and *furnished* all have unordered types. Their permissible values have no obvious ordering that would be relevant to product recommendation. For these attributes to participate in either kind of retrieval, we will need the similarity measures in Figure 2.

In our experiments in Section 5, we use all 794 cases and all six attributes. But our examples in Section 4 are rendered more intelligible by confining our attention to just three attributes: *price*, *bdrms* and *location*. Furthermore, in Section 4's simple examples, we use some invented cases, which are shown in Figure 3. (These cases have been invented for the way they demonstrate different aspects of the behaviour of the operators in our query language.)

4 Retrieval Examples

In this section, we explain and exemplify some of Order-Based Retrieval's operators. We will also show that OBR has greater expressiveness than pure similarity-based retrieval by handling some examples that contain soft constraints.

4.1 Pure Similarity-Based Retrieval

We start with an example in which the customer specifies only 'ideal' values. Suppose the customer desires a two bedroom property in Battersea. Suppose also that these two requirements are equally important to the customer.

Let q be the customer's query, let $\mathrm{Attr}(q)$ be the attributes mentioned in this query (in this case, *bdrms* and *location*) and let π_a be a projection function that obtains the value of attribute a from a case or a query. Then, pure

identifier	price	bdrms	location
A	325	3	*Clapham*
B	330	2	*Hounslow*
C	400	2	*Chelsea*
D	400	3	*Hounslow*
E	500	3	*Chelsea*
F	550	1	*Richmond*
G	600	1	*Richmond*
H	600	4	*Clapham*

Fig. 3. Example Property Case Base

similarity-based retrieval would retrieve cases c from the case base using a similarity measure such as the following:

$$\text{Sim}(c, q) \triangleq \frac{\sum_{a \in \text{Attr}(q)} (w_a \times \text{Sim}_a(\pi_a(c), \pi_a(q)))}{\sum_{a \in \text{Attr}(q)} w_a} \qquad (1)$$

This is a weighted average of attribute-specific similarity measures. In our experiments (Section 5), we are going to assume that all requirements are equally important, and so all weights will be one.

If we evaluate the similarity of each case in Figure 3 to the query, we find that the cases are ordered as follows: A (0.78), C (0.75), H (0.71), E (0.68), B (0.65), D (0.58) and F & G (0.43 each). Conventionally, only the best k of these cases would be recommended to the customer.

4.2   Order-Based Retrieval

We do not use Equation 1 to encode our example query using OBR. In particular, for ordered types, we do not need the attribute-specific similarity measures.

The *bdrms* attribute has an ordered type and we use its ordering, rather than using a similarity measure. The customer wants two bedrooms, so we construct a new ordering from $<$ using the AO operator. The ordering $<_{\text{AO}(<,2)}$ is shown as Figure 4. (The diagram is abbreviated for values greater than 5.)

The *location* attribute has an unordered type so in this case we do use its similarity measure, $\text{Sim}_{location}$, from Figure 2. But we construct an order from it using the SO operator. The order $<_{\text{SO}(\text{Sim}_{location}, Battersea)}$ applied to some sample

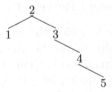

Fig. 4. $<_{\text{AO}(<,2)}$

$Battersea$

|

$Clapham$

|

$Chelsea$

|

$Hounslow$

|

$Richmond$

Fig. 5. $<_{\mathrm{SO}(\mathrm{Sim}_{location}, Battersea)}$

data is shown as Figure 5. To combine the customer's requirements equally, we use the CPO operator. The final query expression is:

$$<_{\mathrm{CPO}(<_{\mathrm{AO}(<,2)}, <_{\mathrm{SO}(\mathrm{Sim}_{location}, Battersea)})}$$

Diagrams such as those in Figures 4 and 5 show the effects of the ordering relations that we have constructed when they are applied to a sample of representative data values. OBR software does not have to build data structures corresponding to these diagrams. It uses the query expressions directly to compare pairs of cases in the case base. An algorithm for finding the maxima of the case base for a given query expression is shown as Figure 6. Figure 7 shows how the case base in Figure 3 is ordered by our query expression.

As can be seen from the diagrams, we are dealing with partial orders. In Figure 7, case A, for example, is neither lower in the ordering nor higher in the ordering than case C: they are incomparable. This is because case A comes closer to the query on *location*, but case C does better on *bdrms*. This illustrates that, in our partially-ordered approach, a set of candidates is often retrieved where each is to be preferred on a different respect. This leads naturally to a diverse set, with the size of the set providing an indication of the number of distinct

```
maxima := {}
for each c ∈ CB
    shouldInsert = true
    for each case in maxima, m
        if c < m
            shouldInsert = false
            break
        else if m < c
            remove m from maxima
        end if
    end for
    if shouldInsert
        insert c into maxima
    end if
end for
```

Fig. 6. Naïve query evaluation algorithm applying $<$ to CB

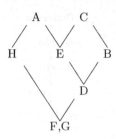

Fig. 7. Ordering the Case Base using the Query

'directions' in which alternatives lie in the case base. We discuss this inherent diversity in Section 5.

It follows too that the maxima is a set: the set of cases that are equal or incomparable to each other and bettered by no other cases. In the example, the maxima is the set $\{A, C\}$. If more cases are to be recommended to the customer, we can display the second 'rank' of cases: $\{H, E, B\}$. This is the maxima when A and C are taken out of the picture. The next rank is $\{D\}$ and the final rank is $\{F, G\}$. This is a similar outcome to that obtained for pure similarity-based retrieval in Section 4.1, although in general there can be considerable differences. Our experiments in Section 5 reveal some of these differences.

One objective comparison, however, is that CPO straightforwardly treats the two requirements in the customer's query equally. In weighted averages, setting the weights to one is not sufficient for treating requirements equally: the values returned by the similarity measures are sensitive to other factors [4] [3]. For example, suppose we decided that the range of permissible values for *bdrms* was not 7 but 11. Cases C & H would swap places in the similarity ranking that we gave in Section 4.1. This new normalisation factor reweights the similarity measure so that case H's similarity to the query changes from 0.71 to 0.76. Changes to normalisations cannot affect the behaviour of CPO.[3]

4.3   Soft Constraints

Suppose customer Ann wants a 2 bedroom property in Battersea as in the previous two subsections, but the maximum she is prepared to spend is £400. Customer Ben also wants a 2 bedroom property in Battersea but he can only afford £200. In product recommender systems that use pure similarity-based retrieval, customers can specify only 'ideal' values; they cannot specify constraints, such as a maximum price.

One solution to this, of course, is to use a hybrid system which first filters the case base, eliminating products that do not satisfy the constraints. A result set is

---

[3] Of course, the main use of weighting is to make one requirement more important than another, although here again the interaction with normalisation can make it hard to achieve definite effects. In OBR, the PO operator and its special cases such as LSPO (Section 2) offer a variety of ways of doing the same thing, again without concerns about normalisation [3].

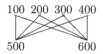

Fig. 8. $<_{\mathrm{FO}(\lambda x[\pi_{price}(x)\leq 400])}$

retrieved from the remaining products using similarity-based retrieval. For Ann's query, cases E, F, G and H would be eliminated, and she would be recommended the remaining cases in the order A, C, B, D.

The problem is that there is now a risk that the customer's requirements are so demanding that all products are eliminated and so none is recommended to the customer. For Ben's query, for example, no products are recommended at all. This is the problem that motivated the use of similarity-based retrieval in recommender systems; traditional database retrieval, using exact matching, can give empty result sets [10] [11].

In OBR, we would take Ann's maximum value and construct a unary predicate from it: $\lambda x[\pi_{price}(x) \leq 400]$. We do not filter away products using this predicate. Instead, we construct an order from it using the FO operator: $<_{\mathrm{FO}(\lambda x[\pi_{price}(x)\leq 400])}$. This says that values that satisfy the predicate are higher in the ordering than ones that do not. We show this in Figure 8 for a handful of different prices.

We can combine this with the rest of Ann's requirements. It is likely that a constraint (even a soft one) should be treated as more important than other requirements, so we will combine using a form of prioritisation. This is a case where we can use LSPO. The final query expressions is therefore

$$<_{\mathrm{LSPO}(<_{\mathrm{FO}(\lambda x[\pi_{price}(x)\leq 400])},<_{\mathrm{CPO}(<_{\mathrm{AO}(<,2)},<_{\mathrm{SO}(\mathrm{Sim}_{location},Battersea)})})}$$

The set of maxima is now $\{A, C\}$ and the subsequent ranks are $\{B\}, \{D\}, \{H, E\}$ and $\{F, G\}$. Cases E, F, G and H can still be recommended. But they are now lower in the ordering than products whose prices fall into Ann's budget.

The effect is more stark for Ben. His query is the same as Ann's, except the predicate that he feeds into the FO operator uses a value of £200 instead of £400. No products satisfy this predicate. But, since no products are eliminated, all products remain eligible for recommendation to Ben and will be recommended on the basis of how well they satisfy his other criteria (bedrooms and location).[4]

4.4   Tweaks

The Entrée system offers a natural form of query refinement [6]. The specific mechanism used for this by Entrée-style systems is known as the *tweak* or *critique*. The customer selects from the result set a product that is at least partly

---

[4] Ben might prefer it if the recommended products exceed his budget to the smallest extent possible. A more complex query can be used for this.

acceptable. The next query will, at heart, use similarity-based retrieval to find products that are similar to this selected product while satisfying the tweak (products that are *"like this but. . . "*). Interaction becomes a process of *navigation* through the product space based on critiques of selected products.

In [3], we argue that OBR gives a better semantics to tweaks than other approaches. Very simply, tweaks are encoded as filters but then converted into orders using Filter-Ordering, FO. As we saw earlier, this turns a hard constraint into a soft constraint. The system will prefer products that satisfy the filter but will not eliminate products that do not satisfy the filter. For example, suppose the customer likes the look of property E in Figure 3 but desires something cheaper. Since E's price is £500, we encode the tweak as $<_{FO(\lambda x[\pi_{price}(x)<500])}$. This tweak would be prioritised over the rest of the query, which is based on trying to match E's location and number of bedrooms:

$$<_{LSPO(<_{FO(\lambda x[\pi_{price}(x)<500])},<_{CPO(<_{AO(<,3)},<_{SO(Sim_{location},Chelsea)})})}$$

5   Diversity

As mentioned in Section 1, diversity is a property of a result set as a whole. Approaches to increasing diversity have incorporated a selection criterion additional to similarity [8] [9] & [1]. However, we believe that some of the query operators in Order-Based Retrieval have a semantics which, in the absence of exact matches, automatically selects diverse products.

For example, consider the AO operator, and an example of its use, Figure 4. One can easily imagine an alternative operator, which we will refer to as the Distance-Ordering operator, in which a distance function is used so that items are ordered solely by their distance from the 'ideal' value, v. With Distance-Ordering, one and three bedroom properties would appear *equal* second in the ordering, whereas in AO they are incomparable.

The reason AO can deliver a more diverse maxima can be explained by thinking further about the example. Suppose a case base of properties contains no two or three bedroom properties, but does contain one and four bedroom properties; and suppose that the query consists only of a requirement for a two bedroom property. If we apply Distance-Ordering and return only the maxima, the customer is shown only one bedroom properties. But, if we apply AO and return only the maxima, the customer is shown one and four bedroom properties. Thus, with AO, customers are shown properties to either side of their 'ideal'.

A more fundamental example is the CPO operator. Suppose we combine two orders $<_1$ and $<_2$ using CPO. Suppose case c_1 is better than case c_2 and is indeed the best case with respect to order $<_1$ but that case c_2 is better than case c_1 and indeed is the best case with respect to order $<_2$. In the ordering given by CPO, they will be incomparable and so, in some sense, they will be as good as each other. If one is in the maxima, the other will also be in the maxima. Similarity-based retrieval will only find these two cases to be indistinguishably good if they have exactly the same degree of similarity to the query, which is

not very likely and is hard to design for. We saw an example of exactly this
in Figure 7 where cases A and C were both in the maxima because case A
does best on *location* and C does best on *bdrms* (and no case does better on
both requirements). Hence, as a means of combining requirements, CPO can
give inherently more diverse results than weighted average, even if it is used to
combine conventional similarity measures.

We now report the results of an investigation into the diversity of result sets.

5.1   Order-Based Retrieval Experiments

We take each of the 794 properties in the whole case base in turn and use each
to construct a query. We use all six of its attributes. For the attributes that
have ordered types (*pricc*, *bdrms* and *bthrms*), we take the value from the case
and construct an order using AO, e.g. $<_{AO(<,2)}$. For the attributes that have
unordered types (*location*, *propType* and *furnished*), we take the value from
the case and construct an ordering using the similarity measure and SO, e.g.
$<_{SO(Sim_{location}, Battersea)}$. We combine all six order expressions using CPO.

For a given query, the remaining 793 cases are the case base, and we retrieve
the maxima from the case base for that query. As we explained previously, the
maxima is a set and may be different in size and contents for each query. For
some queries, the maxima was size 1, for others it was 2, and so on up to 39.
The nice thing about judging the quality of only the maxima (rather than some
best k) is that the maxima is the set that (according to OBR) best matches the
query; its size and contents are not open to arbitrary manipulation.

In Figure 9, for the numbers 1 to 39, we show the number of queries (out of
the 794) whose maxima were of that size.

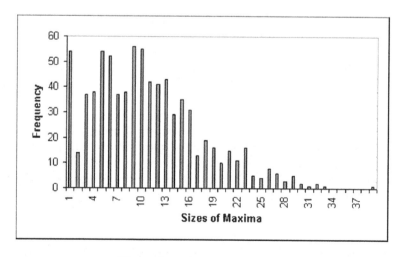

Fig. 9. Size of Maxima for OBR

```
Candidates := bk cases in CB that are most similar to q
R := {}
for i = 1 to k
    best := the c ∈ Candidates for which Quality(c, q, R) is highest
    insert best into R
    remove best from Candidates
end for
return R
```

Fig. 10. The Bounded Greedy (BG) Selection Algorithm

5.2 Bounded Greedy Selection Experiments

We compare OBR with an algorithm from [9] & [1]. Of several algorithms investigated in [9] & [1], the Bounded Greedy Selection algorithm (henceforth BG) gave the most improved retrieval quality while remaining cost-effective. BG retrieves bk cases using pure similarity-based retrieval. From these bk cases, it selects k cases, which will be the result set to be displayed to the customer. It selects the k cases based on their quality relative to the cases selected so far, see Figure 10.

Given query q, the quality of case c relative to the result set so far, R, is defined as follows [1]:

$$Quality(c, q, R) \,\hat{=}\, (1 - \alpha) \times \mathrm{Sim}(c, q) + \alpha \times RelDiversity(c, R) \qquad (2)$$

α is a factor that allows the importance of similarity and diversity to be changed. In line with [9] & [1], we use $\alpha = 0.5$. In Equation 2, similarity, Sim, is measured as per Equation 1. Diversity relative to the result set so far is defined as follows:

$$RelDiv(c, R) \,\hat{=}\, \begin{cases} 1 & \text{if } R = \{\} \\ \dfrac{\sum_{i=1...|R|} (1 - \mathrm{Sim}(c, r_i))}{|R|} & \text{otherwise} \end{cases} \qquad (3)$$

In the experiments, we use $b = 2$. The values we use for k are the sizes of the maxima found using OBR. For example, if some case c is taken to be the query and in OBR the maxima is of size 5, then when we do our experiments using BG, $k = 5$.

5.3 Evaluation Criteria

Having retrieved a result set for a given query q using OBR or using BG, we must evaluate the result set. We want to know whether the result set contains cases that are close to q, but we also want the set to be diverse.

Following [9] & [1], we will measure the average similarity of the result set to query q:

$$AvSim(R, q) \,\hat{=}\, \frac{\sum_{i=1...|R|} \mathrm{Sim}(r_i, q)}{|R|} \qquad (4)$$

There is a sense in which this is unreasonably helpful to BG. BG selects its cases in part using Sim and now we are evaluating its selection using Sim; as in [9]

& [1], we are measuring what we have already partly optimised for. Ideally a different measure (some kind of measure of how satisfied the customer is from a similarity point of view) should be used. But this is not available.

This advantage is given only to BG. OBR's result set will be the set of maxima; they are therefore, in some sense, the best matches to the query, but Sim will not necessarily judge them to be so. In particular, as highlighted in Section 4.2, due to the effects of normalisation, Sim, unlike OBR, is not treating all requirements as equally important.

We will also measure the diversity of the result set. The measure used here is the average dissimilarity between all pairs of cases in the result set [9] & [1] (taking the diversity of a singleton set to be 1):

$$Div(R) \hat{=} \begin{cases} 1 & \text{if } |R|= 1 \\ \dfrac{\sum_{i=1...|R|} \sum_{j=i...|R|}(1-Sim(r_i,r_j))}{\frac{n}{2}(n-1)} & \text{otherwise} \end{cases} \qquad (5)$$

For similar reasons, there is again an experimental bias towards BG.

5.4 Discussion of Results

The results are shown in Figures 11 and 12. For each maxima size, we take the *AvSim* and *Div* values of the queries that gave rise to maxima of that size and plot the average values.[5]

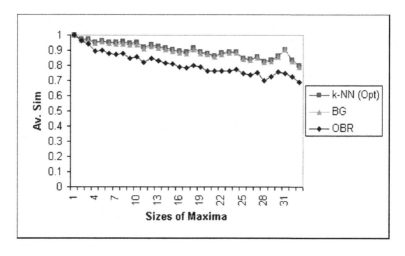

Fig. 11. Average Similarity

---

[5] Some queries gave rise to maxima of sizes 1-33. No queries gave rise to maxima of sizes 34-38. One query gave rise to a maxima of size 39. To avoid a 'gap' in the graphs, the *AvSim* and *Div* for this final query are not included in Figures 11 and 12. These unplotted values do not contradict the rest of the graphs.

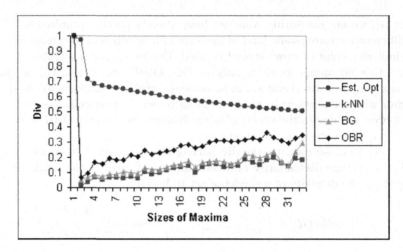

Fig. 12. Diversity

We also plot on the graphs some figures for comparison. In Figure 11, we plot the optimal average similarity. For query q, this is obtained by taking the k cases that are most similar (using Sim) to q (where, again, k is the size of OBR's maxima for q) and computing their average similarity. This is, of course, the familiar k-NN retrieval algorithm.

In Figure 12, we plot the diversity for k-NN but this time this is not the optimal value. So we also plot an estimated optimal diversity (where 'optimal' here simply means 'highest'). Our optimal diversity figure is computed differently from the way that Bradley & Smyth compute theirs [1]. They take the bk cases that are most similar to q, they form all subsets of size k from these cases, they compute the diversity of these subsets and they report the highest. We found that the diversity figure given by OBR frequently outperformed Bradley & Smyth's optimum. Their optimum is, of course, an optimum relative only to the bk most similar cases that they have retrieved for query q. It is not an optimum with respect to the case base as a whole. Since our diversity performance was so often higher than their optimum, we thought it better to plot a truer optimum in Figure 12. Ideally, we would obtain this by taking all subsets of size k from the entire case base, computing their diversity and plotting the highest. This is computationally very expensive, so we estimated it with a greedy algorithm. We take the most dissimilar pair of cases, then we add the next case that will most increase diversity. We keep doing this until we have a set of size k. Its diversity is our estimated optimum.

Figure 11 shows that BG generally outperforms OBR for average similarity and does extremely well compared to the optimum (k-NN). Indeed, on average over the 794 queries, the difference between the optimum and BG average similarities is only 0.009; the differences are so small that the two lines virtually coincide on the graph. This may be explained by the fact that in this case base there will often be regions comprising many properties having much the same location, much the same price and much the same facilities. When BG retrieves bk candidate cases ($b = 2$), these regions are often of a sufficient size that BG suffers only a small decrease in average similarity to the query.

The difference between the optimum and OBR is, on average, 0.081; the figures for OBR are, on average, 0.073 lower than those for BG. These results are perhaps unsurprising given the way the experiments favour BG.

As can be seen in Figure 12, despite the experimental bias, OBR outperforms BG quite considerably when it comes to diversity. The difference between the estimated optimum diversity and OBR's is, on average, 0.386, whereas for BG is it 0.479. OBR's diversity is, on average, 0.12 higher than k-NNs, whereas for BG it is 0.02. The difference between OBR's diversity and BG's is, on average, 0.093. The regions of similar cases that keep BG's average similarity figures high make it harder for BG to increase diversity; it does not decisively outperform k-NN. This is especially interesting because OBR is getting its diversity as a natural consequence of the way the operators are defined, rather than through some additional selection criterion.

Which of the two algorithms is better will depend, to some extent, on the trade-off to be made, in a particular context, between similarity to the query and diversity. No satisfactory way yet exists to measure this trade-off.

Efficiency will also be relevant. In the worst case, the OBR algorithm in Figure 6 carries out $n(n-1)/2$ comparisons. In other work, in the context of a distinct system concerned only with similarity-based retrieval [5], we describe a refinement of this algorithm which gives an improved complexity behaviour: the number of comparisons is bounded above by nm, where m is a constant for each given query, equal to the maximum 'width' of the partial order denoted by the query, e.g., in Figure 4, $m = 2$. In [9] the cost of BG is given as $n + \frac{k^3(b-1)}{4}$ comparisons. In practice, the performance of both algorithms is acceptable.

6   Conclusion

In conclusion, we believe that Order-Based Retrieval is a new, promising approach. It is more expressive than pure similarity-based retrieval; it gives a natural implementation to tweaks; and it can give diverse result sets.

There is much future work to be done, and we mention one major issue here. In OBR, the maxima is the set of best cases; its size is not open to manipulation. But there may be a requirement in a recommender system to present the customer with a minimum or maximum number of cases. If OBR's maxima is too small, subsequent 'ranks' can be displayed. But it will take further research to investigate ways of proceeding when the set of retrieved cases is too large. Options include: incorporating community-wide or customer-specific default orders to narrow the set; asking the customer a dynamically-chosen question to elicit a further customer requirement to narrow the set; or the use of a presentation strategy that requires less than the full set of cases to be displayed on the screen.

References

1. Bradley, K. & B. Smyth: Improving Recommendation Diversity, In D. O'Donoghue (ed.), *Procs. of the Twelfth Irish Conference on Artificial Intelligence and Cognitive Science*, pp.85–94, 2001.
2. Bridge, D.: Product Recommendation Systems: A New Direction, In R. Weber & C.G. von Wangenheim (eds.), *Procs. of the Workshop Programme at the Fourth International Conference on Case-Based Reasoning*, pp.79–86, 2001.
3. Bridge, D. & A. Ferguson: An Expressive Query Language for Product Recommender Systems, *Artificial Intelligence Review*, to appear, 2002.
4. Ferguson,A. & Bridge,D.G.: Partial Orders and Indifference Relations: Being Purposefully Vague in Case-Based Retrieval, in Blanzieri,E. & Portinale,L. (eds.), *Advances in Case-Based Reasoning (Procs. of the 5th European Workshop on Case-Based Reasoning)*, LNAI 1898, pp.74–85, Springer, 2000
5. Ferguson, A. & D. Bridge: Weight Intervals: Conservatively adding quantified uncertainty to similarity, In D. O'Donoghue (ed.), *Procs. of the Twelfth Irish Conference on Artificial Intelligence & Cognitive Science*, pp.75–84, 2001.
6. Hammond, K.J., R. Burke & K. Schmitt: Case Based Approach to Knowledge Navigation, In D.B. Leake (ed.), *Case-Based Reasoning — Experiences, Lessons and Future Directions*, pp.125–136, MIT Press, 1996.
7. Osborne, H.R. & D.G. Bridge: A Case Base Similarity Framework, In I. Smith & B. Faltings (eds.), *Advances in Case-Based Reasoning (Procs. of the Third European Workshop on Case-Based Reasoning)*, Lecture Notes in Artificial Intelligence 1168, pp.309–323, Springer, 1996.
8. Smyth, B. & P. Cotter: Surfing the Digital Wave: Generating Personalised TV Listings Using Collaborative, Case-Based Recommendation, In K.D. Althoff, R. Bergmann & L.K. Branting (eds.), *Case-Based Reasoning Research and Development (Procs. of the Third International Conference on Case-Based Reasoning)*, Lecture Notes in Artificial Intelligence 1650, pp.5612–571, Springer, 1999.
9. Smyth, B. & P. McClave: Similarity vs. Diversity, In D.W. Aha & I. Watson (eds.), *Case-Based Reasoning Research and Development (Procs. of the Fourth International Conference on Case-Based Reasoning)*, Lecture Notes in Artificial Intelligence 2080, pp.347–361, Springer, 2001.
10. Vollrath, I., W. Wilke & R. Bergmann: Case-Based Reasoning Support for Online Catalog Sales, *IEEE Internet Computing*, vol.2(4), pp.45–54, 1998.
11. Wilke, W., M. Lenz & S. Wess: Intelligent Sales Support with CBR, In Lenz, M., B. Bartsch-Spörl, H.-D. Burkhard & S. Wess (eds), *Case-Based Reasoning Technology: From Foundations to Applications*, Lecture Notes in Artificial Intelligence 1400, pp.91–113 Springer, 1998.

Digital Image Similarity
for Geo-spatial Knowledge Management

James D. Carswell[1], David C. Wilson[2], and Michela Bertolotto[2]

[1] Digital Media Centre, Dublin Institute of Technology, Dublin 2, Ireland
`jcarswell@dit.ie`
[2] Smart Media Institute, Department of Computer Science,
University College Dublin, Belfield, Dublin 4, Ireland
{`david.wilson,michela.bertolotto`}`@ucd.ie`

Abstract. The amount and availability of high-quality geo-spatial image data, such as digital satellite and aerial photographs, is increasing
dramatically. Task-based management of such visual information and
associated knowledge is a central concern for organisations that rely on
digital imagery. We are developing geo-spatial knowledge management
techniques that employ case-based reasoning as the core methodology. In
order to provide effective retrieval of task-based experiences that center
around geo-spatial imagery, we need to forward novel similarity metrics
for directly comparing the image components of experience cases. Based
on work in geo-spatial image database retrieval, we are building an effective similarity metric for geo-spatial imagery that makes comparisons
based on derived image features, their shapes, and the spatial relations
between them. This paper gives an overview of the geo-spatial knowledge
management context, describes our image similarity metric, and provides
an initial evaluation of the work.

1 Introduction

Advances in sensor/scanner technology have resulted in the constantly increasing volume and availability of geo-spatial datasets, such as collections of digital
satellite and aerial photographs. Moreover, the available imagery is becoming
more complex, depicting characteristics of the earth surface and topography that
are only visible in the near-infrared or microwave spectrum. The geosciences
and spatial information engineering have been greatly affected by this information explosion. Geo-spatial information systems, in particular, have become
crucial for addressing the problem of visual information overload by delivering
on-point geographic image data combined with relevant associated information,
and they play a key role in supporting the overarching task-based needs of organisations that rely on such information. Moreover, as geo-spatial information
systems are used to address specific tasks, the expert interactions, analyses, and
conclusions—based on relevant visual information—come to represent a substantial organizational knowledge asset.

For example, a company that uses geo-spatial data for architectural development projects may employ such a system to assist in selecting the optimal

S. Craw and A. Preece (Eds.): ECCBR 2002, LNAI 2416, pp. 58–72, 2002.

location for a new hanger at a major airport. From a task-based standpoint, the most relevant work product lies not merely in the applicable visual data, but in descriptions of why and how the information has been collected and to what ends it has been successfully (or unsuccessfully) employed. A clear advantage is provided by capturing and leveraging not only essential underlying information but also a measure of the human expertise involved in seeking out, distilling, and applying the information required for organisational tasks. This serves both to facilitate workflow by providing access to best-practice examples, as well as to grow a repository of task-based experience as a resource for support, training, and minimizing organisational knowledge-loss as a result of workforce fluctuations.

As part of an overall effort in intelligent geo-spatial information systems, we are developing case-based knowledge management support for libraries of geo-spatial imagery. The research draws on a substantial body of work in case-based knowledge management [39,35,18,46,6,7,32]. Our approach addresses task-based geo-spatial knowledge management by providing:

- digital image libraries for effective data organisation and efficient transmission to distributed clients
- sketch-based user interaction to provide a more natural mode of interaction in describing the context for retrieval
- a flexible task environment to support analysis and elucidation of relevant geo-spatial image information that can easily be integrated as part of existing workflow
- case-based tools to support intelligent capture and re-use of encapsulated task-based interactions and context

The challenges in the work are to integrate and tailor existing case-based methods to address specific needs for geo-spatial image information management, as well as to develop hybrid similarity measures that seamlessly integrate very different types of contextual knowledge afforded by query sketches, result images and metadata, image annotations, textual rationale, and other potential resource annotations (e.g., user voice/video recordings).

In order to provide effective retrieval of task-based experiences that center around geo-spatial imagery, we need to forward similarity metrics for directly comparing query sketches and image components of experience cases. Thus, in the first stage of the work, we are adapting and refining techniques developed for geo-spatial image database retrieval for use in the case-based components of the overall system. This paper describes our initial case-based similarity metric for geo-spatial imagery, which makes comparisons based on derived image features, their shapes, and the spatial relations between them. It is a straightforward derivation of work developed for image database retrieval [9,2,5]. Section 2 provides background on geo-spatial imagery, image retrieval, and integrations of CBR with imagery and GIS, and section 3 gives an overview of the task-based image retrieval context. Section 4 describes our approach to image indexing, while sections 5 and 6 respectively describe shape-based and relational components of image similarity. The paper goes on to describe the combined image similarity metric with a working example image query, and it concludes with brief discussion of future directions.

2 Background

This research draws on background in geo-spatial imagery, general approaches to image retrieval, and integrations of CBR with imagery and GIS.

2.1 Geo-spatial Imagery

Geo-spatial information represents the location, shape of, and relationships among geographic features and associated artifacts, including map and remotely sensed data. Two different formats are generally used to represent geo-spatial information: *raster* (digital images, with spatial position implicit in pixel ordering) and *vector* (layered coordinate representations with topographic and associated information, such as geographic maps and digital terrain models). In this research, we focus on managing the large quantities of geo-spatial information available in raster format, primarily digital aerial photos, satellite images, and raster cartography. Geo-spatial imagery is employed in a wide range of applications, such as intelligence operations, recreational and professional mapping, urban and industrial planning, and touristic systems. Typically, geo-spatial imagery will also include *metadata* information, such as: date and time of image acquisition; date and time of introduction to system; scale/resolution; location of the image, expressed in hierarchically arranged geographic entities (e.g., state, country, city); sensor information; and imagery type (e.g., black & white, colour, infrared).

2.2 Image Retrieval

Substantial research efforts within the computer vision community have been focused on retrieving specific images from a large database by querying the properties of these images [10,25,37,41,45]. Some notable prototypes for intelligent image retrieval have been developed, including [8,17,16,19,42,47]. Most of these efforts address the problem in the context of general-use applications, where the images stored in the database display substantial differences in their low-level properties, such as: colour (histogram matching), texture (image coarseness and contrast matching), and composition (dividing an image into homogeneous colour/texture regions and analysing the relative positions of those regions).

An inherent characteristic with geo-spatial images, however, is that they are usually very similar in terms of general low-level properties. Thus in geo-spatial applications, image retrieval approaches based on low-level properties are not very effective. In geo-spatial applications, images are better distinguished by the shape and spatial configuration of the objects they contain. Consequently, a better approach to measuring similarity in geo-spatial datasets relies on the use of queries based on these higher-level properties.

2.3   Case-Based Reasoning

A number of research efforts have investigated case-based reasoning as applied to tasks involving imagery, such as medical diagnosis [36,22,44], face recognition [40], architectural support [11], protein crystallization [29], and remotely sensed data [48]. Previous research in case-based reasoning has examined image recognition [38] and segmentation [43]. For an overview of the issues involved in integrating imagery with case-based reasoning, see [20]. Case-based reasoning has also been applied in sketch-based retrieval of architectural data [12,23], as well as for prediction in GIS applications [31,30,33,27,26].

Many of these case-based approaches rely on low-level image properties that are not appropriate for geo-spatial imagery. The spatial component in our domain also implies that there should not been any processing applied to the imagery (e.g., Fast Fourier Transforms) that transforms the raster image into the frequency domain before further operations begin. Closest in spirit to our work is [28], in which edge-image representations are used to index satellite imagery. While we plan to integrate some of the general techniques described in previous CBR research where applicable, we have chosen to base our image similarity metric on established work that defines measures tailored for geo-spatial imagery [9,2,5].

3   Task-Based Image Retrieval and Knowledge Management

A typical task-based query to our image repository is a straightforward request to a geo-spatial image database, and it could consist of specified metadata, semantic information, and a sketched configuration of image-objects [3,4]. The metadata criterion would include such information on image scale or location, while the semantic criterion would match against previously entered annotations (if any) about the type (purpose, etc.) of objects that should be contained within images of interest. The sketch would include information on desired image-objects and their configuration. For example, if the user decided to retrieve all images with airplanes, airplane hangers, and runways that match to a particular configuration, the query would:

- Process the metadata to retrieve all images that match to the specified criteria (e.g., images from Dublin).
- From this subset of images, use any available semantic information (e.g., airplanes, terminal) to further constrain the result set.
- From this subset of images, select imagery indexed by object-features that best match the user sketch.
- Process the spatial relations of the sketch scene on the last image subset and return a prioritized list of imagery as the query result.

The task-based image retrieval tools under development are an effective means for locating geo-spatial image information, and they provide the core

of the overall system. Alongside, we are developing tools for direct image manipulation, such as filters, transformations, highlighting, sketching, and post-it
type annotations. These will allow the user to identify regions of interest that
can be linked to clarifications, rationale, and other types of annotations (e.g.,
multimedia). The manipulations and annotations will not alter the underlying
images or geo-spatial information, rather they will be layered to provide a task-
specific view. This enables the capture and refinement of more general task-based
ideas and rationale. A typical interaction with the system, then, can capture the
sketch and geo-spatial query or queries posed by the user, the results that were
found to be useful, as well as the user's annotations of the results. All of the
contextual knowledge required to address the task goal can thus be captured as
an experience case, enabling an increasingly powerful cycle of proactive support,
with case-based suggestions based on task context.

As part of case-based retrieval of task experiences, we need to define a measure of similarity for directly comparing image components of experience cases,
one which works in conjunction with the task-based image retrieval system. In
doing so, we focus on the last two steps of the task-based retrieval.

4   Image Indexing

Image metadata and semantic information are used as part of the overall image
indexing scheme, but from the standpoint of computing image-level similarity
there are two main indexing dimensions: the edge-image representation and the
feature library representation [9].

4.1   Image Pre-processing

Upon insertion into the image library, images are pre-processed automatically
by first applying a high-pass edge enhancement filter and then applying a binary
threshold to the resulting image, such that only black or white pixels remain.
Spurious edges (of insignificant length) are also then removed by an additional
filtering step. This process produces the edge-image representation (of a given
raw image) on which shape similarity is computed. The edge-image (e.g., Figure 1b) thus contains only the boundary outlines of image-objects inherent to
its corresponding raw image (e.g., Figure 1a). The original raw image is then
stored along with its corresponding edge representation image.

4.2   Image Feature Library

The image feature library is a hierarchical arrangement of distinct feature outlines (i.e. image-object shapes) with links to image files where such features
appear. It can be likened to an inverted term index in collaborative filtering. At
the task-based level of retrieval, the feature library is used to reduce the search
space of a query from the entirety of a large image library to a substantially
reduced image set containing an abridged group of object-features.

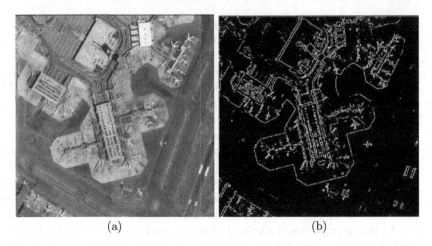

(a)   (b)

Fig. 1. Raw and Edge Representation Images.

From the standpoint of image-level similarity, the feature library defines a reduced vocabulary of canonical image-objects, subsets of which are used as image indices. This index is used as a proxy for the actual image in computing image-level similarity. The individual feature outlines that comprise the library are smaller edge-images representing individual features of interest. They are derived through interaction with the system, either from user query sketches or explicitly identified image regions of interest. The feature library is itself an internal case-based component [34], but a full description is beyond the scope of this paper.

When a new image is inserted into the image library, all of the features in the feature library are matched (using the similarity metric defined in section 7) against the new image to see if and where they match. If a feature-to-image match is above a system threshold, a link from this feature to this image (and vice versa) is established along with its location (i.e. the coordinates of the feature centroid within the image), and the coordinates of the minimum bounding rectangle (MBR) of this feature within the image.

When a new query feature is added to the feature library, it is matched against the entire image library to establish indexing links. Because the indexing process can be computationally expensive, index maintenance is an off-line process.

5   Matching Image-Objects: S_{sh}

An image is composed of spatial objects and their relations with the similarity between scenes described as a function of object similarity plus relation similarity [21]. Our similarity metric is based on a measure of object shape similarity (S_{sh}) and three measures of relational similarity: topology (S_{top}), orientation (S_{or}), and distance (S_{dist}).

The method we employ to match image-object features is derived from least-squares "area-based" matching [1], which involves the extraction and matching of conjugate patches of pixels according to a correlation of summed squared pixel gray-level density differences [24]. In essence, the query patch slides across the library image (translating, rotating, and scaling), until a best-matching position is found.

In contrast to the gray-level matching in traditional least-squares methods, we reduce the comparison to essential shape information content by considering only those pixels that carry image-object information (i.e., image-object edges). This is facilitated by the binary edge-image representation and provides for good shape matching at a substantially reduced computational cost.

In our similarity metric, individual query image-objects are matched against a library image, and the results are combined in the overall image level similarity measure. Given an image-object query (from a user sketch or the feature library), its number of rows and columns are noted along with the total number of pixels representing edges. The centroid of the image feature is calculated using the center of mass. The coordinates of the centroid pixel are then used as the origin for translation, rotation, and scaling during matching.

In order to account for local maxima, the library image is divided into a parameterized number (9 in practice) of disjoint regions, of equal or larger size to the query patch. The query patch is then matched within each of these regions in turn. In order to account for a feature being split across these regions, the query patch is also matched within each of the (16) overlap regions between the original divisions.

In matching a region, the query patch is divided into quadrants by its centroid. Each quadrant, then, measures the degree of match to its current location in the library image region by the extent of overlap in edge-pixels. Each edge-pixel in the quadrant contributes a vote either to stay (if it is already overlaps an image edge) or to move a certain distance in one of the cardinal directions (if it does not overlap). Move distance and direction are determined by the closest image edge. The individual pixel votes for direction and distance are summed, with higher weights given to shorter distances, to determine an overall shift for each quadrant.

From analysis of the edge pixel voting patterns, a decision is made to translate (quadrant votes in the same direction), scale (opposite quadrants vote in opposite directions), or rotate (quadrant votes follow a circular pattern) the query patch within the image region in order to acquire a better match. Typical distance values range from 0 to 10s of pixels in any direction with the maximum distance allowed being half the dimension of the query patch itself. Thus initial approximations for positioning the patch within the region are not required; if the patch is not in a suitable position within the image region, it will automatically move to the image content. This method also allows for occlusions of up to half of the query patch to be detected, as the patch can shift its origin (centroid pixel) right up to the border of the edge-image.

Once the patch is shifted into a new position, the process is repeated. Similar to the traditional least-squares approach, the solution is obtained after a set of iterations with parameterized boundary conditions on goodness of match (number of votes to stay exceed votes to move) and number of iterations (e.g., 20). The best-matched position for each library image region is recorded and the overall is used as the final matching position and percentage for the query patch in the library edge-image. When the query patch has settled on a match, its accuracy is determined by its matching percentage (i.e., by how many of its pixels continue to vote to stay put compared to the total number of pixels that constitute its edges).

6   Matching Image-Object Scenes

When query image-objects are matched to an image, their centroid coordinates within the image are recorded as well as the top left and bottom right coordinates of the query feature's minimum bounding rectangle, after scaling and rotation have taken place. Similarity for spatial relations on the image are determined through the use of the matched query features MBRs.

6.1   Matching Topology: S_{top}

Perhaps the most important of all spatial relations from a user's perspective is topology [14]. It is often more important, in composing a spatial query sketch, for a user to show that objects are positioned correctly relative to each other (disjoint, touching, overlapping, etc.) than to show their relative sizes or distances. It has been shown that topological relations can be derived automatically between pairs of simply connected regions (i.e., regions without holes, by determining their 4 intersection relations between their respective borders and interiors) [13]. More specifically, a 2x2 matrix is generated through the determination of whether the border b or interior i of region A intersects either the border or interior of region B. Taking into consideration the inconsistent relations, we are left with only 8 possible relations, shown in Figure 2. The 4 intersection method can be extended to describe a scene of n objects by building a nxn connectivity matrix whose elements consist of the relations between individual pairs of objects in the scene [15]. The result of such an operation gives a mathematical description of the topology of a scene that can be queried against for similarity. In defining our similarity measure, the degree of topological match is computed as a function of the number of steps between topological relation types (e.g., $disjoint \rightarrow meets$ is one step).

6.2   Matching Orientation: S_{or}

To overcome the lack of exterior orientation information in the query and image scenes, we use an intrinsic reference frame where the query/image-object orientation is in respect to *left-of* or *right-of* the features themselves. To do this, a

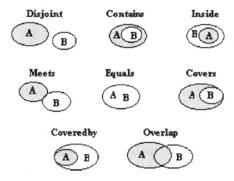

Fig. 2. Binary Topological Relations for Simply Connected Regions.

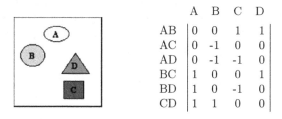

	A	B	C	D
AB	0	0	1	1
AC	0	-1	0	0
AD	0	-1	-1	0
BC	1	0	0	1
BD	1	0	-1	0
CD	1	1	0	0

Fig. 3. Example Image Scene and Corresponding Position Relation Matrix.

position relation matrix is built for each query/image scene. Since a scene comprised of two (or less) objects is trivial to discern (i.e., a scene could be rotated to suit any orientation), our approach assumes three (or more) scene objects. To build the position relation matrix for the scene depicted in Figure 3, an imaginary line connecting the centroid of Feature A to the centroid of Feature B is drawn. Feature A is arbitrarily considered as the *top* feature and Feature B the *bottom* feature. For every other feature (C through n) in the scene it is determined whether they lie *left-of* or *right-of* this line. Fixing the same features in both the query and image scenes to be either top or bottom renders any rotations in the scenes immaterial. The calculation of *left-of* or *right-of* is straightforward, given that we know (from the shape matching algorithm) the pixel coordinates of each feature's MBR in the image scene and each features actual boundary outline in the query scene. For example, if the MBR of Feature C in the image scene lies *left-of* this line, a value of -1 is placed in the position relation matrix. If Feature C's MBR lies *right-of* this line, a value of 1 is entered in the matrix and if Feature C's MBR lies somewhere along this extended line, a 0 is placed in the matrix.

After the remaining features of the scene are likewise added to the matrix, the imaginary line between Feature A and Feature B is deleted and redrawn between Feature A and Feature C with the process of determining *left-of* and *right-of* for the remaining features in the scene repeated. This entire procedure is repeated for every combination of features in the scene, i.e. there are $n(n-1)/2$ combinations

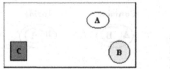

	AB	AC	BC
AB	1	1.74	2.3
AC	.57	1	1.32
BC	.44	.76	1

Fig. 4. Example Image Scene and Corresponding Distance Ratio Matrix.

of extended, imaginary lines that need to be tested against. For example, in the image scene of Figure 2, with 4 image-objects, there are 6 combinations of imaginary lines to be tested against, resulting in a 6x4 position relation matrix.

A position relation matrix is constructed for the query scene and image scene. A normalized correlation coefficient for the query/image scene is then calculated using Equation 1, to describe their respective similarities. This coefficient is scaled between 0 and 1 to give a total scene position matching percentage between the query and image-object configuration, independent of any arbitrary scene rotations.

$$NC = \frac{\sum ((I - \overline{I}) \cdot (Q - \overline{Q}))}{\sqrt{\sum (I - \overline{I})^2 \cdot \sum (Q - \overline{Q})^2}} \tag{1}$$

I and Q are the position relation matrices for the image and query scenes respectively. Similar to the extrinsic reference frame approach, distance is also required in order to distinguish properly between these configurations of spatial entities.

6.3   Matching Relative Distance: S_{dist}

Where no scale information on the query/image scene is provided a-priori, it is necessary to analyze the relative distances between image-objects. A square matrix of rank $n(n-1)/2$ (where n is the number of objects in the scene) can be built for every query/image scene. Each combination of image-object connection is set to a distance of 1 unit, and the distances to the other objects in the scene determined relative to this unit distance. Assuming an example scene of 3 objects, a 3x3 distance ratio matrix would be built (Figure 4).

The ratio approach to calculating the relative distances between objects does not require absolute scale information and is possible of course because the pixel coordinates of the image-object centroids are returned from the shape matching algorithm. The similarity between various query and image scenes, or more specifically their respective distance ratio matrices, is then determined through analysis of their normalized correlation coefficients (Equation 1) scaled between 0 and 1.

7   A Similarity Metric for Image Scenes

Our image-level similarity metric combines similarity measures for individual object shapes, as well as the topological, orientation, and relative distance relations between them [2]. We define a similarity function S that assesses the similarity between an image query scene Q and an image scene I in the image library as follows:

$$S(Q, I) = S_{sh}(Q, I) \cdot w_{sh} + S_{top}(Q, I) \cdot w_{top} + \qquad (2)$$
$$S_{or}(Q, I) \cdot w_{or} + S_{dist}(Q, I) \cdot w_{dist}$$

where:

- S_{sh} measures the degree of shape similarity between objects in Q and the corresponding objects in I. For example, assuming that $obj_1 \ldots obj_n$ are the objects in Q,

$$S_{sh}(Q, I) - \frac{\sum_{i=1}^{n} match\%(obj_i)}{n} \qquad (3)$$

  where $match\%(obj_i)$ is the matching percentage between object obj_i in Q and the corresponding object in I. We might further constrain the match by imposing that for each $i = 1 \ldots n$ $match\%(obj_i) > \epsilon$, with a given threshold ϵ;
- S_{top} measures the degree of similarity between the set of topological relations characterizing objects in Q and the topological relations among corresponding objects in I;
- S_{or} measures the degree of similarity between the set of orientation relations characterizing objects in Q and the orientation relations among corresponding objects in I;
- S_{dist} measures the degree of similarity between the set of distance relations characterizing objects in Q and the distance relations among corresponding objects in I;
- w_{sh}, w_{top}, w_{or}, and w_{dist} are positive weights that establish the relative importance of the individual similarity criteria; their sum must equal 1.

7.1   A Working Example

In this section we show an example of how four different query scenes (Figure 5), sketched by the user, match to a given image I (Figure 6). The query scenes comprise differing configurations of the same three object shapes; i.e. an outline of an airplane (obj_1), airplane hanger (obj_2), and runway (obj_3). A summary of the results of the similarity metric calculations for this example can be found in Table 1. For each of the four query scenes, Q_1, Q_2, Q_3, Q_4, we calculate the value of S using Equation 2.

From these results it can be seen that Query Scene 2 is the best-matched configuration for the given image. This agrees with what a human observer would choose as the best matched configuration since Query Scene 2 is plainly a rotation of the image, sketched at a significantly reduced scale. This demonstrates the ability of our approach to differentiate between arbitrary rotations and scaling of varying query/image scenes in addition to the capacity to distinguish between configurations and shapes of individual image-objects.

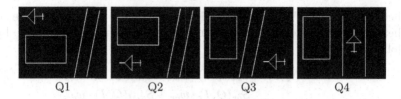

Fig. 5. Four Query Scenes.

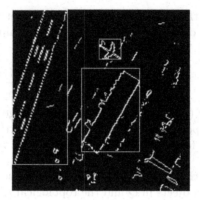

Fig. 6. Edge-Image with Superimposed MBRs.

Table 1. Similarity Results for the Four Query Scenes

	Query Scene			
	1	2	3	4
S_{sh}	82.3	82.3	82.3	82.3
S_{top}	100	100	100	66.7
S_{or}	.5	100	79	81
S_{dist}	81.2	86.7	33.7	35
S	66	92.3	73.8	66.3

8 Conclusion

We have introduced a case-based reasoning approach to knowledge management in the context of task-based geo-spatial imagery retrieval. As a foundation
for the building the overall case-based knowledge management component, we
have derived an effective image-level similarity metric for directly comparing
the image components of experience cases. The similarity metric operates in the
raster/spatial domain and uses the shape of single image-object features together
with their topological, orientation, and distance relations as matching primitives.
We went on to present a working example as a practical illustration of how the
similarity metric evaluates four query scenes for a given image.

While our first priority is to fully realize case-based support at the geo-spatial
task-based level, our long-term goals include an extension of the image-matching

technique for temporal analysis. By relaxing object/relation constraints and analyzing matching percentages, we expect to develop the temporal change detection in areas such as: object elimination, changes in object shape, and change in location. With the increasing use of geo-spatial information both in professional and recreational contexts, we expect that case-based approaches will prove invaluable in ameliorating problems of visual information overload.

References

1. F. Ackerman. Digital image correlation: Performance and potential application in photogrammetry. *Photogrammetric Record*, 11(64):429–439, 1984.
2. P. Agouris, M. Bertolotto, J. D. Carswell, C. Georgiadis, and A. Stefanidis. Scale and orientation-invariant scene similarity metrics for image queries. *International Journal of Geographical Information Science*, 16, 2002.
3. P. Agouris, J. Carswell, and A. Stefanidis. An environment for content-based image retrieval from large spatial databases. *ISPRS Journal of Photogrammetry & Remote Sensing*, 54(4):263–272, 1999.
4. P. Agouris, J. Carswell, and A. Stefanidis. Sketch-based image queries in topographic databases. *Journal of Visual Communication and Image Representation*, 10(2):113–129, 1999.
5. Peggy Agouris, Michela Bertolotto, James D. Carswell, and Anthony Stefanidis. A scene similarity metric for matching configurations of image objects. In *Proceedings of the XIX ISPRS Congress*, Amsterdam, 2000.
6. D. Aha, I. Becerra-Fernandez, F. Maurer, and H. Muñoz-Avila, editors. *Proceedings of the AAAI-99 Workshop on Exploring Synergies of Knowledge Management and Case-Based Reasoning*. AAAI Press, 1999.
7. I. Becerra-Fernandez and D. Aha. Case-based problem solving for knowledge management systems. In *Proceedings of the Twelfth Annual Florida Artificial Intelligence Research Symposium*, pages 219–223. AAAI, 1999.
8. C. Carson, S. Belongie, H. Greenspan, and J. Malik. Region-based image querying. In *Proceedings of the IEEE Workshop on Content-Based Access of Image and Video Libraries*, pages 42–49, San Juan, Puerto Rico, 1997.
9. J. Carswell. *Using Raster Sketches for Digital Image Retrieval*. PhD thesis, University of Maine, Orono, Maine, USA, 2000.
10. S.D. Cohen and L.J. Guibas. Shape-based indexing and retrieval; some first steps. In *Proceedings of the 1996 ARPA Image Understanding Workshop*, volume 2, pages 1209–1212, 1996.
11. Carl-Helmut Coulon. Image retrieval without recognition. In *First European Workshop on Case-Based Reasoning (EWCBR'93), Posters and Presentations*, volume 2 of *SEKI-Report 93-12-2*, pages 399–402, 1993.
12. Ellen Yi-Luen Do and Mark D. Gross. Reasoning about cases with diagrams. In *American Society of Civil Engineers (ASCE) 3rd Congress on Computing in Civil Engineering*, pages 314–320, 1996.
13. M. Egenhofer and R. Franzosa. Point-set topological spatial relations. *International Journal of Geographical Information Systems*, 5(2):161–174, 1991.
14. M. Egenhofer and D. Mark. Naive geography, spatial information theory - a theoretical basis for gis. In A. Frank and W. Kuhn, editors, *Lecture Notes in Computer Science*, pages 1–15, 1995.

15. M. Egenhofer and J. Sharma. Topological consistency. In *Proceedings of the 5th International Symposium on Spatial Data Handling*, pages 335–343, 1992.
16. D.A. Forsyth et al. Finding pictures of objects in large collections of images. In *Proceedings of the ECCV 96 Workshop on Object Representation*, 1996.
17. M. Flickner et al. Query by image and video content: The QBIC system. *IEEE Computer*, 28(9):23–32, 1995.
18. Kurt Fenstermacher and Carsten Tautz, editors. *Proceedings of the ICCBR-01 Workshop on Case-Based Reasoning Approaches for Process-Oriented Knowledge Management*. 2001.
19. C. Frankel, M. Swain, and W. Athitsos. Webseer: An image search engine for the world wide web. Technical Report TR-96-14, Department of Computer Science, University of Chicago, 1996.
20. J. Glasgow and I. Jurisica. Integration of case-based and image-based reasoning. In *Proceedings of the AAAI-98 Workshop on Case-Based Reasoning*, 1998.
21. R. Goyal and M. Egenhofer. Cardinal directions between extended spatial objects. *IEEE Transactions on Knowledge and Data Engineering*, 2000.
22. Morten Grimnes and Agnar Aamodt. A two layer case-based reasoning architecture for medical image understanding. In *Proceedings of EWCBR-96*, pages 164–178, 1996.
23. M. Gross, C. Zimring, and E. Do. Using diagrams to access a case library of design. In *Proceedings of the 1994 International Conference on Artificial Intelligence in Design*, pages 129–144. Kluwer, 1994.
24. A.W. Gruen and E.P. Baltsavias. Geometrically constrained multiphoto matching. *Photogrammetric Engineering and Remote Sensing*, 1987.
25. V.N. Gudivada and V.V. Raghavan. Design and evaluation of algorithms for image retrieval by spatial similarity. *ACM Transactions on Information Systems*, 13(2):115–144, 1995.
26. A. Holt and G. L. Benwell. Case-based reasoning and spatial analysis. *Journal of the Urban and Regional Information Systems Association*, 8(1):27–36, 1996.
27. A. Holt and G. L. Benwell. Applying case-based reasoning techniques in GIS. *The International Journal of Geographical Information Science*, 13(1):9–25, 1999.
28. B. Jose, B. P. Singh, S. Venkataraman, and R. Krishnan. Vector based image matching for indexing in case based reasoning systems. In *Proceedings of GWCBR-96*, 1996.
29. I. Jurisica, P. Rogers, J. Glasgow, S. Fortier, J. Luft, D. Bianca, and G. DeTitta. Image-feature extraction for protein crystallization: Integrating image analysis and case-based reasoning. In *Proceedings of the Thirteenth Annual Conference on Innovative Applications of Artificial Intelligence (IAAI-2001)*, pages 73–80, 2001.
30. Daniel Kaster, Heloisa Vieira Rocha, and Claudia Bauzer Medeiros. Case-based reasoning applied to environmental modeling with GIS. In *Proceedings of GIScience 2000*, 2000.
31. A. Khattak and H. Renski. PLAN<>HOV: A case-based reasoning planning tool for high-occupancy-vehicle lane analysis in a GIS environment. *Transportation Research Record*, 1682:18–27, 1999.
32. H. Kitano and H. Shimazu. The experience sharing architecture: A case study in corporate-wide case-based software quality control. In D. Leake, editor, *Case-Based Reasoning: Experiences, Lessons, and Future Directions*, pages 235–268. AAAI Press, Menlo Park, CA, 1996.

33. Yu Ting Hung Ko-Wan Tsou, Yao-Lin Chang. A case-based urban planning support system using an integrated combination of geographical information systems and remote sensing. In *Proceedings of the 21st Asian Conference on Remote Sensing*, 2000.
34. D. Leake. Case-based CBR: Capturing and reusing reasoning about case adaptation. *International Journal of Expert Systems*, 1997.
35. David B. Leake and David C. Wilson. A case-based framework for interactive capture and reuse of design knowledge. *Applied Intelligence*, 14(1), 2001.
36. R. T. Macura and K. J. Macura. MacRad: Case-based retrieval system for radiology image resource. In *Proceedings of ICCBR-95*, 1995.
37. R. Mehrotra and J. Gray. Similar-shape retrieval in shape data management. *IEEE Computer*, 28(9):57–62, 1995.
38. Alessandro Micarelli, Alessandro Neri, and Giuseppe Sansonetti. A case-based approach to image recognition. In *Proceedings of EWCBR-2000*, pages 443–454, 2000.
39. Mirjam Minor and Steffen Staab, editors. *Proceedings of the German Workshop on Experience Management*. 2002.
40. A. D. Narasimhalu. CAFIIR: An image based CBR/IR application. In *Proceedings of the 1993 AAAI Spring Symposium on Case-Based Reasoning and Information Retrieval*, pages 70–77, 1993.
41. V.E. Ogle. Chabot: Retrieval from a relational database of images. *IEEE Computer*, pages 23–32, September 1995.
42. A. Pentland, R. W. Picard, and S. Scarloff. Photobook: Content-based manipulation of image databases. *International Journal of Computer Vision*, 18(3):233–254, 1996.
43. P. Perner. An architeture for a cbr image segmentation system. *Engineering Applications of Artificial Intelligence*, 12(6):749–759, 1999.
44. P. Perner. CBR-based ultra sonic image interpretation. In *Proceedings of EWCBR-2000*, pages 479–481, 2000.
45. R.W. Pickard and T.P. Minka. Vision texture for annotation. *Multimedia Systems*, 3(1):3–14, 1995.
46. *Proceedings of GWCBR-01: Knowledge Management by Case-Based Reasoning: Experience Management as Reuse of Knowledge*. 2001.
47. S. Sclaroff, L. Taycher, and M. La Cascia. Imagerover: A content-based image browser for the world wide web. In *Proceedings of the IEEE Workshop on Content-Based Access of Image and Video Libraries*, pages 2–9, 1997.
48. S. Venkataraman, R. Krishnan, and K. Rao. A rule-rule-case based system for image analysis. In *First European Workshop on Case-Based Reasoning (EWCBR'93), Posters and Presentations*, volume 2 of *SEKI-Report 93-12-2*, pages 410–414, 1993.

Poetry Generation in COLIBRI

Belén Díaz-Agudo, Pablo Gervás, and Pedro A. González-Calero

Dep. Sistemas Informáticos y Programación
Universidad Complutense de Madrid, Spain
{belend, pgervas, pedro}@sip.ucm.es

Abstract. CBROnto is an ontology that incorporates common Case-Based Reasoning (CBR) terminology and serves as a domain-independent framework to design CBR applications. It is the core of COLIBRI, an environment to assist during the design of knowledge intensive CBR systems that combine cases with various knowledge types and reasoning methods. CBROnto captures knowledge about CBR tasks and methods, and aims to unify case specific and general domain knowledge representational needs. CBROnto specifies a modelling framework to describe reusable CBR Problem Solving Methods based on the CBR tasks they solve. This paper describes CBROnto's main ideas and exemplifies them with an application to generate Spanish poetry versions of texts provided by the user.

1   Introduction

Even though any Case-Based Reasoning (CBR) system relies on a set of previous specific experiences, its reasoning power can be improved through the explicit representation and use of general knowledge about the domain. Our approach to CBR is towards integrated knowledge based systems (KBS) that combine case specific knowledge with models of general domain knowledge. Our ongoing work is the development of COLIBRI (Cases and Ontology Libraries Integration for Building Reasoning Infrastructures), an environment to assist during the design of knowledge intensive CBR (KI-CBR) systems [2,4] that combine concrete cases with various knowledge types and reasoning methods.

COLIBRI's architecture is influenced by knowledge engineering approaches such as Role Limiting Methods [11], CommonKADS [12] or Components of Expertise [13], where a KBS is viewed as consisting of separate but interconnected collaborating components. Typically, components of a KBS include domain knowledge and Problem Solving Methods (PSMs), that represent commonly occurring, domain-independent problem-solving strategies.

COLIBRI views KI-CBR systems as consisting of collaborating knowledge components, and distinguishes different types of knowledge [14]. *Ontologies* describe the structure and vocabulary of the *Domain Knowledge* that refers to the actual collection of statements about the domain. *Tasks* correspond to the goals that must be achieved. *PSMs* capture the problem-solving behavior required to perform the goals of a task. And *Inferences* describe the primitive reasoning steps during problem solving.

S. Craw and A. Preece (Eds.): ECCBR 2002, LNAI 2416, pp. 73–87, 2002.

The core of the COLIBRI architecture is CBROnto, an ontology that incorporates common CBR terminology and problem solving knowledge that serves as a domain-independent framework to design KI-CBR systems [5]. CBROnto is formalized in LOOM [10] a Description Logics (DLs) system on top of which COLIBRI is built. From a general perspective CBROnto can be considered a knowledge representation ontology [14] that captures representation primitives commonly used in the case-based representation languages. Our aim is to propose a rich framework to represent cases based on the terminology from the CBROnto together with a reasoning system that works with such representations. We work with a structured case representation where individuals are concept instances and concepts are organized in a hierarchy with inheritance. In our approach, cases are linked within a semantic network of domain knowledge and will be described by using both the domain vocabulary provided by the domain model, and the CBR vocabulary provided by CBROnto. Another facet of CBROnto is as an unifying framework that structures and organizes different types of knowledge in KI-CBR systems according to the role that each one plays. CBROnto terms serve as a bridge that allows the connection between expert knowledge and previously defined domain ontologies, and helps in discovering and modelling the knowledge needed for a CBR system. As a last facet, CBROnto is a task and method ontology whose contents are described in the next section.

2   CBROnto as a Task and Method Ontology

A useful way of describing problem solving behavior is in terms of the tasks to be solved, the goals to be achieved, the methods that will accomplish those tasks, and the domain knowledge that those methods need. A description along these lines is referred to as a *knowledge level description*. Although various authors have applied knowledge level analysis to CBR systems, the most important of these efforts is the well-known CBR task structure developed by Agnar Aamodt and Enric Plaza [1] influenced by the Components of Expertise Methodology [13]. At the highest level of generality, they describe the general CBR cycle by four tasks: *Retrieve* the most similar case/s, *Reuse* its/their knowledge to solve the problem, *Revise* the proposed solution, and *Retain* the experience. The four CBR tasks each involve a number of more specific subtasks. There are methods to solve tasks, that either decompose a task in subtasks or solve it directly. CBROnto includes a task ontology influenced by Aamodt and Plaza's structure at the first level and identifies a number of alternative methods for each task, where each one of the methods sets up different subtasks, that must be solved in their turn. This kind of task-method-subtask analysis is carried on to a level of detail where the tasks are primitive with respect to the available knowledge.

CBROnto includes a library of PSMs associated to the CBROnto tasks. The CBROnto PSMs are described by relating them to terms within its ontology of tasks, methods and domain characteristics. The method ontology includes method description language terms used to formalize PSMs and defines concepts and relationships that are used by the methods. In [5] CBROnto's method description language is described together with a mapping mechanism to bridge the gap between domain knowledge and PSMs based on a DLs classification strategy. The explicit representation of knowledge requirements based on the CBROnto terminology makes easy to identify and solve the PSM's lack of knowledge.

COLIBRI uses an automatic, general and recursive task resolution mechanism that starts with the task to solve, and finds the alternative methods whose competence subsumes this task. Decomposition methods divide the task in subtasks and the resolution process is applied recursively for each subtask. Resolution methods finalize recursion and solve the task:

Resolve (iT)
1. Get the method individual to resolve the task: iM
2. Get the method functional specification iFS
3. Get the method requirements iReq
4. If iM is a decomposition_method,
        Applying iFS answers with the sequence of subtaks
        to solve: iST$_1$, ..., iST$_n$
        ResolveSeq(iST$_n$, ResolveSeq(iST$_n$ $_1$, ... , ResolveSeq(iST$_2$, Resolve(iST$_1$))...))
    Else   % iM is a resolution method
        Applying iFS with iReq solves the task

When designing a new CBR application, COLIBRI offers alternative methods whose competence subsumes this task. The CBR system designer fixes one (or more) preferred method to solve the task in the application, and configure it according to the required behavior. We distinguish between three types of inputs (or requirements) to configure a method:

- The method *knowledge requirements* represent knowledge elements that the method uses and that must be defined before the method can work, such as similarity measures or relevance criteria for retrieval.
- The method *input requirements* are external inputs to the method, i.e., they are not represented as explicit elements integrated within the domain knowledge. These inputs are fixed by the CBR application designer and will be shared by all the method executions.
- The method *parameter requirements* are also external inputs to the method, but they change within different executions of the method (for example, the query). They are specified by the final user of the CBR application.

The following sections introduce some of the CBROnto methods organized around the tasks they resolve, i.e. their competence.

2.1   Retrieval Methods

Retrieval methods are those whose competence is the retrieval task. CBROnto formalizes several retrieval methods that have been described in [3,4] and that are summarized here. Each retrieval method decomposes the retrieval task into one or more of the following subtasks that are solved themselves by methods that depends on the retrieval method:

- *Obtain cases.* Select the initial case set (CS) to apply the following subtasks.
- *Assess similarity.* Assess the similarity between the query and each one of the cases in CS.

– *Select cases.* Select the case or cases to be returned as retrieval result based on the similarity assessment.

The *computational method* computes all the similarity values during the retrieval process. The CBROnto similarity framework allows representing, in a declarative way, several alternatives to compute numerical similarity values for complex case representations, where the similarity knowledge contained in the domain knowledge base participates in the similarity assessment.

The *relevance criteria method* uses the query language to enable the user to describe the current situation and interests. Relevance criteria are defined as the criteria according to which the system asserts that a case is relevant to a problem and more relevant than any other cases. CBROnto uses relevance criteria expressed in first order logic using LOOM, which allows to express complex conditions that involve any number of cases interrelated by multiple relationships.

Other method used in the example is the *representational method* that assigns similarity meaning to the path joining two cases in the case organization structure and the domain knowledge base, and retrieval is accomplished by traversing that structure starting from the position of the query. We have applied this choice using an *instance classification method* [4] that uses the subsumption links to define the distance between two individuals. The usefulness of this kind of approach will depend on the knowledge structure where the cases are located.

Besides the retrieval methods, CBROnto –mainly through its relation hierarchy– allows to represent different *similarity types* depending on the contributing terms, namely it allows defining different similarity types depending on a semantic classification of the attributes –relations– below the CBROnto terms.

2.2   Adaptation and Revision Methods

CBROnto's adaptation methods are based on using domain independent knowledge in the form of transformation operators [8]. Adaptation knowledge is made up of a set of abstract transformation operators (as SUBSTITUTE, ADD and REMOVE) and memory search strategies to find the information in the domain knowledge, needed to apply these operators.

In this paper we describe one adaptation method that is based on substituting some elements in the retrieved case according to the query. Substitutes are searched in the domain model by using memory search strategies. CBROnto provides domain independent strategies and the mechanisms for the domain expert to add specific domain memory search strategies. Besides, other memory search strategies are learned from user's interactions. A memory search strategy goal is to find an item satisfying certain restrictions. That is why some of the methods used to solve the memory search task are shared with the case retrieval task. For example, to find candidates to substitute element i in the solution we can use the computational method with domain specific similarity measures using i as the query, or use the instance classification method to get instances classified near i in the hierarchy, or use the relevance criteria method to retrieve instances satisfying a given criteria of similarity regarding i.

The method of adaptation by substitution leads to the following subtasks:

- *Copy solution task*
- *Modify solution task* leads to the subtasks (cycle):
  - *Find adaptable parts task*
  - *Apply substitution* leads to the subtasks (cycle):
    * *Find substitutes task*
    * *Select substitute task*
    * *Substitute item task*
    * *Validate task*

If the memory search process performed during the find substitutes task does not find acceptable items, the substitute item task will not be performed. After adaptation, the revision task (when manual) allows the user to substitute an item. The learning methods learn both the failed and the successfully applied memory search strategies, and the manually added substitute. Revision Methods are those whose competence is the *Revise task*, that is decomposed in two subtasks: system revision and user revision. Only one of them is mandatory, when both are specified they are solved in sequence.

The revision task leads to the following subtasks (cycle). Note that each loop of the cycle finds one problem and tries to repair it.

- *Evaluation task*
- *Repair task* leads to the subtasks:
  - *Find repair strategy task*
  - *Apply repair strategy task*

In this paper we do not explain user revision method, but exemplify the self revision method where the evaluation and repair tasks are solved by the self evaluation and repair methods, respectively. Self evaluation is based on DLs classification as it compares the classification between the adapted case and the retrieved case. The concepts under which the retrieved case is classified in the domain model are used as declarative descriptions of the properties that should be maintained by the adapted case after transformations. Namely, substitutions must not alter the classification of the case. If they do, the case requires reparation. the repair needs are identified by the automatic classification of the adapted case under a certain type of problem. Repair strategies are linked to the concepts representing adaptation problems, and, thus, can be directly obtained after every classification of the problem case. When it fails the user will be in charge of repairing the case. Our approach is related with the one proposed in [9] where adaptation cases include knowledge about one-step transformations to solve a type of problems.

This generic method depends on the type of problems and repair strategies that are specifically identified and represented for each domain. We are using an idea that is common for other automatic revision methods, namely, the need of an explicit representation of the system task, i.e., the goals that are required for a case to be correct. Our explicit model of the domain allows representing these goals as classification properties over the adapted case, i.e., the case is correct if it is classified according to certain concepts. We typically use the classification of the retrieved case as the goals to be satisfied by the adapted case. The adapted case is initialized to an exact copy of the retrieved case that, classified under the concepts; after the resolution of the modify task it might not be recognized as an instance of some of these concepts. The repair task is in charge of repairing these failures. The semantic definitions of the domain concepts allows to know why the individual has not be recognized as an instance of a certain concept.

The self repair method uses as the correction measure the conjunction of the concept definitions that must be satisfied by a correct case after adaptation. The evaluation method is based on the LOOM instance recognition mechanism.

3   Implementing Poetry Generation with COLIBRI

Composing poetry is an art not particularly well suited for algorithmic formulation. However, for the specific case of formal poetry, it does have certain overall characteristics that have to be met by any candidate solution. What is particularly interesting from the point of view of illustrating the operation of COLIBRI is the fact that the description of these characteristics involve a complex set of interacting concepts that have to be taken into account.

Another reason involved in the choice of poetry generation as an example of the use of COLIBRI is the existence of previous work along similar lines [6,7] –developed in terms of CBR but not adhering to the CBROnto concepts and the COLIBRI way of chaining them together to form a CBR application– provides a useful reference point from which to discuss the possible advantages and disadvantages of the approach.

The specific process that has been chosen to illustrate this point is conceptually based on a procedure universally employed when not-specially-talented individuals need to personalise a song, for instance, for a birthday, a wedding, or a particular event: pick a song that everybody knows and rewrite the lyrics to suit the situation under consideration. This particular approach to the problem of generating customised lyrics or poetry has the advantage of being easily adapted to a formal CBR architecture. No claims whatsoever regarding the general suitability of this approach for poetry composition in a broad sense should be read into this particular choice.

3.1   Basic Rules of Spanish Poetry

Formal poetry in Spanish is governed by a set of rules that determine a valid verse form and a valid strophic form. A given poem can be analysed by means of these rules in order to establish what strophic form is being used. Another set of rules is applied to analyse (or *scan*) a given verse to count its metrical syllables.

Given that words are divided into syllables and each word has a unique syllable that carries the prosodic stress, the constraints that the rules have to account for are the following:

Metric Syllable Count. Specific strophic forms require different number of syllables to a line. Metric syllables may be run together thereby shortening the syllable count of the line involved. When a word ends in a vowel and the

```
(defconcept Poem :is                    (defconcept Word-occurrence :is
  (:and Domain-concept                    (:and Domain-concept
        (:all has-stanza Stanza)                (:all precedes Word-occurrence)
        (:at-least 1 has-stanza)))              (:at-most 1 precedes)
                                                (:the of-word Word)))
(defconcept Stanza :is
  (:and Domain-concept                  (defconcept Non-final-word-occurrence :is
        (:all has-line Poem-line)         (:and Word-occurrence
        (:at-least 1 has-line)))                (:exactly 1 precedes)))

(defconcept Poem-line :is               (defconcept Word :is
  (:and Line                              (:and Domain-Concept
        (:all has-word Word-occurrence)         (:the text String)
        (:at-least 1 has-word)                  (:the syllables Number)
        (:the first-word Word-occurrence)       (:the stress Number)
        (:the rhyme String)                     (:the rhyme String)
        (:the syllables Number)                 (:the stVowel Number)
        (:all follows-on Poem-line)             (:the endVowel Number)
        (:at-most 1 follows-on)))               (:all has-POSTag POSTag)
                                                (:at-least 1 has-POSTag)))
```

Fig. 1. Structural definitions for the poetry domain.

following word starts with a vowel, the last syllable of the first word and the first syllable of the following word constitute a single syllable. This is known as *synaloepha*, and it is one of the problems that we are facing.

Word Rhyme. Each strophic form requires a different rhyming pattern.

Stanza or Strophic Form. For the purpose this application only poems of the following regular strophic forms are considered: *cuarteto*, a stanza of four lines of 11 syllables where the two outer lines rhyme together and the two inner lines rhyme together; and *terceto*, a stanza of three lines of 11 syllables where the either the two outer lines rhyme together or the three lines have independent rhymes.

3.2   Poetry Domain Knowledge Ontology

The COLIBRI approach to building KI-CBR systems takes advantage of the explicit representation of domain knowledge. allowing to integrate existing ontologies about a particular domain of application. To our regret, we were unable to locate an existing ontology about formal Spanish poetry. An initial sketch of such an ontology has been developed for purposes of illustration, resulting in a knowledge base containing 86 concepts, 22 relations and 606 individuals.

Figure 1 shows the LOOM definitions needed to represent the structure of a poem, a text made up of words, and built up as a series of stanzas, which are groups of a definite number of lines of a specific length in syllables, satisfying a certain rhyme pattern. Going from the parts to the whole, each word is represented as an individual which is an instance of the domain concept *Word* and is described in terms of the following attributes: the name of that particular word (*text*), the number of syllables that the word has (*syllabes*), the position of the stressed syllable of the word counted from the beginning of the word (*stress*), the rhyme of the word (*rhyme*), whether the word begins with a vowel (*stVowel*), whether the word ends in a vowel (*endVowel*), and the part-of-speech tags associated with that word (*has-POSTag*).

```
(defconcept Terceto :is                    (defconcept Terceto-uno-tres :is
  (:and Stanza                               (:and Terceto
        (:exactly 3 has-line)                      (:relates rhymes-with first-line
        (:the first-line Endecasilabo)                                  third-line)))
        (:the second-line Endecasilabo)
        (:the third-line Endecasilabo)))   (defrelation rhymes-with :is
                                             (:satisfies (?x ?y)
(defconcept Endecasilabo :is                 (:and (Poem-line ?x)
  (:and Poem-line                                  (Poem-line ?y)
        (:fillers syllables 11)))                  (:for-some ?z
                                                     (:and (rhyme ?x ?z)
(defconcept Rhymed-poem-line :is                          (rhyme ?y ?z)))))
  (:and Poem-line
        (:exactly 1 rhymes-with)))
```

Fig. 2. Definition of a *terceto* stanza

In our model of the domain we distinguish between words –instances of *Word*– and particular word occurrences –instances of the domain concept *Word-occurrence*. In the representation of the poems we use a different individual for each occurrence of a particular word, though various individuals may be referring back to the same instance of *Word*. Each occurrence is related to the word it represents through the *of-word* relation, and with the word occurrence that follows it in a line through the *precedes*.

A line is represented as an instance of *Poem-line*, which, in addition to a number of word occurrences, represents the rhyme, the number of syllables, whether the sentence follows on onto the next line of the poem, and, for efficiency reasons, which one is the first word of the line. Each *Stanza* is built up from a number of *Poem-lines*, and each *Poem* is related to the stanzas that make it up.

Using the basic vocabulary we can define different types of stanza such as the one shown in Figure 2. A *Terceto* is defined as a stanza of three lines of eleven syllables. Although not shown in the figure, the relation *has-line* subsumes *first-line*, *second-line* and *third-line*, and, therefore, *Terceto* is a *Stanza* with *at-least* 1 *has-line*. The lines of a *Terceto* are *Endecasilabos* defined as *Poem-lines* where 11 is the value of the attribute *syllables*. Finally, a *Terceto-uno-tres* is a *Terceto* where the two outer lines rhyme together. The model identifies that two lines rhyme together when a common rhyme exists between them.

3.3   The Cases

Cases describe a solved problem of poem composition. We describe cases using the CBROnto case description language and domain knowledge terminology. Although different possibilities can be explored, for the sake of simplicity we choose a case where both description and solution is a given poem.

In COLIBRI the definition of the structure of the cases is part of the process of integrating the domain knowledge within CBROnto, in order to bridge the gap between domain terminology and CBR terminology. Integration is based on classification, domain concepts and relations are marked as subconcepts and subrelations of CBROnto concepts and relations. In this way, the domain-independent PSMs can be applied to the domain-specific information.

slgt2:PoetryCase								
description	poe-slgt2:Poem							
solution	poe-slgt2:Poem							
	has-stanza	st1-poe-slgt2:Stanza						
		first-line	l1-st1-poe-slgt2:Poem-line					
			first-word	no221:Word-occurrence				
			rhyme	ada				
			syllables	11				
			follows-on	l2-st1-poe-slgt2:Poem-line				
			has-word	no221:Word-occurrence				
			has-word	so_lo243:Word-occurrence				
			has-word	en413:Word-occurrence				
			has-word	plata485:Word-occurrence				
					precedes	o484:Word-ocurrence		
					of-word	plata:Word		
							text	plata
							syllables	2
							stress	1
							rhyme	ata
							stVowel	0
							endVowel	1
							has-POSTag	ADJGMS:POSTag
							has-POSTag	ADJGFS:POSTag
							has-POSTag	NCFS:POSTag
							has-POSTag	ADJGMP:POSTag
							has-POSTag	ADJGFP:POSTag
					has-word	o484:Word-occurrence		
					has-word	viola321:Word-occurrence		
					has-word	truncada122:Word-occurrence		
			second-line	l2-st1-poe-slgt2:Poem-line				
			third-line	l3-st1-poe-slgt2:Poem-line				

Fig. 3. Case Representation Example

The first thing to do in the design phase is to define a new type of case, i.e an specialization of the concept *Case*, and choose which concept within the domain model will represent a case description (mandatory) and which one will represent a solution (optional). Figure 3 shows a partial view of a case representing a poem (Each case that is added to the system adds an average of 50 individuals to the knowledge base). In the example, the new case type is *PoetryCase* whose *description* and *solution* are both the same instance of the *Poem*:

> no sólo en plata o viola truncada
> se vuelva mas tú y ello juntamente
> en tierra en humo en polvo en sombra en nada [1]

Although no semantic information about the attributes is used here, the integration phase could also determine that, for instance, *precedes* and *follows-on* relations are a kind of *before* attribute, or that the relations *has-stanza*, *has-word*, and *has-line* are a kind of *has-part* attribute. That integration would provide the semantic roles to be used in the predefined *similarity types*. For adaptation purposes, we could also classify *follows-on* under *depends-on* CBROnto relation,

---

[1] not just to silver or limp violets // will turn, but you and all of it as well // to earth, smoke, dust, to gloom, to nothingness

to indicate that if a line which follows onto the next is modified, then the next one may be affected, and its adaptation should be considered.

3.4   Retrieval

The query is given as a sequence of words that we want to inspire our poem, and it is represented as an instance of *PoetryCase* with *description* but, obviously, without *solution*, consisting of just one line with the given *Word-occurrences*.

In the example, the cases with the largest number of POS tag in common with the query should be retrieved. This way, it will be easy to substitute words in the retrieved poem with words from the query without loosing syntactic correctness. Therefore, the *obtain cases* retrieval subtask is easily defined as a LOOM query –a relevance criterion– that retrieves poems based on this requirement.

To solve the *select cases* retrieval subtask we select the cases to be retrieved by computing the similarity between the query and every retrieved case. For the example, we associate a similarity measure with the concept *PoetryCase* that collects the similarity among the *Words* of the *descriptions* of two poems. A similarity measure for the concept *Word* is also needed, taking into consideration all of the word attributes.

Given this configuration of the tasks, if we –carefully– choose as reference words to inspire our poem *"una boca ardiente pase techo y suelo"* we will retrieve the poem used as example in the previous section.

3.5   Adaptation

The high level idea of the adaptation process is to substitute as many words from the poem with words from the query, if possible in the same order as appearing in the query, without loosing the syntactic structure of the poem lines. We assume that the query is a meaningful sentence and, therefore, if we can accommodate those words into the poem in a similar order it is plausible to think that the new poem will reflect, to a certain extent, the original message in the query. In order to maintain the syntactic correctness of the poem, and taking into account that the system has no additional syntactic knowledge, we constrain substitutions to words with exactly the same POS tag. The adaptation algorithm runs, then, as follows: for every word in the poem, the first word in the query with the same POS tag is chosen as its substitute, if none exists then the word in the poem remains unchanged; for every substitution, the word from the query is removed so it is used only once. This process iterates until a whole cycle is done without substitutions or all the words in the query have been included in the poem. In the example this process results, in just one cycle, in:

no sólo en *boca* y viola *ardiente*
se *pase* mas tú y ello juntamente
en tierra en *techo* en *suelo* en sombra en nada [2]

---

[2]   not just to mouth or burning violets // will pass, but you and all of it as well // to earth, shelter, dirt, to gloom, to nothingness.

where all the words from the query (italicized text) have been arranged except *una* because there was no determiner in the original poem.

In order to make this process possible, the designer needs to choose and configure the generic adaptation methods. The method of adaptation by substitution is chosen, which, as described in Section 2.2, leads to the subtasks: copy solution, find adaptable parts, and apply substitution.

There is only one method available for copying the solution, and it does not need any customization. The method for finding adaptable parts in the solution needs to know where in the solution can be accessed the candidates for substitution which, in this case, are the poem words. This information is provided to a new instance of the generic method through the input requirement *toadapt*. *toadapt* is parameterized with the chain of attributes which has to be composed in order to access to the poem words from the entity representing the whole case:

```
(put-input-requirements 'ifind_adaptable_parts_method
 '((toadapt '((solution)(stanza)(has-line)(has-word)(of-word)))))
```

Notice how we can profit from the *is-a* hierarchy of attributes, by using *has-line* which subsumes *first-line*, *second-line* and *third-line*. More sophisticated configurations could be provided for this method to indicate, for example, that only non final words are to be considered for substitution

```
(put-input-requirements 'ifind_adaptable_parts_method
 '((toadapt '((solution)(stanza)(has-line)
              (has-word Non-final-word-occurrence)(of-word)))))
```

which could be useful if we would like to maintain the rhyme of the final words.

The output of the previous method is the input to the method responsible for applying the substitutions. This method, as described in Section 2.2, is a cycle which iterates through the list of candidates for substitution: finding substitutes, selecting one of them, making the substitution, and validating it. Notice that this local validation –word-based– is different to the global validation described in the next section –poem line or poem-based–. The process terminates when the list of candidates gets exhausted, or when an iteration ends without substitutions.

In order to solve the task of finding substitutes, we need to choose and configure one of the available retrieval methods. In the example we are interested on finding words in the query with the same POS tag. We may choose the method to obtain items by classification in representational retrieval, where we look for words which POS tag attribute is classified under the same concept as the candidate for substitution. And, then, further parameterize this method to consider only those words included in the query, instead of the whole vocabulary:

```
(put-input-requirements
 'ifind_substitutes_items_by_classification_method
 '((unique_source '(query solution stanza has-line has-word of-word))))
```

If more than one substitute have been retrieved we need to apply a selection method to choose one of them. Applicable methods are: user selection, random selection, and similarity based selection. Since there is a similarity function associated with the concept *Word*, we could choose the similarity based selection method, so that the substitute would be selected taking into consideration all of the word attributes, apart from the POS tag which serves as the filter in the task of finding substitutes. Nevertheless, since substitutes are restricted to those appearing in the query, it is unlikely to find more than one, and, for the example to work, we just need random selection.

The last two tasks of making the substitution and validating it, are trivial in the example, since the old value is directly substituted by the new one, and no local validation is needed when we only want to maintain syntactic correctness which is guaranteed by employing words with the same POS tag.

The problem with this adaptation process is that, although it preserves the syntactic structure of the retrieved poem, its metric characteristics will be probably lost. As discussed above, this includes number of syllables per line, and rhyme of the final words of lines 1 and 3. The revision process repairs, whenever possible these characteristics.

3.6   Revision

After adaptation, the self revision method is used to solve the revision task, and is in charge of evaluating and, if needed, repairing the proposed solution. As it was described in Section 2.2, the self evaluation method compares the classification between the adapted case and the retrieved case. The concepts under which the retrieved case is classified in the domain model are used as declarative descriptions of the properties that should be maintained by the adapted case after transformations. In the example the retrieved case is recognized as *PoetryType*, the solution is recognized as *Poem*, the stanza is recognized as a *Terceto-uno-tres*, and each one of its poem lines are recognized as *Endecasilabos*. Besides, the first and third poem lines are recognized as *Rhymed-poem-line*.

Before substitutions, the copy of the retrieved case that will be adapted has the same classification. If substitutions provokes a change in the concepts the system recognizes for a certain individual, the evaluation task classifies this individual below a concept representing a type of problem. The type of problems (subconcepts of the *FailureType* CBROnto concept) have associated a repair strategy that tries to put the individual back as an instance of the goal concept.

In the example, we have substituted a word by other of the same POS tag but possibly different rhyme, or number of syllables. Two problem types has been identified during the design of the application. The first one is called *Rhyme-failure* meaning that a poem line should rhyme and it does not. The domain concepts involved in this failure are the concepts that represent the rhyming strophic forms *Terceto-uno-tres* and *Cuarteto*, and the *Rhymed-poem-line* concept. When an individual leaves these concepts it is recognized as an instance of *Rhyme-failure*. The second one is called *Syllables-count-failure* and the domain concepts involved are *Endecasilabo* –11 syllables– and *Octosilabo* –8 syllables.

Next step is to define repair strategies associated to problem types. Each strategy is represented as an instance of the concept *Repair-strategy*, that are linked to the *FailureType* concept through the relation *has-repair-strategy*. The self repair method divides the repair task into two subtasks: find strategy and apply strategy. The two subtasks are solved in a loop that finishes when no failures are found and no strategies can be applied. To find the next strategy that will be applied, the find strategy method searches in the hierarchy rooted by *FailureType* and finds the strategy that is associated to the most specific concept in the hierarchy of problem types. The next step is applying the strategy to the individual that is classified below the problem type concept.

The revision is implemented as the process of substituting words in the adapted poem so that the detected problems can be repaired. For the example, we are defining a repair strategy to the problem type *Rhyme-failure*. The instances of this problem type are the stanzas where we want to modify certain words. We can take advantage of the CBROnto PSMs whose competence is the adaptation task. The method splits the task into subtasks whose methods has to be configured (as we did to configure them for the adaptation task). In order to repair the rhyme of the final words we have to select a word to substitute and then find its replacement:

- The items to be substituted in the stanza are the final word occurrences of the poem lines that belong to the *Rhyme-failure* concept. Besides, in order not to loose the effects of the adaptation, in the revision we are constrained to substitute only those words which do not appear in the query. This is configured as:

  ```
  (put-input-requirements 'ifind_adaptable_parts_method
    '((toadapt '((has-line rhyme_failure)
                 (has-word (:and Final-word-occurrence
                                 Not-query-component)) (of-word)))))
  ```

- The find substitutes method is configured to use a relevance criteria method that finds substitutes with the same POS tag and the proper rhyme depending on the strophic form. The algorithm is to select the first word of the broken rhyme which does not come from the query, and if both words were in the query then to ask the user.

In the example we have lost the rhyme of the final words of first and third lines, and the first line has 9 syllables instead of 11. The word *nada* is the one to be substituted as it does not belong to the query. In order to find a replacement for this word, we search for a word with the following requirements: has the same POS tag as *nada*, and rhymes with *ardiente*. If more than one word were retrieved then the selection process would come into play, and the most similar to *nada*, according to the rest of word attributes, would be selected. If there is no word under the given requirements, then the process fails and the user could be asked for help. In the example, the only word retrieved is *serpiente*, which substitutes *nada* and repairs the rhyme of the final words of first and third lines.

The next loop tries to repair the number of syllables of the poem lines. The order between the repairing processes depend on the classification of the problem types and is important because the solution to a problem may cause a new problem of different type. In the example, since *serpiente* has 1 more syllable than *nada* the third poem line is not an *endecasilabo* (11 syllables) any more.

When fixing the number of syllables of a poem line we take into account that this is the second process of revision, and therefore an additional constraint is not to substitute the last word of a rhymed line.

In order to repair the first line, we select as candidate for substitution the shortest word which was not in the query and is not a final word: *no* and *en*. Then we search for words with one more syllable than the candidate one, and the same POS tag. For *no* we find no candidate, but we find *para* as a substitute for *en* (both are prepositions). With this substitution, the number of syllables is automatically recomputed, and although *para* has only one more syllable than *en*, the new line is an *endecasilabo* because by substituting *en* we have also break the synaloepha between *sólo* and *en*.

In order to repair the third line, we select as candidate for substitution the longest word which was not in the query and is not a final word: *tierra* and *sombra*. We choose the first one and then search for a word with one syllable (one less than *tierra*), with the same POS tag, and ending with a vowel in order not to break the synaloepha. The retrieval word is *tía* which repairs the poem line into 11 syllables, leading to poem (words marked with * were obtained in the revision process):

no sólo para* *boca y* viola *ardiente*
se *pase* mas tú y ello juntamente
en tía* en *techo* en *suelo* en sombra en serpiente* [3]

4   Conclusions and Future Work

We have described CBROnto's task and method ontology and its application to a CBR system to generate Spanish poetry versions of texts provided by the user. The problem chosen as an example had already been tackled elsewhere using CBR. The approach described here presents several advantages with respect to the original one. First, the use of the frame of tasks and methods of CBROnto allows a very clear explicit representation of all the decisions that need to be taken. The domain allows many possible ways of solving the problem at each of the stages, and ad hoc development without a systematic approach run a risk of losing sight of where a design decision has been taken; thereby closing off a possible avenue of exploration for a solution. Second, this very set of tasks and methods provides a set of useful tools that may help to solve particular problems, or provide ideas for developing new solutions.

Two lines of research are now open for further work. First, more than one case may be used for adaptation. For instance, one case may be used to provide the structure of the result, whereas other cases are used to provide the required vocabulary. The variety of methods of CBROnto allow different criteria to be applied when retrieving cases for each of the possible purposes.

An important improvement that is envisaged is the incorporation of an ontology for the terms of the language being employed. As the reader may have

---

[3] not just to mouth or burning violets // will pass, but you and all of it as well // to girl, shelter, dirt, to gloom, to snake.

noticed, the example presented in the paper has been carefully chosen to exemplify the available mechanisms, and, of course, not every query would result in a meaningful poem with the right metric. Having a representation of the meanings of words as well as the other information already in use in the system would present several important advantages: 1) The ontology may provide the information needed to modify the structure selectively, for instance by replacing a masculine singular noun with a feminine singular noun if they refer to the same concept; 2) During retrieval a semantic description for words introduces the possibility of recovering cases where a similar meaning is conveyed with completely different syntactic constructions; 3) Additionally, it could act as a mechanism for extracting from particular cases the relevant relations between case description and case solution, to be used in selecting an adequate vocabulary.

References

1. A. Aamodt and E. Plaza. Case-based reasoning: Foundational issues, methodological variations, and system approaches. *AI Communications*, 7(i), 1994.
2. B. Díaz-Agudo and P. A. González-Calero. An architecture for knowledge intensive CBR systems. In E. Blanzieri and L. Portinale, editors, *Advances in Case-Based Reasoning – (EWCBR'00)*. Springer-Verlag, Berlin Heidelberg New York, 2000.
3. B. Díaz-Agudo and P. A. González-Calero. Classification based retrieval using formal concept analysis. In *Procs. of the (ICCBR 2001)*. Springer-Verlag, 2001.
4. B. Díaz-Agudo and P. A. González-Calero. A declarative similarity framework for knowledge intensive CBR. In *Procs. of the (ICCBR 2001)*. Springer-Verlag, 2001.
5. B. Díaz-Agudo and P. A. González-Calero. CBROnto: a task/method ontology for CBR. In *CBR Track (FLAIRS) accepted to be published*. 2002.
6. P. Gervás. Wasp: Evaluation of different strategies for the automatic generation of spanish verse. In *Proceedings of the AISB-00 Symposium on Creative & Cultural Aspects of AI*, pages 93–100, 2000.
7. P. Gervás. An expert system for the composition of formal Spanish poetry. *Journal of Knowledge-Based Systems*, 14(3–4):181–188, 2001.
8. P. A. González-Calero, M. Gómez-Albarrán, and B. Díaz-Agudo. A substitution-based adaptation model. In *Challenges for Case-Based Reasoning - Proc. of the ICCBR'99 Workshops*. University of Kaiserslautern, 1999.
9. D. B. Leake, A. Kinley, and D. C. Wilson. Acquiring case adaptation knowledge: A hybrid approach. In *Proceedings of the thirteenth National Conference on Artificial Intelligence*, pages 684–689, Menlo Park, CA, 1996. AAAI Press.
10. R. Mac Gregor and R. Bates. The loom knowledge representation language. ISI Reprint Series ISI/RS-87-188, University of Southern California, 1987.
11. J. McDermott. Preliminary steps towards a taxonomy of problem-solving methods. In S. Marcus, editor, *Automating Knowledge Acquisition for Knowledge-Based Systems*. Kluwer Academic Publishers, Boston, 1988.
12. T. Schreiber, B. J. Wielinga, J. M. Akkermans, W. V. de Velde, and R. de Hoog. CommonKADS: A comprehensive methodology for KBS development. *IEEE Expert*, 9(6), 1994.
13. L. Steels. Components of expertise. *AI Magazine*, 11(2):29–49, 1990.
14. G. Van Heijst, A. Schreiber, and B. Wielinga. Using explicit ontologies in knowledge based systems development. *International Journal of Human and Computer Studies*, 46(2/3), 1997.

Adaptation Using Iterated Estimations

Göran Falkman

Department of Computer Science, University of Skövde,
PO Box 408, SE–541 28 Skövde, Sweden
goran.falkman@ida.his.se

Abstract. A model for adaptation in case-based reasoning (CBR) is presented. Similarity assessment is based on the computation and the iterated estimation of structural relationships among representations, and adaptation is given as a special case of the general process.

Compared to traditional approaches to adaptation within CBR, the presented model has the advantage of using a uniform declarative model for both case representation, similarity assessment and adaptation. As a consequence, adaptation knowledge can be made directly available during similarity assessment and for explanation purposes. The use of a uniform model also provides the possibility of a CBR approach to adaptation. The model is compared with other approaches to adaptation within CBR.

1 Introduction

Adaptation plays a fundamental role in the general case-based reasoning (CBR) process. Because every new situation is unique, a CBR system must adapt retrieved previous cases to be able to use them in the new situation. The flexibility of a problem-solving CBR system depends to a large extent on its ability to adapt old solutions to solve novel problems.

Adaptation has typically been separated from the retrieval of similar cases. However, recent work on adaptation has blurred the boundaries between similarity assessment, retrieval and adaptation [17,18,13,3,4], and treat all three steps as parts of the more general process of finding re-useful cases [7,8,14].

Integrating similarity assessment with adaptation leads to adaptation-guided retrieval [17,18,4], in which cases are retrieved on the basis of their adaptability. A similar approach is to use adaptability-based similarity measures, in which the similarity between two cases is measured in terms of how easy it is to adapt one case to the other [3,12,10]. The observation that the adaptation of a case to a new situation can be solved by remembering previous similar adaptations leads to a CBR approach to adaptation, in which *adaptation cases* are used [11].

The MedView project was initiated in 1995 to support evidence-based oral medicine. The overall goal of the project is to develop models, methods and tools to support clinicians in their daily work and research. The formal declarative model of MedView is given by a theory of *partial inductive definitions* [9]. The model constitutes the main governing principle in MedView, not only in the formalisation of clinical terms and concepts, but in visualisation models and in

S. Craw and A. Preece (Eds.): ECCBR 2002, LNAI 2416, pp. 88–102, 2002.

the design and implementation of individual tools and the system as a whole as well. Tools are provided for knowledge acquisition, visualisation and analysis of data, and knowledge sharing. One analysis tool in MedView would be a general CBR system that should assist clinicians within the field of oral medicine.

In [6], a framework for similarity assessment for definitional representations was presented. This paper adds to this research by presenting a model for adaptation in CBR. Adaptation is given as a special case of the iterative process of computing and estimating structural relationships among representations. Compared to traditional approaches to adaptation, our model has the advantage of using a uniform declarative model for both case representation, similarity assessment and adaptation. As a consequence, adaptation knowledge can be made directly available during similarity assessment and for explanation purposes. A uniform model also provides the possibility of a CBR approach to adaptation.

The rest of this paper is organised as follows: In Sect. 2, the definitional framework used is presented. Section 3 briefly reviews the similarity model for definitional representations. Similarity assessment and estimations as a basis for adaptation are discussed in depth in Sect. 4. The paper is concluded in Sect. 5 with a general discussion.

2   Definitional Representations

2.1   Overview

Programs consist of three types of definitions: data definitions, method definitions and state definitions. The data definitions describe the declarative content of the program, e.g., the contents of a case base. The method definitions describe the computation methods (algorithms) used to compute solutions, and, thus, constitute the procedural part of the program. State definitions provide input and output of computations. Computations are initiated by posing queries, which are built using method definitions and an initial state definition, where the method definitions describe how to compute an answer from the initial state definition and given data definitions. The result of a computation is a new definition, a result definition, which describes the answer to a query, as well as information about how the answer was computed. A query can be understood as if we want to know if it is possible to move from the initial state definition to the result definition (if it is possible to transform the initial state definition to the result definition) using the given data definitions and method definitions.

2.2   Definitions

Intuitively, a definition defines possible connections between objects in a given universe. Formally, a *definition* D is given by

1. two sets: the *domain*, denoted $\mathrm{Dom}(D)$, and the *co-domain*, denoted $\mathrm{Com}(D)$, where $\mathrm{Dom}(D) \subseteq \mathrm{Com}(D)$,
2. and a *definiens* operation: $D : \mathrm{Com}(D) \to \mathcal{P}\big(\mathrm{Com}(D)\big)$.

A definition can be presented as a (possibly infinite) system of equations:

$$D \begin{cases} a_0 = C_0 \\ \quad \vdots \\ a_n = C_n \\ \quad \vdots \end{cases} n \geqslant 0 \ .$$

The *atoms* $a_0, \ldots \in \mathrm{Dom}(D)$ and the *conditions* $C_0, \ldots \in \mathrm{Com}(D)$. Given an equational presentation of a definition D, we assume that D is uniquely determined with respect to the objects in the domain: $\mathrm{Dom}(D) = \{a \mid (a = C) \in D\}$, $\mathrm{Com}(D) = \mathrm{Dom}(D) \cup \{C \mid (a = C) \in D\}$ and $D(a) = \{C \mid (a = C) \in D\}$.

We will use some primitive operations on definitions:

- $(C/_A)D$ is the definition: $\mathrm{Com}((C/_A)D) = \mathrm{Com}(D) \cup \{C\}$, $\mathrm{Dom}((C/_A)D) = (\mathrm{Dom}(D) \setminus \{A\}) \cup \{C\}$, $(C/_A)D(A) = \emptyset$ and $(C/_A)D(C) = D(A) \cup D(C)$.
- $D(C/_A)$ is the definition: $\mathrm{Com}(D(C/_A)) = \mathrm{Com}(D) \cup \{C\}$, $\mathrm{Dom}(D(C/_A)) = \mathrm{Dom}(D)$ and if $A \in D(B)$ then $D(C/_A)(B) = (D(B) \setminus \{A\}) \cup \{C\}$ else $D(C/_A)(B) = D(B)$.
- The *identity* definition for a given set S, $\mathrm{I}(S)$: $\mathrm{Com}(\mathrm{I}(S)) = \mathrm{Dom}(\mathrm{I}(S)) = S$ and $\mathrm{I}(S)(A) = \{A\}, \forall A \in S$.
- $D_1 \subseteq D_2$ if and only if $\mathrm{Dom}(D_1) \subseteq \mathrm{Dom}(D_2)$, $\mathrm{Com}(D_1) \subseteq \mathrm{Com}(D_2)$ and $D_1(a) = D_2(a), \forall a \in \mathrm{Dom}(D_1)$.
- $_eD$ denotes the left-hand side of a given equation $e \in D$.
- D_e denotes the right-hand side of a given equation $e \in D$.

2.3 Data Definitions

A *data definition* is a definition D such that $\top \in \mathrm{Com}(D)$, $\bot \in \mathrm{Com}(D)$ and $D(\top) = D(\bot) = \emptyset$.[1]

2.4 State Definitions

A *state definition* with respect to given data definitions $D_1, \ldots, D_n$, $n > 0$, is a definition S such that $\mathrm{Dom}(S) = \mathrm{Com}(S) \subseteq \bigcup_{i=1}^{n}(\mathrm{Com}(D_i))$.

2.5 Method Definitions

Let $\mathcal{V}$ be a set of atoms. Let $\mathcal{O}$ be a set of formal notations $\overline{D}$ and $\underline{D}$ for all definitions D over $\mathcal{V}$. Further, let $\mathcal{W} = (\mathcal{V} \cup \mathcal{O})^*$ be the set of *computation words*.

The set $\mathcal{CC}$ of *computation conditions* is now defined as follows: If $W \in \mathcal{W}$ then $W \in \mathcal{CC}$, and if $C_1 \in \mathcal{CC}$ and $C_2 \in \mathcal{CC}$ then $C_1 C_2 \in \mathcal{CC}$ and $(C_1, C_2) \in \mathcal{CC}$.

A *guard* is a boolean function that restricts the applicability of the definiens operation. Using guards, the set $\mathcal{MC}$ of *method conditions* is defined as follows: If $W \in \mathcal{CC}$ then $W \in \mathcal{MC}$, and if $W \in \mathcal{CC}$ and G is a guard then $W \# G \in \mathcal{MC}$.

---

[1] These are the data definitions used in this paper. In general, data definitions include constructed conditions, e.g., conditions corresponding to ordinary logic connectives.

A *method definition* is a definition M such that $\text{Dom}(M) = \mathcal{V}$, $\text{Com}(M) = \mathcal{MC}$, $M(m) = \{W \mid (m = W) \in M\} \cup \{W \mid (m = W \# G) \in M \wedge G\}$ and $M(A) = \emptyset$, $\forall A \neq m$.[2]

2.6   Result Definitions

Answers to computations are given by *result definitions*. Computation results may contain the results of sub-computations nested within itself, as given by the rules in Sect. 2.7. Thus, the right-hand sides of result definitions can be other result definitions. The following is an example of a result definition:

$$X_1 \left\{ m\overline{D_1} = \begin{cases} (a_1 = b) = \{mD_2 = \{\epsilon = \{a_1 = b_1 \\ (a_2 = c) = \{m\underline{D_2} = \{\epsilon = \{a_2 = c_1 \end{cases} \right. . \tag{1}$$

The right-most equations of (1) are the final equations of the computation. In addition to the final equations, (1) contains information about the branching points of the computation. A result definition, X, can be simplified using the operation $flat(X)$, which gives a definition containing the final equations of X only, e.g., $flat(X_1) = \{a_1 = b_1, a_2 = c_1\}$. If not otherwise stated, we will in the following assume that all result definitions have been flattened in this manner.

Note that a flattened result definition is a valid state definition, and can therefore be used as the starting point for a new computation. Also, flattened result definitions where all left-hand sides are atoms are valid data definitions.

2.7   Computations

Let $\mathcal{CS}$ be the set of *computation states*: If S is a state definition then $S \in \mathcal{CS}$, and if $W \in \mathcal{CC}$ and $C \in \mathcal{CS}$ then the *nested* invocation $(W \, C) \in \mathcal{CS}$.

If $W \in \mathcal{CC}$ and $S \in \mathcal{CS}$, the application of W to S, written $W \, S$, is referred to as a *query*. The purpose of a query $W \, S$ is to compute a result definition X from a given computation condition W and a given computation state S. We write $W \, S \Rightarrow X$ to denote that $W \, S$ can be computed to X. If the computation is successful, we consider X to be the answer to the query.

The operational semantics is given by the following inference rules:

1. *Termination:*

$$\frac{}{\epsilon \, S \Rightarrow S} .$$

2. *Nested Method Invocation:*

$$\frac{W_2 \, C \Rightarrow X_1 \quad W_1 \, flat(X_1) \Rightarrow X}{W_1 \, (W_2 \, C) \Rightarrow X} .$$

---

[2] We assume that each computation method is defined in a method definition with the same name. That is, the only atom defined in a method definition M is m.

$$E_1 \left\{ \begin{array}{l} status = direct \\ direct = mucos \\ direct = palpation \\ mucos = mucos\text{-}site \\ mucos = mucos\text{-}col \\ mucos = mucos\text{-}txt \\ mucos\text{-}site = l735 \\ mucos\text{-}col = white \\ mucos\text{-}col = brown \\ mucos\text{-}txt = plaque \\ palpation = palp\text{-}site \\ palp\text{-}site = l735 \end{array} \right. \qquad E_2 \left\{ \begin{array}{l} status = direct \\ direct = mucos \\ direct = palpation \\ mucos = mucos\text{-}site \\ mucos = mucos\text{-}col \\ mucos = mucos\text{-}txt \\ mucos\text{-}site = l122 \\ mucos\text{-}col = white \\ mucos\text{-}txt = ulcus \\ palpation = palp\text{-}site \\ palp\text{-}site = l122 \end{array} \right.$$

Fig. 1. Two partial cases in MedView

3. *Method:*
$$\frac{WW_1 \, S \Rightarrow X_1 \cdots WW_n \, S \Rightarrow X_n}{WM \, S \Rightarrow X} \, ,$$
where $M(m) = \{W_1, \ldots, W_n\}$, $n > 0$. The results of the sub-computations are collected in the indexed result definition $X = \{W_1 = X_1, \ldots, W_n = X_n\}$.

4. *Choice:*
$$\frac{WW_i \, S \Rightarrow X}{W(W_1, W_2) \, S \Rightarrow X} \, ,$$
where $W_i \in \{W_1, W_2\}$. The elements of $\{W_1, W_2\}$ are tried by backtracking. This rule introduces a non-deterministic choice between possible results.

5. *Domain Left:* In the following, all equations e of the current state definition S are tried by backtracking. Let $a = {}_e S$:
$$\frac{W \left({A_1}/{a}\right)S \Rightarrow X_1 \cdots W \left({A_n}/{a}\right)S \Rightarrow X_n}{W\overline{D} \, S \Rightarrow X} \, ,$$
where $D(a) = \{A_1, \ldots, A_n\}$, $n > 0$, and X is the indexed result definition $\big\{(a = A_1) = X_1, \ldots, (a = A_n) = X_n\big\}$.

6. *Domain Right:* In the following, all equations e of the current state definition S are tried by backtracking. Let $a = S_e$:
$$\frac{W \, S({A}/{a}) \Rightarrow X}{W\underline{D} \, S \Rightarrow X} \, ,$$
where $A \in D(a)$. All elements of $D(a)$ are tried by backtracking. This rule introduces a non-deterministic choice between possible results.

3   Definitional Similarity Assessment

3.1   The Canonical Method

Consider the two data definitions E_1 and E_2 in Fig. 1. E_1 and E_2 both define a small subset of the information contained in a typical case in MedView. In

$$X \left\{ can\overline{E_1} = \left\{ \begin{array}{l} (white = mucos\text{-}col) = \left\{ can\underline{E_2} = \{\epsilon = \{white = white \\ (brown = mucos\text{-}col) = \left\{ can\underline{E_2} = \{\epsilon = \{brown = white \end{array} \right. \right. \right.$$

Fig. 2. The result of computing $can_{E_1,E_2} S$

E_1 and E_2, clinical examination terms, e.g., *direct* and *mucos-col*, are defined in terms of other examination terms, e.g., *mucos* and *palpation*, or in terms of observed values, e.g., *white*.

Suppose we want to compare the definition of *mucos-col* in E_1 with the definition of *mucos-col* in E_2. Assuming that we do not know anything about the structure of E_1 and E_2, a reasonable approach is to 'expand' E_1 and E_2 as much as possible, exploring the whole structure of E_1 and E_2, i.e., to use a computation method that continues as long as anything in the state definition is defined in E_1 or E_2.

This basic behaviour is captured by the following method definition:

$$can_{D_1,D_2} \left\{ \begin{array}{ll} can = can_{D_1,D_2}\overline{D_1} & \text{\# if } \exists(A = B) \in S : A \in \text{Dom}(D_1) \\ can = can_{D_1,D_2}\underline{D_2} & \text{\# if } \exists(A = B) \in S : B \in \text{Dom}(D_2) \\ & \quad \wedge \neg(\exists(A = B) \in S : A \in \text{Dom}(D_1)) \\ can = \epsilon & \text{\# otherwise} \end{array} \right. , \quad (2)$$

where S is the state definition to which the method is applied.

We can read (2) as follows: If the left-hand side of some equation in the current state definition S is defined in D_1 then replace the left-hand side with its definition in D_1, and continue the computation. Otherwise, if the right-hand side of some equation in S is defined in D_2 then replace the right-hand side with one of its definitions in D_2, and continue the computation. Otherwise, end the computation. Thus, we repeatedly replace some left- or right-hand side of S with its definition in D_1 or D_2 respectively, until no left- or right-hand side of S is defined in D_1 or D_2, in short, until no additional changes can be made to S.

3.2 Similarity Assessment

Result definitions contain final equations as well as information about how the equations were established. In this way, computation results describe both structural and computational similarities and differences among data definitions. Our approach to measuring the similarity between data definitions is based on the idea of using computation results as the basis for similarity assessment.

Definition 1 (Similar). *Let D_1 and D_2 be two data definitions. If $\exists X \subseteq I(\text{Com}(D_1) \cup \text{Com}(D_2))$ such that $can_{D_1,D_2} S \Rightarrow X$ for some $S \subseteq I(\text{Com}(D_1) \cup \text{Com}(D_2))$, we say that D_1 is similar to D_2 (through X).*

We will refer to the application of can_{D_1,D_2} to S as a *similarity measure* over D_1 and D_2. Definition 1 can be extended to encompass ordinal and cardinal similarity measures by taking structural properties of the result definition X (e.g., cardinality or the number of identity equations) into account [6].

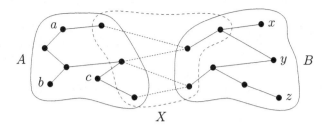

Fig. 3. Using the result definition X as the basis for measuring the similarity between data definitions A and B with respect to initial state definition $\{a = x, b = y, c = z\}$

Example 1. We want to compare E_1 and E_2 with respect to *mucos-col*. To base the comparison on *mucos-col*, we start by defining an initial state definition $S = \{mucos\text{-}col = mucos\text{-}col\}$. We then instantiate the method *can* with E_1 and E_2 and apply the result to S. In the first step of the computation of $can_{E_1,E_2} S$, the computation is split up into two sub-computations using the first equation of (2), and S is transformed into $S_1 = \{white = mucos\text{-}col\}$ and $S_2 = \{brown = mucos\text{-}col\}$ respectively. After two more applications of the second equation of (2) we get $S_3 = \{white = white\}$ and $S_4 = \{brown = white\}$. Since no left- or right-hand side of either S_3 or S_4 is defined in E_1 or E_2, the computation ends. The result of computing $can_{E_1,E_2} S$ is given by the result definition in Fig. 2.

The result definition X in Fig. 2 tells us that only one value of *mucos-col* in E_1 is also a value of *mucos-col* in E_2. In other words, E_1 has only one of its colours in common with E_2. Since $flat(X)$ is not a subset of $\mathrm{I}(\mathrm{Com}(E_1) \cup \mathrm{Com}(E_2))$, E_1 is not similar to E_2.

We may think of the initial state definition as a number of properties of the data definitions on which the similarity assessment should be based, connections between conditions in the domain that we want to establish. The computation method is simply the algorithm we use to compare the data definitions. The result definition defines the connections between conditions in the domain that must already exist in order to establish the connections in the initial state definition. Definition 1 states that all we have to know from the start is that every condition is similar to itself, a quite reasonable assumption.

Figure 3 depicts the idea of using result definitions as the basis for measuring the similarity between data definitions.

3.3   Estimations

If an interpretation of a result definition cannot immediately be found, the result definition can be used as the starting point for further estimation. If necessary, the result of this second step can be used as the starting point for a third step and so on. Thus, the computation of a similarity measure is really only the first step in a more general estimation process.

$$D_1 \begin{cases} anamnesis = common \\ common = drug \\ common = allergy \\ common = smoke \\ drug = no \\ allergy = oranges \\ smoke = 8\ cig/day \end{cases} \quad D_2 \begin{cases} anamnesis = common \\ common = drug \\ common = allergy \\ common = smoke \\ drug = no \\ allergy = lemons \\ smoke = 4\ cig/day \end{cases} \quad D_3 \begin{cases} anamnesis = common \\ common = drug \\ common = allergy \\ common = smoke \\ drug = no \\ allergy = apples \\ smoke = 4\ cig/day \end{cases}$$

Fig. 4. Three partial cases in MedView

Example 2. Consider the two cases D_1 and D_2 in Fig. 4. If we want to define a similarity measure that is based on the pair-wise comparison of the individual common attributes then we can define the initial state definition as $S = \{ drug = drug, allergy = allergy, smoke = smoke \}$.

If we compute $can_{D_1, D_2} S$, we get the (flattened) result definition $X = \{ no = no, oranges = lemons, 8\ cig/day = 4\ cig/day \}$. Perhaps we know that X means that D_1 and D_2 are indeed very similar. However, if that is not the case, since X is a valid state definition, we can estimate X itself using a data definition D_4:

$$D_4 \begin{cases} oranges = citrus \\ lemons = citrus \\ 8\ cig/day = < 10\ cig/day \\ 4\ cig/day = < 10\ cig/day \end{cases} .$$

Intuitively, since both oranges and lemons are examples of citrus fruits, we can get an interpretation of the non-identity $oranges = lemons$ in X in terms of D_4. The non-identity $8\ cig/day = 4\ cig/day$ can be explained in terms of D_4 as well, since $8\ cig/day$ and $4\ cig/day$ are both defined as $< 10\ cig/day$ in D_4.

If we compute $can_{D_4, D_4} X$ we get the result $X_2 = \{ no = no, citrus = citrus, < 10\ cig/day =< 10\ cig/day \}$. Thus, since the result definition of the nested computation $can_{D_4, D_4} (can_{D_1, D_2} S)$ is a subset of $I(Com(D_1) \cup Com(D_2) \cup Com(D_4))$, we conclude that D_1 and D_2 are similar after all.

The basic idea in Example 2 is to use the result definition of the first computation as the starting point (as a new initial state definition) for a second computation in which a new data definition is used. What we are looking for is, so to speak, an interpretation of the result definition in terms of the new data definition; the new data definition can be said to define the model in which the equations of the original result definition should be interpreted.

Since the goal is to get an interpretation of the result definition in terms of a data definition, it would be natural to use a method that, starting at the result definition, expands the data definition as much as possible. Thus, the method *can* could be used. But, we only want to compute until an interpretation of the state definition in terms of the data definition is found, if ever. In particular, we are only interested in the non-identities of the original result definition. A natural assumption is then that state definitions consisting of equations between identical conditions of the involved data definitions are the only state definitions that have an a priori interpretation. In other words, we only want to compute as long as the state definition does not consist of identities only.

The above behaviour is defined in the following variant of the method *can*:

$$can'_D \begin{cases} can' = can'_D \overline{D} \ \# \ \text{if} \ \exists (A = B) \in S \ : \ A \neq B \land A \in \text{Dom}(D) \\ can' = can'_D \underline{D} \ \# \ \text{if} \ \exists (A = B) \in S \ : \ A \neq B \land B \in \text{Dom}(D) \\ \qquad\qquad\qquad \land \neg (\exists (A = B) \in S \ : \ A \in \text{Dom}(D)) \\ can' = \epsilon \qquad\qquad \# \ \text{otherwise} \end{cases} \tag{3}$$

3.4   The Estimation Process

Estimations consist of a number of computation steps. The general structure of these *estimation steps* is a computation method, m_i, followed by a test, t_i, on the result definition.

The general form of an estimation step C_i is given by two method definitions:

$$c_i \ \{ c_i = t_i m_i \qquad \text{and} \qquad t_i \ \{ t_i = \epsilon \ \# \ \textit{if} \ S \subseteq T_i \ ,$$

where S is the state definition to which the method is applied and T_i is a 'test definition'. Thus, C_i corresponds to the computation of c_i, which consists of the computation of m_i, followed by the computation of the 'test method' t_i. The computation of t_i succeeds if and only if the state definition is a subset of T_i.

C_1 equals the computation of an initial similarity measure over given data definitions, i.e., $m_1 = can$ and T_1 is the identity definition over the co-domains of the involved data definitions.

Apart from the initial step, in general, we cannot be more specific about the structure of the estimation steps: The computation method m_i could be any method, of any complexity, and T_i could be any definition. However, according to the reasoning in Sect. 3.3, (3) is a natural choice for m_i, and T_i is typically the identity definition over the co-domains of the involved data definitions.

The above procedure is generalised into the following *estimation process*:

1. The first step is the computation of a similarity measure S.
2. Examine the result definition of the previous step. If the meaning of the result definition is known then the process stops.
3. The current result definition is used as the starting point for another computation, C_i.
4. The result definition, X_i, from the previous step is tested against a test definition T_i. If $X_i \subseteq T_i$ then the meaning of X_i is assumed to be known, and the process stops. Otherwise, repeat from step 3.

The use of estimation processes can be seen as a generalisation of Definition 1: If a given estimation process succeeds for two data definitions D_1 and D_2 then D_1 and D_2 are similar (through that process).

Example 3. Consider the case D_3 in Fig. 4. If we compute $can'_{D_4} (can_{D_1, D_3} S)$, we get $X_3 = \{no = no, citrus = apples, < 10 \ cig/day = < 10 \ cig/day\}$, and since $X_3 \not\subseteq \text{I}(\text{Com}(D_1) \cup \text{Com}(D_3) \cup \text{Com}(D_4))$, D_1 is not similar to D_3.

Now, assume we know that both citrus fruits and apples are fruits:

$$D_5 \begin{cases} citrus = fruits \\ apples = fruits \end{cases}.$$

We can then estimate X_3 using can' and the data definition D_5. If we compute $can'_{D_5} X_3$ we get $X_4 = \{no = no, fruits = fruits, < 10 \ cig/day =< 10 \ cig/day\}$, and, since the result of the computation $can'_{D_5} (can'_{D_4} (can_{D_1,D_3} S))$ is a subset of $I(\text{Com}(D_1) \cup \text{Com}(D_3) \cup \text{Com}(D_4) \cup \text{Com}(D_5))$, D_1 is similar to D_3.

4   Adaptation as Estimation

Result definitions are explicit declarative explanations of why two data definitions are similar or why they are dissimilar: equations between non-identical conditions represent what we do not know, connections between conditions which have to be established, or what must be shown to be true. In other words, result definitions contain information of which conditions need to be adapted and what they should be adapted to.

To select cases that are adaptable, some form of adaptation knowledge is needed. In our model, adaptation knowledge is added by defining data definitions like the definitions D_4 and D_5 in Example 2 and Example 3 respectively.

In Example 2, the adaptation is trivial, only one extra estimation step is needed, but, as we saw in Example 3, in general, adaptation may require more complex estimations. Thus, adaptation in the form of an estimation process may be a costly operation, and the general problem is how adaptable cases can be retrieved without actually performing the adaptation [17]. Our solution to this problem is to define and use special computation methods, like can_{D_4,D_4} in Example 2, and index these methods according to the adaptation they perform.

4.1   Adaptation Knowledge

We discriminate between two types of adaptation knowledge: knowledge about possible adaptations and knowledge about when and how a specific adaptation should be used.

In general, the fact that a value v_i can be adapted to a value v_{i_a} is defined in an *adaptation definition* $D_A = \{v_1 = v_{1_a}, \ldots, v_n = v_{n_a}\}$.

The knowledge about an equation $a_{i_j} = b_{i_j}$ being adaptable by the computation method m_i (i.e., applying m_i to $\{a_{i_j} = b_{i_j}\}$ eventually leads to an identity) is defined in an *adaptation method*:

$$m_A \begin{cases} m_A = m_A m_1 \ \# \ \text{if} \ \bigvee_{1 \leqslant j \leqslant n}((a_{1_j} = b_{1_j}) \in S) \\ \quad \vdots \\ m_A = m_A m_k \ \# \ \text{if} \ \bigvee_{1 \leqslant j \leqslant m}((a_{k_j} = b_{k_j}) \in S) \wedge \\ \qquad \neg(\bigvee_{1 \leqslant j \leqslant n}((a_{1_j} = b_{1_j}) \in S)) \wedge \cdots \wedge \\ \qquad \neg(\bigvee_{1 \leqslant j \leqslant r}((a_{k-1_j} = b_{k-1_j}) \in S)) \\ m_A = \epsilon \qquad \# \ \text{otherwise} \end{cases},$$

where S is the state definition to which the method is applied.

Example 4. Returning to Example 2, *oranges* and 8 *cig/day* can be replaced by *lemons* and 4 *cig/day* respectively, i.e., we define the adaptation definition $AD = \{oranges = lemons, 8\ cig/day = 4\ cig/day\}$. The method can'_{D_4} adapts both $oranges = lemons$ ($lemons = oranges$) and 8 $cig/day = 4\ cig/day$ (4 $cig/day = 8\ cig/day$). Thus, we define the adaptation method:

$$ad \begin{cases} ad = ad\,can'_{D_4} & \#\ \text{if}\ (oranges = lemons) \in S \vee (lemons = oranges) \in S \\ & \vee (8\ cig/day = 4\ cig/day) \in S \\ & \vee (4\ cig/day = 8\ cig/day) \in S \\ ad = \epsilon & \#\ \text{otherwise} \end{cases},$$

where S is the state definition to which the method is applied.

4.2   Adaptation

Adaptation is performed in two steps: First, the adaptation definition D_A is used during case retrieval in the form of a one-step estimation. In this way, v_i will be replaced by v_{i_a} in a single step, and we conclude that v_i *can* be adapted to v_{i_a}. Then m_A is used as a table: For every non-identity $a_{i_j} = b_{i_j}$ in the original result definition, if m_A is defined in the adaptation method m_A, we can adapt v_i to v_{i_a} using $m_A m_i$, i.e., we can *compute* the adaptation needed. In this way, new adaptation knowledge is directly available during case retrieval, and changes in the adaptation capabilities are immediately reflected in the retrieval step.

Adding some details to the above:

1. First, an initial similarity measure over two data definitions D_1 and D_2 is computed, giving X as result.
2. If D_1 and D_2 were not similar (i.e., $X \not\subseteq I(\text{Com}(D_1) \cup \text{Com}(D_2))$), we find out if D_1 can be adapted to D_2 using a single estimation step consisting of the instantiation of can' with the adaptation definition D_A and the application of the result to X, i.e., we compute $can'_{D_A} X \Rightarrow X_2$.
3. If $X_2 \subseteq I(\text{Com}(D_A) \cup \text{Com}(D_1) \cup \text{Com}(D_2))$ then we know that D_1 can be adapted to D_2, and the actual adaptation needed is then computed by applying m_A to X: $m_A X \Rightarrow X_a$.

The final result, X_a, contains the computation steps that adapt D_1 to D_2; X_a encodes (part of) the adaptation knowledge contained in D_A and m_A. This knowledge could be used for different purposes. For example, X_a could be used as an explanation of why D_1 could be adapted to D_2.

Example 5. In Example 2, we saw that the initial similarity measure $can_{D_1,D_2} S$ computes to $X = \{no = no, oranges = lemons, 8\ cig/day = 4\ cig/day\}$. Continuing with Example 4, we check if D_1 can be adapted to D_2 by computing $can'_{AD} X$ to $X_5 = \{no = no, lemons = lemons, 4\ cig/day = 4\ cig/day\}$. Since $X_5 \subseteq I(\text{Com}(AD) \cup \text{Com}(D_1) \cup \text{Com}(D_2))$, D_1 can be adapted to D_2.

To compute the adaptation needed, we compute $ad\,X$, and since $(oranges = lemons) \in X$, this amounts to computing $ad\,can'_{D_4}\,X$:

$$ad\,X \Rightarrow ad\,can'_{D_4}\,X$$
$$\Rightarrow \cdots$$
$$\Rightarrow ad\,\{no = no, citrus = citrus, < 10 \; cig/day = < 10 \; cig/day\}$$
$$\Rightarrow \{no = no, citrus = citrus, < 10 \; cig/day = < 10 \; cig/day\} \;.$$

In the above example, the same computation method was used for adapting all inequalities in the original result definition. The following example shows how to use different computation methods for different adaptations:

Example 6. If we instantiate *can* with D_1 from Example 2 and D_3 from Example 3, applying the result to the initial state definition S from Example 2, we get the result definition $X_6 = \{no = no, oranges = apples, 8 \; cig/day = 4 \; cig/day\}$.

Suppose we know that *oranges* and $8 \; cig/day$ can be replaced by *apples* and $4 \; cig/day$ respectively: $AD_2 = \{oranges = apples, 8 \; cig/day = 4 \; cig/day\}$. We know that $8 \; cig/day = 4 \; cig/day$ can be adapted to $< 10 \; cig/day = < 10 \; cig/day$ using can'_{D_4} and that $apples = citrus$ can be adapted to $fruits = fruits$ using can'_{D_5}:

$$ad_2 \begin{cases} ad_2 = ad_2\,can'_{D_4} \quad \text{\# if } (8 \; cig/day = 4 \; cig/day) \in S \\ \qquad\qquad\qquad \lor (4 \; cig/day = 8 \; cig/day) \in S \\ ad_2 = ad_2\,can'_{D_5} \quad \text{\# if } (citrus = apples) \in S \lor (apples = citrus) \in S \\ \qquad\qquad\qquad \land \neg((8 \; cig/day = 4 \; cig/day) \in S \\ \qquad\qquad\qquad \lor (4 \; cig/day = 8 \; cig/day) \in S) \\ ad_2 = \epsilon \qquad\qquad\quad \text{\# otherwise} \end{cases} ,$$

where S is the state definition to which the method is applied.

We compute $can'_{AD_2}\,X_6$ to $X_7 = \{no = no, apples = apples, 4 \; cig/day = 4 \; cig/day\}$, and, thus, we know that D_1 can be adapted to D_3. To actually compute the adaptation needed, we then compute $ad_2\,X_6$:

$$ad_2\,X_6 \Rightarrow ad_2\,can'_{D_3}\,X_6$$
$$\Rightarrow \cdots$$
$$\Rightarrow ad_2\,\{no = no, citrus = apples, < 10 \; cig/day = < 10 \; cig/day\}$$
$$\Rightarrow ad_2\,can'_{D_5}\,\{no = no, citrus = apples, < 10 \; cig/day = < 10 \; cig/day\}$$
$$\Rightarrow \cdots$$
$$\Rightarrow ad_2\,\{no = no, fruits = fruits, < 10 \; cig/day = < 10 \; cig/day\}$$
$$\Rightarrow \{no = no, fruits = fruits, < 10 \; cig/day = < 10 \; cig/day\} \;.$$

In the above examples, the same method (can') was used for computing all the adaptation needed. Of course, in general, this need not be the case.

5 Discussion

Two advantages of using a definitional model are simplicity and flexibility. A conceptually simple and uniform model is used: cases and all parts of the similarity assessment model, including comparison methods, estimations and adaptation knowledge, are given as definitions. As a consequence, the output of the model, i.e., the result definition, can be used as input in any part of a new computation, and not just as a new initial state definition. In addition, result definitions contain traces of the computation of an adaptation, and, since they are definitions in the formal sense, they can directly be added to the representation of cases, e.g., for providing explanations. This also means that adaptation knowledge can easily be added to the case base and that similarity measures over adaptation definitions and adaptation methods can be defined, thus providing the possibility of a CBR approach to adaptation.

The similarity model in Sect. 3 is general enough to capture many different types of similarity measures: ordinal, cardinal and asymmetric measures. The model is not limited to measures between just two data definitions, any number of definitions could be used.

The idea of using the structure and complexity of result definitions for deciding whether a data definition D_1 is similar to a data definition D_2, can be generalised by taking the structure and complexity of estimation processes (e.g., the number of steps) into account. This can be used for deciding whether D_1 is *more* similar (more adaptable) to D_2 than to a third definition D_3.

We use iterated estimations to interpret result definitions: estimation steps are applied until an interpretation of the state definition is found. This is similar to the view adopted in [3], in which modification rules will be chosen and applied to a given problem and the selected candidate cases, until a common structure of the problem and one candidate case is found.

The adaptation definitions and adaptation methods of Sect. 4.1 play much the same roles as the *adaptation specialists* and *adaptation strategies* respectively in [17,18]: Adaptation definitions define which conditions can be adapted and adaptation methods define which estimation should be used to adapt which condition.

In the work of Fuchs and Mille [8], the matching task produces a set of *matching relations* between source and target cases. Just as our result definitions, these relations can express either the similarity or dissimilarity between the two cases. A matching relation is a triple $\langle d_s, d_t, R_{st} \rangle$, where d_s is a source descriptor, d_t a target descriptor and R_{st} is an explanation linking d_s and d_t. Thus, a matching relation contains the same information as our result definitions. Fuchs and Mille adopts a view where the adaptation of a case is performed by an *enrichment process* all along the CBR-cycle, a view which is very similar to our notion of a coherent estimation process.

In [7], adaptation is viewed as plan adaptation, and the adaptation process itself is considered as a planning process. A plan, in this view, is a triple consisting of an initial state I, a goal statement G and a set of operations O allowing to satisfy G given I. The roles played by I, O and G are very similar to the roles played by the initial state definitions, method definitions (and estimations) and test definitions in our model.

A similar approach to adaptation is proposed in [15,14], where adaptation is modeled by reformulation. To assess the similarity between two problems a *similarity path* is built. The similarity path consists of small reformulation steps, and two problems are similar if there exists a similarity path between them. The building of a similarity path using reformulation steps is similar to the construction of an estimation using individual estimation steps in our model.

In [5], a uniform similarity framework that is used by both retrieval and adaptation processes is presented. In this framework, case retrieval is regarded as interactive refinement of queries, in which those cases that satisfy the given relevance criteria are selected. This is similar to our notion of an iterated estimation process, aiming at satisfying given test definitions. As in our model, [5] uses explicit *similarity terms*, which provide explanations in a declarative way.

For simple adaptations, in which mutually exclusive values are to be replaced by other values, adaptation methods (like ad and ad_2) can automatically be constructed, given suitable computation methods for the different replacements. An open question is how these computation methods can be acquired.

An interesting solution to the problem of acquiring adaptation knowledge is presented in [16]. An interaction model is given, in which *ripple-down rules* are used to encode adaptation knowledge. The model requires the domain expert only to provide simple explanations of the decision taken in a given situation. It would be interesting to investigate if our result definitions could be used in a similar way. The chain of ripple-down rules, with its *except* and *is-not* links, in which objects are classified by the first 'successful' node, is similar to the way our estimation process, in which exceptions are given in the form of guarded choices, interprets a state definition by the first 'successful' estimation step.

References

1. K.-D. Althoff, R. Bergmann, and K. L. Branting, editors. *Case-Based Reasoning: Research and Development. Proceedings of the Third International Conference on Case-Based Reasoning, ICCBR-99, Seeon Monastery, Germany, July 1999*, volume 1650 of *Lecture Notes in Artificial Intelligence*. Springer-Verlag, 1999.
2. E. Blanzieri and L. Portinale, editors. *Advances in Case-Based Reasoning. Proceedings of the 5th European Workshop, EWCBR 2000, Trento, Italy, September 6-9, 2000*, volume 1898 of *Lecture Notes in Artificial Intelligence*. Springer-Verlag, 2000.
3. K. Börner. Structural similarity as guidance in case-based design. In Wess et al. [20], pages 197-208.
4. K. Börner et al. Structural similarity and adaptation. In I. Smith and B. Faltings, editors, *Advances in Case-Based Reasoning. Proceedings of the Third European Workshop, EWCBR-95, Lausanne, Switzerland, November 1996*, volume 1168 of *Lecture Notes in Artificial Intelligence*, pages 58-75. Springer-Verlag, 1996.

5. B. Díaz-Agudo and P. A. González-Calero. A declarative similarity framework for knowledge intensive CBR. In D. W. Aha and I. Watson, editors, *Case-Based Reasoning: Research and Development. Proceedings of the 4th International Conference on Case-Based Reasoning, ICCBR 2001, Vancouver, BC, Canada, July 30–August 2, 2001*, volume 2080 of *Lecture Notes in Artificial Intelligence*, pages 158–172. Springer-Verlag, 2001.

6. G. Falkman. Similarity measures for structured representations: A definitional approach. In E. Blanzieri and L. Portinale, editors, *Advances in Case-Based Reasoning. Proceedings of the 5th European Workshop, EWCBR 2000, Trento, Italy, September 6–9, 2000*, volume 1898 of *Lecture Notes in Artificial Intelligence*, pages 380–392. Springer-Verlag, 2000.

7. B. Fuchs, J. Lieber, A. Mille, and A. Napoli. Towards a unified theory of adaptation in case-based reasoning. In Althoff et al. [1], pages 104–117.

8. B. Fuchs and A. Mille. A knowledge-level task model of adaptation in case-based reasoning. In Althoff et al. [1], pages 118–131.

9. L. Hallnäs. Partial inductive definitions. *Theoretical Computer Science*, 87(1):115–142, 1991.

10. D. B. Leake. Constructive similarity assessment: Using stored cases to define new situations. In *Proceedings of the Fourteenth Annual Conference of the Cognitive Science Society*, pages 313–318, Hillsdale, NJ, USA, 1992. Lawrence Erlbaum.

11. D. B. Leake. Toward a computer model of memory search strategy learning. In *Proceedings of the Sixteenth Annual Conference of the Cognitive Science Society*, pages 549–554, Hillsdale, NJ, USA, 1994. Lawrence Erlbaum.

12. D. B. Leake. Adaptive similarity assessment for case-based explanation. *International Journal of Expert Systems*, 8(2):165–194, 1995.

13. D. B. Leake, A. Kinley, and D. Wilson. Learning to improve case adaptation by introspective reasoning and CBR. In Veloso and Aamodt [19], pages 229–240.

14. J. Lieber and B. Bresson. Case-based reasoning for breast cancer treatment decision helping. In Blanzieri and Portinale [2], pages 173–185.

15. E. Melis, J. Lieber, and A. Napoli. Reformulation in case-based reasoning. In B. Smyth and P. Cunningham, editors, *Advances in Case-Based Reasoning. Proceedings of the 4th European Workshop, EWCBR-98 Dublin, Ireland, September 23–25 1998*, volume 1488 of *Lecture Notes in Artificial Intelligence*, pages 172–183. Springer-Verlag, 1998.

16. A. Salam Khan and A. Hoffmann. Acquiring adaptation knowledge for CBR with MIKAS. In M. Stumptner, D. Corbett, and M. Brooks, editors, *AI 2001: Advances in Artificial Intelligence. Proceedings of the 14th Australian Joint Conference on Artificial Intelligence, Adelaide, Australia, December 10–14, 2001*, volume 2256 of *Lecture Notes in Artificial Intelligence*, pages 201–212. Springer-Verlag, 2001.

17. B. Smyth and M. T. Keane. Retreiving adaptable cases: the role of adaptation knowledge in case retrieval. In Wess et al. [20], pages 109–220.

18. B. Smyth and M. T. Keane. Experiments on adaptation-guided retrieval in case-based reasoning. In Veloso and Aamodt [19], pages 313–324.

19. M. Veloso and A. Aamodt, editors. *Case-Based Reasoning: Research and Development. Proceedings of the First International Conference, ICCBR-95, Sesimbra, Portugal, October 1995*, volume 1010 of *Lecture Notes in Artificial Intelligence*. Springer-Verlag, 1995.

20. S. Wess, K.-D. Althoff, and M. M. Richter, editors. *Topics in Case-Based Reasoning. Selected Papers of the First European Workshop, EWCBR-93 Kaiserslauten, Germany, November 1993*, volume 837 of *Lecture Notes in Artificial Intelligence*. Springer-Verlag, 1994.

The Use of a Uniform Declarative Model in 3D Visualisation for Case-Based Reasoning

Göran Falkman

Department of Computer Science, University of Skövde,
PO Box 408, SE–541 28 Skövde, Sweden
goran.falkman@ida.his.se

Abstract. We present an information visualisation tool, The Cube, as a solution to the problem of visualising cases derived from large amounts of clinical data. The Cube is based on the idea of dynamic 3D parallel diagrams, an idea similar to the notion of 3D parallel coordinate plots. The Cube was developed to provide interactive visualisation of the case base in terms of relationships between and within cases, in order to enhance the clinician's ability to intelligibly analyse existing patient material and to allow for pattern recognition and statistical analysis.

The design and use of The Cube are presented and discussed. We show how the declarative model used and the tight coupling between different visualisation tools directly led to a similarity assessment-based solution to the problem of finding a proper arrangement of dimensions in 3D parallel coordinate displays. The declarative, user-centered nature of The Cube makes it suitable for interactive case-based reasoning (CBR) and opens up for the possibility of case-based visualisation for CBR.

1 Introduction

Computer power increases by the day. Together with increased bandwidth of sensory equipment this leads to increased amounts of collected data in many scientific fields. This in turn increases the need of information visualisation in order to communicate, explore, analyse, understand and learn from data [11].

Clinical medicine is not an exception to this. On the contrary, the compulsion to visualise large volumes of clinical information has been emphasised as a sequel to the immense increase in medical information during the last decades [3].

The MedView project was initiated in 1995 to support evidence-based oral medicine. The central question in MedView is how the chain 'formalise–collect–view–analyse–learn' should be understood and clinically implemented. The basis of MedView is a formalisation of clinical concepts and clinical procedures providing a possibility for recognising patterns and trends otherwise hidden in the monumental amount of clinical data. Tools are provided for collecting clinical data into a case base. However, it is clear that clinicians also somehow want to view the clinical experience gathered by collecting formalised clinical data.

Traditionally, the above chain of clinical tasks involves different models and tools for the different links in the chain. For the user this does not only imply

S. Craw and A. Preece (Eds.): ECCBR 2002, LNAI 2416, pp. 103–117, 2002.
© Springer-Verlag Berlin Heidelberg 2002

the practical problem of switching between different tools, but also a constant cognitive shift between different models. For the developer of medical information systems, the diversity of tools and models that have to be integrated into the system poses a great challenge. Recent work on component-based [13,14] and user-centered [7] visualisation tries to solve these problems by emphasising the tight coupling between users, visualisation and data. A similar trend can be observed within case-based reasoning, in the form of increased interest in *interactive* CBR [1].

The above leads to the following design goals for information visualisation in MedView:

1. The visualisation models should be based on the declarative model used throughout MedView, thereby decreasing the distance between users and visualisation, and facilitating component-based visualisation and integration.
2. To provide an interaction model that allows users to take active part in the various CBR processes, and especially in similarity assessment.
3. To provide a tool for interactive visualisation of the case base in terms of relationships *between cases*.
4. To provide a tool for interactive visualisation of the case base in terms of relationships *within individual cases*.

Solutions to the first three steps have been presented elsewhere [6] and are only briefly reviewed here.

In this paper, we present an information visualisation tool, The Cube, as a solution to the problem of visualising clinical experience derived from large amounts of clinical data. The Cube is based on the idea of dynamic 3D parallel diagrams, an idea similar to the notion of 3D parallel coordinate plots. The Cube was developed to provide interactive visualisation of the case base in terms of relationships between and within cases, in order to enhance the clinician's ability to intelligibly analyse existing patient material and to allow for pattern recognition and statistical analysis.

The design and use of The Cube are presented and discussed. We also show how the declarative model used and the tight coupling between The Cube and another visualisation tool directly led to a similarity assessment-based solution to an inherent problem in multidimensional analysis, namely the problem of finding a proper arrangement of dimensions in 3D parallel coordinate displays.

The Cube has been tested on a case base containing about 1500 cases obtained from different clinics. Clinical practice has indicated that the basic ideas are conceptually appealing to the involved clinicians as The Cube can be used for generating and testing of hypotheses.

The rest of this paper is organised as follows: The next section presents the knowledge representation used in MedView. Section 3 briefly reviews SimVis, a tool for interactive exploration of case bases. The design and use of The Cube are discussed in depth in Sect. 4. Section 5 describes how The Cube can be used in conjunction with SimVis to handle the problem of finding a proper arrangement of dimensions. The paper is concluded in Sect. 6 with a general discussion.

2   Knowledge Representation in MedView

In MedView, knowledge is formalised using a theory of *partial inductive definitions* [9]. Intuitively, a definition defines possible connections between objects in a universe of objects. The conceptual view of a definition is that of a system of equations, where the left-hand sides of the equations (atoms) are defined in terms of the right-hand sides (conditions). For example, the following is a small part of a case in MedView:

$$D \begin{cases} anamnesis = common \\ common = drug \\ common = smoke \\ drug = levaxin \\ smoke = 4\ cigarettes/day \\ diagnosis = diag\text{-}def \\ diag\text{-}def = gingival\ lichen\ planus \end{cases}.$$

In the definition D, the term *anamnesis* is defined by the term *common*, which in turn is defined by the terms *drug* and *smoke*. To find out how something is defined, we use the *definiens* operation. For example, the definiens of *common* in D is $\{drug, smoke\}$.

Clinical data is seen as definitions of clinical terms. Abstract clinical concepts, like diagnosis, examination and patient, are all given by definitions of collections of specific clinical terms. For example, the terms *anamnesis, common, drug, smoke, diagnosis* and *diag-def* are all part of the general structure that defines the basic concept 'examination'. A concrete instance of an examination record (a case) is given by defining terms like *drug* and *diag-def* in terms of observed values, e.g., *levaxin* and *gingival lichen planus* respectively.

Values can be grouped into classes in a hierarchical manner using grouping definitions. For example, diseases such as Herpes labialis, Herpetic gingivostomatitis, Shingles etc., can be grouped into viral diseases. The grouping definitions are definitions in the same sense as the definitions containing the case data, and they are expressed in the same format as the cases.

3   Interactive Visualisation of Case Bases

In this section, we give a brief overview of SimVis, a tool designed to help clinicians to classify and cluster clinical examination data. SimVis is based on a similarity assessment-based interaction model for exploring case bases, and user interaction is supported by 3D visualisation of clusters and similarity measures.

SimVis clusters cases, i.e., definitions in the meaning of Sect. 2. Thus, the basis of SimVis is a model for defining and computing *similarity measures* between definitional structures [5]. The result of computing the similarity between a number of definitions, $D_1, \ldots, D_n$, is another definition, which describes both structural and computational similarities between $D_1, \ldots, D_n$.

The approach is purely declarative, and all parts of a similarity measure, including the computation method used, are given as definitions.

The similarity model forms the basis of a similarity assessment-based interaction model. Since all parts of the similarity model are given as definitions, in principle the user can use the output of the model, i.e., the computed similarity, as input in any other part of the model. The idea is then to let the user interact with the different steps of the similarity assessment process.

The interaction model has been implemented in SimVis, a tool for classifying cases. With SimVis, a clinician can interactively define a similarity measure between cases, apply the measure to a case base, classify the cases according to this measure and visualise the resulting classification in the form of a 3D hierarchical clustering.

4   Multidimensional Analysis of Cases

In this section, we present a declarative model for visualisation of clinical case data based on the notion of multiple parallel diagrams with support for direct manipulation. User interaction is provided by three complementary views of the case data. The model has been used in The Cube, a tool for interactive multidimensional data analysis.

4.1   Design

As was noted in Sect. 2, a case can be seen as a set of definitions of specific examination terms (examination attributes). Clearly, for a given collection of cases, an attribute can be viewed using a two-dimensional diagram with the x-axis as a sort of time line, e.g., by ordering the cases by examination date, and with the values of the attribute on the y-axis. Thus, if we want an overview of the total set of attributes it is natural to think in terms of multiple parallel diagrams (this is similar to the scatter matrix of [4]). This view was then generalised into dynamic 3D parallel diagrams with support for direct manipulation, an idea similar to the concept of 3D *parallel coordinate plots* [10,18].

The Cube consists of a number of planes, one for each attribute that was selected when The Cube was defined. Any number of planes can be selected (e.g., Drugs, Diagnoses, Allergies and Diseases). These planes are presented along the x-axis of The Cube. An individual plane (e.g., Diseases) displays individual values (e.g., Diabetes, Psoriasis and SLE), for the selected attribute. The values are listed along the y-axis of the plane in some order, e.g., in alphabetical or numerical order. The z-axis of The Cube is common to all planes. It is typically used as a time-line, i.e., as an ordering on the examination identification attribute, but an arbitrary attribute can be used as the unit on this axis.

In any case, each case is represented by a line connecting individual values in the different attribute planes. If a case has more than one value for an attribute, the values are connected with a line in the plane. In this way, attribute values generate an information profile for a case. Several parallel lines can be interpreted

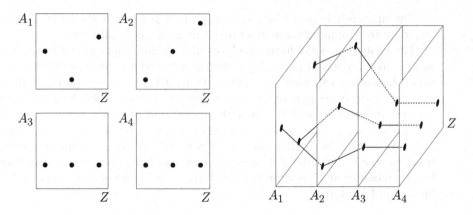

Fig. 1. Four diagrams for the attributes $A_1, \ldots, A_4$ respectively, with the common attribute Z (left), and the corresponding Cube (right)

as a group of patients with a similar information profile, which may indicate an identical diagnosis.

The construction of a generic Cube is depicted in Fig. 1.

Declarative Model. The declarative model of The Cube is that of a hierarchy of nested definitions. A Cube consists of a number of planes, a number of lines and a number of points, where each plane corresponds to an attribute, each line corresponds to a case (examination) and each point corresponds to an attribute-value pair. Cubes, planes, lines and points are all given by definitions.

The planes of a Cube are positioned along the x-axis of the display using an axis definition. A cube definition also defines a z-axis component that maps values of the common z-attribute to positions.

An axis uses a table definition that maps the values of an attribute to relative positions and relative positions to absolute positions, the latter being the actual coordinates used in the 3D display. An axis may also define a grouping definition, which classifies values into groups. Axes use groupings prior to the mapping of values to positions: first, the definition of the value is looked up in the grouping definition of the axis, and then the definition of the result, i.e., the class, is looked up in the table definition of the axis, giving us the position of the class as result.

A plane definition defines a number of point definitions, in which the x-, y- and z-coordinates of the point are defined, and a y-axis, whose attribute gives the attribute of the plane.

Each line definition defines a z-value, i.e., the definiens of the common z-attribute in the corresponding case definition, and a subset of the points defined in the plane definitions.

Figure 2 shows the respective forms of cube, plane and line definitions.

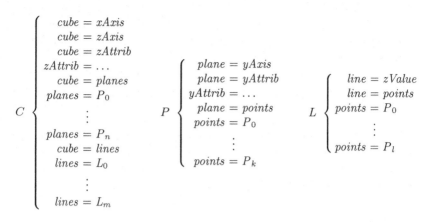

Fig. 2. A cube definition (left), a plane definition (middle) and a line definition (right)

Example 1 (Construction of Point Definitions). Let X and Z be the definiens of $xAxis$ and $zAxis$ respectively, in a cube definition C. Also, let z be the definition of $zAttrib$ in C. For each plane definition P defined in C: Let y be the definiens of $yAttrib$ in P and let Y be the definiens of $yAxis$ in P. Look up the definition of y in the definiens of $axisTable$ in X (i.e., find the position of the attribute of the plane on the x-axis of the Cube). This gives us the common x-coordinate for all the points in the plane. Then, for each definition D in the case base: First, look up the definiens of y in D in the definiens of $axisTable$ in Y (i.e., look up the value of the attribute of the plane in the case, and then find the position of the value on the y-axis of P). This gives us the y-coordinate of the point. Second, look up the definiens of z in D in the definiens of $axisTable$ in Z (i.e., look up the value of the common z-attribute in the case, and then find the position of the value on the common z-axis). This gives us the z-coordinate of the point.

Data-Based Manipulation of Cases. The parallel diagrams display of The Cube provides selection of lines, points and planes, and other manipulations, on a visual basis. This 3D visual presentation is useful for getting an overall picture of the case base, for quickly finding global patterns and trends.

However, a more detailed presentation of the case base is needed as well. This presentation should serve two purposes: First, it should be used for analysing, in detail, visual elements in the Cube, e.g., the selected lines or planes. Second, it should be used for data-based manipulations, e.g., filtering and brushing. The data-based presentation should complement the 3D presentation, and operations made in any presentation should immediately be reflected in the other.

Structure-Based Manipulation of Cases. Manipulating the structure of a Cube, e.g., rearranging the planes, selecting all points in a plane and changing visual properties of planes, lines and points, can be cumbersome using a 3D visual presentation. Thus, there is also a need for a more detailed presentation of the structure of the visualisation model (i.e., of the cube definition).

Just as the data-based presentation, the structure-based presentation should serve two purposes: First, it should be used for manipulating the structure of a Cube and for changing properties of the components of a Cube. For example, the planes could be rearranged, i.e., the x-axis could be redefined, selected points could (temporarily) be hidden and the grouping definitions used could be changed. Second, it should be used as a basis for structure-based manipulations of the underlying data. For example, selecting a plane would select all points defined in that plane. The structure-based presentation represents a third view of the data, which should complement the other two.

4.2   The Cube

The visualisation model described in the previous section has been implemented in a tool called The Cube.

Defining a Cube.   The user defines a new Cube by defining the axes and the planes of the Cube. To define an axis, the user selects the attribute to be used as the unit on the axis and a corresponding axis definition. In the default axis, values are defined by their position in alpha-numerical order. To get other orderings and classifications of values, other axis definitions can be defined, or the axis definition may be augmented with a grouping definition. The user also defines the (common) z-axis of the Cube in the same manner; in this case, the default is to use the personal identification attribute as the unit of the axis.

The upper left window in Fig. 3 is the panel for defining a new Cube.

Working with The Cube.   The user interacts with the 3D parallel diagrams using the main window of The Cube (middle window in Fig. 3). The Cube can be rotated, translated and zoomed using the mouse and the keyboard. Shortcuts are also provided for common views, e.g., front, top, left and right.

The user can change the appearance of a Cube in many ways: The Cube can be viewed in 3D parallel or perspective projection and the elements of the Cube, i.e., the lines, points and planes, can temporarily be hidden. In order to enhance contrast, the background color can be set. In addition, lines and planes can be rendered as wire-frames and planes can be set to be semi-transparent.

The Data Explorer.   It is possible to get statistics about a Cube using the *Data Explorer* presentation of the parallel diagrams display (right window in Fig. 3). In the Data Explorer, each plane is presented as a histogram composed of rectangles, each rectangle associated with one of the cases in the Cube. The number of rectangles corresponds to the number of cases having this particular value for the plane's attribute.

The Data Explorer has two modes of operation: By moving the mouse pointer over the bars in the histograms, the rectangle under the pointer is painted in a

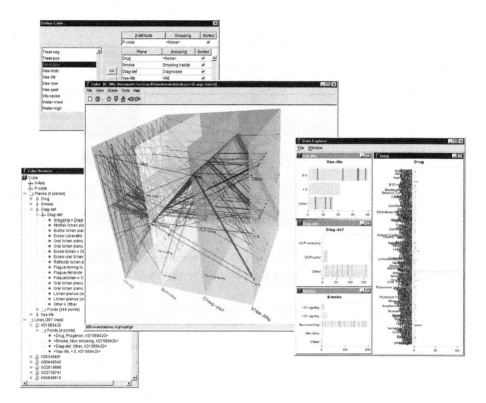

Fig. 3. The Cube: the panel for defining new Cubes (upper left), the visualisation of 3D parallel diagrams (middle), the data explorer window (right) and the window for browsing the structure of the Cube (lower left)

contrasting color, and all rectangles corresponding to this case are highlighted in all other histograms as well. Thus, cases are dynamically linked within and between histograms. Quickly brushing with the mouse over a specific value in one of the histograms, e.g., over the 'Other' bar in the 'Diag-def' histogram, highlights the values of the corresponding cases for the other attributes.

The user can also select all cases having a particular value by double-clicking with the mouse in the corresponding bar, thereby highlighting all rectangles corresponding to these cases in all histograms. By dynamically extending and contracting the selection of values, the user can get an overview of how attribute values are distributed among cases.

The Cube Browser. The structure of a Cube can be examined in detail using the *Cube Browser* (left window in Fig. 3).

In the Cube Browser, the structure of a Cube (i.e., a cube definition) is presented using a dynamic tree display: The root of the tree corresponds to the whole Cube; the x-axis, the z-axis, the lines and the planes constitute the

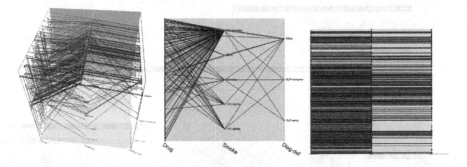

Fig. 4. A Cube showing the relation between medication, smoking habits and diagnoses: seen from the right and above (left), front view (middle) and top view (right)

children of the first level; the second level consists of the z-axis attribute, the z-axis definition, the points of the planes, the points of the lines and so on.

4.3   Applications

The Cube is used for finding patterns and correlations. If the case base is homogenous from the aspect of the chosen attributes, the lines will appear parallel to each other within the Cube. Consequently, heterogeneity and outliers in the case base for a certain attribute will cause the lines to diverge from each other in the corresponding plane. By using the various selection possibilities, a step-wise procedure may be performed where hypotheses are continuously refined.

Example 2. Oral lichen planus (OLP) is a disease with unknown aetiology that affects the oral mucosa. In its most severe form, the disease presents with erosions and ulcerations, which interfere with, e.g., eating of citrus fruits and spicy food. Some of the OLP lesions transform into a malignant disease of the oral mucosa. In this example, The Cube was used to examine drug and smoking habits for symptomatic (ulcerated) and non-symptomatic (non-ulcerated) OLP, information that has not previously been reported.

A Cube with three planes was defined: on the first plane, the drugs taken by the patients were presented, the smoking habits were presented on the second plane and on the third plane the diagnoses of the patients were displayed. The display was simplified by classification of smoking habits into non-smokers, patients not smoking on a daily basis, patients smoking less than 10 cigarettes/day, patients smoking more than 10 cigarettes/day and other smoking habits, and by classification of diagnoses into symptomatic OLP (OLP-symp), non-symptomatic OLP (OLP-nonsymp) and other diagnoses (see Fig. 4).

It was revealed that nearly all patients with OLP-symp were non-smokers compared to patients affected by OLP-nonsymp (81% non-smokers). The opposite was found for medication where only 47% of the patients with OLP-nonsymp used drugs compared to 65% of the patients diagnosed with OLP-symp.

These findings instigate thoughts about how different factors may influence the development of the two clinical forms of the disease. The reported observations have now to be statistically evaluated, and further investigations by using The Cube have to be conducted to examine if patients with OLP-symp take other types of drugs than patients with OLP-nonsymp.

5   Arrangement of Dimensions

The order and arrangement of dimensions is crucial for the effectiveness of multidimensional visualisation techniques like the parallel coordinate plot [15,17]. Often dimensions are arranged, more or less, arbitrarily. Compared to the two-dimensional case, the arrangement problem is even more problematic in the case of The Cube, due to the extra third dimension: not only do we have to consider the proper arrangement of planes, but the arrangement of lines as well.

In this section, we describe an approach to arrange the dimensions of a 3D parallel coordinate plot according to their similarity, where we take advantage of the fact that The Cube and SimVis share the same formal declarative model.

Since the planes and the lines of a Cube are definitions, and since SimVis clusters definitions, the basic idea is to use the similarity framework of SimVis to rearrange the planes of the Cube in such a way that 'similar' planes are positioned next (or close) to each other, and then to do the same thing with the lines. Thus, we must first define similarity measures that determine the similarity between two plane definitions (two line definitions). Then we use the SimVis tool from Sect. 3 to cluster plane definitions (line definitions). The arrangement of planes (lines) is finally given by the clustering order.

We demonstrate the effect of different arrangements in visualising a Med-View case base containing 551 cases using The Cube. The original arrangement of planes and lines can be seen in Fig. 5: From left to right we had drugs ('Drug'), diagnoses ('Diag-def') and smoking habits ('Smoke'). The diagnoses were grouped into the two clinical forms of lichen planus and other diseases, the drugs were sorted alphabetically, but they were not grouped, and the smoking habits were divided into the same classes as in Example 2. Not surprisingly, potential correlations between the use of drugs and smoking habits were not easily discerned. Even the known correlations between the two clinical forms of lichen planus and smoking habits, as was reported in Sect. 4.3, were not easy to discover. Seen from above (the right picture in Fig. 5), the original visualisation also suggested that most cases had values for all three attributes.

5.1   Arrangement of Planes

To be able to cluster the three plane definitions of the Cube in Fig. 5, we must estimate the similarity between the plane definitions. Although this can be done in many ways, the most obvious way is to just compare the relative positions of the points of the planes with each other. In other words, we estimated the similarity of the planes in terms of the relative z-positions for which points existed, and the relative y-positions of these points.

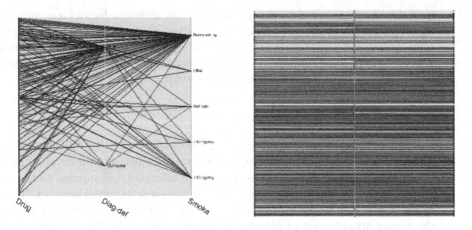

Fig. 5. Original arrangement of planes: front view (left) and top view (right)

In the constructed similarity measure, we compared the y-position of each z-position with each other. Each identity (each pair of identical y-positions) contributed with a small amount to the overall similarity. The clustering in SimVis revealed that 'Smoke' and 'Drug' are the most similar planes, and that 'Diag-def' is slightly more similar to 'Smoke' than to 'Drug'. Thus, the order of the planes should be: 'Drug', 'Smoke' and 'Diag-def', or the reverse.

A new Cube was then defined. The new Cube was identical to the one in Fig. 5 apart from that the planes had been rearranged according to the order given by the above clustering. Figure 4 in Sect. 4.3 shows the new arrangement. Compared to the original visualisation, the even distribution of non-smokers among drugs was more apparent with the new arrangement (the middle picture in Fig. 4). The fact that patients with OLP-symp are, with a few exceptions, non-smokers, was also more clearly seen in the new visualisation. In contrast to the original arrangement, the new arrangement also clearly revealed that quite a few cases lack a value for one of the attributes (the right picture in Fig. 4).

5.2 Arrangement of Lines

Just as the planes, the lines of a Cube are definitions as well. The idea was to cluster the line definitions of the Cube in Fig. 5 using SimVis, to define the resulting clustering order in a grouping definition (see Sect. 2) and, finally, to use this definition as the grouping definition of the z-axis of a new Cube, thereby effectively ordering the lines according to the clustering order.

However, before we can cluster the line definitions, we must define a similarity measure between line definitions. Just as in Sect. 5.1, the natural choice was to compare the individual points of the lines with each other. In other words, we estimated the similarity of the lines in terms of the relative x-positions for which points existed, and the relative y-positions of these points.

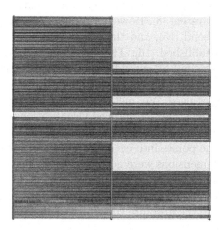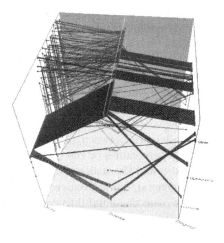

Fig. 6. A new Cube with lines rearranged: seen from above (left) and seen slightly from the right and above (right)

In the constructed similarity measure, each identity (each pair of identical y-positions) contributed with a small amount to the overall similarity. Similarly, each non-identity reduced the overall similarity by the same amount. The similarity depended on which of the, possibly several, y-positions of the first line definition was compared with which y-position of the second line definition. In this example, the comparison that maximised the overall similarity was used. The resulting clustering was then saved into a grouping definition.

A new Cube was then defined. The new Cube was identical to the Cube in Sect. 5.1 apart from that the lines had been rearranged according to the order given by the above clustering, by the use of the saved grouping definition as the grouping definition of the z-axis. Figure 6 shows the new arrangement of lines.

Compared to Sect. 5.1, an improvement was achieved by rearranging the lines according to their similarity. As can be seen in the left picture in Fig. 6, lines that showed a similar behavior in terms of their x-coordinates, i.e., in terms of for which attributes they had defined values, were clearly grouped together more tightly compared to the Cube in Fig. 4. If we compare the left picture in Fig. 4 with the right picture in Fig. 6, it is clear that the rearrangement of the lines also improved the overall visualisation, with 'bands' of similar lines being formed.

6   Discussion

The Cube has been used on a regular basis for a couple of years now. Clinical practice indicates that the basic ideas are conceptually appealing to the involved clinicians as The Cube can be used for generating and testing of hypotheses.

The parallel coordinate plot is a well-known visualisation technique for multi-dimensional analysis. Within the medical domain, parallel coordinate plots have been used as the single geometrical representation of both quantitative and qualitative clinical information in the BAIK system [8]. However, parallel coordinate plots take practice for users to comprehend [15], and the interaction with parallel coordinate plots is not yet well established [16]. Therefore, the work on a methodology for clinical use of The Cube will be extended and carried further.

The examples in Sect. 5 showed that, even for this small number of dimensions and the simple similarity measures used, our method of rearranging the dimensions according to their similarity resulted in improved visualisations. The similarities between planes and lines were measured without taken the actual attribute values or the coordinates of the points into account, i.e., the value domains and the scales of the respective dimensions were not considered. Since we, in general, cannot expect to find a common domain for all dimensions, it does not seem meaningful to consider the actual attribute values of the points during similarity assessment. But, we could take the absolute coordinates into account, i.e., use a common relative scale for all dimensions.

We could also use more complex similarity measures. For example, when measuring the similarity between lines, we could try to capture similarities between the overall form of the lines, as opposed to capturing similarities between properties of individual points. Lines, i.e., cases, showing the same behavior would then be clustered together. We would also be interested in finding an arrangement in which negatively correlated dimensions are positioned next to each other.

Our similarity framework for definitional structures can, of course, be used as a basis for other, non-cluster-based, arrangements of dimensions and lines.

In [2], a solution to the problem of finding a proper arrangement of the dimensions of a two-dimensional parallel coordinate plot is presented. In this approach, dimensions showing a similar behavior are positioned next to each other. Just as in our approach, the finding of an effective ordering of dimensions is based on the idea of arranging dimensions according to their similarity. On the basis of an Euclidian distance measure, or another metric distance measure, a one-dimensional arrangement of a number of dimensions is found. The arrangement is optimal, in the sense that the sum of the similarities between all pairs of dimensions is maximised. Compared to our approach, the fundamental difference is that [2] adopts a purely numeric, non-declarative approach.

The interest in interactive CBR has recently increased [1]. Our approach to visualisation for CBR conforms well to this trend: The interaction model of SimVis supports the visualisation of the similarity assessment process and of the case base as a whole [12,19]. The Cube complements SimVis by visualising the case base in terms of relationships between cases. In fact, the visualisation model of The Cube is also used in SimVis for visualising relationships between atoms *within* individual cases. Our solution to the arrangement problem is an example of how integration issues can be addressed using a uniform declarative model.

Integrating the similarity framework of SimVis with The Cube would enable automatic rearrangement of dimensions: in addition to user-definable axis and grouping definitions, The Cube could also provide user-definable libraries of similarity measures over planes and lines.

Even more interesting is the observation that, since The Cube essentially is a definition, instances of The Cube can be added to the case base and similarity measures *over Cubes* could be defined. When confronted with a new visualisation problem (i.e., we want to construct a new Cube for a given set of attributes), we could search the case base for previous *similar Cubes* that provide a solution in terms of properly arranged dimensions. Thus, the uniform model used opens up for the possibility of *case-based visualisation* for CBR.

7   Summary and Conclusions

- An information visualisation tool, The Cube, was presented as a solution to the problem of visualising cases derived from large amounts of clinical data. The Cube was based on the idea of dynamic 3D parallel diagrams, an idea similar to the notion of 3D parallel coordinate plots.
- A uniform declarative model was used for both knowledge representation and as the basis for visualisation and implementation models.
- The declarative, user-centered nature of The Cube makes it suitable for interactive CBR and opens up for the possibility of case-based visualisation for CBR.
- Known visualisation techniques were modeled using the conceptual model of the underlying data, enabling close interaction with the user and tight coupling between two different visualisation tools.
- The declarative model used and the tight coupling between The Cube and SimVis directly led to a similarity assessment-based solution to the problem of finding a proper arrangement of dimensions and lines in 3D parallel coordinate displays.

References

1. D. W. Aha and H. Muños-Avila. Applied intelligence: Special issue on interactive case-based reasoning. *Applied Intelligence*, 14(1):1–2, 2001.
2. M. Ankerst, S. Berchtold, and D. A. Keim. Similarity clustering of dimensions for an enhanced visualization of multidimensional data. In G. Wills and J. Dill, editors, *Proceedings of the IEEE Symposium on Information Visualization (InfoVis'98), October 19–20, 1998, Research Triangle Park, North Carolina, USA*, pages 52–59, Los Alamitos, CA, USA, 1998. IEEE Computer Society Press.
3. L. Chittaro. Information visualization and its application to medicine. *Artificial Intelligence in Medicine*, 22(2):81–88, 2001.
4. T. Chomut. Exploratory data analysis in parallel coordinates. Research report, IBM Los Angeles Scientific Center, 1987.
5. G. Falkman. Similarity measures for structured representations: A definitional approach. In E. Blanzieri and L. Portinale, editors, *Advances in Case-Based Reasoning. Proceedings of the 5th European Workshop, EWCBR 2000, Trento, Italy, September 6–9, 2000*, volume 1898 of *Lecture Notes in Artificial Intelligence*, pages 380–392. Springer-Verlag, 2000.

6. G. Falkman. Information visualization in clinical odontology: Multidimensional analysis and interactive data exploration. *Artificial Intelligence in Medicine*, 22(2):133–158, 2001.

7. J. Fechter, T. Grunert, L. M. Encarnação, and W. Straßer. User-centered development of medical visualization applications: Flexible interaction through communicating application objects. *Computers & Graphics: Special Issue on Medical Visualization*, 20(6):763–774, 1996.

8. A. J. W. Goldschmidt, C. J. Luz, W. Giere, R. Lüdecke, and D. Jonas. Multidimensional visualization of laboratory findings and functional test-results for analyzing the clinical course of disease in medicine. *Methods of Information in Medicine*, 34(3):302–308, 1995.

9. L. Hallnäs. Partial inductive definitions. *Theoretical Computer Science*, 87(1):115–142, 1991.

10. A. Inselberg. The plane with parallel coordinates. *The Visual Computer*, 1:69–91, 1985.

11. B. McCormick, T. A. DeFanti, and M. D. Brown. Visualization in scientific computing. *Computer Graphics*, 21(6), 1987.

12. E. McKenna and B. Smyth. An interactive visualisation tool for case-based reasoners. *Applied Intelligence*, 14(1):95–114, 2001.

13. C. L. North and B. Shneiderman. Snap-together visualization: Can users construct and operate coordinated views? *Int. J. of Human-Computer Studies*, 53(5):715–739, 2000.

14. C. L. North and B. Shneiderman. Component-based, user-constructed, multiple-view visualization. In *CHI 2001 Video Program*. ACM Press, 2001.

15. B. Shneiderman. *Designing the User Interface: Strategies for Effective Human-Computer Interaction*. Addison-Wesley Longman, Inc., Reading, MA, USA, 3 edition, 1998.

16. H. Siirtola. Direct manipulation of parallel coordinates. In E. Banissi, M. Bannatyne, C. Chen, F. Khosrowshahi, and A. Ursyn, editors, *Proceedings of the IEEE International Conference on Information Visualisation (IV 2000)*, pages 373–378. IEEE Computer Society Press, 2000.

17. R. Spence. *Information Visualization*. Addison-Wesley, Harlow, England, 2001.

18. J. W. Tukey. *Exploratory Data Analysis*. Addison-Wesley, Reading, MA, USA, 1977.

19. Q. Yang and J. Wu. Enhancing the effectiveness of interactive case-based reasoning with clustering and decision forests. *Applied Intelligence*, 14(1):49–64, 2001.

Experiments on Case-Based Retrieval
of Software Designs

Paulo Gomes, Francisco C. Pereira, Paulo Paiva, Nuno Seco, Paulo Carreiro,
José L. Ferreira, and Carlos Bento

CISUC – Centro de Informática e Sistemas da Universidade de Coimbra.
Departamento de Engenharia Informática, Polo II, Universidade de Coimbra. 3030 Coimbra
{pgomes, camara, zeluis, bento}@dei.uc.pt,
{paiva, nseco, carreiro}@student.dei.uc.pt,
http://rebuilder.dei.uc.pt

Abstract. Software systems are becoming increasingly complex, demanding for more computational resources and better software development methodologies. The software engineer and the CASE tool must work like a team. For this to happen, the CASE tool must be able to understand the user, and to provide new functionalities, such as flexible retrieval of old designs. We think that Case-Based Reasoning can provide a reasoning framework capable of meeting these demands. One important task that a CASE tool based on Case-Based Reasoning can perform adequately, is the retrieval of relevant designs. These designs can be stored in a case library, central to the software development company, thus enabling knowledge sharing through out the company. In this paper we present an approach to case-based retrieval of software designs, and experimental results achieved with this approach.

1 Introduction

The need for intelligent CASE (Computer Aided Software Engineering) tools has grown in the last decade. This is due to the increase in software complexity and to the rigorous demands that clients put on software developing companies. Software engineers have to develop better software in less time and with tight budgets. A possible solution to this problem is the use of intelligent CASE tools that provide functionalities for knowledge sharing instead of just code sharing. The good news are that the introduction of intelligent CASE systems creates an opportunity for the corporation to share among all its engineers, the knowledge acquired along the development of previous projects. This knowledge can be stored in a central repository, that enables the intelligent CASE tools to use it. This repository can also be updated, by adding new knowledge, or by removing outdated one, thus evolving with the corporation experience.

---

[1] This work was partially supported by POSI - Programa Operacional Sociedade de Informação of Portuguese Fundação para a Ciência e Tecnologia and European Union FEDER, under contract POSI/33399/SRI/2000, by program PRAXIS XXI.

S. Craw and A. Preece (Eds.): ECCBR 2002, LNAI 2416, pp. 118–132.

Software reuse [1, 2] is an engineering field that studies the use of knowledge gathered from previous developed software, in new projects. Several types of development knowledge can be reused. Ranging from the project specifications [3], to software designs [4], with code [5-7] being the most reused knowledge. Case-based reasoning [8, 9] is a field with shy similarities to software reuse. Both reuse knowledge, with the difference that in software reuse this knowledge relates to one specific domain – software development. Bringing both of these areas together has been done by some research works [10-14]. Software reuse can take advantage of several reasoning techniques developed in case-based reasoning (CBR). The knowledge repository mentioned before can be a case library, with cases describing knowledge related to a specific software project. Cases can then be indexed such that they can be reused in an efficient way. Retrieval capabilities can be added to the intelligent CASE tools allowing the use of the case library. New cases can also be learned from the interaction with the software designers or from the system's reasoning. One of the most important tasks in a CBR tool for software reuse is the retrieval of relevant knowledge. The retrieval of irrelevant cases hinders the remaining phases of CBR. Two important issues must be dealt with in case retrieval: cases must be indexed correctly, meaning that indexes must be discriminatory so that the retrieval algorithm can make use of them; and the similarity metric must be accurate.

We have developed an intelligent CASE tool (REBUILDER), which brings together CBR and Software Reuse. Our approach is intended to aid the software engineer in the design phase. We use the Unified Modeling Language (UML) [15] to represent the design knowledge. Being UML a commonly used design language for most of the software engineers, users interact with the system through an UML editor. From the user point of view, this editor has extra functionalities that can help the design task. These functionalities enable the reuse of knowledge stored in a knowledge base, which comprises a case library along with other knowledge repositories. One of the functionalities developed in our system is the retrieval of designs (complete designs or objects). Our approach to design retrieval combines a general ontology for object classification and indexing, with an object-oriented similarity metric. In this paper we present our approach, and experimental results obtained with our system concerning design retrieval.

The remaining of this paper presents the architecture of REBUILDER. We describe in detail the knowledge base, the retrieval algorithm, the similarity metrics, and the experimental results obtained with REBUILDER. We compare our approach with systems for software reuse, and finally we discuss the experimental results, the advantages and disadvantages of our system.

2 REBUILDER's Architecture

REBUILDER is a CASE tool that provides intelligent support for the software engineer in the design phase. REBUILDER is a tool intended to be used at a corporate level, centralizing the corporation past designs in its knowledge base. There are two types of users interacting with the system. Software designers, using REBUILDER as an intelligent UML editor, and system administrators with the main task of keeping the knowledge base (KB) consistent and updated.

In order for a CASE tool to be used, the design language must be intuitive and human-centered. This is also true for software design where it is common the use of visual languages to represent software modules. One of the worldwide used software design languages is UML [15]. This language provides a representation for all the software development phases. By choosing UML as the representation language, we are providing the user with a design standard.

Figure 1 presents the architecture of REBUILDER. It comprises four main modules: UML editor, KB manager, KB, and CBR engine. The UML editor is the system front-end to the software designer, comprising the working space for design. The KB manager is the interface with the KB and system administrator. It provides access to the various sub modules of knowledge, allowing the administrator to add, delete, or change knowledge in the KB.

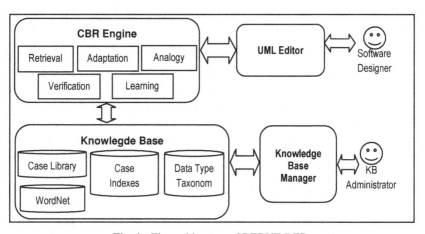

Fig. 1 - The architecture of REBUILDER.

The KB comprises four sub modules: data type taxonomy, case library, case indexes, and WordNet knowledge. The data type taxonomy provides *is-a* relations between data types used in UML. The case library stores the design cases, each one representing a software design. Software designs are stored in UML files created in the editor. The case indexes are used for case retrieval, making retrieval more efficient. WordNet is a lexical reference system [16], used in REBUILDER as a general ontology that categorizes case objects.

The CBR engine performs all the inference work in REBUILDER. There are five sub modules: retrieval, analogy, adaptation, verification, and learning. The retrieval module searches the case library for designs or design objects similar to the query. The most similar ones are presented to the user, allowing the user to reuse these designs, or part of them. Retrieved designs can also suggest new ideas to the designer, helping her/him to explore the design space. The analogy module maps candidate designs from the case library to the query design. The resulting mapping establishes how the knowledge transfer takes place from the old design to the designer query.

Analogy goes further than case retrieval, creating new designs. The adaptation module adapts a past design (or part of it) to the designer query. The main usage of this module is in combination with retrieval. The verification module checks the current design for inconsistencies. The learning module acquires new knowledge from the user interaction, and from the system interaction. This paper focus on the retrieval module.

3 Knowledge Base

As said before, the Knowledge Base comprises four components: Case Library, Case Indexes, WordNet, and Data Type Taxonomy.

The case library is a repository of software designs in the format of UML models. Cases are represented as UML class diagrams defining the software design structure. Class diagrams can comprise three types of objects (packages, classes and interfaces) and four kind of relations between them (associations, generalizations, realizations and dependencies). Each class diagram has a main package named root package. Packages can contain other packages, classes and interfaces. Classes can comprise attributes and methods, interfaces only have methods. Class diagrams are very intuitive, and are an effective visual way of communication between software development members. Though UML has several other diagrams each one representing the software system in a different aspect, only class diagrams are used (see Fig. 2). We have selected this type of diagrams because they are the most used diagrams in UML. Cases are stored as XMI/XML files, which can be used by other CASE tools.

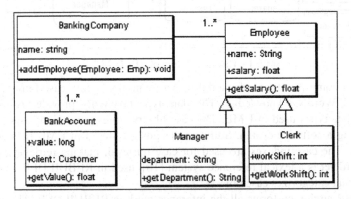

Fig. 2 - Example of an UML class diagram.

WordNet is used in REBUILDER as a common sense ontology. It uses a differential theory where concept meanings are represented by symbols that enable a theorist to distinguish among them. Symbols are words, and concept meanings are called synsets. A synset is a concept represented by one or more words. If more than one word can be used to represent a synset, then they are called synonyms. But there is also another word phenomenon important for WordNet: the same word can have different meanings (polysemy). For instance, the word mouse has two meanings, it can denote a rat, or it can express a computer mouse. WordNet is built around the concept of synset. Basically it comprises a list of word synsets, and different semantic relations between synsets. Each element of the word list comprises a word and a list of synsets that the word represents. Semantic relations between synsets are: *is-a* relations (rat *is-a* mouse), *part-of* relations (door *part-of* house), and other relations. In REBUILDER we use the word synset list (which is essential) and four semantic relations: *is-a*, *part-of*, *substance-of*, and *member-of*. Synsets are classified within four different types: nouns, verbs, adjectives, and adverbs. REBUILDER uses synsets for categorization of software objects. Each object has a context synset which represents the object meaning. In order to find the correct synset, REBUILDER uses the object name, and the names of the objects related with it, which define the object context. The description of this computation is out of this paper scope. The object's context synset can then be used for computing object similarity (using the WordNet semantic relations), or it can be used as a case index, allowing rapid access to objects with the same classification.

As cases can be large, they are stored in files, which makes case access slower then if they were in memory. To solve this problem we use case indexes. These provide a way to access the relevant case parts for retrieval without having to read all the case files from disk. Each object in a case is used as an index. REBUILDER uses the context synset of each object to index the case in WordNet. This way, REBUILDER can retrieve a complete case, using the case root package, or it can retrieve only a subset of case objects, using the objects' indexes. This allows REBUILDER to provide the user the possibility to retrieve not only packages, but also classes and interfaces.

The data type taxonomy is a hierarchy of data types used in REBUILDER. Data types are used in the definition of attributes and methods. The data taxonomy is used to compute the conceptual distance between two data types.

4 Retrieval Algorithm

REBUILDER can retrieve three types of objects (packages, classes and interfaces) based on the WordNet object classification. Suppose that the *N* best objects are to be retrieved, *QObj* is the query object, and *ObjectList* is the universe of objects that can be retrieved (usually *ObjectList* comprises all the library cases). The retrieval algorithm is:

```
ObjsFound  ← ∅
PSynset ← Get context synset of QObj
PSynsets ← {PSynset}
ObjsExplored ← ∅
WHILE (#ObjsFound < N) AND (PSynsets ≠ ∅) DO
    Synset ← Remove first element of PSynsets
    ObjsExplored ← ObjsExplored + Synset
    SubSynsets ← Get Synset hyponyms / subordinates
    SuperSynsets ← Get Synset hypernyms / super ordinates
    SubSynsets ← SubSynsets - ObjsExplored - PSynsets
```

```
    SuperSynsets ← SuperSynsets - ObjsExplored - PSynsets
    PSynsets ← Add SubSynsets to the end of PSynsets
    PSynsets ← Add SuperSynsets to the end of PSynsets
    Objects ← Get all objects indexed by Synset
    Objects ← Objects ∩ ObjectList
    ObjsFound ← ObjsFound ∩ Objects
ENDWHILE
ObjsFound ← Rank ObjsFound by similarity
RETURN Select the first N elements from ObjsFound
```

Object retrieval has two distinct phases. First the WordNet *is-a* relations are used as an index structure to find relevant objects. Then a similarity metric is used to select the best N objects. This process is a compromise between a first phase, which is inexpensive from the computational point of view, and a second phase that demands more computational resources, but much more accurate in the object selection and ranking.

In the first phase the object's context synset works like an index. Starting by *QObj* context synset, the algorithm searches for objects indexed with the same synset. If there are not enough objects, the algorithm uses the hypernyms and hyponyms of this synset to look for objects, going in a spreading activation kind of algorithm. When it has found enough objects, it stops and ranks them using the similarity metric. In the next section we present the similarity metrics used for object ranking.

5 Similarity Metrics

There are three similarity metrics: for classes, for interfaces, and for packages. The class and package similarity metrics are based on WordNet categorization and in the object structure. The interface metric is equal to the class metric with the difference that it does not have attributes.

5.1 Class Similarity

The class similarity metric is based on three components: categorization similarity, inter-class similarity, and intra-class similarity (see also [17]). The similarity between class C_1 and C_2, is:

$$S(C_1, C_2) = \omega_1 \cdot S(S_1, S_2) + \omega_2 \cdot S(Ie_1, Ie_2) + \omega_3 \cdot S(Ia_1, Ia_2) \tag{1}$$

Where $S(S_1, S_2)$ is the categorization similarity based on the distance, in *is-a* relations, between C_1 context synset (S_1) and C_2 context synset (S_2), see equation (3). $S(Ie_1, Ie_2)$ is the inter-class similarity based on the similarity between the diagram relations of C_1 and C_2. $S(Ia_1, Ia_2)$ is the intra-class similarity based on the similarity between attributes and methods of C_1 and C_2. W_i are constants, and we use 0.6, 0.1, and 0.3 as the default values of these constants, based on experimental work.

5.2 Interface Similarity

The interface similarity metric is the same as the class metric with the difference that the intra-class similarity metric is only based on the method similarity, since interfaces do not have attributes.

5.3 Package Similarity

The package similarity between packages PK_1 and PK_2 is:

$$S(Pk_1, Pk_2) = \begin{bmatrix} \omega_1 \cdot S(SPs_1, SPs_2) + \omega_2 \cdot S(OBs_1, OBs_2) \\ + \omega_3 \cdot S(T_1, T_2) + \omega_4 \cdot S(D_1, D_2) \end{bmatrix} \tag{2}$$

This metric is based on four items: sub package list similarity – $S(SPs_1, SPs_2)$, UML class diagram similarity – $S(OBs_1, OBs_2)$, categorization similarity – $S(T_1, T_2)$, and dependency list similarity – $S(D_1, D_2)$. These four items are combined in a weighted sum. The weights used in our experiments are: 0.07, 0.4, 0.5, 0.03, respectively. These values are supported on experimental work. From the weight values it can be seen that the most important factors for package similarity are the categorization similarity and the class diagram similarity.

5.4 Object Categorization Similarity

The object type similarity is computed using the context synsets of the objects. The similarity between synset S_1 and S_2 is:

$$S(S_1, S_2) = \frac{1}{\ln(Min\{\forall Path(S_1, S_2)\} + 1) + 1} \tag{3}$$

Where *Min* is the function returning the smaller element of a list. $Path(S_1, S_2)$ is the WordNet path between synset S_1 and S_2, which returns the number of relations between the synsets. *Ln* is the natural logarithm.

5.5 Inter-Class Similarity

The inter-class similarity between two objects (classes or interfaces) is based on the matching of the relations in which both objects are involved. The similarity between objects O_1 and O_2 is presented in equation (4).

$$S(O_1, O_2) = 2 \cdot \begin{pmatrix} \omega_1 \cdot \left(\dfrac{\sum_{i=1}^{n} S(R_{1i}, R_{2i})}{n} \right) - \omega_2 \cdot \dfrac{Unmatched(R_1)}{\#R_1} \\ - \omega_3 \cdot \dfrac{Unmatched(R_2)}{\#R_2} + \omega_2 + \omega_3 \end{pmatrix} - 1 \tag{4}$$

Where R_i is the set of relations in object i, R_{ij} is the j element of R_i, n is the number of matched relations, $S(R_{1i}, R_{2i})$ is the relation similarity, and w_1, w_2 and w_3 are constants, with $\Sigma w_i = 1$ (default values are: 0.5; 0.4; 0.1). Unmatched(R_i) returns the number of unmatched relations in R_i.

5.6 Intra-Class Similarity

The intra-class similarity between objects O_1 and O_2 is:

$$S(O_1, O_2) = \omega_1 \cdot S(As_1, As_2) + \omega_2 \cdot S(Ms_1, Ms_2) \tag{5}$$

Where $S(As_1, As_2)$ is the similarity between attributes, $S(Ms_1, Ms_2)$ is the similarity between methods, and w_1 and w_2 are constants, with $\Sigma w_i = 1$ (default values are: 0.6; 0.4).

5.7 Sub-Package List Similarity

The similarity between sub package lists SPs_1 and SPs_2 is:

$$S(SPs_1, SPs_2) = 2 \cdot \left(\begin{array}{l} \omega_1 \cdot \left(\dfrac{\sum_{i=1}^{n} S(SPs_{1i}, SPs_{2i})}{n} \right) - \omega_2 \cdot \dfrac{Unmatched(SPs_1)}{\#SPs_1} \\ - \omega_3 \cdot \dfrac{Unmatched(SPs_2)}{\#SPs_2} + \omega_2 + \omega_3 \end{array} \right) - 1 \tag{6}$$

Where w_i are constants, and $\Sigma w_i = 1$ (default values are: 0.5; 0.4; 0.1), n is the number of sub packages matched, $S(Pk_{1i}, Pk_{2i})$ is the similarity between packages, Unmatched(Pk_i) is the number of unmatched packages in Pk_i, SPs_{ij} is the j element of SPs_i, and $\#Pk_i$ is the number of packages in Pk_i.

5.8 UML Class Diagram Similarity

The similarity between lists of UML objects OBs_1 and OBs_2 is:

$$S(OBs_1, OBs_2) = 2 \cdot \left(\begin{array}{l} \omega_1 \cdot \left(\dfrac{\sum_{i=1}^{n} S(OB_{1i}, OB_{2i})}{n} \right) - \omega_2 \cdot \dfrac{Unmatched(OBs_1)}{\#OBs_1} \\ - \omega_3 \cdot \dfrac{Unmatched(OBs_2)}{\#OBs_2} + \omega_2 + \omega_3 \end{array} \right) - 1 \tag{7}$$

Where w_i are constants, and $\Sigma w_i = 1$ (default values are: 0.5; 0.4; 0.1), $\#OBs_i$ is the number of objects in OBs_i, Unmatched(OBs_i) is the number of objects unmapped in OBs_i, n is the number of objects matched, OB_{ij} is the j element of OB_i, and $S(OB_{1i}, OB_{2i})$ is the object categorization similarity.

5.9 Dependency List Similarity

Dependency is a UML relation type, and is commonly used to describe dependencies between packages. The similarity between dependency lists D_1 and D_2 is given by:

$$S(D_1, D_2) = \left[\omega_1 \cdot \frac{\left| \#ID_1 - \#ID_2 \right|}{Max\{\#ID_1, \#ID_2\}} + \omega_2 \cdot \frac{\left| \#OD_1 - \#OD_2 \right|}{Max\{\#OD_1, \#OD_2\}} \right] \tag{8}$$

Where w_1 and w_2 are constants, and $\Sigma w_i = 1$ (default values are: 0.5; 0.5), ID are the input dependencies, and OD are the output dependencies.

6 Retrieval Example

In this section a simple retrieval example is given to illustrate the used algorithm and similarity metrics. Suppose that the diagram of is Fig. 3 a diagram developed in REBUILDER's UML editor. Imagine that this diagram represents part of a banking company information system. It comprises three classes: Banking Company, Customer and Bank Account. They are all related by associations with multiplicity.

The user then selects the retrieval command over the banking company diagram. What the retrieval module does, is to search WordNet for indexes of packages similar to the query. Fig. 4 shows part of the WordNet indexing structure and the package indexes found. The retrieval algorithm starts in the Banking Company synset, where

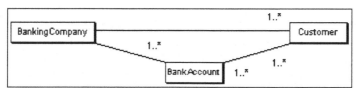

Fig. 4 - The class diagram of the query problem representing a banking company.

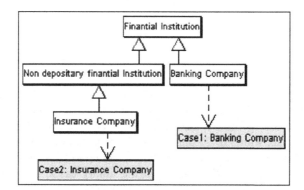

Fig. 4 - Part of the WordNet structure that is used in the retrieval example. White boxes represent WordNet synsets and gray boxes represent case indexes, in this case indexing packages. Links between synsets represent *is-a* relations.

it founds a first package to be retrieved: Case1 – Banking Company (suppose Fig. 2 is Case1). If only two are be retrieved, then the algorithm continues the search expanding to the neighbor synsets, until it reaches the Insurance Company synset. There it finds the Case2 – Insurance Company package (see Fig. 5).

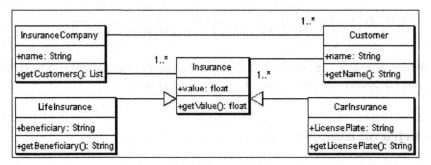

Fig. 5 - The class diagram of Case2.

The next phase is to rank the retrieved cases: Case1 – Banking Company, and Case2 – Insurance Company. The similarity used is the package similarity, since we are retrieving packages. Then the similarity between the problem (P) and Case1 (C1) is given by: $S(P,C1) = w1 * 0 + w2 * S(OBs_P, OBs_{C1}) + w3 * S(T_P + T_{C1}) + w4 * 0$. There are no sub packages and no dependencies between packages, so the first and the last terms are zero. The class diagram similarity: $S(OBs_P, OBs_{C1})$ is: $2 * (w1 * 2 / 2 - w2 * 1/3 - w3 * 3/5 + w2 + w3) - 1 = 0.61$. Two exactly mapped classes BankingCompany to BankingCompany, and BankAccount to BankAccount yielding a score of 2. There is only one unmapped object in the problem, out of 3, and there are 3 unmapped objects in Case1 out of 5. The type similarity, $S(T_P + T_{C1})$, is 1 since the two packages have the same synset. Then $S(P,C1) = 0.74$. Doing the same computations for Case2 yields that $S(P,C2) = 0.41$, $S(OBs_P, OBs_{C1}) = 0.5$ (since there are three mappings: Customer – Customer, Bank – InsuranceCompany, and BankAccount – Insurance, each one of similarity 1, 0.42 and 0.31 respectively), and $S(T_P + T_{C1}) = 0.42$ (since the packages have different synsets). Thus Case1 is more similar to P than Case2.

7   Experimental Work

We have performed two types of experiments: package retrieval and class retrieval. In the Package retrieval experiments the case library used comprises 60 cases. Each case comprises a package, with 5 to 20 objects (total number of objects in the knowledge base is 586). Each object has up to 20 attributes, and up to 20 methods. Three sets of package problems were specified, based on the library cases. Incomplete set P20, with 25 problems, each problem is a case copy with 80% of its objects deleted, attributes and methods are also reduced by 80%. The other sets are the same problems but with 50% (P50) and 20% (P80) deleted.

One of the experimental goals is to define the best weight configuration for package retrieval. For each problem a best case and a set of relevant cases were defined before the runs were executed. These sets are used to evaluate the accuracy of the algorithm. For each problem set, the following weight configurations were used:

	w1	w2	w3	w4
Configuration 1 (C1)	0	1	0	0
Configuration 2 (C2)	0	0.75	0.25	0
Configuration 3 (C3)	0	0.5	0.5	0
Configuration 4 (C4)	0	0.25	0.75	0
Configuration 5 (C5)	0	0	1	0

Because each case has only one package, weights w1 and w4 are not used, leaving only weights w2 (diagram similarity) and w3 (categorization similarity), which concern class diagram similarity and package type similarity. For each problem run the best twenty retrieved cases were analyzed. The data gathered was: best case is first (yes or no), best case is selected (yes or no), percentage of the relevant cases retrieved, computing time, memory used, and the best 20 cases ranked by similarity.

Table 1 - The package retrieval results obtained for the percentage of: best cases in the first ranking place, relevant cases retrieved, and best case retrieved by number of cases retrieved.

	C1	C2	C3	C4	C5
% Relevant Cases Retrieved	82.03	84.15	84.75	85.12	83.95
% Best Case First	81.33	85.33	88.00	88.00	61.33
% Best Case Retrieved (in 5 cases)	88.00	92.00	92.00	92.00	85.33
% Best Case Retrieved (in 10 cases)	89.33	93.33	93.33	93.33	93.33
% Best Case Retrieved (in 15 cases)	92.00	93.33	93.33	93.33	93.33
% Best Case Retrieved (in 20 cases)	93.33	93.33	93.33	93.33	93.33

From the results presented in Table 1, it can be inferred that configuration C4 has the higher percentage of relevant case retrieval, though results obtained for C2, C3 and C5 are very near. In terms of best case retrieval (among the first 20 relevant cases) all the configurations retrieve it 93.3 % of the runs, though results for the retrieval of the best case in the first ranking position are clearly different, with C3 and C4 having the best results. In terms of performance there are no significant differences between the configurations.

In class retrieval experiments we used the same case library as before. Three sets of class problems were specified, based on cases. The strategy used for problem definition is the same that was used in the problem packages. An incomplete set P20, with 50 problems, each problem is a copy of a class from the Knowledge Base with 80% of its methods and attributes deleted. The other sets are the same problems but with 50% (P50) and 20% (P80) deleted. For each class a set of relevant classes was defined before the runs were executed. These sets are used to evaluate the accuracy of the algorithm. For each problem set the following weight configurations was used:

	w1	w2	w3
Configuration 1 (C1)	0	0	1
Configuration 2 (C2)	0	0.5	0.5
Configuration 3 (C3)	0	1	0
Configuration 4 (C4)	0.25	0.25	0.5
Configuration 5 (C5)	0.25	0.5	0.25
Configuration 6 (C6)	0.5	0	0.5
Configuration 7 (C7)	0.5	0.25	0.25
Configuration 8 (C8)	0.5	0.5	0
Configuration 9 (C9)	1	0	0

Weight $w1$ concerns the class categorization similarity, $w2$ the inter-class similarity, and $w3$ the intra-class similarity. For each run the best twenty retrieved classes were analyzed. The data gathered was: percentage of the relevant classes retrieved, computing time, memory used, and the best 20 classes ranked by similarity.

The class retrieval accuracy results are shown in Figure 4. Configurations C1, C6 and C7 have the best results, though the difference with C8 and C5 is small. These results show a correlation between better accuracy and the categorization similarity first, and then with less importance the inter-class similarity. If configurations are ordered first by $w1$, and then by $w2$, it can be seen that the retrieval accuracy values decrease (with the exception of C6 to C7, and C2 to C4): C1 – 80.17; C6 – 80.12; C7 – 80.15; C5 – 79.83; C8 – 79.54; C9 – 78.77; C2 – 76.13; C4 – 76.59; C3 – 73.28. The average computing time is the same for all the configurations, but the average of memory used decreases from C1 to C9.

Table 2 - The accuracy results obtained for class retrieval.

	C1	C2	C3	C4	C5	C6	C7	C8	C9
Retrieval Accuracy	73.28	76.59	76.13	78.77	79.54	79.83	80.15	80.12	80.17

As the experimental results show, in class retrieval the categorization similarity is determinant for finding the right classes, which is consistent with software development knowledge.

8 Related Work

There are several important works on retrieval in case-based design. From these we selected two families of systems for comparison with our approach: CBR design systems, and CBR software design systems.

One relevant CBR design system is FABEL [18]. It is a case-based design system in the domain of architecture intended to work as an intelligent CAD tool. Cases have a complex representation, combining object-based with graph-based representation. Case retrieval comprises several methods, which are used to help the designer to retrieve and explore different aspects of the design. One aspect of FABEL, similar to REBUILDER, is that it uses a visual editor as a means for communication with the designer. In this way, both systems represent cases as diagrams, FABEL in the architecture domain, and REBUILDER in the software design domain.

The work developed by Ashok Goel in the KRITIK family [19] combines CBR with model-based reasoning (MBR). In his work, Goel uses a case representation that describes a design at three different levels: function, behavior, and structure, which allows cases to be indexed and retrieved using these three aspects of design. REBUILDER uses only functional indexes (object synsets), but it provides a functional taxonomy for the indexing mechanism allowing the computation of similarity distances between these indexes. KRITIK does not provide this taxonomy, enabling only a boolean match of indexes.

Mary Lou Maher has developed several case-based design systems in the architectural domain (CASECAD, CADSYN, WIN, DEMEX, [20]). CASECAD has two main working modes: browsing and retrieving. It allows the designer to explore the design space by browsing a case base, and it can retrieve the designs using a user query in the form of attribute/value pairs. CADSYN is very similar to CASECAD but it can also search for subsystems, using a requirements hierarchy. In WIN the case retrieval is an iterative and interactive process that uses MBR retrieval besides doing the attribute/value pair case retrieval. Finally DEMEX addresses the issues of flexible retrieval and memory exploration using three different types of memory: associative memory, model memory and case memory. REBUILDER shares some of the features of these systems, namely the ability to explore the memory of previous designs (the case library).

González et. al. [21] presented a CBR approach for software reuse based on the reuse and design of Object-Oriented code. Cases represent three types of entities: classes, methods and programming recipes, thus allowing the retrieval of these types of objects. Cases comprise a lexical description (problem), code (solution) and code properties (justification). It uses a lexical retrieval algorithm using a natural language query, and conceptual retrieval using an entity and slot similarity measures. One difference between REBUILDER and this approach is that our system works at the design level, González approach deals with the coding level.

Déjà Vu [11] is a CBR system for code generation and reuse using hierarchical CBR. Déjà Vu uses a hierarchical case representation, indexing cases using functional features. The main improvement of this system is the adaptation-guided retrieval which retrieves cases based on the case adaptation effort instead of the similarity with the target problem. This work has several points in common with REBUILDER, some being the hierarchical case representation and reasoning, and the functional indexing of cases. Despite these similarities, Déjà Vu deals with the coding phase of software development.

CAESER [10] is another code reuse CBR tool. It works at the code level and uses data-flow analysis to acquire functional indexes. The user can retrieve cases from the case library using a Prolog-like query goal, which is used by the system to retrieve similar functions. This system like González approach deals with the coding phase, and has some drawbacks in the query generation mode. Althoff and Tautz [3] have a different approach to software reuse and design. Instead of reusing code, they reuse system requirements and associated software development knowledge.

9 Discussion

In this paper we present REBUILDER a CASE tool that uses CBR to expand the software designer cognitive capabilities. It uses several reasoning functionalities, one of them being the ability to retrieve relevant designs from a case library. We describe the retrieval algorithm and how it uses a general ontology – WordNet – as an indexing structure. We also present the similarity metrics used in the system. Experimental work was also described and analyzed.

Concerning the pros and cons of our system, most of the software reuse systems work at the code reuse level, thus having different approaches to retrieval. REBUILDER deals with concepts at a more abstract level than in code reuse systems. WordNet is used to establish a classification structure for design objects, at code level this is more difficult. Query generation in REBUILDER is natural for the designer, and involves no additional effort, while in code reuse, the user must issue a natural language query or one with a specific format (prolog-like or frame-like). Another advantage of REBUILDER is the low effort in case acquisition. In our approach a case is an UML model, just as it was created by the UML editor. Most of the reuse systems must do some type of analysis to create a case. Like some of the systems presented in this paper, REBUILDER provides flexible retrieval through the use of two indexing levels: it can index cases, and parts of cases.

Some limitations of REBUILDER have to do with WordNet. This ontology provides a general way of dealing with most of the names that appear in a design, but there are some situations where it fails to find the meaning of an object's name, in particular when: there is no context, or it can not find the word. In the first situation the user can choose the correct synset solving the problem. WordNet provides a glossary for each synset that can be used to give a synset's description. The second situation can also be solved this way but most of the times it has to do with spelling errors or the name does not follow the naming rules. This can be easily overcome if the user follows the naming rules, used by most of the software development companies.

References

1. Coulange, B., *Software Reuse*. 1997, London: Springer-Verlag.
2. Prieto-Diaz, R., *Status Report: Software Reusability*. IEEE Software, 1993(May).
3. Tautz, C. and K.-D. Althoff. Using Case-Based Reasoning for Reusing Software Knowledge. in *International Conference on Case-Based Reasoning (ICCBR'97)*. 1997. Providence, RI, USA: Springer-Verlag.
4. Liao, S.Y., L.S. Cheung, and W.Y. Liu, *An Object-Oriented System for the Reuse of Software Design Items*. Journal of Object-Oriented Programming, 1999. **11**(8, January 1999): p. 22-28.
5. Prieto-Diaz, R., *Implementing Faceted Classification for Software Reuse*. Communications of the ACM, 1991(May).
6. Burton, B.A., *et al.*, *The Reusable Software Library*. IEEE Software, 1987. **4**(July 1987): p. 25-32.
7. Basset, P.G., *Frame-Based Software Engineering*. IEEE Software, 1987(July): p. 9-16.

8. Aamodt, A. and E. Plaza, *Case-Based Reasoning: Foundational Issues, Methodological Variations, and System Approaches.* AI Communications, 1994. **7**(1): p. 39-59.

9. Kolodner, J., *Case-Based Reasoning.* 1993: Morgan Kaufman.

10. Fouqué, G. and S. Matwin. *Compositional Software reuse with Case-Based Reasoning.* in *9th Conference on Artificial Intelligence for Applications (CAIA'93).* 1993. Orlando, FL, USA: IEEE Computer Society Press.

11. Smyth, B. and P. Cunningham. *Déjà Vu: A Hierarchical Case-Based Reasoning System for Software Design.* in *10th European Conference on Artificial Intelligence (ECAI'92).* 1992. Vienna, Austria: John Wiley & Sons.

12. González, P.A. and C. Fernández. *A Knowledge-Based Approach to Support Software Reuse in Object-oriented Libraries.* in *9th International Conference on Software Engineering and Knowledge Engineering, SEKE'97.* 1997. Madrid, Spain: Knowledge Systems Institute, Illinois.

13. Katalagarianos, P. and Y. Vassiliou, *On the reuse of software: a case-based approach employing a repository.* Automated Software Engineering, 1995. **2**: p. 55-86.

14. Gomes, P., *et al.* Case Retrieval of Software Designs using WordNet. in *European Conference on Artificial Intelligence (ECAI'02).* 2002. Lyon, France: IOS Press, Amsterdam.

15. Rumbaugh, J., I. Jacobson, and G. Booch, *The Unified Modeling Language Reference Manual.* 1998, Reading, MA: Addison-Wesley.

16. Miller, G., *et al., Introduction to WordNet: an on-line lexical database.* International Journal of Lexicography, 1990. **3**(4): p. 235 - 244.

17. Bergmann, R. and A. Stahl. *Similarity Measures for Object-Oriented Case Representations.* in *4th European Conference on Case-Based Reasoning.* 1998. Dublin, Ireland: Springer.

18. Voss, A., *et al. Retrieval of Similar Layouts - About a very Hybrid Approach in FABEL.* in *Artificial Intelligence in Design, AID'94.* 1994. Lausanne, Switzerland: Kluwer Academic Publishers, Netherlands.

19. Goel, A., S. Bhatta, and E. Stroulia, *Kritik: An Early Case-Based Design System,* in *Issues and Applications of Case-Based Reasoning to Design,* M.L. Maher and P. Pu, Editors. 1997, Lawrence Erlbaum Associates.

20. Maher, M.L., *Developing Case-Based Reasoning for Structural Design.* IEEE Expert, 1996. **11**(3, June 1996).

21. Fernández-Chamizo, C., *et al. Supporting Object Reuse through Case-Based Reasoning.* in *Third European Workshop on Case-Based Reasoning (EWCBR'96).* 1996. Lausanne, Suisse: Springer-Verlag.

Exploiting Taxonomic and Causal Relations
in Conversational Case Retrieval

Kalyan Moy Gupta[1], David W. Aha[2], and Nabil Sandhu[1]

[1]ITT Industries, AES Division, Alexandria, VA 22303
[2]Navy Center for Applied Research in Artificial Intelligence,
Naval Research Laboratory (Code 5515), Washington, DC 20375
{Gupta, Aha, Sandhu}@aic.nrl.navy.mil

Abstract. Conversational case-based reasoning (CCBR) systems engage their users in a series of questions and answers and present them with cases that are most applicable to their decision problem. In previous research, we introduced the Taxonomic CCBR methodology, an extension of standard CCBR that improved performance by organizing features related by abstraction into taxonomies. We recently extended this methodology to include causal relations between taxonomies and claimed that it could yield additional performance gains. In this paper, we formalize the causal extension of Taxonomic CCBR, called *Causal CCBR*, and empirically assess its benefits using a new methodology for evaluating CCBR performance. Evaluation of Taxonomic and Causal CCBR systems in troubleshooting and customer support domains demonstrates that they significantly outperform the standard CCBR approach. In addition, Causal CCBR outperforms Taxonomic CCBR to the extent causal relations are incorporated in the case bases.

1 Introduction

Case-based reasoning (CBR) involves retrieving and reusing stored cases to solve problems and make decisions (Kolodner, 1993). Conversational CBR (CCBR) is a methodology for case retrieval that engages a user in a dialog to incrementally formulate a *query* or *problem description* (Aha *et al.*, 2001). CCBR has been successfully applied, for example, to customer support (Acorn & Walden, 1992), troubleshooting (Gupta, 1998), and e-commerce tasks (Shimazu *et al.*, 1994).

Despite the commercial success of CCBR applications, several issues limit their performance. From the end user's perspective, a key issue is that the conversations should be natural, valid, and efficient (Aha *et al.*, 1998). A related issue is the need to reduce the information load experienced and the cognitive effort required during a problem-solving session (Shimazu, 2001). From the knowledge engineer's perspective, methodologies are needed to simplify case library development and improve its quality (Gupta, 1997).

Cognitive effort and conversational naturalness were addressed by developing models that anticipate user needs (e.g., Göker and Thompson, 2000) and those that automatically answer questions on the user's behalf (e.g., Aha *et al.*, 1998). Gupta (2001) addressed the issues of conversational naturalness and efficiency by developing a novel methodology called *Taxonomic CCBR*, which exploits feature

S. Craw and A. Preece (Eds.): ECCBR 2002, LNAI 2416, pp. 133–147.

taxonomies to support efficient retrieval for users at any level of expertise. Gupta argued that this methodology also improves CCBR performance from the knowledge engineer's perspective by simplifying case library development and improving its consistency and quality. Aha & Gupta (2002) subsequently proposed an enhancement of Taxonomic CCBR, named *Causal* CCBR, and predicted that further improvements in CCBR performance could be realized by its combined taxonomic and causal representation.

In this paper, after reviewing CCBR and Taxonomic CCBR (Section 2), we formalize the Causal CCBR extension of Taxonomic CCBR (Section 3). We introduce an evaluation technique for fine-grained comparison of alternative CCBR methodologies, and use it to compare the Standard (i.e., non-taxonomic), Taxonomic, and Causal CCBR variants (Section 4) on two application domains. In Section 5, we report significant performance gains for Taxonomic and Causal CCBR over Standard CCBR. We discuss the implications of these results, and related work, in Section 6.

2 Conversational Case-Based Reasoning Methodologies

2.1 Standard CCBR

A CCBR system conducts a mixed-initiative *conversation* with the user to incrementally develop a query. A user initiates a conversation by providing a brief textual statement, although alternative modalities can be used (Shimazu *et al.*, 1994; Göker *et al.*, 1998; Giampapa & Sycara, 2001). The system *matches* this query with the stored cases, each of which comprises a problem description, consisting of a text component and a set of *conditions* (i.e., <question, answer> pairs), and a corresponding solution. The system responds by displaying an ordered set of closely matching cases. A set of unanswered questions is also displayed that, if answered by the user, enables them to revise the query. These questions can be ranked by a variety of procedures (Aha *et al.*, 2001; Yang & Wu, 2001; McSherry, 2001a; 2001b). The system uses the revised query to update case similarities and rankings. This cycle of answering questions, case retrieval, and question prompting continues until there are no more questions to answer or the user is satisfied with the set of retrieved cases.

In the Standard CCBR approach, each case's list of conditions tends to be ordered from most general to most specific (i.e., they are related by abstraction) (Gupta, 2001). However, conditions can also be related temporally, causally, or by other types of dependencies (Aha & Gupta, 2002). This is because CCBR cases, such as those used for troubleshooting, customer support, and equipment configuration applications, often represent sequential decision-making, sequential information gathering, or sequential problem solving processes. For example, in an application that assists users with solving problems concerning TV remotes, it is necessary to ascertain *Are there batteries in the remote?* prior to checking *Are the batteries in the remote fresh?* or checking *Are the batteries positioned correctly?* Clearly, this strict dependency dictates that the latter two questions should not be asked prior to receiving the first question's answer. Furthermore, the first question should not be asked if either of the latter two questions *have* been answered. While this example illustrates strict dependencies, there can be non-strict dependencies that reflect a desired *partial* ordering. For example, an e-commerce application for selecting an apartment may require that the number of bedrooms be specified before specifying the number of baths and parking spots. In the remainder of this paper, we limit our discussion to strict dependency relations.

Because the Standard CCBR approach does not represent *abstraction* and *dependency* relations, the conversation can be lengthy and unnatural, similarity assessment can be inaccurate, case representation's can be inconsistent, and conversations can fail to adapt to the user's problem statement (Gupta 2001). Attempts to address some of these problems have been isolated and partial. For example, *dialog inferencing* techniques were developed that allow application developers to write inferencing rules and encode taxonomic relations between conditions. However, maintaining a distributed set of rules is difficult. Aha *et al.* (1998) proposed an alternative approach for developing a centralized model to simplify knowledge maintenance. They summarized empirical benefits, assuming automatically extracted rules could be obtained from a user-provided domain model, but did not formalize their model representation, nor provide a rule-extractor. Montazemi and Gupta (1996) demonstrated how belief networks could be used to support dialog inferencing in sequential diagnosis processes so that CCBR could adapt to the degree of detail preferred by a user. Carrick *et al.* (1999) instead used pre-stored query elaboration plans, triggered by user-supplied conditions during a conversation, to conduct dialog inferencing. However, these approaches do not adapt to a user's abstraction level, which requires displaying only those questions that are appropriate to their demonstrated level of understanding, nor simplify and improve case representations.

2.2 Taxonomic CCBR

To address these problems, Gupta (2001) introduced the Taxonomic CCBR approach, which explicitly represents abstraction relations among conditions. He noticed that each case is typically described by one or more *factors*. Taxonomic CCBR models each factor as an independent subsumption taxonomy, where nodes are conditions (i.e., <question, answer> pairs), and problem descriptions are represented by a set of incoming pointers from leaves in distinct factor taxonomies. This distributed case representation, which is more structured than some alternative approaches (e.g., case retrieval nets (Lenz & Burkhard, 1996)), trades off representational flexibility for improved support of question generation.

Gupta (2001) argued that factor taxonomies can facilitate retrieval by focusing attention; if the query is interpreted as identifying a node in a taxonomy, then Taxonomic CCBR deduces that all of its ancestor nodes in that taxonomy have been implicitly answered. Thus, Taxonomic CCBR can provide the following benefits:
- *Improved representational efficiency* by decreasing the number of conditions needed in a case's problem description,
- *Improved conversational efficiency* by decreasing the number of questions that the user needs to answer for effective case retrieval,
- *Improved retrieval accuracy* by limiting similarity comparisons to only the most detailed conditions/leaves, and
- *Adaptive conversations* by tailoring conversations based on the locations of the taxonomic nodes corresponding to the user's query, enforcing a downward taxonomic traversal, and pruning questions deemed irrelevant by the taxonomies.

However, contrasted with Standard CCBR, Taxonomic CCBR requires the development of taxonomies. Furthermore, it also has no knowledge of *inter-factor* dependencies, and ignoring them causes some of the problems presented in Section 2.1. We propose a solution to this problem in Section3.

3   Causal Extensions of Taxonomic CCBR

Aha and Gupta (2002) proposed a Causal CCBR methodology that extends a Taxonomic CCBR approach with causal dependencies. In this section, we formalize the CCBR processes for the combined taxonomic and causal representation.

3.1 Relating Condition Taxonomies with Dependencies

A factor taxonomy *T* is a tree comprising nodes that are conditions. Figure 1 shows two taxonomies from the Printer troubleshooting domain that include a dependency relation. In a taxonomy, an *is-a-type-of* relation relates a child node to its parent. For example, *Power source voltage correct?=No* is-a-type-of *Power source problem?=Yes*. We denote a strict dependency relation *D* as a directed link from a precedent condition to a dependent condition (e.g., from the precedent *Printer plugged in?=Yes* to the dependent *Power source problem?=Yes*.

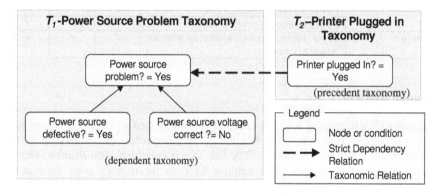

Fig. 1. Example of a strict dependency relation between taxonomies

We constrain the representation of inter-taxonomic dependency relations as follows: ***Only the root nodes from different taxonomies can be related via a strict dependency relation***. This rule ensures that a taxonomy's nodes that are already interrelated by an *is-a-type-of* relation cannot be related in any other way. Also, when interior nodes from different taxonomies are related it implies that there is a dependency relation between taxonomies . Figure 1 illustrates the application of this rule.   The root node of the power source problem taxonomy, *Power source problem?=Yes*, depends on the taxonomy with only one node, *Printer plugged in?=Yes*. Consequently, the child nodes in the former taxonomy depend on the latter.

3.2 Augmenting Case Representations with Strict Dependency Relations

The representation of a case C in Taxonomic CCBR comprises a problem P and a solution S. P is represented by a set of conditions (i.e., <question, answer> pairs) from distinct taxonomies. In addition, we impose the following rule: *The precedent nodes of the dependency relations are excluded from the case representation.* Including the precedent nodes in the case is redundant because they are always traversed prior to locating the dependent nodes during a conversation. Table 1 demonstrates the application of this rule to an example case from a printer troubleshooting application, parts of which were shown in Figure 1, and compares it with Taxonomic and Standard CCBR representations. In this example, Causal CCBR requires only two conditions to represent the case compared to the five conditions in Standard CCBR. This illustrates the representational efficiency achieved by a Causal CCBR methodology.

Table 1. Comparing Causal, Taxonomic, and Standard CCBR case representations from a printer troubleshooting application

Field	Example Text	Std.	Tax.	Caus.
Case Title	Outlet wired improperly or power failure	✓	✓	✓
Text Description	Printer's power fails to come on	✓		
Problem:	Problem type?=Power	✓		
Conditions	Printer comes on?=No	✓	✓	✓
	Printer plugged in?=Yes	✓	✓	
	Power source problem?=Yes	✓		
	Power source defective?=Yes	✓	✓	✓
Solution	Try a different power source or wait for power to come on.	✓	✓	✓

3.3 Causal Retrieval

The Causal CCBR process for case retrieval is summarized in Figure 2, where the user begins a conversation by providing the query's initial text qt, and has access to the taxonomies T and case library L. The first step is *condition identification*, which involves matching qt against all conditions in T to locate each most applicable <question, answer> pair (condition), Q_q, which are added to the query Q. Next, the main loop proceeds by locating, for each $Q_q \in Q$, its set of descendent leaf nodes' conditions (both in its taxonomy and in its dependent taxonomies). The set of retrieved cases are all those in L that contain any of these conditions. Each retrieved case $C \in L$ is then ranked, in descending order, using the following similarity function:

$$sim(Q,C) = \frac{\sum_{Q_q \in Q} sim(Q_q, C_q)}{\#T}$$

where $\#T$ is the number of unique factor taxonomies that contain conditions in Q and C, $Q_q \in Q$, and $C_q \in C$ (i.e., C_q is a condition in C's list of conditions). The similarity of two conditions, whose common question is q, is computed as follows with similarity values ranging in $[-1,1]$:

$$\text{sim}(Q_q, C_q) = \begin{cases} 1 & \textit{is-a-descendent-of}(C_q, Q_q) \\ -1 & \textit{is-in-the-same-taxonomy-as}(C_q, Q_q) \\ 0 & \textit{is-a-dependent-of}(C_{q'}, Q_q) \\ -1 & \exists\, C_{q'} \in \textit{complementary\_nodes}(C_q): \\ & \{\textit{is-a-dependent-of}(C_{q'}, Q_q)\} \end{cases}$$

where *is-a-descendent-of*, *is-in-the-same-taxonomy*, and *is-a-dependent-of* are self-explanatory and the function *complementary_nodes* yields the set of all conditions that have the same question.

Causal_CCBR(qt,T,L) =
   Q := find_most_similar_conditions(qt,T);
   Repeat:
      Leaves := identify_descendant_conditions(Q,T);
      C_r := rank_cases(identify_candidate_cases(Leaves,L));
      Q^Q = rank_questions(C_r);
      Question := user_select_displayed_question(Q^Q);
      Answer := prompt_for_answer(Question);
      Q := add_to_query(Q, Question,Answer);
   Until (user terminates conversation)

Fig. 2. The Causal CCBR retrieval cycle, where the variables are described in the text

Conversation. A Causal CCBR conversation involves presenting the user with a rank ordered set of questions Q^Q derived from the ranked cases C_r. Questions in Q^Q are selected and ranked as is done in Taxonomic CCBR, namely using taxonomy selection for selecting candidate questions, question scoring and selection using a backward-propagation scoring scheme, and question ranking (Gupta 2001). We present an enhancement to the question-scoring and selection step, focusing on its taxonomy-scoring substep resulting from the inclusion of dependency relations.

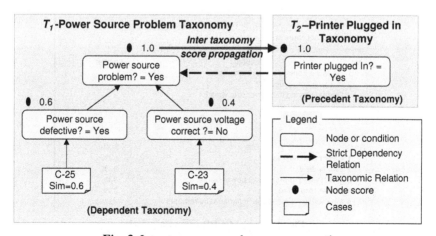

Fig. 3. Inter-taxonomy node score propagation

The inclusion of strict dependency relations requires *inter-taxonomy node score propagation* to compute the node scores for the precedent taxonomy. This is similar to activation propagation in distributed connectionist networks. The root node score from the dependent taxonomy is propagated to the precedent taxonomy using a transitive and additive function. For example, Figure 3 shows a root node score of 1.0 propagated from taxonomy T_1 to taxonomy T_2, where we assume cases C-25 and C-23 have similarities of 0.6 and 0.4, respectively to the query and contain the conditions as shown in the Figure 3.

Question selection is performed in Causal CCBR as follows. If the nodes from the precedent taxonomy have not been answered, then their questions are selected for presentation and the questions from the dependent taxonomies are excluded. For example, the question *Printer plugged in?* will be selected if it has not been answered and the questions from the nodes in taxonomy T_1 will be withheld until this question is answered with *Yes*.

The questions in the selected set Q^Q are rank ordered by descending taxonomy and node scores. We illustrate the reasoning of Causal CCBR in Section 4.

4   Implementation

We implemented Standard, Causal, and Taxonomic CCBR components in a software system called TCRS (**T**axonomic **C**ase **R**etrieval **S**ystem), whose architecture comprises the *User Interface*, the *TCRS Reasoning Engine*, and a case library. The reasoning engine processes a user's query using the *Text Matcher*, retrieves and presents cases using the *Case Retriever,* and selects questions using the *Conversation Generator*. The *Case Base Viewer* enables a knowledge engineer to view the contents of the case base.

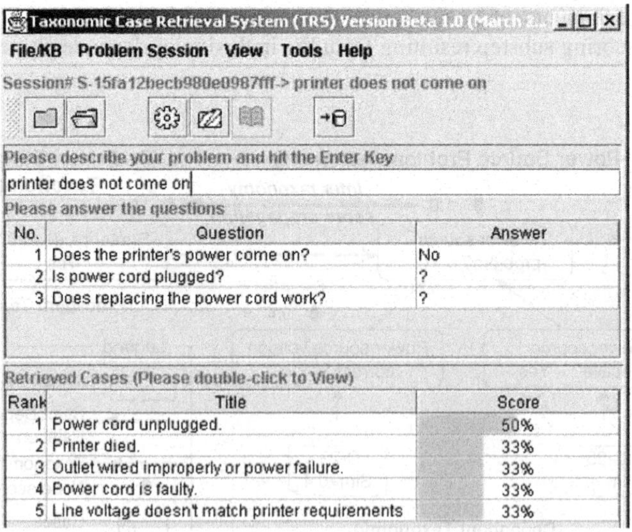

Fig. 4. Causal CCBR reasoning session

Figure 4 shows a problem session where the user has entered the text description *printer does not come on* to the printer troubleshooting case base with a Causal CCBR representation. Figure 4 also demonstrates how the questions from the dependent taxonomy shown in Figure 3 were withheld in the reasoning iteration, thereby reducing the information load on the user. Figure 5 shows a TCRS reasoning session operating under the same conditions but using a Taxonomic representation. It demonstrates that, while it can appropriately select the starting question *Does the printer's power come on?* from the printer power taxonomy, it superfluously presents the question *Do you have a power source problem?* because it ignores the strict dependency relations. Figure 6 shows the same session using the Standard CCBR approach. It demonstrates that four irrelevant questions (i.e., 2, 5, 6, and 7), given the state of the problem solving session, were presented to the user, thereby substantially increasing the information load.

Please describe your problem and hit the Enter Key

Printer does not come on

Please answer the questions

No.	Question	Answer
1	Does the printer's power come on?	No
2	Is power cord plugged?	?
3	Does replacing the power cord work?	?
4	Do you have a power source problem?	?

Retrieved Cases (Please double-click to View)

Rank	Title	Score
1	Power cord unplugged	50%
2	Printer died.	25%
3	Outlet wired improperly or power failure	25%

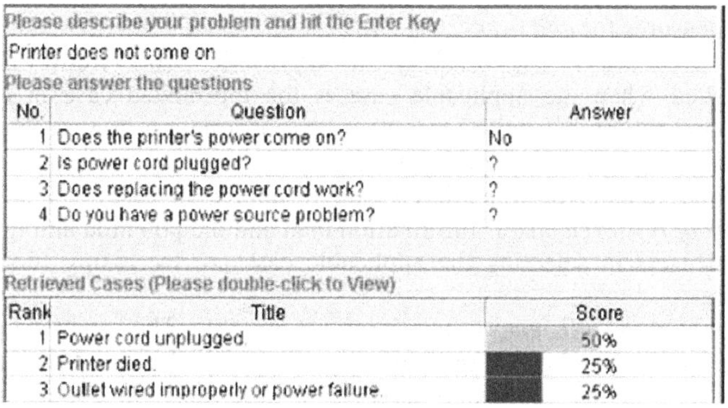

Fig. 5. Taxonomic CCBR reasoning session

Please describe your problem and hit the Enter Key

printer does not come on

Please answer the questions

No.	Question	Answer
1	Does the printer's power come on?	No
2	What are you having a problem with?	?
3	Is power cord plugged?	?
4	Does replacing the power cord work?	?
5	Do you have a power source problem?	?
6	Is power outlet working?	?
7	Does line voltage from power outlet match printer r	?

Retrieved Cases (Please double-click to View)

Rank	Title	Score
1	Power cord unplugged	33%
2	Printer died.	16%
3	Outlet wired improperly or power failure	16%

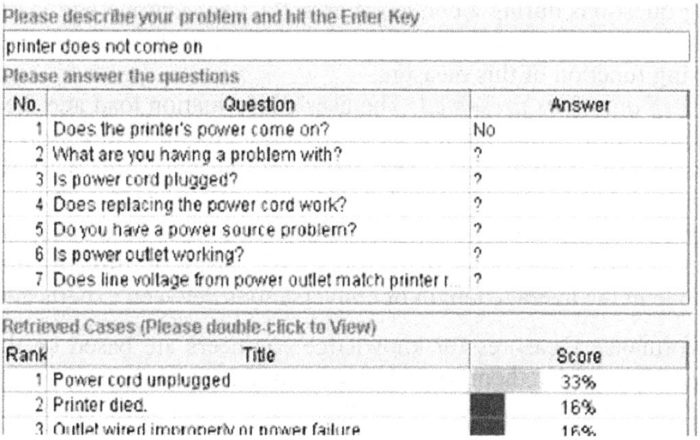

Fig. 6. Standard CCBR reasoning session

5   Empirical Evaluation

5.1 Methodology

Performance Measures: Our objective was to assess the improvement in CCBR performance derived from Taxonomic and Causal CCBR in comparison to Standard CCBR. CCBR performance can be measured from three perspectives: *business process owner*, *end-user*, and *knowledge engineer*. A business process owner's (e.g., a call center manager) goals may include improving their organization's performance by deploying a CCBR application. End users want to retrieve the best solution to their problem most efficiently and with minimal cognitive effort, while knowledge engineers want to minimize their development and maintenance effort. In this paper, we focus on and develop measures from the latter two perspectives. We propose the following measures for *end users*:

1. *Retrieval accuracy (avg. rank of the applicable case):* Retrieval accuracy is maximized when the applicable case is the top-ranked case in C_r. Cognitive effort, and the time required to review the information in a reasoning iteration, are increasing functions of this measure (i.e., we assume that users scan C_r from top to bottom and stop when they locate the applicable case).
2. *Number of retrieved cases:* Information load and the potential ambiguity faced by the end users in selecting the applicable case are increasing functions of this measure.
3. *Conversational efficiency (conversation length):* The number of iterations required (i.e., number of questions answered by the user) to attain a 100% similarity with the applicable case.   The time taken to complete a problem-solving session is an increasing function of this measure.
4. *Conversational accuracy (avg. rank of answered questions):* Answering top ranking questions during a conversation reflect an accurate and realistic question ordering.   The time needed to review questions prior to answering them is an increasing function of this measure.
5. *Number of questions presented:* The user's information load and the time needed to complete a CCBR iteration is an increasing function of this measure.
6. *Conversational adaptiveness*: This measures the ability of a CCBR system to adapt its conversation to the user's level of domain expertise. We conjecture that experts have more efficient conversation because they are likely to issue more precise queries than non-expert users. We measure this by the percentage difference in the average length of conversations between experts and novices.

Our performance measures for knowledge engineers are based on the number of operations performed by them to complete a particular case base maintenance task. We assume that different types of operations require the same amount of effort. we use the following two measures from *knowledge engineer's* perspective:

1. *Effort to insert a case in the case base:* This is measured by the number of conditions in the new case.
2. *Effort to insert a condition in the case base*: This is measured by the total number of operations required to insert a condition, as summarized in Table 2.

Table 2. Measures for computing the effort to insert a condition

Operation	Effort Measure		
	Standard	Taxonomic	Causal
Taxonomy location/creation	-	Scan/create taxonomies[1]	Scan/create taxonomies[1]
Insert into a taxonomy	-	Modify taxonomy[2]	Modify taxonomy[2]
Insert causal Links	-	-	Number of links[3]
Locate affected cases	Scan all cases	-	-
Modify affected cases	Indexed Cases	-	-

1. Scan all taxonomies with more than one node (i.e., number of such taxonomies), under the simplifying assumption that taxonomies are the same size; Effort to create =1
2. Requires removing existing links and inserting new links for this condition. Effort = 2*number_of_children (condition) + 1 (i.e., for the parent link).
3. Effort = number_of_dependents (condition) + number_of_precedents (condition)

Hypotheses: We evaluated the following three hypotheses:

1. Taxonomic and Causal CCBR methodologies outperform standard CCBR from the end user's perspective.
2. They also have better performance from the knowledge engineer's perspective.
3. Causal CCBR outperforms Taxonomic CCBR from the end user's perspective.

The original CCBR case bases for these applications were used to develop three versions for each application: (1) Standard (non-taxonomic), (2) Taxonomic, and (3) Causal. We implemented the standard version in a taxonomic format by ignoring the taxonomic relations. Due to time constraints, for the Electronics case base, 20 cases pertaining to TV, VCR, and TV remote problems were selected from the original case base. Table 3 presents a summary of these six case bases along eight dimensions.

Table 3. Summary of case bases

Case Library Dimension	Printer			Electronics		
	Std.	Tax.	Causal	Std.	Tax.	Causal
Total number of questions	28	28	28	33	33	33
Average number of answers per question, (Min-Max)	1.92, (1-9)	1.92, (1-9)	1.92, (1-9)	3.67, (2-15)	3.67, (2-15)	3.67, (2-15)
Number of taxonomies	50*	25	25	96*	68	68
Avg. number of conditions per taxonomy, (Min-Max)	1,* (1-1)	2.0, (1-11)	2.0, (1-11)	1,* (1-1)	1.41, (1-26)	1.41, (1-26)
Avg. depth of taxonomy, (Min-Max)	1*	1.28 (1-3)	1.28 (1-3)	1*	1.07 (1-5)	1.07 (1-5)
Number of dependencies	0	0	3	0	0	10
Number of cases	26	26	26	20	20	20
Avg. number of conditions per case, (Min-Max)	3.92, (2-6)	2.57, (1-5)	2.42, (1-5)	5.2, (3-8)	2.6, (1-5)	2.5, (1-4)

* Taxonomies with one node each are equivalent to a CCBR system without taxonomies

The Electronics case base is more complex than Printer and has a wider subject matter. Its complexity is reflected by its taxonomies, which are up to five levels deep, and include a greater number of strict dependency relations (10 vs. 3).

Test Procedures: We conducted two simulations (one per perspective), executing each three times per application corresponding to the three CCBR methodologies. Ideally, an evaluation from the end user's perspective would involve testing with human users. However, due to time and resource constraints we gathered experimental data using a simulated user interacting with TCRS. Because each case in our evaluation case base was unique, we used the leave-one-in method (Aha *et al.*, 2001). For each "target" case, the simulated user submitted, for each of its conditions, one query for its node and for each of that condition's ancestor nodes. For each query, a simulated TCRS conversation iterated until the target case attained a similarity value of 100% and all its questions were answered. The simulated user answered exactly one question per iteration by selecting the highest-ranking question that is answered in the target case. For each iteration, we recorded the rank of the target case, number of retrieved cases, rank of the answered question, and the total number of questions presented. TCRS retrieved all cases with similarities greater than zero and presented all eligible questions selected by the methodologies.

We simulated a knowledge engineer's behavior to gather performance data from their perspective. We measured the simulated effort required to insert each case into the case base once. In addition, each condition in the case base was removed and inserted, and the corresponding effort measured using the procedures presented above.

5.2 Analysis

End user perspective: For each application and CCBR methodology, average performance measures were computed, for each query, over the number of iterations required to complete it. The per-query results were then averaged to obtain a case average, and the case library average was obtained by averaging the case averages over total number of cases in the case base. We also performed one-tailed T tests to assess the statistical confidence in our conclusions.

To investigate a CCBR system's ability to adapt to a user's background and expertise, we computed the case base averages for experts and novices as follows. We assumed that expert users are more likely to present queries that are deeper in the taxonomies than those by novices. For experts, we simulated this by applying a probability distribution to the queries that assigned probabilities in direct proportion to the depth of their location in the taxonomy and in inverse proportion to the query depth for novices. The results are shown in Tables 4 and 5 for the two applications.

In Table 4 and 5, statistically significant differences between Standard and Taxonomic ($p < 0.05$, i.e., 95% confidence) are indicated in the Taxonomic Average column by **bold face** and the statistically significant differences between Taxonomic and Causal are shown in bold in the Causal Average column. The Average column in Table 4 shows that Taxonomic CCBR significantly outperformed standard CCBR on all measures except the rank of the retrieved case in Printer application. Likewise,

Table 4. Comparing Standard, Taxonomic, and Causal CCBR on Printer

Measures*	Standard			Taxonomic			Causal		
	Exp	Nov	Avg	Exp	Nov	Avg	Exp	Nov	Avg
Rank of Ret. Case	1.50	1.78	1.66	1.5	1.76	1.63	1.47	1.76	1.63
No. of Ret. Cases	4.31	5.09	4.73	2.7	3.41	**3.11**	2.67	3.43	**3.06**
Length of Conversation	3.92	3.92	3.92	2.86	3.11	**3.0**	2.67	3.03	**2.92**
Rank of Ans. Ques.	1.14	1.26	1.19	0.90	0.91	**0.90**	0.86	0.98	0.89
No. of Ques. Pres.	3.79	4.71	4.28	2.01	2.49	**2.27**	1.93	2.41	**2.19**

* Averaged over 26 cases, Exp = Expert, Nov=Novice, 25 Degrees of freedom for T-Tests

Table 5. Comparing Standard, Taxonomic, and Causal CCBR on Electronics

Measures*	Standard			Taxonomic			Causal		
	Exp	Nov	Avg	Exp	Nov	Avg	Exp	Nov	Avg
Rank of Ret. Case	2.03	2.48	2.25	1.59	2.39	**2.12**	1.59	2.37	2.10
No of Ret. Cases	6.02	7.06	6.54	2.85	4.80	**4.09**	2.83	4.80	4.04
Length of Conversation	5.20	5.20	5.20	2.67	4.09	**3.83**	2.67	4.09	3.83
Rank of Ans. Ques.	1.10	1.12	1.11	1.00	1.05	1.04	0.96	1.0	**0.97**
No, of Ques. Pres.	7.30	8.90	8.10	3.62	5.02	**4.35**	3.34	4.39	**3.80**

*Averaged over 20 cases, Exp = Expert, Nov=Novice, 19 Degrees of freedom for T-Tests

Table 5 shows that Taxonomic CCBR significantly outperformed standard CCBR on all measures except the rank of answered questions on the Electronics application.

Conversation length was reduced by 23.4% using Taxonomic CCBR and by 25.6% using Causal CCBR on the Printer application. Furthermore, Causal CCBR reduced conversation length by 2.67% over Taxonomic CCBR. For Electronics, the reduction in conversation length was 26.4% for both Taxonomic and Causal CCBR.

Retrieval accuracy (i.e., rank of the retrieved case) marginally improved for Taxonomic and Causal CCBR vs. standard CCBR (1.8% in Printer and 5.7% in Electronics). Conversational accuracy (i.e., rank of the answered question) significantly improved for Causal CCBR by 12.6% and 25.2% for Electronics and Printer, respectively, while for Taxonomic CCBR the improvements are 6.3% and 24.3%. There is a significant reduction in the information load and the potential cognitive effort as measured by the number of questions and cases presented to the user. For example, the number of questions presented dropped by 47.0% and 48.8% for Taxonomic and Causal CCBR for Printer. The reduction was even larger for Electronics (i.e., 48.3% and 53.1%). Likewise, the number of cases presented to the user decreased by 34.2% and 35.3% for Taxonomic and Causal CCBR in Printer and by 37.5% and 38.2% for Electronics. Larger performance gains over Electronics suggest that Taxonomic and Causal CCBR might yield greater gains over more complex domains.

The conversational adaptiveness measures of the three CCBR versions are summarized in Table 6. We note that Standard CCBR is not adaptive to the user's experience level, while Taxonomic and Causal CCBR expand and reduce their conversation length to adequately support expert and novice users. Table 6 indicates that adaptivity is higher in Electronics than Printer, again suggesting that the methodologies adequately compensate for an increase in application complexity.

Table 6. Comparing conversational adaptiveness

Applications	Standard	Taxonomic	Causal
Printer	0.0	8.3%	11.8%
Electronics	0.0	37.1%	37.1%

Knowledge Engineer's Perspective: For both applications, using Table 3 we conclude that the effort to insert a case (i.e., average number of conditions per case) in Causal CCBR is the lowest, followed by Taxonomic CCBR, and finally the standard CCBR approach. This is due to the representational efficiency attributed to the methodology (Gupta, 2001; Aha & Gupta, 2002). Causal CCBR provides an effort saving of 38.26% and 51.92% over standard CCBR for the two applications. These

Table 7. Average effort for inserting a condition, computed as described in Table 2

Operation	Printer			Electronics		
	Stan.	Tax.	Caus.	Stan.	Tax.	Caus.
Locate or create Taxonomy	0.00	4.08	4.15	0.00	1.41	1.42
Insert condition	0.00	1.53	1.53	0.00	2.06	2.08
Insert causal Links	0.00	0.00	0.17	0.00	0.00	0.35
Locate affected cases	3.95	0.00	0.00	3.55	0.00	0.00
Modify affected cases	0.76	0.00	0.00	1.55	0.00	0.00
Total Effort	4.71	5.61	5.85	5.1	3.47	3.85

results suggest that the savings in effort for inserting a case increases with the increase in domain scope and complexity, as indicated by taxonomy depth.

Table 7 summarizes the effort for inserting a condition. The total effort in Printer is smaller for standard CCBR by 19% (4.71 vs. 5.61) compared with Taxonomic CCBR, but higher by 31.9% (5.1 vs. 3.47) for Electronics. This is because Printer has more shallow taxonomies, which increase the taxonomy location effort, as opposed to the smaller number of deep taxonomies in Electronics, which lowers this effort. Also, the effort to modify cases is lower in Printer because cases are distributed among the many shallow taxonomies. In contrast, in Electronics, cases are more densely distributed among the few deep taxonomies, thereby greatly increasing the effort to modify affected cases. Overall, Taxonomic and Causal CCBR may be less effort intensive to maintain than regular CCBR for complex applications in which there are many closely related cases. Finally, Causal CCBR applications are only marginally more effort intensive to maintain than the Taxonomic CCBR approach.

6   Discussion

The work described in this paper complements our earlier work. More specifically Gupta (2001) introduced Taxonomic CCBR, and Aha and Gupta (2002) introduced the Causal CCBR extension, but neither of these earlier publications presented a comparative empirical evaluation.

Few researchers have developed CCBR methods that respond appropriately to users, independent of their level of domain expertise. However, Doyle and Cunningham (2000) described how their I-CBR approach, also with the goal of reducing dialog length, can dynamically adapt to a user's query by iteratively re-ranking questions according to an information-gain metric and a spreading activation algorithm. Like their implementation of I-CBR, most CCBR approaches dynamically re-rank questions throughout a conversation. However, Causal CCBR assumes that additional knowledge is available for structuring conditions in factor taxonomies and for linking conditions, which it exploits to select and order questions for conversation.

Kohlmaier *et al.* (2001), in the context of automated e-commerce dialogs, considered how to adapt dialogs to different kinds of customers, with similar goals as ours (i.e., to reduce dialog length and improve dialog quality). Their utility-based attribute-selection strategy, which assumes that attributes are independent, combines probability estimates for a customer's ability to answer questions with similarity variance, which ranks questions based on their influence on a given set of cases. These estimates are updated, after each dialog, using a Bayesian network that accumulates evidence regarding the user's domain knowledge. Their approach, like some others (e.g., Montazemi & Gupta, 1996; Göker & Thompson, 2000), creates user models to tailor conversations. In contrast, Taxonomic and Causal CCBR approaches exploit taxonomies to adjust to the level of expertise displayed by a user, rather than create user models.

In addition to those we already mentioned, other researchers have also contributed suggestions on improving conversation quality. For example, McSherry (2001a) suggested using a structured, rationale-based approach inspired from work on expert systems. Shimazu (2001) investigated *navigation by proposing*, which prompts the user with only three case's solutions at one time, where the cases are selected so as to cover the space of similar neighbors (to the user's query). Again, neither approach explicitly represents nor exploits the type of abstract and causal information used by Causal CCBR.

7 Conclusion

We described how causal links between taxonomies could be used to improve CCBR performance. We introduced a new methodology for evaluating CCBR and presented empirical evidence that Causal CCBR, an extension of the Taxonomic CCBR approach (Gupta, 2001), significantly outperforms both Standard and Taxonomic CCBR approaches across a range of pertinent measures. We are currently investigating approaches to induce taxonomies and we intend to investigate the complementary use of additional dialogue inferencing strategies that link Causal CCBR to a wide variety of information sources.

Acknowledgements. We thank the Naval Research Laboratory for funding this research. We also thank the anonymous reviewers and Francesco Ricci for their helpful comments on an earlier version of this paper.

References

Acorn, T.L., & Walden, S.H. (1992). SMART: Support management automated reasoning technology for COMPAQ customer service. *Proceedings of the Fourth Annual Conference on Innovative Applications of Artificial Intelligence*. San Jose, CA: AAAI Press.

Aha, D.W., & Gupta K.M. (2002). Causal query elaboration in conversational case-based reasoning. In *Proceedings of the Fifteenth Conference of the Florida AI Research Society* (pp. 95-100). Pensacola Beach, FL: AAAI Press.

Aha, D.W., Breslow, L.A., & Munoz-Avila, H. (2001). Conversational case-based reasoning. *Applied Intelligence, 14*(1), 9-32.

Aha, D. W., Maney, T., & Breslow, L. A. (1998). Supporting dialogue inferencing in conversational case-based reasoning. *Proceedings of the Fourth European Workshop on Case-Based Reasoning* (pp. 262-273). Dublin, Ireland: Springer.

Carrick, C., Yang, Q., Abi-Zeid, I., & Lamontagne, L. (1999). Activating CBR systems through autonomous information gathering. *Proceedings of the Third*

International Conference on Case-Based Reasoning (pp. 74-88). Seeon, Germany: Springer.

Doyle, M., & Cunningham, P. (2000). A dynamic approach to reducing dialog in on-line decision guides. *Proceedings of the Fifth European Workshop on Case-Based Reasoning* (pp. 49-60). Trento, Italy: Springer.

Giampapa, J.A., & Sycara, K. (2001). Conversational case-based planning for agent team coordination. *Proceedings of the Fourth International Conference on Case-Based Reasoning* (pp. 189-203). Vancouver, Canada: Springer.

Göker, M., Roth-Berghofer, T., Bergmann, R., Pantleon, T., Traphoner, R., Wess, S., & Wilke, W. (1998). The development of HOMER: A case-based CAD/CAM help-desk support tool. *Proceedings of the Fourth European Workshop on Case-Based Reasoning* (pp. 346-357). Dublin, Ireland: Springer.

Göker, M., & Thompson, C.A. (2000). Personalized conversational case-based recommendation. *Proceedings of the Fifth European Workshop on Case-Based Reasoning* (pp. 99-111). Trento, Italy: Springer.

Gupta K.M. (2001). Taxonomic case-based reasoning. *Proceedings of the Fourth International Conference on Case-Based Reasoning* (pp. 219-233). Vancouver, Canada: Springer.

Gupta, K.M. (1998). Knowledge-based system for troubleshooting complex equipment. *International Journal of Information and Computing Science*, *1*(1), 29-41.

Gupta, K.M. (1997). Case base engineering for large-scale industrial applications. In B.R. Gaines & R. Uthurusamy (Eds.) *Intelligence in Knowledge Management: Papers from the AAAI Spring Symposium* (Technical Report SS-97-01). Stanford, CA: AAAI Press.

Kohlmaier, A., Schmitt, S., & Bergmann, R. (2001). A similarity-based approach to attribute selection in user-adaptive sales dialogs. *Proceedings of the Fourth International Conference on Case-Based Reasoning* (pp. 306-320). Vancouver, Canada: Springer.

Kolodner, J. (1993). *Case-based reasoning.* San Mateo, CA: Morgan Kaufmann.

Lenz, M., & Burkhard H. D. (1996). *Case retrieval nets: Basic ideas and extensions.* In G. Görz & S. Hölldobler (Eds.) *KI-96: Advances in Artificial Intelligence.* Berlin: Springer.

McSherry, D. (2001a). Interactive case-based reasoning in sequential diagnosis. *Applied Intelligence, 14*(1), 65-76.

McSherry, D. (2001b). Minimizing dialog length in interactive case-based reasoning. *Proceedings of the Seventeenth International Joint Conference on Artificial Intelligence* (pp. 993-998). Seattle, WA: Morgan Kaufmann.

Montazemi A.R., & Gupta K.M. (1996), An adaptive agent for case description in diagnostic CBR systems. *Computers in Industry, 29*(3), 209-224.

Shimazu, H. (2001). ExpertClerk: Navigating shoppers' buying process with the combination of asking and proposing. *Proceedings of the Seventeenth International Conference on Artificial Intelligence* (pp. 1443-1448). Seattle, WA: Morgan Kaufmann.

Shimazu, H., Shibata, A., & Nihei, K. (1994). Case-based retrieval interface adapted to customer-initiated dialogues in help desk operations. *Proceedings of the Twelfth National Conference on Artificial Intelligence* (pp. 513-518). Seattle, WA: AAAI Press.

Yang, Q., & Wu, J. (2001). Enhancing the effectiveness of interactive case-based reasoning with clustering and decision forests. *Applied Intelligence, 14*(1), 49-64.

Bayesian Case Reconstruction

Daniel N. Hennessy[1], Bruce G. Buchanan[1], and John M. Rosenberg[2]

[1] Intelligent Systems Program, University of Pittsburgh, Pittsburgh, PA
{hennessy, buchanan}@cs.pitt.edu
[2] Dept of Biological Sciences, University of Pittsburgh, PA
jmr@jmr3.xtal.pitt.edu
http://www.xtal.pitt.edu

Abstract. Bayesian Case Reconstruction (BCR) is a case-based technique that broadens the coverage of a case library by sampling and recombining pieces of existing cases to construct a large set of "plausible" cases. It employs a Bayesian Belief Network to evaluate whether implicit dependencies within the original cases have been maintained. The belief network is constructed from the expert's limited understanding of the domain theory combined with the data available in the case library. The cases are the primary reasoning vehicle. The belief network leverages the available domain model to help evaluate whether the "plausible" cases have maintained the necessary internal context. BCR is applied to the design of screening experiments for Macromolecular Crystallization in the Probabilistic Screen Design program. We describe BCR and provide an empirical comparison of the Probabilistic Screen Design program against the current practice in Macromolecular Crystallization.

1 Introduction

For the past eight years we have been exploring the use of intelligent, electronic assistants for crystallographers via the XtalGrow suite of software that facilitates the trial-and-error process of growing diffraction quality crystals of biological macromolecules. Experimental crystallography, like many other experimental scientific and medical domains can be characterized by: (1) a large number of variables, (2) a large number of possible values for most of the variables, (3) strong interdependence among those variables, (4) a set of "given" variables that have limited predictive value, (5) a complex theory that is not applicable in the laboratory, including an incomplete domain theory and an incomplete case library, and (6) time, material and human resource limitations.

Such domains create a series of competing challenges. The incompleteness of the domain theory implies we do not have the understanding to directly compute a solution to the problem. Machine Learning techniques provide mechanisms for augmenting domain models with knowledge extracted from the case library. However, the incompleteness of the case library is such that the additional knowledge would still be insufficient to compute a solution. Furthermore, the complexity of the domains sug-

S. Craw and A. Preece (Eds.): ECCBR 2002, LNAI 2416, pp. 148–158.
© Springer-Verlag Berlin Heidelberg 2002

gests it would be prohibitively expensive to compute such a solution even if we had the understanding.

Case-Based Reasoning (CBR) is an alternative approach that is often applicable to problems with incomplete domain theories. However, the combination of the large search space and limited case library makes it necessary to expand the coverage of the cases if CBR is going to be a viable solution.

Bayesian Case Reconstruction (BCR) is a case-based technique that attempts to address these issues. BCR broadens the coverage of a case library by sampling and recombining pieces of existing cases to construct a large set of "plausible" cases. It employs a Bayesian Belief Network to evaluate whether implicit dependencies within the original cases have been maintained. The belief net is constructed from (1) the limited structure available in the incomplete domain model, (2) assumptions about the probability distributions (again derived from the limited understanding of the domain), and (3) the data available in the case library. In BCR, the cases are the primary reasoning vehicle. The belief network leverages the available domain model to help evaluate whether the "plausible" cases have maintained the necessary internal context.

Bayesian Case Reconstruction is used in the Probabilistic Screen Design (PSD) program that is the core of the XtalGrow software. In the rest of this paper we will provide a brief background in Macromolecular Crystallography, describe the BCR process and how it is employed in the Probabilistic Screen Design program. We will provide results of an empirical comparison of the Probabilistic Screen Design program against the current approaches in Macromolecular Crystallography. Finally we will discuss the rationale behind BCR versus other alternatives.

2   Background and Methods

2.1   Background: Macromolecular Crystallography

Starting with Sumner's crystallization of urease, crystals have been central to our understanding of biological macromolecules. Currently, crystallization is the essential first step in macromolecular structure determination by X-ray crystallography. This is the only method capable of revealing high-resolution structures for most proteins, protein-DNA complexes, viruses, etc. The high-resolution structural information is critical for modern molecular biological methods that rely on knowledge of the geometrical interrelationships of the various components that comprise the overall structure.

The rate-limiting step in X-ray structure determination is the crystallization itself. It takes anywhere between a few weeks to several years to obtain macromolecular crystals that yield good diffraction patterns. The theory of forces that promote and maintain crystal growth is preliminary, and crystallographers systematically search a large parameter space of experimental settings to grow good crystals. The process is described as follows:

"This [macromolecule crystallization] is done by conducting a long series of crystallization trials, evaluating the results, and using information obtained to improve matters in successive rounds of trials. Because the range of variables is so broad, intelligence and intuition in designing and evaluating individual and collective trials becomes essential." [16]

To be useful for crystallographic analysis, the molecule of interest must not merely be converted to the crystalline state; it must be converted into a single crystal with a high degree of internal order. These two parameters, size and order, are the critical measures of the success of a crystallization experiment because together they determine the quality of the X-ray diffraction pattern that can be obtained from the crystal. Unfortunately, neither is under the direct control of the experimenter. They can be manipulated by changing the "environmental" parameters of the experiment that include macromolecular concentration, pH, salt concentration, etc. To make matters worse, the precise relationships among the environmental parameters on the one hand and size and order on the other is generally different for each macromolecule. Thus each individual case has to be worked out empirically.

The basic scheme to induce crystallization is to slowly reduce the solubility of the macromolecule in a sample solution by one of several established methods. The solubility is determined by all the environmental parameters, one of which is usually the concentration of a "precipitating agent", such as polyethylene glycol. The "crystallization method", such as vapor diffusion, slowly raises the concentration of the precipitating agent (and almost everything else). If all the conditions are favorable, a point is reached where a crystal nucleates and grows.

The basic experiment is repeated with different parameters until either success is obtained or until the experimenter abandons the effort. Typically, many experiments (between 200 and 400) are started simultaneously and allowed to run for several weeks to several months. During this time the experimenter attends to other projects. Then, the results are evaluated and a new series begun (to run concurrently with the older ones).

2.2 Methods: BCR

As its name suggests, Bayesian Case Reconstruction consists of two primary components, a case library and a Bayesian Belief Network. The case library consists of descriptions of previous problem solving episodes, typically in the form of a list of features and their values. The case library for macromolecular crystallization contains considerably more structure including hierarchical data values and hierarchically organized cases of projects comprised of sets of trays each comprised of sets of experiments or wells. The features can be categorized into three types: (1) givens, which are known prior to the start of problem solving, (2) observables, which are controlled or discovered during the problem solving process, and (3) outcomes, which describe the results of the problem solving process (e.g., success or failure).

The second component of the design is the Bayesian Belief Network (BBN). It is assumed that the expert designs the structure of the network relating the interdependencies of the variables that describe the cases. The expert may also specify any or all of the prior and conditional probabilities. Any prior or conditional probabilities the expert does not specify are extracted from the data in the case library. It is important to note that in conformity with the characteristics of the domain described in Section 1, the accuracy and completeness of the belief network are assumed to be very limited.

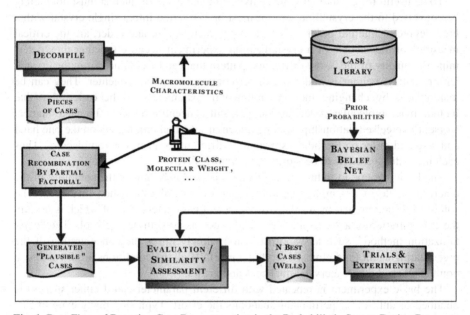

Fig. 1. Data Flow of Bayesian Case Reconstruction in the Probabilistic Screen Design Program

Problem solving begins with the user specifying the values for the given characteristics (i.e., features of the problem known prior to problem solving). The given characteristics are used to select a set of cases that have similar givens to the new problem. There is not enough information for the system to select a set of sufficiently on-point cases to directly solve the problem because of the limited predictive value of the givens and the incompleteness of the case library. However, the pieces of the selected cases can be used to define a limited subspace in which to search.

Therefore, the second step of the process is to generate a set of plausible cases from pieces of the selected cases (see Fig. 1). First, the selected cases are "decompiled" into pieces of cases. These case pieces may be single components or large chunks of the case retaining as little or as much, respectively, of the original internal context of the case as desired. By recombining or "mixing & matching" these pieces of cases the system can generate a set of plausible cases that more uniformly explore the problem space. Additionally the user can edit the pieces of cases based on their knowledge and preferences.

The belief network, learned using the data in the case library and a network structure engineered by the domain expert, evaluates the plausible cases. When the cases were decompiled, critical implicit dependencies between variables in the case were lost. Hennessy & Hinkle [7] and Redmond [8] demonstrate that pieces of cases can only be combined when their original contexts (i.e., implicit dependencies) have been properly considered. The belief network is used to "recompile" those dependencies back into the plausible cases. The nodes corresponding to the givens and observables are set to the values for the corresponding features in a plausible case. The BBN is then used to infer the probability distribution for the outcome node. The result is a score for each plausible case that can be viewed as a crude estimate of the probability of success. In evaluating the plausible cases, those that **implicitly** violate dependencies that are **explicitly** encoded in the BBN will produce a low probability of success and can be removed from consideration. Conversely, those plausible cases that implicitly maintain the dependencies that are explicitly encoded in the BBN will produce a high probability of success.

As is always the situation, the quality of the evaluation (and therefore the preservation of the implicit dependencies) is dependent on the quality of knowledge underlying the inference (in this case, the BBN and case library). However, this weakness is only a factor at the points where the cases have been broken apart and recombined. The implicit dependencies within the case pieces remain intact, providing an additional source of a critical, limited resource in this class of problems: domain knowledge.

The set of "best" plausible cases are selected as the potential solution to the problem. The rough probability of success is a primary factor in determining the "best" cases, but it is not the only one. In macromolecular crystallography, a group of experiments (typically in groups of 24 or 96) are performed in parallel. This is essential due to the combination of time limitations and weakness of the data and theory (simultaneously exploring multiple possible solutions mitigates the risk of the underlying theory steering the system down the wrong path). Therefore, other factors in determining the "best" cases include maintaining an appropriate breadth of cases (in order to explore the problem space efficiently), grouping the cases so that difficult variations are minimized (e.g., varying the temperature within a single tray of experiments) and other domain specific considerations.

The result of BCR is the selection a set of cases that will maximize the probability of obtaining the desired outcome for the specified givens. In the terms of our features types, we are looking for the set $\{X_1, ..., X_n\}$ where X_i is an instantiation of the observables such that the probability P(Outcome = o | Givens = g, Observerables = X_i) is near the maximum. A more detailed examination of how these probabilities are computed can be found in [4].

2.3   The Probabilistic Screen Design Program

The Probabilistic Screen Design (PDS) employs the BCR approach to design crystallographic screening experiments. The case library is a database of the previous crystallization experience of the system. Crystallization experiments are added and edited thru the Crystal Notebook interface (Fig. 2) described in [4]. This includes both historical data, such as the BMCD and paper lab notebook data, as well as data originally generated and tracked by the Crystal Notebook interface. The case library is hierarchically organized around crystallization projects, which consist of a series of trays, which in turn are 4x6 or 8x12 grids of individual experiments or cells. Cells organize the information about the chemical additives in the experiment and the observed and measured results over time.

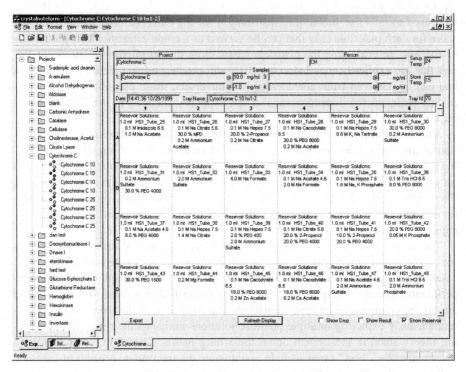

Fig. 2. Crystal Notebook User Interface

For the initial version of this program, the set of parameters that defines the crystallization trials is fixed to include pH, temperature, macromolecular concentration, buffer, two additives (one of which is generally a salt), and precipitating agent. A listing of potential values for the parameters and the extent to which they are represented in the database is provided at the bottom of the window. The parameter values support the use of wildcards ('*' and '?') for matching partially specified names in the database. This is useful, for instance, when the user is interested in the impact of using a "phosphate" buffer regardless of the anion. Binning ranges are supported for the numeric values to aid in matching numeric values against a database. The binning range specifies how strict of a numeric match is required. For instance, a binning range of +/-0.2 for the pH allows 7.5 to match any value between 7.3 and 7.7 inclusive.

The experiments generated by the partial factorial are evaluated by a belief net using the Crystallization Parameter Dependency Graph (see Fig. 3) constructed by a Crystallography expert. As discussed in Section 2.2, the belief network is used to "recompile" lost dependencies back into the case. The result is a score for each generated experiment that can be viewed as a rough probability of success. The list of experiments, including the additives and their concentrations, rank order and computed probability of success, is presented to the user for selection and grouping into trays.

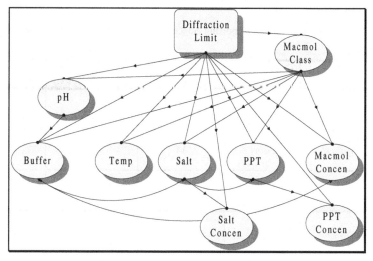

Fig. 3. Crystallization Parameter Dependency Graph

3   Empirical Results

An empirical evaluation of the Probabilistic Screen Design (PDS) was performed by applying the screens generated by the PDS to a set of 10 test proteins. The proteins were chosen for their commercial availability (which included consideration of their price), recognition within the field and representation of a cross section of the Macromolecular Hierarchy. The appropriate PDS screen (i.e., the screen generated for the class of the protein being tested) was applied under the same conditions as two standard screens. The first, Hampton's Crystal Screen I & II, is the most widely used commercial crystallization screen. The second is a grid screen that is routinely applied to new proteins in Dr. Rosenberg's lab that is derived from a published screen frequently cited in the literature.

The individual experiments were visually inspected and scored on a scale of 1 to 5:
1. **Clear** - showing no signs of aggregation of any form.
2. **Precipitates** - aggregation of the protein coming out of solution not in crystalline form.
3. **Microcrystalline showers/microcrystals** - very small crystals that are useless per se but demonstrating promise that, with refinement, larger crystals may be possible.

4. **Crystals probably not suitable for diffraction (thin needles, plates, too small, aggregates)** - often a good starting point for refinement to a diffraction quality crystal.
5. **Crystals apparently suitable for diffraction** - Crystals that by visual inspection appear to be suitable for diffraction.

Table 1. Number of Experiments Reporting Successful Results in Probabilistic Screen Design Evaluation.

Protein	Quality Class		Probabilistic Screen Design	Crystal Screen I & II (Hampton)	Grid Screens
Lysozyme	5	(Good)	15	10	7
	4	(Poor)	4	8	1
	3	(Shower)	15	0	0
Alcohol dehydrogenase	5	(Good)	8	1	0
	4	(Poor)	14	2	0
	3	(Shower)	15	10	10
Catalase	5	(Good)	8	1	3
	4	(Poor)	14	1	15
	3	(Shower)	15	3	21
Lactate dehydrogenase	5	(Good)	1	1	1
	4	(Poor)	2	1	2
	3	(Shower)	0	5	0
DNase	5	(Good)	0	0	0
	4	(Poor)	6	0	0
	3	(Shower)	9	1	0
RNase	5	(Good)	0	1	0
	4	(Poor)	6	2	4
	3	(Shower)	3	3	3
Trypsinogen	5	(Good)	0	0	0
	4	(Poor)	3	0	0
	3	(Shower)	0	0	0
Cytochrome C	5	(Good)	0	0	0
	4	(Poor)	4	0	0
	3	(Shower)	0	0	0
Hemoglobin	5	(Good)	0	0	0
	4	(Poor)	6	4	0
	3	(Shower)	1	2	0
Insulin	5	(Good)	2	2	4
	4	(Poor)	29	7	21
	3	(Shower)	17	14	6
Ten Proteins	5	(Good)	22	16	15
	4	(Poor)	59	35	43
	3	(Shower)	55	50	40

The number of experiments that produced successful results are presented in **Table 1**. Result scores of 1 and 2 are omitted as they represent results that are not considered useful. PDS outperformed the other screening methods virtually across the board. Of particular exception is RNase for which the commercial screen produced a direct hit (a score of 5 representing a crystal which is apparently immediately suitable for diffraction) while PDS and the grid screen failed to find a similarly successful result. However, PDS did produce more results at the 4 and 3 level that could potentially be refined to a diffraction quality crystal.

As the goal of the screening process is to detect useful starting points for further refinement, scores of 3, 4 and 5 are all considered useful results. Analysis of the data in **Table 1** shows that PDS obtained useful results in all ten test proteins where the commercial screens identified useful starting conditions in only eight of the ten proteins and the grid screen derivative provided useful results in only six of the ten test proteins. High quality results (scores of 4 or 5) were again obtained by PDS for all ten (10) test proteins, while the commercial screen had only seven "hits" and the grid screen had only five hits. The commercial screen had one more direct hit (a score of 5) than PDS (six versus five) while both outperformed the grid screen with only four. These results are summarized in **Table 2**.

Table 2. Proteins with at least one "hit" as a function of screen type and quality class.

Quality Class	XtalGrow (Bayesian)	Crystal Screen I & II (Sparse Matrix)	Grid Screens
5	5	6	4
5 + 4	10	7	5
5 + 4 + 3	10	8	6

The data for these preliminary results are based primarily on the data extracted and reengineered from the Biological Macromolecule Crystallization Database (BMCD) [3]. The significant limitations of the BMCD data have been discussed by Jurisica et al [5] and in our own previous analysis [4]. However, it is interesting to note the promising experimental success (albeit initial and limited in scope) despite these limitations. Furthermore, whereas the BMCD data is a static component of the case library, we are actively expanding the case library via the Crystal Notebook, an electronic experimental notebook we have designed. As the number of directly captured experiments, including more precise and accurate crystallization conditions and both success and failure results, the limitations of the BMCD data will incrementally decrease. We expect that this should only enhance the results we have seen so far.

4   Discussion

4.1   BCR vs BBN

We believe that in domains with a complex domain theory, including an incomplete domain model and incomplete case library, BCR provides strong advantages over directly applying a BBN. In constructing a belief network from the data, whether it is the structure, parameters or both, there is inherent loss in the compilation of the cases into the BBN. Implicitly captured in a case is the complex "first-principles" reasoning necessary to generate the solution for the given context. The structure and conditional probabilities in the BBN (whether learned from the data or provided by the domain expert) represent a rough approximation of this first-principles reasoning. In fact, it is known for the crystallographic model that due to the limitations of our understanding of the domain, the BBN does not reflect all of the possible knowledge of the cases. Furthermore, the more complex the domain and incomplete the case library, the poorer the approximation will be.

However, the BBN does provide a convenient mechanism for representing relationships between the variables that are well established in the domain. The formalism of belief networks offers an intuitively appealing approach for expressing inexact causal relationships between domain concepts [13, 14]. The graphical tools that are readily available to represent and manipulate these relationships makes creating and refining a domain model practical for domain experts. The resulting domain model, albeit incomplete, provides an effective mechanism for "recompiling" known relationships back into the composite cases. Such a model is required to expand the coverage of an incomplete case-library via the combination of pieces of cases [7, 8].

The BCR approach described above provides a balance. The implicit first-principles reasoning is retained through the direct use of the cases and their pieces. The available domain theory is incorporated through the use of the BBN to evaluate potential changes in the implicit context when pieces of cases are combined. The combination of pieces of cases is necessary to make available a broader coverage of the problem space. As such we would expect this combined approach to out perform a direct application of the BBN. Kasif et.al. [12] provide an analysis supporting a similar conclusion, however for an approach that does not use pieces of cases. We are currently in the process of evaluating this hypothesis for the BCR approach.

4.2   Related Work

Hennessy and Hinkle [7] used pieces of cases to configure the layout of composite airplane parts for curing in an autoclave. However, it used an offline human evaluation of the combined pieces of cases to confirm the validity of the combination. Redmond [8] also used pieces of cases called snippets for automobile maintenance. However the domain model was much more complete and better understood than in the class of domains explored here.

Breese & Heckerman [9] and Myllymaki & Tirri [10] both compile the case completely in the bayes or neural network. As discussed in Section 4.1, we believe that there is inherent loss in such a compilation that the use of the original cases and their pieces can help avoid. The "domain expert" acknowledges theoretical limitations in the current BBN that are difficult/impossible to correct at this level of complexity. However, BCR, with its empirical data represents a significant step in that direction. Aha & Chang [11] and Kasif et.al. [12] use a probabilistic model to chose relevant cases from the database. Both of these techniques are using the probabilistic model to choose existing cases from the database rather than reconstruct and evaluate cases recombined from pieces of cases.

References

1. Carter Jr., C.W. & Carter, C.W. (1979) Protein Crystallization Using Incomplete Factorial Experiments. J. Biol. Chem., **254**: p. 12219-12223.
2. Hennessy, D., Gopalakrishnan, V., Buchanan, B.G., Rosenberg, J.M., and Subramanian, D., (1994) "Induction of Rules for Biological Macromolecular Crystallization", Proceedings of the Second International Conference on Intelligent Systems for Molecular Biology, pp. 179-187, Stanford, CA
3. Gilliland, G.C. (1987) A biological macromolecule crystallization database: a basis for a crystallization strategy. In Proceedings of the Second International Conference on Protein Crystal Growth; A FEBS Advanced Lecture Course. Bischenberg, Strasbourg, France: North Holland
4. Hennessy, D., Buchanan, B.G., Subramanian, D., Wilkosz, P.A., & Rosenberg, J. M., (2000). "Statistical Methods for the Objective Design of Screening Procedures for Macromolecular Crystallization", Acta Crystallographica Section D D56, 817-827.
6. Jurisica, I., Rogers, P., Glasgow, J., Fortier, S., Luft, J., Wolfley, J., Bianca, M., Weeks, D., DeTitta, G.T. (2001) Intelligent Decision Support for Protein Crystal Growth. To appear in *IBM Systems Journal, Special issue on Deep Computing for Life Sciences*, **40**(2): 394-409
7. Hennessy, D.N. & Hinkle, D. (1992). Applying case-based reasoning to autoclave loading. *IEEE Expert* 7(5): 21-26.
8. Redmond, M.A. (1990). What should I do now? Using goal sequitor knowledge to choose the next problem-solving step. In *Proceedings of the Twelfth Annual Conference of the Cognitive Science Society*. Northvale, NJ: Erlbaum.
9. Breese, J. S., & Heckerman, D. (1995). Decision-theoretic case-based reasoning. *Proceedings of the Fifth International Workshop on Artificial Intelligence and Statistics* (pp. 56-63). Ft. Lauderdale, FL: Unpublished.
10. Myllymaki, P, & Tirri, H. (1993). Massively parallel case-based reasoning with probabilistic similarity metrics. *Proceedings of the First European Workshop on Case-Based Reasoning* (pp. 145-154). Kaiserlautern, Germany: Springer-Verlag.
11. Aha, D. W. & Chang, L. W. (1996). Cooperative Bayesian and Case-Based Reasoning for Solving Multiagent Planning Tasks. NCARAI Technical Report AIC-96-005.
12. Kasif, S., Salzberg, S., Waltz, D., Rachlin, J. & Aha, D. W. (1998). *A probabilistic framework for memory-based reasoning*. Artificial Intelligence, 104(1-2), 297-312.
13. Kim, J. H. & Pearl, J. (1983). A computational model for causal and diagnostic reasoning in inference systems, in: *Proceedings of the 8th International Joint Conference on Artificial Intelligence* (pp. 190-193), Karlsruhe, West Germany
14. Pearl, J. (1988). *Probabilistic Reasoning in Intelligent Systems: Networks of Plausible Inference*. Morgan Kaufman Publishers, San Mateo, California.
15. Kolodner, J. (1993). *Case-Based Reasoning*. Morgan Kaufman Publishers, San Mateo, California.
16. McPherson, A. (1990). *Current Approaches to Macromolecular Crystallization*. European Journal of Biochemistry, 189, 1-23.

Relations between Customer Requirements, Performance Measures, and General Case Properties for Case Base Maintenance

Ioannis Iglezakis and Thomas Reinartz

DaimlerChrysler AG, Research & Technology, RIC/AM,
P.O. Box 2360, 89013 Ulm, Germany
{ioannis.iglezakis,thomas.reinartz}@daimlerchrysler.com

Abstract. The ultimate goal of CBR applications is to satisfy customers using this technology in their daily business. As one of the crucial issues in CBR for practical applications, maintenance is important to cope with demands changing over time. Review and restore are the two steps in CBR that deal with tasks of maintenance. In order to perform these tasks, we suggested case and case base properties, quality criteria, and restore operators in earlier publications. In this paper, we specify concrete performance measures that correspond to general customer requirements, and analyze the relations between these performance criteria, case properties, and restore operators. We present initial results on theoretical analyzes on these relations, and report on examples of experimental studies that indicate that the suggested case properties and the respective restore operators help to identify maintenance strategies in order to optimize performance of CBR systems over time.

1 Introduction

In earlier publications, we established review and restore as two additional steps that enhance the 4–RE CBR process consisting of retrieve, reuse, revise, and retain [1]. The review step checks the CBR system quality and tests if this quality still meets desired quality criteria, whereas the restore step uses different operators to modify the system to get back to a desired level of quality.

The review step consists of three different tasks. First, the *assess* task evaluates the quality of one of the knowledge containers of a CBR system. Second, the *monitor* task displays or visualizes the results of the assess task and, for example, compares the assessment outcome with thresholds. At the end of the review step, it is the goal of the *notify* task to initiate actions on the results of the monitor task.

The restore step again consists of three tasks. First, the *suggest* task computes potential restore operations that are able to modify the affected knowledge container in order to get back to the desired level of quality. Second, the *select* task ranks the suggested restore operations according to some pre–defined preference criterion. Finally, the goal of the *modify* task is the execution of the selected restore operations.

In previous papers, we defined case and case base properties to detect conflicts between cases and quality measures to assess the quality of the case base, and specified

S. Craw and A. Preece (Eds.): ECCBR 2002, LNAI 2416, pp. 159–173, 2002.
© Springer-Verlag Berlin Heidelberg 2002

several restore operations for the case base along with initial heuristics for their application [4,5]. In this paper, we follow up these ideas for case base maintenance and enhance the previous concepts in several ways.

First, we define performance measures for using a CBR system that reflect customer requirements in practical applications. Second, we generalize the case properties to similarity–based properties that no longer rely on specific similarity measures but allow any similarity measure. We will then show how customer requirements, performance criteria, and case properties relate to each other in the context of case base maintenance. Therefore, we present some theoretical results as well as examples for experimental studies that indicate the correctness of the theoretical analyzes.

2   Customer Requirements

Assume typical customers of a help–desk for IT support. They call help–desk agents when they come along a problem with their computer system which they are not able to solve by themselves.[1] Then, the customer describes the problem, and the help–desk agent normally asks additional questions to get a clearer picture of the problem. As soon as the problem is concrete enough, the help–desk agent aims at supporting the customer with a solution, often by remembering similar situations with similar problems.

In terms of case–based reasoning, such a scenario is a typical diagnosis application. The customer problem forms the problem component of a query to the CBR engine. The problem description together with answers to additional questions construct symptoms of the problem definition, often in terms of an attribute–value representation. And finally, the overall solution of the problem corresponds to the solution component of a new case, or matches the solution component of an existing case in the case base (or an adaptation thereof).

In those and similar scenarios, customer requirements are relatively clear:

1. *Customers want an answer to their problem at all.*
   If customers ask a query to some support or a CBR system, either directly or indirectly, they expect an answer. If customers do not get an answer to their query, they get an impression of incompetence, either of the support or of the CBR system.
2. *Customers want correct answers to their problem.*
   Obviously, customers are additionally interested in getting a correct answer. It is possibly not necessary to provide the best correct answer, but it is essential to offer a correct answer.
3. *Customers want fast answers to their problems.*
   Customers with problems are impatient; they want solutions fast. Although, for example, in case of help–desks, there usually exists a complex management for priorities of problems, customers perceive their own problem as the most important and urgent problem.
4. *Customers want confident answers to their problems.*
   In addition to correct and fast answers, customers often expect that the support has a specific confidence. They do not want to try out many solutions until they really get

---

[1] For the moment, we ignore that it is possible to contact modern help–desk organizations in multiple ways beyond telephone calls.

the right answer to their original problem, but insist on that the first solution is already the correct one. Alternatively, if the support is not able to provide a correct solution, customers want to be confident that the support is in no doubt of its decisions.

Unfortunately, these general customer requirements refer to criteria that we are only able to measure if we really use the CBR system in practice. It is hardly possible to estimate the quality of the CBR system according to these requirements by simply looking at the different knowledge containers. Hence, we are looking for a way firstly to measure some criteria that reflect these customer requirements, and then secondly to estimate the values of these criteria before really using the system in practice. For the first purpose, we now specify concrete measurable performance criteria; and for the second need, we identify relations between performance and case properties.

3   Case Representation and Similarity Measure

Before we start with the definition of performance measures, we specify the case representation as well as the similarity measure which we use subsequently. These definitions follow up the representation which we have defined in previous publications. For a detailed discussion, we refer to [5].

Definition 1 (Cases and Case Base).

a) *An attribute a_j is a name accompanied by a set $V_j := \{v_{j1}, \ldots, v_{jk}, \ldots, v_{jN_j}\}$ of values. We denote the set of attributes as $A := \{a_1, \ldots, a_j, \ldots, a_N\}$.*

b) *A problem is a set $p_i := \{p_{i1}, \ldots, p_{ij'}, \ldots, p_{iN_i}\}$ with $\forall j' \in [1; N_i] \exists a_j \in A$ and $\exists v_{jk} \in V_j : p_{ij'} = v_{jk}$, and $\forall j \in [1; N] : |(p_i \cap V_j)| \leq 1$. We denote the set of problems as $P := \{p_1, \ldots, p_i, \ldots, p_M\}$.*

c) *A solution s_i is any item.*

d) *A case is a tuple $c_i := (p_i, s_i)$ with a problem p_i and a solution s_i. A case base is a set of cases $C := \{c_1, \ldots, c_i, \ldots, c_M\}$.*

e) *We further assume a separation of C into a training set T and a test set (or query set) Q with $C = T \cup Q$ and $T \cap Q = \emptyset$.*

The auxiliary functions in definition 2 count coincidence and difference between values of two problem definitions, e.g., of a case and a query. $S_{\leftrightarrow}$ is the number of values for the same attribute with local similarity 1. For example, for symbolic attributes, this number equals the number of identical values; for numeric attributes, this is the number of values with only small differences, e.g., in comparison to a pre–defined threshold ϵ. $S_{\leftrightsquigarrow}$ is the contrary function and corresponds to the number of unequal or more discriminant values. $S_{\leftarrow}$ and $S_{\rightarrow}$ count the number of values for attributes that occur in the case but not in the query, and vice versa, respectively. Finally, S_{-} depicts the amount of information that is missing in both problem definitions, i.e., it counts the number of attributes without values, neither in the case nor in the query.

Definition 2 (Auxiliary Functions). *Assume a local similarity measure $sim_j : V_j \times V_j \mapsto [0; 1]$.*

a) $S_{\leftrightarrow} : P \times P \mapsto \{1..N\}$,
   $S_{\leftrightarrow}(p_i, p_{i'}) := \left| \{ j \in \{1..N\} : |p_i \cap V_j| = |p_{i'} \cap V_j| = 1 \wedge sim_j(p_{ij}, p_{i'j}) = 1 \} \right|$

b) $S_{\rightsquigarrow} : P \times P \mapsto \{1..N\}$,
   $S_{\rightsquigarrow}(p_i, p_{i'}) := \left| \{ j \in \{1..N\} : |p_i \cap V_j| = |p_{i'} \cap V_j| = 1 \wedge sim_j(p_{ij}, p_{i'j}) \neq 1 \} \right|$

c) $S_{\leftarrow} : P \times P \mapsto \{1..N\}$,
   $S_{\leftarrow}(p_i, p_{i'}) := \left| \{ j \in \{1..N\} : |p_i \cap V_j| > |p_{i'} \cap V_j| \} \right|$

d) $S_{\rightarrow} : P \times P \mapsto \{1..N\}$,
   $S_{\rightarrow}(p_i, p_{i'}) := \left| \{ j \in \{1..N\} : |p_i \cap V_j| < |p_{i'} \cap V_j| \} \right|$

e) $S_{-} : P \times P \mapsto \{1..N\}$,
   $S_{-}(p_i, p_{i'}) := \left| \{ j \in \{1..N\} : |p_i \cap V_j| = |p_{i'} \cap V_j| = 0 \} \right|$

We use the auxiliary functions for two different purposes. First, we define the overall similarity measure by a weighted cumulation of these auxiliary values, and second we use them to specify the general case properties later.

The overall similarity in definition 3 is the normalized weighted sum of above auxiliary values. We definitely consider values that coincide for the same attribute $(S_{\leftrightarrow}(p_i, p_{i'}))$ as positive. Different values $(S_{\rightsquigarrow}(p_i, p_{i'}))$ instead do not contribute positive local similarity values and is therefore not considered. For all of the other values $(S_{\leftarrow}(p_i, p_{i'}), S_{\rightarrow}(p_i, p_{i'}),$ and $S_{-}(p_i, p_{i'}))$, weights $w_{\leftarrow}, w_{\rightarrow}$, and w_{-} decide whether we consider their relations as positive $(w = 1)$ or negative $(w = 0)$.

Definition 3 (Similarity Measure). *Assume* $w_{\leftarrow}, w_{\rightarrow}, w_{-} \in \{0, 1\}$.
$$sim : P \times P \mapsto [0; 1],$$
$$sim(p_i, p_{i'}) := N^{-1} \cdot \left(S_{\leftrightarrow}(p_i, p_{i'}) + w_{\leftarrow} \cdot S_{\leftarrow}(p_i, p_{i'}) \right.$$
$$\left. + w_{\rightarrow} \cdot S_{\rightarrow}(p_i, p_{i'}) + w_{-} \cdot S_{-}(p_i, p_{i'}) \right).$$

For example, if we suppose $w_{\leftarrow} = 0$ and $w_{\rightarrow} = 1$, we implement the following strategy for unknown values. Assume p_i is a problem component of a case whereas $p_{i'}$ is a problem component of a query. If a case specifies a value which is not part of the query, we assume that the known problem is more specific than the query. We either have a more general new problem or we have not yet tested the respective missing symptom for the query. In both cases, we do not increment the overall similarity. In contrast, if a case does not specify a value which is part of the query, we assume that the known problem is more general and hence covers all problems which are more specific. In these situations, we increment the overall similarity. If both values are unknown, w_{-} decides whether we count this coincidence as a positive or negative aspect of similarity.

4   Performance Measures

The previously described customer requirements reflect expectations of customers using a CBR system in any practical setting. For the following more precise considerations, we focus on diagnosis as the broad range of applications. We define four different performance measures that correspond to the customer requirements as we will discuss thereafter.

4.1 Coverage

The first performance measure is coverage. A set of cases covers a (query) case if and only if there exists a case within the set of cases that is at least as similar to the (query) case as a pre–defined similarity threshold τ. This similarity threshold τ corresponds to the minimum required similarity that CBR systems use to decide whether to suggest the solution of the most similar case as the solution of a query or not. For example, using a similarity threshold of 0.5 with a simple similarity measure basically counting matching values, this definition of coverage requires that at least half of the values of a case match the values of a query until we accept that this case covers this query.

Definition 4 (Coverage). *Assume* $q = (q_p, q_s) \in Q$, $t = (t_p, t_s) \in T$, $T' \subseteq T$, *and* $\tau > 0$.[2]

a) *T' covers* $q :\Longleftrightarrow \exists t \in T' : sim(t_p, q_p) \geq \tau$.
b) *T' correctly covers* $q :\Longleftrightarrow \exists t \in T' : sim(t_p, q_p) \geq \tau \wedge t_s = q_s$.[3]
c) *The* coverage set *of T' is* $V(T') := \{q \in Q : T' \text{ covers } q\}$.
d) *The* correct (or positive) coverage set *of T' is* $V^+(T') := \{q \in Q : T' \text{ correctly covers } q\}$.
e) *The* coverage *of T' is* $P_V(T') := |Q|^{-1} \cdot |V(T')|$.
f) *The* correct (or positive) coverage *of T' is* $P_V^+(T') := |Q|^{-1} \cdot |V^+(T')|$.

Pure coverage only requires a case with sufficient similarity; it does not necessarily expect that this case is also able to correctly classify the respective query. For the latter situation, we also define a notion of correct (or positive) coverage (see definition 4). For further discussions and specifications, we also define the coverage set of a set of cases and its correct (or positive) pendant. The (correct or positive) coverage as a performance measure is then the relative number of (correctly) covered cases in Q.

4.2 Accuracy

Accuracy is probably the most prominent performance measure that many researchers use to evaluate their approaches. Accuracy (or classification accuracy) counts the number of correct solutions of a CBR system using a case base to solve a set of queries. In classification domains, this number of solutions is compatible to the number of correct classifications.

First, we define when a case (correctly) classifies a query, namely, when this case is the most similar case in the case base in comparison to the query (and the solution components coincide). Furthermore, we specify the (correct or positive) classification set of a case (see definition 5). The accuracy is then the relative number of correctly classified cases in Q.

---

[2] q_p and t_p are the problem components of q and t, and q_s and t_s are the solution components of q and t, respectively. If it is clear that we mean q_p or t_p rather than q_s or t_s, we also use q and t instead of the more detailed notation q_p and t_p.

[3] Note, in real applications we do not know whether $t_s = q_s$ in advance. However, for experimental purposes, we assume a separated original case base into training and test cases (see above) such that we know the solution of queries beforehand.

Definition 5 (Accuracy). *Assume* $q = (q_p, q_s) \in Q$, $t = (t_p, t_s), t' = (t'_p, t'_s) \in T$, *and* $T' \subseteq T$.

a) $t \in T$ classifies $q \iff \nexists t' \in T, t \neq t' : sim(t'_p, q_p) > sim(t_p, q_p)$.[4]
b) $t \in T$ correctly classifies $q \iff t$ *classifies* $q \wedge t_s = q_s$.
c) T' *(correctly) classifies* $q \iff \exists t \in T' : t$ *(correctly) classifies* q.
d) *The* classification set *of* T' *is* $A(T') := \{q \in Q : \exists t' \in T' : t'$ *classifies* $q\}$.
e) *The* correct (or positive) classification set *of* T' *is* $A^+(T') := \{q \in Q : \exists t' \in T' : t'$ *correctly classifies* $q\}$.
f) *The accuracy of* T' *is* $P_A^+(T') := |Q|^{-1} \cdot |A^+(T')|$.

Note, the crucial difference between coverage and accuracy is the desired minimum similarity τ and the relation between solutions of cases and queries. For pure coverage, we demand a minimum similarity τ between cases and queries but do not state any constraints on solutions. For accuracy, we count any correct solution of the most similar case in comparison to a query regardless the exact value of similarity. Hence, coverage is stronger in a sense that it requires a minimum similarity but accuracy is stronger in a sense that it expects correct solutions.

4.3   Retrieval Time and Storage Space

The retrieval time and exact storage space that is needed to cope with the case base depends on the machine used for retrieval and the number of cases in the case base. Since we are not able to change machine characteristics by maintenance, we identify retrieval time with storage space which in turn corresponds to the number of cases for simplicity. Consequently, the respective performance measure P_T only counts the number of cases in the case base.

Definition 6 (Retrieval Time and Storage Space).
   The retrieval time *and* storage space *(indicator) of* T *is* $P_T(T) := |T|$.

4.4   Confidence

Finally, the confidence of a CBR system in its decisions is a fourth performance measure. Thereby, we presume that observed similarities are appropriate as an indication of confidence. The higher the similarity of a case that classifies a query in comparison to the query is, the more confident we assume the CBR system is in its decision.

Definition 7 (Confidence). *Assume* $T' \subseteq T$, $t_q^* \in T'$ *is the case that classifies* $q \in Q$, *and* $sim^+(t_q^*, q) := sim(t_q^*, q)$ *if* t_q^* *correctly classifies* q *as well as* $sim^+(t_q^*, q) := 0$ *if* t_q^* *does not correctly classify* q.

a) *The* (average) confidence *of* T' *(on* Q*) is* $P_C(T) := |Q|^{-1} \cdot \sum_{q \in Q} sim(t_q^*, q)$.[5]

---

[4] In case of ties, i.e., two different cases have the same highest similarity in comparison to the query, we assume some order on T such that *the* case which classifies $q \in Q$ is always unique.
[5] We assume that T always classifies any $q \in Q$.

b) The (average) correct (or positive) confidence *of T' (on Q) is* $P_C^+(T) := |Q|^{-1} \cdot \sum_{q \in Q} sim^+(t_q^*, q)$.

Since we are barely interested in confidence of single decisions, we average confidence over all classifying cases and queries. For regular confidence, we count all similarities between classifying cases and the respective queries, whereas correct (or positive) confidence only takes into account similarities between cases and queries with correct classifications. Hence, we are able to distinguish between the average confidence of a CBR system in general, and the average confidence in its correct decisions. The related average wrong (or negative) confidence is simply the difference between average confidence and average correct (or positive) confidence.

4.5   Related Performance Measures

The most closely related work on similar performance measures is the research by Smyth and colleagues [7]. They define the local competence contribution of individual cases by two sets, the coverage set and the reachability set. The coverage set of a (training) case is the set of (query) cases that this case is able to solve, whereas the reachability set of a (query) case corresponds to the set of cases which are able to solve it. For both sets, Smyth and colleagues use a notion of 'solves'. If we assume that 'solves', for example, means in terms of our terminology $s_i = s_{i'}$ for a case $c_i = (p_i, s_i)$ and a (test) query $c_{i'} = (p_{i'}, s_{i'})$, and we additionally require that case and query have at least a similarity to each other of τ, then their coverage set definition is the same as $V^+(\{c_i\})$ in terms of our concepts.

The correct (or positive) classification set here is also comparable to the coverage set by Smyth et al. However, a classification set only considers queries that were really classified by a case rather than cumulating all cases that were potentially able to correctly classify the query. At the moment, we do not have any corresponding concept to Smyth et al.'s reachability set but it is easily possible to extend our definitions along these ideas and specify comparable sets as soon as we encounter a concrete need for them.

If we compare the definitions here and those of Smyth and colleagues, we observe that their notion of 'solves' is more general than the definitions for coverage and classification sets here, but on the other hand coverage, accuracy, and, especially, confidence cover more general aspects of performance than Symth et al.'s concepts do. Furthermore, their resulting maintenance strategies directly refer to their competence models whereas we only use these concepts to indirectly measure performance but rely on case and case base properties for maintenance purposes.

For more discussion of related work, we refer to earlier publications on case and case base properties (e.g., see [4,5]) and discussions in directly related papers (e.g., see discussions of related work in [6] and [7]).

5   General Case Properties

In previous work, we defined several case properties and used them to specify different quality measures [4]. These properties and measures were based on a simple similarity

Table 1. Examples for Pairs of Cases with Conflicts with respect to General Case Properties

	p_i	s_i	$p_{i'}$	$s_{i'}$	conflict	$S_\leftrightarrow$	$S_\leadsto$	$S_\leftarrow$	$S_\rightarrow$	S_-	Δ
1	$v_{11}\ v_{21}\ v_{31}$	s_1	$v_{11}\ v_{21}$	s_2	¬ sim–consistent	2	0	1	0	2	–
2	$v_{11}\ v_{21}\ v_{31}$	s_1	$v_{11}\ v_{21}\ v_{31}$	s_1	¬ sim–unique	3	0	0	0	2	–
3	$v_{11}\ v_{21}\ v_{31}$	s_1	$v_{11}\ v_{21}$	s_1	¬ sim–minimal	2	0	1	0	2	–
4	$v_{11}\ v_{21}\ v_{31}\ v_{41}$	s_1	$v_{11}\ v_{21}$	$v_{42}\ v_{51}\ s_1$	¬ sim–incoherent$_2$	2	1	1	1	0	2

measure that only compares coincidence between values, i.e., local similarities yield 1 if two values of two cases (or a case and a query) for the same attribute are identical and 0 if they are not the same. The set–oriented notation for problems and solutions, which comprise cases, enabled definitions of properties and measures that mainly used set operations to compute the necessitated conditions and relations.

By now, we generalized these concepts and generated new definitions of general case properties and resulting quality measures that only use the general concept of a similarity measure rather than assuming a specific instantiation of such a measure. In this section, we cite these more general definitions which in their nature are comparable to the previous specifications. The original simple properties and measures are specializations of the general ones presented here. For detailed explanations of case properties and quality measures, we refer to [5].

Definition 8 (General Case Properties). *Assume* $G \subseteq C$, $c_i \in G$, *and* $1 \leq \Delta \in \mathbb{N}$.

a) c_i *sim–consistent within* G $\quad:\Longleftrightarrow\quad \nexists c_{i'} \in G : s_i \neq s_{i'} \ \wedge\ S_\leftrightarrow(p_i, p_{i'}) + S_\leftarrow(p_i, p_{i'}) = N_i \geq N_{i'} \ \wedge\ S_\leftrightarrow(p_i, p_{i'}) > 0 \ \wedge\ S_\leftarrow(p_i, p_{i'}) \geq 0 \ \wedge\ S_\rightarrow(p_i, p_{i'}) = 0.$

b) c_i *sim–unique within* G $\quad:\Longleftrightarrow\quad \nexists c_{i'} \in G, c_{i'} \neq c_i : s_i = s_{i'} \ \wedge\ S_\leftrightarrow(p_i, p_{i'}) = N_i = N_{i'} \ \wedge\ S_\leftrightarrow(p_i, p_{i'}) > 0.$

c) c_i *sim–minimal within* G $\quad:\Longleftrightarrow\quad \nexists c_{i'} \in G : s_i = s_{i'} \ \wedge\ S_\leftrightarrow(p_i, p_{i'}) + S_\leftarrow(p_i, p_{i'}) = N_i > N_{i'} \ \wedge\ S_\leftrightarrow(p_i, p_{i'}) > 0 \ \wedge\ S_\leftarrow(p_i, p_{i'}) > 0 \ \wedge\ S_\rightarrow(p_i, p_{i'}) = 0.$

d) c_i *sim–incoherent$_\Delta$ within* G $\quad:\Longleftrightarrow\quad \nexists c_{i'} \in G : s_i = s_{i'} \ \wedge\ S_\leftrightarrow(p_i, p_{i'}) + S_\leadsto(p_i, p_{i'}) + S_\leftarrow(p_i, p_{i'}) = N_i = N_{i'} \ \wedge\ S_\leftrightarrow(p_i, p_{i'}) > 0 \ \wedge\ S_\leadsto(p_i, p_{i'}) \geq 0 \ \wedge\ S_\leftarrow(p_i, p_{i'}) \geq 0 \ \wedge\ S_\rightarrow(p_i, p_{i'}) \geq 0 \ \wedge\ S_\leftarrow(p_i, p_{i'}) = S_\rightarrow(p_i, p_{i'}) \ \wedge\ S_\leadsto(p_i, p_{i'}) + S_\leftarrow(p_i, p_{i'}) = \Delta.$

Table 1 shows examples of pairs of cases, their conflict to each other, and the resulting values for the auxiliary functions in definition 2.

6   On Relations between Customer Requirements, Performance Measures, and General Case Properties

The ultimate goal in any CBR application is to fulfill customer expectations. In section 2, we briefly characterized the probably most important customer requirements. However, these requirements and the corresponding performance measures rely on true performance of the system, and an ad–hoc estimation of the degree of fulfillment of the requirements by a CBR system is not possible without using the CBR system in practice.

In this section, we first show how customer requirements, performance measures, and case properties relate to each other, and then argue that we are able to use case properties as early indicators for later performance, and hence for the degree of fulfillment of customer requirements by a CBR system.

6.1 Customer Requirements and Performance Measures

If we consider customer requirements, we observe the following correspondence to performance measures:

a) The first customer requirement corresponds to coverage. Customers want an answer to their query, and if a CBR system covers a query it is able to provide an answer, even if we demand a minimum similarity between classifying cases and queries as many CBR systems do.

b) The second customer requirement corresponds to correct coverage or accuracy. Obviously, customers want correct answers; if a CBR system correctly covers a query, it provides a solution that is correct, if the case base does not contain a more similar case in comparison to the query that results in an incorrect solution. Therefore, it is important to additionally measure accuracy. The higher the accuracy of the CBR system is, the more correct solutions it really provides, no matter if the similarity between cases and queries is high or low.

c) The third customer requirement corresponds to retrieval time, and hence to storage space. Customers want fast answers, and if retrieval time is short, answers are fast. There is always a trade–off between coverage, correctness, and speed. A customer is probably willing to wait longer for a correct answer rather than having a wrong solution fast.

d) The fourth customer requirement corresponds to confidence. Customers are interested in confident answers. For example, in a help–desk setting customers want to know how likely the provided solution is going to be the correct solution before they invest time and possibly money in realizing the suggested solution.

According to these relations, we are able to measure customer requirements and the degree of fulfillment for any specific CBR system by analyzing the respective performance measures. However, these performance measures rely on characteristics of retrieval and an a–priori knowledge on expected queries. Retrieval is costly, and a–priori knowledge on expected queries is usually not available in real-world applications.

Therefore, we aim at other criteria that we are able to measure without using the CBR system and testing its retrieval results, and without knowing anything about expected queries in advance. In the following, we argue that it is possible to approximate some expectations on relative performance (with respect to the previously defined performance measures) by analyzing the case properties within a case base. In addition, we also aim at rules that indicate how the performance measures change over time when we apply restore operations to modify cases in the case base for maintenance purposes.

6.2   Performance Measures and Case Properties

Ideally, we want theoretical relations between performance measures and case properties. For example, if we take into account coverage as the performance measure, uniqueness as the case property, and assume a 1–nearest–neighbor algorithm for retrieval, we theoretically know that conflicts that violate uniqueness do not influence coverage. If there exists a case that covers a query, it does not matter if this case exists more than once, and similarly, if there does not exist any case that covers a query, the situation does not change if we have cases multiple times. Likewise, it does not make any difference in terms of coverage if we utilize restore operations to remove conflicts that contradict uniqueness.

However, as extensive theoretical analyzes that we conducted show, relations between performance measures and case properties are not always that clear, and moreover these relations are usually not independent of other assumptions, for example, on similarities between cases and queries. In order to exemplify the relatively complex theoretical relation between performance measures and case properties, we again consider coverage.

Performance Measures and Similarity.   First of all, if we take coverage, when does coverage change? The coverage of a set T' of cases changes if the number of queries that T' covers changes. This number again changes if either T' after modification by maintenance operators does not cover a query q anymore, or if T' then additionally covers an extra query q' which it did not cover before. In terms of the definition of coverage, we reveal the following conditions:

(i) $P_V(T) > P_V(T')$
$$\Longleftrightarrow \exists q \in Q : \exists t \in T : sim(t_p, q_p) \geq \tau \wedge \nexists t' \in T' : sim(t'_p, q_p) \geq \tau$$
$$\Longleftrightarrow \exists q \in Q : \exists t \in T : sim(t_p, q_p) \geq \tau \wedge \forall t' \in T' : sim(t'_p, q_p) < \tau.$$
(ii) $P_V(T) < P_V(T')$
$$\Longleftrightarrow \exists q \in Q : \nexists t \in T : sim(t_p, q_p) \geq \tau \wedge \exists t' \in T' : sim(t'_p, q_p) \geq \tau$$
$$\Longleftrightarrow \exists q \in Q : \forall t \in T : sim(t_p, q_p) < \tau \wedge \exists t' \in T' : sim(t'_p, q_p) \geq \tau.$$

Both conditions mean if we modify a case by any restore operator and this modification in turn changes the coverage of the case base, then the modified case *before* its modification is the only case which covers q for the first condition (if it is not, there exists still another case which covers q), and the modified case *after* its modification is the only case which covers q for the second condition, respectively. We further assume that one of these conditions is true subsequently. [6]

If the modified case is the only case that is responsible for changes of coverage, this change is only possible if modification changes the similarity between the case and the respective query; for the first condition, this modification must decrease this similarity, for the second condition, it must increase the similarity.

---

[6] Otherwise, relations have to consider more cases and the relation of similarities between those cases, the modified case, and queries.

Performance Measures and Restore Operators. If we now assume that we are only interested in positive effects of maintenance in terms of the performance measures, we are able to restrict further analyzes to the second condition. When does modification increase similarity between a case and a query? For modification, we consider restore operators `remove`, `specialize`, `generalize`, `cross`, and `join` [5]. We neither take into account `adjust` and `alter` since both operators are only concatenations of `specialize` and `generalize`, nor `abstract` and `combine` since these two operators state additional assumptions on representation and retrieval which we can not expect in general diagnosis applications. The following definition 9 recapitulates the restore operators which we consider here from earlier publications for completeness.

Definition 9 (Restore Operators). *Assume $C^{\subseteq}$ is the set of all subsets of C, $G \subseteq C$, and $c_i = (p_i, s_i), c_{i'} = (p_{i'}, s_{i'}) \in G$.*

a) `remove`: $C^{\subseteq} \times C \mapsto C^{\subseteq}$, $\text{remove}(G, c_i) := G \setminus \{c_i\}$
b) *Assume $p_i \cap V_j = \emptyset$ and $v_{jk} \in V_j$.*
   `specialize`: $C \times V \mapsto C$, $\text{specialize}(c_i, v_{jk}) := (p_i \cup \{v_{jk}\}, s_i)$
c) *Assume $p_i \cap V_j = \{v_{jk}\}$.*
   `generalize`: $C \times V \mapsto C$, $\text{generalize}(c_i, v_{jk}) := (p_i \setminus \{v_{jk}\}, s_i)$
d) *Assume $1 \leq \Delta \in \mathbb{N}$, $|p_i \cap p_{i'}| + \Delta = N_i = N_{i'}$ or $p_i \subsetneq p_{i'}$ or $p_{i'} \subsetneq p_i$, and $s_i = s_{i'}$.*
   `cross`: $C \times C \mapsto C$, $\text{cross}(c_i, c_{i'}) := (p_i \cap p_{i'}, s_i)$
e) *Assume $1 \leq \Delta \in \mathbb{N}$, $|p_i \cap p_{i'}| + \Delta = N_i = N_{i'}$ and $\forall a_j \in A : |[(p_i \cup p_{i'}) \setminus (p_i \cap p_{i'})] \cap V_j| \leq 1$ or $p_i \subsetneq p_{i'}$ or $p_{i'} \subsetneq p_i$, and $s_i = s_{i'}$.*
   `join`: $C \times C \mapsto C$, $\text{join}(c_i, c_{i'}) := (p_i \cup p_{i'}, s_i)$

The `remove` operator is certainly the strongest operation that maintenance allows. However, `remove` does not directly influence coverage in terms of changing similarities between the modified case and queries, since the modified case no longer exists after its removal. Nonetheless, simple analyzes show that removal of a case always results in the same or lower coverage but it does not positively influence coverage at all.

Now, assume two cases $t, t' \in T$, a query $q \in Q$, and $w_\leftarrow = 0$, $w_\rightarrow = 1$, and $w_- = 1$ for the definition of similarity measure sim (see definition 3). If we consider `specialize`, `generalize`, `cross`, and `join`, we observe the following characteristics:

- $sim(\text{specialize}(t, v_{jk}), q) = sim(t, q)$ if $V_j \cap q = v_{jk}$,[7]
- $sim(\text{specialize}(t, v_{jk}), q) = sim(t, q) - N^{-1}$ if $V_j \cap q = v_{jk'} \neq v_{jk}$, and
- $sim(\text{specialize}(t, v_{jk}), q) = sim(t, q) - N^{-1}$ if $V_j \cap q = \emptyset$.
  All in all, $sim(\text{specialize}(t, v_{jk}), q) \leq sim(t, q)$.
- $sim(\text{generalize}(t, v_{jk}), q) = sim(t, q)$ if $V_j \cap q = v_{jk}$,
- $sim(\text{generalize}(t, v_{jk}), q) = sim(t, q) + N^{-1}$ if $V_j \cap q = v_{jk'} \neq v_{jk}$, and
- $sim(\text{generalize}(t, v_{jk}), q) = sim(t, q) + N^{-1}$ if $V_j \cap q = \emptyset$.
  All in all, $sim(\text{generalize}(t, v_{jk}), q) \geq sim(t, q)$.
- $sim(\text{cross}(t, t'), q) = sim(t, q) = sim(t', q)$ if $t = t'$, and

---

[7] For simplicity, we identify sets with only a single element with this element, i.e., $\{x\} = x$.

- $sim(\mathtt{cross}(t, t'), q) = sim(t, q)$ if $t \subseteq t'$ (similar for t').
  Other general relations are not possible since similarity can increase and decrease depending on the specific relation between values of cases and query.
- $sim(\mathtt{join}(t, t'), q) = sim(t, q) = sim(t', q)$ if $t = t'$, and
- $sim(\mathtt{join}(t, t'), q) = sim(t', q)$ if $t \subseteq t'$ (similar for t).
  All in all, $sim(\mathtt{join}(t, t'), q) \leq sim(t, q)$ and $sim(\mathtt{join}(t, t'), q) \leq sim(t', q)$.

In conclusion, if we are interested in positive effects on coverage by maintenance using the specified restore operations, we conclude that the only operator which ensures — without additional assumptions — that the similarity does not decrease is $\mathtt{gener-}$ $\mathtt{alize}$. Hence, if we want to positively influence coverage by maintenance, it is wise to test $\mathtt{generalize}$ as the first modification operator.

6.3 Further Analyzes

For all performance measures beyond coverage which we used as an example here, similar analyzes are possible, and the results of such analyzes are comparable to those presented here. In some situations, it is possible to derive general theoretical relations between case properties, the resulting conflicts between cases, restore operators, and performance measures. In other situations, it is necessary to state additional assumptions, for example, on similarities between cases and queries, to make the analyzes tractable. We are currently elaborating on such investigations as part of our overall research on maintenance.

An extra type of analysis which we have not yet extensively pushed forward considers relations between the specific type of conflict and changes of the performance measures if we conduct maintenance using restore operators to modify affected cases. Again, initial results on these analyzes show that, in some situations, it is possible to derive general heuristics in case of specific conflicts which type of operator is preferable, and which of the affected cases to modify first, in order to get best results in terms of performance. However, in other situations, again additional assumptions are necessary to make these theoretical analyzes feasible.

7   Experimental Evaluation

Up to this point, the theoretical analyzes show that it is hardly possible to infer general relations between case properties and performance measures for any type of situation without additional assumptions. In order to further check if conflicts indicate not only quality problems within the case base but also indirectly demonstrate that performance measures currently do not yield optimal values, and to see if it is possible to positively manipulate performance values by modifying cases with restore operations when we observe violated case properties, we now turn to an experimental evaluation.

7.1 Experimental Set–Up

Figure 1 outlines the experimental procedure. For each of the ten different data sets from the UCI repository, we initially separate the original data set into five folds of 20

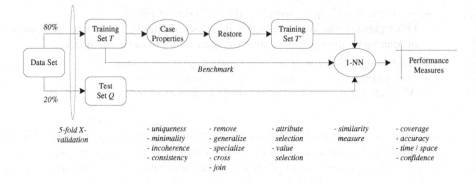

Fig. 1. Experimental Procedure

percent of the entire data each. Thereafter, we split the data into a training set T that consists of four folds and a test set Q that contains the remaining fifth fold. We apply the case properties uniqueness, minimality, incoherence, and consistency to detect conflicts between cases which violate these properties. Then, we utilize the restore operators `remove`, `specialize`, `generalize`, `cross`, and `join` separately to maintain the case base by modifying cases in order to eliminate conflicts. The result of the restore step forms the modified training set T'.

Now, we apply a simple 1–nearest–neighbor algorithm as the CBR mechanism for retrieval and classification with similarity measure sim with $w_\leftarrow = 0, w_\rightarrow = 1, w_- = 1$, and $\epsilon = 0.05$ for local similarity between numeric attributes. Thereafter, we compute the four performance measures $P_V(T')$ with $\tau = 0.75$, $P_A^+(T')$, $P_T(T')$, and $P_C(T')$ and their positive pendants as the overall results of our experiment. The benchmark for comparing these results is the application of the same 1–nearest–neighbor algorithm and computation of the performance measures using the original training set T. We repeat the entire experimental procedure five times, using each of the five folds as the test set once; hence, we implement a 5–fold cross validation experimental design.

For operators `generalize` and `specialize`, we conduct the following strategy to select attributes and values for manipulation. We assess all attributes with information gain ratio as if we were estimating the quality of an attribute for creating the first split in building a decision tree [3]. We then choose the least important attribute according to this selection criterion as the attribute for which we eliminate the value in case of `generalize`, or identify the most important attribute for which we add a value for `specialize`. For the latter operator, we additionally have to decide which value forms the new value for the selected attribute. Therefore, we assume that the most often occurring value for the respective attribute for cases with the same class is the most promising value for our purposes.

7.2   Experimental Results

Table 2 shows experimental results for operator `generalize` in order to eliminate conflicts that violate one of the case properties uniqueness, minimality, incoherence,

Table 2. Experimental Results

Data Set	P_V	P_V^+	P_A^+	P_C	P_C^+
australian	94.6(94.5)	92.0(91.9)	89.4(88.6)	85.9(85.5)	76.7(75.6)
breast-cancer	94.8(94.4)	88.8(88.5)	81.8(80.8)	86.4(85.8)	70.4(69.1)
bridges-version1-ms	81.3(80.3)	60.5(59.5)	66.8(66.8)	83.6(83.5)	55.5(55.4)
bupa	76.5(72.5)	70.1(65.2)	83.5(83.8)	83.9(81.2)	69.0(67.1)
hayes-roth	68.1(68.1)	65.0(55.9)	93.9(84.8)	73.5(73.5)	69.2(61.9)
hepatitis	98.1(98.1)	87.1(87.1)	75.5(75.5)	88.6(88.6)	67.0(67.0)
ionosphere	38.7(38.7)	38.7(38.7)	92.9(92.9)	70.7(70.7)	66.9(66.9)
pima-indians-diabetes	78.9(76.2)	69.9(65.7)	81.9(81.5)	76.7(75.4)	62.5(61.1)
processed-hungarian	94.2(93.5)	89.1(88.1)	86.4(86.1)	83.4(83.2)	72.0(71.6)
voting-records	100.0(100.0)	99.5(99.5)	91.0(91.2)	98.5(98.5)	89.6(89.9)

and consistency in their general similarity–based definition. The table lists five different performance criteria: Coverage P_V, correct coverage P_V^+, accuracy P_A^+, confidence P_C, and correct confidence P_C^+. Left–hand of each column, we see results for the modified case base T' after maintenance, whereas right–hand in brackets we observe the respective benchmark results for the entire training set T before maintenance. Note, we do not report on P_T in this table, since we only list results for operator `generalize` which does not modify the case base size at all.[8]

For coverage, we perceive that the experimental results exactly fit our expectations resulting from the theoretical analysis. Coverage as well as correct coverage remain constant or increase if we apply `generalize` as the maintenance operator. This is coherent with the theoretical analysis that similarities between generalized cases and queries do not decrease.

For accuracy, maintenance has a positive effect on five data sets, a neutral relation holds for three data sets, and we see slightly worse results on the remaining two data sets. Hence, we also infer that maintenance using `generalize` for cases which violate the defined case properties yields promising results in terms of the second performance criterion.

Finally, for confidence, we notice that values again remain constant or increase as for coverage except for data set voting records and correct confidence. It is interesting to see that in most cases it looks like accuracy and confidence are highly correlated, i.e., both performance measures vary in comparable orders of magnitude. Hence, we tend to infer that confidence increases when accuracy does; the more correct classifications a CBR system provides, the more confident it is in its decisions.

All in all, we conclude that the theoretical analyzes give correct hints which operator to test first for maintenance and optimization of performance, and that the suggested general case properties and restore operators are a promising instrument to maintain CBR systems in practical applications when we aim at optimization of performance criteria that correspond to customer requirements.

---

[8] We refer to [2] for some results on P_T and P_A^+ using operator `remove`.

8   Conclusions

In this paper, we presented extensions of our research on case base maintenance. We discussed several customer requirements and defined different performance criteria that are equivalent computable measures for these requirements. Since we are not able to estimate specific values of the performance criteria for any CBR system in advance, and we are also not able to predict changes in performance if we maintain the case base using restore operations, we argued that it is possible to estimate values and changes of performance by considering case properties and their changes after maintenance operations on the case base.

Theoretical analyzes showed that it is hardly possible to derive general rules for the relations between customer requirements, performance criteria, and case properties without making additional assumptions — for example, on the specific similarity measure used for retrieval — to keep the analyzes feasible. However, initial experimental results show that application of restore operators indeed positively influences the performance measures, and that the theoretical analyzes provide first hints which operator is likely to perform best in terms of increasing performance values.

Future research aims at extensions of both, the theoretical analyzes and the experimental studies. The whole research currently offers many parameters to vary, and additional calibrations for all methods seem to have the potential for further examinations. For example, we plan to vary the used similarity measure and the various thresholds such as τ and ϵ, as well as to conduct further experiments with combinations of different restore operators. We strongly believe that we are able to derive more heuristics for appropriate applications of the right restore operators depending on the type of conflicts and the desired effect in performance.

References

1. Agnar Aamodt and Enric Plaza. Case–based reasoning: Foundational issues, methodological variations, and system approaches. *AI Communications*, 7(1):39–59, 1994.
2. Ioannis Iglezakis. The conflict graph for maintaining case–based reasoning systems. In *Proceedings of the 4th International Conference on Case–Based Reasoning*, pages 263–275. Springer–Verlag, 2001.
3. J. Ross Quinlan. *C4.5: Programs for Machine Learning*. Morgan Kaufmann, 1993.
4. Thomas Reinartz, Ioannis Iglezakis, and Thomas Roth–Berghofer. On quality measures for case base maintenance. In *Proceedings of the 5th European Workshop on Case–Based Reasoning*, pages 247–259. Springer–Verlag, 2000.
5. Thomas Reinartz, Ioannis Iglezakis, and Thomas Roth–Berghofer. Review and restore for case–base maintenance. *Computational Intelligence: special issue on maintaining CBR systems*, 17(2):214–234, 2001.
6. Barry Smyth and Elizabeth McKenna. Competence guided incremental footprint-based retrieval. *Knowledge–Based Systems*, 14(3):155–161, 2001.
7. Barry Smyth and Elizabeth McKenna. Competence models and the maintenance problem. *Computational Intelligence: special issue on maintaining CBR systems*, 17(2):235–249, 2001.

Representing Temporal Knowledge
for Case-Based Prediction

Martha Dørum Jære[1], Agnar Aamodt[2], and Pål Skalle[3]

[1] Borak S.L., Ronda de Poniente N4, Tres Cantos, CP 28760, Madrid, Spain
[2] Artificial Intelligence Research Institute, IIIA, Spanish Council for Scientific Research, CSIC,
08193 Bellaterra, Barcelona, Spain.
[3] Department of Petroleum Technology, Norwegian University of Science and Technology,
NO-7491, Trondheim, Norway.

Abstract. Cases are descriptions of situations limited in time and space. The
research reported here introduces a method for representation and reasoning
with time-dependent situations, or temporal cases, within a knowledge-
intensive CBR framework. Most current CBR methods deal with snapshot
cases, descriptions of a world state at a single time stamp. In many time-
dependent situations, value sets at particular time points are less important than
the value changes over some interval of time. Our focus is on prediction
problems for avoiding faulty situations. Based on a well-established theory of
temporal intervals, we have developed a method for representing temporal
cases inside the knowledge-intensive CBR system Creek. The paper presents
the theoretical foundation of the method, the representation formalism and basic
reasoning algorithms, and an example applied to the prediction of unwanted
events in oil well drilling.

1 Introduction

Most current CBR systems represent episodes as distinct snap-shots in time.
Wherever temporal relationships may exist between parameters in a case, they are
either ignored or implicitly handled within the reasoning algorithms. Two current
trends are strengthening the need for explicit representation of temporality. Firstly,
CBR is continuously addressing increasingly challenging problems, and in particular
problem solving in a real world context. Examples are process supervision and control
[17, 20], event prediction from trends [18, 19], and temporal planning [5]. Even
"classical" problems, such as diagnosis and treatment, involve extensive temporal
reasoning when moving beyond the simple classification approach [14, 21]. Secondly,
CBR systems, as well as decision support systems in general, are becoming more
interactive and user-transparent. The trend is away from self-contained problem
solvers and towards user-interactive assistants, where the sequentiality of interactions
often becomes an important piece of information. Both these trends call for an explicit
representation of temporal relationships.

Creek [2, 23] is a CBR system that integrates cases with general domain
knowledge within a single semantic network. Each feature and feature value of a case
is a concept in the semantic network. They are interlinked with other concepts (which

S. Craw and A. Preece (Eds.): ECCBR 2002, LNAI 2416, pp. 174–188.

may be case features or not) through semantic relations specified by the general domain model. Typical relations include subclass and instance relations, part-subpart, process-subprocess, causal and functional relations, as well as particular domain relations (e.g. "has color" or "owes money to"). The general domain knowledge is used as a model-based reasoning support to the case based reasoning processes Retrieve, Reuse, and Retain [1]. Case retrieval, for example, becomes partly an explanation process, in which the initial matching based on index links are justified or criticized. Reuse becomes a process of explaining the adaptation of a past case within the context of the current problem, and Retain the process of explaining/justifying what to retain from a problem just solved. The research described here extends Creek's representation to include temporal relationships, which in turn are utilized by the explanatory mechanisms that underlie the system's reasoning method [12]. Creek addresses problem solving and learning in weak theory, open, and changing domains, such as medicine and most engineering domains. Hence, relations are generally uncertain, and most concepts are described by typical features rather than universally quantified assertions.

In addition to the theoretical and methodological interesting aspects of temporal cases, another motivation for developing a temporal representation within this system comes from a type of application we have been addressing over the last years: Decision support for oil well drilling tasks. While our past work on diagnosis and treatment of unwanted events have utilized cases in order to find out what did happen in the past (such as the cause of a drill string getting stuck) [3, 23], we wanted to utilize the growing case base as a resource for avoiding unwanted events in the future. As the basis for our method, we have adopted James Allen's theory of temporal intervals [4]. This is a well worked-out theory for temporal representations, accompanied by an efficient inference method.

The paper first briefly reviews some of the related research in representing and reasoning about temporality in CBR. This is followed by a summary of James Allen's theory on temporal intervals. The subsequent section introduces the problem of predicting unwanted events in an industrial process, exemplified by the oil drilling domain. Section five presents the temporal representation in our system, and section six describes how the representation is utilized for matching of temporal intervals. Then an example of case-based prediction of a drill-sticking situation is given. The conclusion sums up the results and discusses strengths and weaknesses of the method.

2   Temporal Reasoning and CBR

Early AI research on temporal reasoning makes a distinction between *point-based* and *interval-based* approaches (also referred to as instants-based and period-based approaches [25]). Many well-known theories and systems, such as the Situation Calculus and the early Time Specialist [13], are based on instants as the temporal primitive. Allen's theory of temporal intervals [4], on the other hand, advocates that the interval is the appropriate temporal primitive for reasoning about time.

Although reports of research on temporal representations for CBR in general are scarce, some interesting results have been published. Jaczynski and Trousse propose a method based on so-called time-extended situations [10]. Example applications developed are plant nutrition control and prediction of user behavior for Web navigation. Temporal knowledge is represented as temporal patterns, i.e. multiple streams of data related to time points. The representation holds cases as well as general knowledge, which both are taken into account during retrieval. Cases are represented in one of three different forms, abstract, potential or concrete. Abstract cases, also called domain scripts, capture general or prototypical combinations of data. Concrete cases are explicit situations that have been reused at least one time in the CBR-cycle. Potential cases are case templates whose contents have to be filled from records in the database. Potential cases are stored as concrete cases once they get activated and used. The retrieval method first tries the abstract case, then the concrete case and at last the potential case.

Melendez and his group suggest a method for supervising and controlling the sequencing of process steps that have to fulfill certain conditions [16, 17]. Their main domain is the control of sets of recipes for making products, such as plastic or rubber pieces, from a set of ingredients. A case represents a recipe, and the temporal problem is the control of a set of recipes – a batch – in order to fulfill process conditions and achieve a production goal. A deviation from a normally operating condition is called an event, and consists of actions and reactions. Together, the events represent significant points in the history of a product. An episode contains information related to the behavior between two consecutive events. The retrieval method first matches general conditions such as the initial and final sub-processes, and then the initial conditions of the corresponding episodes.

Hansen [8] presents a method for weather prediction in which a point-based representation of whether observations are utilized in a combined case-based and fuzzy set system. Time is included in the similarity metric, together with other weather parameters. Branting and Hasting's knowledge-intensive CBR system for pest management [6] incorporates a method called "temporal projection". The method aligns two cases in time, by projecting a retrieved case forward or backwards in order to match on other parameters (such as the development stage of an insect).

All the above systems are essentially point-based. We are not aware of other research on temporal reasoning in CBR that take an interval-based approach (in the sense of Allen). The type of problems addressed by our research, where we need to deal with large and complex data sets, as well as the explanatory reasoning methods underlying our CBR approach, strongly indicate that a qualitative, interval-based framework for temporal reasoning is preferable. At least this is our hypothesis.

3 Allen's Temporal Intervals

James Allen [4] introduces a way to represent temporal knowledge in an interval-based temporal logic. An important characteristic of Allen's intervals is that they are decomposable; they can always be decomposed into sub-parts, including time points. Intervals may be open or closed. If they are closed they meet each other exactly, if they are open there will be a point between them that has an empty state when neither of them are true. Intervals can be described in a hierarchy connected by temporal relations: *If interval X is during an interval Y, and P holds during X, then P holds during Y.* Within a "during" hierarchy propositions can hence be inherited. This type of hierarchy allows reasoning processes to be constrained so that irrelevant facts are not considered.

Table 1. The thirteen possible relationships. Adapted from [4].

Relation	Symbol	Inverse Symbol	Pictorial Example
X before Y	<	>	XXX YYY
X equal Y	=	=	XXX YYY
X meets Y	m	mi	XXXYYY
X overlaps Y	o	oi	XXX YYY
X during Y	d	di	XXX YYYYYY
X starts Y	s	si	XXX YYYYYY
X finishes Y	f	fi	XXX YYYYYY

Allen proposes a model of thirteen ways in which an ordered pair of intervals can be related with mutually exclusive temporal relations. The temporal relations are shown in Table 1, where the columns of Symbol and Inverse Symbol define the thirteen relations. In the rightmost column future time is to the right and past time to the left. Together, these relations can be used to express any relationship that can exist between two intervals. They are maintained in a network where nodes represent individual intervals. Allen proposes an algorithm that creates missing temporal relations (temporal constraints) from existing knowledge. The set of transitivity relations on all possible subsequent pairs of temporal primitives is presented in Table 2. When new temporal relations are entered in a temporal network all possible temporal relationships can be derived by use of the transitivity table.

In order to reduce the complexity of a growing number of temporal constraints, Allen proposes a generalization method using *reference intervals*. A reference interval represent a cluster of intervals where the temporal constraints have been computed.

4   Prediction of Unwanted Events

We are addressing the prediction problem within oil well drilling, and our example task is to avoid the situation that a drill string gets stuck in the borehole, and stops the drilling process. Due to high hourly cost of drilling operations and the long time involved in freeing a stuck pipe, this is one of the most costly drilling problems [11, 22]. There is abundant literature on this topic describing how to identify a stuck-pipe situation and free it (e.g. [9]). Still, in order to deal with stuck pipe situations and to avoid them, extensive experience by the crew on the platform is needed. The situation when a driller or a system identifies that something may happen is a continuous process, where qualitative changes of particular parameters are strong indicators.

Table 2. Transitivity table for the twelve temporal relations (omitting "="). A, B, and C are the time intervals. The possible relations, r1 and r2, are listed in the first column and the top row, respectively. Table cells list the inferred relations from a combination of A r1 B and B r2 C. Adapted from [4].

B r2 C / A r1 B	<	>	d	di	o	oi	m	mi	s	si	f	fi
"before" <	<	no info	< o m d s	<	<	< o m d s	<	< o m d s	<	<	< o m d s	<
"after" >	no info	>	> oi mi d f	>	> oi mi d f	>	> oi mi d f	>	> oi mi d f	>	>	>
"during" d	<	>	d	no info	< o m d s	> oi mi d f	<	>	d	> oi mi d f	d	< o m d s
"contains" di	< o m di fi	> oi di mi si =	o oi dur con	di	o di fi	oi di si	o di fi	oi di si	di fi o	di	di si oi	di
"overlaps" o	<	> oi di mi si	o d s	< o m di fi	< o m	o oi dur con =	<	oi di si	o	di fi o	d s o	< o m
"overlapped-by" oi	< o m di fi	>	oi d f	> oi mi di si	o oi dur con =	> oi mi	o di fi	>	oi d f	oi > mi	oi	oi di si
"meets" m	<	> oi mi di si	o d s	<	<	o d s	<	f fi =	m	m	d s o	<
"met-by" mi	< o m di fi	>	oi d f	>	oi d f	>	s si =	>	d f oi	>	mi	mi
"starts" s	<	>	d	< o m di fi	< o m	oi d f	<	mi	s	s si =	d	< m o
"started by" si	< o m di fi	>	oi d f	di	o di fi	oi	o di fi	mi	s si =	si	oi	di

We want our system to give warnings to the user when an unwanted event may be approaching. Two types of system states are defined: *alert state* and *alarm state*. A retrieved case should trigger an *alert state* if a matching past experience indicates an upcoming unwanted event. This happens if the past case was an actual stuck pipe situation, or a situation in which stuck pipe was indicated but avoided. An *alarm state* should be triggered when a seemingly unavoidable unwanted event is about to happen. The alert state is a warning about the alarm state, and ideally the alert state will be discovered in time to avoid the alarm state.

Figure 1 shows a simplified example of some of the parameter-curves in a stuck pipe situation. It shows the magnitude of three different parameters as a function of time. These parameters are continuously being logged by sensors in the well or on the platform. Assume a CBR system that has continuous access to the parameters, and whose task is to identify potential stuck pipe situations based on early indications. The system has two sources of knowledge, the general model and the case-base. The erratic pump pressure at measurement 1300 triggers the system, which starts to look for similar cases in its case-base, and finds two cases above the similarity threshold. Both cases indicate an upcoming occurrence of stuck pipe, and the system executes an alert state warning. One of the two cases contains a cause for the stuck, while in the other case – the best matching case - the cause was not established. The system tries to find a possible explanation for the cause of that case (the latter) within the general knowledge. The explanation structure contains the following explanation:

Erratic Pump Pressure *indicates* Flow Restriction in Annulus
Flow Restriction in Annulus *indicates* Unstable Wellbore
Unstable Wellbore *indicates* Solids Build Up
Solids Build Up *causes* Stuck Pipe

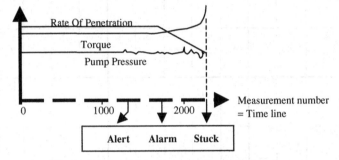

Fig. 1. Temporal development of a stuck pipe case.

The system accepts Solids Build Up as the strongest supported hypothesis for the failure cause, and gives the user advice on how to avoid it on that basis. In addition it presents the other case whose match is above the threshold, as an alternative possible development to be validated by the user.

During this case, taken from a real drilling process, the drill actually got stuck at measurement 2200. Using a system as described, this event should have been avoided. An advantage of using a CBR system here, compared to existing trend analysis [11], is that the latter is based on single parameter analysis. The complexity of the interaction between a drilling process and its surrounding geological formation is too complex to be effectively handled with such a method.

5 Temporal Representation in Creek

Allen's approach is simple, transparent and easy to implement. It allows knowledge to be imprecise and uncertain which is necessary for problems in open domains. In our representation intervals are stored with temporal relationships inside cases. In the same way as Allen's reference intervals (see section 3), the cases restrict the computational complexity by limiting the amount of temporal relations resulting from transitivity rules.

From a cognitive perspective, the application of the transitivity rules leads to a high degree of regularity that becomes visible through the created relations. It is argued that this does not to correspond to the human, relative way of thinking about time [7].

An extended, more explanation-based way of reasoning about temporal relationships would be preferred. We have made an effort to combine the temporal knowledge inside a case with explanations in the general domain knowledge.

As an illustration of how temporality is represented in the Creek system, consider the following story:

> When Juan was in the room, the room was tidy. Juan was there for ten minutes. Maria entered the room thirty minutes after Juan. Then the room was a complete mess and Maria's stereo was stolen.

This story can be represented in a temporal network as shown in Figure 2. We can also formalize the representation as a structured frame with intervals, which in turn is contains their findings, as shown in Table 3. CaseX is related to the intervals, and the intervals are related to the findings, i.e. the observations.

Table 3. Frame object representation of a case and its intervals.

CaseX	Interval1	Interval2	Interval3
hasInterval Interval1	hasFinding JuanInRoom	hasDuration 30Min	hasFinding MariaInRoom
hasInterval Interval2	hasFinding RoomTidy		hasFinding RoomMessy
hasInterval Interval3	hasDuration 10Min		hasFinding StereoStolen

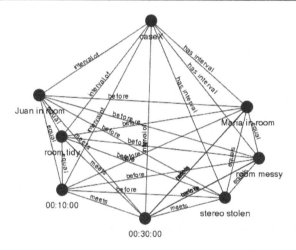

Fig. 2. Illustration of the temporal network of a CaseX where all the findings are related to the other findings directly. We can see that even this very simple temporal situation will create a very dense network.

An example of how this frame-based representation looks in a network perspective is illustrated in Figure 3. This is how temporality is represented in Creek. The clarity and representational efficiency of using intervals within cases are clearly seen. The graphs shown are screen dumps from the Creek Knowledge Editor. Each relation in Creek has a corresponding inverse relation (e.g., has interval / interval of), and in the graphs the direction of a relation is from left to right, then top to bottom.

As illustrated in Figure 3, the temporal intervals are connected to each other with temporal relations: Interval1 (I1) *meets* Interval2 (I2) and Interval2 (I2) *meets* Interval3 (I3). An example of an inferred temporal relation is the relation from I1 to I3. When the two meets intervals are added to the system, it infers, by using the transitivity rules, that I1 is before I3. New intervals are incorporated according to the following procedure:

> For every new interval that is added to the network
> (1) Create a <has interval> relationship
> (2) Create <has finding> relationships
> (3) Create <Temporal Relation> relationships
> (4) Infer new <Temporal Relation> relationships

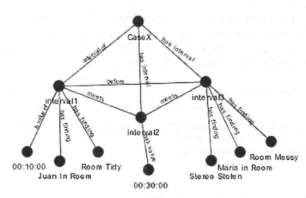

Fig. 3. Illustration of the temporal network of CaseX. All the findings are related to CaseX via intervals. The temporal network is very small but still keeps all of the information of the network in Figure 2.

There are methods for making intervals with or without dating. When we make a case with time-information, the temporal relations are made automatically (third step). For instance, if we make one interval that lasts from 12:00:00 until 12:10:00 and one that lasts from 12:30:20 until 14:20:30, the system will take care of creating the *<before>* relation between them. In the final step the system uses its transitivity rules to infer possible additional temporal relations between the intervals.

6   Temporal Paths and Dynamic Ordering

During case matching in the original (non-temporal) Creek system, three similarity values are computed: The *activation strength* is based on direct index matching, the *explanation strength* is based on similarity explained in the general domain model (where each relation has a certain explanatory strength), while the *matching strength* combines the two former into a resulting similarity degree.

For temporal cases, we refer to the additional temporal similarity measurement as the *temporal path strength*. For each such path the matching degree of corresponding findings is calculated (examples are given in section 7. Comparing the temporal paths is not trivial because there are often many possible temporal paths for a combination of two primitive relations (see table 2). The search space is reduced by a goal-directed search, guided by what to predict. What we in particular are interested in for our prediction task is to foresee possible warning states as early as possible. We developed an algorithm referred to as *dynamic ordering* [12] that enables intervals to be related to each other so that a similarity assessment of parameters can be made in order to predict particular states. The dynamic ordering algorithm uses two procedures in order to follow the temporal paths *{getNextInterval}* and *{getSameTimeIntervals}*. The dynamic ordering algorithm is as follows, where IC is the input case and CC the current case:

> (1) Find first interval in IC and CC (intervalIC and intervalCC)
> (2) Check intervalIC and intervalCC for matching or explainable findings
> (3) If match - Update temporal path strength
> (4) Check {getSameTimeIntervals} for new information and special situations
>   If special situations - Perform action
> (5) {getNextInterval} from CC and IC
> (6) Unless {getNextInterval} is empty - Go to (2)
> (7) Return temporal path strength

(1) The system finds the starting point. Figure 4 illustrates the temporal relationships related to past and future from the viewpoint of one interval. The first interval is found by selecting the interval that ends most to the left on the scale on Figure 4, and has no temporal relationships to intervals more to the left of the scale. The primary preference is a *<Before>* interval without any intervals connected to it with *<Before>*, *<Meets>*, *<Contains>*, *<Overlaps>* or *<Finished-by>* relationships. This interval is guaranteed to be the first one in time, since no other intervals can have an earlier starting point.

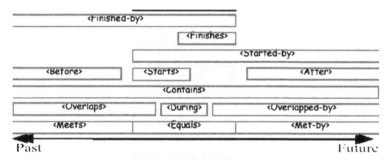

Fig. 4. The thirteen possible relationships between intervals placed on a timeline. The marked square in the middle is the interval connected to, and the two white areas are intervals connected from. The relation names inside the bars show the relationship from an interval to the interval in the middle square.

(2) After recognition of the first intervals within IC and CC, the two intervals are checked for matched findings. The activation strength, the explanation strength and the matching strength are computed as they are in non-temporal cases. If the matching shows that the intervals are not similar, the second interval in CC is compared with the first in the input case. The process of finding the first similar interval may continue all through the CC-case, or a limit can be set for how far it is relevant to try, depending on the type of domain and on the duration of cases. (3) If a match is found, the matching strength, representing the path strength of this temporal path, is added to the temporal path strength. (4) *{getSameTimeIntervals}* finds all the intervals in CC that are at the 'same time' as intervalIC. That is, all findings in intervalCC which share some time-points with intervalIC. This step is special for temporal cases. It keeps the current time-perspective of the input case while matching corresponding findings. It looks for the intervals of CC that are fully contained in or cover any of the

temporal relationships inside the middle square of Figure 4 (*<Contains>*, *<During>*, *<Equals>*, *<Starts>*, *<Started-by>*, *<Finishes>* and *<Finished-by>*). (5) The procedure *{get-NextInterval}* selects the interval that is closest to the current in future time, using the scale in Figure 4. (6) The dynamic ordering continues until *{getNextInterval}* returns an empty value and the case is completely compared with all its intervals. When the input case is fully compared, the accumulated temporal path strength is normalized.

7   An Example of Prediction in Oil-Well Drilling

The exemplified domain is Stuck Pipe, and the cases are reconstructed on the basis of logged data from a Statoil well in the North Sea [24]. The case retrieval step incorporates the prediction goal of being warned about a possible drill-sticking situation sufficiently early to be able to prevent it.

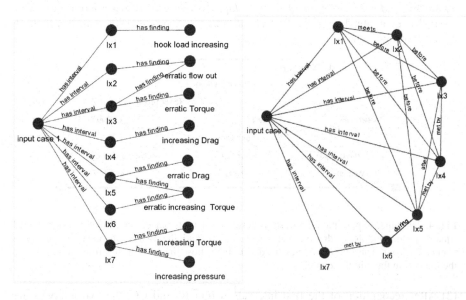

Fig. 5. The input case with findings (left) and temporal relations (right), split in two for readability.

Figure 5 shows the input case after the raw data have been transformed into qualitative findings (currently a manual process). The intervals are named IX1, IX2, IX3, IX4, IX5, IX6 and IX7 (the numbers are just labels and do not necessarily correspond to temporal sequence). The relationship, IX1 *has-finding* HOOK LOAD INCREASING describes that the finding when hook load is increasing is in the time of interval Ix1, and IX2 *has-finding* ERRATIC FLOW OUT describes that the finding when flow out is erratic is in the time of interval Ix2. The relationship IX1 *meets* IX2 describes that the end of IX1 is the time-point before IX2. The entities of the two intervals can hence be temporally described as; HOOK LOAD INCREASING *meets* ERRATIC FLOW OUT.

The system starts by retrieving similar cases from the case-base in a non-temporal way. It retrieves two cases that have matching strength above a set threshold, from which the case "SPCase#1" has the highest strength. The two retrieved cases are then compared in order to find the temporal path strength, by means of dynamic ordering. It turns out that SPCase#1 also has the strongest temporal path strength. We will now trace the temporal matching of findings in the two cases. For simplicity, the activation strength for direct value matching is set to 1.0, while explained matches are set to 0.5.

The process starts by comparing the first intervals in time, and finds the matching finding HOOK LOAD INCREASING. The first interval of SPCase#1 also has the findings ERRATIC INCREASING TORQUE and DECREASING PRESSURE (see Figure 6, note that the inverse of the "has finding" relation is "reminding"), but they are neither directly matched nor explained by input case 1. The temporal path strength is now updated with the value of a direct match for one finding, i.e. it is increased with 1.0.

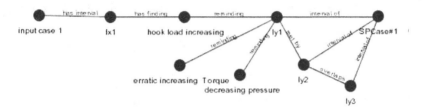

Fig. 6. Comparing the first intervals of the input case and retrieved case.

The next step is to compare the set of intervals retrieved from the procedure *{getSameTimeIntervals}* in order to improve the match and look for occurrences of situations related to the prediction goal. From Figure 5 we see that Ix1 only contains *<before>* and *<meets>* relationships. Hence there are no intervals that share time with Ix1, and no additional intervals are retrieved.

The next intervals in the two cases are then found (procedure *{getNextInterval}*). The next interval to Ix1 is Ix2, determined by the *meets* relationship. One matching finding, ERRATIC FLOW OUT, is found in the second interval of the retrieved case (Iy2). The temporal path strength is updated with the value of one matching finding, and becomes 2.0. Ix2 and Iy2 are then compared in *{getSameTimeIntervals}*. Iy3 and Iy2 in SPCase#1 is found to share a time span, due to their *<overlaps>* relationship. All the findings in interval 2 and 3 are then compared, but no similarities are found. Interval Ix3 and Iy3 are then found to be similar, as they both have the findings ERRATIC FLOW OUT and ERRATIC TORQUE, see Figure 7. The combined value of two matching findings is used to update the path strength, which becomes 4.0. Iy4 has the finding HOOK LOAD INCREASING and Ix4 has the finding INCREASING DRAG. They are explained similar by the relationship INCREASING DRAG *causes* HOOK LOAD INCREASING. The temporal path strength is increased with the value of the explanation, and becomes 4.5.

Ix5 and Iy5 has one matching finding ERRATIC INCREASING TORQUE and one explained similar finding, INCREASING DRAG *causes* INCREASING HOOK LOAD. The temporal path strength is updated with 1.5, and becomes 6.0.

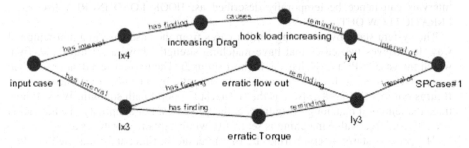

Fig. 7. Direct and explained matches of Ix3/Iy3 and Ix4/Iy4.

When *{getSameTimeIntervals}* is used on Ix5 and Iy5, and these are checked for goal-related situations, an alert state is found. Iy7 (linked by a *<during>* relation from Iy5) has a warning related to it, indicating that at this stage of the past case there was a possibility of an upcoming stuck pipe situation. The following intervals are found with similar time points: Iy5 *during* Iy7, Iy5 *overlaps* Iy6, Ix6 *during* Ix5 (see figure 8).

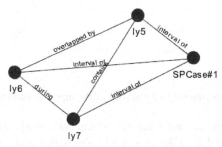

Fig. 8. Temporal relations between I5, I6, and I7 in the retrieved case.

The set of intervals from input case 1 (Ix5 and Ix6) and from SPCase#1 (Iy5, Iy6 and Iy7) are then compared. The following findings are found similar in the two cases: Ix5 and Iy5 has one explained finding; ERRATIC DRAG *causes* HOOK LOAD ERRATIC, and one direct matched finding; ERRATIC INCREASING TORQUE.

Ix5 and Iy7 has one explained finding; ERRATIC DRAG *causes* HOOK LOAD ERRATIC, and one direct matched finding; ERRATIC INCREASING TORQUE.

Iy5 and Ix6 have a direct matched finding; ERRATIC INCREASING TORQUE, and Ix6 and Iy7 the direct match ERRATIC INCREASING TORQUE.

From the combination of the similar findings, Creek has computed a temporal path strength that indicates that the cases are similar at this stage and decides that the warning in Iy7 should be given to the user. Creek warns the user about a possible upcoming stuck pipe situation. Note that by using *{getSameTimeIntervals}* the system is able to find the alert state before Ix7 is directly compared with Iy7.

Relationships between SPCase#1 and input case 1 are visualized in Figure 9. We see that Iy7 and Ix7 have the two direct matching findings INCREASING TORQUE and INCREASING PRESSURE, which further increase the temporal path strength by 2.0. It finally becomes 8.0. The path strength is now divided on all the features of SPCase#1 that have been compared with the input case (22 features are counted). It gives the value 0.36 of the temporal path strength of SPCase#1.

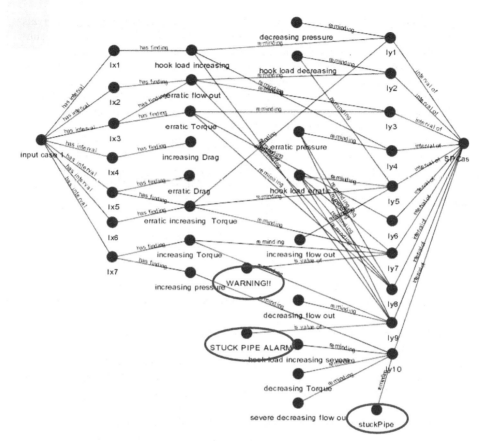

Fig. 9. SPCase#1 and input case 1 compared with each other

8   Conclusion

We have presented a method for representation of temporal intervals in a CBR
system, and how the representation is utilized in case retrieval. The method is aimed
at supporting prediction of events for industrial processes. The paper has shown how
Allen's temporal intervals can be incorporated into the semantic network
representation of the Creek system. An algorithm for matching a sequence of findings
that occur during an oil well drilling process was described, and exemplified. The
research presented has shown that the interval-based approach is suitable for
qualitative temporal reasoning in this context. An advantage of using intervals is that
the representation becomes close to the way the human expert reasons in domains
where qualitative changes of parameters over time are important. Another advantage
is its easy integration into a model-based reasoning system component, as shown in
our example. However, as shown by the two-step retrieval method of Creek, the
interval-based approach will also work with pure syntax-based retrieval methods (i.e.
the activate step only).

A weakness of the representation is that it only enables one fixed layer of intervals in the cases. A more flexible way of handling intervals, in terms of intervals with sub-intervals, etc., would be interesting for some applications. We have done initial research into enabling dynamic structuring of Creek cases [15] that may be useful for that. So far, the system has not undergone a systematic evaluation. Even if Allen's algorithm in principle has nice complexity properties, its integration into the Creek method needs to be more thoroughly investigated. The system, implemented in Java, has only been tried on small knowledge bases.

To run the system in a real operational setting, the problem of transforming raw data into the qualitative changes used by our method needs to be solved. A strong motivation for our method is that many processes are too complex to be predicted by standard trend analysis. Temporal interval-based CBR methods, as exemplified in this paper, should have a high potential for revealing such complex problems.

References

1. Agnar Aamodt, Enric Plaza: "Case-based reasoning: Foundation issues, methodological variation, and system approaches", AICOM, Vol. 7, no. 1 (Mar. 1994) 39-59.2.
2. Agnar Aamodt: Explanation – driven-case-based reasoning. Topics in case-based reasoning, edited by S. Wess et al., Springer Verlag (1994) 274-288.
3. Agnar Aamodt, Helge A. Sandtorv, Ole M. Winnem: Combining Case Based Reasoning and Data Mining - A way of revealing and reusing RAMS experience. In Lydersen, Hansen, Sandtorv (eds.), Safety and Reliability; Proceedings of ESREL '98, Trondheim, June 16-19, 1998. Balkena, Rotterdam, 1998. pp 1345-1351.
4. James F. Allen: Maintaining Knowledge about Temporal Intervals. Communications of the ACM 26, 11, 832-843. The University of Rochester. Nov. 1983.
5. Ralph Bergmann, Hector Muñoz-Avila, Manuela Veloso and Erica Melis: CBR applied to planning. In Case-Based Reasoning Technology; From Foundations to Applications, (chapter 7), pages 169--200. 1998.
6. Branting, L.K., Hastings, J.D.: An empirical evaluation of model-based case matching and adaptation. *Proceedings of the Workshop on Case-Based Reasoning, AAAI-94.* Seattle, Washington, July 1994.
7. Christian Freksa: Temporal reasoning based on semi-intervals. In Artificial Intelligence 54 (1992) pp 199-227. 1992.
8. Bjarne K. Hansen: Weather Prediction Using Case-Based Reasoning and Fuzzy Set Theory, Master of Computer Science Thesis, Technical University of Nova Scotia, Halifax, Nova Scotia, Canada. 2000
9. Inrock Drilling Fluids: IDF Training Manual, Chapter Six - Drilling Problems, Rev2 1989.
10. Michel Jaczynski: A Framework for the Management of Past Experiences with Time-Extended Situations. In ACM Conference of Information and Knowledge Management (CIKM'97), Las Vegas, November 1997. INRIA Sophia-Antipolis, France. 1997.
11. Jardine, McCann and Barber: An Advanced system for the early detection of Sticking pipe. Sedco Forex Schlumberger ADC/SPE 23915. 1992.

12. Martha Dørum Jære: Time sequences in case-based reasoning. Master of Computer Science Thesis, Norwegian University of Science and Technology, Trondheim, Norway, 2001.
13. K. M. Kahn and A. G. Gorry: Mechanizing temporal knowledge. Artificial Intelligence 9,2 (1977). pp 87-108.
14. E.T. Keravnou: Modeling medical concepts as time-objects. In M. Stefanelli and J. Watts, eds., Lecture Notes in Artificial Intelligence, vol. 934. Springer, 1995, pp. 67-90.
15. Ellen Lippe: Learning support by reasoning with structured cases. M.Sc. Thesis, Norwegian University of Science and Technology, Trondheim, Norway, 2001.
16. Joaquim Melendez, Josep Lluis de la Rosa, Daniel Macaya, Joan Colomer: Case Based Approach for generation of recipes in Batch Process Control. Institut d'Infor-matica i Aplicacions -Universitat de Girona, Spain. 1999.
17. Joaquim Melendez, Daniel Macaya, Joan Colomer: Case Based Reasoning Methodology for Supervision. eXiT Group IliA & LEA-SICA, Univeristat de Girona, Spain. 2000.
18. S. Rougegrez. Similarity evaluation between observed behaviors for the prediction of processes. In Topics in Case-Based Reasoning, vol 873 of Lecture Notes in Artificial Intelligence, pp 155-166. Springer 1994.
19. Katarina Sachse: Domain model of drilling fluid problems. (Diploma thesis) Department of Petroleum Engineering, Norwegian University of Science and Technology. Dec. 2000.
20. Rainer Schmidt, Bernard Pollwein, Lothar Gierl: Medical multiparametric time course prognoses applied to kidney function assessments. In International Journal of Medical Informatics 53 (1999), pp 253-263.
21. Yuval Shahar: Timing is everything: Temporal Reasoning and Temporal Data Mainte-nance Medicine. In W Horn et al. (Eds.): AIMDM'99, LNAI 1620, pp30-46, 1999. Springer Verlag.
22. Pål Skalle, Agnar Aamodt and Jostein Sveen: Case-based reasoning - a method for gaining experience and giving advise on how to avoid and how to free stuck drill strings. Proceedings of IADC Middle East Drilling Conference, Dubai, Nov. 1998.
23. Paal Skalle, Josein Sveen and Agnar Aamodt: Improved Efficiency of Oil Well drill-ing through Case Based Reasoning. Proceedings of PRICAI 2000, The Sixth Pacific Rim International Conference on Artificial Intelligence, Melbourne August-September 2000. Lecture Notes in Artificial Intelligence, Springer Verlag, 2000. pp 713-723.
24. Statoil, Boreavdeling, Stavanger, Mud logging data, Gullfax, 1994.
25. Luis Vila: A survey of temporal reasoning in artificial intelligence. AI Communications, Volume 7, Number 1, March 1994, pp 4-28.

Local Predictions for Case-Based Plan Recognition

Boris Kerkez and Michael T. Cox

Department of Computer Science and Engineering
Wright State University, Dayton, OH
{bkerkez,mcox}@cs.wright.edu

Abstract. This paper presents a novel case-based plan recognition system that interprets observations of plan behavior using a case library of past observations. The system is novel in that it represents a plan as a sequence of action-state pairs rather than a sequence of actions preceded by some initial state and followed by some final goal state. The system utilizes a unique abstraction scheme to represent indices into the case base. The paper examines and evaluates three different methods for prediction. The first method is prediction without adaptation; the second is predication with adaptation, and the third is prediction with heuristics. We show that the first method is better than a baseline random prediction, that the second method is an improvement over the first, and that the second and the third methods combined are the best overall strategy.

Introduction

In trying to interpret the world, an agent must be able to explain the events that take place as the world changes. Most important is the explanation of volitional events caused by other actors in the environment. Other actors have goals and plans to achieve these goals, but the observer often has access to only a stream of actions and events that occur. Case-based reasoning attempts to use experience of past events to interpret current events, and moreover tries to infer the goals of the observed actor and to predict what the actor will do next. Plan recognition is another technique that attempts to match current actions to known plans in order to predict the actions and goals of an actor. The research presented here combines both methods in a very novel manner to perform the same inferential tasks (to perform goal and action prediction).

Although the case-based approach to plan recognition is not new (Bares *et al.*, 1994), the novelty of our approach primarily arises from the manner in which we represent a plan (i.e., a case) that records past observations and the representation of indices by which we store and retrieve such old observations when interpreting a current observation. Unlike most plan recognition systems (e.g., Kautz, 1991) that represent a plan as a sequence of actions bracketed by an initial state and a goal state, we represent a plan as a sequence of action-state pairs such that the initial pair is (<null-action>, <initial-state>), and the last action is (<final-action>, <goal-state>) (Kerkez and Cox, 2001). Therefore unlike traditional representations, our plans contain intermediate state information. By saving this intermediate state information, we can find past cases that match a current observation at arbitrary points in a stream of observed actions by maintaining the states that result from the observed actions.

S. Craw and A. Preece (Eds.): ECCBR 2002, LNAI 2416, pp. 189–203.
© Springer-Verlag Berlin Heidelberg 2002

However, because we maintain intermediate state information, the structure of a plan is far more complex. Furthermore many more past cases will match a single observation, because given a current observed state, the state may match multiple intermediate states in multiple past cases. In order to compensate for this additional complexity, we take advantage of a smaller abstract state-space that corresponds to the much larger concrete state space existing in a given domain.

Consider for example the logistics (i.e., package delivery) domain (Veloso, 1994) that contains trucks that transport packages from one location to another. A single state in this domain might be the case where one package (say Package-1) is located at a post office (perhaps PostOffice-1) and a truck (Truck-1) is located at the same post office. The concrete representation for this state is the set of two ground literals {(*at-obj Package-1 PostOffice-1*), (*at-truck Truck-1 PostOffice-1*)}. An alternate state might be { (*at-obj Package-1 PostOffice-2*), (*at-truck Truck-1 PostOffice-1*) }. These are different states, because in the first example both the truck and package are at the same location and in the second state they are at separate locations. But note that the literal (*at-truck Truck-1 PostOffice-1*) is shared by both states. The difference between the two states comes from the *at-obj* literals. Now if we replace the ground literal with the respective generalized literal (*at-obj package location*), the two states are the same.

Fig. 1. A simple example of the logistics planning scenario with two cities

A more complex state is shown in Figure 1. The objects in this state include three packages, three trucks, and two planes (see legend). The figure also shows two cities, each with an airport and a post office. The literals that exist in the domain include *at-truck*, *at-airplane*, *at-obj*, *inside-truck*, and *inside-airplane*.[1] The literals are shown in Table 1. In this domain an abstract state is represented as a feature vector having dimensionality equal to the number of generalized literals. If the dimensions are listed in the order that the literals are enumerated immediately above, then the abstract state for Table 1 is [3 2 2 1 0]. The reason is that the state contains three *at-truck* literals, two *at-airplane* literals, and so on for the remainder of the vector. If we encode the simple states from the previous paragraph likewise, they would both be represented by the vector [1 0 1 0 0].[2]

Table 1. Ground literals representing the state in Figure 1

AT-TRUCK	TRUCK A	POST-OFFICE A		AT-AIRPLANE	PLANE B	AIRPORT B
AT-TRUCK	TRUCK B	AIRPORT B		AT-OBJ	OBJECT A	POST-OFFICE A
AT-TRUCK	TRUCK C	AIRPORT A		AT-OBJ	OBJECT C	POST-OFFICE B
AT-AIRPLANE	PLANE A	AIRPORT A		INSIDE-TRUCK	OBJECT B	TRUCK B

---

[1] The literals in Table 1 are actually *dynamic* predicates. Three *static* predicates also exist. Static predicates never change, because no operators exist that can change them.

[2] Like the abstract vector formed from Table 1, this vector excludes static predicates.

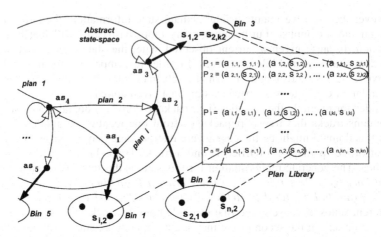

Fig. 2. Indexing and storage structures. Abstract states (as_i) point to bins (bold lines), containing world states (s_j), which point (dashed lines) to past plans (P_j) in which they occurred

As detailed in Kerkez and Cox (2001), a plan can be represented in abstract form as a graph within an abstract space. A particular plan contains a vertex for each abstract state and edges between vertices to represent actions that transition the plan from one abstract state to another (see Figure 2). Each abstract state then points to a bin containing all previously observed concrete states that share the same abstract representation. Furthermore, each concrete state in a given bin points to its location within all cases having that concrete state. The benefit of using this abstract state representation is that a case library is thereby partitioned into a relatively small number of bins such that each bin is a unique abstract state. When retrieving old cases given a new observation, a system need only transform the currently observed concrete state to its corresponding abstract state (linear time), find the bin that is equivalent to the abstract state (constant time), and return those cases indexed by each concrete state in the bin (linear). As described in (Kerkez, 2001), our system does not operate with a complete plan library, but rather it incrementally builds its library from the observed planning behavior. Such incremental construction further decreases the complexity of the state-space and minimizes the existence of extraneous plans (Lesh and Etzioni, 1996).

The case-based plan recognition system introduced here can be classified with respect to the abstraction framework for the case-based reasoning (Bergmann and Wilke, 1996). The system explicitly stores concrete cases and abstract states, while the abstraction generation process is automatic. Although complete abstract cases are not used for indexing, abstracted situations form the basis of the indexing and the retrieval. Past abstract solutions are reused, because the next action prediction is first formed at the abstract level, after which the action is refined by specifying the action arguments. Case deletion policy is not yet implemented and therefore the system could have storage problems given a limited storage space.

Although the abstraction scheme in the case-based reasoning is not a novel concept, it is certainly novel in a way in which it is used in the context of the case-based plan recognition. The abstraction scheme is extremely simple in nature and applicable to a wide variety of planning domains. One requirement for the recognizer presented in this work is the ability to monitor the intermediate planning states, along with a prerequisite that the states are represented as collections of literals with domain objects as literal arguments. The only other requirement is an associated object type hierarchy in order to be able to abstract the concrete states. Although our work utilizes two levels of abstraction, it is certainly possible to extend the abstraction on as many different levels as the object type hierarchy allows.

Similar to the approach in the PARIS system (Bergmann and Wilke, 1995), the recognizer does not form abstraction by simply dropping sentences. However, the simplicity of our abstraction scheme allows for the minimal abstraction theory, since we are simply counting a number of occurrences of a literal of a certain type among a collection of literals representing a world state. Because the state abstraction is used as a way to quickly trigger appropriate past memories, this approach does not require a domain expert to specify the abstract language either, besides the object type hierarchy. When recognizing the plans from the PRODIGY planner, the recognizer automatically extracts the object hierarchy from the domain description, shielding the end user of any knowledge engineering details.

This paper reports the results of an empirical evaluation of the recognition with the abstract indexing scheme. Given the observation of an action-state pair in a new plan, the system's task is to predict the next action that will be observed. First the system retrieves all cases that match the abstract representation of the observed state. Note that each case may contain more than one concrete state whose abstract representation is equal to the abstracted observed state. Therefore many candidate actions may exist across the retrieved cases that can serve as a prediction for the action to be observed next. Such predictions are local to a specific location in a plan, as opposed to a global prediction such as a goal for the entire plan.

We evaluate three different ways in which the action can be selected from the available candidates. The first and most simple method is to select the most common action in the candidate set. If more than one action is most frequent, the system chooses among the most frequent at random. Given that many candidates may still exist among this chosen action, the system chooses from the reduced set, again at random. A somewhat more intelligent method is to choose the most frequent action (randomly if needed), but then to compute an argument substitution for the action rather than to simply re-use the same arguments in the past case. The action with new arguments constitutes an adaptation of the old case element. The former method described above we call prediction without adaptation, whereas the latter we call prediction with adaptation. A third method is to use the knowledge of cases that worked already in the current sequence of predictions to bias the choice of candidate-action selection. We call this method prediction with heuristics. After a prediction is made using one of these three methods, the system will receive the next observation to determine the accuracy of the prediction and to provide the next state for subsequent predictions.

Given this description, the next section in this paper will examine the prediction without adaptation method. It will also present empirical results that show that the method outperforms the baseline performance that randomly chooses an action and arguments without the use of past cases. The following section will present results for prediction with adaptation. The subsequent section examines and shows results for prediction with heuristics. The paper ends with a brief summary and conclusion.

Local Action Prediction without Adaptation

The case-based plan recognition system presented in this work utilizes the indexing scheme described in the previous section as the basis for its reminding processes. After the planning agent executes a planning step, the recognizer observes the executed action, along with the world state of the planner reached by that action. The recognition cycle is initiated upon every observation of a planning action. The current planning situation (represented by the current world state of the planner) is transformed into its abstract form and subsequently matched to a bin. In case of a successful match, retrieval is focused on past situations within the single indexing bin.

The work presented here focuses on the local predictions of the planner's intent, in particular, the predictions of the next immediate action. The action predictions are formed at the two levels. Although concrete action predictions are much more informed than abstract predictions, the latter can also be very useful. For example, it is somewhat successful to recognize that the planner is about to load a truck, although we may not be able to tell with certainty which package is to be loaded. Our future research efforts will explore the predictions of the intermediate world states and the predictions of goals.

When the recognizer is able to find a unique past case having only one concrete state that matches the current abstract state, prediction is determined to be the past action following the matching state. However, when multiple past actions exist, the recognizer needs to determine which action is the most probable current intent of the planner. The next section describes the benefits of the abstract indexing in predicting the next action and evaluations of two different action-choosing strategies.

Experimental Results

To illustrate the practical benefits of next action prediction utilizing abstract indexing and retrieval, we present the evaluations of the action predictions in the logistics planning domain. The experimental evaluation focused on randomly generated planning problems with 3, 5, and 7 cities in the logistics domain. Evaluations presented in this paper concentrate mostly on the results for problems with three cities. This is because asymptotic behavior of the recognizer can clearly be observed given the smaller state-space for three cities. Next, two different problem sets with 5000 problems each were randomly generated for each number of cities. The random problem generator in each of these two problem sets was initialized with a different random seed. Generated problems were solved by the PRODIGY state-space planner (Carbonell *et al.* 1992) that generated solutions to about 80% of the input problems.[3]

The solved planning problems and the generated solutions were then given as the input into the case-based plan recognition system. The system simulates plan execution by parsing the input data and by sending the planning steps to the recognizer one at the time. As described in the previous section, the system is concerned with predictions of the local planning behavior. The recognizer first

---

[3] The reason for the 20% planning failure rate is due to the fact that some random problems are impossible to be solved. In these situations the planner returns from its execution cycle without creating a plan once appropriate maximum execution time threshold is reached.

predicts the next action at the abstract level. Subsequently, the recognizer refines it into a concrete action. Therefore, the accuracy of the concrete action predictions is bounded-above by the accuracy of the abstract action predictions.

We evaluated two different strategies for choosing the past planning action for the prediction in light of multiple action matches. Both of these strategies employ the abstract indexing scheme. The first strategy randomly selects the past planning action among all of the matches within a single bin, while the second strategy considers only the most frequently pursued past actions within the bin. Note that there may exist multiple most frequent past actions when many actions in a given past situation were pursued with an equal frequency. In the logistics domain with 3 cities, multiple most frequent actions are found in about 10% of cases, while in the domain with 7 cities, multiple most frequent actions were found in about 30% of cases. When multiple most frequent past actions are found, the recognizer randomly chooses among them.

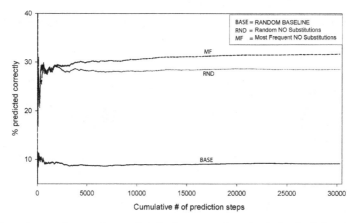

Fig. 3. Percentages of correctly predicted *abstract* actions in 3-city logistics domain with abstract indexing scheme over 30,000 recognition steps

Figures 3 and 4 show the percentages of correctly predicted actions at the abstract and at the concrete level, respectively, for the two past action choice strategies and the baseline test. The baseline test consists of randomly choosing the past action out of all previously observed planning actions without the utilization of the abstract indexing and retrieval scheme. These results as well as all subsequent results in this paper are averages of the two problem sets that use different random seeds in the three-city logistics domain. It is clear from these figures that utilization of the abstract indexing scheme indeed focuses the prediction choices and significantly improves the prediction accuracy with respect to the baseline. The most frequent action strategy performs slightly better than random selection of a past action extracted from the cases retrieved using the abstract indexing scheme as shown in Figures 3 and 4.

Although the most frequent strategy performs better than the random action choice, the improvement is not very significant. This is because of the fact that at this point the recognizer does not perfom argument substitutions in the chosen action. That is, the recognizer perfoms the next action prediction from a previous case without adaptation of the arguments of a previous case. The next section discusses the problems with argument substitutions in general and proposes a feasible, non-optimal method for detecting argument substitutions.

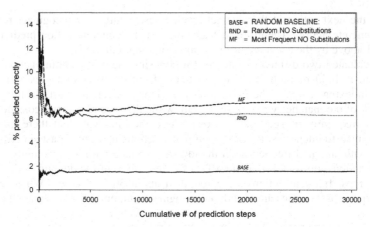

Fig. 4. Percentages of correctly predicted *concrete* actions in 3-city logistics domain with abstract indexing scheme over 30,000 recognition steps

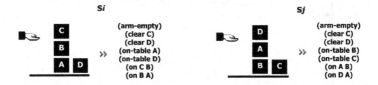

Fig. 5. Two world states s_i and s_j from the simple blocksworld planning domain

Local Predictions with Adaptation

Instead of re-using an action selected from a retrieved case as is, adaptation involves calculating a set of new arguments that can be substituted for the old arguments. In certain complex domains, however, the cost associated with finding an argument substitution for an action can outweigh the benefits of substitutions themselves. To illustrate the predicate argument substitutions, consider Figure 5 with two different world states from a simple blocksworld planning domain. The two states in the figure have the same abstract representation and the same structure, but the positions of the blocks are not identical. Substitution of arguments provides a means of relating the two structurally identical world states in predicate representation. In case of Figure 5, the substitution σ defined by

$$\sigma = \{A/B, B/A, C/D, D/C\} \tag{1}$$

represents the unique substitution of arguments of state s_i into arguments of state s_j. If state s_i is the currently observed state and state s_j is the matching state from an old case, then substitutions can provide more accurate predictions than simply using the corresponding old action. If the planner performed a *"pick-up blockC"* action in the previous situation, then the substitution mechanism enables the recognizer to adapt the argument of the predicted *pick-up* action from *blockC* to *blockD*, because *blockD* from state s_j substitutes for *blockC* in state s_i. The argument substitution can also help the recognizer find the most similar previous situation among potential multiple matches. For example, a past state with most identity substitutions ($\sigma(a)=a$) can be considered the most similar past situation for the currently observed planning state.

Fig. 6. An example of a state from the blocksworld domain where the complexity of the substitution scheme is large

When the state-space for a planning domain is more complex, calculating an argument substitution can   face computational complexity problems. Consider the state shown in Figure 6 in which all fifty different blocks are laying unstacked on the table. When two such states are considered for the argument substitutions, it is clear that any block from one state can be substituted for any block from the other state, resulting in exponential number of possible substitutions. These possible substitutions are essentially all possible permutations of fifty objects, the size of which is not practical for a computer implementation. Another example is shown in

Figure 7 where two different states that have an identical abstract representation are considered for the argument substitutions. Because the two states are structurally different, no exact argument substitutions are possible. In the worst case situation, the reasoner will need to check all possible combinations of substitutions in order to determine that no substitutions are actually possible. Again, the overhead associated with such a failed search is very costly. In case of the example in Figure 7, we may simply check the stacked blocks first and realize that no substitutions are possible. This particular heuristic, however, does not generalize across all planning domains.

Fig. 7. Two structurally different blocksworld states with identical abstract representations

Our approach of coping with the problem of the argument substitutions utilizes techniques common for handling intractable problems. We introduce a simple and computationally effective, sub-optimal process that enables the recognizer to perform argument substitutions. This process utilizes a change of representation technique in which world states represented by ground literals are transformed into corresponding graphs, called *state graphs* (Kerkez and Cox, 2001; Kerkez, 2001). Such representational change facilitates the complexity analysis of the argument substitution scheme.

Practical Adaptation with Argument Substitution

It is possible to utilize knowledge about a domain theory to assure that the argument substitution scheme for state predicates is feasible. When all state graphs in a given planning domain belong to a class of graphs for which efficient isomorphism algorithms exist, then equivalence classes can be efficiently used to group similar past situations inside the bins. If we consider the logistics planning domain without the static state predicates, then the state graphs are always planar. Finding isomorphisms for planar graphs is efficient, and it may help focus the retrieval of past situations in the logistics domain. However, this approach does not generalize to other planning domains, because the state graphs of these may not all be planar (Kerkez, 2002).

Another approach to cope with the need for the argument substitution is to limit the substitutions to a subset of all domain objects. A natural choice is to limit the substitution to include only the arguments of a predicted planning action. Because the number of arguments of a typical planning action is small, substitutions for the action arguments may be found much easier. In terms of the state graph representation, we attempt to find the isomorphism mapping of two graphs induced by the vertices that are the arguments of the considered action. Because the induced graphs can be much smaller then the complete state graphs, finding isomorphism among induced graphs could be simpler. In extreme cases, a vertex representing an action argument can be adjacent to a large number of vertices or even to every other vertex. In such situations, the complexity associated with the argument substitutions is still too great.

For the limited approach to substitution, the recognizer focuses on the next action prediction and attempts to find all possible substitutions of the action arguments only. The substitution process that we chose uses the information contained in the transformed state graphs, concentrating on those vertices that represent the currently matched action arguments. The substitution finding process is neither correct nor complete, because it is not guaranteed to find any correct substitutions when one exists. On the other hand, the process is linear in the number of arguments, and it is therefore very efficient

To explain the substitution algorithm, consider an example with two states s_1 and s_2 with their corresponding state graphs G_1 and G_2, respectively. Let $G_1=(V_{G1}, E_{G1})$, $G_2=(V_{G2}, E_{G2})$, with

$$V_{G1} = \{v_1,...,v_k\}, V_{G2} = \{u_1,...,u_k\}.$$

Let us assume that state s_1 is the currently observed state, while state s_2 is the previously observed state that needs to be adapted. Further assume that the action taken in the state s_2 was action A with arguments $u_{A1},...,u_{Aq<=k}$. Given two states graphs G_1 and G_2, the process of finding the argument substitutions proceeds as follows:

For each action argument u_{Ai},
- Find all of the edges in the graph G_2 incident to u_{Ai}.
- Find all vertices v_j in G_1 that have exactly the same edge incidency set as u_{Ai}.
- If no such vertices can be found, no substitutions exist. Otherwise, vertices v_j in G_1 are possible substitutions for the vertex u_{Ai} in action A.

The above process is linear in the number of edges and vertices in the subgraph induced by the vertices acting as the action arguments. This process enables the recognizer to quickly determine that no substitutions exist between the two given states, because the edge incidency set of some vertex u_{Ai} in G_2 may not have a match in the graph G_1. The process may also find some substitutions that are not applicable outside the subgraph induced by the action arguments and therefore are not feasible substitutions between the two states. This sub-optimal behavior is compensated by the efficiency and the simplicity of the proposed substitution finding process.

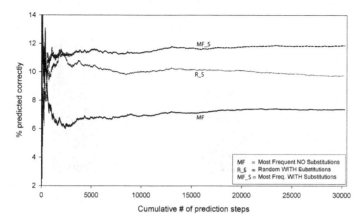

Fig. 8. Percentages of correctly predicted concrete actions in the three-city logistics domain, with the simple and effective argument substitutions scheme

Experimental Results

The substitution finding process described in the previous section was tested on the same two problems sets from the logistics planning domain discussed in the previous results section. The choice of the action at the abstract level remains the same as before, thus the substitution scheme affects only the effectiveness of the action predictions at the concrete level.

Although the process of finding the substitutions is quite simple, it helps the recognizer increase the concrete action prediction accuracy. Figure 8 shows the percentages of the correctly predicted concrete actions over 30,000 recognition steps. The bottom line represents the best performer from previous evaluations in Figure 4. As it can be seen from Figure 8, the random action choice strategy with the substitution scheme outperforms the most frequent action choice strategy without substitutions in a long run. As expected, the most frequent action choice strategy with adaptation significantly outperforms both of its two rivals. Figure 9 shows the comparison of the total numbers of correctly predicted concrete actions over 30,000 prediction steps. In each case it can be seen that the usage of the argument substitutions increases the recognizer's prediction accuracy regardless of the action choice strategy used. The substitution finding technique is also domain-independent, as long as the states and actions can be represented in a predicate form.

Although the improvements introduced by the sub-optimal substitution finding mechanism are evident, the overall prediction accuracy is still not very high. Because a concrete action selection is made only after the abstract action selection, the abstract action prediction accuracy serves as an upper bound for the concrete action prediction accuracy. We can see from the figures that in the best case, about 2/5 of correctly predicted abstract actions remain correct at the concrete level. The next section introduces additional ways in which the concrete action prediction accuracy may come closer to the upper bound determined by the abstract prediction accuracy.

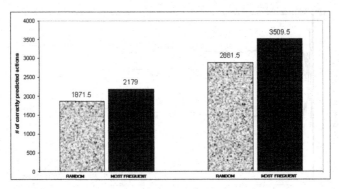

Fig. 9. Number of correct concrete action predictions without (left) and with (right) action argument substitution strategies

Local Predictions with Failure-Driven Heuristics

We have demonstrated that the use of a simple and efficient argument substitution finding scheme improves the accuracy of the recognizer. The simplicity of the recognition scheme leaves a lot of room for the improvement. The accuracy of the action predictions at the concrete level is bounded above by the accuracy at the abstract level, because the choice of the abstract action determines the choice of the concrete action. Therefore, we are interested in improving the prediction accuracy at both levels of abstraction.

Currently, there are two different strategies for choosing the next action at the abstract level: random and most frequent strategies. The former strategy randomly chooses an action extracted from the retrieved cases, while the most frequent strategy chooses the action that was pursued with the greatest frequency in previous situations. As before when multiple most frequent actions exist, the recognizer randomly chooses one. One way of improving the abstract prediction accuracy is to replace the random choice of an abstract action in a case of a tie with a better selection technique. An example includes preferring the last recently used actions.

At the present time, choosing the concrete actions is accomplished both with and without the action arguments substitution. As the previous results show, the substitution scheme is better in predicting the planner's next action. However, in cases where multiple substitutions are possible, the recognizer simply picks a single substitution at random. One obvious way of improving the concrete action predictions is to explore alternative methods of breaking this tie. Our future research will further address the techniques for improving the prediction accuracy at the both levels of abstraction.

It is certainly true that there exist numerous heuristics, whose application may improve the prediction accuracy. In attempt to improve the recognition accuracy, we constrain the recognition process to attempt retrieval of previous cases only in light of a prediction failure. Learning from failure is a cornerstone of many artificial intelligence systems (e.g., Cox and Ram, 1999; Pazzani, 1994). When the recognizer's previously made prediction turns out to be accurate, the recognizer assumes that the correct past case has been found and chooses to form subsequent predictions on the basis of the correct past case. This past case is utilized for the recognition for as long as the recognizer's predictions are valid. As soon as the recognizer makes an incorrect prediction, the retrieval phase starts again and the past matching case is discarded.

Although the use of the heuristic that initiates the retrieval only when predictions fail is fairly simple, the improvement is the prediction accuracy are evident. The next section discusses an evaluation of this simple yet effective heuristic.

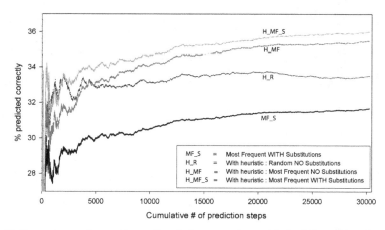

Fig. 10. Percentages of correctly predicted *abstract* actions with the failure-driven heuristic

Experimental Results

To evaluate the effectiveness of failure-driven retrieval, we present the prediction results based on the two three-city logistics problem sets we used in previous evaluations. Unlike the substitution finding scheme that only improves the predictions at the concrete action level, the failure-driven heuristics influences predictions at the abstract action level. Because the abstract actions are chosen before the concrete actions, the failure-driven heuristic affects predictions at both levels of abstraction.

Figure 10 shows the action prediction percentages at the abstract action level. The bottom line in the graph is the scheme that utilizes the most frequent action selection and substitutions of action arguments. This is the best performer from previous evaluations. Note that even the random action selection scheme without substitutions and with the failure-driven heuristic outperforms the best performer from previous evaluations. Because concrete action prediction accuracy is bounded above by the abstract action prediction accuracy, there is even more room for the improvements in predicting the concrete actions.

Figure 11 shows the two different random strategies with the failure-driven heuristic compared to the best performer from previous graphs with the most frequent action selection. These evaluations show that while the failure-driven heuristic increases the accuracy percentages of the random predictions initially, in the long run the randomness brings the slope of the curves down to the accuracy level of the most frequent action selection strategy. This is because over a long period of time the density of the concrete states in the indexing bins increases and the random selection strategy is less likely to pick the correct next action. On the other hand, the slopes of the curves representing the most frequent action selection strategy do not decrease in a long run.

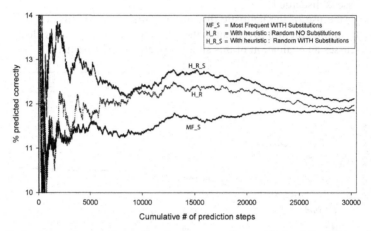

Fig. 11. Percentages of correctly predicted *concrete* actions with the failure-driven heuristic and the random action selection strategies

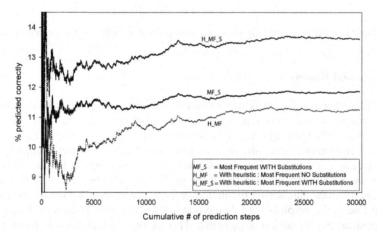

Fig. 12. Percentages of correctly predicted *concrete* actions with the failure-driven heuristic and the most frequent action selection strategies

Figure 12 shows the accuracy percentages of the most frequent prediction strategies with and without the failure-driven heuristic. Unlike random, the most frequent strategy only gets better with the increased number of observations, because the action frequency distribution becomes more uniform. Figure 13 shows the total numbers of the correctly predicted next concrete actions over 30,000 recognition steps. Two best performers from previous evaluations are shown on the left, both with and without the argument substitution schemes. Note from Figure 12 and Figure 13 that the prediction accuracy of the best performer from the previous evaluations is slightly better than the most frequent action selection strategy with the failure-driven heuristic and without substitutions. But unlike the random selection strategies, the most frequent strategies maintain the prediction percentage curves with a small positive slope in a long run. Future research efforts will increase the size of the problem sets in order to analyze the asymptotic behavior of the plan recognition system. As it can be seen from the graphs, the failure-driven heuristic along with the most frequent action selection strategy and substitutions is superior to the all other strategies on this particular dataset.

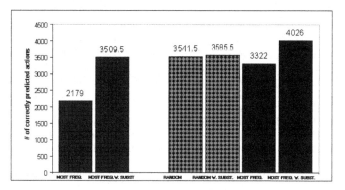

Fig. 13. Number of correct *concrete* action predictions with (right) and without (left) the failure-driven heuristic strategies.

The evaluation results presented in this paper show that the utilization of the abstract indexing scheme along with the argument substitutions and the failure-driven heuristics is the best recognition strategy among all other evaluated strategies. In general, the increase in the prediction accuracy of the argument substitutions scheme alone is more beneficial for the recognition than the failure-driven heuristic alone. However, when these two strategies are used side by side, the prediction accuracy is better than any one of them used alone.

Conclusions

This paper presented an approach to the recognition of the planning actions utilizing a novel indexing scheme in the context of the case-based plan recognition with incomplete plan libraries. The application of the abstract indexing scheme increases the prediction accuracy with respect to the baseline test, while the argument substitution mechanism further improves the recognition accuracy. The failure-driven heuristic further increases the recognizer's accuracy and indicates the potential of the heuristic-driven approaches. Future research efforts will explore the global (goal) predictions, as well as other potentially promising and efficient heuristics.

Acknowledgments

This paper is supported by the Dayton Area Graduate Studies Institute (DAGSI) under grant #HE-WSU-99-09 (ABMIC), by a grant from the Information Technology Research Institute (ITRI), and by the state of Ohio.

References

Bares, M., Canamero, D., Delannoy, J. F., & Kodratoff, Y. (1994). XPlans: Case-based reasoning for plan recognition. *Applied Artificial Intelligence* 8, 617-643.
Bergmann, R., & Wilke, W. (1995). Building and Refining Abstract Planning Cases by Change of Representation Language. *Journal of Artificial Intelligence Research*, 3:53—118.
Bergmann, R., & Wilke, W. (1996). On the Role of Abstractions in Case-Based Reasoning. In *EWCBR-96 European Conference on Case-Based Reasoning*. Springer, 1996.
Carbonell, J. G., Blythe, J., Etzioni, O., Gil, Y., Joseph, R., Kahn, D., Knoblock, C., Minton, S., Perez, A., Reilly, S., Veloso, M., & Wang, X. (1992). *PRODIGY 4.0: The Manual and Tutorial* (Tech. Rep. No. CMU-CS-92-150). Carnegie Mellon University, Department of Computer Science, Pittsburgh, PA.
Cox, M. T., & Ram, A. (1999). Introspective multistrategy learning: On the construction of learning strategies. *Artificial Intelligence*, 112, 1-55.
Kautz, H. (1991). A formal theory of plan recognition and its implementation. In J. Allen, *et. al., Reasoning about plans*. San Francisco: Morgan Kaufmann.
Kerkez, B. (2001) *Incremental case-based keyhole plan recognition*. Technical Report, WSU-CS-01-01, Department of Computer Science and Engineering, Wright State Univ.
Kerkez, B., & Cox, M. (2001). Case-based plan recognition using state indices, In D. W. Aha & I. Watson (Eds.), *Case-based Reasoning Research and Development: Proceedings of 4th international conference on case-based reasoning* (pp. 227-242). Berlin: Springer.
Kerkez, B. (2002). Learning Plan Libraries for Case-based Plan Recognition. In *Proceedings of the 13th Midwest Artificial Intelligence and Cognitive Science Conference*. IIT, Chicago, IL.
Lesh, N., & Etzioni, O. (1996). Scaling up goal recognition. In *Proceedings of the Fifth Internat. Conference on Principles of Knowledge Representation and Reasoning* (pp 178-189).
Pazzani, M. (1994) Learning causal patterns: Making a transition from data-driven to theory-driven learning, in: R. Michalski and G. Tecuci, eds., *Machine learning IV: A multistrategy approach* (Morgan Kaufmann, San Francisco, 1994) 267-293.
Veloso, M. (1994). *Planning and learning by analogical reasoning*. Berlin: Springer.

Automatically Selecting Strategies
for Multi-Case-Base Reasoning[*]

David B. Leake[1] and Raja Sooriamurthi[2]

[1] Computer Science Department, Indiana University, Lindley Hall 215
150 S. Woodlawn Avenue, Bloomington, IN 47405, U.S.A.
leake@cs.indiana.edu
[2] Kelley School of Business, Indiana University, BU540,
1309 East 10th Street, Bloomington, IN 47405, U.S.A.
raja@indiana.edu

Abstract. Case-based reasoning (CBR) systems solve new problems by retrieving stored prior cases, and adapting their solutions to fit new circumstances. Traditionally, CBR systems draw their cases from a single local case-base tailored to their task. However, when a system's own set of cases is limited, it may be beneficial to supplement the local case-base with cases drawn from external case-bases for related tasks. Effective use of external case-bases requires strategies for *multi-case-base reasoning* (MCBR): (1) for deciding when to *dispatch* problems to an external case-base, and (2) for performing *cross-case-base adaptation* to compensate for differences in the tasks and environments that each case-base reflects. This paper presents methods for automatically tuning MCBR systems by selecting effective dispatching criteria and cross-case-base adaptation strategies. The methods require no advance knowledge of the task and domain: they perform tests on an initial set of problems and use the results to select strategies reflecting the characteristics of the local and external case-bases. We present experimental illustrations of the performance of the tuning methods for a numerical prediction task, and demonstrate that a small sample set can be sufficient to make high-quality choices of dispatching and cross-case-base adaptation strategies.

1 Introduction

Case-based reasoning systems solve new problems by retrieving cases from a case-base of prior experiences, and adapting their solutions to fit new circumstances. As a CBR system initially builds up experiences, its case library may be small, potentially limiting its performance. If external case-bases already exist for similar tasks, drawing on those case-bases may help overcome the system's initial knowledge gaps. Even in a system with an extensive case library, external case-bases may contain specialized expertise that would be useful when handling problems outside of the system's normal range of tasks. Unfortunately, it may be difficult to know when to draw on an external case-base and which external case-bases to access. It may also require additional effort to apply cases from an external case-base, due to inter-case-base differences reflecting differences in tasks or execution environments. For example, if an e-commerce application quotes

---

[*] This research is supported in part by NASA under award No NCC 2-1216.

S. Craw and A. Preece (Eds.): ECCBR 2002, LNAI 2416, pp. 204–218, 2002.
© Springer-Verlag Berlin Heidelberg 2002

prices based on the product case-bases of different stores, one of which lists prices in dollars and the other in euros, adjustments will be needed to convert prices from the American case-base for European use. Thus, making effective use of the information in multiple case-bases requires a reasoning process that we call *multi-case-base reasoning: reasoning* about when to access external case-bases and how to apply their cases. The two central requirements are *case dispatching* processes, to determine the case-base to which to send a problem, and *cross-case-base adaptation* processes, to adjust solutions from one case-base in response to differences between the two case-bases. The success of these processes depends on selecting the right strategies for particular case-bases and task domains. This paper develops methods by which an MCBR system can automatically choose between case-bases and select useful cross-case-base adaptation strategies, and tests them for a numerical prediction task.

In principle, developing high-quality case dispatching and cross-case-base adaptation strategies could require arbitrarily-large amounts of knowledge about the task domain and available case-bases. However, MCBR may be useful even with imperfect dispatching strategies and cross-case-base adaptation knowledge. If the local case-base has only sparse coverage of the problem space, and an external case-base has extensive coverage, the benefits of accessing cases for more similar problems can sometimes counterbalance errors introduced by differences in solution characteristics, with a net performance improvement compared to relying on the local case-base alone [5]. The central question examined in this paper is how an MCBR system can predict whether MCBR will be useful and which MCBR strategies will be most effective. The paper presents and evaluates strategies for automatically tuning an MCBR system by determining case dispatching criteria and choosing between alternative cross-case-base adaptation strategies. The self-tuning methods calibrate a multi-case-base reasoning system by testing alternative methods on a small set of cases in the problem-stream and selecting strategies that do well on those tests.

The paper begins by discussing the motivations for multi-case-base reasoning and the factors affecting its performance. It then describes two dispatching strategies, and three simple methods for cross-case-base adaptation of cases with numerical solutions. These cross-case-base adaptation methods are applicable to cases which share a common representation, but whose suggested solutions differ due to differences in their task environments. The paper then presents experiments illustrating some of the factors involved in the performance of MCBR and the benefits of self-calibration. The paper closes with a discussion of the broader ramifications of this type of approach to maintaining case-based reasoning systems.

2   Motivations for Multi-Case-Base Reasoning

The success of CBR systems depends on their access to relevant stored cases. CBR research and applications generally assume that the only case source is the reasoner's own case-base, and focus on developing and refining a single, unified case-base. However, growing numbers of deployed case-based reasoning systems promise new opportunities for CBR systems to supplement their local case-bases, by drawing on the case-bases of other CBR systems addressing related tasks. Just as thousands of topic-specific information sources are now available on the Web, multiple case-bases may eventually provide large-scale distributed, sharable information resources for CBR.

One way to exploit multiple case-bases might be to take an "eager" approach, merging and standardizing all their cases in preparation for future use. This is not always possible—the owners of different case collections will not necessarily be willing to contribute. Even when case-bases could be merged, however, MCBR's "lazy" approach of on-demand access may provide significant advantages [5,6]. For very large case-bases, or when local storage is inadequate to store all cases (e.g., for a substantial case-base stored in a PDA), MCBR enables storing frequently-used cases locally and storing less-commonly-used cases externally. When different sources generate the different case-bases, keeping the case-bases distinct also facilitates a natural division of maintenance effort, with each source maintaining its own case-bases, and other users automatically benefitting as they retrieve their cases from the latest versions of the external case-bases. If the relationships between local and external case-bases change, adjustments are simple: only cross-case-base adaptation policies must be changed, rather than all the stored cases (e.g., if the dollar-euro exchange rate changes, only the cross-case-base adaptation procedure for prices must be changed).

The primary focus of this paper, however is on a use of MCBR that applies regardless of case-base size and maintenance concerns: using MCBR to guide case acquisition from related external case-bases, when a CBR system is building up its initial case-base. Compared to simply gathering and merging cases from all available case-bases, MCBR has three main advantages for this task. First, MCBR selectively adds only those cases needed to solve the problems the system actually encounters, keeping the case-base more compact. (For example, a New Yorker with a case-based restaurant advisor on a PDA may only need cases for New York; cases for other regions need not be merged unless—and until—the need arises.) Second, avoiding eager merging gives the flexibility to draw on any new case-bases that may become available, possibly enabling the system to choose to use higher-quality cases than would have been imported by eager merging. Third, when cross-case-base adaptation is required, using MCBR to import cases as needed can improve solution quality compared to performing cross-case-base adaptation on all external cases and eagerly merging them. Because cross-case-base adaptation may be imperfect, sometimes solving a problem using a local case for a less-similar problem will give better results than solving it using a cross-case-base-adapted version of an external case generated for a more similar problem. The case-dispatching strategies of MCBR take this into account in their decisions about when to draw on external case-bases, but eager merging—by simply performing cross-case-base adaptation on all cases and merging the case-bases—looses that capability.

3   Factors Affecting Performance of Multi-Case-Base Reasoning

Whether it is beneficial to draw on an external case-base depends primarily on five factors. The usefulness of MCBR is increased if:

1. **The external case-base has needed competence that the local case-base lacks:** If the local case-base lacks cases sufficiently similar to a problem, it can be worthwhile to dispatch the problem to a case-base with similar cases, even if cross-case-base

adaptation is weak—the benefits of more similar prior cases may counterbalance errors introduced by cross-case-base adaptation.

2. **The local and external case-bases have similar representations:** If local and external case-bases use dissimilar representations, conversion from one to another may significantly increase the burden for MCBR. Our methods assume matching representations, to focus on issues in dispatching and cross-case-base adaptation, but we return to this issue in Section 6.

3. **Cases for similar problems in the local and external case-bases have similar solutions:** In this situation, minimal cross-case-base adaptation will be needed.

4. **Cross-case-base adaptation is strong and/or local adaptation is weak:** High-quality local adaptation procedures can provide good solutions despite sparse local coverage, decreasing the need for dispatching. Conversely, high-quality cross-case-base adaptation can effectively augment the local case-base with high-quality external cases, increasing the benefit of dispatching, and helping to overcome problems with weak local adaptation knowledge.

5. **External case-bases are easily accessible:** Accessing an external case-base may impose additional costs reflecting factors such as access fees, access delays, and bandwidth used. These factors must be balanced with quality considerations when deciding whether to dispatch cases to external case-bases.

The experiments in Section 5 will explore how different levels of local competence affect the overall benefits of dispatching, given weak cross-case-base adaptation knowledge, and how learning can assist in automatically selecting dispatching and cross-case-base adaptation strategies. The next section describes our strategies for cross-case-base adaptation, case dispatching, and automatic self-calibration.

4   Strategies for Multi-Case-Base Reasoning

Applying MCBR requires augmenting standard CBR with mechanisms to decide when to dispatch problems to external case-bases, where to dispatch them, and how to perform cross-case-base adaptation of the returned cases.

4.1   Samples of Knowledge-Light Cross-Case-Base Adaptation Strategies: Global and Local Interpolations

To illustrate the self-calibration process, we consider how it can be used to choose between four cross-case-base adaptation strategies for the task of case-based numerical prediction. One of these is the baseline of the identity (i.e., no cross-case-base adaptation); the other three are simple "knowledge-light" methods that can be derived from the case-bases involved, without requiring domain-specific knowledge.

1. **No cross-case-base adaptation (ID):** This uses the identity function for cross-case-base adaptation, giving a baseline for comparison with other methods.

2. **Linear interpolation, based on global min and max (Minmax):** This method pairs the minimum and maximum solution values in both case bases, and estimates conversions of values in the external case-base by linear interpolation to the local

CBA1(P, *local_CB*, *external_CB*)

   1   ▷ Calculate solution in external CB
   2   *external_soln* ← solution to P using *external_CB*
   3   ▷ Calculate scale factor for cross-case-base adaptation
   4   *reference_external_case* ← $argmin_{C \in external\_CB} dist(P, C)$
   5   *reference_external_prob* ← problem part of *reference_external_case*
   6   *reference_external_soln* ← soln to *reference_external_prob* using *external_CB*
   7   *reference_local_soln* ← solution to *reference_external_prob* using *local_CB*
   8   *scale_factor* ← *reference_local_soln*/*reference_external_soln*
   9   ▷ Return external solution scaled for consistency with *local_CB*
  10   Return *external_soln* ∗ *scale_factor*

Algorithm 1. CBA1. This method scales external solutions to fit the local case-base, using a scale factor based on comparing the external and local solutions for a similar reference problem already in the external case-base.

case-base. This strategy will be usable if the extreme values of the case-bases are available, and will be effective to the extent that (1) there is a correspondence between extremes in both case-bases, and (2) the correspondence between intermediate values can be approximated as globally linear.

3. **Local approximation, based on calculating a scale factor starting from the most similar external case (CBA1):** This method calculates a new scale factor for each problem. Given an input problem, it retrieves the external case C for the most similar problem. The problem solved by C is then re-solved in the local case-base, and a scale factor is determined by the ratio of the local and external solutions. The solution of the input problem is calculated by solving it in the external case-base, and multiplying the result by the scale factor (Algorithm 1).

4. **Local approximation, based on calculating a scale factor starting from the most similar local case (CBA2):** This method is analogous to CBA1, but calculates the scale factor based on the most similar local case.

4.2   Case Dispatching and Calibration

We consider two case dispatching strategies. The first, *threshold-based dispatching* [5], dispatches problems to an external case-base if local cases are not available for sufficiently similar problems. This method can be used to decide whether a problem is processed locally or dispatched to an external case-base. Because performance depends on setting the right dispatching threshold for the case-bases and cross-case-base adaptation strategies, we also describe an algorithm for setting the dispatching threshold based on a set of test problems. The second strategy, *case-based dispatching*, dispatches problems to the case-bases that best solved similar problems in the past. This strategy can be used to dispatch to an arbitrary number of case-bases, and—because it bases its choices on tests using the current case-bases—automatically reflects the characteristics of the specific case-bases and cross-case-base adaptation strategies.

Threshold-Based Dispatching: In threshold-based dispatching, a fixed threshold $T \geq 0$ determines the maximum acceptable distance between new problems and the problems

THRESHOLDDISPATCH(P, k, $local\_CB$, $external\_CB$)

1    $local\_soln\_dist \leftarrow$ average distance from P to the k nearest cases in $local\_CB$
2   **if** $local\_soln\_dist \leq dispatch\_threshold$
3   **then** *solve P using* $local\_CB$
4   **else** $external\_soln\_dist \leftarrow$ avg. dist. from P to k nearest cases in $external\_CB$
5   **if** $local\_soln\_dist \leq external\_soln\_dist$
6   **then** *solve P using* $local\_CB$
7   **else** *solve P using* $external\_CB$

Algorithm 2. Distance-threshold-based case dispatching algorithm.

in stored local cases. A problem P is dispatched to the external case-base if and only if both (1) P is judged too dissimilar to the problems solved by local cases, and (2) the external case-base contains more similar cases than the local case-base. Algorithm 2 summarizes our dispatching method. Because it is designed for systems using k-NN retrieval, it considers the average similarity between P and the k most similar cases.

Calibrating threshold-based dispatching: Our method for selecting a dispatching threshold examines a test set of problems (e.g., the first problems in the problem-stream), and selects a threshold value to maximize a pre-defined function assessing the utility of solutions. If the goal is simply to maximize the number of problems solved correctly, the utility function assigns a value of 1 if the problem is solved correctly, and 0 if it is solved incorrectly. However, the utility function could also reflect factors such as percent error, solution generation time, bandwidth use, fees to access a particular case-base, etc.

The calibration algorithm first sorts the test problems p_i in ascending order according to their average distance d_{p_i} from the nearest case in the local case-base. The midpoints between d_{p_i} values for adjacent problems are taken as candidate dispatching thresholds; two additional possible thresholds are 0 and infinity. The choice of the threshold can be seen as dividing this ordered set: When a threshold is chosen, all problems with smaller d_{p_i} values will be processed locally, and all other problems will be dispatched. A threshold of zero results in all problems being dispatched; a threshold of infinity corresponds to all problems being solved locally.

The calibration algorithm computes the solution for each test problem in both the local and external case-base and applies the utility function to determine the utility of the resulting solution. It chooses the threshold T to maximize the sum of the utility function values when each problem is solved in the case-base determined by the threshold. In the following experiments, our utility function measures prediction performance.

Case-Based Case Dispatching and Calibration: In our case-based case dispatching method, a *dispatching case-base* is generated by solving the test problems in different case-bases and recording the utilities of the solutions from those case-bases. The dispatching case-base is then used to predict the performance of each candidate case-base (local or external) for similar future problems. Given a new problem to solve, the local or external case-base to use is determined by a weighted voting scheme, in which each problem in the dispatching case-base votes for the local case-base or an external case-base, whichever solved it most effectively, and the votes are weighted according to the similarity of each problem in the dispatching case-base to the new problem to be solved. The dispatching case-base is built by solving each test problem in the local case-base and in each external case-base, and storing cases containing the test problem, case-base identifier, and utility value.

When an input problem is received during normal processing, the problem is dispatched to the case-base (local or external) with highest expected utility, according to the following formula. Let P be an input problem, let k-reference_probs(P) be the k nearest neighbors of P in the dispatching case-base, and $soln\_utility(R, CB)$ be the utility of solving reference problem R using case-base CB. The expected utility of using case-base CB_i to solve P is calculated by:

$$CB\_utility(CB_i, P) = \tfrac{1}{k}\Sigma_{R \in k\text{-}reference\_probs(P)} soln\_utility(R, CB_i).$$

P is dispatched to the case-base CB_i that maximizes $CB\_utility(CB_i, P)$.

4.3   Combining Dispatching with Selection of Cross-Case-Base Adaptation Strategies

A variant of the threshold-based calibration algorithm can be used to select both a dispatching method and a cross-case-base adaptation strategy. In that method, the calibration process applies each cross-case-base adaptation strategy to each problem in the test set, and sets the threshold and cross-case-base adaptation procedure to the combination that maximizes the sum of the utilities for the test problems.

Because the case-based dispatching method makes its choices based on performance on similar problems, it can also easily be extended to simultaneously select the external case-base and cross-case-base adaptation strategy most applicable to a particular type of problem. To build the dispatching case-base, each test problem is solved using all combinations of case-bases and adaptation strategies, with the best case-base and cross-case-base adaptation strategy stored in the dispatching case-base. When the system processes a new problem, the voting procedure then votes for pairs (case-base, cross-case-base adaptation strategy). The application of this type of approach to federations of case-bases is discussed in [6].

5   Experimental Illustrations

We conducted experiments both to study the effects of case dispatching and cross-case-base adaptation methods, and to explore the calibration strategies of the previous section. Our experiments explored the following questions:

1. How do dispatching threshold and cross-case-base adaptation strategies affect system performance? This provides a baseline illustration, replicating results from [5] using a different case-base.
2. Can threshold-based dispatching with a small calibration set select the right cross-case-base adaptation strategy?
3. Can case-based dispatching with a small calibration set predict the right external case-base and cross-case-base adaptation strategy?
4. How does the size of the calibration problem set affect the performance of case-based dispatching and selection of cross-case-base adaptation strategies?

Questions (1) and (2) address dispatching to a single external case-base; (3) and (4) consider dispatching to a set of external case-bases.

5.1   Experimental Setup

The task for our experiments was predicting median housing prices, using a publicly-available data set published on the web by the Delve group (Data for Evaluating Learning in Valid Experiments).[1] This data set includes 22,784 cases from the 1990 U.S. census, divided by states. The experimental task was predicting prices from partial case-bases for one state, augmented by drawing on the complete case-base for another state (or states) as the external case-base(s). Here all cases use the same representation scheme, but the price for a given set of property features will change based on differences in the housing markets in different states. Intuitively, this prediction task can be seen as related to what a real estate appraiser might do after moving to a new area, when it is necessary to reason from a combination of local and non-local experience. The state case-bases used (with their abbreviations and sizes) are Alabama (AL, 470 cases), Arkansas (AK, 471 cases), Florida (FL, 752 cases), Indiana (IN, 590 cases), Illinois (IL, 1308 cases), Kentucky (KY, 471 cases), Ohio (OH, 1051 cases) Mississippi (MI, 500 cases), and Nevada (NV, 56 cases).

We expect multi-case-base reasoning to be most useful early on, when the reasoner has a limited local case library. To model the stages in the growth of a case-base, sparse versions of the local case-bases were generated by randomly selecting varying percentages of the original local case-base. In what follows, the initial case-bases are designated by CB_1, and the sparse versions of these case-bases as $CB_1^\star$. Prediction performance is evaluated using all problems in the full CB_1 case-base as test problems (except those used as test problems for selecting the dispatching threshold or for case-based dispatching), with leave-one-out cross validation. Performance is measured by counting the number of cases whose prices were predicted correctly to within an error margin of 20%. All predictions are done using a distance weighted 3-nearest-neighbor algorithm (3-NN). Note that no effort was made to tune feature weights to achieve better performance; the goal was to study the comparative value of MCBR, rather than to maximize performance.

5.2   How Do Dispatching Threshold and Cross-Case-Base Adaptation Strategies Affect System Performance?

In this experiment, the system determined whether to handle the case locally within $CB_1^\star$ or to dispatch it to an external case-base CB_2, based on the problem's similarity to cases in $CB_1^\star$ and CB_2 and on the dispatching threshold. If the problem was dispatched, cross-case-base adaptation was applied to the predicted value from CB_2 before evaluating its accuracy. Figure 1 illustrates the impact of dispatching criteria and choice of adaptation strategies on performance. Here the local and external case-bases both reflect somewhat similar tasks (predicting house prices in AL and KY), but with very different competences—the local case-base of AL cases is very sparse. $CB_1^\star$ contains only

---

[1] http://www.cs.toronto.edu/~delve/data/census-house/desc.html.

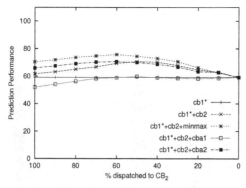

Fig. 1. Prediction accuracy for AL housing prices, using a sparse case-base of AL census data supplemented with dispatching to a full case-base of KY prices, with cross-case-base adaptation.

5 cases, drawn randomly from census data for AL, compared to the full KY case-base CB_2.

Figure 1 shows prediction accuracies of the four different cross-case-base adaptation strategies from Section 4.1 (ID, Minmax, CBA1 and CBA2). Identity cross-case-base adaptation is indicated by $CB_1^\star + CB_2$; linear adaptation based on global min and max is indicated by $CB_1^\star + CB_2$ + minmax; the two local adaptation methods are indicated by $CB_1^\star + CB_2$ + cba1 and $CB_1^\star + CB_2$ + cba2, respectively. The horizontal line, marked $CB_1^\star$, shows baseline performance with no case dispatching. For other conditions, problems are dispatched when no "sufficiently similar" cases are available in $CB_1^\star$, following Algorithm 2.

These experiments were run for a wide range of sparse case-bases. When the distance threshold is too low, problems are dispatched when they could be solved locally, and performance may be degraded by flaws in cross-case-base adaptation. When the threshold is too high, cases are solved locally even when they are outside of the local case-base's competence. However, for the right choice of threshold, as in the 60% dispatched condition of the graph, performance noticeably surpasses the local case-base alone. This pattern appears primarily in sparse case-bases—in our experiments, dispatching had less benefit as the density of the local case-bases increased.

We note that performance depends on both the dispatching threshold and the cross-case base adaptation strategies chosen. For this sample data, performance is actually worse with CBA1 adaptation than if problems are dispatched with no cross-case-base adaptation at all. This example shows that the choice of appropriate strategies is crucial to the success of MCBR.

5.3 Can Threshold-Based Dispatching with a Small Calibration Set Predict the Right Cross-Case-Base Adaptation Strategy?

To explore the feasibility of automatically selecting strategies to tune case dispatching and cross-case-base adaptation, we performed a series of experiments, the results of some of which are shown in Figure 2. These show two samples of the effects of the calibration process for selecting the cross-case-base adaptation strategy to use for two

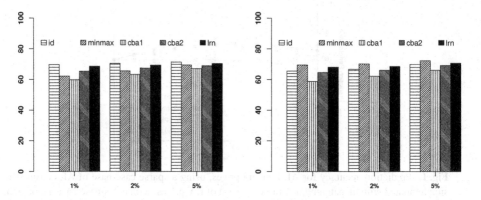

Fig. 2. Left: Predicting AL median house prices, using a sparse AL case-base as the local case-base, with an external case-base of MI census data. Right: Predicting AL prices, using a sparse AL case-base as the local case-base and and an external case-base of KY census data.

different external case-bases, MI and KY. For both graphs, the local case-bases are randomly-selected subsets of the AL case-base. Tests were run for subsets containing 1%, 2%, and 5% of the AL cases, to simulate effects as the local case-base grows over time. For each density, the first bar shows predictive accuracy with no cross-case-base adaptation (ID), the second with minmax, the third and fourth with CBA_1 and CBA_2, and the last (LRN) with the learned method selected by the threshold-based calibration process described in Section 4.2. Graphs represent the average of 10 runs, each using a 10-problem test set for calibration and the remaining 460 AL cases for testing.

For both examples, the case-bases are sufficiently similar that the identity cross-case-base adaptation gives good performance. However, better performance is sometimes achieved with other methods, and the best methods vary. For example, for the MI external case-base and 1% local case-base, the identity outperforms all other methods, and is noticeably superior to minmax. For the KY external case-base and 1% local case-base, minmax outperforms the identity. Thus, selecting a single fixed strategy will sometimes give poor performance, and the question is whether calibration can consistently give performance close to that of the optimal strategy, whichever that strategy may be. In these experiments, calibration resulted in performance close to that of the optimal strategy. Although these choices were surpassed on individual runs, calibration resulted in better average performance than any fixed strategy, even though calibration was based on only 10 test problems.

5.4 Can Case-Based Dispatching with a Small Calibration Set Predict the Right External Case Base and Cross-Case-Base Adaptation Strategy?

The overall goal of MCBR with self-calibration is to automatically adjust the MCBR system's dispatching and cross-case-base adaptation to make the best use of multiple case-bases. To test this ability, we compared the performance of a variety of strategies: using the local case-base only, using one of 12 fixed combinations of external case-bases

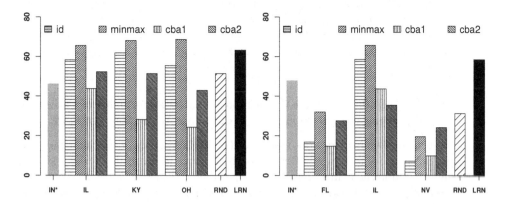

Fig. 3. . Comparison of performance of a sparse local case-base (IN*) with two sets of external case-bases (IL, KY, OH, left, and FL, IL, NV right) for four cross-case-base adaptation strategies. RND designates random dispatching and cross-case-base adaptation; LRN designates the choices learned from the test problems by building up the dispatching case-base.

and strategies (3 external case-bases × 4 cross-case-base adaptation strategies), using randomly-chosen combinations of case-bases and cross-case-base adaptation strategies, and using the case-based method of Section 4.2 to learn to select case-bases and cross-case-base adaptation strategies from the calibration process. All runs used sparse versions of the Indiana case-base (IN*) as the local case-base, and test problems drawn from the full IN case-base, with leave-one-out cross-validation. One set of runs used MCBR with the external case-bases IL, KY, and OH, all of which were expected to have property valuation characteristics similar to the local case-base. Another used the external case-bases FL, IL, and NV, in which two case-bases, FL and NV, were expected to have quite different characteristics. 10 randomly-selected versions of the local case-base were tested as local case-bases, with 5 runs for each one using different randomly-selected calibration sets, for each of the four densities 1%, 2%, 5%, and 10%, for a total of 200 test runs.

As expected, the average benefits of MCBR were greatest for sparse local case-bases. Figure 3 shows average results for the sparsest local case-base tested (1%). The left-hand graph shows results when the local case-base and external case-bases make similar predictions (in fact, the IL case-base with no cross-case-base adaptation outperforms the sparse local case-base IN*). We note that for each of the external case-bases, there is a cross-case-base adaptation strategy for which dispatching markedly outperforms the sparse local case-base. On average, even random dispatching and selection of adaptation outperform the sparse local case-base, but this is outperformed by the learned strategy, whose performance is close to the maximum observed.

In the right-hand graph, the cases in the FL and NV case-bases are dissimilar to those in IN*, and the cross-case-base adaptation strategies are insufficient to compensate. Here random dispatching is much worse, but performance with learned dispatching again surpasses the local case-base and is close to that of the best external case-base and cross-case-base adaptation strategy. In our tests, the learned method consistently approximated or surpassed the optimal single-method performance. As the local case-base became less sparse, the advantage of dispatching decreased, but learning still approximated the best performance, by sending problems to the local case-base. Thus the calibration method appears to be robust enough not only to guide dispatching when external case-bases are helpful, but also to shift to the local case-base when appropriate.

5.5   How Does the Size of the Calibration Set Affect Performance of Case-Based Dispatching and Selection of Cross-Case-Base Adaptation Strategies?

The benefit of tuning strategies will depend on the sufficiency of the calibration set to guide dispatching and choice of cross-case-base adaptation methods. Ideally, a small set would be sufficient, both to minimize calibration effort and to decrease the cost of case-based dispatching. However, we expect smaller sample sizes to degrade performance. Thus an important question is how the calibration set size affects performance: whether the methods can make good dispatching decisions with limited-size samples.

To explore the effects of sample size on system performance, we performed an experiment to compare the performance of case-based dispatching/cross-case-base adaptation selection for different calibration set sizes. As the local case-base, we used a 1% version of the sparse Indiana case-base (IN*). Calibration sets of all sizes ranging from 1–30 cases were randomly selected from the IN case-base, resulting in calibration set sizes ranging from 0.2%–5% of the total problem set. Additional calibration sets were generated up to size 200, in steps of 10. Performance was tested on all remaining cases in the original IN case-base, by leave-one-out cross validation. Runs were performed 15 times, selecting random subsets of IN for calibration, and the results were averaged.

Figure 4 compares the performance achieved with these sample sets to the performance that would be achieved by case-based selection of dispatching and cross-case-base adaptation, if the entire problem set were available for calibration. The figure compares five scenarios: (1) standard CBR with no dispatching, (2) calibration used to guide MCBR (dispatching and cross-case-base adaptation), to draw on three external case-bases expected to have similar characteristics to the local case-base (IL, KY, and OH), (3) random choice of case-bases between the local case-base IN* and the IL, KY, and OH case-bases, with random choice of cross-case base adaptation strategies when external case-bases are used, (4) calibration used to guide MCBR (dispatching and cross-case-base adaptation) to draw on three external case-bases including two case-bases expected to have characteristics divergent from the local case-base (IL, FL, and NV), and (5) random choices, as in (3), with the external case-bases IL, FL, and NV.

For a single case in the calibration set, performance is noticeably below that with the local case-base alone. Surprisingly, calibration on only two cases was sufficient to surpass the local case base on average. As expected, there is an increasing performance trend as the size of the calibration set increases. With 30 cases in the calibration set, performance was 96% of the performance achieved by calibrating on the entire case base, with the improvement curve leveling out for larger calibration set sizes.

When the external case-bases are similar to the local case-base (for external case-bases IL, KY, OH), the average performance of the local case base alone (line 1) is similar to that achieved by random dispatching (line 3). However, when some of the external

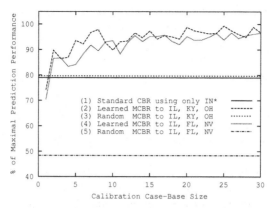

Fig. 4. The effects of calibration sample size on performance, with performance expressed as a percentage of the performance obtained when the entire case-base is used for calibration.

case-bases are quite different (IL, FL, NV), random dispatching results in poor performance (line 5). Either way, the learned strategies (lines 2 and 4) markedly outperform both the local case-base alone and random dispatching. These results are encouraging both for the value of learning MCBR strategies and for the ability to do so from limited sample sets.

6   Perspective

Relationship to distributed CBR: Previous research has proposed approaches in which multiple CBR agents share contents of their individual case-bases as needed [11,7,10] and have studied fundamental issues for efficient access of distributed case-bases [4], with the assumption that the case-bases are standardized. Recent research has also observed the benefits of strategically accessing case-bases with specialized coverage [8]. *Multi-case-base reasoning* differs in addressing questions of applying case-bases that may have been accumulated in other contexts, for somewhat different tasks, and consequently involve tradeoffs.

Most relevant to this paper is Ontañón and Plaza's [9] work on collaborative case-based reasoning. Their Bounded Counsel Policy uses a *termination check* to determine when a local agent's solution is unreliable, prompting consultation with other agents; they also develop methods for learning the termination check. Differences include that termination checks form judgments based on solutions, rather than problems, and that their focus is on deciding when no more solutions need be sought from external case-bases, rather than on learning which external case-bases are the best to consult.

Relationship to Case-Base Maintenance: The self-tuning approach to adjusting dispatching and cross-case-base adaptation can be seen as a form of *case-based reasoner maintenance* [12]. Case-based reasoner maintenance goes beyond maintaining the case-base, to automatically adjust other aspects of the CBR system. The calibration process proposed here for cross-case-base adaptation, for example, could be applied to select adaptation strategies in a single-case-base system. Although prior CBR systems have learned to refine certain characteristics (e.g., their indexing criteria), to our knowledge, our project is the first effort to develop CBR systems that can choose from a repertoire of processing strategies based on current circumstances. We consider work in this area to be a promising future direction for developing self-maintaining CBR systems that can dynamically adjust themselves to new circumstances.

Relationship to Distributed Databases and KDD: Research in IR, KDD, and distributed databases is pursuing a number of areas that may prove useful to MCBR. For example, the question of how large a sample to use to predict data streams, which may be important in selecting a test set for self-calibration, has been studied in [3]. In the IR community, strategies have been developed for estimating the contents of data sets with small samples of their data [1]. Analogous strategies may be useful for making more informed choices about which case-bases to access—by estimating their areas of competence—as well as for choosing test sets of cases for calibration.

An important issue beyond the scope of this paper is how to establish correspondences between case representations, if the representations used by different case-bases differ. Recent databases research on enabling automatic transformation of XML documents, and on learning to map between structured representations (e.g., [2]) promises to be useful for this task.

7   Conclusions

When external case-bases are available to supplement local case knowledge, they can provide a valuable additional resource, especially during the early stages of the growth of a case-base. However, unless the external case-base addresses precisely the same task, cases from external case-bases may not be immediately applicable, necessitating cross-case-base adaptation. Unfortunately, it may not be clear which external case-bases to draw on, which cross-case-base adaptation strategies to apply, or whether the results of applying those strategies will be adequate. The benefits of MCBR depend strongly on the specifics of the problem at hand and how increased case similarity balances against differences in the tasks and environments for which different case-bases were gathered. Unless it is possible to determine when and how to apply MCBR, there is no guarantee that MCBR will be advantageous.

This paper has presented methods that enable an MCBR system to learn when and how to draw on external case-bases, based on testing a small sample of domain problems. Given a set of possible strategies and a utility function to compare alternative solutions, these methods select the strategies that give the best performance. The calibration methods may be applied to any task for which the utility of solutions can be evaluated; the paper has presented experiments on applying self-calibration to choose between knowledge-light strategies for a numerical prediction task, showing that simple methods can be sufficient to achieve good performance. For our test examples, performance of learned strategies far exceeds the performance of local sparse case-bases alone, and performance with learned strategies is close to the performance achieved by the optimal external case-base and cross-case base adaptation strategies. This establishes the promise of the approach.

More broadly, an interesting area for future research is the application of analogous methods to enable traditional CBR systems to tune themselves by testing which strategies work best for samples of the problems that they encounter. Thus we believe that the current results are promising not only for self-tuning in multi-case-base reasoning, but as a step towards CBR systems that can adjust themselves to their tasks.

References

1. J. Callan. Query-based sampling of text databases. *ACM Transactions on Information Systems*, 19(2):97–130, 2001.
2. A. Doan, P. Domingos, and A. Halevy. Reconciling schemas of disparate data sources: A machine learning approach. In *Proceedings of the ACM SIGMOD Conf. on Management of Data (SIGMOD-2001)*, Menlo Park, 2001. ACM Press.
3. P. Domingos and G. Hulten. Mining high-speed data streams. In *Knowledge Discovery and Data Mining*, pages 71–80, 2000.
4. Conor Hayes, Pádraig Cunningham, and Michelle Doyle. Distributed CBR using XML. In *Proceedings of the KI-98 Workshop on Intelligent Systems and Electronic Commerce*, 1998.
5. D. Leake and R. Sooriamurthi. When two case bases are better than one: Exploiting multiple case bases. In *Proceedings of the Fourth International Conference on Case-Based Reasoning, ICCBR-01*, Berlin, 2001. Springer-Verlag.
6. D. Leake and R. Sooriamurthi. Managing multiple case-bases: Dimensions and issues. In *Proceedings of the Fifteenth FLAIRS Conference*, pages 106–110, Menlo Park, 2002. AAAI Press.
7. F. Martin, E. Plaza, and J.-L. Arcos. Knowledge and experience reuse through communications among competent (peer) agents. *International Journal of Software Engineering and Knowledge Engineering*, 9(3):319–341, 1999.
8. L. McGinty and B. Smyth. Collaborative case-based reasoning: Applications in personalised route planning. In *Proceedings of the Fourth International Conference on Case-Based Reasoning*, Berlin, 2001. Springer Verlag.
9. S. Ontañón and E. Plaza. Learning when to collaborate among learning agents. In *Machine Learning: ECML 2001*, pages 395–405, Berlin, 2001. Springer-Verlag.
10. E. Plaza and S. Ontañón. Ensemble case-based reasoning: Collaboration policies for multiagent cooperative CBR. In *Proceedings of the Fourth International Conference on Case-Based Reasoning, ICCBR-01*, Berlin, 2001. Springer-Verlag.
11. M. V. Nagendra Prasad, V. Lesser, and S. Lander. Reasoning and retrieval in distributed case bases. *Journal of Visual Communication and Image Representation*, 7(1):74–87, 1996.
12. D. Wilson and D. Leake. Maintaining case-based reasoners: Dimensions and directions. *Computational Intelligence*, 17(2):196–213, 2001.

Diversity-Conscious Retrieval

David McSherry

School of Information and Software Engineering, University
of Ulster, Coleraine BT52 1SA, Northern Ireland
dmg.mcsherry@ulst.ac.uk

Abstract. There is growing awareness of the need for recommender systems to offer a more diverse choice of alternatives than is possible by simply retrieving the cases that are most similar to a target query. Recent research has shown that major gains in recommendation diversity can often be achieved at the expense of relatively small reductions in similarity. However, there are many domains in which it may not be acceptable to sacrifice similarity in the interest of diversity. To address this problem, we examine the conditions in which similarity can be increased without loss of diversity and present a new approach to retrieval which is designed to deliver such *similarity-preserving* increases in diversity when possible. We also present a more widely applicable approach to increasing diversity in which the requirement that similarity is fully preserved is relaxed to allow some loss of similarity, provided it is strictly controlled.

1 Introduction

Recommender systems for helping customers to select a product or service (e.g. a car, restaurant, or personal computer) are increasingly common in electronic commerce [1-3]. A major advantage of case-based reasoning (CBR) as an approach to product recommendation is the ability to suggest alternatives that may be acceptable when there is no solution that exactly matches a user's query. However, there is growing awareness of the need for recommender systems to offer a more diverse choice of alternatives than is possible by simply retrieving the cases that are most similar to a target query [4-8]. The problem is that the cases that are most similar to the target query also tend to be very similar to each other, with the result that the user may be offered a very restricted choice. The need for a more *diversity-conscious* approach to retrieval is highlighted by the growing trend towards the use of Internet-enabled mobile phones, with screen sizes capable of displaying only a few recommendations [4,8].

Some authors have combined CBR with other recommendation techniques that are less susceptible to the so-called diversity problem [7]. More recent research has focused on approaches to increasing diversity that remain within the CBR paradigm. One such approach is Smyth and McClave's BG algorithm, which combines measures of similarity and diversity in the retrieval process to achieve a better balance between these often conflicting characteristics of the retrieved cases [8]. BG has been shown to provide major gains in diversity at the expense of relatively small reductions in similarity. However, there are many domains in which it may not be

S. Craw and A. Preece (Eds.): ECCBR 2002, LNAI 2416, pp. 219–233.

acceptable to increase diversity at the expense of similarity, for example when the recommended items (e.g. jobs, rental apartments, bargain holidays) are limited in number, available for a limited period, or sought in competition with other users. One need only consider the likely reaction of an apartment seeker to a system that replaces one of three apartments that exactly match her requirements by one that is less suitable. Thus it may often be necessary to insist that similarity is given priority to the extent that any increase in diversity must not be at the expense of similarity.

In recent work we have shown that it is sometimes possible to increase diversity without loss of similarity [5]. In this paper, we extend our analysis of the diversity problem to show that the ability to increase diversity without loss of similarity depends on the underlying similarity measure on which retrieval is based. We present a new approach to retrieval which is designed to deliver such *similarity-preserving* increases in diversity when possible. We also present a more widely applicable approach to increasing diversity in which the requirement that similarity is fully preserved is relaxed to allow some loss of similarity provided it is strictly controlled. Contributions of the research presented include two new algorithms for diversity-conscious retrieval called DCR-1 and DCR-2.

In Section 2, we examine measures of similarity and diversity and introduce the example case library that we use to illustrate our similarity-preserving approach to increasing diversity. Our new retrieval algorithms are presented in Sections 3 and 4. In Section 5, we present empirical evaluations of DCR-1 and DCR-2 in comparison with BG. Our conclusions are presented in Section 6.

2 Similarity and Diversity

The objective of diversity-conscious retrieval is to increase the diversity of the retrieved cases while minimising the impact on their similarity to the target query.

2.1 The Standard Retrieval Set

We refer to the set of cases that are retrieved and presented as alternatives to the user as the *retrieval set*. In a typical recommender system, the standard retrieval set (SRS) for a target query consists of the k cases that are most similar to the target query. An important parameter is k, the required size of the retrieval set. In practice, the value of k may be limited by the available screen size, chosen by system designers in accordance with HCI principles, or configurable by the user [8-11]. For example, the number of restaurants retrieved by Entree [10] is never more than ten.

2.2 Measures of Similarity and Diversity

Increasing diversity in the retrieval set for a target query often means decreasing the average similarity of the retrieved cases to the target query relative to the SRS. Average similarity of the cases in a given retrieval set $R = \{C_1, C_2, ..., C_k\}$ is defined below in terms of the target query Q and the underlying similarity metric Sim on which retrieval is based.

$$similarity(R) = \frac{\sum_{i=1}^{k} Sim(C_i, Q)}{k} \tag{1}$$

Often in practice, queries are *incomplete* in the sense that preferred values are specified for only some of the case attributes, thus reducing the number of attributes available for retrieval [12]. Given a query Q, we denote by A_Q the set of attributes for which preferred values are specified in Q. We refer to $|A_Q|$ as the *length* of the query. One of the similarity measures used in our experiments is the well-known *matching features* similarity measure:

$$Sim_{MF}(C, Q) = \frac{\left|\{a \in A_Q : \pi_a(C) = \pi_a(Q)\}\right|}{\left|A_Q\right|} \tag{2}$$

where for each $a \in A_Q$, $\pi_a(C)$ is the value of a for C and $\pi_a(Q)$ is the preferred value of a as specified in Q. This is a special case of the standard *weighted-sum* measure in which all attributes in the target query are equally weighted and the similarity score assigned to two values of the same attribute is 1 if they are equal and 0 otherwise.

The measure of diversity used in our retrieval algorithms is the measure proposed by Smyth and McClave [8]. Given a target query Q and retrieval set $R = \{C_1, C_2, ..., C_k\}$, the diversity of R is:

$$diversity(R) = \frac{\sum_{i=1}^{k-1} \sum_{j=i+1}^{k} (1 - Sim(C_i, C_j))}{k \frac{(k-1)}{2}} \tag{3}$$

An important point to note is that we measure similarity, and hence diversity, with respect to the attributes in the target query only.

2.3 Increasing Diversity

We refer to the process of constructing a retrieval set for a given query that is more diverse than the SRS for that query as *diversification*. The algorithm we use as a benchmark in our experiments is BG [8]. In BG, cases are sequentially selected for addition to a retrieval set initially containing only the most similar case until the retrieval set reaches the required size k. The case selected at each stage is the one that maximises the product of its similarity to the target case and its diversity *relative* to the cases that have been selected so far. Given a case C and non-empty set of cases $R = \{C_1, C_2, ..., C_n\}$, the diversity of C relative to R is:

$$relative\_diversity(C, R) = \frac{\sum_{i=1}^{n} (1 - Sim(C, C_i))}{n} \tag{4}$$

BG is *bounded* in the sense that candidates for addition to the retrieval set are restricted to the $2k$ cases that are most similar to the target query, where k is the required size of the retrieval set.

The effectiveness of a diversification technique can be measured in terms of the *relative benefit* it provides, defined as the average increase in diversity relative to the SRS divided by the average decrease in similarity. BG has been shown to give better relative benefits than an equivalent unbounded algorithm [8].

2.4 Example Case Library

The case library that we use to illustrate our similarity-preserving approach to increasing diversity is an artificial case library in the property domain containing 50 cases. Attributes in the case library are bedrooms (2, 3, 4 or 5), building style (det, sem or ter), reception rooms (1 or 2) and location (a, b, c or d). The similarity measure on which retrieval is based in our example is Sim_{MF}. Table 1 shows the ten most similar cases for the incomplete query: beds = 4, style = det, loc = a. The similarity of each case to the target query is also shown.

The 1's in the last three columns show the cases in the SRS for $k = 5$ and in retrieval sets of the same size constructed by BG and DCR-1, the diversity-conscious retrieval algorithm we present in Section 3.

Table 1. Ten most similar cases for the incomplete query: beds = 4, style = det, loc = a

Case No.	beds	style	rec	loc	Sim_{MF}	SRS	BG	DCR-1
29	4	det	2	a	1.00	1	1	1
5	4	det	2	a	1.00	1	0	1
48	2	det	2	a	0.67	1	1	1
40	3	det	2	a	0.67	1	1	0
38	3	det	1	a	0.67	1	0	0
31	4	sem	2	a	0.67	0	0	1
16	4	det	1	c	0.67	0	1	1
8	4	sem	2	a	0.67	0	0	0
50	4	sem	2	d	0.33	0	1	0
49	2	det	2	c	0.33	0	0	0
Similarity:						0.80	0.67	0.80
Diversity:						0.26	0.60	0.40

The similarity and diversity characteristics of the SRS and the retrieval sets constructed by BG and DCR-1 for the example query are shown in Table 1. For example, the average similarity of cases in the BG retrieval set is:

$$similarity(BG) = \frac{1.00 + 0.67 + 0.67 + 0.67 + 0.33}{5} = 0.67$$

The diversity of the BG retrieval set is:

$$diversity(BG) = \frac{(0.33 + 0.33 + 0.33 + 0.67) + (0.33 + 0.67 + 1) + (0.67 + 1) + 0.67}{5 \times \frac{(5-1)}{2}} = 0.60$$

While BG has increased diversity from 0.26 to 0.60, the trade-off for this increase in diversity is a 16% reduction in average similarity relative to the SRS. However, the increase in diversity (0.34) is much greater than the corresponding loss in similarity (0.13). This equates to a relative benefit of 2.6. The increase in diversity provided by DCR-1 (0.14) is much less than that provided by BG. On the other hand, there is *no* loss of similarity in DCR-1, which means that the relative benefit it provides is infinite (or immeasurable).

3 Similarity-Preserving Diversification

In Section 2 we have seen that diversity can sometimes be increased without loss of similarity, at least with Sim_{MF} as the underlying similarity measure. In this section, we present the algorithm for diversity-conscious retrieval (DCR-1) used to construct a retrieval set for the example query that was more diverse than the SRS but no less similar. In general, we refer to the process of constructing a retrieval set that is more diverse than the SRS for a given query but no less similar as *similarity-preserving* diversification.

3.1 Maximally-Similar Retrieval Sets

Obviously, no retrieval set (of the same size) can have greater average similarity to a given target query than the SRS for that query. However, it is possible for other retrieval sets to equal the SRS in average similarity to the target query. We say that a retrieval set of the same size as the SRS is *maximally* similar to a target query if it has the same average similarity to the target query as the SRS. Thus the objective in similarity-preserving diversification is to identify a maximally-similar retrieval set (if one exists) that is more diverse than the SRS. Adapted from [5], our approach to this problem is based on the concept of similarity *layers*.

3.2 Similarity Layers

A target query Q partitions the case library into subsets $L_1, L_2, ..., L_n$ such that, for $1 \leq i \leq n$ -1, all cases in L_i are equally similar to Q, and more similar to Q than any case in L_{i+1}. We refer to $L_1, L_2, ..., L_n$ as the similarity layers associated with Q. The *highest* similarity layer associated with a target query, L_1, is the set of cases that are equally most similar to the target query. The highest similarity layer for the example query in Table 1 contains 2 cases while the second highest layer contains 6 cases.

The three highest similarity layers for another target query are shown in Fig. 1. Cases in the SRS for $k = 5$ are shown as filled circles. In this example, the *lowest* similarity layer that contributes to the SRS is L_2. In general, it can be seen that the SRS must include all cases from any similarity layer that is higher than the lowest contributing similarity layer.

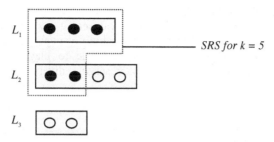

Fig. 1. Similarity layers for an example query

The importance of similarity layers in the context of similarity-preserving diversification can be seen from the following theorem.

Theorem 1. *A maximally-similar retrieval set for a given query can differ from the SRS only in the cases it includes from the lowest similarity layer that contributes to the SRS.*

Proof. Let R be a maximally-similar retrieval set of the required size k and let L_x be the lowest similarity layer that contributes to the SRS. It suffices to show that R, like the SRS, must include all cases from similarity layers (if any) that are higher than L_x and can include no cases from lower similarity layers.

If any case C_1 in a similarity layer that is higher than L_x is not in R, then R must include at least one case C_2 from L_x or from a similarity layer that is lower than L_x. So if C_2 is removed from R and replaced by C_1, this will increase the average similarity of R. But this contradicts our assumption that R is maximally similar. Similarly, if R includes any case C_3 from a similarity layer that is lower than L_x, then there must be a case C_4 in L_x, or in a higher similarity layer, that it does not include. So if C_3 is removed from R and replaced by C_4, this will increase the average similarity of R. Again this contradicts our assumption that R is maximally similar.

It follows from Theorem 1 that if all cases in the lowest similarity layer that contributes to the SRS are needed to fill the SRS, then no other retrieval set can be maximally similar to the target query. In this case, no increase in diversity is possible without loss of similarity.

3.3 Maximising Diversity

An algorithm that attempts to maximise diversity in a retrieval set, MaxD, is outlined in Fig. 2. In this algorithm, k is the required size of the retrieval set, and *Initial* is a non-empty set of cases that is to be extended to provide a retrieval set *RetrievalSet* of the required size. *Candidates* is a set of candidate cases for addition to the retrieval set.

If our aim were simply to construct a retrieval set of high diversity then we could apply MaxD with an initial retrieval set containing only the most similar case, and all other cases as candidates for addition to the retrieval set. Of course, we do not propose the use of MaxD in this way as a solution to the diversity problem. Though capable of constructing highly-diverse retrieval sets, MaxD ignores the similarity of the cases it selects for addition to a retrieval set, thus failing to address the *trade-off* between similarity and diversity. The retrieval sets it constructs (when used as described above) are therefore likely to have low average similarity to the target query. Nevertheless, MaxD has an important role to play as a supplementary algorithm in the algorithm for similarity-preserving diversification that we now present.

---

algorithm *MaxD(Initial, RetrievalSet, Candidates, k)*

begin
        RetrievalSet ← *Initial*
    while |*RetrievalSet*| < *k* **do**
    begin
      C_{best} ← *first(Candidates)*
      D_{max} ← *relative_diversity(C_{best}, RetrievalSet)*
      for all $C \in$ *Candidates* **do**
      if *relative_diversity(C, RetrievalSet)* > D_{max}
      then begin
        C_{best} ← *C*
        D_{max} ← *relative_diversity(C, RetrievalSet)*
      end
      RetrievalSet ← {C_{best}} ∪ *RetrievalSet*
      Candidates ← *Candidates* - {C_{best}}
    end
end

Fig. 2. Algorithm for maximising diversity

3.4 DCR-1

Our algorithm for similarity-preserving diversification is called DCR-1. Given a target query Q and the required size k of the retrieval set, it first constructs the SRS and identifies the lowest similarity layer L_x that contributes to the SRS. It then calls MaxD with an initial retrieval set and a set of candidate cases that depend on whether $C_{max} \in L_x$, where C_{max} is the case that is most similar to the target query (or one of the cases that are equally most similar). If $C_{max} \in L_x$, the initial retrieval set is {C_{max}} and the set of candidate cases is L_x - {C_{max}}. If $C_{max} \notin L_x$, the initial retrieval set consists of all cases (including C_{max}) in similarity layers above L_x and the set of candidate cases is L_x.

For the example query in Table 1, the lowest similarity layer that contributes to the SRS is the second similarity layer. The second similarity layer contains 6 cases but does not include the most similar case. The initial retrieval set for the example query thus consists of the two cases in the first similarity layer and candidates for addition to the retrieval set are the 6 cases in the second similarity layer.

3.5 Discussion

It can be seen from our theoretical analysis that DCR-1's ability to increase diversity without loss of similarity is likely to depend on the underlying similarity measure. With Sim_{MF} as the similarity measure on which retrieval is based, it is not unusual for two or more cases to be equally similar to a target query, one of the conditions necessary for it to be possible to increase diversity without loss of similarity. However, with a more *fine-grained* similarity measure, opportunities for similarity-preserving diversification are likely to occur less frequently. In this case, insisting that similarity is fully preserved may mean that no increase in diversity is possible.

It might be considered that a reasonable strategy would be to 'round off' the similarity values produced by a fine-grained similarity measure, thus creating larger groups of cases of equal similarity to the target query. However, a problem with rounding (see [11] for a more detailed discussion) is that cases with similarity values that differ quite a lot (e.g. 0.66, 0.74) are assigned the same value (0.7) while cases with similarity values that differ much less (e.g. 0.74, 0.76) are assigned different values.

In Section 4 we present a more widely-applicable approach to increasing diversity in which the requirement that similarity is fully preserved is relaxed to allow some loss of similarity provided it is strictly controlled.

4   Similarity-Protected Diversification

The second of our diversity-conscious retrieval algorithms, DCR-2, offers a compromise between the extremes of insisting that similarity is fully preserved and tolerating arbitrary losses in similarity (as in MaxD). An existing algorithm that offers such a compromise is BG [8]. However, DCR-2 adopts a more conservative approach which we refer to as *similarity-protected* diversification. Its objective is to construct a retrieval set that is more diverse than the SRS while ensuring that the loss of similarity is less than a predefined threshold. An important role in the approach is played by the concept of similarity intervals that we now introduce.

4.1   Similarity Intervals

We assume in this discussion that the similarity measure *Sim* on which retrieval is based is such that

$$0 \bullet Sim(C, Q) \bullet 1 \tag{5}$$

for any case C and target query Q. Given a positive integer r, a target query Q partitions the set of cases with non-zero similarity into "intervals" $I_1, I_2, ..., I_r$ of width $\alpha = \dfrac{1}{r}$. That is, for $1 \leq n \leq r$,

$$I_n = \{C : 1 - n\alpha < Sim(C, Q) \bullet 1 - (n-1)\alpha\} \tag{6}$$

The *leftmost* similarity interval, I_1, is the set of cases whose similarity to the target query is greater than $1-\alpha$.

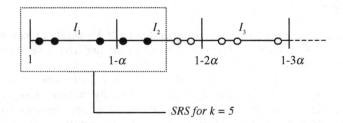

Fig. 3. The similarity intervals associated with a target query

Cases in the first three similarity intervals for a target query (or strictly speaking their similarity scores) are shown in Fig. 3. Cases in the SRS for $k = 5$ are shown as filled circles. In this example, the *rightmost* similarity interval that contributes to the SRS is I_2. In general, it can be seen that the SRS must include all cases from any similarity interval to the left of the rightmost contributing similarity interval.

We are now in a position to present the second of our diversity-conscious retrieval algorithms, DCR-2.

4.2 DCR-2

DCR-2 works in a similar way to DCR-1 except that retrieval is based on the similarity intervals, rather than similarity layers, associated with a target query. Given a target query Q, the required size k of the retrieval set, and the required width α of the similarity intervals, DCR-2 first constructs the SRS and identifies the rightmost similarity interval I_x that contributes to the SRS. It then calls MaxD with an initial retrieval set and a set of candidate cases that depend on whether $C_{max} \in I_x$, where C_{max} is the case that is most similar to the target query (or one of the cases that are equally most similar).

If $C_{max} \in I_x$, the initial retrieval set is $\{C_{max}\}$ and the set of candidate cases is $I_x - \{C_{max}\}$. If $C_{max} \notin I_x$, the initial retrieval set consists of all cases (including C_{max}) in similarity intervals to the left of I_x and the set of candidate cases is I_x. In either case, the DCR-2 retrieval set can differ from the SRS only in the cases it includes from I_x.

In the following theorem, we establish a strict upper bound for the loss of similarity in DCR-2.

Theorem 2. *In* DCR-2, *the loss of average similarity relative to the SRS is always less than* α, *the width of the similarity intervals on which retrieval is based.*

Proof. The DCR-2 retrieval set can differ from the SRS only in the cases it includes from I_x, the rightmost similarity interval that contributes to the SRS. Let S be the average similarity of the cases in the similarity intervals, if any, to the left of I_x. Let $s_1, s_2, ..., s_m$ be the similarities of the cases from I_x that contribute to the SRS, and let $s'_1, s'_2, ..., s'_m$ be the similarities of the cases from I_x that contribute to the DCR-2 retrieval set. If k is the required size of the retrieval set, then:

$$similarity(\text{SRS}) - similarity(\text{DCR-2}) = \frac{(k-m)S + \sum_{i=1}^{m} s_i}{k} - \frac{(k-m)S + \sum_{i=1}^{m} s'_i}{k}$$

$$= \frac{\sum_{i=1}^{m}(s_i - s'_i)}{k} < \frac{m\alpha}{k} \leq \alpha$$

In the following theorem, we show that for recommender systems in which retrieval is based on Sim_{MF}, DCR-2 can be seen as a generalisation of DCR-1.

Theorem 3. *In a recommender system with* Sim_{MF} *as the similarity measure,* DCR-1 *is equivalent to* DCR-2 *with* $\alpha = \frac{1}{r}$, *where r is the number of case attributes on which retrieval is based.*

Proof. It suffices to note that with the specified value of α, and Sim_{MF} as the underlying similarity measure, the similarity intervals on which retrieval is based in DCR-2 coincide with the similarity layers on which retrieval is based in DCR-1.

4.3 Discussion

We have described the strategy that DCR-2 uses to limit the impact of diversification on average similarity. It might be considered that an easier way to achieve this objective would be to insist on a minimum level of similarity to the target query among the retrieved cases; see [5] for an algorithm that uses this approach. However, one limitation of the approach is that depending on the required level of similarity, there may not be enough eligible cases to fill the retrieval set. Another potential problem is that if the number of candidate cases is large, constructing the retrieval set may require considerable computational effort. An important factor contributing to the efficiency of DCR-2 is the restriction of candidates for addition to the initial retrieval set to cases in a single similarity interval.

We have shown that the loss of similarity in DCR-2 is always less than α, the width of the similarity intervals on which retrieval is based. In practice, the loss of similarity is often much less than α. While the optimum value of α is likely to depend on the domain, we have obtained good results with $\alpha = 0.05$ as the width of the similarity intervals in our experiments.

5 Experimental Results

In this section we present empirical evaluations of DCR-1 and DCR-2 in comparison with BG, an existing retrieval algorithm that has been shown to provide major gains in diversity at the expense of relatively small reductions in similarity [8]. The 'Travel' case library used in our experiments is a standard benchmark (*www.ai-*

cbr.org) that contains over 1,000 holidays and their descriptions in terms of features such as holiday type, region, and method of transport. Our experiments are based on a *leave-one-out* approach in which each case is removed from the case library in turn and its description presented as a query to a recommender system running each of the retrieval algorithms to be compared. Of particular interest in the evaluation is the performance of DCR-1 and DCR-2 when the size of the retrieval set is necessarily restricted, for example by the available screen size in Internet-enabled mobile phones [4,8].

5.1 Similarity-Preserving Diversification

Our first experiment compares the performance of DCR-1 and BG when applied to the Travel case library with Sim_{MF} as the underlying similarity measure. To facilitate matching on the numeric attributes price and duration, the values of these attributes were divided into ranges that seemed most appropriate for the expression of user preferences. For each query (generated as described from the description of an actual case) and retrieval-set size k in the range from 2 to 10, we measure the similarity and diversity of the SRS and the retrieval sets constructed by BG and DCR-1. The results presented in Figs. 4 and 5 are averages over 1,024 queries.

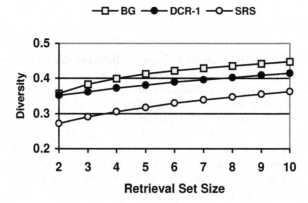

Fig. 4. Diversity gains provided by BG and DCR-1

Diversity Gains. DCR-1 can be seen from Fig. 4 to have provided good increases in diversity over the SRS throughout the range of retrieval-set sizes. With percentage increases ranging from 29% ($k = 2$) to 15% ($k = 10$), its performance is particularly good for small retrieval sets. Given its requirement that similarity must be fully preserved, it is not surprising that DCR-1 gives smaller increases in diversity than BG, though only by a very slight margin for the smallest retrieval-set size ($k = 2$).

Similarity Losses. Fig. 5 shows the similarity losses sustained by BG in order to increase diversity. It is interesting to note that the similarity losses roughly equate to the *additional* increases in diversity that BG provides in comparison with DCR-1.

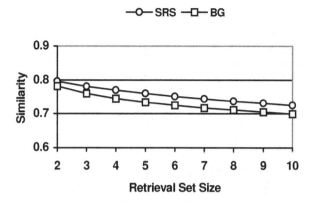

Fig. 5. Similarity losses sustained by BG

Relative Benefits. As there is no loss of similarity in DCR-1, its performance cannot be compared with that of BG in terms of relative benefits. However, it is interesting to note that the relative benefits provided by BG were never less than 3, with best results (6.1 and 4.4) for the smallest retrieval-set sizes $k = 2$ and $k = 3$.

5.2 Similarity-Protected Diversification

Our second experiment compares the performance of DCR-2 and BG when applied to the Travel case library with retrieval based on a *fine-grained* similarity measure. A local similarity measure is defined for each of the eight attributes in the case library and each attribute is assigned a different importance weight. DCR-2 is applied with $\alpha = 0.05$ as the width of the similarity intervals. Also included in the evaluation is a retrieval strategy in which cases in the retrieval set are *randomly* selected from those with non-zero similarity to the target query. Once again, the results presented are averages over 1,024 cases.

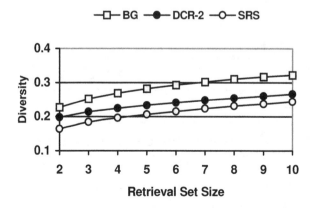

Fig. 6. Diversity gains provided by BG and DCR-2

Diversity Gains. For each retrieval-set size from $k = 2$ to $k = 10$, Fig. 6 shows the diversity of the SRS and the retrieval sets constructed by BG and DCR-2. Average diversity of the retrieval sets constructed by the random strategy (not shown in Fig. 6) was slightly higher than 0.5 for all retrieval-set sizes. Though providing smaller increases in diversity than BG for all retrieval-set sizes, DCR-2 gives good results for very small retrieval sets, with percentage increases of 21% for $k = 2$ and 16% for $k = 3$.

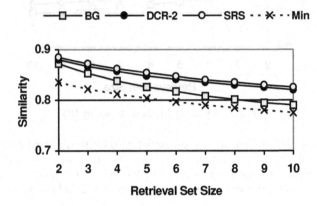

Fig. 7. Similarity losses sustained by BG and DCR-2

Similarity Losses. For each retrieval set-size from $k = 2$ to $k = 10$, Fig. 7 shows the average similarity of the SRS and the retrieval sets constructed by BG and DCR-2. Lower bounds for the average similarity of the DCR-2 retrieval sets, based on our theoretical analysis, are also shown (Min). It is interesting to note that the similarity losses actually sustained by DCR-2 are well within these limits, as indeed are those sustained by BG. However, the similarity losses for DCR-2 are, in general, much less than those for BG. The performance of the random strategy (not shown in Fig. 7) was predictably poor, with average similarity of less than 0.5 for all retrieval-set sizes.

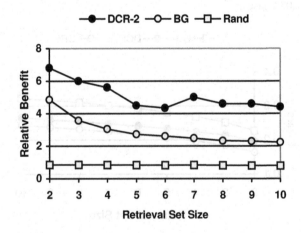

Fig. 8. Relative benefits provided by BG, DCR-2, and Rand

Relative Benefits. For each retrieval-set size k from 2 to 10, we measured the relative benefit, on average, provided by each retrieval strategy; that is, the increase in diversity relative to the SRS divided by the decrease in similarity. DCR-2 can be seen from Fig. 8 to have provided much better relative benefits than BG for all retrieval-set sizes. Both algorithms gave highest relative benefits for the smallest retrieval-set sizes $k = 2$, 3 and 4. However, it is noticeable that DCR-2 continues to provide high relative benefits as the size of the retrieval set increases, approximately doubling the relative benefits that BG provides for $k = 7$, 8, 9 and 10. None of the relative benefits provided by DCR-2 is less than four, which means that the average increase in diversity is never less than four times the average decrease in similarity. Relative benefits provided by the random strategy (Rand) are slightly less than one for all retrieval-set sizes, which means that increases in diversity are balanced by roughly equal decreases in similarity.

6 Conclusions

Increasing diversity at the expense of similarity may not always be acceptable, for example when the items recommended are available only for a limited period or sought in competition with other users. To address this problem, we have presented a new retrieval algorithm called DCR-1 that attempts to increase recommendation diversity while ensuring that similarity is fully preserved. In experiments with Sim_{MF} as the underlying similarity measure in the Travel domain, we have demonstrated DCR-1's ability to deliver *similarity-preserving* increases in diversity. Diversity gains for very small retrieval sets were only slightly less than those provided by BG, an existing algorithm that aims to optimise the trade-off between similarity and diversity but in which similarity is not fully preserved [8].

While the results for Sim_{MF} are very positive, our theoretical analysis shows that DCR-1's ability to increase diversity without loss of similarity depends on the underlying similarity measure. With the more fine-grained similarity measures that are common in practice, insisting that similarity is fully preserved may mean that no increase in diversity is possible. The second of our diversity-conscious algorithms, DCR-2, offers a compromise between the extremes of insisting that similarity is fully preserved and tolerating arbitrary losses in similarity. Experiments with a fine-grained similarity measure in the Travel domain demonstrate the effectiveness of DCR-2 as an algorithm for *similarity-protected* diversification. Though diversity increases provided by DCR-2 were considerably less than those provided by BG, they were gained at the expense of much smaller losses in similarity, with the result that DCR-2 provided much higher relative benefits.

In summary, the research presented in this paper extends our ability to increase recommendation diversity to domains in which similarity must be fully preserved, or in which loss of similarity must be strictly controlled.

References

1. Bergmann, R., Breen, S., Göker, M., Manago, M. Wess, S.: Developing Industrial Case-Based Reasoning Applications: The INRECA Methodology. Springer-Verlag, Berlin Heidelberg New York (1999)
2. Hammond, K.J., Burke, R. Schmitt, K.: A Case-Based Approach to Knowledge Navigation. In: Leake, D.B. (ed.): Case-Based Reasoning: Experiences, Lessons & Future Directions. AAAI Press/MIT Press, Menlo Park, CA (1996) 125-136
3. Wilke, W., Lenz, M., Wess, S.: Intelligent Sales Support with CBR. In: Lenz, M., Bartsch-Spörl, B., Burkhard, H.-D., Wess, S. (eds.): Case-Based Reasoning Technology,. Springer-Verlag, Berlin Heidelberg (1998) 91-113
4. Bradley, K., Smyth, B.: Improving Recommendation Diversity. Proceedings of the Twelfth Irish Conference on Artificial Intelligence and Cognitive Science, Maynooth, Ireland (2001) 85-94
5. McSherry, D.: Increasing Recommendation Diversity Without Loss of Similarity. Proceedings of the 6th UK Workshop on Case-Based Reasoning (2001) 23-31
6. Shimazu, H.: ExpertClerk: Navigating Shoppers' Buying Process with the Combination of Asking and Proposing. Proceedings of the Seventeenth International Joint Conference on Artificial Intelligence. International Joint Conferences on Artificial Intelligence (2001) 1443-1448
7. Smyth, B., Cotter, P.: A Personalised TV Listings Service for the Digital TV Age. Knowledge-Based Systems 13 (2000) 53-59
8. Smyth, B., McClave, P.: Similarity vs. Diversity. In: Aha, D.W., Watson, I. (eds.): Case-Based Reasoning Research and Development. LNAI, Vol. 2080. Springer-Verlag, Berlin Heidelberg (2001) 347-361
9. Branting, L.K.: Acquiring Customer Preferences from Return-Set Selections. In: Aha, D.W., Watson, I. (eds.): Case-Based Reasoning Research and Development. LNAI, Vol. 2080. Springer-Verlag, Berlin Heidelberg New York (2001) 59-73
10. Burke, R.: Ranking Algorithms for Costly Similarity Measures. In: Aha, D.W., Watson, I. (eds.): Case-Based Reasoning Research and Development. LNAI, Vol. 2080. Springer-Verlag, Berlin Heidelberg New York (2001) 105-117
11. Ferguson, A., Bridge, D.: Partial Orders and Indifference Relations: Being Purposefully Vague in Case-Based Retrieval. In: Blanzieri, E., Portinale, L. (eds.): Advances in Case-Based Reasoning. LNAI, Vol. 1898. Springer-Verlag, Berlin Heidelberg New York (2000) 74-85
12. McSherry, D.: The Inseparability Problem in Interactive Case-Based Reasoning. In: Bramer, M., Coenen F., Preece, A. (eds.): Research and Development in Intelligent Systems XVIII. Springer-Verlag, London (2001) 109-122

Improving Case Representation and Case Base Maintenance in Recommender Agents

Miquel Montaner, Beatriz López, and Josep Lluís de la Rosa

Institut d'Informàtica i Aplicacions
Universitat de Girona
Campus Montilivi
17071 Girona, Spain
{mmontane, blopez, peplluis}@eia.udg.es

Abstract. Recommendations by salespeople are always based on knowledge about the products and expertise about your tastes, preferences, interests and behavior in the shop. In an attempt to model the behavior of salespeople, AI research has been focussed on the so called recommender agents. Such agents draw on previous results from machine learning and other advances in AI technology to develop user models and to anticipate and predict user preferences. In this paper we introduce a new approach to recommendation, based on Case-Based Reasoning (CBR). CBR is a paradigm for learning and reasoning through experience, as salesmen do. We present a user model based on cases in which we try to capture both explicit interests (the user is asked for information) and implicit interests (captured from user interaction) of a user on a given item. Retrieval is based on a similarity function that is constantly tuned according to the user model. Moreover, in order to cope with the utility problem that current CBR system suffer from, our approach includes a forgetting mechanism (the drift attribute) that can be extended to other applications beyond e-commerce.

1 Introduction

In the real world, if you always go to the same grocery store to buy your food, then the salespeople there will get to know a great deal about you. Based on the products that you normally buy, they might recommend new items that they think might interest you. For instance, if you always buy a certain brand of milk, a salesperson might recommend, with a good chance of success, another similar product that has a discount that particular week. They will also notice the changing interests of the customers over time. If you do not buy a given product for a long time, salespeople gradually stop recommending similar products. They guess that you are not interested in them anymore. The recommendations of salespeople are always based on knowledge about the products as well as about your tastes, preferences, interests and behavior in the grocery store. In short, your activity in the grocery guides salespeople to improved sales.

S. Craw and A. Preece (Eds.): ECCBR 2002, LNAI 2416, pp. 234–248, 2002.

In an attempt to model the behavior of salespeople, AI research has been focussed on the so-called *recommender systems* [19]. The main task of a recommender system is to locate items, information sources and people related to the interest and preferences of a single person or a group of people [20]. This involves the construction of user models and the ability to anticipate and predict user preferences.

In addressing these types of tasks, recommender systems draw on previous results from machine learning and other AI technology advances. Among the various machine-learning technologies we concentrate on Case-Based Reasoning (CBR) as a paradigm for learning and reasoning through experience, as salespeople do. Previous recommender systems based on CBR include, for example, the Broadway approach [10,24], WebSell [6], Adaptive Place Advisor [9] and Entree [2].

Recently, a quite exhaustive experimentation on similarity metrics, performed with Entree, showed that the quality of recommendations increases if they are based on knowing the reasons behind user preferences rather than on simply having large amounts of information [2]. So, learning that user A does not like an item that was recommended because it was successfully recommended to a similar user B, and knowing the reasons for such a difference between these similar users, increases accuracy. The experiments performed with Entree lend support to the case representation approach presented in this paper, based on two main parts: objective attributes of items (the problem) and subjective attributes (the solution), in which we capture the user's explicit interests (the user is asked) as well as his/her implicit interests (the user interaction is recorded) for a given item. Moreover, in order to cope with the utility problem, our CBR approach includes a forgetting mechanism that can be extended to other applications beyond e-commerce. Our view is in line with current trends in recommender systems development and follows agent-based approaches, and so we speak about personal recommender agents. The agent acts as the grocery salespeople: proactively recommending new products to the user and giving prompted answers to queries from the user.

The outline of this paper is as follows: the next section introduces a new approach to applying CBR to the recommendation domain. The following sections define the case base structure and each CBR phase of this new approach. Finally, section 8 presents related work and section 9 concludes this article.

2   Overview of the CBR Approach to Recommendation

The core of CBR is a case base which includes all the previous experiences that can give us information about new problems. Then, through the similarity concept, the most similar experiences are retrieved. However, similarity is not a simple or uniform concept. Similarity is a subjective term that depends on what one's goals are. For instance, two products with the same price would get maximum similarity if the user was interested in products with that same price, but would get very different similarity for other concepts, such as quality or trademark.

In our approach, the case base consists of a set of previous items explicitly and/or implicitly assessed by the user. Assuming that the user's interest in a new item is similar to the user's interest in similar items, in order to evaluate whether a new item could interest the user, the agent searches the case base for similar items. If the interest the user showed in them is high enough, the new item is recommended to the user.

With regard to the CBR cycle:

1. In the retrieval phase, as from a new item, the system searches similar items in the case base in order to find out whether the user might be interested in it. Local similarity measures are based on item attributes, the relevance of which is computed in each retrieval time. Thus, the similarity metric is automatically maintained.
2. In the reuse phase, as from the retrieved set of similar items, the system calculates a confidence value of interest, to recommend the new item to the user, based on explicit and implicit interests and the validity of the case according to the current user's interests.
3. In the revision phase, as from the relevance feedback of the user, the system evaluates the user's interest in the new item. The idea is to track user interaction with the system to get to know relevant information about the user's interest in the recommended item, as well as explicit and implicit information, in order to retain the new case.
4. In the retain phase, the new item is inserted in the case base with the interest attributes that were added in the revision phase. In order to control the case base size, it is also important to know whether the user never gives new feedback about items in the case base. In such a case, it is necessary to forget these interests with time. We propose the use of a new attribute that we call the *drift attribute*, that will be aware of such changes in the user preferences and contribute to case maintenance.

The CBR cycle is applied both when the agent gives prompted recommendations in the course of answering the user's queries, as well as when the agent proactively recommends something to the user looking for new products. For example, the latter case happens periodically when the recommender agent contacts the restaurants server looking for new restaurants similar to the one that best fits the user preferences.

In the following sections the structure of the case base and the different CBR phases of the new approach are described.

3   The Case Base

A case-based reasoner is heavily dependent on the structure / representation and content of its collection of cases. Moreover, the size of the case base is also an open problem, since it affects the performance of the system. Below, we introduce

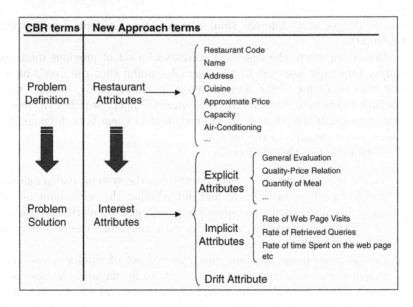

Fig. 1. An Example of Case Representation in the Restaurants Domain

the case base representation we use for recommendation and how we solve the
utility problem with a control attribute called the drift attribute.

3.1   The Case Base Representation

In our approach a case is split into two parts: the first, a set of attributes describing the item (the definition of the problem in CBR terminology) and the second,
a set of attributes describing the user's interest (the solution to the problem in
CBR terminology). We decided to make the agent handle items from just one
topic (e.g., restaurants). Extending the recommender system to other topics can
be carried out in a cooperative environment (see for example [18]). In order to
constrain the domain, we simplify the case base, since items from the same topic
have the same attributes. As shown in Figure 1 from the restaurants recommendation domain, the case representation consists of a set of **item attributes**
describing the restaurant (product description) and a set of **interest attributes**
describing the opinion of the user about the restaurant (product assessment).

Firstly, in order to create a set of attributes for an item, we must use whatever available information there is about the item's qualities. Item descriptions
in general do not tend to be very complex, consisting largely of descriptive adjectives, nouns or values. For example, when the CBR goal is to recommend
restaurants, the system can deal with features of capacity (e.g., "100 places" or
"150 places"), qualities of the cuisine (e.g., "traditional", "creative" or "bland")
or approximate price (e.g., "from $10 to $15" or "from $20 to $30").

Secondly, interest attributes keep all the information the agent gathers from
the user. These attributes depend on the technique used to obtain the relevant

feedback: explicit or implicit [17]. Explicit feedback relies on the fact that any information can be asked of the user explicitly, such as quality-price relation or quantity of food. On the other hand, implicit information can be captured from the interaction between the user and the system, for example, the consulted items, the time spent consulting items, the number of visits to the web page or the number of queries made where the restaurant was retrieved as an answer.

Explicit attributes are the most relevant and accurate, since the user states his opinion. However, it can be a great nuisance to the user and, therefore, it is not always possible to obtain [5]. Implicit attributes are a lot less accurate, but there is no annoyance to the user, since the system just tracks his or her behavior and learns about it. Thus, we deal with both kinds of feedback and we represent the case interests through both explicit and implicit attributes.

Finally, if a case represents the user interest on a given item, the complete case base constitutes the user profile representation which models the user. So, each recommender agent keeps a case base that is the representation of the user on whose behalf the agent is acting.

3.2 The Case Base Maintenance

The main idea of the CBR is to solve new problems by adapting the solutions given for old ones. It should be remarked that, presumably, with a larger set of cases the system gives better results as long as cases cover a wide range of problems. However, several authors claim that when the case base reaches a certain number of cases, the performance of the system remains the same and sometimes decreases [12].

Thus, one of the main drawbacks of the CBR is the utility problem: the uncontrolled growth of case bases may degrade system performance as a direct consequence of the increased cost in accessing memory.

Therefore, a need arises for a technique that controls the case base size by forgetting irrelevant cases. Some approaches handle this problem by storing new cases selectively (for example, only when the existing cases in memory lead to a classification error) and deleting cases occasionally [11]. Other approaches incorporate a restricted expressiveness policy into the indexing scheme by planning an upper bound on the size of a case that can be matched [8]. More recently, McKenna and Smyth [15] proposed a competence model for CBR that has been followed by other researchers defining different performance-based metrics (e.g., [13]). Most of the measures proposed are based on case base coverage.

In the context of recommender agents, however, maintenance is even harder since it is necessary to handle the change of the human interests over time. Mitchell et al proposed learning the description of the user's interests only from the latest observations, with a time window [16]. Maloof and Michalski suggested giving examples an age and deleting instances from the partial memory that are older than a certain age [14]. Billsus and Pazzani implemented a dual user model consisting of both a short-term and a long-term model of user's interests [1]. Finally, Webb and Kuzmycz introduced forgetting old interests with the gradual forgetting function [26]. The main idea behind this, is that natural forgetting is a gradual process.

Based on this last approach, we propose the **drift attribute** in order to adapt to the user interests over time and to solve the utility problem of the CBR systems. The drift attribute is one of the interest attributes (see Figure 1) and its function is to age the cases in the case base. There is one drift attribute per case and it is updated according to the user-system interaction.

The drift attribute works as follows:

- The drift attribute value is confined to the [0-1] interval.
- New items are inserted in the case base with the maximum drift value when the user shows some interest about them.
- The value of the drift attribute is decreased over time, emulating the gradual process of people losing interest in something. The decreasing function is a simple one where the drift attribute δ_q of a case q is decreased by multiplying the last drift value by a factor β of between 0 and 1 (see Equation 1).

$$\delta_q = \delta_q * \beta \tag{1}$$

The key issue then, is when to apply the decreasing function. We have to take into account that different users interact with the system more frequently than others. Therefore, the decreasing function should depend on the user interaction, rather than on a certain number of days or weeks. Our system decreases drift attributes each time a new item is incorporated into the case base.

- The value of the drift attribute is increased (rewarded) if the retrieved case results in a successful recommendation. The rewarding function is as simple as the decreasing one. The drift attribute δ_q of a case q is increased by dividing the last drift value by a factor λ of between 0 and 1 (see Equation 2).

$$\delta_q = \delta_q / \lambda \tag{2}$$

When a case reaches a drift value under a certain threshold (ξ), it is discarded. If the drift value is low enough, it does not make sense to retain the item in the case base. The confidence value for the interest that this item gives is insignificant and it is a useless case that only contributes to increasing the size of the case base and decreasing the performance of the system. Therefore, removing cases with a low drift value is the best solution for automatically controlling the size of the case base.

Initiating the case base adaptation needs a setup phase where the parameters are optimized to get the best performance out of the system. In other words, we will obtain different results by changing the rewarding function (λ), the decreasing function (β) and the threshold (ξ). Finding out the optimal values is an empirical task based on metrics to evaluate the system.

Finally, we want to point out that other authors have applied a gradual forgetting function to their systems in order to adapt the user profile to new interests [26,21]. However, they have a weight/age for all the items of a given topic and when some event affects one of the items in the topic this weight/age is modified in such a way as to affect all the items in that topic. We think that this reduces system performance, especially when the same topic includes a large set of items. Because if in the same interest topic there is one single item that the user is interested in, the topic never drifts, even if the user is not interested in all the other items in the set. Alternatively, in our approach we assign a weight to each item, thus, every case is treated individually, hence solving this problem.

3.3   The Initial Case Base Generation

It is desirable to find out as much as possible from the user so that recommender agents provide satisfactory results from the very beginning. In our approach, the training set [17] seems to be the best technique to generate the initial profile (case base), since the training set list of items given by the user with the appropriate attributes of interest can be the initial case base.

Analyzing the initial profile generation techniques stated in [17], we found different advantages and drawbacks. In manual generation, the user tailors his or her own profile, thus it is a really transparent method. But it bothers the user to have to do this and it is difficult for users to define their preferences explicitly. The empty approach needs potentially a long time to get to know the user's preferences, that is, the initial recommendations are low quality. But in this case, the user is not bothered. The usual approach is to interview the user with a quick manual questionnaire that won't annoy him or her too much, but people are reluctant to give personal data. Typically, the user does not fill in the questionnaire or provides false data. The training set approach depends totally on the profile learning technique (case retain in CBR), since the user just gives a list of items that he likes and/or dislikes, and the learning technique generates the profile. There is nothing to annoy the users and the users easily define their preferences.

4   The Retrieval Phase

In CBR terminology, the retrieval task starts with a new problem description and ends when best matching set of previous cases has been found. When we apply CBR to recommendation, this phase has the same purpose, but instead of retrieving similar problems, the system retrieves similar items. Thus, the retrieval task ends when the set of best matching previous items has been found (see Figure 2).

The most important step in the retrieval phase of CBR is to define the degree of similarity between cases. The success of CBR systems widely depends on the capacity of the system to exhibit how similar two cases are. With an efficient similarity measure, given a case, we can obtain an ordered list of similar cases. Taking advantage of this concept, when a user likes an item, his/her recommender agent can recommend to him/her a list of similar items that the user should like.

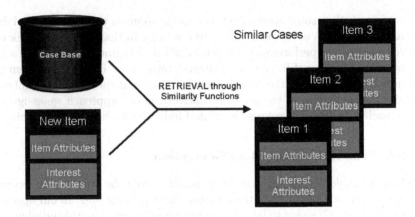

Fig. 2. Retrieve Phase

The degree of similarity between two items is computed by a global similarity function. Typically, the global similarity function is a weighted ponderation of the different attribute similarities based on the user model. For example, a particular user considers that two restaurants are similar if they have a similar price, but another user considers that they are similar if they have a similar cuisine. To get these attribute preferences you can ask the user explicitly when he /she asks the recommender agent for advice. However, such preferences are not available when a recommender agent proactively looks for new items. Therefore, we distinguish two roles of the agent that enforce two different similarity functions:

– Making prompted recommendations to the user when answering his/her queries. In our system the user can explicitly give his/her preferences on the attributes of the restaurant with a numerical value in [1-5] when he/she is looking for a new one. Then, we implement the global similarity function as a Weighted Average (WA) [23], since we can use a normalization in [0,1] of the preference values $pref_i$ given explicitly by the user as weights. In our model, we use the following function:

$$Sim(q,c) = \sum_{i=1}^{n} w_i * sim(q_i, c_i) \tag{3}$$

where:

- n is the number of item attributes of a case,
- q_i are the item attributes of case q,
- c_i are the item attributes of case c,
- $sim(q_i, c_i)$ are the different attribute similarities between q_i and c_i,
- and w_i are the weights of the ponderation, so that $w_i \in [0,1] \forall i$ and $\sum_i w_i = 1$.

In order to calculate the weights w_i based on the preference values $pref_i$, we use the following function:

$$w_i = \frac{pref_i}{\sum_{i=1}^{n} pref_i} \qquad (4)$$

- Making proactive recommendations to the user who is looking for new products. When acting proactively, the agent has no information about the preferences of the user on item attributes. Thus, we implement the global similarity function as an Ordered Weighted Average (OWA) [28], since we are dealing with different preferences of the user and such preferences can be ordered according to their importance. Then, the similarity between cases q and c is calculated as:

$$Sim(q, c) = \sum_{i=1}^{n} w_i * sim_{\sigma(i)}(q_i, c_i) \qquad (5)$$

where:

- n, q_i, c_i and w_i have been already explained in equation 3,
- $sim_{\sigma(i)}(q_i, c_i)$ are the different attribute similarities between q_i and c_i and
- $\sigma(i)$ is a permutation of the values $1, ..., n$ so that $sim_{\sigma(i-1)}(q_{i-1}, c_{i-1}) \geq sim_{\sigma(i)}(q_i, c_i) \; \forall i = 2, ..., n$.

Thus, the key of the global similarity function is to define the weights w_i. In our model, we use the following function:

$$w_i = \begin{cases} \frac{1}{n-i} & if \; i < \frac{n}{2} \\ \frac{1}{n} & if \; i = \frac{n}{2} \\ \frac{1}{n+2*(i-\frac{n}{2})} & if \; i > \frac{n}{2} \end{cases} \qquad (6)$$

Attribute similarities $sim(q_i, c_i)$ depend on the type of attribute. In our case base, we deal with both numerical and labelled attributes, thus, we consider the typical similarity metrics for both kind of attributes [27,7].

Once the similarities between the new case and the cases in the case base are calculated, a set of best matches is chosen. In our implementation, we select the n best cases provided which exceed a minimum selection threshold.

5   The Reuse Phase

The reuse phase consists of adapting the old solutions of the retrieved cases to the new problem based on the differences among them. Once the system has retrieved a set of previous items (the most similar ones), the system knows the user's interest in similar items through the interest attributes (solution in CBR terminology). Assuming that the user's interest in a new item is similar to the user's interest in similar items, in the reuse phase, the recommender agent calculates an interest confidence value for the new item. This value is used to decide whether to recommend the new item to the user.

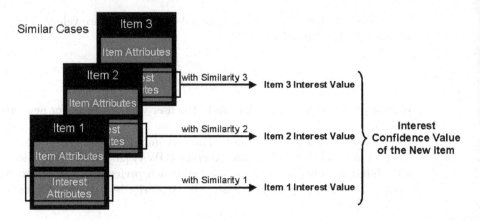

Fig. 3. Reuse Phase

The interest confidence value is a composite of the item interest value of the similar items selected in the retrieve phase (see Figure 3). We calculate it in a two-step process.

First, the item interest value V of each case is computed based on its interest attributes (see Equation 7). Given the following case representation:

Case/ Item	Problem/ Item Attributes	Solution / Interest Attributes		
		Explicit	Implicit	Drift Attribute
p	$p_1, p_2, ..., p_n$	$p_1^e, p_2^e, ..., p_{n_e}^e$	$p_1^i, p_2^i, ..., p_{n_i}^i$	δ_p
q	$q_1, q_2, ..., q_n$	$q_1^e, q_2^e, ..., q_{q_e}^e$	$q_1^i, q_2^i, ..., q_{n_i}^i$	δ_q

where p and q are items, $p_1, p_2, ..., p_n$ and $q_1, q_2, ..., q_n$ are the item attributes, $p_1^e, p_2^e, ..., p_{n_e}^e$ and $q_1^e, q_2^e, ..., q_{n_e}^e$ are explicit attributes, $p_1^i, p_2^i, ..., p_{n_i}^i$ and $q_1^i, q_2^i, ..., q_{n_i}^i$ are implicit attributes and da_p and da_q are drift attributes; the item interest value of the item p is calculated as follows:

$$V_p = \delta_p * g(f^e(p_1^e, ..., p_{n_e}^e), f^i(p_1^i, ..., p_{n_i}^i)) \tag{7}$$

where f^e is the function that combines the explicit interest, f^i is the function that combines the implicit attributes, g is the function that combines the results of f^e and f^i, and finally δ_p is the drift attribute (the temporal parameter related to the relevance of the product explained above). Aggregation techniques like [23] can be used for implementing f^e and f^i. We use the OWA operator for both f^e and f^i (see equation 5), applying the same procedure to obtain the weights that we showed in equation 6.

Finally, function g is a weighted arithmetic average (WA):

$$g(e, i) = \alpha_e * e + \alpha_i * i \tag{8}$$

The explicit attributes are the most relevant, since the user stated his/her opinion. Therefore, g gives more importance to explicit attributes (objective ones) than to the implicit ones (subjective). For instance, we use $\alpha_e = 0.7$ and $\alpha_i = 0.3$.

Second, the interest confidence value I of a new item r is a weighted ponderation function of the item interest value of each similar item:

$$I_r = \frac{\sum_{i=1}^{x}(Sim(r,i) * V_i)}{\sum_{i=1}^{x} Sim(r,i)} \tag{9}$$

where x is the number of similar items, Sim_i is the similarity between the item r and the item i (computed in the retrieve phase) and V_i is the item interest value of the item i. In this way, the most similar items are the most relevant in the final result.

Finally, if the interest confidence value of the new item is greater than a certain value (a confidence threshold), the item is recommended to the user. Otherwise, in the prompted role, the agent provides negative advice to the user regarding the queried item, while on the proactive role, the agent ignores it, the CBR cycle finalizes and there is no recommendation to the user. The item is not interesting enough to the user and the agent should not bother him/her with it.

6   The Revision Phase

Typically, the revision phase consists of evaluating the case solution generated by the reuse phase and learning about it. If the result is successful, then the system learns from the success (case retainment), otherwise it is necessary to repair the case solution using domain-specific knowledge. With regard to our approach, in the revision phase, as in the case of the relevance feedback of the user, the system is able to evaluate the user's interest in the recommended item. The idea is to track the user interaction by filling in the interest attributes of the item (case).

As shown in Figure 1, the interest attributes are distributed in two main groups: implicit and explicit attributes. Obviously, implicit attributes come from implicit feedback from the user, and explicit attributes come from explicit feedback. The idea is to find out the user's interest based on a hybrid relevance feedback system [17]. The user is explicitly asked about the new item, but, taking into account that users are very reluctant to give explicit feedback [5], the system tracks the user interaction with the system and tries to include additional information.

In CBR systems the solution is successful or wrong. When the solution is successful, the system retains the case inserting it into the case base. But when the solution fails, the system is interested in retaining the reason for the failure as well as the good solution, thus, there is an investigation task to find out additional information about the case. In the recommendation field, the user's interest can also be positive or negative, but, oppositely to the previous situation, the system is interested in retaining both positive and negative feedback. It is equally important to keep positive and negative information about the interests of the user, since it is useful to know what the user really "loves" and what the user really "hates". Thus, in this approach, in contrast to what usually happens in CBR systems, there is no investigation task to find out why the user is not interested in the new item, we simply retain the item as not interesting to the user. Therefore, in avoiding the investigation task, typically accomplished by a human expert, we get a completely automatic system.

7   The Retain Phase

In our approach, the new item is inserted into the case base with the interest attributes that were added in the revision phase. But, if the user did not give either explicit or implicit feedback, the item has no interest attributes and the case is not introduced into the case base. Only items with positive or negative interest are retained.

Moreover, when the user gives explicit or implicit feedback about an existing item in the case base, the case is updated. For example, if the user consults the web page of an item, the interest attribute representing the number of visits to the web page, and the attribute representing the time spent looking at the web page, are increased.

In order to control the case base size, it is also important to know whether the user ever gives new feedback about items in the case base. If not, it is necessary to forget these interests with time. This problem is solved with the drift attribute explained in section 3.2.

8   Related Work

A few research groups are investigating the application of CBR concepts and techniques to recommendation. Cunningham et al apply retrieval and adaptation techniques from CBR to intelligent product recommendation agents, particularly to their WebSell system [6]. As in our approach, the core of such application is a product database that describes the specific features of each available product. As a user profile, Websell keeps two selection lists of products which are used for collaborative recommendation service. These selection lists contain both interesting and not interesting products that, as in our approach, are used as a case base to pro-actively recommend new products to the user. Besides the lists, user profiles store more information (e.g., personal information, domain preferences), which can be compared to our approach (explicit information). The main difference is that we explicitly keep a set of interest attributes as a solution for each case, instead of general domain preferences deduced from the lists as WebSell does.

All "FindMe" systems [4] implement a similar CBR. They contain a database from which they retrieve items that meet certain constraints, and they rank the retrieved results by some criteria. For instance, the restaurant recommender Entree [3] makes its recommendations by finding restaurants in a new city similar to restaurants the user knows and likes. The main difference with our system is that Burke et al do not use an interest extensive representation of items in the case base as we do.

The Broadway approach [10,24] also combines explicit and implicit information on cases by means of the use of a behavior summary of the user interaction. Similarly, we keep a detailed information of the user interests and, then, in the reuse phase, we aggregate such information. Moreover, they use interests in retrieval and adaptation while we are only using interests attributes in adaptation.

Adaptive Place Advisor [9] introduces an innovative approach to the retrieval phase based on diversity, which controls the repetition of the same recommendation to a user. Thus, they avoid recommending the same restaurant in a short period of time to the user. In our view, this approach, although innovative, could lead to somewhat suspicious behavior of a system which, with the same inputs, gives different outputs in successive moments, one of which must be untruthful or untrustworthy.

Another important difference between these systems and ours is that they do not handle the change of the user interests over time and, therefore, they do not take into account the maintenance of the case base . Other approaches, outside recommender systems, such as [13,15] deal seriously with the problem of case maintenance since it is the principal drawback of CBR. However, we think that the metrics proposed are far from being useful in open domains as recommender agents. The alternative we propose is the drift attribute, which tackles the problem of maintenance in a way which is as natural as forgetting is for humans. Using the drift attribute is a new idea that we have introduced into the CBR, as applied to recommendation, thus, there is no previous work on this concept. However, this idea is based on the gradual forgetting function that some researchers have applied to other CBR systems. This concept was introduced by [26] and later applied in systems such as SiteIF [22] or LaboUr [21].

9   Conclusions

We have presented a new approach to recommendation based on CBR. The first contribution of this approach concerns case representation. Each case of the case base consists of a first set of attributes describing the item (as a problem definition) and a second set of attributes describing the user's interest (as a solution to a problem). Assuming that the user has a similar opinion about similar items, we can use the interest attributes of old cases to guess whether a new item will be of interest to the user.

The second contribution concerns the similarity metric. The relevance of attributes is computed every retrieval time and is based on information stored in cases. Such an approach reduces the need for maintenance of similarity metrics as well as the fact that no additional learning method is required to acquire the relevance.

Another contribution of this approach is the drift attribute. The drift attribute represents the age of the case in the case base and lets the personal agent distinguish between current and old interests. Consequently, the newest cases will be more confidently recommended than the oldest ones. However, the most important advantage of applying the drift attribute is that the utility problem is mitigated. Drift cases are deleted and the number of cases in the case base becomes stable while the performance of the system is maintained.

We have provided a detailed design of our system. Currently we have a prototype with some of the features implemented. Obviously we need to perform evaluations of the system. We plan to do this in the restaurants domain, based on our previous work [25].

Acknowledgments

This research has been developed within the DAF-DAF Project supported by the CICYT grant DPI2001-2094-C03-01.

References

1. D. Billsus and M. J. Pazzani. A hybrid user model for news classification. In *Kay J. (ed.), UM99 User Modeling - Proceedings of the Seventh International Conference*, pages 99–108. Wien, New York: Springer-Verlag, 1999.
2. R. Burke. A case-based reasoning approach to collaborative filtering. In *E. Blanzieri and L. Portinale (eds.), Advances in Case-Based Reasoning (5th European Workshop, EWCBR 2000)*, pages 370–379. Springer Verlag, New York, 2000.
3. R. Burke. Semantic ratings and heuristic similarity for collaborative filtering. In *AAAI Workshop on Knowledge-based Electronic Markets 2000 (KBEM'00)*. Austin, TX, 2000.
4. R. Burke, K. Hammond, and B. Young. The findme approach to assisted browsing. In *IEEE Expert*, volume 12(4), pages 32–40, 1997.
5. J. Carroll and M. B. Rosson. The paradox of the active user. In *Interfacing Thought: Cognitive Aspects of Human-Computer Interaction*, pages 26–28. J. M. Carroll (Ed.), Cambridge, MA: MIT Press, 1987.
6. P. Cunningham, R. Bergmann, S. Schmitt, R. Traphoner, S. Breen, and B. Smyth. Websell: Intelligent sales assistants for the world wide web. In *e-Business and e-Work 2001 (e-2001)*, 2001.
7. G. Falkman. Similarity measures for structured representations: A definitional approach. In *Blanzieri, E. and Portinale, L., eds., Advances in Case-Based Reasoning. Proceedings of the 5th European Workshop, EWCBR 2000, Trento, Italy*, volume 1898, pages 380–392. Springer-Verlag, Berlin, 2000.
8. A. G. Francis and A. Ram. The utility problem in case-based reasoning. In *CaseBased Reasoning: Papers from the 1993 Workshop. AAAI Press (WS-93-01). Washington*, 1993.
9. M. H. Goker and C. A. Thompson. The adaptive place advisor: A conversational recommendation system. In *Proceedings of the 8th German Workshop on Case Based Reasoning, Lammerbuckel, Germany.*, 2000.
10. M. Jaczynski and B. Trousse. Www assisted browsing by reusing past navigations of a group of users. In *Advanced in Case-based Reaosning, 4th European Workshop on Case-Based Reasoning*, volume 1488, pages 160–171. Lecture Notes in Artificial Intelligence, 1998.

11. D. Kibler and D. W. Aha. Case-based classification. In *Proceedings of the Case-Based Reasoning Workshop at AAAI'88*, pages 62–67, 1988.

12. D. B. Leake and D. C. Wilson. Categorizing case-base maintenance: Dimensions and directions. In *Advances in Case-Based Reasoning: 4th European Workshop, EWCBR-98, Dublin (Ireland)*, 1998.

13. D. B. Leake and D. C. Wilson. Guiding case-base maintenance: Competence and performance. In *Proceedings of the 14th European Conference on Artificial Intelligence Workshop on Flexible Strategies for Maintaining Knowledge Containers*, 2000.

14. M. A. Maloof and R. S. Michalski. Selecting examples for partial memory learning. In *Machine Learning*, volume 41, pages 27–52, 2000.

15. E. McKenna and B. Smyth. A competence model for case-based reasoning. In *9th Irish Conference on Artificial Intelligence and Cognitive Science. Dublin, Ireland*, 1998.

16. T. Mitchell, R. Caruana, D. Freitag, J. McDermott, and D. Zabowski. Experience with a learning personal assistant. In *Communications of the ACM*, volume 37:7, pages 81–91, 1994.

17. M. Montaner. A taxonomy of personalized agents on the internet. In *Technical Report, TR-2001-05-1, Departament d'Electrònica, Informàtica i Automàtica. Universitat de Girona*, 2001.

18. S. Ontañon and E. Plaza. Collaboration policies for case-based reasoning agents. In *Proc. Workshop on Learning Agents Autonomous (Agents'2001). Montreal*, 2001.

19. P. Resnick and H. Varian. Recommender systems. In *Communications of the ACM*, pages 56–58, 1997.

20. R. Sanguesa, U. Cortés, and B. Faltings. W9. workshop on recommender systems. In *Autonomous Agents, 2000. Barcelona, Spain*, 2000.

21. I. Schwab, A. Kobsa, and I. Koychev. Learning user's interests through positive examples using content analysis and collaborative filtering, 2001. Submitted.

22. A. Stefani and C. Strappavara. Personalizing access to web sites: The siteif project. In *Proc. 2nd Workshop on Adaptive Hypertext and Hypermedia HYPERTEXT'98*, 1998.

23. V. Torra. On the integration of numerical information: from the arithmetic mean to fuzzy integrals. In *Torra V. (Ed). Information fusion in data mining. Physiin-Verlag. (Forthcoming)*, 2001.

24. B. Trousse, M. Jaczynski, and R. Kanawati. Using user behavior similarity for recommendation computation: The broadway approach. In *Proceedings of the 8th international conference on human computer interaction (HCI'99), Munich*, 1999.

25. R. Vilà and M. Montaner. Implementació d'un sistema multiagent distribuit format per agents personals que recomanen restaurants aplicant raonament basat en casos i tècniques de trust, May, 2002. Projecte Fi de Carrera en Enginyeria Informàtica, Universitat de Girona.

26. G. Webb and M. Kuzmycz. Feature based modelling: A methodology for producing coherent, consistent, dynamically changing models of agents' competencies. In *User Modelling and User-Adapted Interaction*, volume 5, pages 117–150, 1996.

27. D. R. Wilson and T. R. Martinez. Improved heterogeneous distance functions. In *Journal of Articial Intelligence Research*, volume 6:1, pages 1–34, 1997.

28. R. R. Yager. On ordered weighted averaging aggregation operators in multi-criteria decision making. In *IEEE Transactions on SMC*, volume 18, pages 183–190, 1988.

Similarity Assessment for Generalizied Cases by Optimization Methods

Babak Mougouie[1] and Ralph Bergmann[2]

[1] Max-Planck Institut für Informatik, Saarbrücken, Germany
mbabak@mpi-sb.mpg.de
[2] University of Hildesheim, Data- and Knowledge Management Group
PO-Box 101363, D-31113 Hildesheim, Germany
bergmann@dwm.uni-hildesheim.de

Abstract. Generalized cases are cases that cover a subspace rather than a point in the problem-solution space. Generalized cases can be represented by a set of constraints over the case attributes. For such representations, the similarity assessment between a point query and generalized cases is a difficult problem that is addressed in this paper. The task is to find the distance (or the related similarity) between the point query and the closest point of the area covered by the generalized cases, with respect to some given similarity measure. We formulate this problem as a mathematical optimization problem and we propose a new cutting plane method which enables us to rank generalized cases according to their distance to the query.

1 Introduction

The traditional concept of a cases is that of a point in the problem-solution space, i. e., a problem-solution pair that assigns a single solution to a single problem. During case-based problem solving, cases are retrieved from a case base using a similarity function, which compares the case description with the current query. Driven by examination of several new applications, we proposed the concept of *generalized cases* [6,5,4]. A generalized case covers not only a point of the problem-solution space but a whole subspace of it. A single generalized case immediately provides solutions to a set of closely related problems rather than to a single problem only. The solutions that a generalized case represents are very close to each other; basically they should be considered as (slight) variations of the same principle solution. In general, a single generalized case can be viewed as an implicit representation of a (possibly infinite) set of traditional "point cases".

1.1 Motivation for Generalized Cases

Generalized cases naturally occur in certain CBR applications, such as for the recommendation of parameterized products within electronic commerce or brokerage services. The selection of reusable Intellectual Properties (IPs) of electronic designs is a very concrete example application. Such an IP is a design

S. Craw and A. Preece (Eds.): ECCBR 2002, LNAI 2416, pp. 249–263, 2002.
© Springer-Verlag Berlin Heidelberg 2002

object whose major value comes from the skill of its producer [13], and a re-design of it would consume significant time. IPs usually span a design space because they are descriptions of flexible designs that have to be synthesized to hardware before they actually can be used. More details of this application area for generalized cases is given in section 2.

We also want to make clear, that the idea of generalizing cases is not a radically new concept. It was already implicitly present since the very beginning of CBR and instance-based learning research [12,2,18]. For the purpose of adaptation, recent CBR systems in the area of design and planning [11,17,7] use complex case representations that realize generalized cases. However, in this paper we explore general and more formal view on the concept of generalized cases, which also partially covers the above mentioned related work.

In general, we expect several significant advantages of representing experience in the form of generalized cases [6], which can be summarized as follows:

- experience that naturally covers some space rather than a point can be represented more adequately,
- generalized cases can be integrated with traditional point-cases in a single case base,
- several (possibly an infinite number of) point-cases can be substituted by a single generalized case which helps to reduce the size of the case base,
- case-specific adaptation knowledge can be represented, rather that general case-independent adaptation knowledge.

1.2   The Research Problem: Similarity Assessment and Retrieval

However, the important basic research issues involved when applying generalized cases is related to the representation of generalized cases, the similarity assessment and the retrieval of generalized cases. One serious complication when studying these issues is that they are strongly connected with each other. Depending on the expressiveness of the representation used for generalized cases, the similarity assessment is getting computationally more difficult, which also impacts the overall computational effort for the retrieval from a large case base.

In this paper we address the problem of similarity computation for generalized cases defined over an n-dimensional Real valued vector space through sets of constraints. This extends our previous work that was restricted to linear constraints [5] In particular, we propose two methods for similarity assessment based on numeric optimization methods.[1] We distinguish between convex and non-convex representations of the constraints that define the generalized cases. We first propose the Topkis-Veinott method, which is a feasible direction method, to solve similarity computation problem for convex constraints. However, if the generalized cases includes also non-convex constraints, this method can still be used on a relaxation of the similarity problem to compute an upper

---

[1] We must assume some basic familiarization of the reader with optimizations methods to allow a complete understanding of the methods proposed here. For a comprehensive textbook on optimization see [3].

bound on the similarity. Second, we provide a cutting plane algorithm to compute *approximations* for the similarity of a generalized case. Instead of finding the exact similarity value, the algorithm allows to incrementally find increasing lower and decreasing upper bounds for the similarity of generalized cases. This algorithm works for non-convex and convex constraints. However, its performance decreases for non-convex constraints due to the inherent complexity of the problem of solving a feasibility problem. This algorithm is the foundation for developing retrieval algorithms for ranking generalized cases w.r.t. their similarity to the query similar to the fish and shrink algorithm proposed in [19] or similar to the pivoting-based retrieval [16].

2   Representing Electronic Design IPs as Generalized Cases

Increasingly, electronics companies use IPs ("Intellectual Properties") from third parties inside their complex electronic systems. An IP is a design object whose major value comes from the skill of its producer [13], and a redesign of it would consume significant time. However, a designer who wants to reuse designs from the past must have a lot of experience and knowledge about existing designs, in order to be able to find candidates that are suitable for reuse in his/her specific new situation. Currently, searching electronic IP databases can be an extremely time consuming task because, first, the public-domain documentation of IPs is very restricted and second there are currently no intelligent tools to support the designer in deciding whether a given IP from a database meets (or at least comes close to) the specification of his new application. This is one objective of the current project *IPQ: IP Qualification for Efficient Design Reuse* [2] funded by the German Ministry of Education and Research (BMBF) and the related European Medea project *ToolIP: Tools and Methods for IP* [3].

IPs usually span a design space because they are descriptions of flexible designs that have to be synthesized to hardware before they actually can be used. The behavior of the final hardware depends on a number of *parameters* of the original design description. The valid value combinations for these parameters are constrained by different criteria for each IP.

We developed a representative IP to study issues of representation, retrieval, and parameterization. This IP implements an algorithm for the *discrete cosine transform (DCT)* and its inverse operation *(IDCT)* which is needed as an important part of decoders and encoders of the widely known MPEG-2 video compression algorithm. While the complete electronics design in the VHDL language is described in [21], we now focus only on the variable parameters of the IP, which are shown in Table 1.

---

[2] IPQ Project (12/2000 - 11/2003). Partners: AMD, Fraunhofer Institute for Integrated Circuits, FZI Karlsruhe, Infineon Technologies, Siemens, Sciworx, Empolis, Thomson Multi Media, TU Chemnitz, University of Hildesheim, University of Kaiserslautern, and University of Paderborn. See www.ip-qualifikation.de

[3] See toolip.fzi.de for partners and further information.

Table 1. Selected parameters of the example IP.

parameter	description
frequency f	The clock frequency that can be applied to the IP.
area a	The chip area the synthesized IP will fit on.
width w	Number of bits per input/output word. Determines the accuracy of the DCT. Allowed values are 6, 7, ..., 16.
subword s	Number of bits calculated per clock tick. Changing this design space parameter may have a positive influence on one quality of the design while having a negative impact on another. Allowed values are 1, 2, 4, 8, and no_pipe.

$$f \leq \begin{cases} -0.66w + 115 & \text{if } s = 1 \\ -1.94w + 118 & \text{if } s = 2 \\ -1.74w + 88 & \text{if } s = 4 \\ -0.96w + 54 & \text{if } s = 8 \\ -2.76w + 57 & \text{if } s = \text{no} \end{cases}$$

$$a \geq \begin{cases} 1081w^2 + 2885w + 10064 & \text{if } s = 1 \\ 692w^2 + 2436w + 4367 & \text{if } s = 2 \\ 532w^2 + 1676w + 2794 & \text{if } s = 4 \\ 416w^2 + 1594w + 2413 & \text{if } s = 8 \\ 194w^2 + 2076w + 278 & \text{if } s = \text{no} \end{cases}$$

Fig. 1. Dependencies between the parameters of an example IP

These parameters heavily depend on each other: increasing the accuracy w of the DCT/IDCT increases the chip area consumption a and decreases the maximum clock frequency f in a particular way, shown in Fig. 1. These relationships define a very specific design space that is spanned by the four mentioned parameters. The knowledge about this design space is very central for the selection of the IP during the process of design reuse. When case-based reasoning is applied for IP reuse, the question must be solved how to represent and how to reason with cases that encode design spaces rather than design points.

3   Representing, Similarity Assessment, and Retrieval

To lay the foundation for the remainder of the paper, we now briefly review the basic formal concept of generalized cases and the related similarity assessment described in detail in [5].

Let S be the (possibly infinite) representation space for cases. In the IP application this representation space would include the parameters f, a, w, and s. One could assume that this representation space is subdivided into a problem space and a solution space, but we drop this assumption here since it is less appropriate in design domains. A traditional case c or *point case* is a point in the representation space $\mathcal{S}$, i. e., $c \in \mathcal{S}$. A *generalized case*, can now be extensionally defined as follows:

Definition 1. (Generalized Case) A *generalized case gc* is a subset of the representation space, i. e., $gc \subseteq \mathcal{S}$.

Hence, a generalized case stands for a set of point cases. However, a generalized case should not represent an arbitrary set. The idea is that a generalized case is an abbreviation for a set of closely related point cases that naturally occur as one entity in the real world (e. g. a single IP).

For retrieving generalized cases, the similarity between a query and a generalized case must be determined. As in traditional CBR, we assume that the query is a point in the representation space that may be only partially described. We further assume that a traditional similarity measure $sim(q, c)$ is given which assesses the similarity between a query q and a point case c. Such a similarity measure can be extended in a canonical way to assess the similarity $sim^*(q, gc)$ between a query q and a generalized case gc:

Definition 2. (Canonical Extension of Similarity Measures for Generalized Cases) The similarity measure $sim^*(q, gc) := sup\{sim(q, c) \mid c \in gc\}$ is called the canonical extension of the similarity measure sim to generalized cases.

Applying sim^* ensures that those generalized cases are retrieved that contain the point cases which are most similar to the query. This property is captured in the following lemma.

Lemma 1. Given a case base CB of point cases and a similarity measure sim, then for any case base CB^* of generalized cases such that $CB = \bigcup_{gc \in CB^*} gc$ holds: if c_{ret} is a case from CB which is most similar to a query q w. r. t. sim then there is a generalized case gc_{ret} from CB^* which is most similar to q w. r. t. sim^* such that $c_{ret} \in gc_{ret}$.

This states that if we introduce generalized cases together with sim^*, the same cases are retrieved during problem solving, independent from the clustering of point cases into generalized cases. This provides a clear semantics of generalized cases defined in terms of traditional point cases and similarity measures.

For building CBR systems that reason with generalized cases, efficient representations for generalized cases and efficient approaches for similarity assessment must be developed. Obviously, a straight forward approach by applying the definitions from the previous section (e. g. computing the similarity for each point case covered by a generalized case and determining the maximum of the similarity values) can be quite inefficient if the generalized case covers a large subspace and is impossible of it covers an infinite space. In the following we assume a representation for generalized cases that uses constraints for representing dependencies between attributes of the representation space. Hence, a generalized case is represented by a set of constraints $\{C_1, \ldots, C_k\}$. Such a generalized case represents the set of point cases whose attribute values fulfill all constraints it consists of.

4   Rephrasing Similarity Assessment

In the remainder of the paper we focus on the problem of similarity assessment and retrieval w.r.t. the canonical extension of a given similarity measure. This problem is quite hard if generalized cases are represented by sets of constraints such as shown in Fig. 1. In the following we restrict ourselves to case representation spaces that are n-dimensional Real valued vector spaces, i.e. $\mathcal{S} = I\!\!R^n$ and $gc \subseteq I\!\!R^n$. Further, we assume that the generalized case is intensionally defined by a set of constraints over $I\!\!R^n$, i.e. a point case is within the generalized cases if for this point all constraints are fulfilled. According to our current analysis of the domain of IP reuse, we consider this as a reasonable restriction for IP representation as well as a reasonable restriction for other domains in which generalized cases occur.

4.1   Similarity Assessment as Optimization Problem

We now rephrase the similarity assessment problem for generalized cases as an optimization problem. For this purpose we make use of the well known correspondence between similarity measures and distance measures as discussed for example in [9]. Given a bijective, strictly monotonously decreasing mapping $f : [0,1] \rightarrow [0,1]$ such that $f(0) = 1$, $f(1) = 0$ and $\text{sim}(x,y) = f(dist(x,y))$ then $dist$ is a distance measure. Then we say sim and $dist$ are compatible. Given such a compatible distance measure, the similarity assessment problem for generalized cases can now be formulated as an optimization problem:

$$\textbf{(OP)} \qquad \begin{aligned} &\min\ dist(q,x) \\[4pt] &\text{s.t.} h(x) \leq 0, \end{aligned}$$

where h is a set of m functions $h_1, h_2, \ldots$ that represent gc by $h(x) \leq 0$, i.e., $x \in gc \iff \forall i\ h_i(x) \leq 0$. In this optimization problem, $dist$ is the *objective function* to be minimized.

4.2   Convex Minimization

Certain important classes of optimization problems have the property that every local minimum is a global minimum. A well known example is *convex minimization* where the objective function (here the distance measure) is a convex function and where the feasible set (here the constraints of the generalized case) is a convex set. To be more precise, let's consider some basic definitions.

Definition 3. A set $\mathcal{C} \subset I\!\!R^n$ is called *convex* if for each two points x, y in $\mathcal{C}$ the line segment $[x, y]$ connecting x and y is completely inside $\mathcal{C}$.

Definition 4. Let $\mathcal{C} \subset I\!\!R^n, \mathcal{C} \neq \emptyset, \mathcal{C}$ convex. A function $f : \mathcal{C} \rightarrow I\!\!R$ is called *convex* if for all $x, y \in \mathcal{C}$ and all $\alpha \in (0,1)$

$$f(\alpha x + (1 - \alpha)y) \leq \alpha f(x) + (1 - \alpha)f(y)$$

Geometrically, the line segment connecting $[x, y]$ is above the graph of f.

If both, the objective function *dist* is a convex function and *gc* is a convex set, then using nonlinear programming methods, we can retrieve a global optimal solution. For this important cases we can exactly determine the similarity sim* as we will show in section 5.

4.3 Relaxed Optimization to Find a Lower Bound

We now relax the restriction to convex constraints. If *gc* includes constraints which are also non-convex, we can at least relax the original optimization problem **(OP)** Therefore, we can decompose **(OP)** as follows:

$$\min \quad dist(q, x)$$

(OP)
$$\text{s.t.} \quad h_1(x) \le 0,$$
$$h_2(x) \le 0,$$

where h_1 is a set of m_1 convex functions and h_2 is a set of m_2 non-convex functions and $m_1 + m_2 = m$. As a result, the following problem is again a convex minimization problem:

$$\min \quad dist(q, x)$$
(CP)
$$\text{s.t.} \quad h_1(x) \le 0.$$

It's clear that **(CP)** is a relaxation of **(OP)**, therefore its optimal solution is a lower bound for **(OP)**.

5   The Topkis-Veinott Method

In order to compute the optimal solution to the convex minimization problem, one can apply the well known Topkis-Veinott algorithm [3]. This nonlinear optimization method is basically a feasible direction method that finds the global optimum under the assumption that the objective function *dist* is convex and all constraints h_1 are convex. We have analyzed several similarity and distance measure that typically occur in CBR applications (particularly including the IP reuse domain) and it turned out that all of them are in fact convex. Hence, this algorithm is of some practical importance.

The idea of the Topkis-Veinott method is to improve the value of objective function by moving from one feasible point (a point which fulfills all constraints) to another one. Let's consider the following definition.

Definition 5. Consider the problem $\min f(x)$ subject to $x \in S$, where $f : \mathbb{R}^n \to \mathbb{R}$ and S is a nonempty set in $\mathbb{R}^n$. A nonzero vector d is called a *feasible direction* at $x \in S$ if there exist a $\delta > 0$ such that $x + \lambda d \in S$ for all $\lambda \in (0, \delta)$. Furthermore, d is called an *improving fesible direction* at $x \in S$ if there exists a $\delta > 0$ such that $f(x + \lambda d) < f(x)$ and $x + \lambda d \in S$ for all $\lambda \in (0, \delta)$.

Suppose that x is a given feasible point. If an improving feasible direction d at x exists, we move along d with a step size λ reaching a new feasible point and we do the same iteration for the new point. If such an improving direction does not exist, we conclude that the current point is the optimal solution. Applying this method on (**CP**) we receive the global optimal solution. We now formalize the algorithm as follows:

For the sake of simplicity set $h_1 = h$.

> **Input:** $h = h_i(x) \leq 0$ for $i = 1, .., m_1$,
> $f(x) = dist(q, x)$,
> an initial feasible solution x_1 with $h_i(x_1) \leq 0$.
> **Output:** the optimal solution of (**CP**).

Set $k = 1$ and go to step 1.

1. If (z_k, d_k) be an optimal solution of:

$$\min \quad z$$
$$\text{s.t.} \quad \nabla f(x_k)^t d - z \leq 0$$
$$\nabla h_i(x_k)^t d - z \leq -h_i(x_k) \text{ for } i = 1, ..., m_1$$
$$-1 \leq d_j \leq 1 \qquad \text{for } j = 1, ..., n$$

If $z_k = 0$, stop; x_k is the optimal solution of (**CP**). If $z_k < 0$, go to step 2.

2. Let λ_k be an optimal solution to:

$$\min \quad f(x_k + \lambda d_k)$$
$$\text{s.t.} \quad 0 \leq \lambda \leq \lambda_{max}$$

where $\lambda_{max} = sup\{\lambda : h_i(x_k + \lambda d_k) \leq 0 \text{ for } i = 1, ..., m_1\}$. Let $x_{k+1} = x_k + \lambda_k d_k$, replace k by $k + 1$ and return to step 1.

Remark 1. As we said, the optimal solution of (**CP**) is a lower bound for (**OP**). To make this bound tighter, we can replace the objective function of (**CP**) with its *Lagrangian relaxation* $dist(q, x) + u h_2(x)$ where $u = (u_1, ..., u_{m_2}) \geq 0$ is the *Lagrangian multiplier* associated with $h_2(x) \leq 0$.

Remark 2. In case of non-differentiability of any of the above functions, we can apply the sub-gradient of the function instead of its gradient. It's obvious that Topkis-Veinott algorithm is not the only choice we have. We can apply any other algorithm like sub-gradient algorithm as well.

6   A Cutting Plane Method

Retrieving the most similar case to the query is our ultimate goal. This can be achieved if we are able to rank all gc's such that there is one gc where its upper bound is smaller than the lower bound of all others. Hence it is not necessary to determine the similarity between the query and all generalized cases exactly.

6.1   The Basic Approach

We assume that for each gc, we are given a feasible point, i.e. one point for which we know that all constraints are fulfilled. This feasible point gives us an upper bound for the corresponding gc and the Topkis-Veinott Algorithm on the relaxed problem will give a lower bound for it. This means we can rank gc's using these lower and upper bounds and probably exclude some of them which have lower bounds greater than the upper bound of at least one gc. The problem arises when there is no gc such that its upper bound is smaller than the lower bound of all other gc's. To solve this problem we need to tighten the bounds. Therefore, we propose a cutting plane method which does the task:

> **Input:**   (OP) corresponding to a gc,
>   an upper bound ub and a lower bound lb for (OP).
> **Output:** a better lower or upper bound for (OP).

1. Consider the line segment connecting ub and lb. Retrieve the perpendicular bisector of this line segment and its corresponding half plane including lb. Let's represent this half plane by $H(x) \leq 0$.
2. We want to find a feasible point for the region $\mathcal{R}$ constructed by the following constraints:

$$h(x) \leq 0,$$
$$H(x) \leq 0,$$
$$dist(q, x) - dist(q, ub) \leq 0.$$

Let's call these $m + 2$ constraints $g_i(x) \leq 0$ for $i = 1, ..., m + 2$.
3. Suppose $g_i(ub) \leq 0$ for $i \in I$ and $g_i(ub) > 0$ for $i \notin I$. Now consider the following problem which is a feasibility problem:

$$\min \sum_{i \notin I} z_i$$

$$(\textbf{FP}) \qquad \text{s.t.} \quad \begin{array}{lll} g_i(x) & \leq 0 & \text{for } i \in I \\ g_i(x) - z_i \leq 0 & & \text{for } i \notin I \\ z_i \geq 0 & & \text{for } i \notin I \end{array}$$

If the optimal objective value of the above problem is zero, then there exists a feasible solution of $\mathcal{R}$, since $z_i = 0$ for $i \notin I$, therefore $g_i(x) \leq 0$ for $i = 1, ..., m + 2$. We solve the above problem starting from $(ub, \hat{z})$, where $\hat{z}_i = g_i(ub)$ for $i \notin I$.
4. Assume at termination of (FP) the optimal objective value is zero. Hence we obtain a feasible solution of $\mathcal{R}$. This means we have recognized a point valid in gc which is closer to q than ub. Therefore, we have a new upper bound for (OP).
5. If (FP) has the optimal objective value bigger than zero, we conclude there is no better solution than ub in $H(x) \leq 0$. Therefore, we have to look for the better solution in $H(x) > 0$. We add this constraint to the set of constraints of (CP) and solve the new problem. The new region does not include lb since lb is inside $H(x) \leq 0$ due to the construction of it. So the solution of the new (CP) is a new lower bound for (OP).

With the above method, we tighten the bounds of **(OP)**. Therefore applying it iteratively will not be exhaustive. The only problem is that in each iteration we need to solve two optimization problems which is time consuming. To avoid this, we consider some more intelligent methods.

6.2 Gauges, Unit Balls and Distances

Definition 6. Let $\mathcal{B}$ be a compact set in $I\!\!R^n$ containing the origin in its interior. The *Minkowski-functional* or *gauge* with respect to $\mathcal{B}$ is defined as

$$\gamma_\mathcal{B}(x) = inf\{\lambda \geq 0 : x \in \lambda\mathcal{B}\}, \qquad x \in I\!\!R^n,$$

and $\mathcal{B}$ is called the *unit ball* of the gauge.

The idea to find the distance from x to y is to put the origin of the unit ball on x and enlarge or shrink the unit ball till its boundary touches y,

$$dist(x, y) = \gamma_\mathcal{B}(x - y)$$

As an example for Euclidean distance, the unit ball is a circle.

Remark 3. The unit balls should be subset of $I\!\!R^n$ but not subset of $I\!\!R^{n-1}$ (otherwise we have infinite or undefined distances in some dimensions). Then, we simply say they are *affine unit balls*.

Definition 7. Let the affine polyhedron $\mathcal{B}$ define a gauge in $I\!\!R^n$. Then $ext(\mathcal{B})$ = $\{e_1, ..., e_\sigma\}$ is the set of *extreme points* of $\mathcal{B}$.
Each face of $\mathcal{B}$ is an affine polyhedron in $I\!\!R^{n-1}$ with some extreme points in $ext(\mathcal{B})$. The half-lines starting at the origin and passing through the extreme points of $\mathcal{B}$ are called *fundamental directions* of the gauge, denoted by $d_1, ..., d_\sigma$. The fundamental directions, formed by these points and the origin, produce affine cones in $I\!\!R^n$. These cones are called *fundamental cones in $I\!\!R^n$*.

Remark 4. For the sake of simplicity, we assume the unit ball corresponding to the distant function of **(OP)** is convex. For the remedy of such a problem and more information about unit balls, you can refer to [14], [15] and [20].

Lemma 2. The optimal solution of **(OP)** lies on the boundary of gc if q is not located inside gc.

Proof. Suppose x', inside gc, is the optimal solution such that for all $x \in gc, dist(q, x) \geq dist(q, x')$. Then, there exists $\delta > 0$ such that the ball $B(x', \delta)$ is located completely inside gc. The line segment passing through q and x' cuts the boundary of $B(x', \delta)$ at y and y'. Without loss of generality, assume q, y' and x' are located in this line such that y' is between q and x'.

On the other hand, since q is located out of gc, the unit ball with the origin on q can be chosen small enough such that y' and x' are out it. Then if we enlarge the unit ball, it will first touch y' and then x', since y' is located between x' and q on the line segment passing through them. Therefore

$$dist(q, x') > dist(q, y').$$

This is a contradiction, since y' is feasible in gc is and gives a better objective value than x'. Therefore, the optimal solution lies on the boundary of gc.

Lemma 3. Let x' be a point on the boundary of gc. The unit ball $\mathcal{B}$ with the origin on q will touch x' at one of its faces $\mathcal{F}$. Let H be the hyperplane containing $\mathcal{F}$. Without loss of generality assume q is located in $H(x) \leq 0$. Prove that all the points inside $H(x) > 0$ have a greater distance to q than x'.

Proof. The proof is very trivial. H is the separating hyperplane of $\mathcal{B}$ and the points inside $H(x) > 0$. We know $dist(x', q) \geq dist(x, q)$ for all $x \in B$ and $dist(x', q) < dist(x, q)$ for all $x \notin \mathcal{B}$.

Since $\mathcal{B}$ and $H(x) > 0$ are completely separated therefore $dist(x', q) < dist(x, q)$ for any x in $H(x) > 0$.

These two lemmas will lead us to choose a more intelligent cutting hyperplane.

6.3   The Algorithm

Below, we establish an algorithm using this more intelligent cutting hyperplane.

Input: (OP) corresponding to a gc and a feasible point of gc called ub.

1. We first check wether q is inside the feasible region of **(OP)**, i.e. q is inside the generalized case. Therefore, check whether $h_j(q) > 0$ for some j. Let $J := \{j \mid h_j(q) > 0\}$. If J is empty stop, q is inside the generalized case and the distance is 0.
2. Solve the corresponding **(CP)** with Topkis-Veinott algorithm. Let lb be the determined lower bound.
3. Now, we check whether l_b is also a solution of **(OP)**. For this purpose, we check whether $h_i(lb) \leq 0$ for all $i = 1, ..., m_2$ (remember, these are the non-convex constraints). If this is the case we stop and lb gives the exact distance between q and gc.
4. Now, we move from u_b to the boundary of the feasible region of **(OP)**. Therefore, we intersect the line passing through ub and q with $h_j(x) = 0$ for all $j \in J$. Let x' be the closest intersection point to ub for $j \in J$. Set $ub = x'$.
5. Consider the line segment connecting ub and q. Let mid be a point on this line segment such that

$$dist(q, mid) = (dist(q, ub) + dist(q, lb))/2. \tag{1}$$

6. Retrieve the unit ball $\mathcal{B}$ with origin on q touching mid on a face $\mathcal{F}$. This can be simply done by finding the fundamental cone including mid and moving the face of the unit ball of this cone to mid. Let H be the corresponding hyperplane containing $\mathcal{F}$. Suppose q is located in $H(x) \leq 0$.

7. Consider the following constraints:

$$h(x) \leq 0,$$
$$H(x) \leq 0,$$
$$dist(q, x) - dist(q, mid) \leq 0.$$

Let's call these $m + 2$ constraints $g_i(x) \leq 0$ for $i = 1, ..., m + 2$.

8. Suppose $g_i(mid) \leq 0$ for $i \in I$ and $g_i(mid) > 0$ for $i \notin I$. Solve the corresponding (**FP**) of $g_i(x)$.

9. Consider (x^*, z^*) where z^* is the optimal objective value of (**FP**).
   If $z^* = 0$ set $ub = x^*$ and add $H \leq 0$ to (**OP**),
   else set $lb = mid$ and add $H > 0$ to (**OP**).

10. If a stopping criterion is not satisfied, go to step 4.

The steps 5 to 10 are also shown in Figure 2. The point mid, the unit ball and its face touching mid and H are represented in figure. Here, $H \leq 0$ means the half space to the right hand side of H. The feasible region of (**OP**) or $h(x) \leq 0$ is also represented by its original name gc. If we intersect these spaces together with $dist(q, x) - dist(q, mid) \leq 0$ we get $\mathcal{R}$. If $\mathcal{R}$ is not empty as it is the case in this figure, by solving (**FP**) we will find a point which is the new upper bound. If $\mathcal{R}$ is empty, then mid is the new lower bound.

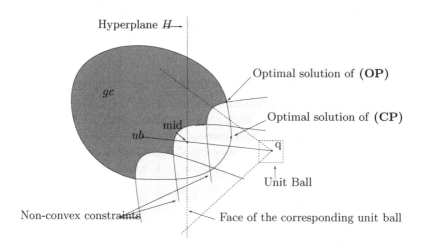

Fig. 2. An instant of the algorithm

Now we apply the algorithm as a black box for tightening the bounds of the (**OP**) for each gc separately and in parallel. We can stop further investigation for a gc whenever its lb is bigger than the ub of another gc. This is going to be our stopping criterion.

Remark 5. It's obvious that mid need not to be exactly as in (1). It can be chosen according to the lower and upper bounds of other gc's.

6.4   Convergence and Complexity

Lemma 4.   Prove that the algorithm is not exhaustive.

Proof. Obviously $lb \neq ub$, otherwise the stopping criterion is satisfied. Due to the construction of mid:

$$dist(q, lb) < dist(q, mid) < dist(q, ub).$$

where $dist(q, mid)$ is exactly in the middle of the interval $[dist(q, lb), dist(q, ub)]$. Suppose $z^* = 0$, then $dist(q, x^*) \leq dist(q, mid)$ and since we set $ub = x^*$, then the new interval has at most half of the length of the old one.
If $z^* > 0$, then $lb = mid$ which again the new interval is exactly half of the old one. Therefore, we have a sequence of intervals getting smaller and smaller. So the algorithm is not exhaustive.

The algorithm is quite flexible in the sense that the first 4 steps or some of them can be omitted. These 4 steps are some heuristical methods that depending on the behavior of the problem might accelerate the procedure of tightening the bounds. To get more insight about the behavior of them, we refer the reader to [14].

Let ub_1 and lb_1 be the initial points giving upper and lower bounds respectively. ub_1 is the initial feasible point and lb_1 might be q itself or the solution of (**CP**). If we set $l = dist(q, ub_1))$ and , $T = O((\mathbf{FP}))$, then the asymptotic running time of the algorithm is $O(T\log(l))$.

6.5   Feasibility Problem

Efficiency of our algorithm is crucially dependent on the feasibility problem. There exist several references considering different methods to solve this problem. In [1] and [3], the standard line search method has been developed. The problem of finding a solution for a nonlinear system of equations is investigated in [8]. Finally some global optimization methods in [10] which solve (**FP**) without considering the nature of it.

We propose to use a line search algorithm for the feaibility problem. This can be done by searching inside H starting from mid. It's enough to search only inside H, since gc is a connective region and if H cuts it somewhere, then there exists a point $\bar{x}$ where $H(\bar{x}) = 0$ and $\bar{x} \in \mathcal{R}$. Note that $H(mid) = 0$, therefore mid is a good starting point.

7   Summary and Conclusion

In this paper, we have analyzed the problem of similarity assessment for generalized cases that are represented through constraints over an n-dimensional Real-valued vector space. We have shown that the difficulty of this problem depends on whether the constraints include just convex constraints or also nonconvex constraints. For the convex constraints and if also the similarity measure is convex, the Topkis-Veinott method can be easily applied to determine exactly the similarity between a point query and generalized cases. If the similarity measure is not convex or the generalized case contains also non-convex constraints, the problem is more difficult. For this situation, we proposed a new algorithm that allows to incrementally compute sequences of upper and lower bounds for the similarity and we show the convergence of the algorithm. This algorithm can be applied to construct a retrieval algorithm for generalized cases similar to the fish and shrink retrieval algorithm [19] or the pivoting-based retrieval [16]. It allows to rank generalized cases without the need to exactly compute all similarity values.

In general this paper is an indication for the fact that optimization theory provides a variety of methods that are useful for similarity assessment for generalized cases. Although, this paper is a very important step towards solving the similarity problem for generalized cases, there are still many open problems to be addressed. First, the feasibility problem that has to be solved as part of the algorithm (see section 6.5) is still a difficult problem in optimization and it has to be analyzed in more details in the context it occurs in our algorithm. Second, the proposed method is limited to Real-valued case representations only. The problem of similarity assessment for generalized cases must also be analyzed for case-representations including discrete types and constraints and also for mixed representations.

Currently, practical experiences with this algorithm concerning efficiency in real domains, such as the IP reuse domain, is still missing and it is an important part of our future work as well.

Acknowledgements

This work has been partially funded by the BMBF project IPQ. The authors want to thank Ivo Vollrath and Michael M. Richter for many discussions on the topic of this paper.

References

1. M. Avriel and B. Golany. *Mathematical Programming for Industrial Engineers.* Marcel Dekker, INC., 1996.
2. Ray Bareiss. *Exemplar-Based Knowledge Acquisition: A unified Approach to Concept Representation, Classification and Learning.* Academic Press, 1989.
3. M. S. Bazaraa, H.D. Sherali, and Shetty C.M. *NonLinear Programming, Theorey and Algorithms.* 2nd Edition, Wiley, 1993.
4. R. Bergmann. *Experience Management: Foundations, Development Methodology, and Internet-based Applications.* Springer, forthcomming, 2002.
5. R. Bergmann and I. Vollrath. Generalized cases: Representation and steps towards efficient similarity assessment. In W. Burgard, Th. Christaller, and A. B. Cremers, editors, *KI-99: Advances in Artificial Intelligence.*, LNAI 1701. Springer, 1999.
6. R. Bergmann, I. Vollrath, and T. Wahlmann. Generalized cases and their application to electronic designs. In E. Melis, editor, *7. German Workshop on Case-Based Reasoning (GWCBR'99).*, 1999.

7. Ralph Bergmann. *Effizientes Problemlösen durch flexible Wiederverwendung von Fällen auf verschiedenen Abstraktionsebenen.* DISKI 138. infix, 1996.
8. L. Blum, F. Cucker, M. Shub, and Smale S. *Complexity and Real Computation.* Springer, 1997.
9. H.-D. Burkhard and M.M. Richter. Similarity in case-based reasoning and fuzzy theory. In S.K. Pal, T.S. Dillon, and D.S. Yeung, editors, *Soft Computing in Case-Based Reasoning,* chapter 2. Springer, 2000.
10. R. Horst and H. Tuy. *Global Otimization: Deterministic Approaches.* Springer, 1993.
11. Kefeng Hua, Ian Smith, and Boi Faltings. Integrated case-based building design. In Stefan Wess, Klaus-Dieter Althoff, and Michael M Richter, editors, *Topics in Case-Based Reasoning. Proc. Of the First European Workshop on Case-Based Reasoning (EWCBR-93),* Lecture Notes in Artificial Intelligence, 837, pages 436–445. Springer Verlag, 1993.
12. Janet L Kolodner. *Retrieval and Organizational Strategies in Conceptual Memory.* PhD thesis, Yale University, 1980.
13. Jeff Lewis. Intellectual property (IP) components. Artisan Components, Inc., [web page], http://www.artisan.com/ip.html, 1997. [Accessed 28 Oct 1998].
14. B. Mougouie. Optimization of distance/similarity functions under linear and non-linear constraints with application in case-based reasoning. Diplomarbeit, Max-Planck Institut für Informatik, Saarbrücken, Germany., 2001.
15. S. Nickel. Convex analysis. Technical report, Department of Mathematics, University of Kaiserslautern, Kaiserslautern, Germany, 1998.
16. L. Portinale, P. Torasso, and D. Magro. Selecting most adaptable diagnostic solutions thorugh pivoting-based retrieval. In David B Leake and Enric Plaza, editors, *Case-Based Reasoning Research and Development, Proc. ICCBR-97,* Lecture Notes in Artificial Intelligence, 1266, pages 393–402. Springer Verlag, 1997.
17. Lisa Purvis and Pearl Pu. Adaptation using constraint satisfaction techniques. Lecture Notes in Artificial Intelligence, 1010, pages 289–300. Springer Verlag, 1995.
18. S Salzberg. A nearest hyperrectangle learning method. *Machine Learning,* 6:277–309, 1991.
19. Jörg W. Schaaf. Fish and shrink: a next step towards efficient case retrieval in large scaled case bases. In Ian Smith and Boi Faltings, editors, *Advances in Case-Based Reasoning,* Lecture Notes in Artificial Intelligence, 1186, pages 362–376. Springer Verlag, 1996.
20. A. Schoebel. Lecture notes in location theory. Technical report, Department of Mathematics, University of Kaiserslautern, Kaiserslautern, Germany, 2000.
21. Thomas Wahlmann. Implementierung einer skalierbaren diskreten Kosinustransformation in VHDL. Diploma thesis, University of Siegen, 1999.

Case Acquisition in a Project Planning Environment

Sasidhar Mukkamalla and Héctor Muñoz-Avila

Department of Computer Science and Engineering
19 Memorial Drive West
Lehigh University
Bethlehem, PA 18015, USA
{sam6,munoz}@cse.lehigh.edu

Abstract: In this paper, we propose an approach to acquire cases in the context of project planning, without any extra effort from the end user. Under our definition, a case has a one to one correspondence with the standard elements of a project plan. We exploit this correspondence to capture cases automatically from project planning episodes. We provide an algorithm for extracting cases from project plans. We implemented this algorithm on top of a commercial project-planning tool and perform experiments evaluating our approach.

Introduction

Knowledge acquisition is a problem frequently faced when using intelligent problem-solving techniques in real-world situations. It is well known that over the years intelligent systems have been developed but failed to be used because it was not feasible to feed such systems with adequate knowledge. Research on this area has typically concentrated on developing interfaces to capture knowledge from users. Although a lot of progress has been made in this direction, it is still difficult to convince users to take advantage of such systems because of the overhead needed to learn how to use those interfaces and then using them to feed the intelligent system with the knowledge needed.

We present an alternative for addressing the knowledge-acquisition problem, namely, to extract knowledge from the same interactive tools that users regularly use in achieving their tasks. By doing so, the knowledge acquisition effort becomes transparent to the user. This alternative derives from our ongoing effort to provide a knowledge-layer to enhance project-planning tools.

Project planning is a business process for successfully delivering one-of-a kind products and services under real-world time and resource constraints. In previous work (Muñoz-Avila et al, 2002), a knowledge-layer for existing tools supporting project planning was proposed; the core idea in this proposal called knowledge-based project planning (KBPP) was to reuse cases containing pieces of project plans when creating new project plans. In this paper, we also report on the first implementation of a KBPP on top of a commercial Project Planning (PP) tool, but our primary focus is on the case acquisition capabilities that we developed.

On the core of our case acquisition effort is the definition of cases. As a result of our definition, a case has a one to one correspondence with the standard elements of a project plan. This notion reflects our believe that by only using standard PP elements

S. Craw and A. Preece (Eds.): ECCBR 2002, LNAI 2416, pp. 264–277.
© Springer-Verlag Berlin Heidelberg 2002

to define cases the intelligent component of the KBPP system will be less intrusive, the cases are more natural from the point of view of the end-user and the case acquisition effort will be simplified.

This paper is organized as follows. In the next section we discuss related work. Then, we summarize the proposal for KBPP presented in (Muñoz-Avila et al, 2002) and discuss the first implementation of these ideas. The following section discusses our case capture approach. Then, we discuss an implementation of our case acquisition ideas in a project-planning tool, Microsoft Project. Next we evaluate our approach and finally we make concluding remarks.

Related Work

Providing tools for knowledge acquisition has been a frequently studied research topic. For example, in the EXPECT project (Blythe et al, 2001), an integrated suit of intelligent interfaces is used to capture knowledge. The EXPECT project shows that by integrating these interfaces it is possible to elicit the context of the users actions, which enhances the knowledge acquisition capabilities. This is somewhat related to our work, since the use of a KBPP tool by the user provides the context for the case capture knowledge. However, the main difference lies in that we are not constructing ad-hoc interfaces to capture, instead we are capturing the cases from the data given by the user during his/her regular interactions with the PP tool.

Authors have long observed that the problem-solving episodes can be captured as cases (e.g., Veloso, 1993). If users develop a project plan using tools such as Microsoft Project, the elements of a project plan could be stored as cases. As we will discuss, our method traverses different elements within a project plan in a process that is similar to the foot-printing process, which is used to identify relevant features of a plan generated (Veloso, 1993).

In the system CaMeL (Elgami et al, 2002), a process is shown that allows automatic elicitation compiled knowledge forms from cases. These compiled knowledge forms are called methods and indicate how to decompose tasks following the hierarchical task network representation (HTN) that we use in this work. A similar process developed by Carrick and Cunnigham (Carrick and Cunningham, 1993) can elicit rules from cases. In our work, we study the acquisition of cases, which is a complementary problem to these two approaches. We envision a two-step process in which cases are learned using the process described in this paper. In the rest of this paper we will concentrate only on the case acquisition process.

Another related research direction is to capture user intent and use this as conditions for case retrieval. For example, by analyzing the input of a user in an interactive system, intent about the rational for user actions can be inferred (El Fattah, 2001).

Knowledge-Based Project Planning

Several software packages for project management are commercially available. These include *Microsoft Project*™ (Microsoft) and *SureTrak*™ (Primavera Systems Inc).

These interactive systems help a planner store a work-breakdown structure (WBS), which indicates how the project's tasks can be decomposed into manageable work units. These packages also contain a suit of tools to control the scheduling of the tasks and the management of resources.

In (Muñoz-Avila et al, 2002), KBPP is proposed to assist planners in the development of WBS by using hierarchical case decomposition techniques. This proposal was based on the recognition that WBS representations, as commonly used in project planning, are very similar to the HTN representations used in the planning community.

Hierarchical Planning

The particular hierarchical planning approach that we use is hierarchical task network planning (HTN). In HTN, high-level tasks are decomposed into simpler tasks, until eventually so-called **primitive** tasks are reached. Primitive tasks indicate concrete actions to be undertaken. Tasks that can be decomposed are called **compound.** For example, creating an advertising strategy can be a high-level task. Giving an advertisement in the local newspaper can be a primitive task. Both tasks can be related, the latter being a descendant of the former, through a hierarchy formed by the task-subtask relations.

The algorithm that we implemented for HTN planning is a variation of an algorithm called SiN (Muñoz-Avila et al, 2001; 2000). SiN uses two sources of information: methods and cases. A **method** has the form (:*method h P ST* <) and indicate the preconditions P to decompose a task h into subtasks ST. < defines an order between the subtasks in ST. Methods are compiled forms of generic knowledge; they are always applicable for any situation for which the preconditions P hold. A method is applicable in a situation or state S, which is defined as a collection of facts, if there is a substitution θ such that the condition $P\theta$ is valid in S. A set of preconditions $P\theta$ is **valid** in S if for each positive precondition, p, p is in S and for each negative precondition, not(q), q is not in S.

Since creating a set of methods, completely describing a domain is in general infeasible, SiN uses cases to enhance the knowledge that a system has about the domain. A **case** has the form *(:case h P ST < Q)* where *h, P, ST* and < play the same role as in the methods and Q are question-answer pairs indicating preferences for the applicability of the case. Cases are examples of decompositions and thus are situation-specific. A knowledge base in SiN consists of cases, methods and operators. Operators indicate the effects of performing the primitive tasks.

As we said before, the algorithm that we implemented for HTN planning is a variation of the SiN algorithm. SiN integrates the SHOP planning system (Nau et al, 1999) and NaCoDAE/HTN, an extension for HTN planning of the NaCODAE conversational CBR (CCBR) system (Aha and Breslow, 1998). To decompose tasks, SiN uses SHOP's methods and NaCoDAE/HTN's cases. At any point of time either SHOP or NaCODAE is decomposing tasks and will cede control to the other one if it reaches a compound task that it cannot decompose.

Our variation is called SHOP/CCBR as it extends SHOP while mimicking the CCBR style interactions of NaCoDAE. The main advantage of SHOP/CCBR over SiN is that it allows simultaneous consideration of cases and methods to decompose a task instead of SiN's approach of considering either cases or methods but not both at the same time. Another advantage is that cases can include variables and complex applicability conditions like numerical constraints that in SiN are only available for methods. An important point is that SHOP/CCBR like SiN, but unlike SHOP does not require either methods or operators to generate task decompositions. That is, SHOP/CCBR can use cases only to generate task decompositions. This is crucial in the context of project planning, where a complete knowledge base might not be available.

Work-Breakdown Structure and HTNs

A WBS is a hierarchically organized set of *elements* that need to be performed to deliver the required goods and/or services (e.g., creating a marketing strategy). Elements in a WBS can be of two kinds: tasks and activities. *Tasks* can contain activities and other tasks. Activities are terminal nodes (e.g., giving an add in the local newspaper). Elements in the WBS can be ordered using precedent constraints. The mapping of WBS to hierarchical plans is straightforward: the WBS tasks map the HTN compound tasks, the WBS activities map the HTN primitive tasks, and the precedence constraints map the ordering constraints. This mapping means that the AI techniques used for hierarchical plan generation could be used for WBS generation. However as pointed in (Muñoz-Avila et al, 2002), the *main condition for using these techniques is that cases and methods are available.* This is precisely the issue we are addressing in this paper.

Case Contents

In the conversational case-based reasoning approach, the case's question-answer pairs and the preconditions were conceived to indicate conditions under which a particular case is applicable. In the context of KBPP, we want the conditions for applicability of a case to correspond to project plan elements. In a project plan, several elements are maintained, including:

1. The hierarchical relation between elements (i.e., tasks and activities) in the WBS
2. The resources available for the project
3. The assignments between resources and tasks
4. The precedence constraints between elements in the WBS

Accordingly we simplified definition of a case to *(:case h C ST <)*. That is, we will have conditions *C* only instead of the preconditions and question-answer pairs defined for cases in CCBR. These conditions state the collection of task-resource assignments that are relevant for the case. In the HICAP system (Muñoz-Avila et al, 1999), basically the same five elements above are represented. The main difference is that cases use question-answer pairs to assess their applicability rather than the task-resource assignments.

Although the simplification in the form of the cases is only slight, it reflects an important goal of our approach for KBPP. We want the cases to have a one to one correspondence with the standard elements of a project plan. This goal reflects our belief that by using only the standard PP elements, the intelligent component of the KBPP system will be less intrusive, the cases fit into the natural perspective of the end-user and the case acquisition effort will be simplified.

One vs. Multi-level Cases

A WBS can be seen as a collection of one-level decompositions. Each one level-decomposition refines a single task into (sub)tasks and/or activities. The whole collection decomposes the most high-level tasks (i.e., tasks having no parent tasks) into activities (i.e., the non-decomposable elements of the WBS). In our approach, each one-level decomposition is stored as a single case. The alternative could have been cases that contain several decomposition levels or even a complete WBS. There are some trade-offs that we consider:

- Cases containing several decomposition levels or the complete WBS provide a better or complete picture of the overall plan. Their main drawback is that the case re-usability is limited, as more levels are added, more constraints should be considered to assess the applicability of the WBS in new situations.
- Cases containing one-level decomposition give no overall picture of the plan. Their main advantage is that they can be reused in several situations as cases from different WBS can be combined. For example, it is possible to decompose a task with a case captured from one WBS and to decompose one of the children tasks with a case captured from another WBS.

We decided to store only one-level decompositions in our cases to maximize the re-usability of the cases. As we will see, our experiments suggest that even after solving few problems the coverage provided by the captured cases is greatly improved.

Concrete versus Generalized Cases

Another question that we explored was whether to store in the knowledge base generalized cases or not. Given a case $CA = (:case\ h\ C\ ST\ <)$, we define the generalization of CA, denoted by **Gen**(CA), as a case obtained by mapping each parameter, ψ, occurring in the arguments of the head, conditions, or subtasks of CA, with a unique variable, $?\psi$. In this way, each occurrence of same parameter in h, C and ST is replaced by the same variable.

Thus, the question was whether CA or Gen(CA) should be stored in the knowledge base. The problem of using Gen(CA) instead of CA is that Gen(CA) might not **correctly model the target domain**. That is, If $X = \{?x_1, ..., ?x_n\}$ is the set of the variables in Gen(CA), there might be instantiations of X for which Gen(CA) that do not reflect the behavior of the target domain. Using CA has its own problems; the most important of which is the coverage of a case base consisting of concrete cases. For each possible task in the domain we will require one concrete case having the same head. If there is a maximum of n task names, with an average number of arguments, m, and each argument can take an average number of values, v. The minimum number of cases required will be n.m^v, one for each possible task. Notice that this is the minimum number, since we compute similarity on the conditions for determining applicability of a case to a given task. So we need several cases for each task to obtain a better coverage.

Our answer to this question was to combine these two approaches; if the **type** for each parameter in the case is known, we generalize the parameter by uniformly replacing it with the same variable. Parameters for which the type is not known are not generalized. In addition we add the following constraints as conditions of the case:

- For each two different variables, ?x and ?y, of the same type, we add the constraint (:different ?x ?y)
- For each constant, c, and each variable, ?x, we add the constraint (:different ?x c)

We denoted by **Gen+(CA)** the procedure that generalizes only typed parameters as indicated above. Our case acquisition strategy adds this kind of generalized cases to the knowledge base. It is possible that this generalization might still not correctly model the target domain. As more cases are added, these kinds of errors can be detected if the heads of the new and the existing case match, the conditions of one is contained in the other one but their subtasks and/or the orderings are different. We plan to address this issue in future work.

Algorithm for Case Capture

The case acquisition process starts on the most high-level tasks as indicated in the *caseAcquisition* algorithm. PL is the current project plan, which includes the four elements indicated in the previous section. KB is the knowledge base consisting cases and methods (operators present in KB, if any, are ignored).

Algorithm: caseAcquisition(PL,KB)

For each most high-level task t do
    captureCase(t, PL, KB)

The caseCapture algorithm is described below. The *assignedResources* function returns the **associations** of a task *t* in the current project plan. The associations of a task is a pair *(t, ra)* where *ra* consists of:

1. The set of resources associated with *t* and their attributes (e.g., type), and
2. The set of resources associated with each child activity of *t*

The rationale for the first set of resources is that those are the ones specified by the user as relevant for the particular task and these resources are stored as conditions for that particular case. Since activities are not stored as separate cases (they have no subtasks), the resources associated with them are stored as conditions for the cases in which activities appear as tasks.

The subtasks and orderings functions return the subtasks/activities of the task and the orderings between the tasks/activities in *ST* respectively.

```
Algorithm: captureCase(t, PL, KB)

    If t is an activity then return
    C ← assignedResources(t, PL)
    ST ← subtasks(t, PL)
    ord ← orderings(ST,PL)
    storeChecking(Gen+((:case t C ST <)),KB)
    for each t' in ST do
            captureCase(t',PL,KB)
```

The procedure storeChecking stores a new case Gen+((:case t C ST <)) in KB if there is no case (:case t' P' ST' <') and there is no method (:method h' P' ST' <') for which the case is an instance of. That is, there is no substitution θ, such that $h'\theta = h$, $P'\theta = C$, $ST'\theta = ST$ and the orderings relations are preserved (i.e., For every t_1 and t_2 in ST if $t_1 <' t_2$ holds then $t_1\theta < t_2$ also holds). The reason being that if the conditions C of the candidate case (:case t C ST <) are applicable in any state S, then the corresponding case or method in KB is also applicable in S. That is, if there is a substitution α such that $C\alpha$ is valid in S, then $P\theta\alpha$ must be valid in S. So essentially storeChecking makes sure that no case or method in KB subsumes the candidate case.

The caseAcquisition algorithm terminates because the task-subtask relation in a WBS is always a collection of trees (one tree for each most high-level task) and thus it cannot contain loops. For example, the WBS view of Microsoft Project only allows the addition of tasks/activities as children of a single task.

The process of traversing the WBS identifying relevant resources at each level is similar to the foot-printing process in Prodigy/Analogy (Veloso, 1993). The key difference is that instead of complete knowledge base, we only use the four elements of the project plan to extract the cases. In Prodigy/Analogy the knowledge base is used to annotate the cases with the operations from which a plan was derived. The whole point of our work is that such a complete knowledge base is not available for many real world problems. This distinction reflects a difference on the role of the cases: in our work cases enhance the knowledge base whereas in prodigy/Analogy (and any other system performing derivational analogy on top of a first-principles planner) cases serve as meta-knowledge to guide the usage of the complete knowledge base.

Case Study: Microsoft Project

Microsoft Project is a popular commercial project management tool. It helps users to store WBS, allocate resources and follow deadlines. It incorporates a Visual Basic editor that allows users to extend its functionality. The WBS is edited in a spreadsheet like window called the **Task View**. All the resources are edited in the **Resource Sheet**. The user can allocate resources to each task separately.

We added a new functionality into Microsoft Project. The user has now the possibility to start a semi-automatic plan generation process. When the user selects a task and chooses the KBPP decompose function, the following steps are performed:

- A KBPP module that is implemented in Microsoft Project reads all the resources and their attributes. Then, it invokes SHOP/CCBR with this task and resources.
- SHOP/CCBR computes all applicable methods and cases for the task and displays them for the user to select one of them.
- The user then selects a case or method and the corresponding decomposition is inserted in Microsoft project.

We used COM (Component Object Model) as the software design model to facilitate the communication between Microsoft Project and SHOP/CCBR.

Figure 1 presents an overview of the information flow of the overall system. The user inputs a project plan, including the resources and resource assignments (label 1 in figure 1). Our case acquisition module implemented within Microsoft Project is used to capture cases from the project plan (label 2 in the figure 1). These cases are used to augment the knowledge base used by SHOP/CCBR. Given a new situation and a task in Microsoft Project (label 3 in the figure 1), SHOP/CCBR is invoked to create a WBS for achieving that task relative to the state.

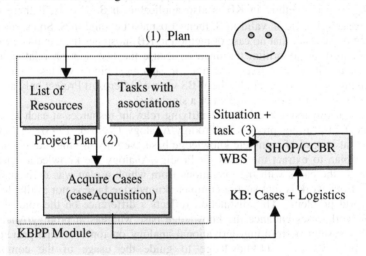

Fig. 1. Information flow in KBPP System

As an example consider Figure 2, which shows the Task View of all the tasks and their associated resources of a partial plan created in Microsoft Project. If the user selects the task *Transport Package1 from NottingHill to Hasenheide* to store as a case, the system can potentially learn 4 cases.

Task Name	Resource Names
⊟ Transport Package1 from Notting Hill to Hasenheide	Package1,Hasenheide,Notting Hill
⊟ Pick-up Package1 from Notting Hill	Package1,Notting Hill
Load Truck1 with Package1	Truck1
⊟ Carry Package1 from Notting Hill to Hasenheide	Package1,Notting Hill,Hasenheide
Drive Truck1 from Notting Hill to Heathrow	Truck1 ,Notting Hill,Heathrow
Unload Package1 from Truck1	Truck1 ,Package1
Load BA-981 with Package1	BA-981 ,Package1
Fly BA-981 from Heathrow to Tegel	BA-981 ,Heathrow,Tegel
Unload BA-981 with Package1	BA-981 ,Package1
Load Truck2 with Package1	Truck2,Package1
Drive Truck2 from Tegel to Hasenheide	Truck2,Hasenheide
⊟ Deliver Package1 at Hasenheide	Package1
Unload Truck2 with Package1	Truck2,Package1 ,Hasenheide

Fig. 2. A plan created in Microsoft Project

The head of the case is *Transport ?Package1 from ?NottingHill to ?Hasenheide.* To compute the conditions, the KBPP module reads all the resources associated with the task and their corresponding attributes. Here, the system reads that Package1 is at NottingHill, NottingHill is a location in London, Hasenheide is a Location in Berlin, London and Berlin are cities. Thus, the resulting conditions of the case are:

(PACKAGE ?Package1)
(PACKAGE-AT ?Package1 ?NottingHill)
(LOCATION ?NottingHill)
(IN-CITY ?NottingHill ?London)
(CITY ?London)
(LOCATION ?Hasenheide)
(IN-CITY ?Hasenheide ?Berlin)
(CITY ?Berlin)
(DIFFERENT ?NottingHill ?Hasenheide)
(DIFFERENT ?London ?Berlin)

The ordering relation < is read from the relation between tasks as stored in Microsoft Project (these orderings can be viewed by the user in the **Gantt Chart View**). The resulting subtasks of the case are:

(Pick-up ?Package1 from ?NottingHill)
(Carry ?Package1 from ?NottingHill to ?Hasenheide)
(Deliver ?Pacakge1 at ?Hasenheide)

Evaluation

We performed an experimental evaluation of our case acquisition strategy. The purpose was to observe the effects of adding more cases to the coverage of the knowledge base. We use the standard definition of coverage i.e. the number of problems that can be solved with the knowledge base (Smyth and Keane, 1995).

Domains

Initially the knowledge base consisted of methods describing the complete HTN version of the Logistics domain (Veloso and Carbonell, 1993). In the Logistics domain, packages need to be moved between different places. Trucks and planes are used to transport objects between different places. We also defined a subset of the UMTranslog (Erols et al, 1994). Our subset of UMTranslog extends the logistics domain by defining objects that can be a combination of the following types: *regular, liquids, perishables* and *hazmat*. For example, milk can be defined as a liquid and perishable object. The transportation means in our extension can be a combination of four types: *regular, tanker, refrigerated* and *hazardous*. Each type is specially suited to transport one object type. For example a refrigerated tanker truck is suitable to transport milk. All the problems solvable by Logistics domain were also solvable by UMTranslog but not the other way around (i.e. only a strict subset of the problems that are solvable with UMTranslog are solvable with Logistics).

Experimental Setup

A random problem generator feeds problems to the HTN planner SHOP that uses our subset of the UMTranslog domain to generate solution plans. The solution plan is passed to Microsoft Project as a WBS because there is a one to one correspondence between HTN plans and WBSs. In addition, a specialized procedure is used to represent the preconditions of the methods as resources allocated to that particular high-level task. SHOP and this specialized procedure form the automatic user which play the role that the human user plays in Figure 1.

Our test data was obtained as follows: 70 problems were randomly generated. These were divided in two groups: one consisting of 50 problems, the learning set, and the other one consisting of 20 problems, the test set. Each of the 70 problems is solvable by UMTranslog but none is solvable by Logistics. The learning set was split in 5 groups of 10 problems each. We did 5 runs with each of these 5 groups. At each run each of the 10 problems within the group was solved using SHOP and UMTranslog and passed to Microsoft Project (label 1 in the figure 1). Cases were captured from each of these plans using the caseAcquisition algorithm and stored in the case base (label 2 in the figure 1). Cases captured from previous runs were kept for the following runs. Then, SHOP/CCBR tried to solve each of the 20 test problems using the augmented knowledge base (label 3 in the Figure 1). We thus ran a total of 100 problem-solving episodes.

Extracting Resources from an HTN Plan

As we saw, getting a WBS from an HTN plan is a straightforward process because of the one-to-one correspondence between them. Feeding the information about the resource usage is another matter. Since the purpose of extracting resources from HTN plan was simply to feed Microsoft Project so we can perform our experiments, we decided to write a simple procedure specialized for this domain. For each compound task *t* in the plan we identified the method that was used to decompose it. For each precondition in the method, we identified the resources mentioned in the precondition and:

- Added each resource to the list of resources in Microsoft Project if the resource was not there already
- Assigned each of these resources to the task *t*

In our previous example, if the precondition stated that the Package1 is at NottingHill, we added Package1 to the list of resources, assigned this resource to the task *Transport Package1 from NottingHill to Hasenheide*. In the entry for Package1 we added 2 columns: "NottingHill" and "Hasenheide". The order guaranteed that when the resources are extracted by the caseCapture procedure, they match the form of the preconditions in the UMTranslog domain and we could verify that the cases correspond to instances of the UMTranslog methods.

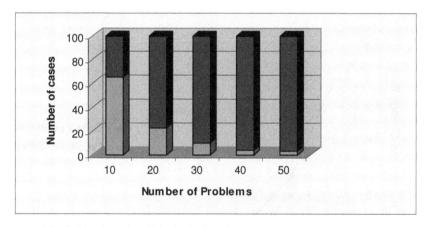

Fig. 3. Number of problem in the learning set vs. Number of cases learnt

Results and Discussion

Figure 3 shows the number of problems in the learning set (x-axis) versus number of cases learnt for each learning set (y-axis). We observe that the number of cases learnt for each learning set decreases rapidly as more problems are solved. Figure 4 shows the number of cases learnt versus number of test problems solved. The percentage of problems that are solved augments rapidly as more runs are made. More interestingly we observe a co-relation between the results of both figures. Namely that at the point where fewer cases are learnt, more problems are solved. This shows that after that point we reach a near saturation point in the coverage of knowledge base. To observe this effect more clearly, Figure 5 shows the normalized change rate of the cases learned and the problems solved. As we can see in the fourth learning set the rate of cases learned and new problems solved is very small.

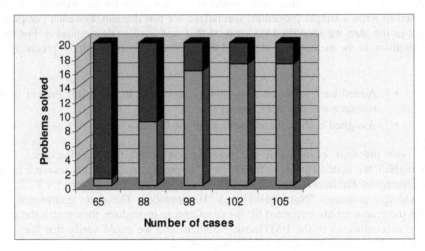

Fig. 4. Number of Cases learnt vs. Number of test problems solved

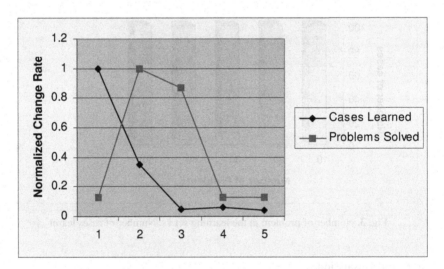

Fig. 5. Normalized change rate for cases learned and problems solved

This illustrates the flexibility of our definition of cases; by making cases consist of one-level decompositions rather than complete plan and by generalizing them, the opportunities for re-usability of the cases are greatly improved.

Our experimental setup was made under the following ideal conditions that may not occur in real-world problems:

- Project plans entered by the automatic user were provable correct. This is the result of using SHOP, which always generates correct plans. In addition, our specialized extraction procedure extracts conditions from HTN plans and enters them as resources in Microsoft Project. In real-world situations users make errors and feed the system with incomplete information. Moreover, explicit criteria might not even exist to determine if a plan is valid or not.
- Each of the plans obtained by SHOP/CCBR with the augmented knowledge base correctly model the target domain. That is, each of these plans could be generated by SHOP using UMTranslog. Again in real-world situations it might not be possible to determine such correctness or as discussed previously, captured cases might not even correctly model the target domain.
- Related to both of the above points, operators were available that indicated the effects of performing the activities (i.e., the primitive tasks). Such effects are needed to ensure correctness of the plans generated by SHOP and SHOP/CCBR. Again, in many real-world situations it is simply not possible to state such operators.

The purpose of these ideal conditions was to allow us to measure the increase in coverage of the knowledge base without any noise in the data.

Conclusions and Future Work

In this paper we present an alternative approach to case capture. Instead of developing a specialized case capture interface, we capture cases by extracting information about the project plans that are created by the user. The key condition for our approach is that the case representation formalism, HTNs, has a one-to-one correspondence with the WBS. We developed the caseAcquisition algorithm that traverses the WBS, creating a case from each one-level decomposition. Conditions about the applicability of the case are extracted by observing the resources associated with the task being decomposed.

We implemented our ideas about case extraction on Microsoft Project and added a task decomposer system, SHOP/CCBR. An important point is that SHOP/CCBR does not require methods and/or operators to be available to generate task decompositions. We performed an experiment under ideal laboratory conditions, namely, starting plans in Microsoft Project being provable correct HTN plans, having operators and methods available in SHOP/CCBR that allow to test the correctness of the plans generated by the augmented knowledge base (consisting of operators, methods and captured cases). We observed the rapid increment in coverage of the augmented knowledge base while there is a rapid decrement of the number of cases learned. We discussed that the rapid increment was due to our strategy of storing one-level decompositions in the cases instead of multi-level decompositions and our case generalization procedure.

We want to explore case base maintenance issues in the near future. In our current implementation, a first step in this direction is made; the storeCheck procedure checks that no candidate case is added to the knowledge base when either a method or a case exists, that subsumes the candidate case. Despite this, redundancy can easily be generated. Another related issue that we want to address is the case over-generalization of the Gen+ function.

References

Aha, D.W., and Breslow, L. Refining conversational case libraries. In: *Proceedings of the Fourth European Workshop on Case-Based Reasoning (EWCBR-98).* Providence, RI: Springer. 1998.

Blythe, J., Kim, J., Ramachandran, S., and Gil, Y. An Integrated Environment for Knowledge Acquisition. In: *Proceedings of the International Conference on Intelligent User Interfaces 2001.*

El Fattah, Y. Structured Representation of Causal Relationships in Template Planning.(A Preliminary Report). Rockwell Scientific Technical Report, 2001.

Erol, K., Nau, D., & Hendler, J. HTN planning: Complexity and expressivity. In: *Proceedings of the Twelfth National Conference on Artificial Intelligence* (pp. 123-1128). Seattle, WA: AAAI Press, 1994

Hanney, K., and Keane, M.T Learning Adaptation Rules from a Case-Base. In: *Proceedings of the Third European Workshop on Case-Based Reasoning (EWCBR-96)*, Lausanne, Switzerland: Springer. 1996.

Ilghami, O., Nau, D.S., Muñoz-Avila, H., & Aha, D.W. (2002) CaMeL: Learning Methods for HTN Planning. To appear in *Proccedings of the The Sixth International Conference on AI Planning & Scheduling (AIPS'02)*, 2002.

Muñoz-Avila, H., McFarlane, D., Aha, D.W., Ballas, J., Breslow, L.A., & Nau, D. Using guidelines to constrain interactive case-based HTN planning. In: *Proceedings of the Third International Conference on Case-Based Reasoning* (ICCBR-99). Munich: Springer, 1999.

Muñoz-Avila, H., Aha, D.W., Nau D. S., Breslow, L.A., Weber, R., & Yamal, F. SiN: Integrating Case-based Reasoning with Task Decomposition. To appear in *Proceedings of the Seventeenth International Joint Conference on Artificial Intelligence (IJCAI-2001).* Seattle, WA: AAAI Press, 2001.

Muñoz-Avila, H., Gupta, K., Aha, D.W., Nau, D.S. Knowledge Based Project Planning. To appear in *Knowledge Management and Organizational Memories.* 2002.

Nau, D., Cao, Y., Lotem, A., & Muñoz-Avila, H. SHOP: Simple hierarchical ordered planner. *Proceedings of the Sixteenth International Joint Conference on Artificial Intelligence (IJCAI-99).* Stockholm: AAAI Press, 1999.

Smyth, B., and Keane, M.T., Remembering to forget: A competence-preserving case deletion policy for case-based reasoning systems. *In: Proceedings of the Fourthteen International Joint Conference on Artificial Intelligence (IJCAI-95).* AAAI Press, 1995.

Veloso, M. *Planning and learning by analogical reasoning.* Berlin: Springer-Verlag, 1994.

Improving Case-Based Recommendation

A Collaborative Filtering Approach

Derry O' Sullivan, David Wilson, and Barry Smyth

Smart Media Institute
University College Dublin
{dermot.osullivan,david.wilson,barry.smyth}@ucd.ie

Abstract. Data Mining, or Knowledge Discovery as it is also known, is becoming increasingly useful in a wide variety of applications. In the following paper, we look at its use in combating some of the traditional issues faced with recommender systems. We discuss our ongoing work which aims to enhance the performance of PTV, an applied recommender system working in the TV listings domain. This system currently combines the results of separate user-based collaborative and case-based components to recommend programs to users. Our extension to this idea operates on the theory of developing a case-based view of the collaborative component itself. By using data mining techniques to extract relationships between programme items, we can address the sparsity/maintenance problem. We also adopt a unique approach to recommendation ranking which combines user similarities and item similarities to provide more effective recommendation orderings. Experimental results corroborate our ideas, demonstrating the effectiveness of data mining in improving recommender systems by providing similarity knowledge to address sparsity, both at user-based recommendation level and recommendation ranking level.

1 Introduction

Due to the large amount of information present in the world today, technologies are required which filter all the available data, leaving us with only the information which is valuable to us. Such technologies must take into account vast quantities of data as well as scalability issues. Even information sources using application-specific market-basket data suffer this problem; hence recommender systems exist to help us find what we want. Modern recommender systems typically employ collaborative, content-based filtering techniques, or some combination thereof [1,2,3,4,5,6,7]. Content-based filtering techniques operate by analyzing item content and providing recommendations based on this. Genre, for example, could be used as a comparative descriptor for items such as television programs, movies, or music (e.g., *"Friends"* is of genre *comedy* as is *"Frasier"*). Given a partial or complete item description as a query, new items with similar descriptions can be usefully recommended. This provides a means of direct access to related items, as soon as they become available, but it does necessitate a knowledge-engineering overhead in building sufficient item descriptions. Another drawback appears when prioritizing the recommendation of items that are similar to those previously preferred; content-based systems may incur a cost in terms of the diversity of items recommended. In contrast,

S. Craw and A. Preece (Eds.): ECCBR 2002, LNAI 2416, pp. 278–291, 2002.

collaborative filtering(CF) techniques make recommendations by comparing user profiles of rated items, according to similarities and differences in the item ratings. These methods require little knowledge-engineering overhead, and there is greater opportunity for recommendation diversity. However, collaborative techniques incur a cost in gathering enough profile information to make accurate user similarity measurements. This *sparsity problem* tells us that, on average, two users are unlikely to have rated many of the same items and so there will be little direct overlap between their profiles. This is problematic when it comes to retrieval, because it means that there may be no direct way to measure the similarity between two profiles unless we have access to additional knowledge that allows us to compare non-identical profile items. There is also a *latency problem* in that new, one-off, or esoteric items will not be recommended until the items have found their way, if ever, into sufficiently many user profiles.

PTV is an established online recommender system deployed in the television listings domain[4]. PTV already combines complementary results from separate user-based collaborative and case-based components for recommending programs to users. In this research, we are interested in improving recommendation accuracy in the overall system by addressing the sparsity problem in the collaborative component. Sparsity (and latency) can be addressed directly by asking users to make additional rankings tailored to increase recommendation breadth (and depth). However, this presents an unwelcome burden for users, and a given user may have no basis for rating targeted items, which could weaken, rather than strengthen, system recommendations. Thus, we would like to base our efforts on the information provided through the normal task-based processing of the system. For example, we might assign genre information to establish comparative relationships between items beyond item overlap. We are mindful, however, that the collaborative filtering component is desirable, in part, because it can provide diverse and high-quality recommendations with minimal knowledge-engineering effort. One of the goals of this research, then, is to strike a good balance between improving collaborative recommendations and the amount of development overhead in doing so. Our approach applies automatic data mining techniques to extend the similarity relationships between programme items. Addressing the sparsity problem faced by collaborative systems is very much in the spirit of our experiences with reasoning knowledge maintenance in case-based reasoning (CBR) [8]. CBR would typically be viewed well within the content-based recommendation camp, but the methodology of retrieving similar user profiles (cases) and adapting them by combining new items with the current profile (case) context lends itself to a case-based view [9]. With this in mind, we propose a case-based perspective on collaborative filtering [10] which enables CF profiles to be used directly as cases, and we approach the problem of reducing sparsity as a similarity coverage problem in CBR, where similarities are based on an incomplete (possibly non-overlapping) space of descriptors that calls for augmentation (c.f., [8,11]).

This paper describes our data mining approach to improving case-based collaborative recommendation, and it presents experiments that show the benefits of mining similarity knowledge to address sparsity, both at the level of user-based recommendation and at the level of recommendation ranking. From the collaborative perspective, this provides a way to address the sparsity problem. From the CBR perspective, it provides a new approach to similarity maintenance.

2   Mining Programme Similarity Knowledge

There are many automated techniques that could be used to derive item similarity knowledge. The initial approach we have chosen is to apply data mining techniques (see [12] for an overview), in particular the *Apriori* algorithm [13], to extract association rules between programmes in PTV user-profile cases. By discovering hidden relationships between TV programmes, we may be able both to cover more potential profile matches and to make more informed recommendations. For example, under conventional collaborative filtering techniques, a person that likes *X-Files* and *Frasier* would not normally be comparable to a person that likes *Friends* and *ER*, but discovering a relationship between *Frasier* and *Friends* would provide a basis for profile comparison.

Association rules are of the form $A \Rightarrow B$, where A and B are sets of items (television programmes). In data mining terms, whenever a transaction (case) contains a certain itemset (set of programmes) A, then the transaction probably contains another itemset B.

The probability that a given rule holds, *rule confidence*, is the percentage of transactions containing B given that A occurs:

$$P(B \subseteq T | A \subseteq T) \tag{1}$$

The *support* of an itemset A is defined as the fraction of transactions supporting A with respect to the entire database. The support of a rule $A \Rightarrow B$, then, is the probability that both itemsets occur together in a transaction:

$$support(A \Rightarrow B) = P((A \cup B) \subseteq T) \tag{2}$$

The measure of rule confidence is related to support, and can be computed as follows:

$$confidence(A \Rightarrow B) = \frac{support(A \cup B)}{support(A)} \tag{3}$$

In mining association rules, the confidence and support values are often used to constrain exponentially large candidate rule sets by setting thresholds.

2.1   Item Similarities

Treating PTV user profiles as transactions and the rated programmes therein as itemsets, the Apriori algorithm can be used to derive a set of programme-programme association rules and confidence levels. We have limited this initial phase of the work to rules with single-programme antecedents and consequents. Table 1 shows some sample rules that were generated by running Apriori on our PTV data set. The resulting confidence values are taken as probabilities and used to fill in a programme-programme similarity matrix, as shown in Table 2, which provides the additional similarity knowledge necessary to compare non-identical profile items.

Since the matter of additional similarity coverage rests in populating the matrix as densely as possible, two natural extensions suggest themselves. First, the directly generated rules can be chained together ($A \Rightarrow B$ and $B \Rightarrow C$ imply $A \Rightarrow C$) to provide

Table 1. Selected rules for PTV

Rule	Support	Confidence
Friends ⇒ Frasier	12%	25%
Friends ⇒ ER	14%	37%
Frasier ⇒ ER	10%	22%

Table 2. Example item similarity matrix

	Friends	Frasier	ER
Friends	1	.25	.37
Frasier	-	1	.22
ER	-	-	1

indirect programme relationships. A choice then has to be made as to how the indirect rule confidence will be calculated (e.g., minimum, maximum, or some combination of the confidences in the potential paths); our experiments present results from a number of different models. Second, while it is not logically implied, we would like to see whether rule symmetry (e.g., *Friends⇒Frasier* supporting *Frasier⇒Friends*) could be exploited to extend coverage. Based on previous experiments [10], we have decided to ignore this aspect at present, noting it instead for future work. Rule similarity knowledge that is generated by Apriori, we refer to as *direct*, and additional derived knowledge as *indirect*.

Building such item-item similarity knowledge to address the sparsity/maintenance problem is similar in spirit to item-based collaborative techniques [14]. The item-based collaborative approach uses rating overlaps to build item-item similarities, and suggested items are then retrieved in direct comparison to the elements that comprise a user profile. The direct nature of such item retrieval recalls direct content-based item recommendation, as well as the potential cost in terms of diversity.

3   Recommendation Strategy

The availability of item similarity knowledge facilitates a new type of similarity-based recommendation strategy that combines elements from case-based and collaborative recommendation techniques. It facilitates the use of more sophisticated CBR-like similarity metrics on ratings-based profile data, which in turn make it possible to leverage indirect similarities between profile cases, and so generate improved recommendation lists. This new recommendation strategy consists of two basic steps:

1. The target profile, t is compared to each profile case, $s_i \epsilon S$, to select the k most similar cases.
2. The items contained within these selected cases (but absent in the target profile) are ranked according to the relevance to the target, and the r most similar items are returned as recommendations.

3.1 Profile Matching

The profile similarity metric is presented in Equation 4 as the weighted-sum of the similarities between the items in the target and source profile cases. In the situation where there is a direct correspondence between an item in the source, s_i, and the target, t'_j, then maximal similarity is assumed (Equation 5). However, the nature of ratings-based profile cases is such that these direct correspondences are rare and in such situations the similarity value of the source profile item is computed as the mean similarity between this item and the n most similar items in the target profile case $(t'_1...t'_n)$ (Equation 6).

$$PSim(t, s, n) = \sum_{s_i \in s} w_i \cdot ISim(t, s_i, n) \tag{4}$$

$$ISim(t, s_i, n) = 1 \ \ if \ t'_j = s_i \tag{5}$$

$$= \frac{\sum_{j=1..n} sim(t'_j, s_i)}{n} \tag{6}$$

Notice, that if $n = 1$ and there is a perfect one-to-one correspondence between the target and source profile cases, then this profile similarity metric is equivalent to the traditional weighted-sum similarity metric used in CBR.

3.2 Recommendation Ranking

Once the k most similar profile cases $(\hat{S})$ to the target have been identified a set of ranked item recommendations can be produced. There are three factors to consider when ranking these recommendations. First, we want to give priority to those items that have a high similarity to the target profile case. Second, items that occur in many of the retrieved profile cases should be preferred to those that occur in few profile cases. Finally, items that are recommended by profiles that are similar to the target should be preferred to items that are recommended by less similar profiles. Accordingly we compute the *relevance* of an item, s_i from a retrieved profile case, s, with respect to the target profile, t, as shown in Equation 7; where $S' \subseteq \hat{S}$ is the set of retrieved profile cases that contain s_i.

$$Rel(s_i, t, \hat{S}) = ISim(t, s_i, k) \cdot \frac{|S'|}{|\hat{S}|} \cdot \sum_{s \in S'} PSim(t, s, k) \tag{7}$$

4   Experimental Evaluation

In order to evaluate our approach to mining and applying similarity knowledge, we conducted a series of experiments using data from 622 PTV user profiles. The first set of experiments were designed to investigate the performance characteristics of our chosen data mining algorithm within the PTV domain. The second set of experiments tested the potential for mining additional similarity knowledge, in terms of relationships between programme items. The third set of experiments tested the potential of the approach for improving actual recommendation quality. We repeated our experiments using 3 further datasets:

1. MovieLens dataset consisting of 659 user profiles from the movie recommender domain;
2. Fischlar dataset consisting of 650 user profiles similar to PTV (Fischlar [15] is a streaming video library which uses PTV's personalization technologies to provide recommendations).
3. Eachmovie dataset consisting of 651 user profiles similar to MovieLens.

For experimental runs, we examined only positively rated items, leaving negative ratings for future work.

4.1 Tuning Data Mining

In our first set of experiments, we applied the Apriori algorithm to both datasets for different parameterizations of the algorithm. Since data mining was the basis for maintaining similarity knowledge, we wanted to determine how rule generation would be influenced by parameter choice, namely confidence and support thresholds. The first experiment tested the number of rules generated for varying levels of confidence and support. In the PTV data, changes in the number of rules across confidence values for different support levels were quite similar, indicating that the parameterization is more dependent on the measure of confidence than on support. This can be seen more clearly in the results of the second experiment which measured how well the generated rules match the entire profile set. This average accuracy is computed as the ratio of antecedent and consequent matches to antecedent matches. There is little change in rule accuracy as the level of support changes across different levels of confidence. A similar pattern emerged in results from the MovieLens and Fischlar data [10]. Based on these results, we chose representative support levels (PTV and Fischlar: 5%, Eachmovie and MovieLens: 20%) for the remainder of the experiments. Having different representative support values highlights an important difference; both the PTV and Fischlar datasets were much sparser than MovieLens. To corroborate this fact, we use a density metric (Equation 8) taken from [14]:

$$Density(Database) = \frac{Number\ of\ nonzero\ entries}{Number\ of\ total\ entries} \qquad (8)$$

where the number of total entries is calculated by multiplying the number of users by the number of items that have been rated at least once; the number of nonzero entries is the total number of ratings overall in the database.

Using this metric, we found PTV is 160% denser than Fischlar, MovieLens 182% denser than Eachmovie and 1100% denser than PTV. This causes lower rule generation at high support values, which necessitates dropping to low support values to find more rules with higher confidences.

4.2 Increasing Similarity Coverage

In the next set of experiments, we were interested in evaluating the degree to which similarity coverage could be improved by the rule sets. For the first experiment, the density of the generated item-item similarity matrix was taken as our measure of similarity coverage. We varied confidence levels from 40% to 5% at 5% intervals. On each run we generated the Apriori direct rule set, as well as a maximal indirect rule set and filled in the item similarity matrix, taking the matrix density relative to the items that participated in the rule set. Results for PTV showed direct item similarities provide an average of 10% coverage, but there is a marked increase for the indirect similarity rules (65% coverage in the best case). Of course, the Apriori method does not generate association rules for every profile programme, and in fact Apriori ignores a great many programmes because their frequency fails the Apriori threshold tests. Nevertheless when we add these newly generated rules to the full item-item matrix, we found an increase in density from 0.6% to 2.6%. Again, a similar pattern was found in the MovieLens (.08% to .36%), Fischlar (.17% to .65%) and Eachmovie (.1% to .35%) datasets [10].

4.3 Improving Recommendations

With encouraging results for increasing the similarity coverage, we designed experiments to test the effect of this new similarity knowledge on recommendation quality. Based on our earlier experiments, we chose representative confidence levels of 10% on the PTV and Fischlar datasets, 60% on Eachmovie and 70% on the MovieLens dataset.

Recommendation Coverage

In the first experiment, we measured the number of profiles in the PTV dataset that could possibly be compared as a percentage of all potential profile comparisons for different similarity metrics. Using our standard collaborative filtering metric gave coverage of 42%, while our similarity metric using direct rules only and then adding indirect rules increased the coverage to 52% and 70% respectively.

Recommendation Accuracy

The final experiment tested the accuracy of recommendation on both datasets. After generating direct and indirect similarity rules, a profile case is selected from the case-base. A parameterized percentage of the items in the selected case are removed from consideration. The remainder of the profile case is then used as the basis for retrieval, using our similarity metric and recommendation ranking. Accuracy was calculated using three metrics:

1. Percentage of removed items that were recommended in each case.
2. Percentage of profiles in which at least one removed item was recommended.
3. A combination of the above: percentage of removed items that were recommended, given a recommendation could be made.

We were most interested in looking for uplift in recommendation quality when comparing our CBR technique (using direct and indirect similarity rules) to a pure collaborative filtering technique. We tested the effect of our recommendation ranking function by correlating rank score/numerical rank and item success. On the PTV dataset, results of the first metric showed that using direct rules (20%) outperformed indirect rules (18%), which in turn outperformed pure CF (8%). A similar pattern was seen in the other metrics

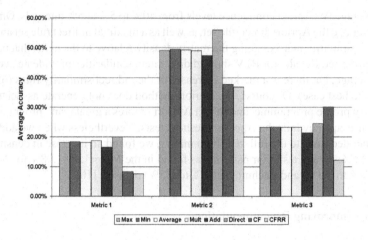

Fig. 1. PTV recommendation accuracy.

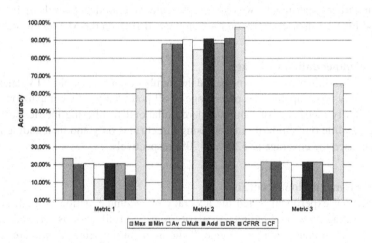

Fig. 2. MovieLens recommendation accuracy.

except for metric 3 which showed pure CF having a higher accuracy (30%) than either CBR method (Direct: 24%, Indirect: 30%) (Figure 1). Fischlar data provided similar evidence to PTV; metric 1 showed rule techniques outperforming their collaborative counterparts (CF: 4%, Direct: 15%, Indirect: 12%). Metrics 2 and 3 confirmed these findings; however metric 3 showed CF (34%) defeating both CBR methods (Direct: 21%, Indirect: 18%) (Figure 3). These results seem to indicate that indirect rules may not be as useful as their direct counterparts; another possibility is that these rules are generating high quality recommendations which are not present in our profile cases.

Eachmovie results showed a similar pattern to the previous two datasets; however, an increase was noted in metric accuracies for all techniques with direct and indirect rules performing better than CF (Figure 4). On the MovieLens dataset, different results

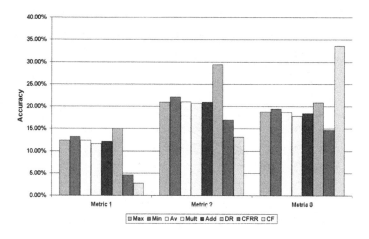

Fig. 3. Fischlar recommendation accuracy.

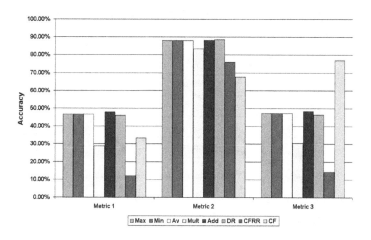

Fig. 4. Eachmovie recommendation accuracy.

were seen. CF outperforms both direct and indirect rules in all three metrics (by almost 30% on average) (Figure 2). These results may indicate that more densely populated profile case-bases favour CF techniques, an issue that bears further study for possible multi-strategy approaches.

Recommendation Ranking Accuracy

In order to test our recommendation ranking function against pure CF methods, we used a simplified version of our recommendation ranking method to test CF ranking: For each unique item in our list of recommended profiles s_i, where $S' \subseteq S$ is the set of retrieved

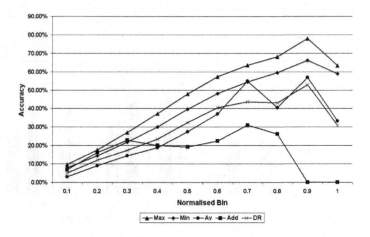

Fig. 5. PTV recommendation rank score accuracy.

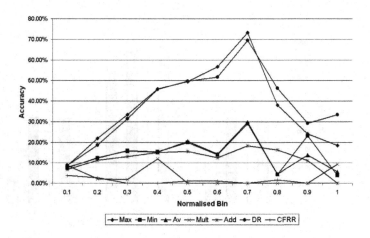

Fig. 6. MovieLens recommendation rank score accuracy.

profiles that contain s_i, and a target t:

$$Rel(s_i, t) = \frac{|S'|}{|S|} \cdot \sum_{s \in S'} CFSim(s, t) \tag{9}$$

We then test our ranking functions by finding correlations between the score/rank of an item and its success over all profiles. For recommendation score, we normalize the score and then find the number of successes in each bin (0 - 1.0 in 0.1 increments); for rank, our bins contain all the successes at each rank position over all profiles. PTV results show that certain models (Maximum, Addition, Average) used in chaining for indirect rule generation give greater correlations over both direct (14% increase rank,

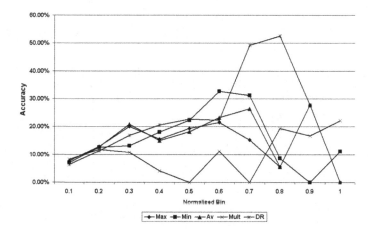

Fig. 7. Fischlar recommendation rank score accuracy.

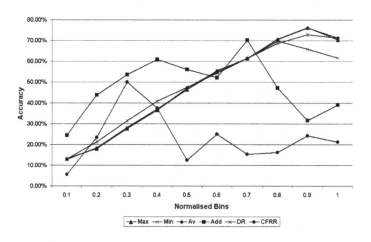

Fig. 8. Eachmovie recommendation rank score accuracy.

19% score) and CF techniques (52% increase rank) (Figure 5). We also found that score binning proved extremely inaccurate under CF with little or no correlation to be found.

With MovieLens data, we again found that certain models provide uplift from direct to indirect rules(8% rank, 4% score) (Figure 6). Again CF results proved inaccurate for use. When comparing both datasets ranking correlations, we also note that using the Maximal model for rule chaining provides the best possible accuracy. Eachmovie results displayed Add, Average and Maximal models performing equally well (Figure 8). With the Fischlar dataset, however, the minimal chaining model gave highest accuracy. Direct rules outperform indirect (14% rank, 24% score) and CF (56% rank) techniques (Figure 7). Future work aims to discover how chaining models affect certain datasets into giving contrasting results.

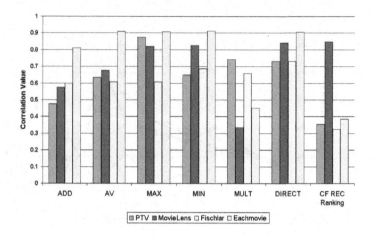

Fig. 9. Recommendation ranking correlations.

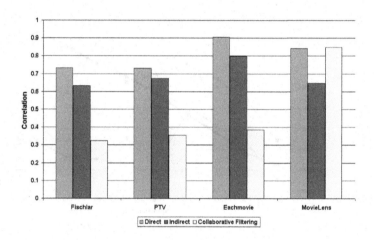

Fig. 10. Accuracy of Techniques.

Figures 10 and 11 confirm a theory discussed previously; the effect of density on techniques used. As the density increases, CF techniques perform comparatively with our techniques; the reverse is true, however, when sparser datasets are used.

5 Conclusion and Future Work

We have described a data mining approach to ameliorating the problem of sparse similarity knowledge in profile-based recommendation systems. From a collaborative filtering standpoint, this provides a means to address the sparsity problem. From a case-based reasoning standpoint, this provides a mechanism for maintaining similarity knowledge. An initial evaluation of the work has been conducted in the domain of TV listing rec-

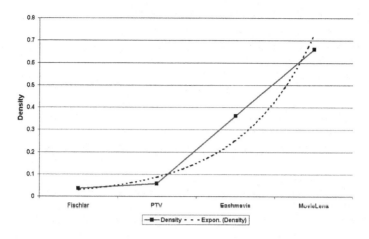

Fig. 11. Dataset Density.

ommendation, using a well known commercial recommender (PTV [4]), and the results are supported by additional experiments, both in the movie recommendation domain and another TV listing recommendation system. The results provide good evidence in support of the view that learning similarity knowledge through profile mining makes it possible to improve overall recommendation quality, especially in sparser datasets.

Our future work will investigate the effects of these algorithms on further data sets to reinforce out theory on density/accuracy, using multiple antecedents and consequents in data mining, inclusion of negative ratings and the use of behavioural data [16] to enhance/test our recommender accuracy. We would also like to compare data mining to item-based collaborative metrics[14], both in measures such as Mean Absolute Error, as well as in terms of recommendation diversity.

References

1. Herlocker, J., Konstan, J., Borchers, A., Riedl, J.: An algorithmic framework for performing collaborative filtering. In: Proceedings of the 1999 Conference on Research and Development in Information Retrieval: SIGIR-99. (1999)
2. Konstan, J., Miller, B., Maltz, D., Herlocker, J., Gordon, L., Riedl, J.: Grouplens: Applying collaborative filtering to usenet news. Communications of the ACM **40** (1997) 77–87
3. Shardanand, U., Maes, P.: Social information filtering: Algorithms for automating "word of mouth". In: Proceedings of ACM CHI'95 Conference on Human Factors in Computing Systems. (1995) 210–217
4. Smyth, B., Cotter, P.: Personalized electronic programme guides. Artificial Intelligence Magazine **21** (2001)
5. Good, N., Schafer, J.B., Konstan, J.A., Borchers, A., Sarwar, B.M., Herlocker, J.L., Riedl, J.: Combining collaborative filtering with personal agents for better recommendations. In: Proceedings of the 1999 Conference of the American Association of Artifical Intelligence (AAAI-99). (1999) 439–446

6. Soboroff, I., Nicholas, C.: Combining content and collaboration in text filtering. In: Proceedings of the IJCAI-99 Workshop on Machine Learning for Information Filtering. (1999)
7. Balabanović, M., Shoham, Y.: Fab: Content-based, collaborative recommendation. Communications of the ACM **40** (1997) 66–72
8. Wilson, D.C., Leake, D.B.: Maintaining case-based reasoners: Dimensions and directions. Computational Intelligence **17** (2001)
9. Watson, I.: CBR is a methodology not a technology. Knowledge Based Systems **12** (1999) 303–308
10. O'Sullivan, D., Wilson, D., Smyth, B.: Using collaborative filtering data in case-based recommendation. In: Proceedings of the 15th International FLAIRS Conference. (2002) To Appear.
11. Fox, S., Leake, D.: Learning to refine indexing by introspective reasoning. In: Proceedings of First International Conference on Case-Based Reasoning, Berlin, Springer Verlag (1995) 431–440
12. Hipp, J., Nakhaeizadeh, U.G.: Mining association rules: Deriving a superior algorithm by analyzing today's approaches. In: Proceedings of the 4th European Symposium on Principles of Data Mining and Knowledge Discovery. (2000)
13. Agrawal, R., Mannila, H., Srikant, R., Toivonen, H., Verkamo, A.I.: Fast discovery of association rules. In Fayyad, U.M., Piatetsky-Shapiro, G., Smyth, P., Uthurusamy, R., eds.: Advances in Knowledge Discovery and Data Mining. AAAI Press (1996) 307–328
14. Sarwar, B.M., Karypis, G., Konstan, J.A., Riedl, J.: Item-based collaborative filtering recommender algorithms. In: Proceedings of the Tenth International World Wide Web Conference. (2001)
15. Donald, K.M.: (Use of the fischlar video library system)
16. Charu Aggarwal, Zheng Sun, P.S.Y.: Finding profile association rules (1998)

Efficient Similarity Determination and Case Construction Techniques for Case-Based Reasoning

David W. Patterson, Niall Rooney, and Mykola Galushka

The Northern Ireland Knowledge Engineering Laboratory
School of Information and Software Engineering
University of Ulster at Jordanstown,
Newtownabbey, County Antrim,
Northern Ireland
{wd.patterson, nf.rooney, mg.galushka}@ulst.ac.uk

Abstract. In this paper, we present three techniques for knowledge discovery in case-based reasoning. The first two techniques D-HS and D-HS+SR are concerned with the discovery of similarity knowledge and operate on an uncompacted case-base while the third technique D-HS+PSR is concerned with the discovery of both similarity and case knowledge and operates on a compacted case-base. All three techniques provide a very efficient and competent means of similarity determination in CBR, which are empirically shown to be up to 25 times faster than k-NN without any loss in competency. D-HS+PSR proposes a novel approach to automatically engineering compact case-bases with a minimal overhead to the system, compared to other approaches such as case deletion/addition. Additionally as the approach provides a means for automatically reducing the number of cases required in the case-base without any loss in problem solving competency it has the greatest implication of the three techniques for reducing the effects of the utility problem in CBR.

1 Introduction

The nearest neighbour (NN) algorithm is a commonly used similarity metric in CBR. Its appeal includes its simplicity, its transparency, its robustness in the presence of noise and the fact that it does not require training. Over the years researchers have studied the nearest neighbour algorithm in detail to try and improve upon its competency. For example its noise tolerance has been improved by retrieving k nearest cases and introducing a 'voting' scheme to combine the various predictions [21]. Attribute values have been weighted according to their significance to help deal with the curse of dimensionality [21], cases themselves have been weighted to increase the retrieval probability of more competent cases ([3,2,10]) and approaches to improving the manner in which symbolic attributes are dealt with by the algorithm proposed [16,2,3]. All of these improvements have focused on improving the competency of the NN algorithm. A major drawback of the algorithm, due to its exhaustive search through the case-base for the most similar case, remains its efficiency. This is poor especially for large case-bases. A serious consequence of this poor efficiency in CBR is an exacerbation of the effects of the utility problem.

S. Craw and A. Preece (Eds.): ECCBR 2002, LNAI 2416, pp. 292–305.
© Springer-Verlag Berlin Heidelberg 2002

The utility problem, which is seen in many problem solving systems, manifests itself as a reduction in the efficiency (average problem solving time) of a problem solving system as new knowledge is learned. It is classically observed in first principles reasoners such as speed up learners [20] but has also been observed in CBR systems which do not have a first principles reasoner at their core [17]. In CBR the time taken to solve a problem is composed of the time required to search the case-base to retrieve an appropriately similar case plus the time taken to adapt the retrieved case's solution. The less similar a target problem and retrieved case are, the more processing is required during adaptation and the longer the problem solving process will be [19]. Therefore to improve efficiency, compelling arguments exist which advocate continually adding cases to a case-base over time to try and maximise problem space coverage thus reducing both the amount of adaptation required and the time taken to solve problems. Although this may initially seem to be logical unfortunately in reality it has not been shown to be true. In general it remains that for small case-bases the addition of a new case improves the problem space coverage (and hence the adaptation efficiency) of the case-base significantly. As the case-base grows in size the improvement on overall problem space coverage caused by the addition of a new case becomes less significant and with it the associated effects of improved problem solving efficiency are less pronounced. Finally there is a point reached (saturation point) where the savings provided by the decrease in adaptation costs, as a result of adding a new case to the case-base, are less than the costs associated with the corresponding increase in the case-base search time. Thus the overall time taken to solve a problem actually increases with the addition of a new case to the case-base. This is known as the utility problem in CBR.

A number of techniques have been applied to reducing the effects of the utility problem in CBR. All can be regarded as knowledge maintenance strategies, which add a considerable overhead to the housekeeping functions of the CBR system and all focus on the improved management of either similarity/retrieval knowledge or case knowledge. Most of these techniques focus on ensuring that the basic problem solving ability (competence) of the CBR system is maintained whilst reducing retrieval time. These techniques fall into two main categories, namely, policies which do not limit the size of the case-base in achieving the maximal problem space coverage possible and those which do. The former use indexing structures to improve search efficiency while the latter, which include case addition and deletion policies, rely on the fact that the number of cases present in the case-base will never be allowed to become so large so as to affect the search efficiency of the retrieval process significantly. That is, they strategically limit the size of the case-base to avoid the saturation point ever being reached. Overviews of these strategies are now presented.

1.1 Case Indexing Policies

Case indexing has been widely applied in CBR as a method of improving search efficiency to combat the effects of the utility problem. As only a selective portion of the case-base is made available during retrieval, search time is reduced and the efficiency of identifying a possible solution is increased dramatically. Unfortunately building and maintaining a competent index is not an easy task as it is highly dependent on the retrieval circumstances, which are constantly changing. Therefore the indexing structure (retrieval knowledge) of the case-base must be maintained to reflect this. This maintenance of retrieval knowledge can be a major burden on CBR systems. If the indexing scheme is poor or maintenance is ignored, cases with good solutions to the target problem may be overlooked as they reside in a different part of the case-base unaccessible under the current indexing scheme. This can lead to the complex adaptation of less suited cases, a reduction in competency and in severe situations, problem-solving failures. Therefore, due to poor retrieval knowledge or insufficient maintenance, in an attempt to improve efficiency, competency is often sacrificed [11].

A number of researchers have applied indexing strategies to CBR. Zhang & Yang [22] take an indexing approach to reducing redundancy in case-bases, based on a neural network model. Aha [1] presented a methodology of continually refining a case library in the domain of conversational case-base reasoning to improve both competency and efficiency. Deangdej [4] devised a dynamic indexing structure to retrieve cases at run time from a case-base of over two million cases. Fox [5] developed an introspective reasoning technique for dynamically refining case indexes based on previous retrievals. Smyth has devised an indexing scheme based on a case competence model [19], which improves retrieval competency and efficiency.

1.2   Case Addition Policies

The basic theory behind this approach is to prevent the case-base from ever becoming so large that efficiency is detrimentally affected. The majority of these techniques focus on some concept of problem space coverage provided by the cases in the case-base and aim to build efficient case-bases with the maximal coverage using the minimal number of cases. For example a novel case addition approach to maintaining competency in case-bases is presented in CaseMaker [8]. Here the best case to add to a developing case-base is selected based on an evaluation of the additional coverage it provides. Zhu & Yang [23] have proposed a case addition policy, also based on coverage, which keeps efficiency high, thus avoiding the utility problem, while at the same time guaranteeing to preserve the competence of a case-base. Additionally they highlight the importance of defining the right similarity metrics in order to define more accurately case-base coverage. Portinale et al. [12,13] also propose a system which determines if a new case should be added to a case-base using adaptability cost as a determinant measure. Racine & Yang [14] describe how contradictions and inconsistencies within a case-base can lead to degradation in efficiency. They advocate validating a new case before it is added to the case-base. As with the indexing strategies there is a large maintenance overhead associated with these techniques and therefore they may need to be carried out off line.

1.3   Case Deletion Policies

Most deletion policies are also based on some notion of the problem space coverage provided by cases. Deletion is a very difficult strategy to implement in CBR as some cases are inevitably more expendable than others. This is due to the fact that cases are the basic unit of both *competency* and *efficiency* in a case-base [17,12]. Techniques applied include the Footprint-Utility Deletion Policy [19], which selects cases for deletion based on their competence *and* utility (efficiency) contributions to the case-base. Hunt et al. [7] propose a system based on the immune system designed to forget cases which were no longer relevant to the problems being solved. This was based on how relevant cases were to recent problems encountered and to other cases in the case-base. Again these strategies add a considerable maintenance burden to the CBR system and therefore may need to be carried out off line. Another problem with case addition and deletion policies is that inevitably case knowledge is excluded from the case-base. It is widely recognised that knowledge can be converted from one knowledge container into another in CBR systems [15]. For example Hanney [6] has demonstrated how case-knowledge can be used as a source of adaptation knowledge. McSherry has done likewise [8]. Anand et al [2] have demonstrated that case-knowledge can also act as a rich source of similarity knowledge. Therefore by excluding some of the cases vital knowledge could be lost to the system.

The main aims of this research were four-fold. The first goal was the development of a means of similarity determination, which was more efficient than the k-NN algorithm. The second goal was that the algorithms should have at least the same competency as k-NN. The third goal was to develop a system which could reduce the effects of the utility problem in CBR. The final goal was to develop an approach, which could automatically and efficiently manage both similarity knowledge and case knowledge in CBR in *real time*, something which most policies designed to reduce the effects the utility problem are inefficient at doing.

Specifically we describe 2 algorithms Discretised-Highest Similarity (D-HS) and Discretised-Highest Similarity with Set Reduction (D-HS+SR) designed to improve the efficiency of the similarity determination process. The second technique is designed to improve upon the competency of the first. We take the view that case knowledge should not be readily excluded from the case-base in an effort to improve efficiency alone but retained to enrich the engineering and maintenance of the other knowledge containers. We present empirical evidence, which shows these novel similarity determination algorithms to have a competency similar to k-NN but an efficiency which is substantially better, especially for larger case-bases. A third technique is also presented Discretised-Highest Similarity with Pattern Solution Reuse (D-HS+PSR) which was designed to improve upon the retrieval efficiency of the first 2 techniques by reducing the number of cases in the case-base. This is in the spirit of the classical case deletion policies of Smyth [18] with the single major advantage of a minimal case-base knowledge engineering overhead. This technique is guaranteed to have the same competency as the D-HS+SR approach but will be faster for large case-bases. In this we propose a 2 tier case-base architecture whereby reasoning is carried out using the reduced case-base (the primary case-base) but the system has the facility to consult the unreduced case-base (the secondary case-base) for knowledge discovery purposes when necessary, and in doing so this architecture ensures no knowledge is lost from the system. All 3 techniques are similarity knowledge discovery techniques with the last one also being a case knowledge discovery and maintenance technique. The research presented here forms part of the M^2 CBR system [9], which was designed to create an architecture wherein the processes of CBR knowledge discovery and maintenance could be automated to reduce the amount of effort that was required from humans and therefore make CBR technology more attractive to industrialists.

2 Methodology

The training cases were processed to create a matrix M where each cell $M(i,j)$ contains a list of cases whose normalised attribute value x for attribute i lies in an interval $1/d_i * (j-1) <= x < 1/d_i * j$. For nominal attributes the value of d_i is simply the number of possible attribute values. For continuous numeric attributes, we chose di to have the value of 10 so in essence numeric attributes are discretised into 10 intervals. The 3 retrieval techniques presented are all based on this matrix structure. The first of these, D-HS, identifies the 5 cases which have the most matching attribute values to a target case. A target case was said to match a case from the case-base on a particular attribute value if both of their attribute values fell into the same discretised interval as defined in equation 1. A count was kept of the number of times the attributes of each case in the case-base case fell into the same discretised intervals as the corresponding attribute of the target. This means that the similarity function has maximal value if two cases agree on all their attribute values and 0 if they agree on none of their attribute values. The 5 cases from the case-base, which had the highest number of matching attributes, were used to predict an average value in the case of a continuous output field, and a majority class for classification problems.

$$similarity(C_1, C_2) = \sum_{n=1}^{d} match(C_1(n), C_2(n)) \qquad (1)$$

where

d is the number of attributes, $C_1(n)$ is the nth attribute value of case C_1

$match(C_1(n), C_2(n)) = 1$ if $C_1(n)$ and $C_2(n)$ lie in the same discretised interval,

0 otherwise

Case-Base:

C1(0.1,0.3, 0.9,0.6)
C2(0.2,0.9, 0.4,0.3)
C3(0.4,0.3 ,0.1,0.2)
C4(0.5,0.9,0.6,0.8)
C5(0.3, 0.1,0.6,0.4)
C6(0.9,0.5,0.3,0.3)
C7(0.3,0.3,0.2,0.4)
C8(0.3,0.3,0.1,0.2)
C9(0.2,0.5,0.5,0.3)
C10(0.1,0.2,0.5,0.3)
T(0.3,0.5,0.5,?)

Matrix:

	1	2	3	4	5
Interval: A1	C1,C10	C2,C5,C7,C8,C9,T	C3,C4		C6
A2	C5	C1,C3,C7,C8,C10	C6,C9,T		C2,C4
A3	C3,C8	C6,C7	C2,C9,C10,T	C4,C5	C1
Interval range:	0.0-0.2	0.2-0.4	0.4-0.6	0.6-0.8	0.8-1

Fig. 1. Matrix Representation of the Cases in the Case-Base

The construction of the matrix in Figure 1 is shown for an artificial sample case-base with 10 cases, each having 3 input attributes (A1,A2,A3) split into 5 discretised intervals and one output field. In addition, the position of a target case T is shown in bold along with those cases with matching attribute values to T.

Figure 2 shows the results of a retrieval for target T which, from Figure 1, can be seen falls into the 2nd interval for A1, the 3rd interval for A2 and the 3rd interval for A3. It also shows the matching count table which holds the counts as described previously. Cases are added to the initial retrieval set in descending order of similarity values, until the initial retrieval set has at least 5 cases. C9, the case with the highest similarity (matching count of 3) was added first, then the next most similar case was C2 (matching count of 2), followed by cases C5, C6, C7, C8 and C10 which all have a similarity of 1.

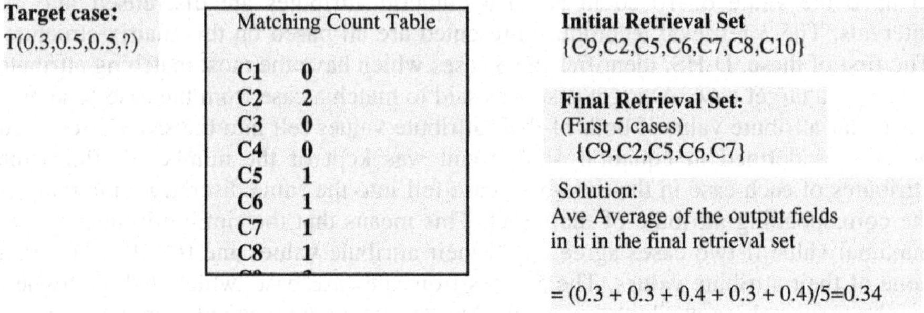

Target case: T(0.3,0.5,0.5,?)	Matching Count Table		Initial Retrieval Set {C9,C2,C5,C6,C7,C8,C10}
	C1	0	
	C2	2	Final Retrieval Set:
	C3	0	(First 5 cases)
	C4	0	{C9,C2,C5,C6,C7}
	C5	1	
	C6	1	Solution:
	C7	1	Ave Average of the output fields
	C8	1	in ti in the final retrieval set

$$= (0.3 + 0.3 + 0.4 + 0.3 + 0.4)/5 = 0.34$$

Fig. 2. D-HS Retrieval

The initial retrieval set now has 7 cases and is reduced to the final retrieval set (consisting of 5 cases) by taking the first five cases in order. The solution was calculated by taking the average value of the individual case solution fields for these cases. Therefore cases C8 and C10 were arbitrarily excluded from the final retrieval set. The situation where the initial retrieval set has more than 5 cases we refer to as Condition 1. This is a limitation of the technique as we are forced to remove cases that have the same similarity value as the *minimum similarity* of the final retrieval set, therefore potentially excluding cases which could lead to a better solution. The minimum similarity is the lowest matching count of the cases in the final retrieval set. In our example this has value 1. This limitation was addressed by the second technique, an adaptation of D-HS called D-HS+SR. In this technique, at least N highest matching cases were added to the initial retrieval set, with cases being added again in descending order of their matching count in a similar fashion to D-HS. The initial retrieval set was reduced to 5 by finding the closest cases to the target case according to a distance metric, which in our experiments was chosen to be Euclidean, and choosing the 5 cases with minimum distance. In Figure 3, this process is shown for a value of N equal to 5[1].

It can be seen that the initial retrieval set is the same as it was with D-HS {C9,C2,C5,C6,C7,C8,C10}. This set was reduced to 5 cases by finding the 5 closest cases based on the distance metric. Notice that the 5 closest cases in the final retrieval set are not the same as the 5 cases selected by D-HS leading to a potentially different solution. If there are only N cases in the initial retrieval set, no reduction is necessary.

---

[1] We set N by empirical means to be 10

Matching Count Table	
C1	0
C2	2
C3	0
C4	0
C5	1
C6	1
C7	1
C8	1
C9	3
C10	1

Initial retrieval set:

{C9,C2,C5,C6,C7,C8,C10 }

Set reduction based on distance:

Case	Distance
C9	0.1
C2	0.42
C5	0.41
C6	0.63
C7	0.36
C8	0.45
C10	0.36

Final Retrieval Set
{ C9,C10,C7,C5,C2}

Solution:

Average of the 5 closest cases =
(0.3 ı 0.3 ı 0.4 + 0.4 + 0.3)/5
= 0.34

Fig. 3. D-HS+SR Retrieval

The D-HS+SR process can be made more efficient by noting that for large case-bases, there is a high probability that a number of different target cases will have the same matrix retrieval pattern (as a result of the attribute value discretisation process) and therefore result in the same initial retrieval set. By using an auxiliary retrieval tree structure, such as the one in Figure 4, it is possible to store a target case's retrieval pattern with its initial retrieval set, thereby negating the need for a matrix lookup the next time the same pattern is encountered by the system. From Figure 4 it can be seen that each level of the tree corresponds to an attribute and each node in the tree is partitioned into the number of discretised intervals for that attribute. Each of the partitions has child pointers to the next attribute. The use of the tree structure is shown in Figure 4 for the same target case and case-base as shown in previous examples. The target's 1st attribute falls into interval 2, its 2nd attribute falls into interval 3 and the 3rd attribute also falls into interval 3, so the tree is descended as shown to find an existing initial retrieval set for pattern {2,3,3}. The matrix is now only required during retrieval if a target case's pattern is not recognised by the tree (that is if it has not been encountered before). In this situation the matrix is used to solve the problem and the new target pattern and respective initial retrieval set are added to the tree and made available for future retrievals. This approach is referred to as D-HS+PSR and is inspired by the basic principals of CBR of reusing old solutions where possible. The tree retrieval patterns therefore were used to construct a new compact *primary* case-base. Figure 4 shows the new structure of a case C' within this primary case-base which can be used to solve target case T. It can be viewed as a generalisation of the case knowledge within the matrix from a target case's perspective. It should be noted that the efficiency of the D-HS+PSR technique will automatically improve over time, as new solutions to unseen target patterns are determined from the matrix and added to the tree for future reuse. In this way the generalized cases form a primary case-base, which the system initially interrogates to form solutions. If it cannot form a solution, it then falls back upon the matrix (the secondary case-base) to form a solution. This technique has an initial overhead in setting up the primary case-base but for large data sets with good problem space coverage this should be compensated for by the improved speed by which problems can be solved by using the primary case-base as opposed to the matrix. Additionally this technique is guaranteed to have the same competency as the D-HS+SR approach because the D-HS+SR algorithm is used to determine the initial retrieval sets, which are being reused, in the first place.

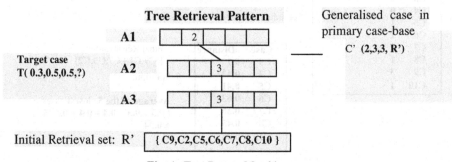

Fig. 4. Tree Pattern Matching

Three Hypotheses were formed based on this theory. The first (H1) was that the retrieval techniques as described will work significantly faster then k-NN for large case-bases. It can be seen that D-HS is linear in time complexity. In the case of uniformly distributed attributes this is of $O(N)$ where N the size of data. In the worse case where each case falls in one attribute interval only for all attributes this requires $O(dN)$ iterations where d is the number of attributes. This may appear similar to the time complexity for k-NN, however there is less numerical calculation required to update the counts array at each iteration, than is required to calculate the distance between a case and the target case using k-NN. The second hypothesis (H2) stated that D-HS +SR will show better competencies than D-HS where Condition 1 is likely to occur. The final hypothesis (H3) stated that D-HS+PSR will show improvement in retrieval times most noticeably for large case-bases with good problem space coverage, as in such situations the frequency of repeated solutions is likely to be high.

3 Experimental Technique

k-NN, D-HS, D-HS+SR and D-HS+PSR were compared for efficiency and competency using a 10-fold cross validation on 15 case-bases to predict the solution for a target case. Thirteen case-bases were taken from the UCI machine learning repository and two, namely DATAHOUSE 1 and DATAHOUSE 2, were taken from a housing domain supplied by a local Housing Agency.

Case-bases were filtered to remove irrelevant attributes as indicated by their case-base descriptions and missing attributes were replaced using a means or modal technique. Mean absolute errors were recorded for each technique after 10 fold cross validation. The absolute difference between the predicted value and the target case's actual solution field gave the absolute error. The Mean Absolute Error (MAE) was the average of the absolute errors over all cross fold validation folds. Two tailed paired t-tests (with a 95% confidence interval) were carried out to see if the difference between the competencies for k-NN and D-HS, k-NN and D-HS+SR and k-NN and D-HS+PSR respectively were statistically significant. The time taken to carry out the cross validation was recorded as an indication of retrieval efficiency for each technique.

4 Experimental Results and Discussion

The MAEs for k-NN, D-HS and D-HS+SR, the percentage change in MAE compared to K-NN and results of t-tests along with their significance values are shown in Table 1. The results for the MAEs for D-HS+PSR are not shown as they are were the same as for D-HS+SR. Statistically significant differences in MAE compared to k-NN are shown in bold font.

Table 1. Retrieval Competencies

Case-base	K-NN	D-HS				D-HS+SR			
		MAE	%	t-val	sig	MAE	%	t-val	sig
SOYBEAN	0.0925	0.006	92.8	0.993	0.347	0	100	1.083	0.307
ECHOCARDIOGRAM	0.1384	0.142	-3.1	-1.93	0.851	0.142	-3.1	-2.94	0.776
IRIS	0.0273	0.026	4.8	0.049	0.962	0.023	15.8	0.325	0.753
GLASS	1.09	1.01	7.3	-0.55	0.95	0.93	14.7	0.478	0.64
DERMATOLOGY	0.0261	0.022	12.6	0.593	0.568	0.020	21.1	0.993	0.347
HOUSING	4.276	3.37	21.2	1.33	0.215	3.15	26.3	1.884	0.092
DATAHOUSE 1	7523	6953	7.6	2.602	**0.029**	6939	7.8	4.252	**0.002**
DATAHOUSE 2	5017	4515	10	4.177	**0.002**	4680	6.7	2.479	**0.035**
BALANCE	0.1481	0.114	23	2.423	**0.038**	0.193	-23.3	-1.826	0.101
BREAST CANCER	0.0435	0.0439	-0.9	-0.029	0.977	0.038	12.6	0.619	0.551
CREDIT	0.224	0.176	21.1	1.883	0.092	0.160	28.2	0.503	0.627
DIABETES	0.31	0.29	6.5	1.182	0.268	0.27	12.9	1.877	0.093
ABALONE	1.63	1.67	-2.4	-0.291	0.778	1.64	-0.6	-0.105	0.101
MUSHROOMS	0.0011	7.4E-4	35.1	1.365	0.205	4.9E-4	56.7	1.224	0.252
ADULT	0.21	0.166	20.7	34.89	**0**	0.173	17.6	40.50	**0**

The results indicate that D-HS gave better MAEs than k-NN for 12 out of 15 of the case-bases. The percentage improvements range from 92.8% (SOYBEAN), 35.1%, (MUSHROOMS), 23% (BALANCE), 21.2% (HOUSING), 21.1% (CREDIT), 20.7% (ADULT), 12.6% (DERMATOLOGY), 10% (DATAHOUSE 2), 7.6% (DATAHOUSE 1), 7.3% (GLASS), 6.5% (DIABETES), and 4.8% (IRIS). 4 case-bases (DATAHOUSE 1, DATAHOUSE 2, BALANCE, ADULT) showed competencies which were better than K-NN and significantly different as indicated by the t-values. The remaining 3 case-bases gave poorer MAEs with D-HS compared to k-NN, none of which were significantly different. The percentage decreases in competency were BREAST CANCER -0.9%, ABALONE -2.4% and ECHOCARDIOGRAM -3.1%. Therefore overall it can be said that with D-HS, 12 case-bases showed an increase in competency, while 3 showed a slight decrease in competency. The average increase in competency, over all the case-bases, provided by D-HS over k-NN was 17%.

Results for the D-HS+SR approach indicate that 12 out of 15 case-bases showed an improvement in MAE compared to k-NN. Of these 11 showed an even greater improvement in MAE than the D-HS approach with only DATAHOUSE 2 and ADULT showing a slight drop in MAE improvement of 3.3% and 3.1% respectively compared to the D-HS results. Of these 12 case-bases with improved MAEs, 3 (DATAHOUSE 1, DATAHOUSE 2 and ADULT) were significantly different in competency to k-NN. For the 3 case-bases which showed a decrease in MAE compared to k-NN, ECHOCARDIOGRAM showed the same decrease in MAE as with the D-HS approach while BALANCE showed a large decrease in competency - 23.3% and ABALONE showed a very small decrease in competency of –0.6%. None of these were deemed significantly different by the t-tests. Therefore with D-HS+SR, 3 case-bases are more competent than k-NN, while none are less competent and 12 can be said to show similar competencies. It is interesting to note that of the case-bases which produced a decrease in competency with D-HS (ECHOCARDIOGRAM –3.1%, BREAST CANCER –0.9% and ABALONE –2.4%) D-HS+SR improved upon the competencies of 2 of these case-bases (BREAST CANCER 12.6% and ABALONE –0.6%) while ECHOCARDIOGRAM produced the same competency.

One anomaly in the results is the decrease in competency for BALANCE with the D-HS+SR technique compared to the D-HS approach, as its competency fell from 23% to –23.3%. This was due to the fact that the case-base BALANCE had a small number (4) of discrete attributes and that when the N most similar cases were retrieved in the initial retrieval set, their ordered Euclidean distances from the target were the same, making the reduction technique ineffective.

The average overall improvement in competency, compared to k-NN, using the D-HS+SR approach over all 15 case-bases was 19.56%, which was higher than the corresponding average overall improvement with D-HS (17%), showing that Condition 1 is in general likely to occur, thus providing support for H2.

Additionally D-HS+SR improved upon the D-HS competencies in 11 of the 15 case-bases with one giving the same competency for both approaches. From this it can be concluded that there is good experimental evidence to suggest that neither D-HS nor D-HS+SR are less competent predictors than k-NN but some instances they are better and that D-HS+SR is the more competent of the two techniques. This provides further support for H2.

Table 2 shows the total retrieval times for each technique and the percentage improvement in retrieval time compared to k-NN. As the case-bases are ordered in increasing size it is clear from Table 2 that increasing the size of the case-base increases the efficiency, over k-NN, for all three techniques, thus providing support for H1.

Table 3 shows the average increase in efficiency (ratio of technique: k-NN efficiency) of each of the techniques for small case-bases up to 400 cases in size (SOYBEAN, ECHOCARDIOGRAM, IRIS, GLASS and DERMATOLOGY), for medium sized case-bases larger than 400 cases but less than 4000 (HOUSING to DIABETES), and for large case-bases having size larger than 4000 cases (ABALONE, MUSHROOMS and ADULT).

All 3 techniques were more efficient than k-NN and the magnitude of the improvement increased as the size of the case-base increased. D-HS+SR showed a slight decrease in efficiency compared to D-HS for all the case-bases irrespective of their size, as is to be expected, due to the increased computational overhead of using the Euclidean distance to ultimately select the 5 closest cases for the Final Retrieval Set. Despite this extra overhead, it always showed better efficiency than k-NN.

Table 2. Retrieval Times and Efficiencies compared to k-NN

Case-base	K-NN	D-HS		D-HS+SR		D-HS+PSR	
	Time (ms)	Time (ms)	Imp.	Time (ms)	Imp.	Time (ms)	Imp.
SOYBEAN	34	27	1.3	29	1.2	31.1	1.1
ECHOCARDIOGRM	47.1	19.1	2.5	23	2	26.1	1.8
IRIS	30.1	12	2.5	19	1.6	17	1.8
GLASS	75	23	3.3	30	2.5	29.1	2.6
DERMATOLOGY	1168.7	161.3	7.2	180.3	6.5	197.3	5.9
HOUSING	472	62.1	7.6	73.1	6.5	80.1	5.9
DATAHOUSE2	690	73.1	9.4	96.2	7.2	88.1	7.8
DATAHOUSE1	643	71.1	9	88.1	7.3	86.1	7.5
BALANCE	404.5	38	10.6	48.1	8.4	53.1	7.6
BREAST CANCER	634	81.1	7.8	101.1	6.3	96.1	6.6
CREDIT	1598.3	172.2	9.3	202.2	7.9	208.3	7.7
DIABETES	703	82.1	8.6	99.2	7.1	99.1	7.1
ABALONE	21720	1120.6	19.4	1380	15.7	881.3	24.6
MUSHROOMS	3.7×10^5	1.9×10^4	19.7	1.9×10^4	19.1	1.9×10^4	18.8
ADULT	3.7×10^6	2.1×10^5	17.7	2.1×10^5	17.4	1.9×10^5	19.4

Table 3. Average Efficiency Improvement for different case-base sizes Compared to k-NN

Case-Base Size	D-HS Average efficiency Improvement	D-HS+SR Average efficiency Improvement	D-HS+PSR Average efficiency Improvement
Small	3.36	2.76	2.64
Medium	8.9	7.24	7.17
Large	18.9	17.4	20.94

D-HS+PSR was less efficient than D-HS for all case-bases smaller than 4000 cases and more efficient for those larger than 4000 cases with the exception of MUSHROOMS. The reason it is less efficient than D-HS for the smaller case-bases is due to the extra time that is required to construct the primary case-base. Where the retrieval patterns of previously solved problems are reused regularly the savings produced from the D-HS+PSR approach will outweigh the cost of constructing the primary case-base. With case-bases with poorer problem space coverage the number of times a case from the primary case-base is reused is less than with case-bases with larger problem space coverage. Therefore we would expect larger case-bases to show better efficiencies using the D-HS+PSR than when not. From the results 2 of the 3 large case-bases (ABALONE and ADULT) gave better efficiencies with the tree retrieval compared to D-HS while MUSHROOMS did not show an improvement. This was an unexpected result, however, on examining the MUSHROOM case-base, it was shown to consist of entirely nominal attributes. The design of the tree structure dictates that there are the same number of intervals in the tree for a nominal attribute as there are distinct values for that attribute. Therefore if there are a large number of nominal attributes in a case, the chances of exactly the same pattern of attributes reoccurring during retrieval is diminished, thus explaining why the D-HS+PSR approach produced a decrease in efficiency for this case-base. From this it can be said that H3 is not in general supported by case-bases where there is a large number of nominal attributes. Further research is required to improve the technique to enable it to better cope with this type of attribute. D-HS+PSR was slightly less efficient than D-HS+SR with 7 case-bases, slightly more efficient than D-HS+SR with 7 case-bases and once it provided identical efficiency results. Excluding the three large case-bases the average improvement in efficiency for D-HS+PSR compared to D-HS+SR was 0.09, indicating, as expected, that for small to medium sized case-bases the technique does not have a large impact. For the three large case-bases, the average efficiency improvement was 3.53%.

5 Conclusions and Future Work

In this paper we have provided 3 algorithms, all designed for the real time, efficient similarity knowledge management in CBR, with one algorithm also designed for efficient case knowledge management. All approaches have empirically been shown to have at least similar competency to the basic k-NN algorithm but with much improved efficiency. The D-HS+PSR algorithm also compacts the case-base without loss of competency. The implications of this for CBR are a reduction of the effects of the utility problem through construction of a smaller primary case-base, the retention of all case-knowledge within the system via the secondary case-base (which is useful for the discovery of knowledge in other containers), more efficient retrievals and a real time approach to knowledge maintenance in CBR. Knowledge maintenance is a major issue when developing CBR systems. Historically most research focuses on the development of the knowledge containers but more recently the need to efficiently maintain that knowledge has been recognised. The D-HS and D-HS+SR techniques provide a simple means of similarity knowledge maintenance. When a new case is added to the case-base the matrix is updated to reflect its attribute values and this case is now immediately available for retrieval. As previously discussed historical approaches to maintaining case knowledge largely focuses on individual case coverage issues, which introduce a large overhead on the system. The D-HS+PSR technique presented here provides a means of case knowledge maintenance which should have a much lower overhead on the system compared to the more classical approaches based on coverage. As this approach reuses knowledge from the matrix to discover cases in the first place, each time a new case is added to the matrix, the primary case-base may have to be updated to reflect this change. This may entail updating the initial retrieval set of the cases in the primary case-base. For example from Figure 2 if a new case, which matched the target case on one attribute were added to the matrix, this would have to be added to the initial retrieval set in the primary case-base for the pattern relating to the target case. The cost of such an update on system efficiency would need to be empirically investigated in future work but as stated should be substantially less than the cost of working out individual case coverages. As D-HS+PSR decreases the number of cases in the case-base without any loss in problem solving competency, it has the most significant effect, of the 3 techniques presented, on the utility problem.

The matrix can also be used to highlight the areas of the problems space, where the system presently lacks knowledge to solve problems, thus drawing attention to these areas for future case knowledge acquisition. Theoretically if all cells in the matrix have values present then there would be complete problem space coverage in that a solution could be found for all target problems. One approach to discovering any missing matrix knowledge would be to rely on the expert to actively acquire it but a more appealing and elegant approach would be to use machine-learning techniques to automatically discover the missing case knowledge. The matrix would be used in this instance as a knowledge acquisition tool. This will be the focus of future work within this system. Other issues for further study include the relationship between case knowledge and adaptation knowledge and an improvement to the D-HS+PSR technique so it can more efficiently deal with nominal attributes. In addition, a study of variable sized matrix intervals and the weighting of attributes and retrieval cases will be carried out.

References

[1] Aha, D. W. and Breslow, L. Refining conversational case libraries. In Proceedings of the 2nd International Conference on Case-based Reasoning,-ICCBR-97, pp 267-276, Providence RI, USA, 1997.
[2] Anand, SS; Patterson, DW and Hughes, JG. Knowledge Intensive Exception Spaces, AAAI-98, pp 574-579, 1998.
[3] Cost, S.; and Salzberg, S. 1993. A Weighted Nearest Neighbour Algorithm for Learning with Symbolic Features. *Machine Learning* 10: 57-78.
[4] Deangdej, J., Lukose, D., Tsui, E., Beinat, P. and Prophet, L. Dynamically creating indices for two million cases: A real world problem. In Smith, I. And Faltings, B. eds., *Advances in Case-Based Reasoning, Lecture Notes in AI*, .Springer-Verlag. 105-119. Berlin: Springer Verlag 1996.
[5] Fox, S. and Leake, D.B. Using Introspective reasoning to refine indexing. In roceedings of the 14th International Joint Conference on Artificial Intelligence. Montreal, Canada, August , pp 391-387. 1995.
[6] Hanney, K. and Keane M. Learning Adaptation Rules from a Case-Base, Proc. Advances in Case-Based Reasoning, 3rd European Workshop, EWCBR-96, pp179-192, Lausanne, Switzerland, November 1996.
[7] Hunt, J.E., Cooke, D.E. and Holstein, H. Case-memory and retrieval based on the immune system. 1st International Conference on Case-Based reasoning (ICCBR-95), pp 205-216,. 1995.
[8] McSherry, D. Automating case selection in the construction of a case library. Proceedings of ES99, the19th SGES International Conference on Knowledge-Based Systems and Applied Artificial Intelligence, Cambridge, pp 163-177, December 1999
[9] Patterson, D., Anand, S.S., Dubitzky, D. and Hughes, J.G. Towards Automated Case Knowledge Discovery in the M^2 Case-Based Reasoning System, *Knowledge and Information Systems*:An International Journal, (1), pp 61-82, Springer Verlag, 1999.
[10] Patterson, D; Anand, SS; Dubitzky, D and Hughes, JG. A Knowledge Light Approach to Similarity Maintenance for Improving Case-Based Competence. Workshop on Flexible Strategies for Maintaining Knowledge Containers 14th European Conference on Artificial Intelligence, ECAI 2000. PP 65 - 77. 2000
[11] Patterson, D., Rooney, N. & Galushka, M. Towards Dynamic Maintenance of Retrieval Knowledge in CBR. Proceedings of the 15th International FLAIRS Conference. AAAI Press. 2002
[12] Portinale, L., Torasso, P. and Magro, D. Dynamic Case Memory Management, Proc. ECAI 98, pp. 73-78, John Wiley and Sons, Brighton, 1998.

[13] Portinale, L., Torasso, P. and Magro, D. Speed up quality and competence in multi model reasoning Proceedings of the 3rd International Conference in Case-Based Reasoning pp 303-317, 1999.

[14] Racine, K. and Yang, Q. Maintaining unstructured case-bases. In the Proceedings of the 2nd International Conference on case-Based Reasoning, ICCBR-97, pp 553-564, Providence, RI, USA. 1997.

[15] Richter, M. The Knowledge Contained in Similarity Measures. Invited Talk, The First International Conference in Case-Based Reasoning, Sesimbra, Portugal, October, 1995.

[16] Stanfill, C.; and Waltz, D. 1986. Towards Memory-based Reasoning. *Communications of the ACM*. 29(12): 1213-1228.

[17] Smyth, B. and Keane, M. Remembering to Forget.: A Competence-Preserving case Deletion Policy for Case-Based Reasoning Systems. Proceedings of 14th IJCAI, pp377-382. 1995.

[18] Smyth, B. Constructing Competent Case-Based Reasoners: Theories, Tools and techniques. Workshop On Automating the Construction of Case-Based Reasoners, Sixteenth International Joint Conference on Artificial Intelligence, Stockholm, Sweden, pp 17-23 1999

[19] Smyth, B. and McKenna, E. Footprint-based retrieval. Proceedings of the 3rd International Conference on Case-Based Reasoning, Munich, Germany, pp 343-357. July 1999.

[20] Tadepalli, P. A theory of unsupervised speedup learning. Proceedings of the 12th National Conference on Artificial Intelligence (AAAI-92), pp 229-234, 1992.

[21] Wettschereck et al 1997. Wettschereck, D.; Aha, D.; and Mohri, T. 1997. A Review of Empirical Evaluation of Feature Weighting Methods for a Class of Lazy Learning Algorithms, *Artificial Intelligence Review Journal*.

[22] Zang, Z. and Yang, Q. Towards lifetime maintenance of case-based indexes for continual case-based reasoning. In Proceedings of the 8th International Conference on Artificial Intelligence: Methodology, Systems, Applications, Sozopol, Bulgaria, 1998.

[23] Zhu, J. and Yang, Q. Remembering to Add: Competence-preserving Case Addition Policies for Case-base Maintenance. In International Joint Conference in Artificial Intelligence 1999 (IJCAI-99), pp. 234-239. 1999.

Constructive Adaptation

Enric Plaza and Josep-Lluís Arcos

IIIA-CSIC - Artificial Intelligence Research Institute
Campus UAB, 08193 Bellaterra, Catalonia, Spain.
Vox: +34-93-5809570, Fax: +34-93-5809661
{enric,arcos}@iiia.csic.es

Abstract. Constructive adaptation is a search-based technique for generative reuse in CBR systems for configuration tasks. We discuss the relation of constructive adaptation (CA) with other reuse approaches and we define CA as a search process in the space of solutions where cases are used in two main phases: hypotheses generation and hypotheses ordering. Later, three different CBR systems using CA for reuse are analyzed: configuring gas treatment plants, generating expressive musical phrases, and configuring component-based software applications. After the three analyses, constructive adaptation is discussed in detail and some conclusions are drawn to close the paper.

1 Introduction

Classically, adaptation methods have been classified as generative reuse versus transformational reuse [1]. Derivational (or analogical) replay is the paradigmatic method of generative reuse and has been used in planning tasks. The basic idea in derivational replay is that the trace of the problem solving process in a retrieved case is obtained and replayed (re-instantiated) into the context of the current problem. In transformational reuse there are a number of transformational operators that are applied to (a copy of) the solution of a retrieved case until a solution consistent with the new problem is achieved. Constructive Adaptation (CA) is a form of generative reuse in that the solution of the new problem is constructed (rather than transformed). For this reason it is similar (but not identical) to derivational replay. However, constructive adaptation uses the solution of retrieved cases as such, not the trace of solving the case.

Constructive adaptation, in abstract terms, can be described as a search process in the space of solutions where cases are used in two main phases: hypotheses generation and hypotheses ordering. Before explaining the technique of constructive adaptation we discuss its relation with other generative and transformational techniques for reuse in §2. Then, we present in §3 the main elements of constructive adaptation and the search process over states (representing partial solutions) that is at the core of CA. For better understanding CA three CBR systems using constructive adaptation as reuse method are analyzed. These CBR systems perform tasks where solutions are complex structures of elements in widely different domains. The three CBR systems have the tasks of configuring gas treatment plants, generating expressive musical phrases, and configuring

S. Craw and A. Preece (Eds.): ECCBR 2002, LNAI 2416, pp. 306–320, 2002.

component-based software applications. After analyzing the CA reuse process in three CBR systems, constructive adaptation is discussed in detail in §4, and finally some conclusions are drawn to close the paper.

2 Reuse in a Nutshell

There have been several studies with the goal to systematize the different adaptation techniques used in CBR [13,14]. In this section we will briefly summarize different approaches to adaptation exclusively with the goal of understanding the relation of constructive adaptation with other existing techniques. We will first discuss the notions of reuse and adaptation, then we will review the major adaptation techniques and compare them with constructive adaptation.

We can distinguish analytical tasks from synthetic tasks; we will see that reuse is quite different for CBR systems performing analytical or synthetic tasks. An analytical task is one in which solutions are expressed as an enumerated collection of elements, typically called classes —and thus the task is usually called classification or identification. A synthetic task is one where the number of solutions is so large that they are not enumerated; instead there are *solution elements* and a solution is a composite structure of these elements. The possible compositions determine the solution search space, and problem solving is a process that is able to find a composition that is a solution. Instead of saying that classification CBR has no adaptation and synthetic CBR has adaptation, the notion of *reuse* was introduced in [1] in order to encompass the processing of knowledge obtained from retrieved cases in synthetic and analytical tasks. Thus, synthetic tasks have adaptation techniques for realizing the reuse process, while analytical tasks have techniques that assess the retrieved cases for deciding which is the solution of a problem. For instance, in k-nearest neighbor the *retrieve* process determines the number k and those cases that are most similar to the problem, while the *reuse* process uses that information with a specific technique—e.g. using retrieved cases to "vote" on classes and taking as solution the class with most votes.

Concerning adaptation techniques for reuse on synthetic tasks, they fall into two families: transformational adaptation and generative adaptation. Transformational adaptation (see [9,10]) takes the description of a problem and a retrieved case (including the solution description) and transfers the retrieved solution by modifying it until a new solution structure is achieved that is "consistent" (or "adequate") for the new problem. Transformational adaptation can be analyzed in more detail, for instance *compositional adaptation* is defined in [13] and [14] as a form of adaptation where solution parts coming from multiple cases are adapted and combined together. For our purposes, we will consider compositional adaptation as a modality of transformational adaptation where the solution structures being transformed originate not from one but several cases. This view is consistent with the fact that both derivational adaptation

Table 1. Comparison of derivational, constructive, and transformational methods for reuse considering the *basis* of information used to take decisions and the way a *solution* is build.

Method		Basis	Solution
Generative	**Derivational**	trace	construct
	Constructive	case	construct
Transformational		case	transform

(e.g. derivational analogy in [11]) and constructive adaptation (as shown later in the paper) may use information from one or several cases[1].

Derivational (or generative, as sometimes is called) adaptation is based on augmenting the case representation to detailed knowledge of the decisions taken while solving the problem, and this recorded information (e.g. decisions, options, justifications) is used to "replay" them in the context of the new problem. As originally defined in *derivational analogy* [6] for planning systems the cases contain *traces* from planning process performed to solve them; also it is stated that in Prodigy/Analogy stored plans are annotated with plan *rationale* and reuse involves adaptation driven by this rationale [12].

Let us define *generative adaptation* as a process that uses information from retrieved cases to *construct* a (new) solution for the current problem. From this point of view, we have two large families of adaptation techniques: transformational adaptation (including compositional, structural, etc varieties) and generative adaptation — that includes both derivational adaptation and constructive adaptation. Table 1 shows the main features of these techniques:

Generation vs. Transformation. The solution is generated (using case information) in generative adaptation while it is derived by transforming old solution(s) in transformational adaptation;

Cases vs. Traces. Derivational adaptation use annotations of the problem solving process (the "trace") in the retrieved cases while constructive adaptation uses just the cases (i.e. a description of the problem and the solution without intermediate information about how the system went from problem to solution during problem solving).

In the following sections we will present constructive adaptation as a reuse method for configuration tasks, where we use *configuration* as a general term for tasks where the solution is a structure of relations among elements. Specifically, we will present applications of constructive adaptation to the design of plants for gas treatment (§ 3.1), generation of expressive musical phrases (§ 3.2) and configuration of CBR systems based on software components (§ 3.3). We will not consider planning tasks in our framework; although it could be included in this generic definition planning involves a very specialized collection of approaches

---

[1] Another distinction is made in [14] between transformational and structural adaptation; since both are based on reorganizing solution elements provided by retrieved cases it will suffice for our purpose here to subsume structural adaptation as a modality that fits in our definition of transformational adaptation

(both in the case-based planning approaches and in the planning community at large) that focus on the *sequential* structure of plans.

3   Constructive Adaptation

Succinctly, constructive adaptation (CA) is a form of best-first heuristic search in the space of solutions that uses information from cases (solved problems) to guide that search. Different modalities of CA can be developed: e.g. the search process can be exhaustive or not, the representation of cases and states can be identical or not. We are now going to characterize CA in more detail by defining its two constitutive processes or functions: *Hypotheses Generation* an *Hypotheses Ordering*. Subsequently, we will show three specific realizations of CA in three different CBR systems.

Let us start defining a case $C_i = (P_i, K_i)$ as a pair of problem description P_i and a solution K_i. The problem description P_i include the problem requirements $Req(P_i)$, usually the input provided by the user. Since the solution is a *configuration*, we can consider that —given a CBR system using a representation language with concepts and relations— a configuration is a *structure* of those concepts and relations. Let us denote $\mathcal{K}$ the set of possible configurations expressible in a language. Notice that the set $\mathcal{K}$ contains both partial and complete configurations; thus we will note the set of complete configurations $\mathcal{K}_C \subset \mathcal{K}$. The solution of a case is a configuration that is both complete and valid. A configuration K_i is complete when $K_i \in \mathcal{K}_C$. Moreover, we say that a solution is *valid* if $Sat(Req(P_i), K_i)$, i.e. if the solution satisfies the input requirements.

Constructive adaptation works upon *states*. A state is a domain-specific representation of the information needed to represent a partially specified solution, in our case a *partial configuration*. We will assume that there is a function $SAC : \mathcal{S} \to \mathcal{K}$ (where $\mathcal{S}$ is the set of states expressible in a CBR system) such that given a state $s \in \mathcal{S}$ as input SAC yields a corresponding (partial) configuration $K \in \mathcal{K}$ in the language used in the case base. Notice that a state contains more information than the partial configuration: it may contain the user input requirements, intermediate values used for problem solving, etc. There are CBR systems that may use the case representation itself as a way to represent a state — this option is often taken in transformational adaptation, since transformation rules and operators are defined upon the structure of cases.

In general, however, representation of state and case need not be identical. We introduce this distinction not only for theoretical clarification, but also for practical purposes: it has been convenient to implement state representation as distinct from case representation. The rationale can be summarized as follows: *cases* have representation biased towards storing and retrieving "experience episodes" of problem solving, while *states* have representation biased towards the search-based problem solving.

After introducing the basic elements of CA (cases, configurations, and states) we will describe the *process* of constructive adaptation shown in Figure 1. The CA process is a best-first search process with two basic functions (*Hypotheses*

```
Initialize OS = (list (Initial-State P_i))
Function CA(OS)
    Case (null OS) then No-Solution
    Case (Goal-Test (first OS)) then (SAC (first OS))
    Case else
        Let SS = (HG (first OS))
        Let OS = (HO (append SS (rest OS)))
            (CA OS)
```

Fig. 1. The search process of constructive adaptation expressed in pseudo code. Functions HG and HO are *Hypotheses Generation* and *Hypotheses Ordering*. Variables *OS* and *SS* are the lists of *Open States* and *Successor States*. The function SAC maps the solution state into the *configuration* of the solution. Function Initial-State maps the input requirement P_i into a state.

Generation and *Hypotheses Ordering*) and two auxiliary functions (*Goal Test* and *Initial State*). *Goal Test* is simply a function that given a state s checks whether or not it is a solution—i.e. if the corresponding configuration $SAC(s)$ is complete and valid. *Initial State* is a function that maps from the input requirements of the system $Req(P_i)$ to the *initial* state received by CA.

The process of *Hypotheses Generation* is domain specific and can use knowledge acquired from cases (CK) and from domain models containing general knowledge (GK), or both. Given s, an *open state*, *Hypotheses Generation* "expands" this state, i.e. generates the *successor* states of s. The essential idea of *Hypotheses Generation* is that when several options exist about elements or relations that can be added to the configuration of the state $SAC(s)$ then each option is considered a possible hypothesis, and a new (successor) state is generated incorporating one hypothesis.

In order to decide which open state s is selected to be expanded the *Hypotheses Ordering* function is used to rank the open states; CA (see Fig. 1) then selects the best one according to this ordering. The process of *Hypotheses Ordering* is domain specific and can use knowledge provided by cases (CK) and from domain models containing general knowledge (GK), or both.

The CA search process is summarized in Fig. 1. CA starts receiving (a list with) an initial state generated from the problem description P_i by auxiliary function *Initial State*. The CA algorithm works with an ordered set of hypotheses, the list of open states OS. Being recursive, CA checks first the termination conditions: a) if OS is empty all possible states have been explored, and CA terminates because there is no solution , and b) if the best state in OS (the first in the ranking of open states) passes the *Goal Test* this state is a solution for P_i. The recursive step in Fig. 1 generates the successor states SS of the best state in OS using the *Hypotheses Generation* function and they are added to the open states OS; then the list OS is re-ordered using the *Hypotheses Ordering* function and this is passed to the recursive call of CA.

Since *Hypotheses Generation* and *Hypotheses Ordering* are both domain-specific (as well as the representation of state) the explanation so far of CA has been very abstract. The best way to understand more concretely CA is through several case studies where specific CBR systems use specific *Hypotheses Generation* and *Hypotheses Ordering* functions. The following sections describe constructive adaptation in several CBR systems focusing on how states a represented, and how *Hypotheses Generation* and *Hypotheses Ordering* use case knowledge (CK) and domain knowledge (GK).

3.1   Design of Gas Treatment Plants

T-Air is a case-based reasoning application developed for aiding engineers in the design of gas treatment plants [2] developed at the IIIA for the Spanish company TECNIUM. The gas treatment is required in many and diverse industrial processes such as the control of the atmospheric pollution due to corrosive residual gases which contain vapors, mists, and dusts of industrial origin. Examples of gas treatments are the absorption of gases and vapors such as SO_2, CLH, or CL_2; the absorption of NO_x with recovering of HNO_3; the absorption of drops and fogs such as PO_4H_3 or $ClNH_4$; dust removal in metallic oxides; and elimination of odors from organic origin.

The main problem in designing gas treatment plants is that the diversity of possible problems is as high as the diversity of industrial processes while the experimental models about them is small. The knowledge acquired by engineers with their practical experience is the main tool used for solving new problems. For the design of gas treatment plants about forty different types of main equipment have been covered. We also started with a case-base comprising one thousand solved problems (cases) involving, each of them, from two to twenty different types of equipment.

A *solution* for a *T-Air* problem (Fig. 2) is a configuration holding the required equipments (mainly scrubbers, pumps, tanks, and fans), the design and working parameters for each equipment, and the topology of the installation (the gas circuit and the liquid circuits). The CBR process is organized on three *task levels:* a) selecting the class of chemical process to be realized, b) selecting the major equipments to be used (and their inter-connections), and c) adding auxiliary equipment and assessing the values for the parameters of each equipment.

A *state* in *T-Air* contains information about a) the input requirements, b) the corresponding partial configuration, c) a collection of *open issues*, and d) hypotheses supporting cases. The open issues represent the collection of decisions pending to be resolved in the state's partial configuration. For every hypothesis incorporated into a state a set of *supporting cases* is recorded; they are the cases from which this particular hypothesis was derived. The initial state is formed by the input requirements plus the initial open issue— namely, selecting the class of the chemical process to be realized.

Hypotheses Generation. The successor function takes the best state (see below how "best" is assessed) and selects as current issue one of the open issues — this selection is based on a domain model (GK). If the issue belongs to the *task level* of chemical process class the new hypotheses are generated using a case-based process (CK). *T-Air* retrieves cases based on the input requirements (and

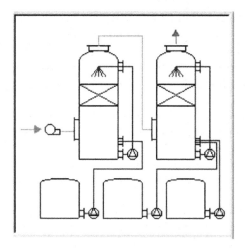

Fig. 2. A solution in *T-Air* is the structure of equipments of a gas treatment plant.

some derived features inferred from the requirements). Then *T-Air* generates one hypothesis (a successor state) for each chemical process class found in the retrieved cases. For instance, odor elimination can be solved by *adsorption*[2] or *absorption*. The successor states for *adsorption* and *absorption* will also record the *supporting cases* corresponding to each hypothesis.

If the open issue belongs to the *task level* of equipment selection the new hypotheses are generated using a case-based process (CK). *T-Air* retrieves cases based on the input requirements and the chemical process class; a new hypothesis is generated by each "core equipment" found in the retrieved cases. A new hypothesis is a new state with a partial configuration that incorporates one of the "core equipments", the new *open issues* corresponding to this equipment, and the supporting cases for the hypothesis. For instance, odor elimination with absorption can be realized with the core equipment "two scrubbers, a pump, and a fan" or "one multiventuri, a pump, and a fan".

If the open issue belongs to the third *task level* the hypotheses to be generated concern auxiliary equipment and parameter assessment. The major parameters are assessed using a case-based process (CK) because there are no analytical models capable of estimating them, and the TECNIUM company experience (represented as cases) is the only available knowledge[3]. However, when a parameter is assessed to have a certain value, this may provoke the rising of new open issues that need to be solved. These open issues can be solved adding auxiliary equipment to the configuration. For instance, when the chemical reaction is exothermic and the gas flow exceeds a certain threshold a new open issue for

---

[2] Adsorption is the use of solids for removing substances from either gaseous or liquid solutions.

[3] There are less critical parameters that can computed using analytical methods, and *T-Air* uses them when available.

refrigerating the involved equipment is generated. This issue can be solved by the addition of a refrigerator as auxiliary equipment.

Hypotheses Ordering. The ordering of hypotheses is performed by an assessment heuristic based on both domain knowledge (GK) and cases (CK). The assessment heuristic takes into account several dimensions: i) estimated overall cost (GK), ii) plant overall reliability (GK and CK), iii) critical parameter values (GK), and iv) supporting cases (CK). The assessment heuristic receives a state as input and estimates these dimensions on the partial configuration that corresponds to that state; the pending states are ordered by this heuristic. This means that, all other things equal, the *T-Air* system will first explore the states corresponding to configurations that have greater number of related cases in the case base.

Finally, the *Goal-Test* function checks whether a state is a solution —i.e. whether the configuration of the state is complete and valid (using domain knowledge). The search process is not *exhaustive* because there is no guarantee that the Hypotheses Generation function will generate all *possible* hypotheses. Hypotheses Generation uses cases retrieved from the case base to pinpoint the hypothesis to be considered.

3.2   Expressive Music Generation

SaxEx [4] is a system for generating expressive performances of melodies based on examples of human performances (currently SaxEx is focused in tenor saxophone interpretations of standard jazz ballads). The input of SaxEx is a musical phrase with a sound track and a score in Midi format plus some affective labels characterizing the intended mood for the expressive performance. In the notation introduced in §3 this input is the *Req(P)* part of the problem description. Two musical theories are used by SaxEx: Narmour's implication/realization (IR) model and Lerdahl and Jackendoff's generative theory of tonal music (GTTM). SaxEx employs IR and GTTM to construct two complementary models of the musical structure of the phrase. While the IR model holds an analysis of melodic surface, the GTTM model concentrates on the hierarchical structures associated with a piece. The problem description *P* is formed both by the input *Req(P)* and the musical structures inferred using these domain models.

A solution for a problem in SaxEx is a sequential structure of notes belonging to a phrase, where each note has an associated *expressive model*. The expressive model holds the following parameters: sound amplitude (dynamics); note anticipations/delays (rubato); note durations (rubato); attack and release times (rubato and articulation); vibrato frequency and vibrato amplitude of notes; articulation mode of each note (from legato to staccato); and note attacks (allowing effects such as reaching the pitch of a note starting from a lower pitch or increasing the noise component of the sound). Summarizing, a solution is achieved when each note has an assigned value for each expressive parameter.

A *state* in SaxEx contains information about i) the input requirements, ii) the expressive models generated up to this point, and iii) the set of *open notes* (the notes in the phrase without an expressive model). The *initial state* is formed by the input requirements and all the notes of the musical phrase as open notes.

Hypotheses Generation. Given a state s Hypotheses Generation selects the next note from open notes and uses cases (CK) for generating several expressive models for that note —each one embodied in a new successor state. Notice that the hypotheses generated are expressive models and not individual expressive parameters. For each note, a set of similar notes is retrieved using the mechanism of perspectives [3]. Analyzing the expressive models of the retrieved notes, with the help of musical knowledge that constrain over the possible combinations of values, several (alternative) expressive models are generated, each with an assessment of *note similarity* —comparing the problem note and the retrieved notes involved in each expressive model.

Hypotheses Ordering. The ordering of hypotheses uses domain knowledge (GK) and case knowledge (CK). Domain knowledge assesses the coherence of the different expressive models in a state. This assessment takes into account that the expressive models represent the way the melody (a sequence) will be performed. SaxEx establishes two kinds of main coherence criteria: smoothness and variation. Moreover, these criteria are established both over single expressive parameters (e.g. pitch, attack) and over the relations among expressive parameters (e.g. the relation between pitch and attack). Smoothness and variation are basically contradictory: the first tends to iron out strong variations, while the second, variation, is against repetition of structures and thus strengthens variations. The resulting expressive performance deals with the trade-offs among them with the aim of striking an overall balance pleasant to the ear. Case knowledge is used to estimate an overall similarity value of a state with respect to the cases used in generating that state. This is done by aggregating the *note similarity* values of the notes with expressive model belonging to the state. The Hypotheses Ordering function combines these two assessment values into a state "goodness" value and ranks the *open states* according to these values.

Finally, the *Goal-Test* function just checks that the solution is complete and valid. Validity in SaxEx is defined by two threshold values of smoothness (min) and variation (max) that have to be satisfied by a final state. Smoothness and variation thresholds can be set by the user according to her particular musical interests.

3.3   Component-Based Software Configuration

Finally, we will present a CBR system using CA for configuring software applications from a library of software components called *CBR broker*. The *CBR broker* only assumes that the software components are expressed in the UPML (Universal Problem-solving Methods Language) formalism [7]. In a nutshell, UPML can describe *tasks* (what is to be achieved), *problem-solving methods* (how can a task be achieved), and *domain models* (knowledge needed to achieve tasks). Task and PSMs (problem-solving methods) are characterized by their input/output signature and their competence; the competence of a task or PSM is described by *preconditions* (statements of what is supposed to hold for the component to be

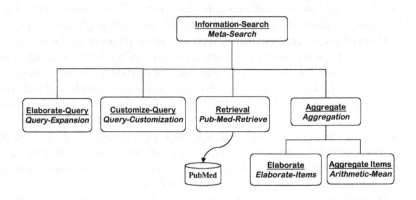

Fig. 3. A configuration in the WIM multiagent system. A box contains the binding of a <u>task</u> and a *PSM*, while a cylinder is a domain model.

applicable) and *postconditions* (statements about what holds after applying the component). A domain model is characterized by properties of the knowledge it contains.

A PSM elementary or be can decomposed into subtasks; when a PSM is a decomposition the *CBR broker* has to find which PSMs can achieve those (sub) tasks and when the PSM is elementary the *CBR broker* has to find which domain models are required. The *CBR broker* receives as input a *competence requirement* specifying the preconditions, postconditions and available domain models for building a target application. The output of the *CBR broker* is a *configuration*: a structure specifying a) for a task, a specific PSM able to achieve that task, and b) for each elementary PSM, which domain models are used — we call those association *bindings* (see Fig. 3). We say a configuration is *complete* when all bindings have been resolved, and *valid* when the input competence requirement is satisfied; a configuration is a solution when it is complete and valid. The *CBR broker* stores in the case base those configurations obtained in the past and CA uses them to guide the search process over the solution space.

The *CBR broker* has been used in a multi-agent system for retrieval and integration of medical information in databases called WIM (Web Information Mediator) [8]. The Problem Solving Agents register their competence as PSMs into a Library using the UPML language. When a User Agent has some particular task to achieve for its user it sends a competence requirement to the broker, that interacts with the Librarian Agent to obtain UPML specifications and finally reaches a complete and valid configuration. Since a configuration is just an abstract specification there is now the need to *operationalize* it into a working system—in this case, a team of agents with the adequate competences. This process of *team formation* is achieved by a negotiation process between the CBR broker and the registered Problem Solving Agents [8].

A *state* in *CBR broker* corresponds to a partial configuration. A state holds information about *tp-bindings* (task/PSM bindings), preconditions and postconditions. The *closed bindings* is the collection of task/PSM bindings in the partial configuration of that state. The *open bindings* are those bindings not yet resolved (tasks without a PSM bound to it). Moreover, a state has open (resp. closed) preconditions and postconditions: they are those pre- and postconditions not yet satisfied (resp. already satisfied) by the current partial configuration. The *initial state* is created from the input competence requirement: the input preconditions are closed preconditions (we assume they are satisfied) and the input postconditions are open postconditions.

Hypotheses Generation. The *CBR broker* takes one task T from the open bindings; several hypotheses can be generated for T, each one a PSM capable of achieving T. The *CBR broker* uses the notion of *component matching* to select PSMs that can meaningfully achieve a task. Component matching is defined as follows: a PSM M matches a task T when a) their input/output signatures are consistent, b) all the postconditions of T are satisfied by M, and c) all the preconditions of M are satisfied by T[4].

For each PSM that matches T a new state is generated where T is bound to one of these PSMs. The new *tp-binding* is called current tp-binding and is added to the closed bindings. Moreover, the rest of the information of the state is updated as follows. If the new PSM has subtasks they are added to open bindings; if the new PSM is elementary the required domain models are associated with it (if some are not available this new state is not valid and is not generated). The open postconditions satisfied by the postconditions of the new PSM are deleted and become closed postconditions, while its new preconditions become open preconditions.

Notice that only general knowledge (GK) is used in Hypotheses Generation, since the options are retrieved from the UPML library using the notion of *component matching*. Because of this, *CBR broker* performs an exhaustive search with respect to the Library of components being used.

Hypotheses Ordering. The *CBR broker* uses only case knowledge (CK) to rank the open states (the partial configurations); the cases are pairs $C_i = (P_i, K_i)$ where P_i is the input competence requirement and K is the configuration found for that input. First, the *CBR broker* computes the similarity between the problem P and each case input description P_i using the LAUD structural similarity distance[5][5]. Thus, LAUD provides a ranking over the set of cases in the case base. The next step is to transfer this knowledge to the set of open states and rank them accordingly. Since each open state incorporates a new hypothesis

---

[4] Notice that this condition is the converse of the previous one. The reason is that preconditions are assumptions about what is true in the world so that a component is applicable. If a PSM can achieve the same postcondition requiring less assumptions than the task specified, the PSM still satisfies that task.

[5] A structural similarity is needed because the problem descriptions are represented as feature terms; in particular, pre- and postconditions are sets of feature terms that require a distance measure capable to deal with relational cases.

Table 2. Dimensions that characterize Constructive Adaptation (CA) in the three CBR systems reviewed. Keywords used in the table: GK = General (Domain) Knowledge, CK = Case (based) Knowledge.

CA Dimensions	T-Air	SaxEx	CBR Broker
Hypothesis Generation	GK & CK	CK	GK
Hypothesis Ordering	GK & CK	GK & CK	CK
Exhaustive Search	No	No	Yes

in the form of the *current tp-binding*, the *CA-broker* searches in the ranked cases which C_i has the same task/PSM binding in the solution. The state is given as *endorsement value* the similarity of the highest ranking case containing the state's current *tp-binding* and all the open states are ranked according to their endorsement values.

Finally, *Goal-Test* checks whether a state is a solution, i.e. there are no open bindings and all input competence requirements pre- and postconditions are satisfied by the closed pre- and postconditions.

4   Constructive Adaptation Revisited

After the description of three CBR systems using constructive adaptation (CA) we can review the basic notions of this reuse technique. Basically, CA is a generative technique for reuse (since CA constructs a solution using case information). We have seen in the exemplified CBR systems that both general domain knowledge (GK) and case knowledge (CK) can be used inside CA and that they can be used for generating hypotheses and/or ordering hypotheses. Table 2 characterizes several dimensions of constructive adaptation, with the columns characterizing the three CBR systems reviewed in §3.

The first dimension, Hypothesis Generation, specifies whether general domain knowledge (GK) and/or case knowledge (CK) is used in generating new hypotheses while generating successor states. We can see that *T-Air* uses both GK and CK while SaxEx and the *CBR Broker* use only CK and GK respectively. The second dimension, Hypothesis Ordering, specifies whether general domain knowledge (GK) and/or case knowledge (CK) is used in ordering the hypotheses to be considered (i.e. ranking the open states). We can see that the *CBR Broker* uses only CK while the other two combine general and case knowledge.

Finally, the Exhaustive Search dimension specifies whether the search process is able to consider all possible solutions. Only the *CBR Broker* performs an exhaustive search (with respect to the totality of the components in the Library). Since the three systems provide just one solution (and not all valid solutions) this means that exhaustivity only assures that when no solution is found it's because it does not exist. The reason for being exhaustive is that Hypothesis Generation uses GK to retrieve *all* components in the Library that match a task specification; retrieved cases are used only to order the hypotheses. *T-Air* and SaxEx are not exhaustive because CK and GK is used to focus the search process only on those hypotheses that have some endorsement from general or case knowledge. Exhaustivity is not a good thing per se, it is a property that a system may or may not need. *T-Air* has as a user an engineer of TECNIUM company that uses past cases (plants engineered by TECNIUM) to achieve rapid prototyping of new plants. There are always several solutions and the system helps to find the good ones in terms of economy and ease of construction. In SaxEx the number of possible solutions is always so large that exhaustivity is not an issue.

5   Conclusions

The overall view of constructive adaptation, at this point, is that it's a flexible technique for using cases and general knowledge in CBR systems for synthetic tasks. The three reviewed CBR systems have quite different application domains, and the only common aspect is that the solution to be built by CBR is a complex structure of elements. Constructive adaptation offers a way to organize reuse processes into the well founded paradigm of state-based search, and clarifies the phases where cases (and general knowledge) can be used, namely generation and ordering of hypotheses. The exact way in which cases are used to make the decisions involved in generation and ordering is open and may vary from one application domain to the other. However, applying CA to these CBR systems, understanding how to use cases was easy once we had a clear idea of what a *state* was in the system. As a lesson learned from these experiments we can say that the main issue to apply CA was to clarify what information was to be present in a state; once this was clear the rest of the elements in CA were easy to design: hypotheses generation and ordering, and goal test.

Let us consider now the relation between constructive adaptation and derivational reply: in §2 we considered both as techniques for generative reuse, the difference being that derivational reply uses cases augmented with problem solving data (the *trace* that is later *replayed* while CA just uses the cases —conceived as (P, S) problem solution pairs. This difference comes from the distinction of *states* and *cases* in CA. When the solution state is found, a solution configuration is built, but no "trace" information is stored— trace information is contained in the search branches that generate, evaluate and discard states, and it is discarded when only the final configuration S is stored in a case. The reason why it is so in CA was simply because this information was not needed. In retrospect, we think this difference is due to the nature of planning tasks and the type of search process required for planning. A plan is a sequential structure with a total or a partial order. Planning can be seen as a search problem but its nature has required that AI researchers developed specific methods, heuristics, and representations for planning tasks. Thus, we think that recording trace information on plans stored as cases comes naturally because it fits this specialized approaches of search processes for planning.

Our approach, however, has been focused on configuration tasks where a solution is a structure of elements and their relations. Constructive adaptation proceeds by adding elements to the solution and relating it to the other elements; if more than one element can be added, these alternative options are interpreted as alternative hypotheses embodied in several states. Cases can be used for generating and ordering hypotheses, and for this purpose there was no need to store in cases information about the trace of the search process. The information needed from the cases can be directly obtained from their solution structures, in a specific way adequate for each application domain.

Finally, there are different types of search processes that can be implemented in the framework of constructive adaptation. The search process in adapting cases can be exhaustive when all options (hypotheses) are always generated and cases are used to rank the order in which each combination of hypotheses (state) is explored— e.g. the *CBR broker* of §3.3. However, in applications where there is no general knowledge available cases can be used to generate alternative hypotheses; this process is performed in the SaxEx system although general (musical) knowledge is also used.

Generating hypothesis from a case base does not imply that the search process of CA is exhaustive or not: it depends on the case base and on the kind of memory search that the retrieval method performs. We have seen that *T-Air* and SaxEx are not exhaustive, but the reason for this concerns the type of CBR system being developed. It is possible to have an exhaustive search process in CA when hypotheses are generated from CK and not GK, as in the following example. Consider a variant of the *CBR broker* where there is no Library of UPML components and just a case base of configurations of components. Let us suppose that the case base has a number of cases that assures that every component originally in the Library is used in at least one configuration case. In this scenario, the *CBR broker* can use the definition of *component matching* in §3.3 to search the memory of configurations and find all components that satisfy some requirements. Therefore, with certain conditions on the case base (when the number and variety of cases are a good sample the possible solutions) and on the retrieval method over cases (finding all items relevant for a specific context) the CA search process can be exhaustive.

Acknowledgments

This research has been supported by the Esprit Long Term Research Project 27169: IBROW *An Intelligent Brokering Service for Knowledge-Component Reuse on the World-Wide Web,* and the TIC Project 2000-1094-C02 Tabasco: *Content-based Audio Transformation using CBR.*

References

1. Agnar Aamodt and Enric Plaza. Case-based reasoning: Foundational issues, methodological variations, and system approaches. *Artificial Intelligence Communications*, 7(1):39–59, 1994.

2. Josep Lluís Arcos. T-Air: A case-based reasoning system for designing chemical absorption plants. In David W. Aha and Ian Watson, editors, *Case-Based Reasoning Research and Development*, number 2080 in Lecture Notes in Artificial Intelligence, pages 576–588. Springer-Verlag, 2001.

3. Josep Lluís Arcos and Ramon López de Mántaras. Perspectives: A declarative bias mechanism for case retrieval. In David Leake and Enric Plaza, editors, *Case-Based Reasoning. Research and Development*, number 1266 in Lecture Notes in Artificial Intelligence, pages 279–290. Springer-Verlag, 1997.

4. J. L. Arcos and R. López de Mántaras. An interactive case-based reasoning approach for generating expressive music. *Applied Intelligence*, 14(1):115–129, 2001.

5. Eva Armengol and Enric Plaza. Similarity assessment for relational CBR. In David W. Aha and Ian Watson, editors, *Case-Based Reasoning Research and Development, 4th International Conference on Case-Based Reasoning, ICCBR 2001*, volume 2080 of *Lecture Notes in Computer Science*, pages 44–58, 2001.

6. Jaime Carbonell. Derivational analogy: A theory of reconstructive problem solving and expertise acquisition. In *Machine Learning: An Artificial Intelligence Approach*, volume 2, pages 371–392. Morgan Kaufmann, 1986.

7. D. Fensel, V. R. Benjamins, M. Gaspari S. Decker, R. Groenboom, W. Grosso, M. Musen, E. Motta, E. Plaza, G. Schreiber, R. Studer, and B. Wielinga. The component model of UPML in a nutshell. In *Proceedings of the International Workshop on Knowledge Acquisition KAW'98*, 1998.

8. Mario Gómez, Chema Abásolo, and Enric Plaza. Domain-independent ontologies for cooperative information agents. In *Proceedings Workshop on Cooperative Information Agents*, volume 2128 of *LNAI*, pages 118–129, 2001.

9. K. J. Hammond. *Case-based planning: Viewing planning as a memory task*. Academic Press, 1989.

10. T. Heinrich and J. L. Kolodner. The roles of adaptation in case-based design. In *Proceedings of the AAAI Worksop on Case-based Reasoning*, 1991.

11. Manuela Veloso and Jaime Carbonell. Toward scaling up machine learning: A case study with derivational analogy in prodigy. In Steven Minton, editor, *Machine Learning Methods for Planning*, pages 233–272. Morgan Kaufmann, 1993.

12. Manuela M. Veloso, Alice M. Mulvehill, and Michael T. Cox. Rationale-supported mixed-initiative case-based planning. In *AAAI/IAAI*, pages 1072–1077, 1997.

13. W. Wilke, B. Smyth, and P. Cunningham. *Using configuration techniques for adaptation*, pages 139–168. Number 1400 in LNAI. Springer Verlag, 1998.

14. W. Wilke and R. Bergmann. Techniques and knowledge used for adaptation during case-based problem solving. In *IEA/AIE (Vol. 2)*, pages 497–506, 1998.

A Fuzzy Case Retrieval Approach Based on SQL for Implementing Electronic Catalogs

Luigi Portinale and Stefania Montani

Dipartimento di Informatica
Università del Piemonte Orientale "Amedeo Avogadro"
Spalto Marengo 33 - 15100 Alessandria (ITALY)
{portinal,stefania}@unipmn.it

Abstract. Providing a flexible and efficient way of consulting a catalog in e-commerce applications is of primary importance in order to guarantee the customer with a set of products actually related to his/her interests. Most electronic catalogs exploit standard database techniques both for storage and retrieval of product information. However, a naive application of ordinary databases may produce unsatisfactory results, since standard query tools are not able to retrieve information (i.e. products) that only partially match the user/customer specification. The use of CBR may alleviate some of the above problems, because of the ability of a CBR system of retrieving products having characteristics similar to the ones specified by the user. While the majority of the approaches is based on k-NN retrieval techniques, in the present paper we propose fuzzy-based retrieval as a natural way for implementing flexible search on electronic catalogs. Since the exploitation of standard DBMS technology is of paramount importance for deploying any E-commerce application, we also propose to use a fuzzy extension to SQL for retrieving a set of products that the customer specifies using precise as well as vague or imprecise features. The proposed implementation is based on a client/server web-based architecture working on top of a relational standard DBMS. A specific example concerning an on-line wine shop is used to demonstrate the capabilities of the approach.

1 Introduction

Building E-commerce applications such as electronic catalogs for e-shops is certainly one of the most important activities over the Internet. A lot of effort is currently devoted to the technological framework for E-commerce implementations [8]; however, despite these technological advances, the construction of e-shops may be a serious problem if the final user needs are not taken into primary account. Electronic catalogs are very often like a "big unknown land" where the customer/user has to search for a given target, very often with no precise idea of what to look for. Most electronic catalogs use standard database technology both for the storage and the retrieval of the product information; relational DBMS are a very mature technology, however their use in electronic catalogs suffers of some drawbacks [20,15]. The main problem with ordinary database is

S. Craw and A. Preece (Eds.): ECCBR 2002, LNAI 2416, pp. 321–335, 2002.

their intrinsic boolean nature: if a query is specified, only the objects that exactly satisfy the query are returned. In case of product retrieval, the user has to precisely know the characteristics of the product he/she is looking for and this is not often the case. As a consequence, if the user under-specifies the product, an excessive number of results are returned, making unuseful the search. On the other hand, if the user over-specifies the product, an empty result set may be obtained. In general, even if a reasonable number of products is returned, only those products that completely satisfy the search parameters are returned, missing those items that only partially match the query parameters, but that may be potentially interesting to the user. This problem is particularly worth in B2C (Business to Customer) applications, where the final user is a customer who is usually not an expert in the product field and is not usually able to precisely specify every characteristic of the desired product.

Case-Based Reasoning (CBR) approaches to product retrieval in electronic catalogs have been proposed as a suitable way of addressing and solving the above problems [23,16,19,22,7]; product recommendation based on case-based retrieval is in fact more flexible, since similarity among products and among users asking the products can be explicitly taken into account. On the other hand current database technology is crucial in any information system and even E-commerce applications should exploit as much as possible the power offered by a DBMS.

The use of database techniques for supporting the construction of case-based systems is recently attracting serious attention; the reasons are twofold: if data of interest are already stored in a database, the database itself can be used as a case base; moreover, part of the technological facilities of a DBMS may be exploited in the CBR cycle, in particular for case retrieval. This is particularly true in E-commerce applications, where the *product database* represents the main data source, which records are easily interpretable as "cases" for a case-based recommendation system [16,17,23]. Database driven proposals focus on the retrieval step of the CBR cycle[1], since similarity-based retrieval is the fundamental step that allows one to start with a set of relevant cases (e.g. the most relevant products), in order to apply any needed revision and/or refinement.

Case retrieval algorithms usually focus on implementing Nearest-Neighbor (NN) techniques, where local similarity metrics, relative to individual features, are combined in a weighted way to get a global similarity between a retrieved and a target case. A k-NN case retrieval algorithm will then return the k most similar cases to the target one. In product selection from electronic catalogs a major issue is to allow for an imprecise description of the products in the retrieval phase; even if a distance-based approach like k-NN may be adopted, we argue that imprecise information and specification may be more adequately modeled through a standard fuzzy-based approach. Fuzzy logic provides a useful way for directly addressing the representation of vague and imprecise concepts and

---

[1] Actually, in [23] a revision of the classical CBR cycle presented in [1] is proposed, by specifically taking into account the e-commerce application; however no particular database technique is specifically proposed for implementing this new cycle.

features, so it is a natural candidate when a retrieval has to be performed on the basis of such an imprecise characterization. In [5], it is argued that the notion of *acceptance* may represent the needs of a flexible case retrieval methodology better than distance (or similarity). As for distance, local acceptance functions can be combined into global acceptance functions to determine whether a target case is acceptable (i.e. it should be retrieved) with respect to a given query. In particular, very often local acceptance functions take the form of fuzzy distributions; in this way, the definition of a fuzzy linguistic term over the domain of a given attribute of a case can be exploited to characterize the acceptance of cases having similar (in the fuzzy sense) values for that particular attribute or feature.

In the present paper, we will present an approach where local acceptance relative to a feature can be expressed through fuzzy distributions on its domain, abstracting the actual values to linguistic terms. The peculiarity of the approach is that global acceptance is completely defined in fuzzy terms, by means of the usual combinations of local distributions through specific defined *norms* [13]. Our main goal is to define a case retrieval approach suitable for query cases expressible (either directly or indirectly) with fuzzy concepts, in such a way that a flexible product selection can be implemented over a standard database of products in an electronic catalog. We concentrate on flexible product selection and on search facilities, without considering other complementary aspects like product customization, user collaboration and user dialog construction [7]. An extended version of SQL, able to deal with fuzzy predicates and conditions, is introduced as a suitable way to directly query a case base stored on a relational DBMS; this approach is based on the **SQLf** language proposed in [4], extending standard SQL in order to deal with *fuzzy queries*. The advantage of this approach is that the whole power of an SQL engine can be fully exploited, with no need of implementing specific retrieval algorithms. Moreover, the use of SQL and of standard DBMS allows us to obtain an efficient retrieval in very large case bases.

The paper is organized as follows. Section 2 introduces the main issues underlying fuzzy-based retrieval and fuzzy querying on relational databases. Section 3 shows how the fuzzy querying framework can actually be exploited to implement fuzzy case retrieval; a client/server architecture able to generate a Fuzzy-SQL query from a case specification is presented in section 4; Section 5 shows how the retrieval architecture introduced in the previous section can be actually exploited in the construction of a product selection application from an on-line catalog: an example concerning bottle selection in an on-line wine shop is used to demonstrate the capabilities of the approach. Finally, conclusions and comparisons with related works are presented in section 6.

2   Fuzzy Case Retrieval

2.1   Fuzzy Acceptability

The Nearest-Neighbor approach to case retrieval is based on distance measures defined on case features (local distance) that are then combined in a suitable way, in order to get the actual distance between a query or target case and a retrieved case (global distance). Case similarity is easily defined as a kind of *inverse* function of case distance (greater is the distance, smaller is the similarity). On the other hand, we can also view case retrieval as a way of accepting a set of cases, by means of some fuzzy measure of acceptance defined on the case features.

Despite their relative differences, fuzzy retrieval (based on acceptance) and Nearest-Neighbor retrieval (based on distance) have some common grounds cite-Burkhard:00. In [5], a correspondence between acceptability and distance has been pointed out through the so-called *characteristics similarity curves* defining acceptability regions in the feature space. Acceptability functions can then be used instead of distance or similarity functions and local acceptability can be combined into global acceptability functions to determine whether the case should be retrieved, that is whether it is acceptable with respect to the query case and a particular acceptability threshold (see [5] for more details).

Fuzzy membership of a feature value with respect to a particular fuzzy set can be viewed as a local acceptance function [6]. The standard notion of α-cut of a fuzzy set (i.e. the set of elements having degree of membership in the fuzzy set greater or equal to α) can then be used to define an acceptability region; as in the case of characteristics similarity curves, different acceptability thresholds (i.e. different αs) give rise to different acceptability regions. Notice that, in case of fuzzy retrieval, the main reference is a linguistic value (i.e. a fuzzy set), while in similarity-based retrieval the reference is a feature value, not defined on a fuzzy set. This essentially means that fuzzy retrieval is more general in use, by allowing the fuzzification of the queries, i.e. query cases can be expressed in terms of both crisp and fuzzy values. We will return on this aspect in section 3.

Finally, in a fuzzy context, global acceptability is easily obtained by using fuzzy combination through suitable t-norms o t-conorms [13]; this means that the standard framework of fuzzy logic provides a sound way of aggregating local information (at the feature level) into a global measure (at the case level). Given the fact that fuzzy logic matching can be formally used to retrieve a set of cases given a particular query, the problem to solve is how to implement this kind of fuzzy retrieval. Our aim is to exploit as much as possible standard data representation and standard query tools. For this reason, we investigated the possibility of exploiting fuzzy extension to SQL for imprecise querying in relational databases.

2.2   Fuzzy Querying in Databases

It is well-known that standard relational databases can only deal with precise information and standard query languages, like SQL, only support boolean queries. Fuzzy logic provides a natural way of generalizing the strict satisfiability of boolean logic to a notion of satisfiability with different degrees; this is the reason why considerable efforts has been dedicated inside the database community toward the possibility of dealing with fuzzy information in a database. Despite the numerous approaches to the problem, in the present paper we are only interested in fuzzy querying on an ordinary database [4,11]. In particular, in [4] standard SQL is adopted as the starting point for a set of extensions able to improve query capabilities from boolean to fuzzy ones. The implementation of the SQL extensions can be actually provided on top of a standard relational DBMS, by means of a suitable module able to transform a fuzzy query into a regular one through the so called *derivation principle* [3].

We are interested in simple SQL statements with no nesting (i.e. we consider the WHERE clause to be a reference to an actual condition and not to nested SQL statements); in our Fuzzy-SQL language, the condition can be a composite fuzzy formula involving both crisp and fuzzy predicates and operators.

Concerning fuzzy predicates, a set of linguistic values can be defined over the domains of the attributes of interest; three different types of fuzzy predicates are considered: (1)*fuzzy predicates on continuous domain*: a set of linguistic values defined on a continuous domain (*continuous scalar attributes*) and through a continuous distribution; (2)*fuzzy predicates on discrete domains*: a set of linguistic values defined on a discrete domain, but with two different possible types of distribution: (2.1)*continuous distribution* for *scalar discrete* attributes (i.e. with ordered values) or (2.2)*discrete distribution* for *nominal* attributes (with unordered values).

Furthermore, a set of fuzzy operators can be defined to relate fuzzy or crisp predicates; also in this case we have different types of operators: *continuous operators* characterized by a continuous fuzzy distribution over a function of the operands (e.g. their difference); *discrete operators* defining a *similarity relation* characterized by a symmetric matrix of similarity degrees.

By allowing fuzzy predicates and operators to form the condition of the WHERE clause, the result of the SELECT is actually a fuzzy relation, i.e. a set of tuples with associated the degree to which they satisfy the WHERE clause. Such a degree can be characterized as follows: let

SELECT A FROM R WHERE fc

be a query with fuzzy condition fc; the result will be a fuzzy relation Rf with membership function $\mu_{Rf}(a) = \sup_{(x \in R) \wedge (x.A=a)} \mu_{fc}(x)$. The fuzzy distribution $\mu_{fc}(x)$ relative to fc must then be computed by taking into account the logical connectives involved and their fuzzy interpretation. It is well known that the general way to give a fuzzy interpretation to logical connectives is to associate negation with *complement to one*, conjunction with a suitable *t-norm* and disjunction with the corresponding *t-conorm* [13]. In the following, we will concentrate on the simplest t-norm and t-conorm, namely the min and max operators such that $\mu_{A \wedge B}(x) = \min(\mu_A(x), \mu_B(x))$ and $\mu_{A \vee B}(x) = \max(\mu_A(x), \mu_B(x))$.

In order to process a query using a standard DBMS, we have to devise a way of translating the Fuzzy-SQL statement into a standard one. The most simple way is to require the fuzzy query to return a boolean relation R_b which tuples are extracted from the fuzzy relation R_f, by considering a suitable threshold on the fuzzy distribution of R_f. We consider, as in [4], the following syntax

SELECT (λ) A FROM R WHERE fc

which meaning is that a set of tuples with attribute set A, from relation set R, satisfying the condition fc with degree $\mu \geq \lambda$ is returned (in fuzzy terms, the λ-cut of the fuzzy relation R_f resulting from the query is returned).

If we restrict attention to the kind of queries previously discussed (which are suitable to model standard case retrieval) and if we adopt min and max operator as norms, then it is possible to derive from a Fuzzy-SQL query, an SQL query returning exactly the λ-cut required[2] [3].

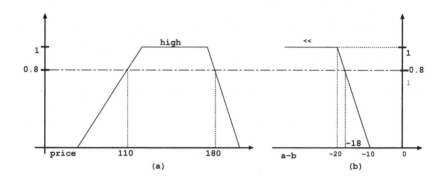

Fig. 1. Fuzzy Distributions

Example. Consider a generic relation PRODUCT containing the attribute price over which the linguistic term high is defined. Figure 1 shows a possible fuzzy distribution for high as well as the distribution of a fuzzy operator $\ll$ (much less than), defined over the difference $(a - b)$ of the operands, by considering the expression $a \ll b$. Let C be a generic condition and $D(C)$ the fuzzy degree of C; $D(\mathtt{price} = \mathtt{high} \wedge \mathtt{price} \ll 100) \geq 0.8$ will hold iff $\min(D(\mathtt{price} = \mathtt{high})$, $D(\mathtt{price} \ll 100)) \geq 0.8$, iff $D(\mathtt{price} = \mathtt{high}) \geq 0.8 \wedge D(\mathtt{price} \ll 100) \geq 0.8$ iff $(110 \leq \mathtt{price} \leq 180) \wedge (\mathtt{price} - 100) \leq -18$. The latter condition can be easily translated in a standard WHERE clause of SQL.

3   Implementing Fuzzy Case Retrieval

In order to make effective a fuzzy retrieval approach on top of a relational database we have defined the following framework for case retrieval implementation:

- cases are defined as collections of $\langle feature, value \rangle$ pairs and then represented as tuples of relations; it could happen that the relevant information for a case is scattered in different relations of a relational scheme, however it is

---

[2] If other norms are used, we are only guaranteed that a superset of the λ-cut is returned and a further filter must be applied to the result [14].

always possible to define a suitable view in order to reconstruct relevant case information in a single (possibly virtual) table or relation; (we will return on this point in the following);
- as a consequence of the previous point, case features are represented by standard relational attributes;
- fuzzy terms and fuzzy operators are defined on the case base scheme (the database scheme of the case base) through a suitable meta-database containing all the fuzzy knowledge;
- a target or query case is defined by specifying values for a set of features in a suitable way (see below);
- retrieval takes place, after specifying a precision level λ, by generating a Fuzzy-SQL query on the case base with threshold λ, returning the set of cases (tuples) within the λ limit of acceptability (i.e. the λ-cut of the resulting relation).

By considering the above framework, we notice that there is no fuzzy information represented in the case base. Cases are stored in the case base (the object database) by using, for each feature, only values from the corresponding attribute domain; on the other hand, query cases may also be specified by using linguistic (fuzzy) abstractions on such values. This means that, for each feature (attribute) to be specified in a query case, three different possibilities can be used:

1. specification of a linguistic value (if the corresponding domain allows for it);
2. specification of a crisp value, to be used *as is*;
3. specification of a crisp value *to be fuzzified*.

In the last case, fuzzification may take place in different ways; for instance, in case of a scalar attribute A which input value is a, the fuzzy expression A **near** a can be used instead of $A = a$[3].

However, more sophisticated fuzzification strategies can also be defined, by constructing a fuzzy distribution from those defined over the domain of the attribute and from the input value (see [24,14]).

In addition to the specification of a crisp or linguistic value, the target case can also specify additional conditions involving specific (possibly fuzzy) operators (e.g. the user can specify that it requires cases with `price=high` and `price` $\ll 100$). Finally, a global retrieval (acceptability) threshold λ has to be specified. A Fuzzy-SQL query can then be generated as follows:

- one or more tables $(R_1, \ldots R_k)$ which rows contain the cases of interest for retrieval are selected: each R_i may be either a view suitably constructed or a table on the original scheme;
- a fuzzy condition fc is created by taking the AND of all the expressions (crisp, fuzzy and fuzzified) specified in the target case[4]; a join condition jc is created over $R_1 \ldots R_k$;

---
[3] A more general solution could be to provide specific operators of nearness **near$_a$** for each individual scalar attribute A.

[4] Notice that such expressions may in principle involve any logical operator (NOT, OR, AND).

– a query of the form SELECT (λ) * FROM $R_1, \ldots R_k$ WHERE fc AND jc
  is generated and executed.

Retrieved cases will then be obtained as the tuples of the result table obtained
from the query.

4   An Architecture for Fuzzy Retrieval

Following the approach outlined in the previous sections, we have implemented
a client/server architecture, able to process Fuzzy-SQL queries on top of a relational DBMS. The system provides a way of generating the relevant fuzzy query
from a target case specification and can be used as a basis for the construction
of specific applications where fuzzy case retrieval is required. In particular, it
represents the core architecture over which an electronic catalog for product selection can be built. Figure 2 shows the main components of the architecture and
their inter-relationships. A case base is implemented using a standard relational
database where cases are stored in a suitable set of tables; in addition to the
object database, a *meta-database* storing all fuzzy information and knowledge is
also required (we have chosen POSTGRESQL (http://www.postgresql.org) as
the DBMS for the current implementation). Two different actors may interact
with the system: the final user who specifies the target case (i.e. the product
specification in case of selection form catalogs) and receiving the most similar
(in fuzzy sense) cases back; the system administrator, who can interact on every
part of the system and in particular with the meta-database for the specification
of the fuzzy knowledge.

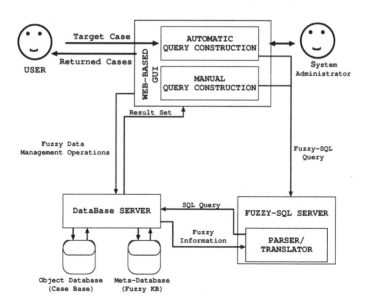

Fig. 2. System Architecture

The actual core of the architecture is a Fuzzy-SQL Server written in Java. It is devoted to the processing of the fuzzy query, by means of a Parser/Translator, implemented using Lex and Yacc; the syntax of the fuzzy query is checked and a standard SQL query is then generated, by deriving the corresponding boolean condition for the λ-cut by using the fuzzy knowledge in the meta-database. The DB server and the Fuzzy-SQL server do not need to run on the same host and communicate via JDBC driver.

Finally, a Web-Based Graphical User Interface has been implemented as a Java applet, exploiting standard browser capabilities. The GUI fulfills the following requirements: automatic Fuzzy-SQL query generation from a target case template specified by the user (in E-commerce applications through the selection of the features of the desired product); manual Fuzzy-SQL query construction (advanced users or administrator); meta-data management operations (definition of fuzzy knowledge) and database administration (administrator).

5 Flexible Product Selection from an On-Line Catalog

The fuzzy retrieval architecture outlined in the previous section may be used as the retrieval engine for a flexible product selection application from an electronic catalog. Starting from the database scheme where product information are usually stored, a standard approach consists in building a suitable *product view* over the original table space reconstructing the relevant product information for the user; such a view can then be used together with the original tables to query the database for a set of products meeting the user requirement as best as possible.

To demonstrate the capabilities of the approach, we present an example of product selection from an electronic catalog of an on-line *wine-shop*[5].

The example involves the construction of a fuzzy retrieval system for wine selection, starting from user requirements that may contain precise (e.g. a wine from that particular producer) as well as vague or fuzzy specifications (e.g. a wine with a cheap price and a medium ageing). The relational scheme for the object database (WINE) is composed by the following tables:

WINE_REGION(region_name,country);
PRODUCER(prod_name,prod_address,prod_email,prod_website,region_name);
WINE_TYPE(wtype_name,type,color);
WINE(wine_name,prod_name,wtype_name,region_name,category,cru);
BOTTLE(wine_name,prod_name,year,availability,price)

Foreign key constraints are defined as follows:

    PRODUCER:foreign key(region_name)
                        references WINE_REGION(region_name)
    WINE:foreign key(prod_name) references PRODUCER(prod_name)
    WINE:foreign key(wtype_name) references WINE_TYPE(wtype_name)

---

[5] We are currently experimenting the architecture in a variety of other domains ranging from on-line travel selection, touristic itinerary selection, etc..., to applications not related to E-commerce like therapy retrieval in medical domains.

```
WINE:foreign key(region_name) references WINE_REGION(region_name)
BOTTLE:foreign key(wine_name,prod_name)
                    references WINE(wine_name,prod_name)
```

The table WINE_REGION stores information about a particular wine region that may be the region of a producer as well as the region where a wine is produced (a producer may produce wines in different regions, while having residence in a particular wine region); table WINE_TYPE concerns information about a generic wine type (e.g. Barolo, Chianti Classico, Chardonnay California, etc...) such as the name, the possible type or classification (e.g. DOCG in Italy, AC in France) and the color; table WINE concerns specific wines of given producers belonging to a given wine_type (wtype_name) and stores information about the category of the wine (dry, sweet, strong sweet, passito) and the possible *cru* from which the wine is produced; table BOTTLE stores the specific information about a particular production of a wine such as the year, the price and the store availability; finally table PRODUCER stores all the specific information of a producer.

As we can notice that database is quite structured since it has been designed by taking into account standard DB design techniques; however, in order to maintain relevant product information in a more compact form, the following view has been defined:

```
CREATE VIEW PRODUCT(wine_name,year,producer,price
                    wtype_name,wtype_type,color,category,
                    region,ageing) AS
     SELECT B.wine_name,B.year,B.prod_name,B.price,
            WT.wtype_name,WT.type,WT.color,W.category,
            W.region_name,($CURRENT_YEAR-B.year) AS ageing
     FROM BOTTLE B, WINE W, WINE_TYPE WT
     WHERE (W.wtype_name=WT.wtype_name) AND
            (B.wine_name=W.wine_name)
```

Notice that, once a suitable product has been retrieved by using the above view, if more details on the producer, the wine region or the wine itself are needed, they can be obtained by joining the view with the suitable tables.

In our example we consider the set of fuzzy predicates shown in table 1. In addition to these predicates, we have also defined a similarity relation *sim* on the attribute region_name of table WINE_REGION and on wtype_name of WINE_TYPE

Table 1. Fuzzy predicates for the wine domain.

Table.Field	Fuzzy Values	Distrib./Domain Type
PRODUCER.prod_name	std_importance, high_importance	discrete/discrete
WINE_TYPE.wtype_name	std_importance, high_importance	discrete/discrete
WINE_REGION.region_name	std_importance, high_importance	discrete/discrete
BOTTLE.ageing	young, medium, old	contin./discrete
BOTTLE.price	very_cheap, cheap, medium, expensive, very_expensive	contin./contin.

modeling a fuzzy similarity among wine regions (with respect to "soil" characteristics) and wine types (with respect to basic oenological characterisitcs). For instance, if the user requires a wine "like" *Barolo*, the system is able to exploit specific similarities in order to propose bottles of *Barbaresco* (and possibly of *Nebbiolo*) as well.

Finally, some fuzzy operators can also be defined; for example the operator *much less than* for the attribute BOTTLE.price (<<p) as defined in fig. 1(b). Notice that all fuzzy knowledge is defined on the original tables of the scheme, but it can be applied to the attributes of the PRODUCT view, since they are derived from the attributes of those tables.

A target or query case is constructed by the user through a suitable template, where the feature he/she is interested in are selected and instantiated (in a mixed crisp and fuzzy way)[6].

Suppose for example that the user is interested in bottles of red young wine, from an important producer, with a medium price much less than 40.00 Euros and with characteristics similar to wines from "Chiantishire"; furthermore, the user is also interested in knowing the country of the proposed bottles.

He/She can select the corresponding features and then specify the values of interest; at this stage, the user has also to specify how strict are the conditions he/she requires for the retrieval; in other words, he/she has to specify how precise he/she wants the results of the retrieval to be with respect to the target case (product) specification. A direct input value or a sliding bar ranging from value 0 (lowest degree of precision) to value 1 (highest degree of precision) can be used to provide such a parameter. The specified value is used by the fuzzy query constructor module as the λ threshold for the query, while the user specified retrieval conditions will be used in the WHERE clause of the generated query.

In this specific example, if a threshold of 0.8 is specified the following query is generated[7]:

```
SELECT (0.8) *
FROM PRODUCT, WINE_REGION
WHERE (PRODUCT.region_name=WINE_REGION.region_name) AND
      (PRODUCT.region_name |sim| 'Chiantishire') AND
      (PRODUCT.prod_name = {high_importance}) AND
      (PRODUCT.price=[medium]) AND (PRODUCT.price <<p 40.00) AND
```

---

[6] In the present paper the emphasis is on the capabilities of the retrieval engine; in a deployed application, the user does not necessarily has to specify each requirement directly. Requirements (and so fuzzy conditions) may be elicited through a guided user-machine dialogue; for example, the system may ask the user something like "Do you need the product for making an important gift?". If the answer is yes the system may add to the retrieval condition something like PRODUCT.wtype_name=high_importance.

[7] Special syntactical notation has been introduced in our Fuzzy-SQL language to identify fuzzy predicates (e.g. square brackets for values from a continouos distribution and curly brackets for values from a discrete distribution) or similarity relations (e.g. '|' symbol).

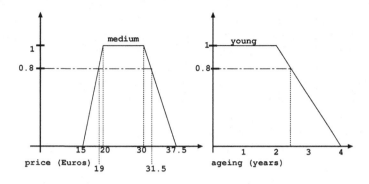

Fig. 3. Fuzzy predicates for `ageing` and `price`

```
(PRODUCT.ageing=[young]) AND
(PRODUCT.color='red')
```

Suppose that fuzzy predicates young on ageing and medium on price are defined as in fig. 3, and that the operator ≪p is defined from the membership distribution of operator ≪ in fig. 1; the corresponding standard SQL query produced by the system will be:

```
SELECT *
FROM PRODUCT, WINE_REGION
WHERE (PRODUCT.region_name=WINE_REGION.region_name) AND
      (PRODUCT.region_name IN ('Chiantishire','Montalcino',
             'Bolgheri') AND
      (PRODUCT.prod_name in ('Prod1',....'Prodk')) AND
      (PRODUCT.price between 19.00 and 31.50) AND
      (PRODUCT.price-40.00 <= -18.00) AND
      (PRODUCT.ageing between 0 and 2) AND
      (PRODUCT.color='red')
```

given that 'Chiantishire','Montalcino' and 'Bolgheri' are the only wine regions having similarity degree grater than 0.8 wrt 'Chiantishire' itself and 'Prod1' ... 'Prodk' are the names of the only k producers having membership degree grater than 0.8 wrt to the fuzzy set *high_importance*.

All the SQL code (either fuzzy or standard) is in principle totally transparent to the end user searching for the suitable travel. The join condition over PRODUCT and WINE_REGION is automatically added by the query construction module once the user has specified a requirement over an attribute not present in the PRODUCT view (i.e. the country of production of the wine)[8]. Notice that the SQL code as produced by the translation from Fuzzy-SQL is susceptible of improvment, since conditions over price may be simplified in (PRODUCT.price between 19.00 and 22.00).

---

[8] Again, in a deployed application the set of the returned attributes can be used to construct a presentation page for the user.

Once a first set of products (i.e. wine bottles) has been returned, the user can iterate the process on the result set until a satisfactory set of products has been found. Such a refinement may occur either by changing selection conditions or by changing the precision threshold or by changing both. For instance, if a more strict threshold is used in the previous example (e.g. 0.9), the selection over `price` will correspondgly change to

(PRODUCT.price between 19.50 and 30.75) AND
(PRODUCT.price-40 <= -19.00)

(or alternatively as `PRODUCT.price between 19.50 and 21.00`).

6 Conclusions and Related Works

We have presented an approach to flexible search on electronic catalogs based on fuzzy retrieval. Cases are identified with product descriptions in terms of specific features; however, instead of resorting to standard similarity-based retrieval based on k-NN techiniques, we argue that fuzzy-based retrieval can be more naturally exploited in this framework, where user product specification are intrinsically vague and imprecise. A case retrieval client/server architecture, exploiting a fuzzy extension to SQL has been presented. The system is able to automatically produce a fuzzy query from a target case template and can exploit the support of a standard relational DBMS for storing and retrieving cases. The use of standard SQL code for the actual retrieval of the relevant cases or products allows the approach to address the problem of retrieval in very large case bases.

The exploitation of CBR for E-commerce applications has been investigated in several ways; the WEBSELL architecture [15,7] is an example of use of CBR in any aspect concerning intelligent assistance on on-line sales: representation of products, customer dialog, product search and product customization. Product search [22,20,16] and product customization [19,2] are the aspects that have received major attention from CBR researchers.

In the present paper we have concentrated on flexible product search, since we argue that the application of fuzzy retrieval is a neglected area in selecting products from electronic catalogs. The problem of characterizing fuzzy retrieval has already been faced in the past, but usually in different contexts. In [10], a difference is pointed out between case filtering (as preliminary to retrieval) and case selection; hierarchical fuzzy classification is proposed for the first step, while a particular pattern matching technique exploiting fuzzy information is used for case selection. More emphasis to the problem of aggregating information is given in [21] where the use of fuzzy integrals is suggested as a suitable methodology for the synthetic evaluation of cases; a financial application is used to present the approach. Fuzzy extension to standard k-NN techniques is presented in [9] as a useful way for dealing with the challenging problem of retrieving cases for wheather prediction. The approach aims at retrieving the k most similar cases, in fuzzy terms of similarity, with respect to a target case description. However, the main goals are slightly different from ours, putting emphasis on classification and prediction via fuzzy weighting.

Concerning the problem of exploiting standard database techniques for case retrieval, some approaches have been proposed in the broad context of knowledge management, for the implementation of corporate-wide case-based systems [12,18]. In the CARET system [18], standard SQL code similar to the one obtained by our approach is derived, starting from a similarity taxonomy over which to implement a standard k-NN approach.

With similar aims, but more related to E-commerce applications is the work presented in [16]. The use of a relational database and of standard SQL is exploited for implementing case retrieval in a commercial CBR toolbox called ORENGE; also in this case no fuzzy extension to SQL is proposed, since the goal is again to implement standard (crisp) k-NN via a query relaxation technique. Commonalities with our approach can be pointed out, since both systems (i.e. CARET and ORENGE) are implemented on top of a relational DBMS and suitable thresholds must be defined for case retrieval through SQL code.

Our future work will concentrate on the possibility of creating more parametric queries, also supporting the different importance a given attribute may have in specific retrievals and in combining product selection with product customization.

References

1. A. Aamodt and E. Plaza. Case-based reasoning: Foundational issues, methodological variations and system approaches. *AI Communications*, 7(1):39–59, 1994.
2. S Aguzzoli, P. Avesani, and P. Massa. Compositional recommender systems using Case-Based Reasoning approach. Technical Report 0111-25, IRST-ITC, Trento (Italy), 2001. Also in Electr. Proc. of ACM SIGIR Workshop on Recommender Systems (www.cs.orst.edu/ herlock/rsw2001).
3. P. Bosc and O. Pivert. Fuzzy queries in conventional databases. In L. Zadeh and J. Kacprzyk, editors, *Fuzzy Logic for the Management of Uncertainty*, pages 645–672. John Wiley, 1992.
4. P. Bosc and O. Pivert. SQLf: a relational database language for fuzzy querying. *IEEE Transactions on Fuzzy Systems*, 3(1), 1995.
5. H-D. Burkhard. Extending some concepts of CBR: foundations of case retrieval nets. In M. Lenz, B. Bartsch-Spoerl, H-D. Burkhard, and S. Wess, editors, *Case Based reasoning Technology: from Foundations to Applications*, pages 17–50. LNAI 1400, Springer, 1998.
6. H-D. Burkhard and M.M. Richter. On the notion of similarity in Case-Based Reasoning and Fuzzy theory. In S.K.Pal, T.S. Dillon, and D.S. Yeung, editors, *Soft Computing in Case Based Reasoning*, pages 29–46. Springer, 2000.
7. P. Cunningham, R. Bergmann, S. Scmitt, R. Traphoener, S. Breen, and B. Smyth. WEBSELL: Intelligent sales assistants for the World Wide Web. Technical Report TCD-CS-2000-42, Trinity College Dublin, 2000.
8. H. Deitel, P. Deitel, and T. Nieto. *E-business and E-commerce: How to Program*. Prentice Hall, 2001.
9. B.K. Hansen. *Whether prediction using CBR and fuzzy set theory*. Master Thesis, Dalhousie University, 2000. http://www.cs.dal.ca/~ bjarne/thesis.pdf.

10. M. Jaczynski and B. Trousse. Fuzzy logic for the retrieval step of a case-based reasoner. In *2nd European Workshop on Case-Based Reasoning - EWCBR94*, pages 313–320, Chantilly, France, 1994.

11. J. Kacprzyck and A. Ziolowski. Database queries with fuzzy linguistic quantifiers. *IEEE Transactions on Systems, Man and Cybernetics*, 16(3), 1986.

12. H. Kitano and H Shimazu. The experience-sharing architecute: a case study in corporate-wide case-based software quality control. In D.B. Leake, editor, *Case Based Reasoning: Experiences, Lessons and Future Directions*. AAAI Press, 1996.

13. C.T. Liu and C.S. George Lee. *Neural Fuzzy Systems*. Prentice Hall, 1996.

14. L. Portinale and A. Verrua. Exploiting Fuzzy-SQL in Case-Based Reasoning. In *Proc. FLAIRS '01*, Key West, FL, 2001.

15. S. Schmitt and R. Bergmann. Applying Case-Based Reasoning technology for product selection and customization in electronic commerce environments. In *Proc. 12th Intl. Bled Electronic Commerce Conference*, Bled, Slovenia, 1999.

16. J. Schumacher and R. Bergmann. An efficient approach to similarity-based retrieval on top of relational databases. In E. Blanzieri and L. Portinale, editors, *Proc. 5th EWCBR*, pages 273–284, Trento, 2000. Lecture Notes in Artificial Intelligence 1898.

17. M. Schumacher and T. Roth-Berghofer. Architectures for integration of CBR systems with databases for e-commerce. In *Proc. 7th German Workshop on CBR (GWCBR'99)*, 1999.

18. H. Shimazu, H. Kitano, and A. Shibata. Retrieving cases from relational databases: another strike toward corporate-wide case-based systems. In *Proc. 13th Intern. Joint Conference on Artificial Intelligence (IJCAI'93)*, pages 909–914, 1993.

19. A. Stahl and R. Bergmann. Applying recursive CBR for the customization of structured products in an electronic shop. In E. Blanzieri and L. Portinale, editors, *Proc. 5th European Workshop on CBR*, Trento, 2000. Lecture Notes in Artificial Intelligence 1898.

20. I. Vollrath, W. Wilke, and R. Bergmann. Intelligent electronic catalogs for sales support. In *Advances in Soft Computing - Engineering Design and Manufacturing*. Springer, 1999.

21. R. Weber-Lee, R. Barcia, and S. Khator. Case-based reasoning for cash flow forecasting using fuzzy retrieval. In *Proc. First International Conference on Case-Based Reasoning - ICCBR95*, pages 510–519, Sesimbra, Portugal, 1995.

22. S. Weibelzahl, R. Bergmann, and G. Weber. Towards an empirical evaluation of CBR approaches for product recommendation in electronic shops. In *Proc. 8th German Workshop on CBR*, 2000.

23. W. Wilke, M. Lenz, and S. Wess. Intelligent sales support with CBR. In M. Lenz, B. Bartsch-Spoerl, H-D. Burkhard, and S. Wess, editors, *Case Based reasoning Technology: from Foundations to Applications*, pages 91–113. LNAI 1400, Springer, 1998.

24. X. Wu. Fuzzy interpretation of discretized intervals. *IEEE Transactions on Fuzzy Systems*, 7(6):753–759, 1999.

Integrating Hybrid Rule-Based
with Case-Based Reasoning

Jim Prentzas and Ioannis Hatzilygeroudis

University of Patras, School of Engineering
Dept of Computer Engin. & Informatics, 26500 Patras, Hellas (Greece)
and
Computer Technology Institute, P.O. Box 1122, 26110 Patras, Hellas (Greece)
{prentzas, ihatz}@ceid.upatras.gr, ihatz@cti.gr

Abstract. In this paper, we present an approach integrating neurule-based and case-based reasoning. Neurules are a kind of hybrid rules that combine a symbolic (production rules) and a connectionist representation (adaline unit). Each neurule is represented as an adaline unit. One way that the neurules can be produced is from symbolic rules by merging the symbolic rules having the same conclusion. In this way, the number of rules in the rule base is decreased. If the symbolic rules, acting as source knowledge of the neurules, do not cover the full complexities of the domain, accuracy of the produced neurules is affected as well. To improve accuracy, neurules can be integrated with cases representing their exceptions. The integration approach enhances a previous method integrating symbolic rules with cases. The use of neurules instead of symbolic rules improves the efficiency of the inference mechanism and allows for drawing conclusions even if some of the inputs are unknown.

1 Introduction

Symbolic rules constitute a popular knowledge representation scheme used in the development of expert systems. Rules represent general knowledge of the domain. They exhibit a number of attractive features such as naturalness, modularity and ease of explanation. One of their major drawbacks is the difficulty in acquiring them. The traditional process of eliciting rules through the interaction with the expert may turn out to be a bottleneck causing delays in the system's overall development. Furthermore, the acquired rules may be imperfect and not covering the full complexities of the domain. Rule induction methods deal with many of these disadvantages but may still be unable to recognize exceptions in small, low frequency sections of the domain [7].

Case-based reasoning offers some advantages compared to symbolic rules and other knowledge representation formalisms. Cases represent specific knowledge of the domain. Cases are natural and usually easy to obtain [1], [14], [17]. New cases can be inserted into a knowledge base without making changes to the preexisting knowledge. Incremental learning comes natural to case-based reasoning. The more

S. Craw and A. Preece (Eds.): ECCBR 2002, LNAI 2416, pp. 336–349.

cases are available the better the domain knowledge will be represented. Therefore, the accuracy of a case-based system can be enhanced throughout its operation, as new cases become available. A negative aspect of cases compared to symbolic rules is that they do not provide concise representations of the incorporated knowledge. Furthermore, the time-performance of the retrieval operations is not always the desirable.

Approaches integrating rule-based and case-based reasoning have given interesting and effective knowledge representation schemes [2], [6], [7], [8], [16], [18], [21]. The goal of these efforts is to derive hybrid representations that augment the positive aspects of the integrated formalisms and simultaneously minimize their negative aspects. In [11] the approaches integrating rule-based and case-based reasoning are distinguished into two basic categories: efficiency-improving and accuracy-improving methods. The former concern integration methods in which rules and cases are dependent, meaning that one representation scheme was derived from the other (i.e., rules derived from cases or vice versa), and the efficiency of the integrated scheme exceeds the efficiency that could have been achieved with rules or cases alone (e.g. [3], [15], [22]). The latter involves approaches in which the two representation schemes are independent and their integration results in improved accuracy compared to each one representation scheme working individually (e.g. [5], [11], [20]).

A popular integration method resulting in accuracy improvement is described in [11]. This approach involves integration of independent rules and cases in an innovative way. The purpose of this integration is to use cases in order to enhance a set of symbolic rules that is only approximately correct. On the one hand, cases are used as exceptions to the symbolic rules filling their gaps in representing domain knowledge. On the other hand, symbolic rules perform indexing of the cases facilitating their retrieval. Experimental results have demonstrated the effectiveness of the integration.

However, the performance of this method can be further enhanced if neurules [12] are used instead of pure symbolic rules. Neurules are a type of hybrid rules integrating symbolic rules with neurocomputing. Their main characteristic is that they retain the modularity of production rules and also their naturalness in a great degree.

One way that the neurules can be produced is from symbolic rules [12]. However, if the symbolic rules, acting as source knowledge to the neurule base, do not cover the full complexities of the domain, the accuracy of the resulting neurule base will be affected as well. Integrating neurules with cases in an approach similar to the one described in [11] can create an effective scheme combining three types of knowledge representation formalisms: symbolic rules, neural networks and cases. Such integration is justified by the fact that the approach described in [11] requires efficient symbolic rule-based reasoning acting as the indexing component of case-based reasoning. Neurules improve the performance of symbolic rules since neurule-based reasoning is more efficient than symbolic rule-based reasoning [12].

In this paper, we present an approach for effectively combining neurule-base and case-based reasoning. This approach improves on the one hand the accuracy of the neurules and on the other hand the performance of the approach presented in [11]. The rest of the paper is organized as following. Section 2 presents neurules, whereas

Section 3 presents the architecture for integrating neurule-based and case-based reasoning. Section 4 presents methods for constructing the indexing scheme of the case library. Section 5 describes the hybrid inference mechanism. Section 6 presents experimental results regarding the performance of the inference process. Finally, Section 7 concludes.

2   Neurules

Neurules are a type of hybrid rules integrating symbolic rules with neurocomputing giving pre-eminence to the symbolic component. Neurocomputing is used within the symbolic framework to improve the performance of symbolic rules [12]. In contrast to other hybrid approaches (e.g. [9], [10]), the constructed knowledge base retains the modularity of production rules, since it consists of autonomous units (neurules), and also retains their naturalness in a great degree, since neurules look much like symbolic rules. Also, the inference mechanism is a tightly integrated process, which results in more efficient inferences than those of symbolic rules. Explanations in the form of if-then rules can be produced [13].

2.1 Syntax and Semantics

The form of a neurule is depicted in Fig.1a. Each condition C_i is assigned a number sf_i, called its *significance factor*. Moreover, each rule itself is assigned a number sf_0, called its *bias factor*. Internally, each neurule is considered as an adaline unit (Fig.1b). The *inputs* C_i ($i=1,...,n$) of the unit are the *conditions* of the rule. The weights of the unit are the significance factors of the neurule and its bias is the bias factor of the neurule. Each input takes a value from the following set of discrete values: [1 (true), -1 (false), 0 (unknown)]. This gives the opportunity to easily distinguish between the falsity and the absence of a condition in contrast to symbolic rules. The *output D*, which represents the *conclusion* (decision) of the rule, is calculated via the standard formulas:

$$D = f(\mathbf{a}), \quad \mathbf{a} = sf_0 + \sum_{i=1}^{n} sf_i \ C_i$$

$$f(\mathbf{a}) = \begin{cases} 1 & if \ \mathbf{a} \geq 0 \\ -1 & otherwise \end{cases}$$

where **a** is the *activation value* and *f(x)* the *activation function*, a threshold function. Hence, the output can take one of two values ('-1', '1') representing failure and success of the rule respectively.

The general syntax of a condition C_i and the conclusion D is:

<condition>::= <variable> <l-predicate> <value>
<conclusion>::= <variable> <r-predicate> <value>

where <variable> denotes a *variable*, that is a symbol representing a concept in the domain, e.g. 'sex', 'pain' etc, in a medical domain. <l-predicate> denotes a symbolic or a numeric predicate. The symbolic predicates are {is, isnot} whereas the numeric predicates are {<, >, =}. <r-predicate> can only be a symbolic predicate. <value> denotes a value. It can be a *symbol* or a *number*. Corresponding symbolic rules have the same syntax as that in Fig.1a, without the significance factors and with ',' denoting conjunction. The significance factor of a condition represents the significance (weight) of the condition in drawing the conclusion(s). Table 1 presents two example rules, a symbolic (R1) and a neurule (N1), from a medical diagnosis domain.

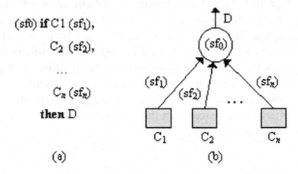

Fig. 1. (a) Form of a neurule (b) a neurule as an adaline unit

A variable in a condition can be either an input variable or an intermediate variable or even an output variable, whereas a variable in a conclusion can be either an intermediate or an output variable. An input variable takes values from the user (input data), whereas intermediate or output variables take values through inference since they represent intermediate and final conclusions respectively. We distinguish between intermediate and output neurules. An intermediate neurule is a neurule having at least one intermediate variable in its conditions and intermediate variables in its conclusions. An output neurule is one having an output variable in its conclusions.

Table 1. An example (a) symbolic rule and (b) neurule

R1	N1
if sex is man,	(-4.2) **if** pain is continuous (3.0),
age > 20,	patient-class isnot man36-55 (2.8),
age < 36	fever is medium (2.7),
then patient-class is man21-35	fever is high (2.7)
	then disease-type is inflammation
(a)	(b)

Neurules can be constructed from symbolic rules thus exploiting existing symbolic rule bases. This process is fully described in [12]. According to the process, symbolic rules having the same conclusion are organized into merger sets and an adaline unit is initially assigned to each one of them. Each unit is individually trained via the Least Mean Square (LMS) algorithm. Its training set is based on the combined logical function of the rules (i.e., the disjunction of the conjunctions of their conditions) in the merger set. When the training set is inseparable, special techniques are used. In that case, more than one neurule having the same conclusion are produced. Section 4.2 contains an example merger set (Table 3) and the corresponding produced neurule (Table 5).

2.2 The Neurule-Based Inference Engine

The neurule-based inference engine performs a task of classification: based on the values of the condition variables and the weighted sums of the conditions, conclusions are reached. It gives pre-eminence to symbolic reasoning, based on a backward chaining strategy [12]. As soon as the initial input data is given and put in the working memory, the output neurules are considered for evaluation. One of them is selected for evaluation. Selection is based on textual order. A neurule fires if the output of the corresponding adaline unit is computed to be '1' after evaluation of its conditions. A neurule is said to be 'blocked' if the output of the corresponding adaline unit is computed to be '-1' after evaluation of its conditions.

A condition evaluates to 'true', if it matches a fact in the working memory, that is there is a fact with the same variable, predicate and value. A condition evaluates to 'unknown', if there is a fact with the same variable, predicate and 'unknown' as its value. A condition cannot be evaluated if there is no fact in the working memory with the same variable. In this case, either a question is made to the user to provide data for the variable, in case of an input variable, or an intermediate neurule with a conclusion containing the variable is examined, in case of an intermediate variable. A condition with an input variable evaluates to 'false', if there is a fact in the working memory with the same variable, predicate and different value. A condition with an intermediate variable evaluates to 'false' if additionally to the latter there is no unevaluated intermediate neurule that has a conclusion with the same variable. Inference stops either when one or more output neurules are fired (success) or there is no further action (failure).

Conditions of neurules are organized according to the descending order of their significance factors. This facilitates inference. When a neurule is examined in the inference process, not all of its conditions need to be evaluated. Evaluation of a neurule's conditions proceeds until their weighted sum exceeds the remaining sum (i.e., sum of the absolute values of the unevaluated conditions' significance factors).

When a neurule base is produced from a symbolic rule base, experimental results have shown that neurule-based inference is more efficient than the corresponding symbolic rule-based inference [12]. The main reason for this is the fact that a neurule is a merger of usually more than one symbolic rule having the same conclusion and thus the total number of rules in the rule base is reduced. In this way, the number of rules participating in the inference process is reduced and so is the number of the evaluated conditions. Another advantage of neurule-based reasoning compared to symbolic rule-based reasoning is the ability to reach conclusions from neurules even if some of the conditions are unknown. This is not possible in symbolic rule-based reasoning. A symbolic rule needs all its conditions to be known in order to produce a conclusion.

3 The Hybrid Architecture

In Fig. 2, the architecture of the hybrid system implementing the method for integrating neurule-based and case-based reasoning is presented. The run-time system (in the dashed shape) consists of the following modules: the *working memory*, the *hybrid inference mechanism*, the *explanation mechanism*, the *neurule base* and the *indexed case library*.

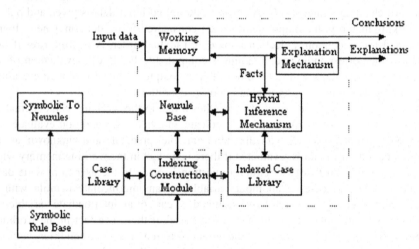

Fig. 2. The hybrid architecture

The neurule base contains neurules. These neurules may be produced by conversion from a *symbolic rule base*. This process is described in detail in [12] and is performed by the *symbolic to neurules* module.

Each case is formalized as a set of attribute values. A few of these attributes are used for descriptive purposes, but most of them in performing inferences. Most of the attributes used in making inferences correspond to input, intermediate and output variables of symbolic rules. The neurule base is used to index a *case library*. In this way, an indexed case library is derived. Special care is required when converting an symbolic rule-base (SRB) that already indexes a case library to a neurule base. The process of acquiring an indexing scheme is performed offline by the *indexing construction module* and is described in Section 4.

The hybrid inference mechanism makes inferences combining neurule-based and case-based reasoning. It takes into account the facts contained in the working memory, the neurules in the neurule base and the cases in the indexed case library. The hybrid inference mechanism is described in Section 5.

4 Indexing

Indexing concerns the organization of the available cases so that combined neurule-based and case-based reasoning can be performed. The neurules contained in the neurule base are used to index cases representing their exceptions. A case constitutes an exception to a neurule if its attribute values satisfy sufficient conditions of the neurule but the neurule's conclusion contradicts the corresponding attribute value of the case. Exception cases to neurules are considered of most importance as they fill gaps in the knowledge represented by neurules. During inference, exceptions may assist in reaching the right conclusion.

The indexing process may take as input the following two types of knowledge:
(a) Available neurules and cases.
(b) Available symbolic rules and exception cases. This type of knowledge concerns an available formalism of symbolic rules and indexed exception cases as the one presented in [11].

The availability of data determines which type of knowledge is provided as input to the indexing module. The indexing process for each one of these types is briefly presented in the following.

4.1 Indexing Process for Available Neurules and Cases

The available neurules must be associated with the cases constituting their exceptions. For each case, this information can be easily acquired as following:

Until all the intermediate and output attribute values of the case have been considered:

1. Perform neurule-based reasoning for the neurules based on the attribute values of the case.
2. If a neurule fires, check whether the value of its conclusion variable matches the corresponding attribute value of the case. If it doesn't, mark the case as an exception to this neurule.

As an example, to demonstrate how the indexing process works, we use neurule N1 presented in Table 1 and the two example cases in Table 2. The cases possess other attributes as well. However, only their most important attributes are shown in Table 2.

Table 2. Example cases

patient-class	pain	fever	ant-reaction	joints-pain	disease-type
human0-20	continuous	medium	high	yes	special-arthritis
human0-20	continuous	high	high	no	inflammation

Disease-type is the attribute of the cases corresponding to the neurule's conclusion. Let ws_1 and rs_1 be the weighted and remaining sum respectively for the first case. Also let ws_2 and rs_2 be the weighted and remaining sum respectively for the second case. Evaluation of conditions for the first case (second case) continues until $|ws_1| > |rs_1|$ ($|ws_2| > |rs_2|$). The final values of these sums are the following:

$ws_1 = (-4.2) + 3.0 + 2.8 + 2.7 = 4.3 > 0$,

$rs_1 = 2.7$,

$ws_2 = (-4.2) + 3.0 + 2.8 - 2.7 + 2.7 = 1.6 > 0$,

$rs_2 = 0$.

Therefore, the attribute values of both cases give a positive weighted sum for the neurule's conditions. Notice that only the first three conditions of the neurule need to be taken into account for the first case since the weighted sum (4.3) exceeds the remaining sum (i.e., the absolute value of the significance factor of the fourth condition), which equals to 2.7. The fact that the weighted sums were positive means that both cases will be classified in the 'inflammation' disease-type. However, only the disease-type observed for the second case complies with the neurule's conclusion. The first case contradicts the neurule. Therefore, it will be indexed as an exception to the neurule.

4.2 Indexing Process for Available Symbolic Rules and Exception Cases

The symbolic rules are converted to neurules using the symbolic to neurules module. The produced neurules are associated with the exception cases of the symbolic rules belonging to their merger sets.

A potential disadvantage of this conversion is the fact that in average a produced neurule will be associated with more exception cases than its merged symbolic rules. This may affect negatively the case-based reasoning part of the inference process. However, the explanation rule produced from the neurule can be used to surpass this deficiency by limiting the exception cases considered by case-based reasoning (see Section 5).

Table 3. Symbolic rules of a merger set

R2
if patient-class is human0-20,
  pain is night,
  fever is no-fever,
  ant-reaction is none
then disease-type is primary-malignant
	R3
	if patient-class is human21-35,
	  pain is night,
	  ant-reaction is none
	then disease-type is primary-malignant

R4
if patient-class is human21-35,
  pain is continuous,
  fever is no-fever,
  ant-reaction is none
then disease-type is primary-malignant	

As an example, consider the three symbolic rules (R2, R3, R4) presented in Table 3. Table 4 presents some of their exception cases. The symbolic rule for which each of these example cases is an exception, is shown in the 'disease-type' column of the table in parenthesis. Merging these three symbolic rules produces the neurule presented in Table 5. The cases in Table 4 are now indexed as exceptions to this neurule. This example demonstrates how the average number of exception cases indexed by a neurule is increased if it is produced from a merger set of symbolic rules indexing exception cases.

Table 4. Exception cases indexed by the symbolic rules in Table 3

patient-class	pain	Fever	ant-reaction	joints-pain	disease-type
human0-20	night	no-fever	none	yes	inflammation (R2)
human21-35	continuous	no-fever	none	no	primary-benign (R4)
human21-35	continuous	no-fever	none	yes	chronic-inflammation (R4)
human21-35	night	no-fever	none	no	arthritis (R3)

Table 5. Neurule produced by merging the symbolic rules in Table 3

NR2-R3-R4

(-7.8) **if** patient-class is human21-35 (6.9),
       pain is night (6.4),
       ant-reaction is none (6.3),
       patient-class is human0-20 (3.0),
       fever is no-fever (2.7),
       pain is continuous (2.6)
   then disease-type is primary-malignant

5   The Hybrid Inference Mechanism

The inference mechanism combines neurule-based reasoning with case-based reasoning. The combined inference process mainly focuses on the neurules. The exception cases are considered only when sufficient conditions of a neurule are fulfilled so that it can fire. If this is so, firing of the neurule is suspended and case-based reasoning is performed for its exception cases. The results produced by case-based reasoning are evaluated in order to assess whether the neurule will fire or whether the conclusion proposed by the exception case will be considered valid.

Case-based reasoning and evaluation of its results is performed as in [11]. Reasoning tries to find similarities between known data and exception cases. If such similarity is found, an analogical rule encompassing the similar attribute values between the indexed case and the input case is produced. The analogy rules produced by case-based reasoning are evaluated. Evaluation is based on two factors: the similarity degree between the input case and the exception cases and how well the analogy rule works (generalizes) on other exception cases. If the analogy between the input case and an exception case proves to be compelling, the conclusion supported by the case is considered valid, whereas the associated neurule becomes 'blocked'.

The basic steps of the inference process combining neurule-based and case-based reasoning are the following:

1. Perform neurule-based reasoning for the neurules.
2. If enough of the conditions of a neurule are fulfilled so that it can fire, do the following:

2.1. If the neurule has no associated exception cases, it fires and its conclusion is inserted into the working memory.

2.2. If the neurule is associated with exception cases suspend its firing. Produce an explanation rule for the neurule and perform case-based reasoning for the neurule's associated exception cases matching the explanation rule.

2.3. If the analogy proposed by case-based reasoning is compelling, insert the conclusion supported by the exception case into the working memory and mark the neurule as 'blocked'. Otherwise, mark the neurule as 'fired' and insert its conclusion into the working memory.

To explain how conclusions are reached, the explanation mechanism described in [13] is used. If a neurule becomes 'blocked', due to an exception case, the explanation rule produced is the analogy rule yielded by the operation of case-based reasoning for the neurule's exception cases. If this is so, the explanation mechanism informs that an exception was triggered and the exception conclusion was produced instead of the normal one.

We now present a simple example. Suppose that the case contained in Table 6 is given as input to neurule NR2-R3-R4 (see Table 5).

Table 6. An input case to neurule NR2-R3-R4

patient-class	pain	fever	ant-reaction	joints-pain
human21-35	night	high	none	no

Only the first three conditions need to be examined. Their weighted sum is (-7.8) + 6.9 + 6.4 + 6.3 = 11.8. This number is greater than the remaining sum of the rest three conditions that equals to 3.0 + 2.7 + 2.6 = 8.3.

The explanation rule (EXR) produced is shown in Table 7. Firing of the neurule is suspended and the exception cases matching the explanation rule are considered in the case-based reasoning process. From the exception cases shown in Table 4, only the fourth one matches the explanation rule.

Table 7. Explanation rule produced from neurule NR2-R3-R4

EXR
if   patient-class is human21-35,
pain is night,
ant-reaction is none
then disease-type is primary-malignant

Suppose that the same input case was given to the three symbolic rules shown in Table 3. In the symbolic rule-based reasoning part of the inference, the order that the rules will be considered is R2, R3, and R4. The conditions of rule R2 are not satisfied. However, all conditions of rule R3 are satisfied. Four rule conditions will have to be examined (one condition for R2 and three conditions for R3) instead of the three conditions examined in neurule-based reasoning. Firing of rule R3 is suspended and its indexed exception cases (i.e., the fourth case in Table 4) will be considered by case-based reasoning.

Therefore, both types of inference mechanisms produce the same results. However, the inference mechanism combining neurule-based and case-based reasoning requires the examination of fewer conditions. This feature is intensified in longer inference chains when much more rules have to be examined.

6 Experimental Results

To test the effectiveness of our approach we used a symbolic rule base concerning a medical application domain. The symbolic rule base contained fifty-eight (58) symbolic rules acquired by interviewing an expert. The symbolic rules were indexing available exception cases in order to improve their accuracy. This combined symbolic rule base and indexed case library will be referred to as SRCL. By using the symbolic-to-neurules module, the symbolic rules were converted to neurules. In total, thirty-four (34) neurules were produced. The exception cases of the merged symbolic rules were indexed accordingly by the produced neurules. The combined neurule base and indexed case library will be referred to as NRCL.

Inferences were run for SRCL and NRCL. Inferences from SRCL were performed using the inference mechanism combining rule-based and case-based reasoning as described in [11]. Inferences from NRCL were performed according to the inference mechanism integrating neurule-based and case-based reasoning. As expected, inferences produced the same conclusions in both SRCL and NRCL for the same variable-value data. However, inferences from NRCL required the evaluation of fewer conditions than the corresponding inferences from SRCL.

Table 8 presents such experimental results regarding inferences from SRCL and NRCL. It presents results regarding the number of visited rules as well as the number of evaluated conditions. The table also presents if the conclusion was derived as an exception or not (column 'Exception Occurred').

As can be seen from the table, there is an average 45% reduction in the rules visited in NRCL. Furthermore, about 25% fewer conditions were evaluated in inferences from NRCL. Finally, the integration with case-based reasoning improved the accuracy of the inference mechanism in about 30% of the inferences.

7 Conclusions

In this paper, we present an approach that integrates neurule-based and case-based reasoning. Neurules are a type of hybrid rules integrating symbolic rules with neurocomputing. In contrast to other neuro-symbolic approaches, neurules retain the naturalness and modularity of symbolic rules. Integration of neurules and cases is done in order to improve the accuracy of the inference mechanism. Neurules are used to index cases representing their exceptions.

The use of neurules instead of symbolic rules as in the approach described in [11] offers a number of advantages. Conclusions from neurules can be reached more efficiently. In addition, neurule-based inference can be performed even if some of the inputs are unknown. This is not possible in symbolic rule-based reasoning. Even an existing formalism of symbolic rules and indexed exception cases can be converted to a formalism of neurules and indexed exception cases.

The presented approach integrates three types of knowledge representation schemes: symbolic rules, neural networks and case-based reasoning. Most hybrid intelligent systems implemented in the past usually integrate two intelligent technologies e.g. neural networks and expert systems [4], neural and fuzzy logic [19], genetic algorithms and neural networks, etc. A new development that should receive interest in the future is the integration of more than two intelligent technologies that can facilitate the solution of complex problems and exploit multiple types of available data sources.

Table 8. Experimental Results

Inference No	Rules Visited	Conditions Evaluated	Exception Occurred
	SRCL / NRCL	SRCL / NRCL	
1	8 / 4	17 / 10	No
2	11 / 6	26 / 17	Yes
3	13 / 8	26 / 21	No
4	17 / 10	33 / 27	No
5	21 / 10	32 / 22	No
6	24 / 11	43 / 32	No
7	26 / 13	48 / 39	Yes
8	29 / 15	57 / 44	Yes
9	32 / 16	58 / 43	Yes
10	40 / 22	59 / 51	No
11	42 / 23	77 / 59	No
12	44 / 24	81 / 63	No
13	47 / 26	86 / 65	No
Total	**354 / 188**	**643 / 493**	

Acknowledgements

This work is supported by the Research Committee of the University of Patras, Program Caratheodoris-2001, project No 2788.

References

1. Aamodt, A., Plaza, E.: Case-Based Reasoning: Foundational Issues, Methodological Variations and System Approaches. Artificial Intelligence Communications 7 (1994) 39-59.
2. Aha, D., Daniels, J.J. (eds.): Case-Based Reasoning Integrations: Papers from the 1998 AAAI Workshop. Technical Report WS-98-15. AAAI Press (1998).
3. Althoff, K., Wess, S., Traphoner, R.: INRECA-A Seamless Integration of Induction and Case-Based Reasoning for Decision Support Tasks. Proceedings of the Eighth Workshop German SIG on Machine Learning (1995).
4. Boutsinas, B., Vrahatis, M., N.: Artificial nonmonotonic neural networks. AI 132 (2001) 1-38.
5. Branting, L.K.: Building Explanations from Rules and Structured Cases. International Journal of Man-Machine Studies 34 (1991) 797-837.
6. Branting, L.K.: Reasoning with Rules and Precedents. Kluwer Academic Publishers. Dordrecht (1999).
7. Cercone, N., An, A., Chan, C.: Rule-Induction and Case-Based Reasoning: Hybrid Architectures Appear Advantageous. IEEE Transactions on Knowledge and Data Engineering 11 (1999) 164-174.
8. Domingos, P.: Unifying Instance-Based and Rule-Based Induction. Machine Learning 24 (1996) 144-168.
9. Gallant, S. I.: Neural Network Learning and Expert Systems. MIT Press (1993).
10. Ghalwash, A. Z.: A Recency Inference Engine for Connectionist Knowledge Bases: Applied Intelligence 9 (1998) 201-215.
11. Golding, A.R., Rosenbloom, P.S.: Improving accuracy by combining rule-based and case-based reasoning. Artificial Intelligence 87 (1996) 215-254.
12. Hatzilygeroudis, I., Prentzas, J.: Neurules: Improving the Performance of Symbolic Rules. International Journal on AI Tools 9 (2000) 113-130.
13. Hatzilygeroudis, I., Prentzas, J.: An Efficient Hybrid Rule-Based Inference Engine with Explanation Capability. Proceedings of the 14th International FLAIRS Conference. AAAI Press (2001) 227-231.
14. Kolodner, J.: Case-Based Reasoning. Morgan Kaufmann Publishers, San Mateo, CA (1993).
15. Koton, P.: Reasoning about Evidence in Causal Explanations. Proceedings of the AAAI-88. AAAI Press (1988).
16. Leake, D.B.: Combining Rules and Cases to Learn Case Adaptation. Proceedings of the 17th Annual Conference of the Cognitive Science Society (1995).
17. Leake, D.B. (ed.): Case-Based Reasoning: Experiences, Lessons & Future Directions. AAAI Press/MIT Press (1996).
18. Marling, C.R., Petot, G.J., Sterling, L.S.: Integrating Case-Based and Rule-Based Reasoning to Meet Multiple Design Constraints. Computational Intelligence 15 (1999) 308-332.

19. Neagu, C.-D., Palade, V.: Modular Neuro-Fuzzy Networks Used in Explicit and Implicit Knowledge Integration, Proceedings of the 15th International FLAIRS Conference (FLAIRS-02). AAAI Press (2002) 277-281.
20. Rissland, E.L., Skalak, D.B.: CABARET: Rule Interpretation in a Hybrid Architecture. International Journal of Man-Machine Studies 34 (1991) 839-887.
21. Surma, J., Vanhoof, K.: An Empirical Study on Combining Instance-Based and Rule-Based Classifiers. Case-Based Reasoning Research and Development, First International Conference, ICCBR-95, Proceedings. Lecture Notes in Computer Science, Vol. 1010. Springer-Verlag, Berlin Heidelberg New York (1995).
22. Veloso, M.M.: Learning by Analogical Reasoning in General Problem Solving. PhD Thesis, Technical Report CMU-CS-92-174, Carnegie Mellon University, Pittsburg, PA (1992).

Search and Adaptation
in a Fuzzy Object Oriented Case Base

Magali Ruet and Laurent Geneste

LGP / ENIT, Avenue d'Azereix, BP 1629,
65016 TARBES Cedex, France
{ruet,laurent}@enit.fr

Abstract. In this paper we propose to represent a case using an object oriented model that enables the description of imprecise knowledge using possibility distributions. The proposed search process is based on this modeling and a fuzzy similarity measure is defined. The adaptation process is achieved with propagation of domain constraints in a neighborhood of the retrieved case. We propose a method to define this neighborhood. We illustrate our proposition by an example in the field of machining operation configuration.

1 Introduction

In many industrial problems such as expert configuration or design, the intrinsic complexity of the problem (many parameters, many technological constraints) has led to the definition of systems in which constraints are explicitly defined and propagated during configuration/design process [3]. However, generally these propagation techniques are rather blind and above all they do not take into account past experiences to guide configuration. Nevertheless in many configuration problems involving expertise, adapting a solution obtained in a previous similar situation may be judicious.

More generally it has been observed that in many firms the reuse and generalization of past experiences (often called "lesson learned") is becoming a key factor for the improvement (in time and in quality) of operational processes. The memory of past experiences proves to be necessary for such a reuse of previously found solutions. Yet when experts appreciation is part of this memory, imprecision may often pervades stored information. Therefore we propose a formalism enabling us to structure experts knowledge with an explicit representation of the imprecision/ inaccuracy. The second major issue consists in providing the system user with convenient tools intended to searching and adapting past solutions to a problem similar to his current problem (target problem). Such a goal can be achieved by mixing case based reasoning (CBR) techniques and constraint propagation techniques.

This paper is divided into four main sections. The first section describes the data structure used for knowledge acquisition. The second section explains the suggested technique for search and the third section details the adaptation mechanisms. The last section presents an illustration in the field of machining operation configuration.

S. Craw and A. Preece (Eds.): ECCBR 2002, LNAI 2416, pp. 350–364.
© Springer-Verlag Berlin Heidelberg 2002

2 Case Modeling

The object oriented modeling language U.M.L. (Unified Modeling Language) [9] has been selected as a standard modeling of domain knowledge. U.M.L. class diagram and object diagram intervene in this analysis to represent field data. The schema of the knowledge base (ontology) is described with a class diagram whereas the knowledge base is an instantiation of the class diagram (object diagram). An example is given in Fig 1.

Cases are represented by an object instantiated from the class diagram. Each object is composed of attributes that characterize the case. These attributes may sometimes require a full object to properly describe a case (composition).

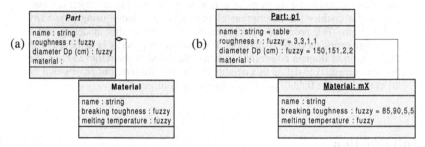

Fig. 1. (a) Excerpt of the class diagram: a part is described by attributes *name*, *roughness*, and *diameter* and by attribute *material* itself described by an object from the class *Material*. (b) A case example: case *p1* is an instantiation of the class *Part*. Some of its attributes are valued and others still have to be valued

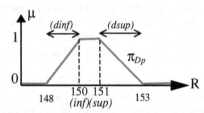

Fig. 2. The attribute *diameter Dp* is defined on a reference domain R by a possibility distribution expressing the possible degree of membership (μ) of each value of R to the attribute. A possibility distribution is a function π of a reference domain R to [0,1] so that: $\sup(\pi(x)) = 1, x \in R$

Beyond the object oriented structure, we allow the description of uncertain and imprecise knowledge. Indeed possibility distributions [5] are used to model an imprecise value of an object attribute. In this paper possibility distributions are represented using trapezoidal fuzzy sets as in Fig 2. A trapezoidal fuzzy set is described by 4 numbers: (inf, sup, dinf, dsup).

The target case is an instance of the class diagram, some of its attributes may be unvalued. The search process is developed in next section, then adaptation techniques are detailed in section 4.

3 Fuzzy Search

A few works include fuzzy logic and possibility theory in the retrieval step of case based reasoning [7] [12] [13] [20]. Therefore the proposal advanced in this section consists in exploiting an object oriented structure in which a search algorithm supporting the possibility theory is recursively propagated [5]. The search result is a necessity degree N and a possibility degree Π showing similarities between cases stored in the object structure and target case (N and Π vary in [0,1]). The search for similar cases is divided into two steps. The first step, described as a filtering process, makes it possible to determine the classes of the model concerned with the problem (section 3.1). Then a similarity measure allows to identify the nearest source case to the target case among cases selected during the former filtering step (section 3.2).

3.1   Rough Filtering

In the literature most CBR systems use indexing techniques to accelerate the filtering of cases stored in the case base. Indexing strategies are numerous and often implemented with difficulty [14]. They are based on the use of an index to be correctly defined in order to find all the cases which may be similar to the target case. The considered filtering mechanism does not use such an indexing strategy but is based on the class structure of the knowledge base.

The exploitation of the object modeling as an indexing base is suggested to allow a fast selection of potentially interesting objects during the similar case search. The filtering process is therefore achieved by comparing attributes of the target case class (o belonging to class O) with each class of the class diagram (class O'). According to the observed similarity between classes O and O' it can be decided to inspect the objects belonging to class O' in more details (section 3.2).

Filtering algorithm `class_similarity(O,O')` determining the similarity of structure of class O (class of target case) and class O' (class of the class diagram).

Procedure `class_similarity(O,O')`	
Input:	O: class of target case,
	O': class of the class diagram.
Output:	S: structural similarity between O and O'.
Notation:	a: attribute of class O,
	w_a: weight of a,
	C: constituent class of class O,
	C': constituent class of class O',
	w_c: weight of C,
	n: number of attributes of class O.

```
begin
   S = 0
   for each a ∈ O
       if a ∈ O'
           S = S + w
   for each C ∈ O
       maxi = 0
```

```
      for each C' ∈ O'
            maxi = max(maxi, class_similarity(C,C'))
         S = S + maxi*w_c
   S = S/∑w_k,k{1,2,...,n}                    /*normalisation*/
end.
```

Weights given by the user to target case attributes are processed by the rough filtering algorithm. When required, it is thus possible to find out similarities between very different classes which have yet common attributes considered as important according to the user requirements.

The result of the filtering process is a class of the class diagram. All objects belonging to this class are potentially similar to the target case. The best case allowing to pursue the process will extracted from the case base using the similarity measure described in next section.

Let us underline that this filtering process may not be relevant when few cases are stored in the library or when few classes specialise the class diagram.

3.2   Fuzzy Similarity Measure

Each case detected during the filtering step is compared to the target case using a similarity measure. The most similar case will then be selected and subsequently adapted. The suggested similarity measure considers the object oriented structure of the knowledge base and allows the use of possibility distributions in order to represent the imprecise and/or uncertain attributes of cases. There are two levels of similarity: the *local similarity* defined at the attribute level (i.e. on a single domain) and the *global similarity* defined at the object level (i.e. on a cartesian product of domains).

The local similarity is modeled using a similarity membership function μ_a allowing the user to associate a specific similarity measure to an attribute. In particular $\mu_a(x,y)=1$ if x is completely similar to y, $\mu_a(x,y)=0$ if x is totally different to y, and $0<\mu_a(x,y)<1$ for intermediate similarities.

The similarity measure is computed as follows:

Notations:

- T denotes the target case and S the source case
- $att_{T,a}$ the name of attribute a of case T, and $val_{T,a}$ its value
- D_a the domain of attribute a and $U = D_a \times D_a$
- w_a the weight associated to attribute a for the search
- n the number of attributes of the target case
- μ_a the similarity membership function describing the local similarity for attribute a: for example the figure 3 represents the membership function called "close to" where the similarity degree of two values of an attribute is expressed. The "close to" membership function is defined by:

$$\mu_a(x,y) = 1 - \frac{|x-y|}{\Delta} \text{ if } 0 \le |x-y| \le \Delta = 1$$

$$\mu_a(x,y) = 0 \qquad otherwise$$

where Δ defines the slope of the "close to" membership function.

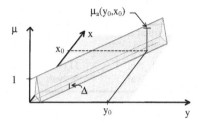

Fig. 3. An example of a membership function. The "close to" membership function represents how two values of an attribute are similar. The value y_0 of y (name of the attribute in the source case) is similar to the value x_0 of x (name of the same attribute in the target case) at a level defined by $\mu_a(y_0,x_0)$

− π_T the possibility distribution describing the attribute value $val_{T,a}$
− π_S the possibility distribution describing the attribute value $val_{S,a}$
− π_D the possibility distribution defined by

$$\pi_D (x,y) = \min (\pi_T(x), \pi_S(y)) \tag{1}$$

At the level of each attribute a, the possibility and necessity degrees corresponding to a local similarity are computed as follows:

$$\Pi_a(val_{T,a},val_{S,a}) = \sup_{u \in U} \min(\mu_a(u),\pi_D(u)) \tag{2}$$

$$N_a(val_{T,a},val_{S,a}) = \inf_{u \in U} \max(\mu_a(u), 1-\pi_D(u))$$

Once each local similarity has been assessed, the evaluation of the global similarity is achieved by considering the weights associated to each attribute of the target object and by computing the min of the max of the obtained similarities. Therefore the possibility and necessity degrees at the object level are:

$$\Pi(T,S) = \min_{i=1,n} \max(1-w_i,s_i) \qquad N(T,S) = \min_{i=1,n} \max(1-w_i,s_i') \tag{3}$$

with :

$$s_i = \begin{cases} \Pi_a(val_{T,i},val_{S,j}) & if \quad \exists j \in \{1,...,n\} \quad att_{T,i} = att_{S,j} \\ 0 & else \end{cases} \tag{4}$$

$$s_i' = \begin{cases} N_a(val_{T,i},val_{S,j}) & if \quad \exists j \in \{1,...,n\} \quad att_{T,i} = att_{S,j} \\ 0 & else \end{cases}$$

The necessity and possibility degrees represent at which level two cases are similar. They respectively correspond to a lower and upper bound of the similarity degree.

Concerning cases endowed with different object structure (e.g. cases composed by objects belonging to different classes) the similarity measure computed between two cases must take their difference of structure into account [1]. The table below (table 1) summarizes how the proposed algorithm will act depending on the difference of structure of the compared two cases.

Table 1. Value of local similarity (Π_a and N_a) depending on the state of attribute in source case

State of attribute a in source case	a is defined and is valued	a is defined but is not valued	a is not defined
Valued attribute a in target case	$\Pi_a(val_{T,a}, val_{S,a})$ $N_a(val_{T,a}, val_{S,a})$	$\Pi_a(val_{T,a}, val_{S,a})=1$ $N_a(val_{T,a}, val_{S,a})=0$	$\Pi_a(val_{T,a}, val_{S,a})=0$ $N_a(val_{T,a}, val_{S,a})=0$

The developed similarity algorithm differentiates cases with the same structure from cases with a different structure. When the target case is compared with a source case, the algorithm systematically reviews each target attribute. Then the value of the local similarity between the value of this attribute in source case and the value of this attribute in target case depends on the state of the attribute in source case.

The same reasoning can apply when target attributes are described by objects. Hence, as shown in both last points the structure of compared cases has an impact on the similarity computed between these cases.

Similarity algorithm `object_similarity(T,S)` computing the necessity of similarity N(T,S) and possibility of similarity Π(T,S) of objects T (target case) and S (source case).

Procedure object_similarity(T,S)

Input:	T: target case (object),
	S: source case (object).
Output:	N: necessity value of resemblance between T and S,
	Π: possibility value of resemblance between T and S.
Notation:	a: name of an attribute,
	w_a: weight of a,
	$val_{T,a}$: value of attribute a in target case T,
	$val_{S,a}$: value of attribute a in source case S,
	C: name of an aggregated class,
	$val_{T,C}$: value of C in object T,
	$val_{S,C}$: value of C in object S,
	Class(T): class of object T,
	$N_a(x,y)$: local necessity measure between attributes x and y (see(2)),
	$\Pi_a(x,y)$: local possibility measure between attributes x and y (see(2)),
	N(X,Y): global necessity measure between classes X and Y (see (3)),
	Π(X,Y): global possibility measure between classes X and Y (see (3)).

```
begin
  N = 1
  Π = 1
  for each a ∈ Class(T)
   if a ∈ Class(S) and val_{s,a} is defined
     then N = min(max(1-w_a, N_a(val_{T,a}, val_{S,a})), N)
          Π = min(max(1-w_a, Π_a(val_{T,a}, val_{S,a})), Π)
   if a ∈ Class(S) and val_{s,a} is not defined
     then N = min(1-w_a, N)              /*N_a(val_{T,a},val_{S,a})=0*/
          Π is unchanged                 /*Π_a(val_{T,a},val_{S,a})=1*/
   if a ∉ Class(S)
```

```
      then  N = min(1-w_a, N)                /*N_a(val_T,a, val_S,a)=0*/
            Π = min(1-w_a, Π)                /*Π_a(val_T,a, val_S,a)=0*/
   for each C ∈ Class(T)
      if C ∈ Class(S) and val_s,c is defined
         then  N = min(max(1-w_c, object_similarity.N(val_T,c, val_s,c)), N)
               Π = min(max(1-w_c, object_similarity.Π(val_T,c, val_s,c)), Π)
      if C ∈ Class(S) and val_s,c is not defined
         then  N = min(1-w_c, N)             /*object_similarity.N(val_T,c, val_s,c)=0*/
               Π is unchanged                /* object_similarity.Π(val_T,c, val_s,c)=1*/
      if C ∉ Class(S)
         then  N = min(1-w_c, N)             /* object_similarity.N(val_s,c, val_s,c)-0*/
               Π = min(1-w_c, Π)             /* object_similarity.Π(val_T,c, val_s,c)=0*/
end.
```

Once the most similar source case to the target case has been found, the adaptation process can begin. This step is described in the next section.

4 Adaptation Process

According to us the adaptation should be carried out in a neighborhood of the found solution and supported by constraint propagation techniques (Fig. 4). Preliminary defining adaptation domains is thus required. Constraint satisfaction techniques can then be used for guiding the adaptation of a past solution to the target problem. Section 4.1 presents previous related works that propose to combine Constraint Satisfaction Problem (CSP) techniques with CBR. Sections 4.2 and 4.3 detail the adaptation suggested. Then section 4.4 presents an adaptability measure based on adaptation domains.

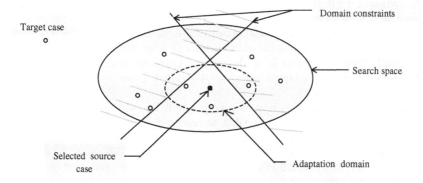

Fig. 4. Search and adaptation of a solution

4.1   Related Works

Several attempts aiming at integrating Constraint Satisfaction and Case-Based Reasoning have been made within the past (refer to [24]). This section details works in which constraint satisfaction techniques are used in the adaptation process of case based reasoning paradigm.

In the COMPOSER system [19] CSP techniques are used to solve the adaptation process of CBR to engineering design domain. The suggested methodology uses cases represented as a discrete CSP. A matching process is applied between source cases and the new problem; several cases emerge from this comparison. These cases, their solutions and their constraints form the new problem: the new CSP which can be solved with CSP algorithms. In COMPOSER each case must be modeled as a CSP to apply constraint satisfaction algorithm and thus to adapt source cases.

The authors of [17] suggest using the CBR paradigm for constraint satisfaction problems concerning product configuration. The case based reasoning process intervenes to help the customer expressing his needs as past cases represent past sales and describe past buyers and bought products. In that case the adaptation process is carried out using an interchangeability criterion [18] [25]. In fact, a value can sometimes be replaced by another value in a CSP. Therefore the issue is to know set of variables concerned by interchangeability and then to properly use this knowledge in order to solve the CSP. This is the purpose of this CBR adaptation process.

The aim of the IDIOM system [15] is to promote interactive design of building by reusing past designs and adapting them according to preferences based on design and case combination. Past design cases are stored and when an architect designs a new building, he selects past cases and may also assign preferences if necessary. Constraint bound to cases combination are also stored with past cases. The latter are combined to form a new design and then are adapted with CSP algorithm according to knowledge they hold and to preferences.

The approach defined in [23] for testing the interoperability of networking protocols suggests representing the knowledge base (Interoperability tests) as a set of CSPs. When a CSP fails according to monitored observations, CBR is used to enhance the CSP with previous cases.

In the configuration field, the authors of [25] have introduced the idea of starting from a previous configuration close to customer's requirements (instead of starting from scratch) before adapting it. In this system cases are modeled according to the CSP representation and adapted using neighborhood, context dependent and meta interchangeability concepts.

However, these approaches rely on a very simple knowledge base structure (CSP formalism) which often does not enable to represent an expert knowledge. In this paper, we suggest a different way to mix CBR and CSP. We propose to use constraint propagation in order to guide the adaptation phase of the CBR cycle. To do so, it is required to determine adaptation domains in which the constraint propagation takes place. This is done in section 4.2.

4.2 Adaptation Domains

To define an area surrounding the retrieved case, we propose to compute an adaptation domain for each attribute with three parameters: the values of the attribute of source case, the similarity membership function of this attribute and a similarity threshold α.

The similarity membership function of an attribute (μ_a) and the value of this attribute in the source case (π_s) are used to determine a new membership function (μ_T): the estimated membership function of the value of the attribute in target case. The latter is calculated by the projection of the intersection of μ_a and π_s (Fig. 5). Then the α-cut is computed in the new membership function μ_T (Fig. 6). The cut of the μ_T function at the α level gives the adaptation domain of the attribute: [$\inf_\alpha$, $\sup_\alpha$]. The value of α is chosen by the user. If $\alpha = 0$, the whole domain of the attribute is selected for adaptation. If $\alpha = 1$, the adaptation domain corresponds to the minimum adaptation domain. The automatic tuning of α remains an unsolved issue and an interactive tuning may provide a first approach.

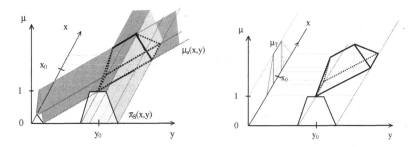

Fig. 5. Intersection between $\pi_s(x, y)$ and $\mu_a(x, y)$

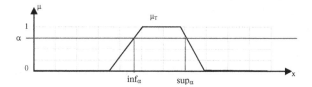

Fig. 6. α-cut of the membership function $\mu_T(x,y)$

Once adaptation domains have been determined for each attribute, the adaptation domain of an object is made of the cartesian product of these attribute adaptation domains.

4.3 Fuzzy Constraint Propagation for Adaptation

Adaptation domains being defined it is now possible to propagate domain constraints on these domains.

Practical constraint problem experiences show that constraint variables are defined on discrete or continuous domains; constraints may be discrete, continuous or both discrete and continuous and constraints may be binary or of arity superior to 2. Many works about constraint propagation techniques deal with these particularities [2] [4] [10] [21] as suggested in [16].

We propose to use fuzzy constraints as described in [6] and CSP techniques to reduce adaptation domains. First the use of soft constraints (constraints modelled by means of a fuzzy set) corroborates the proposal herein which allows to model imprecise and uncertain knowledge. Then prioritised constraints and prioritised soft constraints allow to personalize the constraints description.

For example a soft constraint allows to define the fact that two attributes are constrained by the fact that their values have to be equal. With soft constraint definition this strict equality is transformed to a soft equality (values are equal with a degree).

A constraint propagation algorithm integrating fuzzy constraints (called FAC-3) has been proposed by [6]. Using this filtering algorithm and a Branch and Bound search algorithm it is possible to propagate domain constraints on the adaptation domains and to build the corresponding search tree.

4.4 Adaptability Measure

The adaptability of a case may be an important criterion for the selection of the case to be adapted, as suggested in [22] with the notion of AGR (Adaptation Guided Retrieval). Therefore we propose an adaptability measure based on the specificity measure [8] [26] of fuzzy set. The specificity measure characterizes the fuzziness of the value represented by the fuzzy set. The more the value is fuzzy (*imprecise*) the more the specificity value is close to 0. Opposite when a fuzzy set corresponds to a singleton its specificity is 1.

We can compute the adaptability of an attribute by using the membership function μ_r obtained as described in section 4.2.

For an attribute a, the adaptability is $1-Sp(a)$ where $Sp(a)$ denotes the specificity of the attribute a. We illustrate in figure 7 different adaptability values for an attribute. The adaptability is a value assessed between 0 and 1. Once the adaptability of each attribute of an object is evaluated, it is possible to determine the adaptability of an object as the aggregation of its attribute adaptability using an operator such as minimum, product or average.

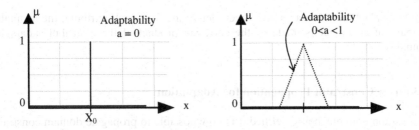

Fig. 7. Examples of adaptability values of an attribute *a*

The specified adaptability measure intervene as a complementary measuring tool of the similarity measure during the search step for the selection of the best past similar case to the target case.

5 Application

In this section the advanced configuration reasoning is illustrated by an example applied to the configuration of a machining operation. This example is taken from a real size knowledge base describing a machining operation, involves more than 30 decision variables and 32 technological constraints [11]. In this example, a machining operation is composed of a part, a tool and a machine. In this example, some attributes are described using fuzzy number (Fig. 8). A machining operation is represented by an object diagram (Fig. 9).

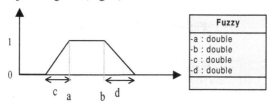

Fig. 8. Fuzzy class model

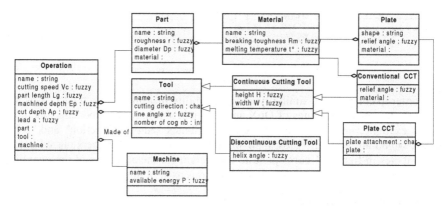

Fig. 9. Partial schema of the knowledge base

A partial instance of the class diagram is described in figure 10. The complete instance of the class diagram contains four different operations recorded in the case library (please note that for reading simplification purposes, attributes are mentioned with abbreviations detailed in figure 9, and operations Op2, Op3 and Op4 have been excluded). The operation to configure, called OpX, is represented in figure 11. This target operation has some known attributes and others that have to be valued. In this example we present the search step for similar operation and the adaptation process.

Based on the four operations of the knowledge base and on the works previously presented, this illustration describes the search for the most similar and adaptable past configuration.

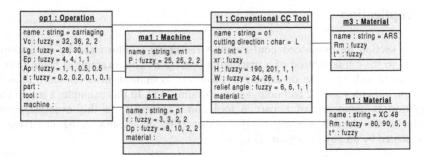

Fig. 10. Partial knowledge base

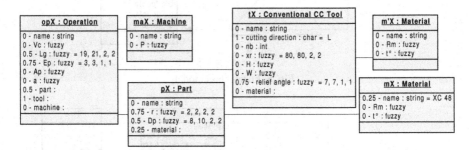

Fig. 11. Operation to configure: target case

In order to compute the similarity and adaptability measures of each past cases it is necessary to weight attributes of OpX and to select similarity membership functions. In this example, importance is allowed to attributes "cutting direction" and "relief angle", which are tool attributes: their weight is valued to 1. Numbers placed before the attributes in figure 11 correspond to the weight for the attributes of the operation to configure. The similarity membership functions used in this example is as follows:

- similarity "close to" defined by: $\mu_a(x, y) = 1 - \dfrac{|x-y|}{\Delta}$ if $0 \le |x - y| \le \Delta = 1$

$$\mu_a(x, y) = 0 \quad otherwise$$

where Δ defines the slope of the "close to" membership function (Fig. 3).

- similarity "true/false" defined by: $\mu_a(x, y) = 1$ if $x = y$

$$\mu_a(x, y) = 0 \quad otherwise$$

- "ad hoc" similarity for instance for the comparison of material   defined as follows:

μ_a	XC18	XC25	XC38	XC48	XC60
XC48	0.7	0.8	0.9	1	0.3

- similarity between objects defined as follows for objects o and o':

$$\mu_\beta(o, o') = \beta.\Pi(o, o') + (1 - \beta).N(o, o')$$

where β enables to tune the strength of required similarity. $\beta=1$ corresponds to a loose requirement on the similarity whereas $\beta=0$ corresponds to a strong requirement on the similarity. In this example, we use this similarity function with $\beta=1$.

Table 2. Similarity and adaptability measures results

	Op1	Op2	Op3	Op4
Similarity with OpX	Π=0.5 N=0.25	Π=0.5 N=0.25	Π=0.33 N=0.25	Π=0.33 N=0.25
Adaptability	0.734	0.748	0.752	0.744

Results of the similarity and adaptability are given in table 2.

From a similarity point of view, operation Op1 and operation Op2 have the same similarity degrees with operation OpX. Nevertheless operation Op1 can not be easily adapted to configure operation OpX (since its adaptability is equal to 0.734 i.e. the weakest adaptability value), while operation Op2 is more adaptable and therefore is an interesting target for our configuration process. Operation Op3 is more adaptable but is less similar and should therefore not be privileged. The same remark applies to operation Op4.

Once operation Op2 has been chosen, it is possible to determine the adaptation domains for the operation at level $\alpha = 0.5$. The values for the example are given for each attribute on figure 12.

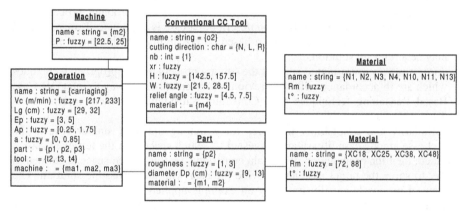

Fig. 12. Adaptation domains

Constraints of the domain have now to be propagated on the adaptation domains to provide a solution to the configuration problem. Three binary constraints are taken into account in this example:

-     an attachment constraint between a machine and a tool: $C_{M\text{-}T}$,
-     a compatibility constraint between a tool and its material: $C_{T\text{-}TM}$,
-     a machining constraint between the name of a tool material and the name of a part material: $C_{TM\text{-}PM}$.

In order to construct the solution's search tree an order for the instantiation of the variables is selected. The first variable to be instantiated is the name of the part material of OpX (PM=XC48). Then the name of the tool material (TM), the tool (T) and the machine (M) are respectively instantiated. At each node of the tree, a value for the variable is chosen and the filtering fuzzy algorithm FAC-3 is applied to reduce variables domains.

Before beginning the constraint propagation process, variables domains are:

$D_M = \{ma_1, ma_2, ma_3\}$ $D_{TM} = \{N1, N2, N3, N4, N10, N11, N13\}$

$D_T = \{t_2, t_3, t_4\}$ $D_{PM} = \{XC18, XC25, XC38, XC48\}$

Using FAC-3 and Branch and Bound algorithms, domain constraints are applied on restricted domains and value for some variables are found. The result of the search is:

$M = ma_3$ $TM = N1$

$T = t_2$ $PM = XC48$

The used CSP algorithm give a confidence degree of the found solution between 0 and 1. In our example this degree is 0.9.

6 Conclusion

This paper aims at introducing our propositions for the definition of a CBR process based on fuzzy and object oriented cases for experience based problem solving.

Three major issues are faced when dealing with experience based problem solving:
- first, an experience base is often complex and needs to be structured in order to facilitate its exploitation and its evolutions. It is suggested to use an enhanced object oriented modeling including the explicit representation of constraints,
- second, when expert knowledge is required in a solving problem process, it is frequently observed that information describing a case is imprecise. Thus providing the user with an attribute description based on possibility distributions if necessary may be a relevant solution,
- third, it is very important to support the solving process with appropriate techniques which are in accordance with the previous representations. A way to integrate Case Based Reasoning techniques with Constraint Satisfaction Problem techniques is described to achieve this goal.

Similarity and adaptability measures for searching the most similar case to the target case among case library are suggested. A search space near the retrieved case is defined, then the propagation of domain constraints on this search space is defined in order to solve the target case and provide the user with an admissible solution. The advanced proposals are illustrated by an example applied to the configuration of a machining operation. This kind of configuration is complex and in many cases, experts solve machining configuration problem using their past configuration experiences.

The suggested solutions have been validated on restricted knowledge bases and their operationalization is under way using a software framework, allowing to consider the extension of this validation to industrial size problems. However, the use of the suggested techniques is not limited to configuration problems and experimentations are carried out in a "Return of Experience" (or "Lesson Learned") application.

References

1. Bergmann, R., Stahl, A.: Similarity measures for object-oriented case representations. Lecture Notes in Computer Science 1488 Springer, (1998) 25-36

2. Bessière, C.: Arc-consistency in dynamic constraint satisfaction problems. 10th AAAI, California (1991) 221-226
3. Brown, D.C.: Some Thoughts on Configuration Processes. AAAI 1996 Fall Symposium Workshop on Configuration, MIT, Cambridge, Massachusetts, USA (1996)
4. Dechter, R., Dechter, A. Structure driven algorithms for truth maintenance. Artificial Intelligence Journal (82) (1996) 1-20
5. Dubois, D., Prade, H.: Fuzzy Sets and Systems. Eds: Academic Press. New York, Fuzzy Logic CDROM Library (1996)
6. Dubois, D., Fargier, H., Prade, H.: Possibility theory in constraint satisfaction problems: Handling priority, preference and uncertainty. Applied Intelligence (6) (1996) 287-309
7. Dubois, D., Esteva, F., Garcia, P., Godo, L., Lopez de Mantaras, R., Prade, H.: Fuzzy set-based models in case-based reasoning. 2nd ICCBR, Providence, Rhode Island, USA (1997)
8. Dubois, D., Kerre, E., Mesiar, R., Prade, H.: Fuzzy interval analysis. Fundamentals of Fuzzy Sets, Dubois & Prade, The Handbook of Fuzzy Sets, Kluwer Acad. Publ. (1999)
9. Fowler, M., Scott, K., Booch, G.: Uml Distilled: Applying the Standard Object Modeling Language. Addison-Wesley Pub Co. (1997)
10. Gelle, E.: On the generation of locally consistent solution spaces inmixed dynamic constraint problems, PhD Thesis, Swiss Federal Institute of Technology (EPFL), Lausanne (1998)
11. Geneste, L., Ruet, M., Monteiro, T.: Configuration of a machining operation. Workshop on Configuration, 14th European Conference on Artificial Intelligence, ECAI, Berlin (2000)
12. Hansen, B.: Weather Prediction Using Case-Based Reasoning and Fuzzy Set Theory. Master of Computer Science Thesis, Technical University of Nova Scotia, Canada (2000)
13. Hüllermeier, E., Dubois, D., Prade, H.: Extensions of a qualitative approach to case-based decision making: uncertainty and fuzzy quantification in act evaluation, 7th European Congress on Intelligent Techniques & Soft Computing, Aachen, Germany (1999)
14. Kolodner, J.: Case Based Reasoning. Morgan Kaufmann Publishers, Inc. (1993)
15. Lottaz, C.: Constraint solving, preference activation and solution adaptation in IDIOM. Technical report, Swiss Federal Institute of Technology (EPFL), Lausanne (1996)
16. Monteiro, T., Perpen, J.L., Geneste, L.: Configuring a machining operation as a constraint satisfaction problem. CIMCA'99, Austria (1999)
17. Neagu, N., Faltings, B.: Constraint satisfaction for case adaptation. Workshop on Case Adaptation of the Int. Conf. on CBR, ICCBR, Kaiserslautern, Germany (1999)
18. Neagu, N., Faltings, B.: Exploiting interchangeabilities for case adaptation. 4th ICCBR, Case-Based Reasoning Research and Development. Aha D.W., Watson I. & Yang Q., Springer, LNCS (2001)
19. Purvis, L., Pu, P.: An approach to case combination. Workshop on adaptation in case-based reasoning, European Conference on Artificial Intelligence, ECAI, Budapest (1996)
20. Salotti, S.: Filtrage flou et représentation centrée objet pour raisonner par analogie: le système FLORAN. (in French) PhD Thesis, University of Paris XI, Orsay, France (1992)
21. Sam, D.: Constraint consistency techniques for continuous domains. PhD Thesis, Swiss Federal Institute of Technology (EPFL), Lausanne (1995)
22. Smyth, B., Keane, M. T.: Experiments on adaptation-guided retrieval in case-based design. 1st Int. Conf. on Case-Based Reasoning, ICCBR, Portugal (1995)
23. Sqalli, M. H., Freuder, E. C.: CBR support for CSP modeling of InterOperability testing. Workshop on CBR Integrations, AAAI, Madison, Wisconsin, USA (1998)
24. Sqalli, M. H., Purvis, L., Freuder, E.C.: Survey of applications integrating constraint satisfaction and case-based reasoning. PACLP, London (1999)
25. Weigel, R., Torrens, M., Faltings, B.V.: Interchangeability for Case Adaptation Configuration Problems. Workshop on CBR Integrations (AAAI-98), Madison, Wisconsin, USA. (1998)
26. Yager, R.R.: On the specificity of a possibility distribution. Fuzzy Sets and Systems (50) (1992) 279-292

Deleting and Building Sort Out Techniques for Case Base Maintenance

Maria Salamó and Elisabet Golobardes

Enginyeria i Arquitectura La Salle, Universitat Ramon Llull,
Psg. Bonanova 8, 08022 Barcelona, Spain
{mariasal,elisabet}@salleurl.edu

Abstract. Early work on case based reasoning reported in the literature shows the importance of case base maintenance for successful practical systems. Different criteria to the maintenance task have been used for more than half a century. In this paper we present different sort out techniques for case base maintenance. All the sort out techniques proposed are based on the same principle: a Rough Sets competence model. First of all, we present sort out reduction techniques based on deletion of cases. Next, we present sort out techniques that build new reduced competent case memories based on the original ones. The main purpose of these methods is to maintain the competence and reduce, as much as possible, its size. Experiments using different domains, most of them from the UCI repository, show that the reduction techniques maintain the competence obtained by the original case memory. The results are analysed with those obtained using well-known reduction techniques.

1 Introduction

Case-Based Reasoning (CBR) systems solve problems by reusing the solutions to similar problems stored as cases in a case memory [12] (also known as case-base). However, these systems are sensitive to the cases present in the case memory and often its accuracy rate depends on the significance of the stored cases. Therefore, in CBR systems it is important to reduce the case memory in order to remove noisy cases and also to achieve a good generalisation accuracy.

This paper presents two approaches, based on a Rough Sets competence model, to reduce the case memory while maintaining the competence. The two approaches are: (1) reduction techniques based on deletion of cases; (2) reduction techniques based on the construction of new competent cases. Both approaches have been introduced into our Case-Based Classifier System called BASTIAN[15]. This paper continues the initial Rough Sets approaches presented in our previous work [14], defining a competence model based on Rough Sets and explaining new approximations to improve weak points.

The reduction techniques proposed for the deletion approach are: Sort out Case Memory (SortOutCM) and Sort Out Internal Case Memory (SortOutInternalCM). The sort out reduction techniques obtain the quality of approximation to each case and separate it in the space of classes. Both techniques contain

S. Craw and A. Preece (Eds.): ECCBR 2002, LNAI 2416, pp. 365–379, 2002.

the same foundations, but the SortOutCM has a more restrictive behaviour on deletion than SortOutInternalCM.

The reduction techniques proposed for the building approach are: SortOut-MeanCM and SortOutMeanInternalCM. These techniques follow the initial approach of sort out techniques but their goal is different: the construction of new competent case memories using the information provided by the original ones.

The paper is organised as follows. Section 2 introduces some relevant related work. Next, section 3 describes the foundations of the Rough Sets Theory used in our reduction techniques. Then, section 4 details the proposed Rough Sets reduction techniques based on the deletion of cases and on the construction of new case memories. Section 5 describes the testbed of the experiments and the results obtained. Finally, section 6 presents some conclusions and further work.

2   Related Work

Case-Based Reasoning systems solve problems by reusing a corpus of previous solving experience stored as a case memory T of solved cases t. A performance goal for any practical CBR system is the maintenance of a case memory T maximizing coverage and minimizing case memory storage requirements.

Many researchers have addressed the problem of case memory reduction [21,20] and different approaches have been proposed. The first kind of approaches are based on *nearest neighbours editing* rule (CNN,SNN,DEL,ENN,RENN)[21]. The second kind of approaches are related to Instance Based Learning algorithms (IBL) [1]. Another approach to instance pruning systems are those that take into account the order in which instances are removed (DROP1 to DROP5)[21].

Another way to approach this problem is to modify the instances themselves, instead of simply deciding which ones to keep. RISE [3] treats each instance as a rule that can be generalised. EACH [16] based on the *Nested Generalized Exemplars* (NGE) theory, uses hyperrectangles to replace one or more instances, introducing a generalization mechanism over the original training set. Another approach is the one proposed by GALE [7]. The goal is to induce a set of compact instances using evolutionary computation.

Finally, researchers have also focused on increasing the overall competence, *the range of target problems that can be successfully solved* [17], of the case memory through case deletion. Strategies have been developed for controlling case memory growth. Several methods such as competence-preserving deletion [17] and failure-driven deletion [10], as well as for generating compact case memories through competence-based case addition [18,23,19]. Leake and Wilson [6] examine the benefits of using fine-grained performance metrics to directly guide case addition or deletion. These methods are specially important for task domains with non-uniform problem distributions. The maintenance integrated with the overall case-based reasoning process was presented in [11]. Finally, a case-base maintenance method that avoids building sophisticated structures around a case-base or complex operations is presented by Yang and Wu [22]. Their method partitions cases into clusters that can be converted to new smaller case-bases.

3   Rough Sets Theory

Zdzislaw Pawlak introduced Rough Sets theory in 1982 [9]. The idea of Rough Sets relies on the approximation of a set by a pair of sets. These sets are known as the lower and the upper approximation. These approximations are generated by the available data about the elements of the set.

We use Rough Sets theory for extracting the dependencies of knowledge. These dependencies are the basis for computing the relevance of instances into the Case-Based Classifier System. We use two measures of case relevance to decide which cases have to be deleted from the case memory applying different policies. The first measure (*Accuracy Rough Sets*) captures the *degree of completeness* of our knowledge. The second one (*Class Rough Sets*) computes the *quality of approximation* of each case. The following sections introduce some concepts and definitions required to define how to extract these two measures.

3.1   Introduction to the Rough Sets Theory

We have a **Universe** (U) (finite not null set of cases that describes our problem, i.e. the case memory). We compute from our universe the **concepts** (cases) that form partitions. The union of all the *concepts* make the entire Universe. Using *all the concepts* we can describe all the **equivalence relations** (R) over the universe U. Let an equivalence relation be a *set of features* that describe a specific concept. U/R is the family of all **equivalence classes** of R. The universe and the relations form the **knowledge base** (K), defined as $K = <U, \hat{R}>$, where $\hat{R}$ is the family of equivalence relations over U. Every relation over the universe is an elementary concept in K. All the concepts are formed by a set of equivalence relations that describe them. Thus, the goal is to search for the minimal set of R that defines the same concept as the initial set.

Definition 1 (Indiscernibility Relations)

$IND(\hat{P}) = \bigcap \hat{R}$ where $\hat{P} \subseteq \hat{R}$. The indiscernibility relation is an equivalence relation over U. Hence, it partitions the concepts (cases) into equivalence classes. These sets of classes are sets of instances indiscernible with respect to the features in P. Such a partition is denoted as $U/IND(P)$. In supervised machine learning the sets of cases indiscernible, with respect to the class attribute, contain the cases of each class.

Approximations of Set. Given a condition set that contains all cases present in the case memory and a decision set that presents all the classes that the condition set has to classify. We are searching for a subset of the condition set able to classify the decision set. The following definitions explain this idea.

Let $K = <U, \hat{R}>$ be a knowledge base. For any subset of cases $X \subseteq U$ and an equivalence relation $R \in \hat{R}$, $R \subseteq IND(K)$ we associate two subsets called: Lower $\underline{R}X$; and Upper $\overline{R}X$ approximations. If $\underline{R}X = \overline{R}X$ then X is an *exact set* (definable using subset R), otherwise X is a *rough set* with respect to R.

Definition 2 (Lower approximation)

The lower approximation, defined as: $\underline{R}X = \bigcup\{Y \in U/R : Y \subseteq X\}$ is the set of all elements of U which can *certainly* be classified as elements of X in knowledge R.

Definition 3 (Upper approximation)

The upper approximation, $\overline{R}X = \bigcup\{Y \in U/R : X \cap Y \neq \emptyset\}$ is the set of elements of U which can *possibly* be classified as elements of X, employing knowledge R.

Reduct and Core of knowledge This part is related to the concept of reduction of the feature search space that defines the initial knowledge base. Next, this reduced space is used to extract the relevance of each case. Intuitively, a **reduct** of knowledge is its essential part which suffices to define all concepts occurring in the knowledge, whereas the **core** is the most important part.

Let $\hat{R}$ be a family of equivalence relations and $R \in \hat{R}$. We will say that:
- R is *indispensable* if $IND(\hat{R}) \neq IND(\hat{R} - \{R\})$; otherwise it is *dispensable*. $IND(\hat{R} - \{R\})$ is the family of equivalence $\hat{R}$ extracting R.
- The family $\hat{R}$ is *independent* if each $R \in \hat{R}$ is *indispensable* in R; otherwise it is *dependent*.

Definition 4 (Reduct)

$\hat{Q} \in \hat{R}$ is a reduct of $\hat{R}$ if : $\hat{Q}$ is *independent* and $IND(\hat{Q}) = IND(\hat{R})$. Obviously, $\hat{R}$ may have many reducts. Using $\hat{Q}$ it is possible to approximate the same concept as using $\hat{R}$. Each reduct has the property that a feature can not be removed from it without changing the indiscernibility relation.

Definition 5 (Core)

The set of all indispensable relations in $\hat{R}$ will be called the *core* of $\hat{R}$, and will be denoted as: $CORE(\hat{R}) = \bigcap RED(\hat{R})$. Where $RED(\hat{R})$ is the family of all reducts of $\hat{R}$. It is the most characteristic part of knowledge and can not be eliminated.

3.2   Measures of Relevance Based on Rough Sets

Accuracy Rough Sets and **Class Rough Sets** measures use the information of reducts and the core to compute the relevance of each case.

Accuracy Rough Sets This measure computes the *Accuracy* coefficient (**AccurCoef**) of each case t in the knowledge base (case memory T) as:

$$For\ each\ instance\ t\ \in\ T\ it\ computes : AccurCoef(t) = \frac{card\ (\ \underline{P}(t))}{card\ (\ \overline{P}\ (t))} \quad (1)$$

Where $AccurCoef(t)$ is the relevance of the instance t; T is the training set; *card* is the cardinality of one set; P is the set that contains the *reducts* and *core* obtained from the original data; and finally $\underline{P}(t)$ and $\overline{P}(t)$ are the presence of t in the lower and upper approximations, respectively.

The accuracy measure expresses the degree of completeness of our knowledge about the set P. The accuracy coefficient explains if an instance is on an internal region or on a border line region, thus $AccurCoef(t)$ is a binary value. When the value is 0 it means an internal case, and a value of 1 means an outlier case. Inexactness of a set of cases is due to the existence of a borderline region. The greater a borderline region of a set, the lower the accuracy of the set. The accuracy expresses the percentage of possible correct decisions made when classifying cases employing knowledge P.

Class Rough Sets   In this measure we use the *quality of classification* coefficient (**ClassCoef**). It is computed as:

$$For\ each\ instance\ t\ \in\ T\ it\ computes: ClassCoef(t) = \frac{card\ (\ \underline{P}(t))}{card\ (T)} \quad (2)$$

Where $ClassCoef(t)$ is the relevance of the instance t; T is the training set; $card$ is the cardinality of a set; P is a set that contains the reducts and core; and finally $\underline{P}(t)$ is the presence of t in the lower approximation.

The $ClassCoef$ coefficient expresses the percentage of cases which can be correctly classified employing the knowledge t. This coefficient has a range of values between 0 to 1, where 0 and 1 mean that the instance classifies incorrectly and correctly, respectively, the range of cases that belong to its class. The higher the quality, the nearer to the outlier region.

4   Reduction Techniques

In this section, we present the competence model and the two approximations techniques to reduce the case memory proposed in this paper: (1) Deletion techniques; (2) Building techniques. All these reduction techniques are based on the Rough Sets measures described in section 3.2. Each measure is a different point of view of the coverage of each case in the case memory. Once we have the coverage measures, we decide to combine both approaches in order to achieve a better competence and compact case memory using them.

The first part of this section describes the competence model in terms of our environment and our coverage measures. The second part assumes a competence model and defines two deletion techniques and two building techniques using this model. The aim is to verify if the model is feasible in its foundations. Therefore, we define the most simple building case memory technique, because we know in advance that if the model does not assure a minimal competence, the building technique will considerably degrade the competence.

4.1   Sort Out Case Memory Techniques: Defining the Model

First of all, we present the key concepts in categorising the cases in the sort out case memory (see figure 1(a)). The *coverage* and *reachability* concepts are modified, for our *coverage* coefficients and to our problem task, with regard to B. Smyth and M. Keane [17]. However, we maintain as far as possible the essence of the original ones. The *coverage* is computed using the Rough Sets coefficients explained in section 3.2. On the other hand, the *reachability* in this case is adapted to classification tasks.

Definition 6 (Coverage)
Let $T = \{t_1, t_2, ..., t_n\}$ be a training set of instances, $\forall\ t_i \in T$:
$Coverage(t_i) = AccurCoef(t_i) \lor ClassCoef(t_i)$

The *coverage* of a case is the accuracy and quality when it is used to solve a target problem. The *coverage* is computed using the $AccurCoef$ if it is 1 else the $ClassCoef$.

Definition 7 (Reachability)

Let $T = \{t_1, t_2, ..., t_n\}$ be a training set of instances, $\forall\, t_i \in T$:

$$Reachability(t_i) = \begin{cases} class\,(t_i) & if\ it\ is\ a\ classification\ task \\ adaptable(t_i, T) & if\ it\ is\ not\ a\ classification\ task \end{cases} \quad (3)$$

The original definition is maintained and extended to classification tasks. The *reachability* of a target problem is the set of cases that can be used to provide its solution.

Definition 8 (Coverage group)

Let $T = \{t_1, t_2, ..., t_n\}$ be a training set of instances and let S be a subset of instances where $S \in T$. For all instances i and j in S:
$CoverageGroup(S) - Coverage(i) - Coverage(j)$

A coverage group (see figure 1(a)) is a set of cases from the case memory where all the cases have the same *coverage* without taking into account the class of each case. The coverage group shows space regions of our knowledge. The bigger a coverage group, the higher outlier the set of cases. The lower the coverage group, the higher an internal set of cases.

Definition 9 (Reachability group)

Let $T = \{t_1, t_2, ..., t_n\}$ be a training set of instances and let S be a subset of instances where $S \in T$. For all instances i and j in S:
$ReachabilityGroup(S) = Reachability(i) = Reachability(j)$

A reachability group (see figure 1(a)) is the set of instances that can be used to provide a solution for the target. The reachability group produce the sort out of the case memory. However, a reachability group can contain different coverage groups. Every coverage group shows the levels of information (border line regions) in the reachability group.

Definition 10 (Master case)

Let $S = \{s_1, s_2, ..., s_n\}$ and $T = \{t_1, t_2, ..., t_n\}$ be two sets of instances, where $S \in T$. For each $CoverageGroup(s) \in ReachabilityGroup(S)$ we have a:
$MasterCase(t) = $ A selected case t from $ReachabilityGroup(S)$
$$\wedge CoverageGroup(s)$$

Each coverage group contains a master case. Thus each reachability group contains as many master cases as coverage groups. The master cases will depend on the selection policies we use in our reduction techniques. These will be explained in the following sections.

4.2   Sort Out Deletion Policies

The reader will notice that algorithm 1 SortOutCM treats all cases using the same policy. The aim is to reduce as much as possible the number of cases in the case memory, and to treat not selected cases as $MasterCase$ as if they were redundant or irrelevant cases. There is no difference between the outlier cases and the internal ones. However, it is known that the outlier cases contribute greatly to the competence of a system. The deletion of outliers reduces the competence of a system.

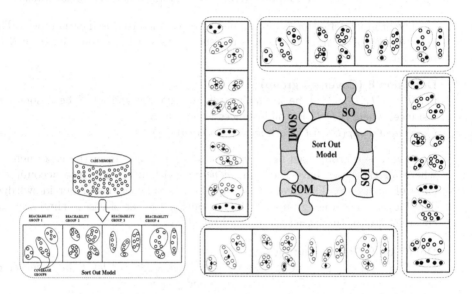

(a) Sort Out Case Memory   (b) Sort Out Techniques

Fig. 1. Figure (a) describes the distribution of a case base for a four classes example using the sort out model and figure (b) describes the behaviour of each Sort Out technique for the previous example, where a ○ represents a deleted case, ● a *MasterCase*, and ◆ a mean *MasterCase*.

This idea promotes a modification of the previous policy. We prefer to maintain or even improve the competence, selecting a fewer number of cases to be deleted from the case memory. The aim is twofold: first, to maintain the competence; second to improve utility of our case memory maintaining its diversity. Thus, an extension of the previous algorithm is algorithm 2 SortOutInternalCM.

Algorithm 1 SortOutCM

SortOutCM (CaseMemory T)
1. Sort out each instance $t \in T$ in its corresponding $ReachabilityGroup(S)$
2. Order decremented each $ReachabilityGroup(S)$ by $CoverageGroup(s) \in$
   $ReachabilityGroup(S)$
3. for each $ReachabilityGroup(S)$
4.   for each $CoverageGroup(s) \in ReachabilityGroup(S)$
5.   Select the first instance as a $MasterCase(t)$ to maintain in T
6.   Delete the rest of instances from CaseMemory T in the $CoverageGroup(s)$
7.   end for
8. end for
9. return CaseMemory T

This algorithm 2 modifies only the internal *CoverageGroups* and maintains all the cases present in an outlier *CoverageGroup*. Therefore, the selection process in this algorithm uses a less restrictive policy. The outlier cases are isolated cases that no other case but itself can solve. Thus, it is important to maintain them because a *MasterCase* can not be a good representative of the *CoverageGroup*. In this case, each case in a outlier *CoverageGroup* is an isolated space region of each class. It could be possible to find an outlier coverage group whose *MasterCase* could be a good representative *MasterCase*, but this part involves further work.

Algorithm 2 SortOutInternalCM

SortOutInternalCM (CaseMemory T)
1. Sort out each instance $t \in T$ in its corresponding *ReachabilityGroup(S)*
2. Order decremented each *ReachabilityGroup(S)* by *CoverageGroup(s)* $\in$ *ReachabilityGroup(S)*
3. for each *ReachabilityGroup(S)*
4.   for each *CoverageGroup(s)* $\in$ *ReachabilityGroup(S)*
5.   Select the first instance as a *MasterCase(t)*
6.   if *Coverage(t)* $\neq$ 1.0, Delete the rest of instances from T in the *CoverageGroup(s)*
7.   elseif *Coverage(t)* = 1.0
             Select the rest of instances as a *MasterCase(t)* to maintain in T
8.   endif
9.   end for
10. end for
11. return CaseMemory T

4.3   Sort Out Building Policies

Deletion techniques prompt a question: What is the reason for selecting the first case as a *MasterCase*? Actually, there is no specific reason but the implementation. The sort out case memory has all the cases ordered by their *coverage* and *reachability*, but when two cases have the same coverage, then the order of the initial case memory is maintained. However, this answer suggests new questions: Could it be possible to build a new case memory based on the original one? Could the sort out case memory be a model that guarantees a minimal competence?

The last question focuses on the assumption that the sort out case memory taken as a model itself enables the CBR system to maintain the competence. Therefore if we apply a building policy, which used without the model will surely decrease the competence, the model has to maintain it.

This section explains the modificacions in the previous algorithms in order to build new case memories using the *coverage*, the *reachability* and on the initial case memory. In order to test the reliability of this option, we use a simple policy. Algorithm 3 called SortOutMeanCM shows the modifications.

The SortOutMeanCM creates a new case for each *ReachabilityGroup* using all the cases that belong to the same *CoverageGroup*, computing the mean value for each attribute of these cases. This policy is based on gravity pointers.

Algorithm 3 SortOutMeanCM

SortOutMeanCM (CaseMemory T)
1. Sort out each instance $t \in T$ in its corresponding $ReachabilityGroup(S)$
2. Order decremented each $ReachabilityGroup(S)$ by $CoverageGroup(s) \in ReachabilityGroup(S)$
3. for each $ReachabilityGroup(S)$
4.   for each $CoverageGroup(s) \in ReachabilityGroup(S)$
5.   for each instance present in the $CoverageGroup(s)$ computes the mean value of
   each attribute a as: $\dfrac{\sum_{i=1}^{F} a_i}{card\ (\ cases\ in\ CoverageGroup(s)\ )}$
6.   end for
7.   Delete all the instances from CaseMemory T present in $CoverageGroup(s)$
8.   Add computed Mean instance t in T with the same $Coverage(s)$ and $Reachability(S)$
9.   end for
10. end for
11. return CaseMemory T

Initially the selection of gravity pointers is not a good policy. However, if the model produces a good distribution of cases, the competence will be maintained.

This algorithm inherits the same problem as the initial deletion algorithm: it treats the outlier cases the same as the internal cases. The case memory generated is a consequence of the previous data and the coefficients extracted using Rough Sets, which also uses the original case memory. Therefore, we modify the previous algorithm to select the set of cases that belong to an internal *CoverageGroup*. The algorithm 4 SortOutMeanInternalCM maintains the outlier cases without changing their content.

Algorithm 4 SortOutMeanInternalCM

SortOutMeanInternalCM (casememory T)
1. Sort out each instance $t \in T$ in its corresponding $ReachabilityGroup(S)$
2. Order decremented each $ReachabilityGroup(S)$ by $CoverageGroup(s) \in ReachabilityGroup(S)$
3. for each $ReachabilityGroup(S)$
4.   for each $CoverageGroup(s) \in ReachabilityGroup(S)$
5.   Select the first instance as a $MasterCase(t)$
6.   if $Coverage(t) \neq 1.0$
7.   for each instance present in the $CoverageGroup(s)$ computes the mean value of
     each attribute a as: $\dfrac{\sum_{i=1}^{F} a_i}{card\ (\ cases\ in\ CoverageGroup(s)\ )}$
8.   Delete $MasterCase(t)$
9.   Delete all the instances from CaseMemory T present in $CoverageGroup(s)$
10.   Add computed Mean instance t in T with the same $Coverage(s)$ and $Reachability(S)$
11.   elseif $Coverage(t) = 1.0$ Select the rest of instances of the $CoverageGroup(s)$ as a $MasterCase(t)$
12.   endif
13.   end for
14. end for
15. return CaseMemory T

Both methods (algorithms 3 and 4) contain the same number of cases as the deletion techniques (algorithms 1 and 2). The only difference between them are the sources of their instances. Deletion policies use the original case memory. However, building policies modify the original case memory to construct or build a new compact competence case memory generating new *MasterCases*. Figure 1(b) shows the behaviour of each algorithm when applied to a case base.

5   Experimental Study

This section is structured as follows. First, we describe the testbed used in the empirical study. Then, we discuss the results obtained using the reduction techniques based on Rough Sets. We compare the results obtained to CBR system working with the original case memory. Finally, we also compare the results with some related learning systems.

5.1   Testbed

In order to evaluate the performance rate, we use ten datasets. These datasets can be grouped in two ways: *public* and *private*. The datasets and their characteristics are listed in table 1. **Public datasets** are obtained from the UCI repository [8]. They are: *breast cancer Wisconsin (Breast-Wisconsin), Glass, Ionosphere, Iris, Sonar and Vehicle*. **Private datasets** come from our own repository. They deal with *diagnosis* of breast cancer and *synthetic* datasets. Datasets related to diagnosis are *Biopsy* and *Mammogram. Biopsy* [4] is the result of digitally processed biopsy images, whereas *Mammogram* consists in detecting breast cancer using the microcalcifications (μCa) present in a mammogram [5]. In *Mammogram* each example contains the description of several μCa present in the image; in other words, the input information used is a set of real valued matrices. We also use two *synthetic* datasets to tune up the learning algorithms, because we knew their solutions in advance. *MX11* is the eleven input multiplexer. TAO-*grid* is a dataset obtained from sampling the TAO figure using a grid [7].

These datasets were chosen in order to provide a wide variety of application areas, sizes, combinations of feature types, and difficulty as measured by the accuracy achieved on them by current algorithms. The choice was also made with the goal of having enough data points to extract conclusions.

Table 1. Datasets and their characteristics used in the empirical study.

	Dataset	Ref.	Samples	Numeric feat.	Symbolic feat.	Classes	Inconsistent
1	*Biopsy*	BI	1027	24	-	2	Yes
2	*Breast-Wisconsin*	BC	699	9	-	2	Yes
3	*Glass*	GL	214	9	-	6	No
4	*Ionosphere*	IO	351	34	-	2	No
5	*Iris*	IR	150	4	-	3	No
6	*Mammogram*	MA	216	23	-	2	Yes
7	*MX11*	MX	2048	-	11	2	No
8	*Sonar*	SO	208	60	-	2	No
9	*TAO-Grid*	TG	1888	2	-	2	No
10	*Vehicle*	VE	846	18	-	4	No

The study described in this paper was carried out in the context of BAS-TIAN, a *case-**BA**sed **S**ys**T**em **I**n cl**A**ssificatio**N**. BASTIAN has been developed in JAVA, for details see [13]. All techniques were run using the same set of parameters for all datasets. The configuration of BASTIAN platform for this paper is set as follows. It uses a 1-Nearest Neighbour Algorithm. The case memory is represented as a list of cases. Each case contains the set of attributes, its class and the AccurCoef and ClassCoef coefficients. Our goal is to test the reliability and feasibility of the reduction techniques. Therefore, we have not focused on the case representation used by the system. The retain phase does not store any new case in the case memory, so the CBR system only contains the initial case memory. Finally, no weighting method is used in this paper in order to test the reliability of our reduction techniques. Further work will consist of testing the influence of these methods in conjunction with weighting methods.

The percentage of correct classifications has been averaged over stratified ten-fold cross-validation runs. We analyse the significance of the performance using paired t-test on these runs.

5.2 Experimental Analysis of the Reduction Techniques

The experimental results for each dataset using CBR system and Rough Sets reduction techniques (SortOutCM (SO), SortOutInternalCM (SOI), SortOut-MeanCM (SOM) and SortOutMeanInternalCM (SOMI)) are shown in table 2.

Table 2. Mean percentage of correct classifications (%PA) and mean storage size (%CM). Two-sided paired t-test (p = 0.1) is performed, where a • and o stand for a significant improvement or degradation of our CBR related to the reduction technique compared. Bold font indicates the best prediction accuracy.

Ref.	CBR		SO		SOI		SOM		SOMI	
	%PA	%CM	%PA	%CM	%PA	%CM	%PA	%CM	%PA	%CM
BI	83.15	100.0	75.17o	0.94	**83.75**	88.74	79.96o	0.94	**83.75**	88.74
BC	**96.28**	100.0	95.59	3.17	95.85	29.42	95.41	3.17	95.99	29.42
GL	**72.42**	100.0	63.64	18.11	64.48	37.89	65.89	18.11	64.37	37.89
IO	90.59	100.0	83.48o	4.71	**91.16**	50.68	88.02	4.71	90.03	50.68
IR	**96.0**	100.0	91.33o	12.44	91.33o	13.18	94.0	12.44	93.33	13.18
MA	**64.81**	100.0	59.75	7.98	58.04	25.36	59.74	7.98	57.19	25.36
MX	**78.61**	100.0	66.74o	0.1	**78.61**	99.9	66.35o	0.1	**78.61**	99.9
SO	84.61	100.0	68.90o	4.45	86.42•	65.15	73.38o	4.45	**87.50•**	65.15
TG	**95.76**	100.0	89.60o	1.37	89.66o	1.37	91.31o	1.37	91.31o	1.37
VE	67.37	100.0	56.79o	3.68	69.70	68.33	58.46o	3.68	**69.95**	68.33

The aim of our reduction techniques is to reduce the case memory while maintaining the competence of the system. This priority guides our sort out reduction techniques based on Rough Sets competence model. Following this criterion, the results related to SortOutCM and SortOutMeanCM are not good because, as predicted in their description, the deletion or building of outlier cases produce a competence loss. However, the sort out internal techniques have a different behaviour. For example, the *Sonar* dataset obtains a good competence as well as it reduces the case memory, in both approximations: SortOutInternalCM (SOI) and SortOutMeanInternalCM (SOMI). Thus, we denote that the sort out case memories need to maintain the outlier cases present in the original case memory.

Comparing deletion versus building reduction techniques, we conclude that both techniques obtain similar competence on all datasets. However, building methods obtain on average the best competence. These results influence our further work because the gravity points policy chosen was the most simple in order to test the reliability of these techniques and the feasibility of the sort out case memories.

To sum up, the results obtained using the sort out reduction techniques, deleting or building policies, on average maintain the competence of the system while reducing as much as possible the case memory. There are some datasets that present competence loss whereas the reduction increases. This occurs because some of the existing *CoverageGroups* must be deleted and not selected to build or maintain a *MasterCase*, because the coverage of the group is so near the outlier space regions that its maintenance prevents the case base reasoning system from separating correctly between different classes. This fact can be observed in some datasets, for example *Mammogram* and *Glass*, where the results obtained using whatever method are similar. The solution of this weak point is part of our further work.

Table 3. Mean percentage of correct classifications (%PA) and mean storage size (%CM). Two-sided paired t-test (p = 0.1) is performed, where a • and ∘ stand for a significant improvement or degradation of our SOMI approach related to the system compared. Bold font indicates the best prediction accuracy.

Ref.	SOMI		SOI		CBR		IB2		IB3		IB4	
	%PA	%CM	%PA	%CM	%PA	%CM	%PA	%CM	%PA	%CM	%PA	%CM
BI	**83.75**	88.74	**83.75**	88.74	83.15	100.0	75.77•	26.65	78.51•	13.62	76.46•	12.82
BC	95.99	29.42	95.85	29.42	**96.28**	100.0	91.86•	8.18	94.98	2.86	94.86	2.65
GL	64.37	37.89	64.48	37.89	**72.42**	100.0	62.53	42.99	65.56	44.34	66.40	39.40
IO	90.03	50.68	**91.16**	50.68	90.59	100.0	86.61	15.82	90.62	13.89	90.35	15.44
IR	93.33	13.18	91.33	13.18	96.0	100.0	93.98	9.85	91.33	11.26	**96.66**	12.00
MA	57.19	25.36	58.04	25.36	64.81	100.0	**66.19**	42.28	60.16	14.30	60.03	21.55
MX	78.61	99.9	78.61	99.9	78.61	100.0	**87.07∘**	18.99	81.59	15.76	81.34	15.84
SO	**87.50**	65.15	86.42	65.15	84.61	100.0	80.72	27.30	62.11∘	22.70	63.06•	22.92
TG	91.31	1.37	89.66•	1.37	**95.76∘**	100.0	94.87∘	7.38	95.04∘	5.63	93.96∘	5.79
VE	**69.95**	68.33	69.70	68.33	67.37	100.0	65.46•	40.01	63.21•	33.36	63.68•	31.66

Sort out internal techniques (SOI and SOMI) obtain on average a higher generalisation on accuracy than IBL, as shown in table 3. The performance of IBL algorithms decline, in almost all datasets (e.g. *Breast-Wisconsin, Biopsy*), when case memory is reduced. SOMI and SOI obtains on average higher prediction accuracy than IB2, IB3 and IB4. On the other hand, the mean storage size obtained is higher in our reduction techniques than those obtained in IBL schemes.

Finishing the experimental study, we also run several well-known reduction schemes on the previous data sets. The reduction algorithms are: CNN, SNN, DEL, ENN, RENN, DROP1, DROP2, DROP3, DROP4 and DROP5 (a complete explanation of them can be found in [21]). We use the same datasets described above but with different ten-fold cross validation sets. We want to analyse the results obtained using the proposed SortOutMeanInternalCM reduction technique with those obtained by these reduction techniques. Tables 4 and 5 illustrate the mean prediction accuracy and the mean storage size for all systems in all datasets, respectively.

Table 4 shows the behaviour of our SortOutMeanInternalCM reduction technique in comparison with CNN, SNN, DEL, ENN and RENN techniques. SOMI results are on average better than those obtained by the reduction techniques studied. RENN improves the results of SortOutMeanInternalCM (SOMI) in

Table 4. Mean percentage of correct classifications (%PA) and mean storage size (%CM). Two-sided paired t-test (p = 0.1) is performed, where a • and o stand for a significant improvement or degradation of our SOMI approach related to the system compared. Bold font indicates the best prediction accuracy.

Ref.	SOMI		CNN		SNN		DEL		ENN		RENN	
	%PA	%CM	%PA	%CM	%PA	%CM	%PA	%CM	%PA	%CM	%PA	%CM
BI	**83.75**	88.74	79.57•	17.82	78.41•	14.51	82.79•	0.35	77.82•	16.52	81.03•	84.51
BC	95.99	29.42	95.57	5.87	95.42	3.72	96.57	0.32	95.28	3.61	**97.00**o	96.34
GL	64.37	37.89	67.64o	24.97	67.73	20.51	64.87	4.47	68.23	19.32	**68.66**o	72.90
IO	**90.03**	50.68	88.89	9.94	85.75•	7.00	80.34•	1.01	88.31	7.79	85.18•	86.39
IR	93.33	13.18	**96.00**	14.00	94.00	9.93	**96.00**	2.52	91.33	8.59	**96.00**	94.44
MA	57.19	25.36	61.04	25.06	63.42	18.05	62.53	1.03	63.85	21.66	**65.32**	66.92
MX	78.61	99.9	89.01o	37.17	89.01o	37.15	68.99•	0.55	85.05o	32.54	**99.80**o	99.89
SO	**87.50**	65.15	83.26	23.45	80.38	20.52	77.45•	1.12	85.62	19.34	82.74	86.49
TG	91.31	1.37	94.39o	7.15	94.76o	6.38	87.66•	0.26	**96.77**o	3.75	95.18o	96.51
VE	**69.95**	68.33	69.74	23.30	69.27	19.90	62.29•	2.55	66.91•	20.70	68.67	74.56

Table 5. Mean percentage of correct classifications (%PA) and mean storage size (%CM). Two-sided paired t-test (p = 0.1) is performed, where a • and o stand for a significant improvement or degradation of our SOMI approach related to the system compared. Bold font indicates best prediction accuracy.

Ref.	SOMI		DROP1		DROP2		DROP3		DROP4		DROP5	
	%PA	%CM	%PA	%CM	%PA	%CM	%PA	%CM	%PA	%CM	%PA	%CM
BI	83.75	88.74	76.36•	26.84	76.95•	29.38	77.34•	15.16	76.16•	28.11	76.17o	27.03
BC	95.99	29.42	93.28•	8.79	92.56•	8.35	96.28	2.70	95.00	4.37	93.28•	8.79
GL	64.37	37.89	66.39	40.86	69.57o	42.94	67.27	33.28	69.18o	43.30	65.02	40.65
IO	90.03	50.68	81.20•	23.04	87.73	19.21	88.89	14.24	88.02	15.83	81.20•	23.04
IR	93.33	13.18	91.33	12.44	90.00	14.07	**92.66**	12.07	88.67•	7.93	91.33	12.44
MA	57.19	25.36	**61.60**	42.69	58.33	51.34	58.51	12.60	58.29	50.77	**61.60**	42.64
MX	78.61	99.9	87.94o	19.02	**100.00**o	98.37	82.37o	17.10	86.52o	25.47	86.52o	18.89
SO	87.50	65.15	84.64	25.05	**87.07**	28.26	76.57•	16.93	84.64	26.82	84.64	25.11
TG	91.31	1.37	94.76o	8.03	**95.23**o	8.95	94.49o	6.76	89.41•	2.18	94.76o	8.03
VE	69.95	68.33	64.66•	38.69	67.16	43.21	66.21•	29.42	68.21	43.85	64.66•	38.69

some data sets (e.g. *Breast-Wisconsin*) but its reduction on the case memory is lower than SOMI.

The results in table 5 report that SortOutMeanInternalCM obtains a balanced behaviour between competence and size. On the other hand, there are some reduction techniques that obtain best competence for some data sets making a smaller reduction of the case memory size. Sort out technique shows better competence for some data sets (e.g. *Biopsy, Breast-w, Vehicle*), although its results are also worse in others (e.g. *MX11*).

All the experiments (tables 3, 4 and 5) lead to some interesting observations. First, it is worth noting that the individual SortOutInternalCM (SOI) and SortOutMeanInternalCM (SOMI) work correctly in all data sets, obtaining better results using SOMI because the gravity pointer selection of *MasterCases* is more representative than the first case of each *CoverageGroup*. Therefore, as a second conclusion, we demonstrate the feasibility of the sort out case memories and the competence model. Finally, the results in all tables suggest that all the reduction techniques work well in some, but not all, domains. This has been termed the *selective superiority problem* [2]. Consequently, future work will consist of improving the selection of *MasterCases* in order to enlarge the outlier cases from the internal ones to improve the overall competence in all the domains.

6   Conclusions and Further Work

This paper presents a competence model defined using Rough Sets theory. Under this competence model it introduces two different approaches to the reduction of the case memory: the first one presents different deletion techniques; the second one relies on building techniques. The aim of this paper was twofold: (1) to denote that the deletion techniques of sort out case memories are reliable, and (2) to reveal that the construction of case memories will be feasible using a competence model and sort out case memories. Empirical studies show that these reduction techniques produce a higher or equal generalisation accuracy on classification tasks. We can conclude that the deletion policies could be improved in some facets and the building policies are a promising area to study. Our further work will be focused on these observations. Firstly, we can modify the selection of *MasterCases* in order to enlarge the distance from internal cases to outlier ones and to obtain a higher competence. Secondly, the building policies have to avoid some gravity points. Therefore, it could be interesting to study different methods to build the case memory. Finally, we want to analyse the influence of the weighting methods and similarity functions in these reduction techniques.

Acknowledgements

This work is supported by the *Ministerio de Sanidad y Consumo, Instituto de Salud Carlos III, Fondo de Investigación Sanitaria* of Spain, Grant No. 00/0033-02. We wish to thank *Enginyeria i Arquitectura La Salle* (Ramon Llull University) for their support to our Research Group in Intelligent Systems. We also wish to thank D. Aha for providing the IBL code as well as D. Randall Wilson and Tony R. Martinez who provided the code of the other reduction techniques. Finally, we wish to thank the anonymous reviewers for their useful comments.

References

1. D. Aha and D. Kibler. Instance-based learning algorithms. *Machine Learning, Vol. 6*, pages 37–66, 1991.
2. C.E. Brodley. Addressing the selective superiority problem: Automatic algorithm/model class selection. In *Proceedings of the 10th International Conference on Machine Learning*, pages 17–24, 1993.
3. P. Domingos. Context-sensitive feature selection for lazy learners. In *AI Review*, volume 11, pages 227–253, 1997.
4. J.M. Garrell, E. Golobardes, E. Bernadó, and X. Llorà. Automatic diagnosis with Genetic Algorithms and Case-Based Reasoning. 13:367–362, October 1999. Elsevier Science Ltd., ISSN 0954-1810.

5. E. Golobardes, X. Llorà, M. Salamó, and J. Martí. Computer Aided Diagnosis with Case-Based Reasoning and Genetic Algorithms. *Knowledge-Based Systems*, (15):45–52, 2002.

6. D. Leake and D. Wilson. Remembering Why to Remember: Performance-Guided Case-Base Maintenance. In *Proceedings of the Fifth European Workshop on Case-Based Reasoning*, pages 161–172, 2000.

7. X. Llorà and J.M. Garrell. Inducing Partially-Defined Instances with Evolutionary Algorithms. In *Proceedings of the 18th International Conference on Machine Learning (ICML'2001)*, pages 337–344. Morgan Kaufmann Publishers, 2001.

8. C. J. Merz and P. M. Murphy. UCI Repository for Machine Learning Data-Bases [http://www.ics.uci.edu/~mlearn/MLRepository.html]. *Irvine, CA: University of California, Department of Information and Computer Science*, 1998.

9. Z. Pawlak. Rough Sets. In *International Journal of Information and Computer Science*, volume 11, 1982.

10. L. Portinale, P. Torasso, and P. Tavano. Speed-up, quality and competence in multi-modal reasoning. In *Proceedings of the Third International Conference on Case-Based Reasoning*, pages 303–317, 1999.

11. T. Reinartz and I. Iglezakis. Review and Restore for Case-Base Maintenance. *Computational Intelligence*, 17(2):214–234, 2001.

12. C.K. Riesbeck and R.C. Schank. *Inside Case-Based Reasoning*. Lawrence Erlbaum Associates, Hillsdale, NJ, US, 1989.

13. M. Salamó and E. Golobardes. BASTIAN: Incorporating the Rough Sets theory into a Case-Based Classifier System. In *Butlletí de l'acia: III Congrés Català d'Intel·ligència Artificial (CCIA'00)*, pages 284–293, Barcelona, Spain, October 2000.

14. M. Salamó and E. Golobardes. Rough sets reduction techniques for case-based reasoning. In *Proceedings 4th. International Conference on Case-Based Reasoning, ICCBR 2001*, pages 467–482, Vancouver, BC, Canada, 2001.

15. M. Salamó, E. Golobardes, D. Vernet, and M. Nieto. Weighting methods for a Case-Based Classifier System. In *LEARNING'00*, Madrid, Spain, October 2000. IEEE.

16. S. Salzberg. A nearest hyperrectangle learning method. *Machine Learning*, 6:277–309, 1991.

17. B. Smyth and M. Keane. Remembering to forget: A competence-preserving case deletion policy for case-based reasoning systems. In *Proceedings of the Thirteen International Joint Conference on Artificial Intelligence*, pages 377–382, 1995.

18. B. Smyth and E. McKenna. Building compact competent case-bases. In *Proceedings of the Third International Conference on Case-Based Reasoning*, pages 329–342, 1999.

19. B. Smyth and E. McKenna. Competence Models and the maintenance problem. *Computational Intelligence*, 17(2):235–249, 2001.

20. D.C. Wilson and D.B. Leake. Maintaining Case-Based Reasoners:Dimensions and Directions. *Computational Intelligence*, 17(2):196–213, 2001.

21. D.R. Wilson and T.R. Martinez. Reduction techniques for Instance-Based Learning Algorithms. *Machine Learning, 38*, pages 257–286, 2000.

22. Q. Yang and J. Wu. Keep it Simple: A Case-Base Maintenance Policy Based on Clustering and Information Theory. In *Proc. of the Canadian AI Conference*, pages 102–114, 2000.

23. J. Zhu and Q. Yang. Remembering to add: Competence-preserving case-addition policies for case base maintenance. In *Proceedings of the Fifteenth International Joint Conference on Artificial Intelligence*, volume 1, pages 234–239, 1999.

Entropy-Based vs. Similarity-Influenced: Attribute Selection Methods for Dialogs Tested on Different Electronic Commerce Domains

Sascha Schmitt[1], Philipp Dopichaj[1], and Patricia Domínguez-Marín[2]

[1] Artificial Intelligence – Knowledge-Based Systems Group
Department of Computer Science, University of Kaiserslautern
67653 Kaiserslautern, Germany
{sschmitt|dopichaj}@informatik.uni-kl.de

[2] Department of Optimization
ITWM – Fraunhofer Institut für Techno- und Wirtschaftsmathematik
P.O. Box 3049, 67618 Kaiserslautern, Germany
dominguez@itwm.fhg.de

Abstract. Recent research activities in the field of attribute selection for carrying on dialogs with on-line customers have focused on entropy-based approaches that make use of information gain measures. These measures consider the distribution of attribute values in the case base and are focused on their ability to reduce dialog length. The implicit knowledge contained in the similarity measures is neglected. In previous work, we proposed the similarity-influenced selection method *simVar*, which selects the attributes that induce the maximum change in similarity distribution amongst the candidate cases, thereby partitioning the case base into similar and dissimilar cases. In this paper we present an evaluation of the selection methods using three domains with distinct characteristics. The comparison of the selection methods is based on the quality of the dialogs generated. Statistical analysis was used to support the evaluation results.

1 Introduction

Companies using Electronic Commerce (EC) systems aim at automating their sales process to a maximum degree. Thereby, they sell products and services providing information to different types of customers. Nowadays, EC happens mainly via the Internet. When a customer enters an electronic sales site, the EC application will interact with her to find out about her requirements concerning her priority objective. Such an interaction phase can contain a more or less sophisticated communication process with respect to the limited possibilities given by the Internet medium that simulates the sales dialog between customers and sales persons. Generally speaking, the purpose of this phase is to elicit the customer's demands such that a search on product databases is well prepared. The overall aim is to find the products that best match the customer's requirements. At the stage of the search process, CBR technology has proven its strengths for intelligent product recommendations [2, 5, 19].

S. Craw and A. Preece (Eds.): ECCBR 2002, LNAI 2416, pp. 380–394.

However, in our opinion the demand elicitation and search process have to interweave, especially when considering EC-specific aspects like the customer should only be asked a minimum of questions, there should be non-redundant questions, etc. Problems of the latter kind increase the risk of the customer leaving the electronic shop without success. The basis for dialogs is the selection of product properties to be specified by the customer. An e-sales system should always try to present a product, which is the best choice with respect to the properties specified so far. The remaining (unspecified) properties have to be examined with respect to their information content. [16]

Several CBR approaches to automated sales dialogs have been suggested so far [7, 10, 12]. The approaches have in common that they concentrate on the reduction of the number of questions a customer is asked by the sales system, i.e. dialog length. The underlying idea is to consider the product distribution within the product database. Questions will be selected according to their relevance for the customer's utility function (decides the usability of a product). The selection mechanism works with a certain selection criterion. Seen from the more technical point of view, the underlying methods are based on an information gain measure that is used to select the next attribute to ask which is maximally discriminating the product database, i.e. limits the number of candidate cases (products). These methods enable the dialog system to react more flexibly to the current sales situation and also to adapt to the customers more individually.

In Kohlmaier et al. [8], we introduced a new measure *simVar*, which better leverages the CBR system-inherent similarities by considering similarity distributions of the candidate cases instead of value distributions only.

A number of evaluation tests have shown that certain domain-dependent factors exist, which decide the quality of the dialogs generated by an attribute selection method used on a domain. In this paper, we will present the results supported by statistical validation models.

Section 2 describes entropy-based attribute selection to generate on-line dialogs in EC applications and gives an overview of the current related work leveraging information gain measures. Section 3 introduces the *simVar* measure motivated by a few drawbacks that had been encountered for the entropy-based heuristics. Section 4 presents the domain aspects that we considered crucial factors for the quality of the applied attribute selection methods. It also summarizes the most important results of our test series. It also briefly describes the statistical validation methods that are the basis for our conclusions on the domain-dependencies. Our conclusions and a short outlook on future work are presented in Section 5.

2   Entropy-Based Attribute Selection

A couple of approaches exist for attribute selection methods that use *entropy*-based measures considering the special aspects of EC, like keeping dialogs as short as possible to reduce the risk of the customer leaving the e-shop early. As entropy respectively *information gain* measures defined on entropy are well-known concepts, we will only briefly introduce the important formulas needed for further proceeding.

The attribute selection method we want to consider in this section originally stem from the ID3 algorithm to build decision trees for classification problems [13].

Building such trees, the central task is to find the attribute that best classifies the examples in each step to grow the tree. The idea is to select the most useful attribute.

Transferring this idea to a CBR context, let us assume C to be a set of classified cases. Each case $c \in C$ is an example for a class. If there are k different classes we can partition $C = C_1 \cup \ldots \cup C_k$ such that each C_i only contains cases of the class i, $i=1..k$. Then we define the entropy of the set C in (1): [11, 14]

$$E(C) := -\sum_{i=1}^{k} \frac{|C_i|}{|C|} \cdot \log_2\left(\frac{|C_i|}{|C|}\right) \tag{1}$$

To find an attribute A that has the highest expected discrimination power, we want to consider the entropy of C under the estimation that a value v for A is given, written $C|A$. If the attribute A has m possible values $v_1, \ldots, v_m$ the case base can be divided into m partitions such that each partition C^{v_j}, $j=1..m$, contains only cases in which the attribute A has the value v_j. Then we can define the entropy of $C|A$ in (2):

$$E(C|A) := -\sum_{v \in \{v_1,\ldots,v_m\}} \frac{|C^v|}{|C|} \cdot E(C^v) \tag{2}$$

With (1) and (2) we can finally define the information gain measure $Gain(C,A)$ in (3). The information gain measures the expected reduction in entropy. In other words, $Gain$ measures the effectiveness of an attribute in classifying the cases in the case base [11]:

$$Gain(C, A) := E(C) - E(C|A) \tag{3}$$

An entropy-based attribute selection method determines the next question by the maximum information gain. The maximum information gain is computed using the structured product descriptions. Those product properties (attributes) that allow us to distinguish (discriminate) between the product descriptions most clearly are selected. The selection process also considers the attribute values already specified. The attribute selection process ignores those product specifications that do not match the customer's (partial) query.

2.1   Entropy Information Gain Measures in EC Scenarios

The most significant difference between an EC scenario and a classification task is usually the lack of explicit classes in EC sales applications. The cases stored in the case base are not examples for classification but possible products. To directly apply an entropy measure for classified cases it would be necessary to pre-cluster the products and produce artificial class labels, e.g., the case (product) ID [10]. Several different algorithms for this clustering process have been investigated [7, 20].

In the construction of decision trees for classification all cases that do not exactly match the specified attribute are excluded from the set of candidates. This assumption is central to the entropy measure. Transferred to the EC dialog model, it means that the proposal of a question leads to a new dialog situation s in which all products that do not exactly match the current attribute value are excluded. If the transition from dialog situation s to s' is reached by assigning a value v_l, $l \in \{1, .., m\}$ to the Attribute A the information gain for this transition can be calculated like (4) with C^{v_l} the subset of C that contains only cases with attribute value v_l for A:

$$gain(s, s') := -\log_2\left(\frac{\left|C^{v_l}\right|}{|C|}\right) \tag{4}$$

Then, the expected information gain for assigning a value v to attribute A is defined by (5):

$$gain(s, A) := - \sum_{v \in \{v_1, ..., v_m\}} p_v \cdot \log_2\left(\frac{\left|C^v\right|}{|C|}\right) \tag{5}$$

The probability p_v that attribute A is assigned the value v can be estimated from the sample of cases in the case base, e.g., $p_v = |C^v|/|C|$.

2.2 Hybrid Approach: Entropy Measure Integrating Similarities

The underlying idea behind the following extension is to weaken the exact exclusion of all cases that are not equal to the specified attribute value. Substituting the case set size $\left|C^{v_l}\right|$ by the similarity sum of all attribute values does this in (6) with $A(c)$ the value of attribute A in case c:

$$\left|C^{v_l}\right| \approx \sum_{c \in C} sim(A(c), v_l) \tag{6}$$

Then, the new extended expected information gain *extgain* results in (7) [12]: [1]

$$extgain(s, A) := - \sum_{v \in \{v_1, ..., v_m\}} p_v \cdot \log_2\left(\frac{\sum_{c \in C} sim(A(c), v)}{|C|}\right) \tag{7}$$

While this at first sight seems like a logical extension, the exact semantics of this estimation have to be considered. In the interpretation of the standard entropy measure, all cases that do not exactly match the query are excluded from the set of candidate cases. With this interpretation all cases remain in the set of candidates but are not counted equally. Two cases with a similarity of 0.5 are considered the same as one perfectly matching case. This interpretation implicitly requires that all used similarity measures model a fuzzy concept of equality and not any other concept of utility [3]. In the context of EC for which this measure especially applies, the similarity measures model a level of customer satisfaction and not equality [8].

---

[1] We named this method *extgain* to refer to it more easily. It should be noted that this is not an official name.

2.3   Enhanced Hybrid Approach

In orenge 3.1, a new attribute selection method was introduced [12]. In our opinion, it is an extension to *extgain* (7), modifying the expected information gain based on the assumption that it is more important to distinguish between the cases that are most similar to the partial query. This idea is similar to our approach to the treatment of irrelevant cases and top performers in *simVar*, later described in Sect. 3.2.

In order to explain this idea, consider the following situation depicted in Table 1. Let c_i be the cases, A_1 and A_2 attributes and q the (partial) query.

Table 1. Example value distribution

	c_1	c_2	c_3	c_4	c_5	c_6
A_1	1	1	1	2	3	4
A_2	2	3	4	1	1	1
$sim(q,c_i)$	0.9	0.9	0.9	0.1	0.1	0.1

The expected information gain of the attributes A_1 and A_2 according to the formula used in older releases of orenge is equal; it is more likely, however, that asking for the value of A_2 helps us find a more suitable product. This is because the best cases so far (c_1, c_2 and c_3) differ in their values for A_2; each of these cases has a high similarity and there is a low number of cases that share the same attribute value, expressed by $n_{c.A} = 1$ with $n_{c.A} := |\{c' \in C : A(c') = A(c)\}|$. This idea is reflected in the following formula for the enhanced extended information gain *engain* [12]:[2]

$$engain(A,C) := extgain(A,C) + \frac{1}{|C|} \cdot \sum_{c \in C} \log_2 \left(\frac{1}{n_{c.A} \cdot sim(q,c)} \right) \qquad (8)$$

As a special exception, the summands corresponding to cases c with $sim(q,c) = 0$ are set to 0 to avoid division by zero. Note also that *engain* can result in negative values in extreme situations, which seems to be a method-inherent bug regarding the definition of entropy-based information gain. Nevertheless, we decided to test this method anyway as it has been successfully used in practice and the negative values are not a problem as far as the tests described in this article are concerned.

2.4   Entropy Measures in CBR Applications

In the field of CBR applications, many publications have dealt with the topic of attribute selection. Most approaches have their origin in classification and traditionally focus on the generation of decision trees. For example, Auriol et al. [1] have suggested advancements of decision trees or combined approaches in the INRECA project. One of the first applications of an information gain measure to reduce the number of questions was introduced by Cunningham & Smyth [6, 17]. They applied incremental CBR in the context of fault diagnosis in technical modules. It was recognised that the complete problem description is not available at the

---

[2] *engain* is also not an official name for this method (cf. remark in footnote 1).

beginning, since problem attributes have to be investigated by tests, which may be expensive.

Doyle & Cunningham [7] have transferred the idea of interactive CBR to the field of on-line decision guides in which usually no classified data exists. Their approach compares several techniques of pre-clustering the available cases, before the entropy information gain measure can be applied. The different approaches are compared in terms of average dialog length. The questioning continues until a manageable set of cases remains. The approach does not consider whether or not the presented results satisfy the customer's requirements. Their tests are run on a leave-one-out basis. An important feature of the *simVar* approach described in the ensuing subsection is that the dialog is dynamically adapted, depending on the customer's answers. So, the induction steps are delayed to run time [7].

McSherry [10] proposed another approach for minimizing the length of dialogs for product selection in EC environments and also faults to be identified in diagnosis systems. He focuses on CBR applications in which the system's task is to identify a single case in the case base. It is proposed to construct a so-called *identification tree*, which is a decision tree with specially adapted splitting criteria that are based on information gain measures. With respect to the common problem in EC applications, i.e. usually there are no product classes defined beforehand, the author also suggests that each product can be treated as a unique outcome class, thus avoiding the need for cases to be clustered.

The information gain extension *extgain* (7) was used in the dialog service of the orenge 3.0 framework [12] and its predecessor CBR-Works, commercial products for the development of CBR applications. The enhanced version *engain* (8) is used since orenge 3.1.

3   Similarity-Influenced Attribute Selection

The conventional approaches described in Sect. 2 bring a couple of disadvantages with respect to their deployment in EC scenarios:

- For the pure entropy-based information gain approaches (5), the system-inherent similarity information is neglected and stays unused in this context. Attributes with a statistically high information gain might not contribute to a similar solution (product). A straightforward counterexample is the unique product ID, which certainly partitions the case base perfectly. If a customer knew the ID of the desired product it would be found with a single question.
- While the extended entropy measure *extgain* is a first approach to similarity-influenced attribute selection, it also has drawbacks:
  - attribute weights are not considered. Since the similarities are only calculated between attribute values, the influence of the selected attribute on the overall similarity is not considered.
  - the similarity measures are restricted to model the concept of fuzzy equality. The estimation of the case set size with the sum of similarities implies that similarities express a degree of equality. This is not always so, especially in an EC situation where similarity models the degree of customer satisfaction.

- The hybrid measure *engain* as a follow-up of *extgain* is a significant improvement with respect to the points mentioned above. However, the consideration of similarity is only focused on the current sales situation, i.e. based on the partial query. The method does not try to predict the influence of a possible attribute value on the overall similarity in the next dialog step. As a consequence, it can happen that an attribute with a wide range of occurring values among the candidate cases is selected but the similarities of the appropriate cases are not distributed well, i.e. the cases have approximately equal similarity values.

3.1   The *simVar* Measure

In order to overcome these problems, we proposed the *simVar* measure based on the variance of similarities [8]. Higher similarity variance in the set of candidate cases implies better discrimination between possible target cases (products) and unsatisfactory products (see Fig. 1: target cases depicted by grey bars). The *simVar* measure is calculated as shown by (9) and (10):

$$simVar(q,A,v,C) := \frac{1}{|C|} \cdot \sum_{c \in C} \left(sim(q_{A \leftarrow v}, c) - \mu \right)^2 \tag{9}$$

Analogously to the information gain measure, we can consider the transition of a dialog situation s to the new situation s' by assigning the value v to the query attribute A of query q (denoted $q_{A \leftarrow v}$); μ is the average value of all similarities, and C again the case base:

$$simVar(q,A,C) := \sum_{v \in \{v_1,...,v_m\}} p_v \cdot simVar(q,A,v,C) \tag{10}$$

Corresponding to the previous considerations, the expected discriminative power of assigning a value v to the attribute A with the probability p_v for the *simVar* measure is reflected by (10).

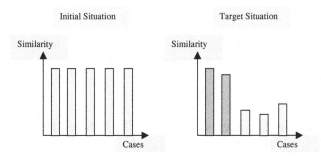

Fig. 1. Target situation characterised by similarity distribution

3.2   Analysis of *simVar*

Most of the time, an increase in similarity variance leads to better discrimination of satisfactory products. At the beginning of the dialog no information about the customer's requirements is available and all products are indistinguishable. If an optimistic interpretation is used all products have a 100% chance of satisfying the customer's demands and this chance decreases, as more information about the customer's requirements is available. [8]

In this initial situation, two possible successor situations can occur. Either, there is only little change in the case distribution when asking for a value of attribute A_m. All products are close to the average value and the target products are not very easily discernible. The questions that led to this transition had no great discrimination power. Or, a different attribute A_n is asked and the target cases can easily be identified. The target cases are the only cases with higher than average similarity. The *simVar* strategy will prefer a situation with higher variance. Here it has to be noted again that the actually assigned value for an attribute cannot be known in advance, but to verify the validity of *simVar* as a heuristic it is sufficient to prove that in dialog situations with higher variance the target cases are better discernible.

EC applications usually feature a huge database of available products. Most of these products are not acceptable for the customer and will have relatively low similarity in a retrieval. If such *irrelevant cases* [15] are considered in the variance calculation they can falsify the results. Such situations can be avoided by utilising a threshold introduced with a partitioning criterion to select the candidate cases after each question.

Near the end of the dialog, another problematic situation can occur. All irrelevant cases have been identified and excluded from the set of candidates by previous questions and only a relatively small set of equally well performing cases remains. Since these cases performed very well so far, they are alike with respect to their similarity value and up to now they have represented good alternatives to the target product. So, they are likely to have identical values in some of the unasked attributes as well and differ only in few attributes. The only way of identifying the target case among these *top performers* [15] is to ask those questions in which the top performers differ, even if this might lead to a decrease in the overall variance. To avoid this, the dialog strategy has to recognise such a situation and switch the attribute selection method to allow a decrease in variance of the top performers. While these situations are relatively sparse, they lead to noticeable decrease in performance near the end of the dialog. A possible solution to the problem is a dialog strategy that switches to maximize a change of variance in the top performing cases if the variance cannot be further increased.

4   Domain Dependencies of the Attribute Selection Methods

In an earlier evaluation of our *simVar* (10) approach, we recognized that the performance of this measure depends on the domain to which it is applied [9]. This has led us to the idea to further investigate into this topic and also to compare the other common methods based on entropy, i.e. *gain* (5), extended entropy combined with similarities *extgain* (7), and the second hybrid approach *engain* (8). As a fifth method we added the *random* attribute selection.

All tests were performed on a leave-one-out basis, i.e. each product was successively taken from the case base and used as reference query. After each question (attribute selection) retrieval was performed again. This retrieval result was compared to the result of the initial retrieval performed with the reference query. Such an ideal retrieval represents the best possible result for the customer, since the reference query contains the complete customer's requirements. A retrieval result is considered successful respectively correct, if it comes sufficiently close to the result of the ideal retrieval (cf. the following subsection). We used the commercial retrieval engine of *orenge* for all tests.

4.1   Test Conditions

Usually, the assessment of the approaches for attribute selection has concentrated on dialog length. It has not been considered how well does the retrieval result fit (quality of the generated dialog) with respect to the information gained by the dialog. Therefore, we defined when we would consider a retrieval to be correct.

Definition 4.1: (Correctness of a retrieval result)
A retrieval result is *correct with respect to an ideal retrieval result* if the best k cases of the current result can be found in the best n cases of the ideal result.

For all our tests we set $k=3$, $n=5$. We have chosen three domains relevant to EC environments to evaluate our approach: Last Minute Travels, Used Cars, and Personal Computers (PCs).

Each domain is described by 28 attributes and consists of 1500 cases without missing values. In order to compare all the methods from an objective point of view, we consider the same number of attributes for all the combinations and the same number of initial products. The cases were taken from real world applications. These applications all contained more products (e.g., in case of the travel domain even more than 600,000) from which we randomly chose the 1500 for each domain. The specific models were also described by more attributes (e.g., in case of the PC domain there were more than 70 attributes). The characteristic difference between the three domains is their number of attributes of Boolean type in the models. Of course, we artificially constructed the new models according to our requirements, i.e. high, medium, and low number of Boolean attributes.

As described in Section 3.2, *simVar* requires the use of a partitioning threshold to dispose of irrelevant cases. Picking a good value for this threshold is crucial for the performance: If it is too high some of the best-matching cases are discarded early in the dialog; on the other hand, if it is too low the irrelevant cases are considered in the variance calculation, resulting in inappropriate dialogs that do not satisfy the customer's demands very well. As this threshold depends on the domain, we examined several values for each domain. It turned out that a range of thresholds between 0.7 and 0.9 was adequate for the respective domains.

Even though we consider the threshold an inherent property of *simVar*, we also applied partitioning to the other methods to find out whether it has a relevant influence. The result was that the threshold made hardly any difference for the other three methods (unless it was so high that too many cases got lost in the dialogs). Considering this, we decided not to use partitioning for these methods.

4.2   Comparing the Different Methods

In order to obtain a good comparison between the methods, we have developed an experimental design with the following *factors* and *levels* [18]:

- *domain*: We propose three kinds of domains depending on the number of Boolean attributes, i.e. the attributes that can only be assigned the values true or false. We consider three levels: *travels* with 26 Boolean attributes (93% of the attributes), *used cars* with 14 (50% of the attributes), and *PCs* with only 1 Boolean attribute (approx. 4% of the attributes).
- *number of products* (*#products*): The amount of the products considered in the domain affects the difficulty of the selection. For this reason, we propose *#products* as a factor. The levels are: 50, 100, 150, 200, and 300 products. Each set of products was randomly taken for each domain.
- *weights*: We consider two levels: with or without weights, depending on the fact if weights are set in the domain for similarity calculation. Weights can play an important role even though they are not an explicit part of the formula for calculation of the appropriate selection method. They can still take an influence in the similarity calculation, which is used to measure correctness.
- *methods*: This factor has five levels according to the methods we compare: *simVar*, *gain*, *extgain*, *engain*, and *random*.

In this way we have a linear model with four factors (domain with three levels, products with five levels, weights with two levels, and methods with five levels) therefore we get 150 different combinations. For each combination we take into account 28 results (one for each attribute: after each question it is registered how many dialogs were correct in the sense of Def. 4.1), thus this design leads to 4200 observations. In our model we have considered a measure based on the successful dialogs after each question as dependent variable, which is a proportion between these successful dialogs and the number of products. We denote the dependent variable as *ratio*.

The presented statistical study does not require any normality assumption. For this reason, the observed responses do not have been tested to be normally distributed. All the factors were tested to be simultaneously meaningful performing an analysis of variance (ANOVA) [4] applied to the model. It should be mentioned that the ANOVA is conservative against normality assumption. Additionally, principal component analysis was also applied in order to check whether some factors may be removed from consideration. Once more, we get the conclusion that none of them is meaningless, as shows Table 2.

Table 2. Principal component analysis

	coefficients			
ratio	domain	#products	weights	methods
-0.882	0.371	0.138	-0.155	0.74

From Table 2 we can conclude that just one component is required to explain the total variance of the dependent variable *ratio*. Moreover, all the factors are significant in the model, since all of them have a non zero coefficient in the component.

The comparison between the methods was made in two steps. First, we compare the results within each combination of factors to test whether the number of successful dialogs after each question shows a statistically similar behaviour for each method. As we mentioned before, we consider just the proportion of the number of successful dialogs after each question with respect to the number of products (*ratio*). In this way, we obtain a measure of the quality of each method that is independent of the levels of the factor *#products*. In order to perform this test we use two kinds of nonparametric methods (for which no normality assumption is required): Mann-Whitney U-test for comparing two independent samples and Kruskal-Wallis test for $r>2$ independent samples [18]. Second, we check which method performs better in each combination using robust statistics (trimmed mean) and confidence intervals for the mean value [4]. Discarding a certain percentage of the lowest and the highest scores and then computing the mean of the remaining scores calculate a trimmed mean. We have considered a mean trimmed to 10%, which is computed by discarding the lower and higher 5% of the scores and taking the mean of the remaining scores.

Table 3. Results for each method depending on the *weights*

weight	trimmed means				
	simVar (1)	gain (2)	extgain (3)	engain (4)	random (5)
without	66.23	60.37	65.85	63.43	27.96
with	80.82	71.95	59.40	72.06	27.53
p-value	0.000	0.000	0.211	0.001	0.880

Table 3 presents the results according to the comparisons of each method with and without the use of weights. The p-value is the probability of getting a result as extreme or more extreme than the one observed if the proposed null hypothesis is correct. In Table 3 our null hypothesis is the assumption of obtaining a similar behaviour for each method with and without the consideration of weights. In this case, we use the Mann-Whitney U-test, since we only compare two independent samples at each time. We can observe that the p-values corresponding to the methods *simVar*, *gain*, and *engain* (denoted by 1, 2, and 4, respectively) do not exceed 0.05. Therefore, the factor *weight* is significant for these methods and moreover, the best performance is obtained by its use (large ratio value represented by the trimmed mean) with a confidence level above 95%. Nevertheless, the behaviour of methods *extgain*, and *random* (denoted by 3 and 5) does not depend on the use of weights, since their p-value is too large.

Depending on the levels of the factor *domain* (*travels*, *used cars*, and *PCs*) we obtain different conclusions about the behaviour of the different methods. In order to facilitate the legibility of these conclusions, we present a summary of them in Table 4 and Table 5. As above we denote the different methods *simVar*, *gain*, *extgain*, *engain*, and *random* by 1, 2, 3, 4, and 5, respectively. Now, our null hypothesis is the assumption of having a combination of two, three, or four methods with a similar behaviour. When we compare more than two methods ($r>2$) we use the Kruskal-Wallis test (r independent samples), otherwise, when we compare only two of them we use the Mann-Whitney U-test (two independent samples).

Table 4. Comparison between the methods depending on the *domains*

domain	trimmed means				
	simVar (1)	gain (2)	extgain (3)	engain (4)	random (5)
all	73.58	66.21	62.64	67.75	27.74
travels	84.22	86.60	85.00	86.54	28.56
used cars	61.69	49.33	47.73	53.09	21.99
PCs	74.82	62.67	55.02	63.50	32.72

Table 5. Obtained p-values depending on the *domains*

domain	p-values										
	(1,2,3,4,5)	(2,3,4,5)	(1,5)	(1,2,3,4)	(2,3,4)	(1,2)	(1,3)	(1,4)	(2,3)	(2,4)	(3,4)
all	0.000	0.000	0.000	0.004	0.244	0.010	0.001	0.046	0.248	0.623	0.103
travels	0.000	0.000	0.000	0.000	0.926	0.000	0.000	0.000	0.934	0.706	0.775
used cars	0.000	0.000	0.000	0.000	0.317	0.001	0.000	0.014	0.632	0.382	0.116
PCs	0.000	0.000	0.000	0.000	0.186	0.000	0.000	0.000	0.140	0.781	0.094

All the tests were performed using SPSS 10.0.6 (Statistical Packages for the Social Sciences)[3].

From Table 5 we can observe that the behaviour between the five methods is never equal with a confidence level above 95% (since the p-value according to (1,2,3,4,5) never reaches the value 0.05). We have not included all the results according to the comparisons between each method and the *random* method. But taking into account that it does not behave as *simVar* nor as the group containing *gain, extgain, engain* (p-value below 0.05 in all the cases) and observing the differences between their trimmed mean values, it is not difficult to see that the *random* method has a very poor performance. Moreover, the remaining four methods do not behave similar, since again the corresponding p-value does not reach 0.05 in any case. Nevertheless, the methods 2, 3, and 4 have a similar performance in all the cases (p-value very large), except for the domain concerning the *PCs*.

In addition, we can draw the following conclusions:

– Considering the results obtained for *all* the domains, we can ensure that *simVar* behaves better than any other method with a confidence level above 95%.
– Considering the results obtained for the domain *travels*, we conclude that *gain, extgain*, and *engain* give similar performance, which is better than that of *simVar* with a confidence level above 95%.
– From the results obtained for the domain *used cars*, we get again that the best method is *simVar* with a confidence level above 95%.
– Finally, for the domain *PCs*, *simVar* performs the best results with a confidence level above 95%. Moreover, *engain* and *gain* behave better than *extgain* with a confidence level above 90% (p-value below 0.1) and 85% (p-value below 0.15), respectively.

---

[3] See http://www.spss.com/

5   Conclusions and Future Work

The statistical evaluations suggest that among our five methods tested there is no single best method for all scenarios. Depending on certain domain-specific parameters, we would prefer one of these methods. However, it is clear that *extgain* and *random* show the worst behaviour. For this reason, we propose to choose *simVar*, *gain*, and *engain* as the best ones in most of the scenarios and even when we consider together all of them. However, it must be mentioned that the simulation models an *ideal customer*, i.e. a customer who can and will answer all the questions, provided all the observations.

For the interpretation of the results, it is important to realize that customers want to find a suitable product without answering too many questions. Therefore, success should be reached in the dialog as early as possible; it hardly makes any difference whether the desired products are found after the 20th or the 28th question, as no normal customer is willing to answer that many questions.

It is obvious that the domain model has a major impact on the relative performance of the methods: *simVar* excels in the *PC* domain with reasonable weights attached to the attributes, and it still outperforms the other methods in the *used cars* domain with weights. It does not perform too well in the *travels* domain – though it should be noted that its behaviour in the first third of the dialogs is about as good as in the other methods – or if all attributes are assigned equal weights (which has been evaluated in additional tests not described here). The reason for this is that the similarities play an important role for the attribute selection in *simVar*, so it is desirable to have attributes with a wide variety of values (Booleans being an extreme counterexample with only two distinct values), and the attributes should also be of different importance (i.e. they should have different weights). Both assumptions usually hold true in 'real' domains.

Surprisingly, *extgain* – which also uses similarities for question selection – appears to perform better if all attributes have equal weights: In these cases it outperforms its ancestor *gain* in the *used cars* and *PC* domains. The performance is very poor in the *PC* domain with weights, reaching only about 25% successful dialogs after the first 15 questions, jumping to about 80% after the 16th question, indicating that this was a very important question that should have been asked earlier.

The bottom line is that *simVar* is well suited for applications in EC, as its strengths lie in domains that are typical for this field, as long as they are modeled reasonably. It should definitely be mentioned that compared to the information gain measures, the *simVar* method is very resource-intensive with respect to calculation time.

Summarizing, it should be remarked again that our experimental design is based on an *ideal customer*. But more realistic customer classes should be taken into account in order to get more general conclusions. For this reason, we propose for future experiments the introduction of a new factor *customer class* with three additional levels: expert, intermediate, and beginner [9]. This factor could have a strong impact on the results and on the selection of a good method. This will require new tests on termination criteria because customers terminate dialogs for different reasons. If the utility function described in [8] is used for these tests, *engain* cannot be used as the underlying information gain measure, as the utility function expects non-negative input values (cf. Sect. 2.3). As a first step, the customers will only be simulated and later on, it should be done with real customers. It has to be noted that the proposed similarity variance *simVar* is only one example of a similarity-influenced measure.

Other metrics have to be investigated which might be even better suited than the variance of similarities.

References

1. Auriol, E., Wess, S., Manago, M., Althoff, K.D., Traphöner, R.: INRECA. A Seamlessly Integrated System Based on Inductive Inference and Case-Based Reasoning. In: Veloso, M., Aamodt, A. (eds.): Case-Based Reasoning Research and Development. Proc. of the 1st Internat. Conf. on Case-Based Reasoning, ICCBR'95. LNAI 1010, Springer-Verlag (1995)
2. Bergmann, R., Breen, S., Göker, M., Manago, M., Wess, S.: Developing Industrial Case-Based Reasoning Applications. The INRECA-Methodology. LNAI 1612, Springer-Verlag (1999)
3. Bergmann, R., Richter, M.M., Schmitt, S., Stahl, A., Vollrath, I.: Utility-Oriented Matching: A New Research Direction for Case-Based Reasoning. In: Vollrath, I., Schmitt, S., Reimer, U. (eds.): Proc. of the 9th German Workshop on Case-Based Reasoning, GWCBR'01, Baden-Baden, Germany. In: Schnurr, H.-P., Staab, S., Studer, R., Stumme, G., Sure, Y. (Hrsg.): Professionelles Wissensmanagement. Shaker Verlag (2001)
4. Cohen, P.R.: Empirical Methods for Artificial Intelligence. The MIT Press (1995)
5. Cunningham, P., Bergmann, R., Schmitt, S., Traphöner, R., Breen, S., Smyth, B.: WEBSELL: Intelligent Sales Assistants for the World Wide Web. In: Weber, R., Gresse von Wangenheim, C. (eds.): Proc of the Workshop Program at the 4th International Conference on Case-Based Reasoning, ICCBR-2001, Vancouver, Canada. Workshop 3: Case-Based Reasoning in Electronic Commerce (2001)
6. Cunningham, P., Smyth, B.: A comparison of model-based and incremental case-based approaches to electronic fault diagnosis. In: Proc. of the Case-Based Reasoning Workshop at AAAI-94 (1994)
7. Doyle, M., Cunningham, P.: A Dynamic Approach to Reducing Dialog in On-Line Decision Guides. In: Blanzieri, E., Protionale, L. (eds.): Advances in Case-Based Reasoning. Proc. of the 5th European Workshop on Case-Based Reasoning, EWCBR 2000. LNAI 1898, Springer-Verlag (2000)
8. Kohlmaier, A., Schmitt, S., Bergmann, R.: A Similarity-based Approach to Selection in User-Adaptive Sales Dialogs. In: Aha, D.W., Watson, I. (eds.): Case-Based Reasoning Research and Development. Proc. of the 4th International Conference on Case-Based Reasoning, ICCBR-2001. LNAI 2080, Springer-Verlag (2001)
9. Kohlmaier, A., Schmitt, S., Bergmann, R.: Evaluation of a Similarity-based Approach to Customer-adaptive Electronic Sales Dialogs. In: Weibelzahl, S., Chin, D., Weber, G. (eds.): Empirical Evaluation of Adaptive Systems. Proc. of the workshop held at the 8th International Conference on User Modeling (2001)
10. McSherry, D.: Minimizing Dialog Length in Interactive Case-Based Reasoning. In: Proc. of the 17th International Joint Conference on Artificial Intelligence, IJCAI-01, Seattle, USA (2001)
11. Mitchell, T.M.: Machine Learning. McGraw-Hill (1997)
12. orenge:dialog. In: orenge: Open Retrieval Engine 3.2 Manual. empolis – knowledge management. http://www.km.empolis.com/
13. Quinlan, J.R.: Induction of Decision Trees. Machine Learning 1 (1986)
14. Quinlan, J.R.: C4.5: Programs for Machine Learning. Morgan Kaufmann, San Mateo, California (1993)
15. Schmitt, S.: simVar:A Similarity-Influenced Question Selection Criterion for e-Sales Dialogs. In: Burke, R., Cunningham, P. (eds.): Special Issue on AI Approaches to User Requirements Elicitation for E-Commerce. Artificial Intelligence Review. To be published

16. Schmitt, S., Bergmann, R.: A Formal Approach to Dialogs with Online Customers. In: O'Keefe, B., Loebbecke, C., Gricar, J., Pucihar, A., Lenart, G. (eds.): e-Everything: e-Commerce, e-Government, e-Household, e-Democracy. Proc. of the 14th Bled Electronic Commerce Conference. Vol. 1: Research (2001)
17. Smyth, B., Cunningham, P.: A Comparison of Incremental Case-Based Reasoning and Inductive Learning. In: Proc. of the 2nd European Workshop on Case-Based Reasoning, EWCBR'94, Chantilly, France (1994)
18. Stoodley, K.D.C., Lewis, T., Stainton, C.L.S.: Applied Statistical Techniques. Halsted Press (1980)
19. Wilke, W., Lenz, M., Wess, S.: Intelligent Sales Support with CBR. In: Lenz, M., Bartsch-Spörl, B., Burkhard, H.D., Wess, S. (eds.): Case-Based Reasoning Technology. From Foundations to Applications. Springer-Verlag (1998)
20. Yang, Q., Wu, J.: Enhancing the Effectiveness of Interactive Case-Based Reasoning with Clustering and Decision Forests. In: Aha, D., Muñoz-Avila, H. (eds.): Applied Intelligence Journal, Special Issue on Interactive CBR (1999).

Category-Based Filtering and User Stereotype Cases to Reduce the Latency Problem in Recommender Systems

Mikael Sollenborn and Peter Funk

Mälardalen University
Department of Computer Science and Engineering
Västerås, Sweden
{mikael.sollenborn, peter.funk}@idt.mdh.se

Abstract. Collaborative filtering is an often successful method for personalized item selection in Recommender systems. However, in domains where items are frequently added, collaborative filtering encounters the *latency problem*. Characterized by the system's inability to select recently added items, the latency problem appears because new items in a collaborative filtering system must be reviewed before they can be recommended. Content-based filtering may help to counteract this problem, but runs the risk of only recommending items almost identical to the ones the user has appreciated before. In this paper, a combination of category-based filtering and user stereotype cases is proposed as a novel approach to reduce the latency problem. Category-based filtering puts emphasis on categories as meta-data to enable quicker personalization. User stereotype cases, identified by clustering similar users, are utilized to decrease response times and improve the accuracy of recommendations when user information is incomplete.

1 Introduction

Personalization on the Internet is today a growing research area, as the information overload problem has created an emerging need for individualized user treatment. By focusing on each visitor's requirements, the user's effort in navigating vast amounts of information can be made more focused, efficient and manageable. The underlying idea of personalization is the assumption that individualized content will satisfy users and increase revenue directly or indirectly, e.g. attract new users and make them more willing to revisit a web site and buy more services and products [1].

For personalization of web pages, Recommender systems are currently the most common approach. Based on the information filtering technique known as automated collaborative filtering (ACF) [2, 3, 4], standard Recommender systems essentially function on a peer review basis. When making recommendations, users with similar preferences are identified, and their item ratings are used to propose items to one another. Implementation of an ACF Recommender system can be divided into three steps [5]:

S. Craw and A. Preece (Eds.): ECCBR 2002, LNAI 2416, pp. 395–405.

1. Record the behavior of a large number of people, e.g. their interest in selected items such as adverts, news, books, etc.
2. Select a number of users who's past behavior is similar to the current user.
3. Recommend personalized items based on preferences of the selected users.

In addition to collaborative filtering, personalized selections based on matching the current user's previous selections with individual items - known as content-based filtering - is also very common [6]. In short, where filtering with ACF involves comparing a user with other users, content-based filtering is performed by comparing the user's preferences with the available information about items, e.g. meta-data or content keywords.

One potential problem with standard Recommender systems is that all reasoning is done online. With impatient users waiting for quick responses, the search for similar users must be very time-efficient. This time restriction also results in fewer possibilities when trying to improve or extend the content filtering strategies. In order to improve both speed and recommendation effectiveness, current approaches to building Recommender systems often try to perform some of the reasoning offline using clustering techniques [7, 8].

Traditional Recommender systems also encounter the *latency* problem [9], i.e. new items incorporated into a Recommender system cannot be used in collaborative recommendations before a substantial amount of users have evaluated it, as the recommendations rely on other users opinions. This problem is especially apparent in domains where new items are often added and old items quickly get out of date. Content-based filtering may be a solution, but runs the risk of only recommending items almost identical to the ones the user has appreciated before [9]. As noted in [10], the most obvious solution to the latency problem is to categorize the items in the system. In this paper we go one step further and assume that for some applications domains, Recommender systems solely based on categories provide sufficient personalization.

Our proposed approach for reducing the latency problem in highly dynamic domains is called category-based filtering. In a category-based filtering system, user preferences reflect attitudes not towards single items, but categories of similar items, both on a collective and an individual level. At the collective level, off-line clustering is used to find user stereotype cases, thus employing a Case-Based Reasoning view of information filtering. Clustered user data enables quicker response times and makes collaborative reasoning possible for meta-data in the form of categories.

In section 2 the category-based filtering approach is explained. Section 3 gives a more detailed exploration of classification, clustering and item selection. The research prototype, a personalization system based on category-based filtering and user clustering, is briefly described in section 4, and the following section gives a conclusion.

2 Category-Based Filtering Approach

In this section we explore how category-based filtering is used in a Recommender system and how it is integrated with clustering and user modeling.

2.1 Rating Technique

Typically, rating methods are divided into invasive and non-invasive techniques. An invasive rating method requires explicit user feedback. A commonly used approach is to let users mark their appreciation of items viewed or purchased on a scale. In contrast, non-invasive methods observes the user's behavior, requiring no more input than the user's normal interaction with the system. As a result, non-invasive methods generate noisier data, but have the benefit of being invisible to the user.

For our purposes, i.e. dynamic domains where data changes frequently, invasive techniques put too much burden on the users. Instead, a simple non-invasive technique was chosen. The system selects a set of items to show, and observes user reactions to these items. The system notes whether the user responds positively, by clicking on one of the currently shown items, or negatively, by ignoring them. We do not consider viewing time following a click, because the number of responses to a category of items will be many times as high as that for single items in a representationless ACF system, making the consequences of a single click less relevant.

2.2 Category-Based Filtering

We refer to the personalization approach proposed in this paper as *category-based filtering*. Its main characteristic is that selection of information is based on category ratings instead of item ratings, in contrast to other content-filtering strategies in general, and representationless collaborative filtering in particular. To function, category-based filtering requires categorization of every item, either manually or by an automated process.

In our implementation of category-based filtering, the selection of items is based partly on individual user models, and partly on collective user stereotypes cases. A *user model* represents the current knowledge about a user's reaction towards shown categories of items. A *user stereotype case*, in contrast, consists of collective information about a group of users.

User stereotypes, as introduced by Rich in [11], require two types of information. The system must know what properties capture a stereotype, and what events or behavior that implies a particular stereotype. On the Internet, this information is highly dynamic and in our domain dependent on both content of categories and population of users. A clustering approach, as described below, is therefore preferable to static stereotypes, since it is able to automatically identify related categories and adapt to a changing population of users and their preferences.

By representing a solution to the problem of supplying a 'typical' kind of user with appropriate information, it is natural to see user stereotype cases as part of a Case-Based Reasoning process. When the information in a user model is insufficient for deciding which items to select, the user stereotype case most closely resembling the user is consulted to make assumptions about the user's expected behavior (Retrieve, Reuse). The case is Revised when the user evaluates the recommended items, and Retained when the user stereotype cases are updated.

The system could also be seen as a hybrid of collaborative and content-based filtering, with strong emphasis on categories as item meta-data. Unlike other such hybrid systems [12, 4], the collaborative selection is also based on meta-data, as the peer reviewing process deals with categories instead of items.

The focus on categories reduces the latency problem, as new items can be recommended as soon as the system knows the user's attitude towards the item's corresponding category. Because of this, selecting items based on category ratings instead of ratings of individual items is especially suited for domains where there is a constant flow of new information (e.g. news and adverts), provided that effective categorization is possible.

As category-based filtering could possibly be seen mainly as an extension to existing filtering strategies, one might feel inclined to propose the terms category-based collaborative filtering and category-based content-based filtering instead. However, apart from the clumsiness of these expressions, the term category-based collaborative filtering has been used for other purposes [13].

The user stereotype cases needed for collaborative selection of items are created offline using clustering methods described in section 3. Each cluster represents a part of the entire user population. Probabilistic nets within the cases, formed from the cluster data, represent collective attitudes towards categories of items.

With the clusters identified, a new user can be assigned a user stereotype case after a short period of initial observation. As the user model matures, the case assignment may change to point out the characteristics of the user in a more precise way.

The frequency of generating clusters and updating the user stereotypes cases depends on the application domain, e.g. the number of visits to the web site it's being used on. All individual user information is always preserved, enabling the system to perform a re-clustering at any time.

2.2.1 User Models
Based on the dimensions identified in [11], a user model in the proposed system has the following properties: each user has a separate user model, the model is built and refined non-invasively by the system on each site visit, and the model contains both specific, short-term information and (limited) long-term information.

A user model is represented by a matrix of choices and preferences For each category, the number of times the user has been approached with items belonging to it is stored, as well as the number of positive responses. Table 1 shows an example preference matrix with a simplified history ("Last ten"-column) that would capture sudden changes of user preferences. In this example, only two clicks the last ten times the user was approached with hunting items may indicate a decline of interest for such adverts.

Table 1. Example preference matrix

	Shown	Clicked	Last ten
Hunting	24	11	2
Fishing	18	4	3
Cosmetics	12	1	0

When the preferences of a user are to be ranked, the value for each category may be reduced, e.g. to one of four levels: positive, neutral, negative, or unknown. The unknown attitude is reserved for categories that have not yet been evaluated.

2.2.2 User Stereotype Cases and Appreciation Nets

User stereotypes cases are representations of common attitudes among a group of similar users. The chosen method of capturing collective interests is to utilize what will be referred to as appreciation nets. Appreciation nets are graphs with nodes and directed edges, where edges represent a probabilistic relationship. If every node in the net has an edge going into every other node, the appreciation net is said to be complete, with n(n-1) node connections. In Figure 1 an example of an appreciation net is given for four item categories. In this example population the likelihood that a person who likes hunting is also interested in motor sports is 60% (indicated by 0,6 at the edge from hunting to motor sports). In the opposite direction, a person that appreciates motor sports also enjoys hunting with a probability of 30%. Of all the persons belonging to this population, 50% enjoy motor sports, but only 20% appreciates hunting, as indicated in the category nodes.

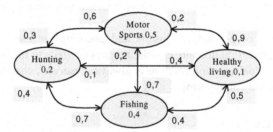

Fig. 1. An appreciation net with four item categories

2.3 System Architecture

Figure 2 shows a schematic view of a system using category-based filtering. Each user visiting the web site is assigned an individual user agent. The agent's task is to handle web page modifications and interaction with the user involving personalized items. The Reasoner uses category-based filtering to select a set of items assumed to be of interest for the current user, based on the user model (the user's preference matrix) and the closest user stereotype case. The user agent tracks all user responses and stores them in the user model. The cases are updated offline (as indicated by the dotted line) by clustering similar user models.

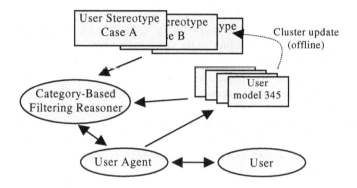

Fig. 2. Example of a personalization system using category-based filtering

3   Clustering and Selection

This section takes a closer look at techniques and algorithms used for personalization in a category-based system.

3.1   Clustering Users

For the creation of user stereotype cases, an agglomerative, hierarchical clustering method was chosen, avoiding partitioning since the number of appropriate clusters will be difficult to guess in advance. The variables determining cluster membership are as many as there are categories in the system, but categories that have not yet been evaluated by a user are not included when comparing him/her to other users. Different values are assigned to the category attitudes negative, neutral, and positive. To measure distance between clusters, the city-block (Manhattan distance) metric is used. Similar clusters are merged using the unweighted pair-group average method [14].

After clustering, the (highly subjective) optimal number of clusters must be determined. Currently, the chosen method is to pick a maximum number of clusters M based on the number of users N registered on the web site. The minimum amount of users U belonging to a cluster is then calculated as $U = N/M$, meaning we treat a group of U or more similar individuals as "statistically significant" to form a collective model. Now, traversing the cluster tree selecting clusters of size U or bigger results in a number of clusters from 1 to M. Although this method produces acceptable results for the limited test domain, more formal approaches for determining the number of clusters, such as LMM or BIC, are considered for the final implementation.

As noted earlier, a user stereotype case contains an appreciation net, with all nodes connected to every other node in both directions. When forming such a net, a joint distribution is made from the ranked category preferences of every user belonging to the group, resulting in a two-dimensional matrix exposing collective preferences. Building the user stereotype case is primarily a question of how much information from the joint distribution to include in the appreciation net.

For each category C the system stores the probability of a positive evaluation by any user belonging to the group, as node values in the appreciation net. This information is very important because for categories where $P(C)$ is high, quick tests can be made to determine whether new users conform to a specific cluster.

Secondly, couplings between pairs of categories are examined. The probability of a user appreciating C in case the user likes D, $P(C|D)$, is preserved for each category-to-category connection, stored as binary relationships between category nodes in the appreciation net.

The dominating preference information can be captured in binary relations between category nodes. Some preference information may also be captured in probability values involving more than two category nodes (e.g. if users are interested in category D and E the likelihood for interest in C is $P(C|D \wedge E)$). A calculation of probability values among all possible n-tuples of relations may have a too high computational price and make the resulting model unnecessarily complex. Considering the possibly increased inference ability gained from probability relations involving three of four categories, such probability values may be worth preserving in the appreciation net if the values are distinctive enough (i.e. exceptionally low or high).

3.2 Classification of Users

Automatic classification is attempted by targeting the user with information corresponding to differential probability values in the user stereotype cases appreciation nets. The goal is to determine which case resembles the new user the most.

Beginning with the biggest cluster is an adequate starting point, because it's where the user most likely belongs. What is sought for is a number of category nodes in the appreciation net with high appreciation probabilities, with these values being as unique as possible compared to the equivalent category values in other cluster models. Categories with unique but low appreciation probabilities are not as interesting, as a positive response can be considered a lot more informational than a negative, i.e. a user showing interest probably *is* interested, but a user that doesn't may simply be temporary ignorant or short of time. The appropriateness of being chosen is calculated for every category node C by comparing it to the corresponding category node C_i in every other case appreciation net, using

$$F = P(C) * \sum_i \left| P(C) - P(Ci) \right| . \tag{1}$$

The three categories with highest F are chosen for testing, meaning information belonging to these categories will be shown to the user, with five items per category. This may or may not take several visits to the site, depending on the type of site and how much information can be shown normally during a visit. When all items have been shown, an initial user stereotype case membership determination is performed. The formula resembles a Naive Bayesian Classifier, but sums probabilities instead of multiplying them to avoid having occasional conditional probabilities close to zero produce an unsuitably low total similarity value. The categories involved in the test are compared to each user stereotype case, putting emphasis on similar categories with high probability values (again because it's more important what is appreciated than what is not), and limiting the comparison to categories already tested. The similarity S is calculated for every user stereotype case, where Ci is category i in the tested user's preference matrix, $Csui$ the corresponding category i for member u in user stereotype s, and M an empirically chosen modification rate, using

$$S = \sum_i P(P(Csui) = (P(Ci) \pm 0.1) \mid s) * (P(Csi) * M + (1-M)) . \tag{2}$$

The case that most closely resembles the initial behavior of the user (highest S) is now chosen for a second pick of categories using (1), separate from the ones chosen before. A new test is done, followed by another comparison using (2). This process continues every time the user visits the site. Eventually, the system will mix the testing data with items selected by assuming that the user does in fact belong to the cluster the user currently resembles the most, as well as re-evaluating categories that were positively responded to before. As more and more categories are evaluated, the amount of testing data ceases gradually. Cluster membership may still change, either because the number of clusters or the user's behavior has changed, but no longer as a result of evaluating "classification-aggressive" testing data.

3.3 Selection of Personalized Items

Once a user is assigned to a user stereotype case, the Reasoner (figure 2) is able to make qualified guesses about what a semi-new user might and might not appreciate. Whenever there is insufficient information about a user as an individual during decision-making, the case connected to the user will be examined to find out how similar users have behaved.

Asked to select personalized information for a specific user, the system initially decides whether or not it knows enough about the user's behavioral patterns to determine cluster membership. If not, the system will try to classify the user as described above. If cluster affiliation can be guessed but not completely determined, the system may alternately pick items it assumes the user will appreciate, while at the same time trying to further strengthen the belief that the user belongs to a specific cluster.

The Reasoner selects two types of information, appreciation-known and appreciation-assumed. A new user is confronted with a lot of appreciation-assumed information, but as the user provides more information, the appreciation-known information gradually replaces it.

Appreciation-known items are chosen only from categories the user has 'sufficiently evaluated'. A sufficiently evaluated category simply means a category that the user has evaluated enough times to be reasonably sure about the individual's attitude towards it. The number labeled sufficient varies however, as the system gradually tries to follow a new or semi-new user when providing more information. The system may also decide that a category needs re-evaluation if the user's last ten responses to it has been significantly different to the corresponding long-term behavior.

Appreciation-known information is selected by ranking the user preferences, picking items from categories that have been positively evaluated. In this process, the system tries to balance the number of shown items among the positive preferences, as well as sometimes picking sufficiently evaluated categories with a less positive ranking to allow for re-evaluation.

When appreciation-assumed items are to be selected, the system chooses a category node starting point in the appreciation net among the users positively ranked preferences. With this node as base, the system examines all connected category nodes. The category to select information from is chosen randomly from a dynamically generated pie chart, where each category not among the user's positive preferences gets a slice size (choice probability) calculated using equation 3. W is the connection weight, C is the number of clicks done on items belonging to this category, S the number of times shown to the user, and L how many of the last H items in the category that has been clicked by the user. H is domain dependent; in our test evaluation the history length is ten items, as shown in Table 1.

$$P = W * ((C + 1)/(S + 1) + (L+1)/H) \tag{3}$$

Another form of appreciation-assumed item selection, used in parallel with the method above, essentially uses the same method as the automatic classification process: picking items from categories in the appreciation net where the probability of a positive response is high. This item selection method is used only if there are still categories with high appreciation probabilities that the user has not yet evaluated.

The items selected by using each of these techniques are finally merged, and presented to the current user.

4   Implementation

The research prototype is currently being implemented, and has so far been tested on a small set of users in a limited surrounding. News and adverts were chosen as item types, as they both represent dynamic domains were items generally change often.

In the testing environment, users are shown a selected number of news summaries, containing approximately 200 letters. These news items are categorized manually in advance. The user is able to receive the full article by clicking on a news item. This information is used to build a preference matrix for the current user to aid in the category-based filtering approach. Adverts are handled similarly. A selected number of adverts are shown to the user and when clicked, additional product information is displayed.

To keep the user models reasonably small, item selections in categories are not given any time stamps, only the number of positive responses for the last ten times the item was shown (se example in Table 1).

A number of user stereotype cases have been initiated in advance, and off-line update of clustering is performed frequently in the form of refinement (a new cluster is generated from the same set of users). The re-clustering algorithm for grouping similar users into new clusters, as discussed in section 3.2, has been implemented but remains to be thoroughly tested and integrated. The appreciation nets currently only capture binary relations between item categories.

The prototype has been evaluated by a number of hypothetical users. The testing of the prototype has shown ability to quickly adapt to users preferences for a small number of categorized news and adverts (50 news and 70 adverts, 5 different hypothetical users with their interest profile predetermined and with a consistent behavior and low amounts of noise).

5   Conclusions

In this paper we have presented an approach to Recommender systems for application domains where items are frequently added. Provided that sufficient categorization is possible, we have shown that category-based filtering enables handling the latency problem.

In the proposed approach, users are represented partly by individual user models, and partly by user stereotypes cases. The cases, which are created offline through clustering, are used when the knowledge about an individual user is too limited to draw the needed conclusions for recommending items. The system will automatically attempt classification of new users by comparing the user's behavior with the user stereotype cases, selecting the most similar one.

Personalized information is divided into two categories: appreciation-known and appreciation-assumed. While the former represents item selections based on a user's known previous behavior, appreciation-assumed items are chosen because of high appreciation probabilities among other users belonging to the same user stereotype case as the current user.

So far, category-based filtering has been tested on hypothetical users in a limited surrounding, where the approach has shown the ability to adapt to user's needs.

Large-scale tests to further confirm the usability of category-based filtering for practical domains are currently being prepared.

References

1. Reichheld, F.F., Sasser, W.E.: Zero defections:quality comes to service. Harvard Business Review, 68:105-7, September-October (1990)
2. Shardanad, U., Maes, P.: Social Information Filtering: Algorithms for Automating 'Word of Mouth'. Proceedings of the ACM Conference on Human Factors in Computing Systems, ACM Press (1995) 210-217
3. Konstan, J.A., Miller, B.N., Maltz, D., Herlocker, J.L., Gordan, L.R., Riedl, J.: GroupLens: Applying collaborative filtering to usenet news. Communications of the ACM 40 (1997) 3:77-87
4. Cotter, P., Smyth, B.: WAPing the Web: Content Personalisation for WAP-Enabled Devices. Proceedings of the 1st International Conference on Adaptive Hypermedia and Adaptive Web-Based Systems, Trento, Italy (2000) 98-108
5. Mukherjee, R., Dutta, S.: MOVIES2GO – a new approach to online movie recommendations. In workshop Intelligent Techniques for Web Personalization, IJCAI-2001, Seattle Washington (2001) 26-34
6. Rafter, R., Smyth, B.: Passive Profiling from Server Logs in an Online Recruitment Environment. In workshop Intelligent Techniques for Web Personalization, IJCAI-2001, Seattle Washington (2001) 35-41
7. Mobasher, B., Dai, H., Luo, T., Nakagawa, M.: Improving the Effectiveness of Collaborative Filtering on Anonymous Web Usage Data. In workshop Intelligent Techniques for Web Personalization, IJCAI-2001, Seattle Washington (2001) 53-60
8. Ungar, L.H., Foster, D.P.: Clustering Methods for Collaborative Filtering. Proceedings of the Workshop on Recommendation Systems. AAAI Press, Menlo Park California (1998)
9. Funakoshi, K., Ohguro, T.: A content-based collaborative recommender system with detailed use of evaluations. In Proceedings of 4th International Conference on Knowledge-Based Intelligent Engineering Systems and Allied Technologies, Volume 1 (2000) 253-256
10. Hayes, C., Cunningham, P., Smyth, B.: A Case-Based Reasoning View of Automated Collaborative Filtering. In Proceedings of 4th International Conference on Case-Based Reasoning, ICCBR2001 (2001) 243-248
11. Rich, E.: User Modeling via Stereotypes. Cognitive Science 3 (1979) 329-354
12. Balabanovic, M., Shoham, Y.: Combining Content-Based and Collaborative Recommendation. Communications of the ACM 40 (1997) 3:66-72
13. Kohrs, A., Merialdo, B.: Using category-based collaborative filtering in the Active WebMuseum. Proceedings of IEEE International Conference on Multimedia and Expo, New York (2000) 1:351-354
14. Jain, A.K., Dubes, R.C.: Algorithms for Clustering Data. Prentice Hall (1988)

Defining Similarity Measures: Top-Down vs. Bottom-Up

Armin Stahl

University of Kaiserslautern, Computer Science Department
Artificial Intelligence - Knowledge-Based Systems Group
67653 Kaiserslautern, Germany
stahl@informatik.uni-kl.de

Abstract. Defining similarity measures is a crucial task when developing CBR applications. Particularly, when employing utility-based similarity measures rather than pure distance-based measures one is confronted with a difficult knowledge engineering task. In this paper we point out some problems of the state-of-the-art procedure to defining similarity measures. To overcome these problems we propose an alternative strategy to acquire the necessary domain knowledge based on a Machine Learning approach. To show the feasibility of this strategy several application scenarios are discussed and some results of an experimental evaluation for one of these scenarios are presented.

1 Introduction

One of the core tasks when developing case-based reasoning (CBR) applications is the definition of similarity measures used to retrieve cases that may help to solve a given problem according to the traditional paradigm of CBR, namely *"similar problems have similar solutions"*. However, this traditional view leads to some limitations and open questions in many current CBR applications:

- Is it always appropriate to interpret similarity as a kind of geometrical distance?
- What is the semantics of the term *similarity* in a particular application?
- What kind of knowledge has to be encoded in the similarity measure?
- How to acquire this knowledge?

In our point of view, the similarity measure has to consider knowledge about the utility of cases for particular problem situations [1]. This means, the role of the similarity measure is to approximate a usually unknown *utility function* as well as possible. Unfortunately, the definition of such *utility-based similarity measures* is more difficult than the definition of pure distance-based measures. Though one motivation of CBR was the avoidance of the knowledge acquisition bottleneck that reduces the commercial applicability of traditional rule-based expert systems, the definition of sophisticated similarity measures leads again to exactly this problem. Nevertheless, many current CBR applications already employ more or less utility-based similarity measures.

S. Craw and A. Preece (Eds.): ECCBR 2002, LNAI 2416, pp. 406–420, 2002.

While case knowledge is often already available in the form of existing or easily collectable data-sets, the knowledge about the utility of cases for new problem situations is usually not available in such an explicit form. Depending on the particular domain and application scenario, for example, it has to be acquired by consulting a domain expert who possesses implicit knowledge about the underlying utility function. Further, the acquired knowledge has to be formalized by using the similarity representation structures provided by the applied CBR tool. This knowledge engineering task is a difficult and time consuming procedure. Though today available CBR tools provide sophisticated graphical user interfaces for comfortably modeling similarity measures, unfortunately there are hardly any approaches to facilitate the definition of domain specific similarity measures in a more intelligent way.

Another aspect is the validation and maintenance of the defined similarity measures to guarantee powerful CBR applications. While a lot of research work was done to ensure high quality of the case knowledge [8,9,11], a corresponding quality management for the similarity measure is still neglected. However, developing approaches that help to guarantee high quality of similarity measures with reasonable effort may further push the commercial success of CBR applications.

The aim of this paper is the comparison of two complementary strategies for defining similarity measures. First, the state-of-art strategy is reviewed. After that an alternative approach is introduced and it is shown how this approach can simplify the mentioned knowledge acquisition task.

To show the practical feasibility of this alternative approach some typical application scenarios are discussed. Further, some results of an experimental evaluation for one of these scenarios are presented. Finally, we close with a discussion of related work and some general conclusions.

2   Approaches to Defining Similarity Measures

In the following we assume an attribute-value based case representation and a corresponding similarity measure consisting of three basic elements:

1. *local similarity functions* used to compute the similarity between query and case attribute values
2. *attribute weights* representing the relevance of each attribute for the similarity assessment
3. an *amalgamation function* responsible for the computation of a final similarity value for a particular query-case pair based on the local similarities and attribute weights

To define a similarity measure that approximates the application specific utility function sufficiently, one has to select appropriate values and functions for the three previously mentioned representation items. In the following sections the state-of-the-art procedure for this knowledge engineering task is reviewed and an alternative approach is introduced. Further, we discuss how these two complementary approaches can be combined to profit from the advantages of both.

2.1 State of the Art: Bottom-Up

The procedure usually employed to define a similarity measure of the assumed structure can be characterized as a "Divide and Conquer" strategy. Because a knowledge engineer is usually not able to formulate a similarity function that approximates the utility of an arbitrary complex case for a given query directly, one tries to decompose this problem. Therefore, the particular attributes of the case representation are first considered separately and are analyzed with respect to their influence on the utility function. To formalize this kind of *local utility*, local similarity measures have to be defined for each attribute.

In fact, in practical CBR systems the local similarity measures are often not really attribute specific but data type specific. For simplicity, we suppose that each attribute possesses its own data type consisting of a description of its value range and the corresponding similarity measure. This combination of value range and similarity measure is useful because the value range has usually a direct influence on the similarity measure. Therefore, the formal representations of local similarity measures also differ depending on the basic data-type of the corresponding attribute. For discrete unordered symbol types a widely used representation are similarity-tables[1]. Mathematical functions based on the difference of the two values to be compared are the common representation for numerical types. To facilitate the definition of local similarity measures CBR tools provide standard functions that are parameterized to be adapted on the application specific requirements. This reduces the similarity definition task on the selection of appropriate parameter values.

After defining the local similarity functions, the knowledge engineer has to estimate the relative importance of each attribute for the entire utility function. The result of this estimation is a set of attribute weights.

To obtain a global similarity measure one has finally to decide how to combine the results of the local similarity measures and the respective attribute weights. Therefore, a special amalgamation has to be defined. In many applications a simple weighted sum is sufficient, however, sometimes other amalgamation functions may lead to more accurate results.

An illustration of the described procedure is shown in Figure 1. Consider one wants to define a similarity measure that estimates the utility of particular personal computers with respect to a requirement specification given by a customer. For simplicity, in the shown example only the attributes Price, CPU-Clock, and CD-Drive are considered. For the attribute Price a local similarity measure is chosen that represents a kind of "less is perfect" semantic, that means the utility of a PC decreases if and only if the price is higher than the price a customer is willing to pay. However, the measure used for the CPU-Clock attribute encodes a complementary measure due to the different semantic of this attribute. Further, the attribute Price has a higher influence on the utility compared with the two technically properties, modeled by the shown attribute weights. Finally, a standard weighted sum is used as amalgamation function.

---

[1] A similarity-table enumerates similarity values for each possible combination of values explicitly.

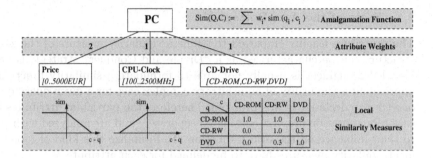

Fig. 1. Defining similarity measures bottom-up

Drawbacks of the Bottom-Up Approach. However, one basic motivation of CBR was the desire for knowledge-based systems that lead even to good results in domains where such a deeper understanding of the coherences is missing. Of course, CBR has already proved its capability to realize powerful applications in such domains. This success can be explained by the fact that very simple similarity measures based on a pure geometrical distance are often sufficient to obtain good results, provided that enough reasonable case data is available. Nevertheless, we argue that the applicability of CBR might be enhanced if it is possible to encode more domain knowledge into the similarity measure even in domains which are not really understood by human experts.

Another drawback of the bottom-up approach occurs in domains where the necessary background knowledge is at least partially available. Because the indispensable formal knowledge representation does usually not reflect the way of thinking of the domain expert, the probability of "knowledge compilation errors" is very high. Consider again the example above with the two complementary similarity functions for the attributes Price and CPU-Speed. These "more is perfect" or "less is perfect" functions are a typical example where errors may occur by selecting the wrong function. On the one hand, the domain expert might be confused about the relation between the difference of the values to be compared and the similarity. On the other hand, the errors might be the result of simple misfortunes. Nevertheless, the errors can lead to significant consequences for the entire similarity computation especially if an above averaged weight is assigned to the corresponding attribute.

Besides such clear true-false errors, a knowledge engineer is also faced with more fuzzy problems when defining a similarity measure. Often, parameters can be used to influence the degree of decrease of similarity with respect to the distance of the values to be compared. However, the assignment of concrete values to such parameters is often a very subjective decision of the particular knowledge engineer.

The basic foundation of the bottom-up approach is that a careful definition of the different representation items will lead to an adequate global similarity measure. However, during the definition process the utility of a particular case with respect to a given query is never estimated. In fact, depending on the application scenario, the knowledge engineer often trusts the values computed by the global similarity measure without any further validation. This is the reason why the previously described errors in the similarity measure may significantly decrease the accuracy of the entire CBR system. If the measured accuracy does not fit the requirements, the most common strategy is to guarantee high quality of the case base [8,9,11]. However, generic approaches to discover relevant errors in the similarity measure are still not in focus of research.

2.2   Alternative Approach: Top-Down

To to be applied successfully, the approach discussed in the preceding section makes an important demand. The knowledge engineer or an additionally consulted domain expert must be able to provide a certain amount of background knowledge about the application domain. This knowledge is a basic requirement for an adequate definition of the various representation elements of the similarity measure. In our example above, very different local similarity functions are selected to represent the particular meaning of each attribute for the entire utility approximation. This presumes at least a partial understanding of the causal relationships in the application domain.

Learning Similarity Measures.   To show a possible way to overcome both problems — the acquisition of the mandatory background knowledge for utility-based similarity measures and the missing validation of already defined measures — we propose a very complementary procedure compared with the discussed state-of-the-art approach. Instead of defining every single representation item of the similarity measure manually, we suggest to estimate the utility of available cases for a given query directly. Of course, mostly it would be very hard to define the utility absolutely, e.g. by assigning a concrete utility value to a case. Therefore, our concept is based on a more relative estimation that we call *case order feedback* (see also [12]). The assumption of this concept is that even if a domain expert is unable to estimate the utility of a given case for a particular problem absolutely, s/he should be able to compare the utility of two given cases. This means, we suppose that an expert is usually able to determine which of two cases is the more suitable one to solve a particular problem. Of course, the situation that both cases are equally useful or that the expert does not possess certain knowledge to decide it, is also imaginable. Nevertheless, we can consider a domain expert as a kind of *similarity teacher* as illustrated in Figure 2.

We assume that the similarity teacher is confronted with a query and an arbitrary set of possibly partially ordered cases. The given partial order S may be determined by an already existing similarity measure. However, the order S may not reflect the real utility of the cases with respect to the query. Therefore, the similarity teacher has to rearrange the cases by using his implicit knowledge about the application domain resulting in a new partial order U. In general, the similarity teacher has not to be represented necessarily by a human domain expert. In Section 3.4 we will discuss a different realization of a similarity teacher.

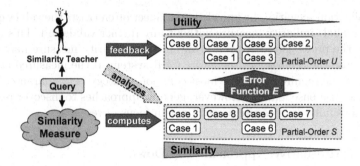

Fig. 2. The role of the similarity teacher

We argue that, in principle, case order feedback can be used by a Machine Learning approach to determine a similarity measure that approximates the utility function of the domain sufficiently. This means, the combination of queries and associated case order feedback can be used as examples to employ a supervised learning algorithm. Unfortunately, this differs from the standard classification problem, due to the structure of these examples. Standard ML algorithms usually are confronted with pairs that consist of a problem description and a class identifier. Here, the query can also be interpreted as a problem description, however, the case order is obviously not a simple class identifier.

To realize this special machine learning task we introduced an *error function* that compares the correct case order determined by the similarity teacher and the perhaps incorrect case order computed by an already predefined similarity measure. This error function computes a value $E \geq 0$ to measure the distance between the two partial orders S and U. By introducing this error function the learning task can also be characterized as an optimization problem. Concretely, we want to optimize the given similarity measure by minimizing the error E.

Depending on the concrete ML algorithm to be used it might be necessary to ensure further properties of the error function E. However, the focus of this paper is not the development of a particular algorithm but a more general motivation why and under which circumstances this alternative approach might facilitate the definition of utility-based similarity measures. The description of a concrete error function and an algorithm based on the presented approach to learn attribute weights is discussed in [12].

Advantages and Problems of the Top-Down Approach. Compared with the bottom-up process described in section 2.1, the previously discussed top-down approach may lead to some significant advantages. One basic property of this approach is that it does not necessarily require a deeper understanding of the causal relationships in the application domain to enable a knowledge engineer to define utility-based similarity measures. Here, an expert must only be able to give a raw estimation of the utility of a case, but he has not to know the causal reasons for this particular utility. We argue that this fact allows a much easier knowledge acquisition in domains where an expert usually estimates the utility of cases by an act of instinct.

However, in other domains like the mentioned PC domain, the bottom-up process is often the more natural way. To decide which of two PCs is the more appropriate one with respect to a set of demands, one would usually analyze and compare the concrete technical properties of the two PCs during the decision process. This procedure matches the utility decomposition procedure when defining local similarity measures in the bottom-up manner.

Another advantage of the top-down approach is the possibility to employ it for a well-defined validation of already defined similarity measures. By comparing the retrieval ranking computed by the similarity measure with the correct case order determined by the similarity teacher, one gets a measure for the quality of the defined similarity function. If this quality, i.e. the value computed by the error function E, does not fit the application requirements, applying the proposed learning algorithm may lead to evidences for detecting possible errors in the similarity measure.

2.3 The Hybrid Approach

Obviously, the bottom-up and the top-down approach are very complementary strategies for defining similarity measures. As already mentioned above, the success of each approach depends primarily on the particular application circumstances. However, to benefit of the advantages of both, sometimes a combination of both strategies seems to be the optimal way.

In a first step, the knowledge engineer can encode some background knowledge into the similarity measure by following the bottom-up procedure. This means, any causal relationships of the application domain that are obvious to the expert should be encoded directly in particular local similarity measures and feature weights. For all other representation elements one can use standard similarity functions based on the geometrical distance of the values to be compared. Such standard functions are even used by many commercial CBR shells as an initial similarity measure.

In a second step, one can apply the top-down approach to encode additional but perhaps difficult to acquire background knowledge into the similarity measure. Therefore, the knowledge engineer has to determine typical example queries that are used for a test retrieval based on the similarity measure defined before. Through analyzing the respective case rankings it is then possible to collect the case order feedback required by the supposed learning algorithm. This training data can then be used to optimize the predefined similarity measure.

Generally, one can consider different strategies how the learning algorithm may handle the partially predefined similarity measure.

Good Starting Point. A quite simple approach is the use of the predefined measure as the start point for the learning algorithm. Many ML algorithms employ local search strategies that usually deliver better results if a good start point is chosen. However, the major disadvantage of this strategy is that the learning algorithm may "override" some of the decisions made by the knowledge engineer before, even though these decisions are based on certain expert knowledge.

Constraints. To overcome the drawback of the precedent approach, one can treat the decisions made by the knowledge engineer as constraints to be considered during the learning process. This means, the learning algorithm is only allowed to change representation elements of the predefined similarity measure that are explicitly marked as uncertain knowledge. Besides a strict distinction between "certain", i.e. unchangeable, and "uncertain", i.e. changeable knowledge, one can also imagine more flexible approaches that guide the search process of the learning algorithm. Therefore, the knowledge engineer may assign every representation element a kind of "trust-level" (e.g., represented by numbers of $[0,1]$) to express her/his uncertainty when defining particular knowledge items. The learning algorithm may treat these numbers as probability values assigned to particular areas of the search space to focus the search process on areas where it is more probable to find a similarity measure that fits the training data.

3   Typical Application Scenarios

The aim of this section is to show the practically applicability of the approaches discussed before. Up to now we have only discussed the possibility to support a domain expert when defining a utility-based similarity measure. In the following we describe several application scenarios where learning the similarity measure (or parts of it), may also facilitate the development of powerful CBR applications.

3.1   Distributed Utility Knowledge

In many application domains the users of a knowledge-based expert system are often more or less experienced experts in the domain themselves. Thus, they are principally able to recognize faulty or suboptimal solutions proposed by the system. If we develop expert systems that give expert users the possibility to communicate these deficiencies back to the system, this feedback can obviously be used to avoid similar errors in the future use of the system.

Consider a typical CBR application that provides the user with a set of alternative solutions ranked by their utility estimated by the system's internal similarity measure. Further, we assume that the system does not perform case adaptation. If the user disagrees with the presented case ranking due to his well-founded domain knowledge, we should give her/him the possibility to comment the unsatisfactory retrieval result. This leads again to the case order feedback required by the top-down approach and can be used to improve the faulty similarity measure.

By employing this feedback possibility, the system will be enabled to acquire domain knowledge from all its users. This means, by and by the system will encode particular background knowledge of several domain experts in its similarity measure. This may enable the system to obtain respective high expertise that may lead to powerful problem solving capabilities. Nevertheless, it must be considered that the feedback from different users may contain an increased amount of contradictions leading to more noisy training data.

3.2   Personalized Utility Requirements

Another situation occurs if different users of a CBR system make different demands on the case retrieval. This means, for identical queries, cases may have different utilities depending on the context of the particular user.

For example, consider a product recommendation system in e-Commerce. Here the users are customers with individual preferences with respect to the offered products. For example, some customers focus more on the price of a product while others are mainly interested in the technical properties. These preferences can be represented in form of attributes weights, i.e. they can be encoded into the similarity measure used to retrieve suitable products. However, this approach may significantly increase the knowledge engineering effort when developing a recommendation system based on CBR. Instead of defining one domain specific similarity measure, one has to define several measures that consider the specific preferences of individual customers or customer classes, respectively. But even if one is willed to put up with this additional effort, it is still an open question how to acquire the required knowledge.

We argue that the presented learning approach is able to facilitate both issues. Firstly, it may reduce the effort to define several similarity measures. Secondly, it is probably the only feasible way to obtain the required knowledge. To apply the approach on the described scenario, one has to define one or several initial similarity measures that approximate the user specific utility measures as well as possible. During the use of the system one has to acquire case order feedback from the users to learn more specific measures for each user or user class. Generally, one can distinguish between two basic possibilities to obtain case order feedback from customers:

Passive Approach: Here, the feedback is only collected implicitly, e.g. by observing the buying patterns of customers.
Active Approach: To obtain more training data with higher quality one can alternatively ask the users for explicit feedback about the presented case ranking. However, this approach is coupled with the risk to annoy the user.

3.3   Maintenance of Utility Knowledge

Another important issue is that the utility function to be approximated by the similarity measure may change with the time. The changing of domain knowledge and the resulting necessity for maintaining this knowledge is a well-known problem in AI. Especially rule-based systems are strongly affected by this maintenance problem. One strength of traditional CBR systems is that a major part of the required knowledge is represented in form of cases. The maintenance of case knowledge is much easier and a lot of respective strategies already have been developed [8,9,11].

However, if we employ utility-based measures instead of pure distance-based measures, we are confronted with an additional maintenance problem. How to ensure the retrieval of the most useful cases even if the underlying utility function is changing with the time?

One idea is to check the retrieval quality in fixed periods by evaluating some example queries. To get a measure for the retrieval quality one can determine the value of the error function E introduced in section 2.2. If the value exceeds a critical threshold it is possible to start the learning approach by using the previously evaluated retrieval results.

Another idea corresponds to the strategies discussed in the two precedent scenarios. If we enable the user to give feedback on the retrieval results computed during the daily use of the system, and if we assume that the users possess implicit knowledge about the changing utility function, it should be possible to adapt the similarity measure continuously.

3.4   Considering Adaptability of Cases

Although most commercial CBR systems still neglect the adaptation phase of the CBR cycle, many researchers have already remarked that performing adaptation makes a special demand on the similarity measure to be used in the precedent retrieval step [7,10]. Instead to guarantee the retrieval of cases that contain a solution that is maximally useful for the current problem directly, the similarity measure has to consider the *adaptability* of cases. This means, under certain circumstances it might be better to select a particular case with a solution that is less useful than the solutions contained in other cases. This situation occurs if this solution can be adapted more easily to solve the given problem compared with the alternative solutions.

However, the definition of similarity measures that approximate this special kind of utility function is a really difficult task due to the complex dependencies between the particular adaptation procedure, the available cases, and the causal relationships in the application domain. We argue that it is mostly easier to define the domain specific similarity measure that estimates the straight utility of a solution than to define the mentioned measure that considers the adaptability of cases. However, if we assume the existence of the *domain specific measure* sim_U, it should be possible to learn the *adaptability measure* sim_A more or less automatically by employing the top-down approach.

Therefore, we initialize sim_A with sim_U and present an example query to the CBR system. The system starts a retrieval on its case base and returns the n most similar cases with respect to sim_A. Then, we apply the adaptation procedure to all these n cases that do not contain an optimal solution. After this adaptation phase we reorder the finally proposed solutions again by using sim_U. The resulting order represents the kind of case order feedback required by the learning algorithm and can be used to optimize sim_A.

Obviously, this application scenario is coupled with a major advantage. If we presume the existence of the measure sim_U and if we have access to a sufficient amount of example queries[2], we are able to generate the training data required for the learning algorithm automatically. Therefore, the amount of available training data is only restricted by the available computation resources. Due to the fact that the amount of training data is one of the most crucial aspects in machine learning, a significant improvement of sim_A should be realistic, provided that our hypotheses space (here, the representation of the similarity measure) contains an appropriate hypotheses (here, an adequate sim_A).

In the next section some results of an experimentally evaluation of an example application corresponding to the recently discussed scenario are presented.

4   Experimental Evaluation

For the evaluation we have used a typical e-Commerce domain where adaptation increases the performance of a CBR system significantly: the recommendation of personal computers[3]. In our domain the case representation consists of 11 attributes describing the basic properties of a PC like price, CPU-clock, RAM-size, etc. To enable the system to perform product customization we have defined about 20 more and less complex adaptation rules, for example, to adapt the size of the RAM or to add additional components (CD-Recorder, DVD-Drive, etc.). As described in Section 3.4, the selection of an adequate case prior adaptation is a crucial issue for the success of the defined adaptation rules due to the impact of technical constraints. To learn a similarity measure sim_A (here only the attribute weights) that considers the adaptability of the personal computers contained in the case base with respect to a given query, we have employed the learning approach discussed before.

4.1   The Experiment

Figure 3 illustrates the performed experiment. Firstly, we have generated case order feedback by creating 600 queries randomly, performing adaptation of all retrieved cases[4] and reordering the cases by using a predefined utility measure sim_U[5]. After that we split the obtained data in a training set S_{train} (33%) and a test set S_{test} (66%). To learn the attribute weights of the measure sim_A, we incrementally applied our learning algorithm based on a gradient search (for details see [12]) by using an increasing subset of the training data S_{train}.

In the evaluation phase we used the learned measure sim_{A_i} (i denotes the number of used training examples) to start new retrievals for all queries contained

---

[2] Example queries may be generated randomly or may be collected within the application domain. However, solutions for these example problems are not required!

[3] The employed recommendation system has been implemented by using the CBR shell CBR-Works. See also http://www.cbr-web.org

[4] The initially used case base contained about 20 cases

[5] sim_U has been defined by employing the bottom-up approach

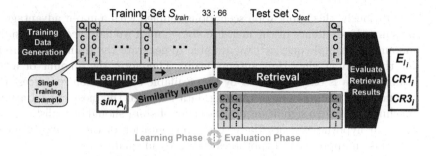

Fig. 3. The Experiment

in S_{test}, whereby we obtained respective case rankings. To get a measure for the quality of these case rankings — and therewith a measure for the success of the learning procedure — we counted the percentage of retrievals where the optimal case was returned as most "similar" case (denoted by $CR1_i$) or within the 3 most "similar" cases (denoted by $CR3_i$), respectively. The information about the optimal cases was available in form of the test data S_{test}. Further, we computed the value of the index error E_I (see [12]) that can be viewed as a measure for the quality of the entire retrieval results. However, for the described application the first two measures are more meaningful, because in practice it is only feasible to adapt some few cases after the retrieval due to the time constraints in the e-Commerce scenario.

To obtain statistical relevant results we have repeated the described experiment 10 times, everytime with newly generated data S_{train} and S_{test}. Finally, we determined the best, the worst and the average values of the introduced quality measures.

4.2   Evaluation Results

Figure 4 shows the results of the described evaluation procedure. The x-axis represents in both charts the number of used training examples. Therefore, the start situation, i.e. the obtained retrieval results when using the initial measure sim_U, is represented on the very left side of the charts. With an increasing amount of used training data a clear increase of all three determined quality measures can be observed. On the one hand, the percentage of retrievals that return the optimal case increased in average from 27% up to 41% w.r.t. the measure $CR1$ and from 52% up to 67% w.r.t. the measure $CR3$. On the other hand, the index error decreased in average from 25.8 down to 21.4. Surprising is the fact that a relative small number of training examples (about 15) was sufficient to reach nearly the optimal results. A decrease of the quality of the learned measure sim_A (probably caused by overfitting the training data) only occurred sometimes when using less than 6 training examples.

In our point of view, these results clearly show the power of our approach, at least for the application scenario discussed in Section 3.4. Firstly, it has to

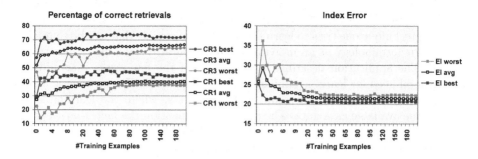

Fig. 4. Evaluation Results

be considered that we have only optimized the attribute weights and not the entire similarity measure. When optimizing the two remaining elements of the similarity measure, a further improvement of the retrieval quality is very likely. Secondly, it has to be considered that the optimization procedure does not lead to any additional effort for the knowledge engineer in this particular application scenario. The required training data is generated by using the already defined utility measure sim_U and therefore the entire optimization can be performed absolutely automatically. Due to the fact that the amount of available training data is only restricted by the available computation time, the risk of overfitting this data is also negligible low. Hence, introducing a specific similarity measure that estimates the adaptability of cases and learning this measure by applying the top-down approach can significantly improve CBR systems that employ adaptation.

5   Related Work

Although a lot of approaches to learn feature weights have been developed ([13,2,14]), these approaches are usually not suited to realize the discussed top-down procedure for learning utility-based similarity measures. The problem is that they address the traditional classification task and therefore presume training examples consisting of problem descriptions and corresponding classes. However, CBR is widely-used for more general problem tasks (e.g. recommendation systems in e-Commerce) where such a kind of training data is not available. An interesting approach to learn customer preferences in e-Commerce is presented in [3]. The training data used here, called *return-set selections*, is comparable with the case order feedback presumed by our approach.

Another research area that is interested in retrieving useful items is Information Retrieval (IR). Here, *relevance feedback* acquired from the system users is used to improve the retrieval capabilities of the system. One difference to our approach is, that this feedback only signs retrieved items either as relevant or not relevant. A finer estimation of the utility, e.g. by comparing different items, is not considered. Further, the IR systems usually do not learn a general representation (comparable with a similarity measure), they rather try to extend the given queries with additional key terms to obtain a more specific query. With this technique one tries to learn the *actual user context* that can be characterized in our terminology as an individual and temporarily valid utility function [5].

The application described in [6] is one of the few works that address the general need for learning similarity measures in CBR. Here, a genetic algorithm is used to learn the index and feature weights, where the learning is driven by the available case data. The authors also mention the fact, that learning the similarity measure can be characterized as knowledge acquisition or maintenance depending on whether knowledge is being created or refined.

6 Conclusion

In this paper we have discussed that the traditional bottom-up procedure to defining utility-based similarity measures can lead to the well-known knowledge acquisition problem. To avoid this problem we have proposed to learn this knowledge by using a special kind of training data, called *case order feedback*. We argue that under certain circumstances this alternative top-down approach can significantly facilitate the definition of similarity measures. In our point of view it is sometimes even the only feasible way to get a good approximation of the underlying utility function with reasonable effort. To show the feasibility of the top-down approach, we have finally presented some evaluation results for one of the previously discussed application scenarios.

Generally, one can point out that a combination of the bottom-up and the top-down approach is possible (see Section 2.3). Such a combination may lead to clear advantages compared with the application of only one of these approaches. The use of a partially predefined similarity measure when applying the top-down approach obviously decreases the hypotheses space to be considered by the learning algorithm, at least when following the constraint strategy. Another aspect is that the comprehension of available well-founded domain knowledge will inevitably reduce the amount of training data required to learn a similarity measure that approximates the utility function sufficiently. Last but not least, the consideration of domain constraints during the learning process reduces the risk that the learned similarity measure overfitts the given training data [4].

In the future we plan to apply the top-down approach to learn the entire similarity measure rather than only the attribute weights. Further, an application of the presented ideas on the other discussed application scenarios is necessary to prove the general power of the top-down approach. Due to the lack of generic approaches to guarantee similarity measures with high quality, we see an urgent need for further research in this area.

References

1. R. Bergmann, M. Michael Richter, S. Schmitt, A. Stahl, and I. Vollrath. Utility-oriented matching: A new research direction for Case-Based Reasoning. In *Professionelles Wissensmanagement: Erfahrungen und Visionen. Proceedings of the 1st Conference on Professional Knowledge Management.* Shaker, 2001.

2. A. Bonzano, P. Cunningham, and B. Smyth. Using introspective learning to improve retrieval in CBR: A case study in air traffic control. In *Proceedings of the 2nd International Conference on Case-Based Reasoning*. Springer, 1997.

3. K. Branting. Acquiring customer preferences from return-set selections. In *Proceedings of the 4th International Conference on Case-Based Reasoning*. Springer, 2001.

4. Pedro Domingos. The role of occam's razor in knowledge discovery. *Data Mining and Knowledge Discovery*, 3(4):409–425, 1999.

5. A. Goker. Capturing information need by learning user context. In *Working Notes of the Workshop on Learning about Users, 16th International Joint Conference in Artificial Intelligence*, 1999.

6. J. Jarmulak, S. Craw, and R. Rowe. Genetic algorithms to optimise CBR retrieval. In *Proceedings of the 5th European Workshop on Case-Based Reasoning*. Springer, 2000.

7. D. Leake, A. Kinley, and D. Wilson. Linking adaptation and similarity learning. In *Proceedings of the 18th Annual Conference of the Cognitive Science Society*. Hillsdale, NJ: Lawrence Erlbaum, 1996.

8. D. Leake and D. Wilson. Remembering why to remember: Performance-guided case-base maintenance. In *Proceedings of the 5th European Workshop on Case-Based Reasoning: Advances in Case-Based Reasoning*. Springer, 2000.

9. T. Reinartz, I. Iglezakis, and T. Roth-Berhofer. On quality measures for case base maintenance. In *Proceedings of the 5th European Workshop on Case-Based Reasoning: Advances in Case-Based Reasoning*. Springer, 2000.

10. B. Smyth and M. T. Keane. Retrieving adaptable cases: The role of adaptation knowledge in case retrieval. In *Proceedings of the 1st European Workshop on Case-Based Reasoning*. Springer, 1993.

11. B. Smyth and E. McKenna. Modelling the competence of case-bases. In *Proceedings of the 4th European Workshop on Case-Based Reasoning*. Springer, 1998.

12. A. Stahl. Learning feature weights from case order feedback. In *Proceedings of the 4th International Conference on Case-Based Reasoning*. Springer, 2001.

13. Dietrich Wettschereck and David W. Aha. Weighting features. In *Proceeding of the 1st International Conference on Case-Based Reasoning*. Springer Verlag, 1995.

14. Z. Zhang and Q. Yang. Dynamic refiniement of feature weights using quantitative introspective learning. In *Proceedings of the 16th International Joint Conference on Artificial Intelligence*, 1999.

Learning to Adapt for Case-Based Design*

Nirmalie Wiratunga[1], Susan Craw[1], and Ray Rowe[2]

[1] School of Computing,
The Robert Gordon University,
Aberdeen AB25 1HG, Scotland, UK
{nw|s.craw}@scms.rgu.ac.uk
[2] AstraZeneca
Macclesfield, Cheshire SK10 2NA, England, UK

Abstract. Design is a complex open-ended task and it is unreasonable to expect a case-base to contain representatives of all possible designs. Therefore, adaptation is a desirable capability for case-based design systems, but acquiring adaptation knowledge can involve significant effort. In this paper adaptation knowledge is induced separately for different criteria associated with the retrieved solution, using knowledge sources implicit in the case-base. This provides a committee of learners and their combined advice is better able to satisfy design constraints and compatibility requirements compared to a single learner. The main emphasis of the paper is to evaluate the impact of specific-to-general and general-to-specific learning on adaptation knowledge acquired by committee members. For this purpose we conduct experiments on a real tablet formulation problem which is tackled as a decomposable design task. Evaluation results suggest that adaptation achieves significant gains compared to a retrieve-only CBR system, but shows that both learning biases can be beneficial for different decomposed sub-tasks.

1 Introduction

Reuse of previously solved problems is attractive because human problem-solving is often also experience-based. However past experiences cannot always be directly applied to new situations without some adaptation to suit the current problem. This is particularly true for design problems because it is unreasonable to expect a case-base to contain all possible design cases. Hence, adaptation is often necessary before a retrieved design can be successfully re-used in new circumstances.

Unlike retrieval, adaptation typically requires a significant knowledge engineering effort. This is a common obstacle for both classification and design tasks. However, adaptation for non-classification tasks is a more challenging problem [18]. For instance, a design solution typically consists of multiple properties rather than a single class label, furthermore design solutions are subject to constraints and compatibility requirements which are often difficult to elicit from domain experts. For these reasons there is a clear need for effective knowledge acquisition tools for design. It is this need that motivates the research presented in this paper.

---

* This work is supported by EPSRC grant GR/L98015 awarded to Susan Craw.

S. Craw and A. Preece (Eds.): ECCBR 2002, LNAI 2416, pp. 421–435, 2002.

We explore how a committee of learners can be employed to acquire adaptation knowledge enabling the committee to predict desirable modifications to a retrieved design. The main thrust of the paper is to investigate how different learning biases influence the committee's advice and the impact of generalised and specialised adaptation knowledge on overall solution accuracy. We use the tablet formulation application [2] to demonstrate our approach to adaptation, but it is more generally applicable to other component-based design tasks. Other examples include formulation more generally (e.g. rubber for Pirelli racing tyres [1]) and configuration (e.g. PC configuration [17]). Tablet formulation is particularly challenging because the formulation for a tablet is not unique, and most importantly as in other real-world problems we have relatively small amounts of formulation data.

In Section 2 we briefly describe different yet complementary algorithms that can be used for learning adaptation knowledge. A description of component-based design in the context of tablet formulation is presented in Section 3. In Section 4, we consider knowledge sources useful for learning adaptation knowledge, and show how these sources can be used to cast learning of adaptation knowledge as a classification task. The committee-based adaptation approach is discussed in Section 5, where multiple learners provide adaptation advice applicable to a retrieved design solution. Experimental results for tablet formulation appear in Section 6. An overview of current trends in the acquisition of adaptation knowledge, and how adaptation techniques introduced in this paper relate to existing techniques, are discussed in Section 7, followed by conclusions in Section 8.

2   Learning Algorithms and Boosting

We look at two different learning algorithms that can be employed to induce adaptation knowledge. In particular we look at RISE [4] a hybrid algorithm that combines induction and instance-based learning, and how it differs from the commonly used C4.5 [12]. Boosting is known to improve the performance of learning algorithms particularly with tasks that exhibit varying degrees of difficulty [5]. Since this is typical of design tasks we also look at how boosting is incorporated with C4.5 and how it can be used with RISE.

2.1   Learning Algorithms

The commonly used C4.5 algorithm induces decision trees by recursively selecting discriminatory attributes by means of the information gain heuristic. The effect of selecting a feature is that the problem space is divided into regions according to its values. The partitions correspond to hyper-planes that are orthogonal to the axis of the selected feature and parallel to all other axes. C4.5 employs a divide and conquer approach, so the number of training examples to which the heuristic is applied decreases with progressive recursive iterations. The approach is top-down, moving in a *general-to-specific* direction. Therefore the tree size, particularly the number of leaf nodes (corresponding to the number of regions in the divided problem space), is a good indicator of the complexity of the task. Indeed, when the problem space does not adhere to orthogonal hyper-plane

Input: ES is the training set

MaxTrials: 10
let trial = 1

Rise (ES)
    Let RS be ES
    Compute Acc(RS)
    Repeat
        Foreach rule R in RS
            find the nearest example E to R
            not covered by R, and of R's class
            let R' = generalised R now covering E
            let RS' = RS with R replaced by R'
            if Acc(RS') $\geq$ Acc(RS)
            then let RS = RS'
                delete duplicate rules in RS
    Until no increase in Acc(RS)
    return RS

boostedRise
    Foreach example, E in ES
        let E's weight, w = 1 / size(ES)
    Repeat
        let rules, RS = RISE (ES)
        let err = 1 - Acc(RS)
        Foreach E in ES
            if E is correctly classified
                let E's weight, w =w*(err/1-err)
        re-normalise all weights
        let ruleset[trial] = RS
        let trial = trial + 1
    Until (err $\geq$ 0.5) or (trial $\geq$ MaxTrials)

Fig. 1. The RISE algorithm

Fig. 2. Boosting RISE

regions it is usual to observe an increased number of leaf nodes. In general though, increased tree size is a sign that a different bias may be appropriate; for instance that of Nearest Neighbour (NN).

The hybrid RISE algorithm combines 1-NN with rule induction and is different from C4.5 in several ways:

- rules are induced in parallel and the hill-climbing heuristic takes into consideration the accuracy on the entire rule set instead of a divide and conquer approach; and
- direction of search is *specific-to-general* where rules are generalised by broadening numeric intervals and dropping conditions, instead of selecting an attribute at each iteration to add as an extra discriminatory condition.

Figure 1 shows pseudo-code for the RISE algorithm. The boosted version in Figure 2 is described in Section 2.2. RISE treats each example in the training set as a specialised rule at the start. For instance given an example e_1 consisting of two features and a class; (f_1=blue,f_2=0.5,class=yes), the corresponding specific RISE rule, r_1 is: if (f_1=blue) and ($0.5 \leq f_2 \leq 0.5$) then yes. Learning is achieved by generalising the rule as follows:

- identify the best match example for the rule that is not already associated with this rule and having the rule's class (see [4] for the modified Euclidean distance measure used to establish distance between an example and a rule); and
- attempt to generalise the rule so that the identified example is covered by the rule; i.e. the rule's conditions are met by the new example's features.

Consider example, e_2, with the following description and class; (f_1=blue, f_2=0.6, class =yes). Assuming this is the best match for r_1, the generalisation of r_1 will result in: if ($f_1 = blue$) and ($0.5 \leq f_2 \leq 0.6$) then yes. If however example e_3 with (f_1=red, f_2=0.5, class=yes) is the best match then the generalised r_1 will be: if (true) and ($0.5 \leq$

$f_2 \leq 0.5$) then *yes*. Notice that dropping antecedent ($f_1 = blue$) is similar to stating that the condition is always satisfied by any example.

A generalised rule is accepted only if the accuracy on the whole training set is not adversely affected. This process is repeated until there is no further increase in accuracy. Since the training examples are treated as rules, initially the accuracy on the training set will be 100%. Therefore, to get around this problem, the accuracy measure ($Acc(RS)$), uses a leave-one-out methodology: when classifying an example, its corresponding rule is left out, unless the rule can also be satisfied by other examples in the training set. In the worst situation no generalisations are accepted, and the final rule set contains the specific rules corresponding to each training example in the training set. This would result in a pure instance-based algorithm or 1-NN. However, it is more likely that the final rule set may contain some generalised rules in addition to the specific ones.

When classifying a test (unseen) example RISE identifies the rules that are nearest to the example. If there is only one such rule then that rule is the winning rule and is applied to generate a solution. If however there are several rules at equal distance to the example, then a conflict resolution strategy is necessary. RISE's strategy is to choose the one with the highest (Laplace) accuracy. However when there are several rules with equal accuracy RISE chooses the rule predicting the most frequent class and breaks any ties randomly. According to this scheme a covering rule does not necessarily become the winning rule, because the winning rule is ascertained by the distance to the example followed by conflict resolution. Figure 3 illustrates a series of test examples represented by two numeric features where classification depends on the distance to 2 generalised and 10 specific rules. The two rectangles represent the generalised rules, and the scattered + and - represent specific rules. The ? indicates various test examples. The text in the figure explains how RISE identifies the winning rule for each circumstance, where the circles represent the search region when NN is employed.

2.2   Boosting

The general idea of boosting is to iteratively generate several learners, with each learner biased by the incorrectly solved training examples in the previous iteration or trial. This is achieved by associating weights with training examples and updating these weights at each trial. Weights of correctly solved training examples are decreased and this has the effect of increasing the weights of incorrectly solved training examples. It means that the learner tries harder to correctly solve these difficult training examples in the next trial. The votes of classifiers formed at each trial need to be combined in order to classify a test example; a majority vote is applied. However it makes sense to trust those classifiers that have a higher accuracy on the training set and therefore the vote is typically weighted by this accuracy.

Boosting has been incorporated with C4.5 [13]. In short C4.5's mechanism that is already in place for dealing with fractional values associated with examples having missing attribute values is exploited. This means that during boosted learning the information gain calculations will be based on weighted examples. Since incorrectly classified examples are given higher weights with boosting, the information gain heuristic will tend to favour features that are discriminatory of examples that were incorrectly solved in previous trials.

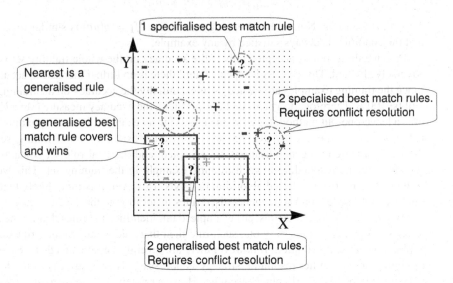

Fig. 3. RISE identifying the winning rule when classifying a test example

We have explored ways to incorporate boosting with RISE (Figure 2). Initially all N training examples are assigned the same weight of $1/N$. At each trial the weights are updated so that weights of correctly classified examples are reduced according to the error rate of the ruleset. In practice once weights are updated, they need to be re-normalised so that their sum remains at one. The impact of updated weights will be reflected by the weighted accuracy in RISE, and this in turn will influence the generalisations that are accepted during learning. Essentially, this means that previously abandoned generalisations may be accepted in subsequent boosted trials due to higher weights associated with the few examples that are now correctly classified and, lower weights associated with examples that are now incorrectly classified. The boosting mechanisms adopted here is similar to AdaBoost.M1 [5], the only difference being that, when classifying a test example, the (Laplace) accuracy of individual rules is used for the weighted vote instead of the learner's accuracy (also suggested in [13]).

3   The Problem Domain

Formulating a tablet for a given dose of a new drug involves choosing inert *excipients* (e.g. Lactose, Maize-Starch, etc.) to mix with the drug so that the tablet can be manufactured in a robust form. A tablet consists of five *components* with distinct roles (Figure 4). However, an excipient can be used as one or more components; e.g. the excipient Maize Starch can not only be used as a filler but also as a disintegrant. The formulation task entails identifying a suitable excipient for each component ensuring that its physical and chemical properties enable it to operate in the desired role. Chosen excipients must also be compatible with each other and the drug.

The tablet formulation task falls within the broader problem category of design, and in particular decomposable design. Unlike classification problems, a design consists of

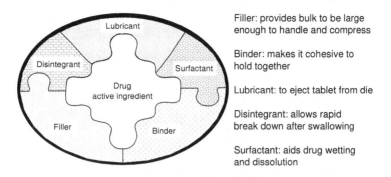

Filler: provides bulk to be large enough to handle and compress

Binder: makes it cohesive to hold together

Lubricant: to eject tablet from die

Disintegrant: allows rapid break down after swallowing

Surfactant: aids drug wetting and dissolution

Fig. 4. The drug and five tablet components

multiple sub-parts that together form the solution. Invariably, solutions are sought by decomposing the task into sub-tasks and then finding compatible sub-solutions to each sub-task. Typically design sub-tasks are solved individually, by invoking a CBR cycle to handle each of the sub-tasks, before combining the sub-solutions. It is often sensible to solve the sub-tasks sequentially, whereby the sub-solutions from previous cycles can guide problem-solving for later sub-tasks [11,14].

Choosing a suitable excipient for each component are the subtasks for tablet formulation. In fact human formulators adopt such an approach. When given a new problem consisting of the drug and its dose, the most constrained component, Filler, and its quantity are chosen first, followed by Binder, then Disintegrant, Surfactant and finally the Lubricant. We found that separate CBR cycles were useful to solve each component and that incremental instantiations of the problem with each progressive iteration ensured that excipients selected later are compatible with previous ones [2]. This meant that when choosing the binder, the filler already chosen in the previous iteration would also contribute towards the problem solving process for the binder.

4   Adaptation Knowledge

Learning adaptation knowledge requires access to a set of past experiences of retrieved solutions and how these solutions were adapted to suit the new problem. For this purpose we exploit the data already in the case-base to form adaptation training examples (Figure 5). A single case from the *original* case-base is used as the *probe* case and the remaining cases form a cut-down case-base which is used for a retrieve-only CBR system. The probe case acts as an unseen problem for this system. In response to each probe case, the system retrieves cases that are above some similarity threshold. Since we know the solutions to all cases in the original case-base (in particular the probe's), each *retrieved* case, together with its probe case are utilised to form an *adaptation training case*. The adaptation training set thus formed is used to induce adaptation knowledge. This new knowledge will be applied at the adaptation stage by the original CBR system when solving new problems.

Task decomposition reduces the complexity of adaptation knowledge because adaptations can now be applied to sub-solutions. However, when inducing adaptation knowl-

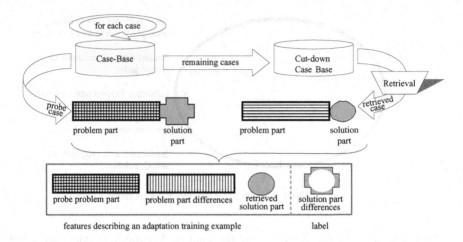

Fig. 5. Forming adaptation training examples

edge for a specific sub-solution, we must ensure that the learner is informed of previous sub-solutions and their interactions. We have identified *Knowledge sources* useful when learning adaptation knowledge for decomposable design problems and briefly outline them here under two broad categories:

Adaptation triggers
- problem properties (e.g. dose and drug properties);
- component interaction properties (e.g. properties of the filler identified in the previous sub-task when solving the binder in the current sub-task); and
- constraining properties (e.g. maximum tablet weight)

Adaptation targets
- component static properties (e.g. filler name, filler solubility); and
- component compatibility properties (e.g. stability of filler with the drug)

The knowledge sources grouped under *adaptation triggers* are useful to describe circumstances that suggest the need for adaptation. For this purpose, problem properties are an obvious knowledge source. Component interaction properties are less obvious but are common with decomposable design tasks; interactions with sub-solutions from previous iterations are useful when determining sub-solutions in future iterations. Constraining properties are typical for design tasks in general. The *adaptation targets* group identifies knowledge sources that collectively describe a component. These are used to express how the necessary adaptations might be realised. The static properties include properties of the component that remain unaffected (by other components or the problem properties), while component compatibility properties refer to properties of the component that change with the new problem properties.

For the tablet formulation task a solution consists of; an excipient name and quantity for each tablet component. Experimental results in [8] were convincing for adaptation of quantities, so in this paper, we concentrate on excipient names. Therefore, when adaptation is triggered the modifications to adaptation targets need to be applied with a view to identifying suitable excipients for components. In the rest of this section we look at how adaptation training examples are created using the knowledge sources just described and how the output of adaptation learning can be utilised to identify desirable modification of retrieved solutions.

4.1   Features of a Training Example for Adaptation

In Figure 5 the first two sets of features for the *adaptation training example* are formed by the problem part of the probe case (cross pattern), and the differences (vertical lines) between this and the problem part of the retrieved similar case (horizontal lines). The problem part consists of properties grouped under adaptation triggers; for tablet formulation these include drug properties including its dose, and properties of excipients selected in previous iterations.

The retrieved solution part (oval shape with uneven outline) consists of component properties; i.e. adaptation targets. For tablet formulation if the sub-task is the filler component then these include the name of the retrieved excipient (such as Lactose) and the excipient's static properties (such as solubility of Lactose), while the excipient's stability with the retrieved case's drug is a compatibility property. However, compatibility properties of the retrieved filler in relation to the new drug must be ascertained. It is the properties of this refined retrieved solution (oval shape with even outline) that is included as the third set of features for the adaptation training example. Any further mention of the retrieved solution refers to this refined solution.

Since we know the actual component solution for the probe case (cross shape), and that for the retrieved case (oval shape), the differences between these two solution parts can also be ascertained. These differences need to be translated into concepts that are meaningful in the context of learning adaptation knowledge before we can label the adaptation training example. For instance with tablet formulation a known design constraint is:

if the drug is insoluble then the filler should be soluble

Accordingly, adaptation knowledge related to the solubility (component property) of the retrieved filler (component) captured by adaptation training examples should ideally have the following flavour:

if the drug is insoluble and the retrieved filler is insoluble then select another filler with an INCreased solubility

Here the translation from retrieved to adapted filler component is facilitated by the *adaptation action*, increase. Accordingly, an adaptation action can be used as the label for the adaptation training example. This is derived from the difference between the probe and retrieved case's solution parts. The learning algorithms can be used to induce knowledge which amounts to predicting adaptation actions. Generating an adapted solution involves the application of the predicted action to the retrieved solution. In this example it would mean selecting a filler with a greater solubility than the retrieved filler, and presenting its name as the adapted solution.

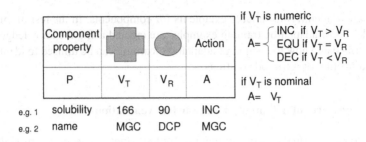

Fig. 6. Deriving adaptation actions to form concepts for adaptation learning

4.2   Adaptation Actions

In Figure 6, the cross and oval shapes correspond to the actual (target) and retrieved solution components from Figure 5. For instance P could be a numeric property, such as the *solubility* of the filler, or it could be a nominal property, such as the *name* of the filler. For numeric P, an adaptation action A is chosen from INC, DEC or EQU. according to the difference between the target value V_T (of P) from the probe case and the retrieved value V_R (also of P) from the retrieved case. In Figure 6, with *solubility*, the derived adaptation action is INC because V_T is greater than V_R. This action indicates that the training example captures a situation when the solubility should be increased. For nominal properties the adaptation action is an explicit mapping from V_R to V_T. The second example in Figure 6 illustrates this with filler *name*. Here DCP, is mapped to the target filler name, MGC.

5   Adaptation with a Committee of Experts

The set of adaptation training examples is utilised by a set of learners $learner_i$, and the result of each learning is an adaptation $expert_i$; an expert that predicts adaptation actions applicable to P_i. Here P_i can be any one of the component properties grouped under adaptation targets. Design constraints typically concern multiple component properties and require balancing of these properties to achieve consistency. A component described using m properties provides a different learning opportunity with each of its properties, i.e. we can learn actions associated with not just one, but all m. Therefore, for a set of component properties, $\{P_1, \ldots, P_m\}$, we have m *learners*, each predicting adaptation actions applicable to a single property. With large m it makes sense to apply feature selection to P_i, thereby reducing the number of classifiers. Presently for a given component role (e.g. filler, binder) we use the n most discriminatory component properties from a C4.5 decision tree that uniquely identifies each of the potential components by predicting the component's name [10].

5.1   Role of an Adaptation Expert

Figure 7 illustrates how adaptation experts are used to solve a new adaptation task. The new task is formed using the problem part of the new probe case, and the differences between this and the problem part of the retrieved case. The solution part which is the component for the retrieved case is represented by the oval (uneven outline). This retrieved solution is refined (oval with even outline) before it is included as part of the new adaptation task; i.e. new compatibilities are derived according to the probe's problem properties. The ? indicates that the component name for the new problem is not known and needs to be established with the aid of the adaptation experts (3 in this case). Each expert predicts an adaptation action applicable to a different property of the retrieved component.

Let us consider $expert_1$ in Figure 7 predicting INC applicable to a numeric property, for instance like $solubility$ in Figure 6. In response to $expert_1$'s suggestion (INC) a component having a greater value for $solubility$ (compared to the retrieved component's value) will be selected. In Figure 7 there are two candidate solutions consistent with $expert_1$'s prediction. When expert predictions are associated with a nominal property then the adaptation selects components having the predicted value for the nominal property. A slightly different situation occurs for nominal predictions when the property concerned is the component's $name$. For instance $expert_2$ in Figure 7 predicts the $name$ of the component. In this situation there is no selection step, because the predicted $name$ explicitly identifies the component.

In addition to predicting an adaptation action an expert also provides the confidence in its prediction. When the expert is generated by a boosted learner, the confidence reflects the weighted proportion of votes for the action with the highest vote. Selected candidates inherit this confidence and so are equally good. In our example the single candidate for $expert_2$ has confidence 0.6, while both candidates compatible with $expert_1$'s prediction have confidence of 0.5. Generally, suggestions made by all experts are considered in order to make an informed choice between candidate components.

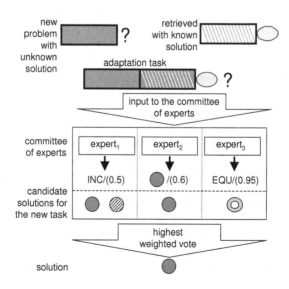

Fig. 7. Applying adaptation experts

5.2   Adaptation According to Majority Consensus

An adaptation committee is formed where each member $expert_i$, an output of $learner_i$, predicts an action applicable to P_i. With n members predicting n actions complete unanimity is unlikely when selecting a candidate. However, we can exploit majority consensus of the committee to select candidates that consolidate as many of the adaptation actions as possible. Credibility of the committee-based approach very much depends on the goodness of the committee, where committee members have an error rate of better than random guessing, and disagreement between members is uncorrelated [3].

The committee of experts is used to adapt a retrieved solution during the adaptation stage within the original CBR system. In Figure 7 the committee consists of three members. For a given adaptation task, each member predicts an adaptation action applicable to a different component property. Once candidate components are identified in step with each member's advice, the name of the candidate component with highest weighted vote is proposed as the best component solution for the new problem.

6   Evaluation

Our tablet formulation data set contains 156 formulations for 39 drugs. It is common for tablets of several doses of the same drug to have quite similar formulations so we apply a leave-N-*drug*-out testing. The test set for a single *test run* contains different doses for 4 randomly chosen drugs ($N = 4$) and the training set contains formulations for the remaining 35 drugs which form the (original) CBR system. Each drug has 4 formulations corresponding to different doses, and so the test set size is 16. The remaining 140 training cases form the case base of the CBR system, and the knowledge-light approach is applied to this set, using a leave-1-drug-out approach.

RETRIEVE, an optimised retrieve-only CBR system [7], is compared with 3 systems that also incorporate adaptation with a committee of adaptation experts: C4.5$_\Delta$ uses boosted C4.5; RISE$_\Delta$ applies boosted RISE; and 1-NN$_\Delta$ employs the 1-NN principle. We report our findings for the binder and filler components because they account for most of the tablet weight and have been found to be difficult [8]. The adaptation committee consisted of 3 adaptation experts for the binder, and 5 for the filler. The graphs show average accuracy for 25 test runs sorted in increasing order of RETRIEVE accuracy. Significance is reported from a one-sided paired t-test with 95% confidence.

Figure 8 shows the results for binder. Improvements in overall average accuracy from adaptation were significant: 34% for RETRIEVE, 65% for C4.5$_\Delta$, 70% for RISE$_\Delta$ and 71% for 1-NN$_\Delta$. Adaptation with all learning algorithms demonstrates substantial improvement over optimised retrieve-only, with accuracy more than doubled for two adaptation methods. The only run where RETRIEVE fairs better is 21, and close examination of this indicates that the various adaptation experts agreed on a single piece of wrong advice, resulting in similar incorrect candidate components being selected. The formulation data sets contain erroneous data, e.g. a value zero can denote "not entered" or "not relevant". Therefore it is likely that these expert errors are the outcome of noise.

The performance of RISE$_\Delta$ and 1-NN$_\Delta$ are significantly better than C4.5$_\Delta$, but are not significantly different from each other. RISE's specific-to-general search direction allows it to identify small exception regions that will go undetected (or be more badly

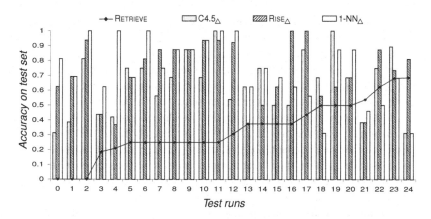

Fig. 8. Accuracy for binder

identified) by general-to-specific learners such as $C4.5$. With a few test runs RISE_Δ has faired worse than 1-NN_Δ. This might be explained by RISE's example generalisation to hyper-rectangles and classification of test examples according to its nearest hyper-rectangle. Since all features describing the adaptation task for tablet formulation consist of numeric features, generalisations can result in overlapping hyper-rectangles and hence be less accurate than 1-NN.

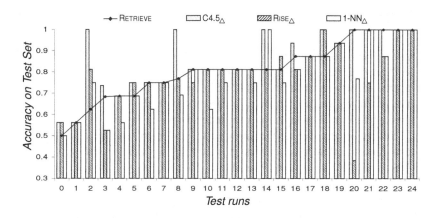

Fig. 9. Accuracy for filler

Figure 9 shows the filler results. Overall RETRIEVE's average accuracy of 81% was improved by $C4.5_\Delta$ to 86%. Although this improvement is significant, it is quite modest since retrieval accuracy is already high. We also found that $C4.5_\Delta$'s improvement is achievable with a single expert based on the component property *name*, instead of a committee. This may suggest that properties of the filler component are not important when solving the filler sub-task, because filler is the first of the decomposable sub-tasks.

RISE_Δ and 1-NN_Δ faired relatively poorly in the filler adaptation task with an overall average accuracy of 78% and 77% respectively. Close examination of test runs such as 3, 16, and 22 indicate that generalisation did not take place with RISE_Δ. Consequently the ruleset consisted of the initial set of specialised rules and RISE_Δ operates as 1-NN_Δ. Generally C4.5_Δ's learning bias of dividing the problem space into regions corresponding to hyper-planes seems to better suit the filler adaptation task compared to RISE_Δ's generalisations of examples into hyper-rectangles. In fact a majority of decision trees built for the filler task had significantly fewer nodes compared to trees formed for the binder adaptation task possibly suggestive that the filler adaptation task to be less specific than the binder adaptation task. Previous experiments with RISE [4] had confirmed RISE's advantage when concepts are highly specific, but had failed to produce the opposite result for general concepts, with both noise-free and noisy datasets.

It is interesting to observe that RETRIEVE works well for the filler task with accuracy at 81%, compared to 34% for the binder task. This is unexpected since the filler task seems harder with 8 potential fillers to choose from compared to 5 potential binders, using a similar training set size. RETRIEVE's inconsistent performance may suggest that the binder task is harder because it has to be compatible with both the drug and the filler. It is encouraging that the different knowledge sources (Section 4) selectively chosen and recorded by adaptation training examples, have nevertheless helped induce adaptation knowledge capable of improving upon RETRIEVE's performance with both decomposed sub-tasks.

7 Related Work

Research into adaptation has increasingly been devoted to developing domain independent knowledge acquisition tools. Our contribution falls within this area of research and is particularly focused on design tasks. Since adaptation knowledge is elicited from cases that are already available in the case-base our work also falls under the *knowledge light* approach to learning adaptation knowledge proposed in [19].

Systems that advocate the knowledge light approach typically apply adaptations according to differences between the new problem and the retrieved case's problem. McSherry's CREST system [9] explicitly finds a case-pair from the existing case-base with similar differences and uses the relationship between the pair to adapt the retrieved case. However we have found that problem differences alone are not sufficient, because the impact of differences often differ in different parts of the problem space. Therefore, our adaptation training examples record both the problem properties and their differences. For design problems the representation of adaptation training cases is further enriched with data from implicit knowledge sources in the case-base, such as component interaction and compatibility properties. While case retrieval is viewed as a search for the best match between the problem properties of the probe and cases in the case-base, adaptation is viewed as a search in the solution space for the right transformations from a retrieved solution to the target solution [16]. Adaptation actions that label our adaptation training examples are like transformations that when applied to the retrieved solution help identify a suitable target solution.

With real domains such as tablet formulation it is typical to operate with an incomplete case-base. In these circumstances generalisation from case-pair differences is an obvious choice. With Hanney & Keane [6]'s rule induction approach, initially each specific rule consists of all feature-value differences. These rules are then generalised in an approach similar to Domingos' RISE system [4]; i.e. specific-to-general rule learning by dropping or by extending antecedents to cover cases with similar solutions. Our evaluation results have shown that a specific-to-general approach need not always be the best approach to adaptation. Certainly the filler adaptation sub-task benefited from C4.5's approach to induction, while RISE's specific-to-general approach was better suited for the binder. This seems to suggest the need for a learner that can both generalise and specialise. The challenge is to identify heuristics that enable such a combined learner to establish the best bias with each induction opportunity.

Three forms of adaptation have been identified: substitutional, transformational and generative [15]. The retrieved tablet formulation needed to be refined so that compatibilities with the new drug are substituted for those of the old. The advice from the committee can be viewed as desirable transformations to a retrieved tablet formulation; for instance selecting an excipient with increased solubility is an indication that changed physical properties are required. Generative adaptation repeats the reasoning that achieved the retrieved solution for the new problem, requiring increasingly complex adaptation knowledge. Acquiring such knowledge using a knowledge-light approach might very well be challenging if not impossible.

8 Conclusions

The evaluation of different learning biases for committee based adaptation applied to a formulation task is a novel contribution of this paper. Adaptation knowledge was acquired by combining the outcome of multiple boosted learning sessions. The advice provided by these learners proved to be useful because multiple learners are better able to deliver the requirements of design tasks which often involve the consolidation of different components to form a plausible solution.

Translating solution differences into adaptation action concepts is particularly useful for design tasks, because predictions such as INC, EQU or DEC, capture adaptation circumstances that pose constraints on solution properties. This reduces significant knowledge engineering effort that would have been required if these constraints had to be elicited explicitly from a domain expert. Delegating adaptation learning associated with a single property to an individual classifier seems plausible. However, there is yet work to be done in order to establish which solution properties provide the best gain for identifying an adapted solution. Presently, expert advice is combined according to majority vote weighted by learner accuracy. This vote may need to be influenced by other CBR knowledge containers such as similarity and case-base indexing knowledge. This may help impose an order on proposed candidates, providing a more informed choice.

The use of multiple learners has been demonstrated using three different learning algorithms on the tablet formulation domain. An adaptation committee when formed with boosted C4.5 performed well for the filler sub-task while boosted RISE and 1-NN did better for the binder sub-task. Given the different learning biases of these algorithms there is a need to investigate how a CBR system can be equipped to differentiate between the varied adaptation needs of decomposed sub-tasks. For this purpose the ability to both specialise and generalise will be useful for automatic acquisition and refinement of adaptation knowledge.

References

1. Bandini, S., Manzoni, S.: CBR adaptation for chemical formulation. In *Proc 4th Int Conf on CBR*, pages 634–647, 2001. Springer.
2. Craw, S., Wiratunga, N., Rowe, R.: Case-based design for tablet formulation. In *Proc 4th European Workshop on CBR*, pages 358–369, 1998. Springer.
3. Dietterich, T.G.: Ensemble methods in machine learning. In *1st Int Workshop on Multiple Classifier Systems*, pages 1–15, 2000. Springer.
4. Domingos, P.: Unifying instance-based and rule-based induction. *ML*, 24:141–168, 1996.
5. Freund, Y., Schapire, R.: Experiments with a new boosting algorithm. In *Proc 13th Int Conf on Machine Learning*, pages 148–156, 1996.
6. Hanney, K., Keane, M.T.: The adaptation knowledge bottleneck: How to ease it by learning from cases. In *Proc of the 2nd Int Conf on CBR*, pages 359–370, 1997. Springer.
7. Jarmulak, J., Craw, S., Rowe, R.: Genetic algorithms to optimise CBR retrieval. In *Proc 5th European Workshop on CBR*, pages 137–149, 2000. Springer.
8. Jarmulak, J., Craw, S., Rowe, R.: Using case-base data to learn adaptation knowledge for design. In *Proc 17th IJCAI*, pages 1011–1016, 2001. Morgan Kaufmann.
9. McSherry, D.: An adaptation heuristic for case-based estimation. In *Proc 4th European Workshop on CBR*, pages 184–195, 1998. Springer.
10. McSherry, D.: Minimising dialog length in interactive case-based reasoning. In *Proc 17th IJCAI*, pages 993–998, 2001. Morgan Kaufmann.
11. Netten, B.D., Vingerhoeds, R.A.: Incremental adaptation for conceptual design in EADOCS. In *ECAI Workshop on Adaptation in CBR*, 1996.
12. Quinlan, J.R.: Induction of decision trees. *Machine Learning*, 1:81–106, 1986.
13. Quinlan, J.R.: Bagging, boosting, and C4.5. In *Proc 13th National Conf on AI*, pages 725–730, 1996.
14. Smyth, B., Cunningham, P.: Déjà Vu: A hierarchical case-based reasoning system for software design. In *Proc ECAI92*, pages 587–589, 1992. Wiley.
15. Smyth, B., Cunningham, P.: Complexity of adaptation in real-world case-based reasoning systems. In *Proc 6th Irish Conf on AI & Cognitive Science*, Ireland, 1993.
16. Smyth, B., Keane, M.T.: Adaptation-guided retrieval: Questioning the similarity assumption. *Artificial Intelligence*, 102:249–293, 1998.
17. Stahl, A., Bergmann, R.: Applying recursive CBR to the customisation of structured products in an electronic shop. In *Proc 5th European Workshop on CBR*, pages 297–308, 2000. Springer.
18. Wettschereck, D., Aha, D.W. (eds.): In *Proc ECML-97 Workshop on Case-Based Learning:Beyond Classification of Feature Vectors*, 1997. http://nathan.gmd.de/persons/dietrich.wettschereck/ecml97-wkshp/ecml97ws2.ps.
19. Wilke, W., Vollrath, I., Althoff, K.D., Bergmann, R.: A framework for learning adaptation knowledge based on knowledge light approaches. In *5th German Workshop on CBR*, 1997.

An Approach to Aggregating Ensembles of Lazy Learners That Supports Explanation[1]

Gabriele Zenobi and Pádraig Cunningham

Department of Computer Science
Trinity College Dublin
{Gabriele.Zenobi,Padraig.Cunningham}@cs.tcd.ie

Abstract: Ensemble research has shown that the aggregated output of an ensemble of predictors can be more accurate than a single predictor. This is true also for lazy learning systems like Case-Based Reasoning (CBR) and k-Nearest-Neighbour. Aggregation is normally achieved by voting in classification tasks and by averaging in regression tasks. For CBR, this increased accuracy comes at the cost of interpretability however. If we consider the use of retrieved cases for explanation to be one of the advantages of CBR then this is lost in an ensemble. This is because a large number of cases will have been retrieved by the ensemble members. In this paper we present a new technique for aggregation that obtains excellent results and identifies a small number of cases for use in explanation. This new approach might be viewed as a transformation process whereby cases are transformed from their feature based representation to a representation based on the predictions of ensemble members. This new representation produces very accurate predictions and allows a small number of similar neighbours to be identified.

1 Introduction

A major development in Machine Learning (ML) research in recent years is the realisation that ensembles of models can offer significant improvements in accuracy over single models. To define an ensemble we need two elements: a set of properly trained classifiers and an aggregation mechanism that composes the single predictions into an overall outcome. Typically, the aggregation process will be a simple average or a simple majority vote over the output of the ensembles, e.g. (Breiman, 1996). However, it may also be a complex linear or non-linear combination of the component predictions, e.g. (Jacobs et al., 1991, Heskes, 1998).

Whatever the aggregation process, it has implications for interpretability if the ensemble is composed of lazy learners (Cunningham & Zenobi, 2001). This is very important for domains such as medical decision support where interpretability plays a fundamental role. For instance Ong et al. (1997) and Armengol et al. (2001) describe CBR systems for medical decision support where the use of retrieved cases in explanation plays a central role (see also (Leake, 1996) on explanation in CBR).

---

[1] This research was carried out as part of the MediLink project funded under the PRTLI programme of the Irish Higher Education Authority.

S. Craw and A. Preece (Eds.): ECCBR 2002, LNAI 2416, pp. 436–447.

CBR allows for the use of the retrieved cases in explanation as follows:

"The system predicts that the outcome will be X because that was the outcome in case C1 that differed from the current case only in the value of feature F which was f2 instead of f1.

In addition the outcome in C2 was also X ..."

Explanation in these terms (i.e. expressed in the vocabulary of the case features) will not always be adequate, but in some situations such as in medical decision support it can be quite useful. However if the prediction is coming from an ensemble of CBR systems rather than a single system there is no longer a small number of cases to use for explanation.

So there appears to be a fundamental incompatibility between the ensemble idea and the interpretability of CBR. By definition, the ensemble is an order of magnitude more complex than a basic CBR system with an extra layer of processing (i.e. aggregation) between the cases and the proposed solution. In (Zenobi & Cunningham, 2001) we have argued that the effectiveness of ensembles stems in part from the ensemble performing an implicit decomposition of the problem space with ensemble members *specializing* in local regions of the space. Presumably an explanation of the output of the ensemble should also reflect the way the ensemble has modeled the problem space.

In this paper we present a new approach to the ensemble aggregation process that obtains excellent results and identifies a small number of cases for use in explanation. This new approach might be viewed as a representation transformation process whereby cases are transformed from their feature-based representation to a representation based on the predictions of ensemble members (see section 3). If this representation is used for prediction using a simple nearest neighbour approach (we call this *Meta k*NN) it has a generalization accuracy comparable to that of the ensemble. We argue that this is because it accesses the model of the problem domain that is implicit in the ensemble. This view is supported by the fact that the *Meta k*NN shows very high fidelity to the ensemble predictions. The evaluation in section 4 also shows that this *Meta k*NN classifier produces very accurate predictions and allows a small number of similar neighbours to be identified. But first, the process of aggregating a set of case-based classifiers into an ensemble is described in the next section.

2   Ensembles of *k*-Nearest Neighbour Classifiers

It is well known that ensembles of predictors can improve on the performance of a single predictor (Hansen & Salmon, 1990; Krogh & Vedelsby, 1995; Breiman, 1996). This improvement depends on the members of the ensemble being diverse; a characteristic that arises naturally with decision trees or neural networks trained using different data sets. Indeed the ensemble has the added advantage of overcoming this instability problem. *k*-Nearest-Neighbour (*k*-NN) classifiers do not have this instability so producing an ensemble that will show an *uplift* requires another approach. The most common way to do this is to base the ensemble members on different feature subsets (Ho, 1998; Guerra-Salcedo & Whitley, 1999a, 1999b). Again, it has been shown that the improvement due to the ensemble depends on the diversity of the members (Ricci & Aha, 1998;Cunningham & Carney, 2000; Zenobi & Cunningham, 2001).

Figure 1 shows how such an ensemble of k-NN classifiers would operate. Assume that the ensemble members are based on different feature subsets and these subsets have been chosen to maximize diversity and minimize error (see section 2.1). In this example there are m classifiers and k is set to 3. The task is binary classification with black corresponding to 1. The first classifier retrieves 2 black and one white example. By simple voting this will predict black (1) as the output; alternatively a fuzzy or probabilistic prediction might be produced as follows:

$$p(c_j|x) = \frac{\sum_{k \in \mathbf{K}} 1(k_c = c_j) \cdot \frac{1}{d(k,x)}}{\sum_{k \in \mathbf{K}} \frac{1}{d(k,x)}} \tag{1}$$

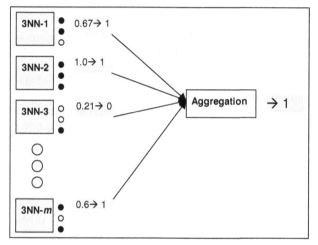

Fig.1. The aggregation process in an ensemble of k-Nearest Neighbour Classifiers.

This is the probability of example x having class c_j, where $\mathbf{K}$ is the set of k nearest neighbours of x, k_c is the class of k, $d()$ is the distance function and $1()$ returns 1 iff its argument is true (Wettschereck et al. 1997). A probabilistic prediction of 0.67 would translate to a prediction of 1 that would be passed to the aggregation process. Alternatively the prediction of 0.67 could be passed for aggregation. The relevance of this is that the aggregation process will perform averaging for continuous predictions and voting for binary predictions. These alternatives generalize to the multi-class situation in a straightforward manner. In the evaluations presented in this paper it is the continuous (probabilistic) value that is passed to the aggregation step. Then the prediction of the ensemble is a weighted sum of the component predictions:

$$p_E(c_j|x) = \sum_{i=1}^{m} w_i p_i(c_j|x) \tag{2}$$

where p_i is the probabilistic prediction of the ith member – in our implementation the weights are equal and sum to 1.

The key point in presenting this example is to show that a large number of cases contribute to the prediction of the ensemble. For example, in an ensemble of 25 classifiers each retrieving 5 neighbours, 125 neighbours will be retrieved. Clearly there will be duplicates in this set but with the prediction from each classifier being made on the basis of a different feature subset, it is very likely that the nearest neighbours for one particular classifier will not be the same as for another. When the neighbours from all members are put together in a "pool" it is not clear which ones are the most representative. We might rank based on frequency of occurrence but that is unlikely to be a complete solution. In section 3 we present our *Meta k*-NN solution to this problem but first we complete the discussion on ensembles with an account of how to train ensembles of *k*-NN classifiers in order to maximise diversity.

2.1 Training with Diversity

It is well known that the potential for an ensemble to be more accurate than its constituent members depends on there being diversity in the ensemble. If all ensemble members agree, there is no *uplift* due to the ensemble; instead it is important for the ensemble members to be right (and wrong) in different areas of the problem space (Zenobi & Cunningham, 2001).

For classification the most commonly used error measure is a simple 0/1 loss function, so a measure of diversity (ambiguity) on a single prediction is:

$$a_i(x_j) = \begin{cases} 0 \text{ if } arg\,max_{c_j}[p_j(c_j \mid x)] = arg\,max_{c_j}[p_E(c_j \mid x)] \\ 1 \text{ otherwise.} \end{cases} \tag{1}$$

where $a_i(x_j)$ is the ambiguity of the ith classifier on example x_j and the two *arg max* functions return respectively the ith classifier and the ensemble predicted class. Thus the contribution to diversity of an ensemble member i as measured on a set of N examples is:

$$A_i = \frac{1}{N} \sum_{j=1}^{N} a_i(x_j) \tag{2}$$

So an ensemble trained to minimize the error of individual members while maximizing this contribution to diversity will be very effective. *AmbHC*, an algorithm to do this for ensembles of *k*-NN classifiers based on different feature subsets is described in (Zenobi & Cunningham, 2001). The details of this algorithm will not be repeated here but the basic principles are as follows. Each ensemble member is defined by a feature mask identifying the features that are 'turned on' in that member. The training of the ensemble involves searching through the space of all feature masks to identify a set of masks that maximizes the diversity and minimizes the error of individual members. This search involves flipping bits in the masks and testing to see if they produce an improvement in error or diversity. Since there is clearly a tradeoff between error and diversity a threshold is used within which small deteriorations in one measure are tolerated for the sake of significant improvements in the other (see (Zenobi & Cunningham, 2001) for details).

This process produces an ensemble of k-NN classifiers based on different feature subsets that is very accurate but difficult to interpret due to the potentially large number of cases involved in generating a solution.

In the evaluation presented in section 4 two different approaches to producing ensembles of k-NN classifiers are evaluated. These are called:

- *AmbHC:* the method described here that uses diversity (i.e. ambiguity+hill-climb)
- *HC:* search for feature masks is based on error only, does not consider diversity.

In both these scenarios the aggregation for the ensemble is done using the weighted sum described in equation 2 (ensemble members are assigned equal weights).

3 The Meta k-Nearest-Neighbour Aggregation Technique

Consider a database consisting of a set of n cases, each one described by f features (see Table 1). For simplicity suppose all the features are normalised numerical and that the outcome is a simple binary classification mapped to the classes 0 and 1.

Table 1. A sample data set of n cases each described by f features.

	Feature 1	**Feature 2**	...	**Feature** f	**CLASS**
Case 1	0.23	0.16	...	0.98	0
Case 2	0.14	0.56	...	0.32	1
Case 3	0.45	0.16	...	0.42	0
...	...	...	...	...	...
Case n	0.56	0.18	...	0.0	1

Suppose we train an ensemble of m k-NN classifiers differing on the feature subset chosen as described in section 2.1. For the training data, each classifier will return a class prediction (in the form of a probability between 0 and 1). It is then possible to associate a new $n \times m$ matrix with this ensemble, where in the position (i,j) is stored the prediction given by the classifier j for the case i. In other words each case is described by a new set of features representing how the ensemble (through each one of its classifiers) *sees* the case. An example of such a matrix is shown in Table 2. The arrows indicate what would have been the final prediction if the classifier were used on its own.

This new matrix is a transformation of the data that in some sense reflects how the ensemble has modelled the problem domain. It also suggests a new two-stage process of classification. In the first stage a target example is presented to the ensemble as before. In the second stage the outputs of the ensemble members is used as a representation of the case in a *Meta* k-NN classification process. The case-base for the *Meta* k-NN process is the transformed data shown in Table 2.

Table 2. A transformation of the data shown in Table 1 based on the outputs of the m classifiers in the ensemble.

	Classifier 1	Classifier 2	...	Classifier m	CLASS
Case 1	0.95 →1	0.08 →0	...	0.21 →0	0
Case 2	0.67 →1	1.0 →1	...	0.0 →0	1
Case 3	0.21 →0	0.19 →0	...	0.69 →1	0
...	...	...	...	...	...
Case n	0.61 →1	0.32 →0	...	0.15 →0	1

This *Meta* k-NN classifier has excellent accuracy − equivalent to that of the ensemble and has the added advantage that a small number of cases are identified for use in explanation.

4   Evaluation and Discussion

In this section we present an experimental study of the aggregation technique we have described in section 3. This evaluation shows two things:

i.   Using the *Meta* k-NN aggregation technique we obtain performance (accuracy) that is comparable to that obtained with the standard weighted average technique. This is shown by a comparison of the generalization errors of both the techniques.

ii.   The *Meta* k-NN technique, which is a single classifier working with a transformed representation produced by the ensemble, models the problem domain in a way that is very similar to the ensemble on which it is based. This is shown by measuring the fidelity of the predictions from the *Meta* k-NN technique to the predictions given by standard aggregation technique.

Since these evaluations are very computationally intensive we present results on only four datasets, three from the UCI repository (Pima Indians, Heart Disease, Cylinder) and the Warfarin data-set described in (Byrne et al., 2000).

We have focused for simplicity on binary classification problems (in the case of Warfarin we have turned it into a 2-class task). The *Meta* k-NN aggregation technique is easily generalized to the case of n-classes. We have also considered datasets that do not have a skewed class distribution, as simple 0/1 error measures are questionable for datasets with very unbalanced class distributions.

In the following set of four figures (Fig. 2, 3, 4 and 5) we show the first of the two studies mentioned above; each figure refers to a different data set. For a complete comparison we have applied to each dataset both the *HC* and *AmbHC* training algorithms described in (Zenobi & Cunningham, 2001). Using these we have trained ensembles of 25 k-NN classifiers (k =5). The generalization error of each ensemble was determined using 5-fold cross validation. This entire process was repeated 2 or 3 times and the results averaged since the hill-climbing strategy is quite sensitive to the initial condition.

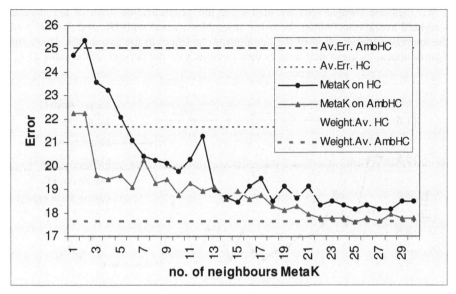

Fig. 2. Results for Heart data

The diagrams show the generalization error of the *Meta* k-NN aggregation strategy (both for ensembles trained with *HC* and *AmbHC*) plotted against the number of retrieved neighbours k_M. It is important to distinguish k_M from k, which is the number of retrieved neighbours for any single classifier in the ensemble. It is worth noting that the choice of this k_M is completely unrelated to the choice of k.

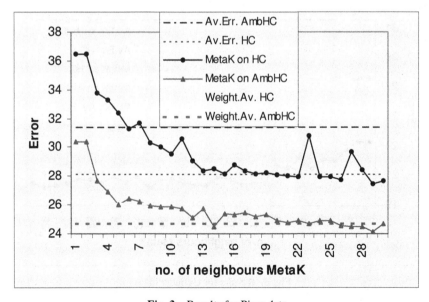

Fig. 3. Results for Pima data

To facilitate comparisons we also show the generalization error of the standard weighted average technique (both for ensembles trained with *HC* and *AmbHC*) and the average generalization of the component classifiers in the ensembles. These four figures appear as horizontal lines as they obviously do not depend on the value of k_M.

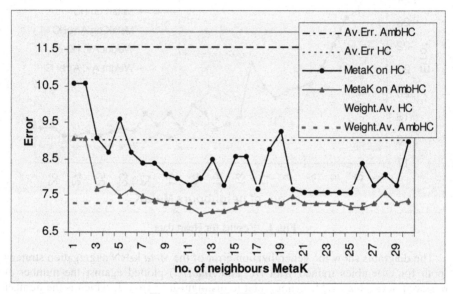

Fig. 4. Results for Warfarin data

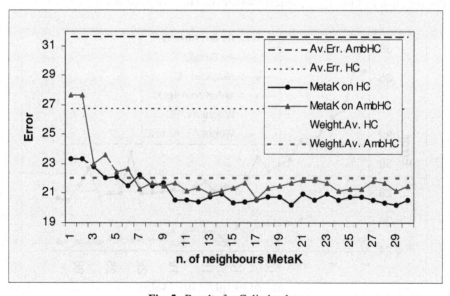

Fig. 5. Results for Cylinder data

From the figures shown above we can make a few observations. First, there is a confirmation of the fact that ensembles trained with *AmbHC* and using the standard aggregation approach have a better generalization error that those trained with a simple *HC*, even though the average error of the component classifiers are considerably worse. This is no surprise, and simply shows once again that diversity plays a crucial role in the ensemble performance.

Second, the *Meta* k-NN aggregation technique performed on ensembles trained with *AmbHC* scores comparable or better results to the weighted average aggregation technique for larger values of k_M. As a general trend we observe that already for values of k_M between 5 and 7 the result obtained by *Meta* k-NN is comparable to a weighted average on ensembles trained with *HC* (i.e. a score about between 1% and 2.5% worse than the one for *AmbHC*), with the great advantage of retrieving a small set of cases for explanation. When we increase the value of k_M up to 25 the *Meta* k-NN technique outperforms (except in the Heart dataset) ensembles trained with *AmbHC* and using the standard aggregation technique. In this case the set of retrieved neighbours is large (but still smaller than that retrieved by a classic aggregation technique) and has the important capability of giving a coherent ranking to the cases retrieved.

Third, the *Meta* k-NN aggregation technique performed on ensembles trained with simple *HC* scores generally worse generalization errors than the one performed on ensembles trained with *AmbHC*. A possible explanation for this phenomenon can be the fact that classifiers trained with *HC* have a lower diversity, so they carry less "rich" information about the problem domain, than the ones trained with *AmbHC*; when the *Meta* k-NN case-base is created it is possible that the columns (classifiers' predictions) show a higher dependence in the case of *HC*. The only exception to this is the Cylinder dataset where the *AmbHC* approach has no clear advantage over the *HC* technique. This is probably due to the large number of features in this dataset (38) and the consequent 'natural' diversity that exists even in ensemble members trained using *HC*.

Figure 6 shows the second study mentioned at the beginning of this section. It compares the fidelity of the *Meta* k-NN classifiers with the corresponding *AmbHC* ensemble. We do not consider the *HC* ensemble because it (and the corresponding *Meta* k-NN classifier) have poorer accuracy.

We have plotted for all four datasets the figures for fidelity between the predictions given by the *Meta* k-NN and standard aggregation technique. This is calculated as a binary error (0 if the two predictions match, 1 if they don't) and is plotted against increasing values of k_M.

From this figure it is clear that the fidelity is high. After $k_M=5$ already all the datasets (except Cylinder) score a fidelity over 95% (error less than 5%) and for two of the datasets the fidelity goes up to 98% and more as k_M increases. We can reasonably argue that the problem domain decomposition in the case of the two different aggregation strategies is nearly equivalent.

5   Conclusions and Future Research

Ensembles have had a big impact on Machine Learning research in recent years because they bring significant improvements in accuracy and stability. Another development in ML research is the emphasis on interpretability explanation. This is probably due to the increased interest in Data Mining where the emphasis is as much on insight as prediction. Because ensembles introduce an extra layer of complexity they make explanation much more difficult. In this paper we have presented a technique that reconciles these two things – at least for lazy learning systems.

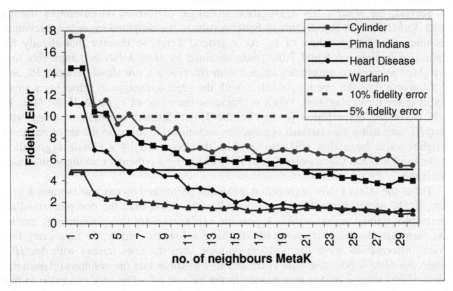

Fig. 6. Fidelity error of the *Meta k*-NN classifiers to the ensemble on which they are based. The 10% and 5% error lines are shown for comparison.

We have introduced a new technique, *Meta k*-NN, that performs the aggregation step when using an ensemble. This technique obtains good results, comparable to the standard averaging approach to aggregation in terms of generalization error, and allows us to identify a small set of cases for use in explanation. Even though large vales of k_M are required to provide good accuracy this is not a problem as the set of cases are ranked and the top ranking cases can be used for explanation.

In conclusion, we have introduced a new aggregation process that might be used in two modes:

i.   Use *Meta k*-NN to produce the prediction *and* to identify cases for use in explanation. This would be appropriate when *Meta k*-NN showed to have a generalization accuracy equal to that of the standard aggregation technique.

ii.   Use the standard aggregation technique to produce predictions and use *Meta k*-NN to identify cases for explanation – the high fidelity would allow for this. This would be appropriate when the accuracy of *Meta k*-NN was poorer than the standard aggregation.

5.1 Future Work

Since the key benefit we claim for this technique is its ability to select cases for use in explanation we need to evaluate the usefulness of the cases retrieved. We have access to domain experts in the Warfarin domain and in other medical domains and we will perform a study where these experts will rate the relevance of the retrieved cases.

The accuracy of *Meta k-NN* might further be improved by performing feature subset selection. Some of the features (i.e. ensemble member predictions) are probably more informative than others and deleting some features may improve performance.

References

Armengol, E., Palaudàries, A., Plaza, E., (2001). Individual Prognosis of Diabetes Long-term Risks: A CBR Approach. *Methods of Information in Medicine. Special issue on prognostic models in Medicine.* vol. 40, pp. 46-51.

Breiman, L., (1996) Bagging predictors. *Machine Learning,* 24:123-140.

Cunningham, P., Carney, J., (2000) Diversity versus Quality in Classification Ensembles based on Feature Selection, 11ᵗʰ European Conference on Machine Learning (ECML 2000), Lecture Notes in Artificial Intelligence, R. López de Mántaras and E. Plaza, (eds) pp109-116, Springer Verlag.

Cunningham, P., Zenobi, G., (2001) Case Representation Issues for Case-Based Reasoning from Ensemble Research, in Proceedings of 4ᵗʰ International Conference on Case-Based Reasoning eds D. W. Aha, I. Watson, LNAI 2080, pp146-157, Springer Verlag.

Guerra-Salcedo, C., Whitley, D., (1999a). Genetic Approach for Feature Selection for Ensemble Creation. in GECCO-99: Proceedings of the Genetic and Evolutionary Computation Conference, Banzhaf, W., Daida, J., Eiben, A. E., Garzon, M. H., Honavar, V., Jakiela, M., & Smith, R. E. (eds.). Orlando, Florida USA, pp236-243, San Francisco, CA: Morgan Kaufmann.

Guerra-Salcedo, C., Whitley, D., (1999b). Feature Selection Mechanisms for Ensemble Creation: A Genetic Search Perspective, in Data Mining with Evolutionary Algorithms: Research Directions. Papers from the AAAI Workshop. Alex A. Freitas (Ed.) Technical Report WS-99-06. AAAI Press, 1999.

Hansen, L.K., Salamon, P., (1990) Neural Network Ensembles, IEEE Pattern Analysis and Machine Intelligence, 1990. **12**, 10, 993-1001.

Heskes, T.M. (1998). Selecting weighting factors in logarithmic opinion pools. *Advances in Neural Information Processing Systems, 10,* 266-272.

Ho, T.K., (1998) Nearest Neighbours in Random Subspaces, Proc. Of 2ⁿᵈ International Workshop on Statistical Techniques in Pattern Recognition, A. Amin, D. Dori, P. Puil, H. Freeman, (eds.) pp640-648, Springer Verlag LNCS 1451.

Kohavi, P. Langley, Y. Yun, (1997) The Utility of Feature Weighting in NearestNeighbor Algorithms, European Conference on Machine Learning, ECML'97, Prague, Czech Republic, 1997, poster.

Krogh, A., Vedelsby, J., (1995) Neural Network Ensembles, Cross Validation and Active Learning, in Advances in Neural Information Processing Systems 7, G. Tesauro, D. S. Touretsky, T. K. Leen, eds., pp231-238, MIT Press, Cambridge MA.

Jacobs, R.A., Jordan, M.I., Nowlan, S.J., & Hinton, G.E., (1991) Adaptive mixtures of local experts, *Neural Computation*, 3, 79-98.

Leake, D., B., (1996) CBR in Context: The Present and Future, in Leake, D.B. (ed) Case-Based Reasoning: Experiences, Lessons and Future Directions, pp3-30, MIT Press.

Ong, L.S., Sheperd, B., Tong, L.C., Seow-Choen, F., Ho, Y.H., Tong, L.C., Ho Y.S, Tan, K. (1997) The Colorectal Cancer Recurrence Support (CARES) System. Artificial Intelligence in Medicine 11(3): 175-188.

Ricci, F., & Aha, D. W. (1998). Error-correcting output codes for local learners. Proceedings of the Tenth European Conference on Machine Learning (280-291). Chemnitz, Germany: Springer.

van de Laar, P., Heskes, T., (2000) Input selection based on an ensemble, Neurocomputing, 34:227-238.

Wettschereck, D., Aha, D. W., & Mohri, T. (1997). A review and empirical evaluation of feature weighting methods for a class of lazy learning algorithms. *Artificial Intelligence Review, 11*, 273-314.

Zenobi, G., Cunningham, P., (2001) Using Diversity in Preparing Ensembles of Classifiers Based on Different Feature Subsets to Minimize Generalization Error, 12th European Conference on Machine Learning (ECML 2001), eds L. De Raedt & P. Flach, LNAI 2167, pp576-587, Springer Verlag.

An Experimental Study of Increasing Diversity for Case-Based Diagnosis

Lu Zhang, Frans Coenen, and Paul Leng

The Department of Computer Science, The University of Liverpool,
Liverpool L69 3BX, UK
{lzhang, frans, phl}@csc.liv.ac.uk

Abstract. Increasing diversity for case-based reasoning (CBR) is an issue that has recently drawn the attention of researchers in the CBR field. Several diversification techniques have been proposed and discussed in the literature. However, whether and to what extent those techniques can bring about benefits to end-users remains in question. In this paper, we report an experiment in applying a diversification technique to a case-based diagnosis tool in a product maintenance domain. The results of this offer some evidence in support of diversification techniques.

Keywords. Diagnosis, Diversification, Product maintenance

1 Introduction

Recently, the issue of increasing diversity for case-based reasoning (CBR) systems has become a focus of discussion (see e.g. [5], [1], [6], and [4] etc.). Most research on this issue has been carried out for recommendation systems. The main reason for addressing this problem is that the retrieved cases are usually similar to each other and thus can only offer very restricted choices to users [6]. However, there is insufficient evidence that end-users of the systems can substantially benefit from increasing diversity techniques.

In this paper, we report an experiment in applying an adaptation of the '*diversification by elimination*' technique proposed in [4] to a case-based diagnosis tool in a product maintenance domain. In case-based diagnosis systems, each retrieved case is used to suggest a possible fault. As different cases may indicate the same fault, eliminating some cases reporting the same fault may substantially increase the number of suggested possible faults in the retrieved cases. Therefore, for a given size of the retrieval set, the diversified retrieval set may lead to an increased probability that the real fault of the case under diagnosis is suggested among the faults of the retrieved cases. This increase may be very valuable for domains in which CBR can only achieve low accuracy.

To evaluate to what extent the diversification strategy in our tool can be beneficial, we performed some experiments on some real data acquired from a commercial domain. From our experiments, we found that, within a certain range of retrieval set sizes, the diversified approach achieved significantly greater success in including the real fault in the retrieve set than did the un-diversified approach, although neither

S. Craw and A. Preece (Eds.): ECCBR 2002, LNAI 2416, pp. 448–459.

achieved a very high success. These results suggest that diversification can be an effective technology for domains in which normal CBR approaches can only achieve low accuracy.

The remainder of this paper is organised as follows. Section 2 provides a general description of the case-based diagnosis tool. Section 3 reports the diversification technique used in the tool. Section 4 reports some experiments based on the tool using real data. Section 5 discusses some limitations of our study. Section 6 concludes this paper.

2 The Case-Based Diagnosis Tool

In this section, we describe the case-based diagnosis tool in a product maintenance domain, on which our case study for diversification has been performed.

2.1 Domain

The diagnosis problem we are facing originates from the needs of a manufacturer of domestic appliances in a flexible manufacturing context, whose name is Stoves PLC. The company concerned can deliver more than 3000 versions of its cookers to customers, making it possible to satisfy a very wide range of different customer requirements. However, this creates a problem for the after-sale service, because of the difficulty in providing its field engineers with the information necessary to maintain cookers of all these different models. In general, field engineers may need to be able to deal with any problem concerning any of the sold cookers, which may include versions previously unknown to them. Producing conventional service manuals and other product documentation for each model variant clearly imposes unacceptable strains on the production cycle, and the resulting volume of documentation will be unmanageable for field engineers. The company periodically issues updated documentation CDs to field engineers as a partial solution, but it has been accepted among its field engineers that more automated and/or intelligent diagnosis support is still needed. This is the broad scope of our research, for which preliminary results have been published (see. e.g. [2], [7], [3], and [8]).

The current system in use for fault diagnosis employs a large after-sale services department consisting of customer call receivers and field engineers. When a customer calls to report a fault, the customer call receiver will try to solve that case through a telephone dialogue. If he/she cannot do so, he/she will record the case in an after-sale services information system as an unsolved case. The system assigns recorded cases to field engineers each day, and field engineers go to the corresponding customers to solve the assigned cases. After solving a case, the field engineer will phone back to the after-sale services department to report the solved case and that case is recorded as completed in the system. All the data about previous cases is stored in the system for quite a long period of time.

It is clear that any system that might make it more likely for a fault to be correctly identified by the customer call receiver, or more rapidly diagnosed by a service engineer, would be of value. In this context, we have designed and implemented a simple case-based diagnosis tool to give the service personnel more intelligent support.

2.2 Diagnosis Process

The diagnosis process of the tool is depicted in Fig. 1. When encountering a new case, the service agent (call receiver or field engineer) will provide a description of the new case according to the customer's report. This description will be matched with the cases in the case base. Some most similar cases will be retrieved, which can be viewed in detail by the service agent to help him/her to identify the fault of the new case. After the new case has been solved, it can be stored into the case base for future diagnosis.

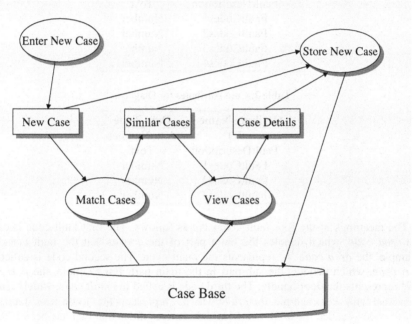

Fig. 1. The diagnosis procedure

2.3 Case Representation

As mentioned above, there is an after-sale services information system for recording maintenance requests of customers and assigning the requests to field engineers. In that system, a case is represented as values in the following attributes (see Table 1).

Among these attributes, most are for identifying the location of the customers and help field engineers to find their customers. As these attributes are irrelevant to diagnosis, we only use five of the above attributes in our diagnosis tool. These attributes are shown in Table 2. An alternative and more sophisticated case structure exploited in the same domain can be found in [8].

Table 1. Original Case Attributes

Attribute Name	Data Type
ID	AutoNumber
CallDate	Date/Time
Surname	Text
HouseNo	Text
StreetName	Text
Town	Text
Postcode	Text
PhoneNo	Text
JobNo	Text
Engineer	Text
FaultDescription	Text
FaultCodes1	Number
FaultCodes2	Number
FaultCodes3	Number
FaultCodes4	Number

Table 2. Case Attributes for Diagnosis

Attribute Name	Data Type
ID	AutoNumber
FaultDescription	Text
FaultCodes1	Number
FaultCodes2	Number
FaultCodes3	Number

The meanings of the four fault codes are as follows. The first fault code is called the *area code*, which denotes the main part of the cooker that the fault is in. For example, the *area code* '6' represents the main oven. The second code is called the *part code*, which denotes the sub-part in the main part. For example, the *part code* '17' represents the door handle. The third code is called the *fault code*, which denotes the actual fault. For example, the *fault code* '55' represents the 'loose wire' fault. The fourth code is called the *action code*, which denotes the action that has been taken to fix the fault. Presently, there are 8 choices for the first code, 194 choices for the second code, 59 choices for the third code, and 26 choices for the fourth code. As our tool is focused on diagnosing the fault, we do not use the *action code* in our tool.

2.4 Case Matching

In this experimental version of our tool, we use a simple case matching strategy. As an engineer can usually find the possible faulty parts in a short time, our tool requires that two similar cases should share the same *area code* and the same *part code*. Another reason of this case matching strategy is that the *area code* and the *part code* are actually representing the location of the fault and therefore cases sharing the same *fault code* under different *area codes* or *part codes* are unlikely to be similar at all. Under this circumstance, the similarity of cases is based only on a matching of the fault descriptions of the cases. As the fault description in a case is in plain English, we simply count the number of matched words between two descriptions as the similarity. The more words are matched, the more similar the two cases are. We require at least one word to be matched, to establish a potential similarity between cases.

3   Diversification in the Tool

3.1 Retrieval Set and Hit Rate

To explain the reason for using diversification techniques in our tool, we first explain the concepts of *retrieval set* and *hit rate*. As the fault descriptions of cases are provided verbally by customers, who may have little knowledge of their cookers, the most similar case identified may not actually exhibit the same fault as the case under diagnosis. To increase the probability that the actual fault will be identified correctly, a set of similar cases is retrieved, rather than just the single most similar case. It is hoped that one of the similar cases may have the same fault as the case under diagnosis. To evaluate the success of the diagnosis, we use the concept '*hit rate*'. The *hit rate* is defined as the number of cases under diagnosis whose faults appear in the faults of their *retrieval set,* divided by the total number of cases under diagnosis. For example, suppose there are 100 cases under diagnosis, and in 80 cases the corresponding retrieval set includes a case that suggests a correct diagnosis of the fault under consideration. Then the *hit rate* is therefore 80%.

Obviously, increasing the size of retrieval sets can usually increase the hit rate. However, as well as the cost of retrieving more cases, a larger retrieval set increases the difficulty in analysing the results to correctly identify the fault, so to general we will aim to restrict the size of the retrieval set. As only those cases that have distinct faults in the retrieval set can actually contribute to an increase in the hit rate, diversification of the retrieval set may also achieve the same effect as increasing the size of the retrieval set. In our tool, we use the following strategy to retrieve only those cases suggesting distinct faults.

3.2 Diversification Strategy

The diversification strategy exploited in our tool is essentially the '*diversification by elimination*' strategy proposed in [4]. However, our strategy is aiming at eliminating cases suggesting the same faults, while the '*diversification by elimination*' strategy is aiming at eliminating *similar cases* (which share the same descriptions with other retrieved cases in most of the attributes).

As discussed in [4], a main limitation of the '*diversification by elimination*' strategy is that it may cause loss in similarity. However, this limitation almost does not exist in our tool, because an eliminated case must have the same values in all the three fault codes (which uniquely identify the actual fault) with a previously retrieved case.

The algorithm for our strategy is depicted in Fig. 2. Supposing the input candidate cases are stored in the variable '*Candidates*' ordered by similarity, and k is the maximum size of the *retrieval set*. The output is the variable '*RetrievalSet*' containing at most *k* cases with distinct faults.

Input: Candidates, k
Output: RetrievalSet
Algorithm:
    Step 1: RetrievalSet←Φ
    Step 2: C←head(Candidates)
                Candidates←tail(Candidates, |Candidates|-1)
                if (has-distinct-fault (RetrievalSet, C))
                        add (RetrievalSet, C)
    Step 3: if (|RetrievalSet |≠k and |Candidates|≠0)
                goto Step 2
            else exit

Fig. 2. Diversification algorithm

3.3 An Example

Fig. 3 and Fig. 4 show the changes between the normal retrieval set and the diversified retrieval set when diagnosing the same case. The sizes of the two retrieval sets are both seven. Fig. 3 depicts the situation without diversification. The fault '*Inoperative*' appears three times in the retrieval set. Fig. 4 depicts the situation after diversification, where the fault '*Inoperative*' only counts once, and two new faults appear in the retrieval set.

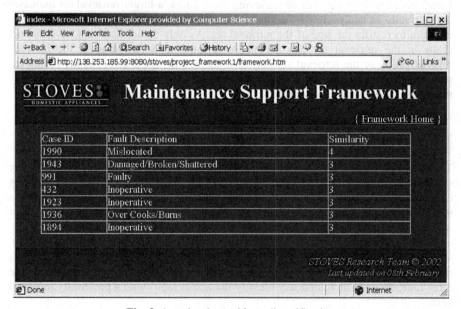

Fig. 3. A retrieval set without diversification

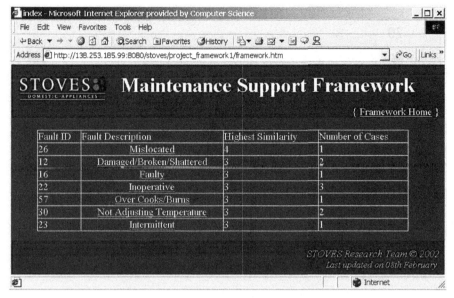

Fig. 4. A retrieval set with diversification

4   Experimental Results

4.1 Experimental Method

To evaluate the benefit of diversification in the tool, we performed some experiments on some real data obtained from the company concerned. We collected 1988 cases recorded in the after-sale services information system during October and November 2001. As the original cases are represented as values in the attributes in Table 1, we extracted only the values in the attributes in Table 2 to form our case base.

We then randomly separated the 1988 cases into a training set containing 1000 cases, used to create the case base, and a test set containing 988 cases. For different retrieval set size k, we recorded both the hit rate of the case-based diagnosis without diversification and the hit rate of the diversified case-based diagnosis. Finally, we represented the relationships between the retrieval set sizes and the two hit rates as a chart containing two lines.

To avoid occasional results, we performed the experiments three times using different random separations. In the following, we report the results of the three experiments.

4.2 Results and Analysis

As the results of the second experiment and the third experiment are similar to those of the first, we report the first experiment in detail, and the other two briefly.

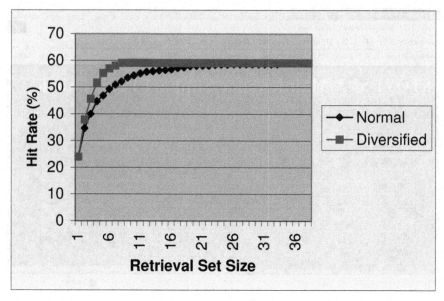

Fig. 5. Results of the first experiment

4.2.1 First Experiment

When the retrieval set size is 1, only the single most similar case is retrieved in both the 'normal' approach and the diversified approach, achieving a hit rate of 23.99%. With the increase of the retrieval set size, both hit rates also increase, but that of the diversified approach increases more rapidly. When the retrieval set size is 5, there is the maximum difference of hit rates between the two approaches – 8.40 percentage points. The diversified approach reaches the highest hit rate (59.11%) when the retrieval set size is 9, while the normal approach reaches the highest hit rate (59.11%) when the retrieval set size is 38. The convergence of the two approaches at this hit rate illustrates the failure of the fault description, in many cases, to provide a good basis for diagnosis. These results show that diversification can help the tool to reach the maximum hit rate when the retrieval set size is still quite small. On average, there is a 7.12 percentage point difference between the two approaches when the retrieval set size is between 4 and 9. The line chart for comparing the hit rates of the two approaches in the first experiment is in Fig. 5.

4.2.2 Second Experiment

The results of the second experiment are similar. When the retrieval set size is 1, both approaches achieve the lowest hit rate of 22.37%. When the retrieval set size is 6, there is the maximum difference of hit rates between the two approaches – 7.59 percentage points. The diversified approach reaches the highest hit rate (60.53%) when retrieval set size is 10, while the normal approach reaches the highest hit rate (60.53%) when retrieval set size is 41. On average, there is a 6.63 percentage point difference between the two approaches when the retrieval set size is between 4 and 9. The line chart for comparing the hit rates of the two approaches in the second experiment is in Fig. 6.

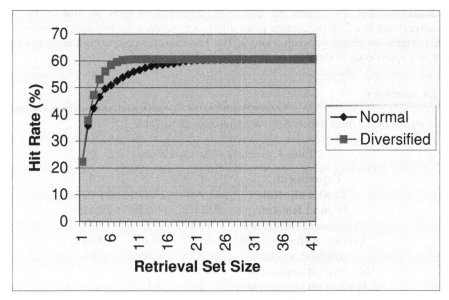

Fig. 6. Results of the second experiment

4.2.3 Third Experiment

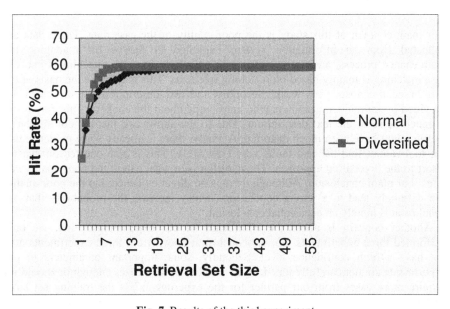

Fig. 7. Results of the third experiment

When the retrieval set size is 1, both approaches achieve the lowest hit rate of 25.00%. When the retrieval set size is 7, there is the maximum difference of hit rates between the two approaches – 5.57 percentage points. The diversified approach reaches the highest hit rate (59.11%) when retrieval set size is 10, while the normal approach reaches the highest hit rate (59.11%) when retrieval set size is 55. On average, there is a 5.06 percentage point difference between the two approaches when the retrieval set size is between 4 and 9. The line chart for comparing the hit rates of the two approaches in the third experiment is in Fig. 7.

4.2.4 Summary

The results of the three experiments are summarised in Table 3.

Table 3. Summary of the experiments

Experiment	1	2	3
Lowest Hit Rate	23.99%	22.37%	25.00%
Highest Hit Rate	59.11%	60.53%	59.11%
Maximum Difference	8.40	7.59	5.57
Average difference (4-9)	7.12	6.63	5.06
Highest set size (diversified approach)	9	10	10
Highest set size (normal approach)	38	41	55

5 Limitations

Our main concern of this study is the poor quality of the case data. These data are collected from an information system exploited in Stoves for managing the maintenance process, and are not planned particularly for case matching. First, our case matching is mainly based on matching free texts. This may make the basis of the case-based diagnosis very weak. Secondly, the text descriptions of the cases are provided by individual customers who know little about the cookers. This may result in much noise in the text descriptions. Due to the above two factors, our similarity metric might have been much distorted. Actually, there is already some evidence that our tool cannot find the real faults very effectively. This is also one reason that we resort to the diversified approach. The question is to what extent the poor quality can affect our main conclusion. Although there is no direct evidence that the poor quality can definitely lead to a wrong conclusion, it may increase the probability that our conclusion is merely an occasional conclusion.

Another concern is about the confidence of our experiments. First, we only performed three experiments. So, the conclusion drawn from three experiments may not have a high confidence level. Secondly, some important parameters in our experiments are not carefully tuned. Is the number of total cases enough or should we acquire more cases from our partner for the experiments? Is the training set large enough or not?

Based on the above two concerns, we think our conclusion should only be tentative and still requires further evaluation.

6 Conclusion

In this paper, we have reported an experiment in applying a diversification technique to a case-based diagnosis tool in a product maintenance domain. The aim of our study is to evaluate whether and to what extent applying the diversification technique in the tool is advantageous over not applying the technique. Our experimental results show that, in the real-life domain we have investigated, the diversified approach is much more effective than the un-diversified approach in successfully including the real fault within a relatively small retrieval set. This result arises, in part, because of the relatively poor quality of the data used for matching cases. In this context, there is a relatively high probability that the correct fault will not appear within a small retrieval set, and, without diversification, it sometimes requires a very large retrieval set to produce the most successful match. We have shown that in this case, use of diversification can be very effective in identifying the best matches without the need for an unmanageably large retrieval set. Therefore, we conclude that diversification may be an effective method to increase the *hit rate* while keeping a rather small retrieval set size in a noisy diagnosis domain.

Acknowledgements

The research described in this paper is supported by the Department of Trade and Industry under the Foresight 'Link' programme. We wish to express our thanks to our partners in the project, Stoves PLC and NA Software Ltd, and in particular to Colin Johnson, Prof Mike Delves, and the Project Monitor, Stan Price.

References

1. Bradley, K., Smyth, B.: Improving Recommendation Diversity. In: Proceedings of the Twelfth Irish Conference on Artificial Intelligence and Cognitive Science, Maynooth, Ireland (2001) 85-94
2. Coenen, F., Leng, P., Weaver, R., Zhang, W.: Integrated online support for field service engineers in a flexible manufacturing context. In: Applications and Innovations in Intelligent Systems VIII (Proc ES2000 Conference, Cambridge), eds A Macintosh, M Moulton and F Coenen, Springer, London, (2000) 141-152
3. Coenen, F., Leng, P., Zhang. L.: Flexible Field Service Support using Multiple Diagnostic Tools. In Proceedings of 5th IEEE International Conference on Intelligent Engineering Systems, (2001) 225-229
4. McSherry, D.: Increasing Recommendation Diversity Without Loss of Similarity. In: Proceedings of the Sixth UK CBR Workshop, 10 December (2001) 23-31
5. Smyth, B., Cotter, P.: A Personalised TV Listing Service for the Digital TV Age. Knowledge-Based Systems, 13 (2000) 53-59.

6.   Smyth, B., McClave, P.: Similarity vs. Diversity. In: Aha, D.W., Watson, I. (eds) Case-Based Reasoning Research and Development. LNAI, Vol. 2080. Springer-Verlag, Berlin Heidelberg (2001) 347-361
7.   Zhang, W., Coenen, F., Leng, P.,: On-Line Support for Field Service Engineers in a Flexible Manufacturing Environment: the Stoves Project. In: Proceedings of IeC '2000 Conference, Manchester (2000) 31-40
8.   Zhang, L., Coenen, F., Leng, P.,: A Case Based Diagnostic Tool in a Flexible Manufacturing Context. In: Proceedings of the Sixth UK CBR Workshop, 10 December (2001) 61-69

Collaborative
Case-Based Recommender Systems

Stefano Aguzzoli*, Paolo Avesani, and Paolo Massa

ITC-IRST,
Via Sommarive 18 - Loc. Pantè, I-38050 Povo, Trento, Italy
{aguzzoli,avesani,massa}@irst.itc.it

Abstract. We introduce an application combining CBR and collaborative filtering techniques in the music domain. We describe a scenario in which a new kind of recommendation is required, which is capable of summarizing many recommendations in one suggestion. Our claim is that recommending one set of goods is different from recommending a single good many times. The paper illustrates how a case-based reasoning approach can provide an effective solution to this problem reducing the drawbacks related to the user profiles. CoCoA, a compilation compiler advisor, will be described as a running example of a collaborative case-based recommendation system.

1 Introduction

The notion of intelligent sale support [3,13] is going to be widely recognized as a new challenge for e-commerce applications. The new scenario promoted by the Internet has increased the opportunities for customizing products; now, it is possible to tailor goods or services closely to a user's needs.

The pre-sale phase in the context of electronic commerce is being revisited, because the role of the customer has changed. In the past, a customer could only select a product from a set catalogue made in advance by the supplier organization. Now, the customer is directly involved in the process of assembling the product, a task that requires the combination of a set of predefined components in accordance with user preferences.

The music market [8] represent one of the most visible scenarios in which this evolution is occurring. In the past, the delivered goods were compact discs containing compilations (that is, selected collections) of audio tracks; nowadays, it is possible to buy individual tracks rather than entire precompiled CDs. In spite of this change, the notion of "compilation" is still relevant, because e-commerce systems enable the purchase of single tracks, but the delivery still relies on compact discs as media. In this scenario, the role of the editor of compilations has moved from the market expert to the final user.

---

* Current address: Computer Science Department, University of Milan; email: stefano@gongolo.usr.dsi.unimi.it.

S. Craw and A. Preece (Eds.): ECCBR 2002, LNAI 2416, pp. 460–474, 2002.

New Web portals devoted to the sale of sound tracks[1] allow users to create their own compilations. Usually, the assembling process is based on an iterative step that adds a sound track selected from the result set of a query to a repository of music.

From this perspective, the advantage introduced by the personalization of the product could hold some drawbacks. Firstly, the simple iterative step of adding one track after another quickly becomes boring, as an average compilation includes some 15 tracks. Secondly, query engines on track repositories are not able to provide querying over many important features of music, because track tagging is time consuming and user dependent. Finally, there is no way to address a query to a repository in which each individual track is enriched with information on what is an appropriate context for its inclusion in a compilation.

Giving the users the opportunity to assemble their own compilations, enables the web portal to collect important knowledge about the sound tracks. Indeed, every single compilation may be considered as an instance of the *genre of use* related to its sound tracks. These kinds of genre are not the usual categories used to classify music (rock, jazz, classical, and so on); the genres of use represents all the different perspectives along which a user can turn to music. Following this approach, one can imagine to have the standard compilations of "rock" rather than "jazz music", but at the same time one could have compilations of "california dreaming music rather than "a night with my girl" music, which may possibly put together tracks that would be kept separated under a traditional classification system.

From this perspective, a repository of compilations may be considered a powerful case base to support both the editing of personalized compilations and the detection of genres of use introduced by customers.

In the following, we examine how recommendation systems can take advantage of case-based reasoning and how the collaborative filtering techniques [6,11] can be extended to support product personalization [15,14,16]. After presenting the motivations for this work, we briefly introduce CoCoA, a recommendation system for music compilations. The following sections gives a detailed explanation of the design of the case-based retrieval engine used by CoCoA, which is based on the collaborative filtering approach. We then give the results of an empirical evaluation carried out on a dataset derived from EachMovie [10]. The paper concludes with a brief discussion of the results, including a comparison with the Singular Value Decomposition technique [7,5].

2   Case-Based Recommender Systems

While case-based reasoning systems and recommendation systems are both related to information retrieval, the way to formulate the query differs. The former allows sketching the goal by example; the latter relies on the notion of user profile and leaves the goal implicit even though it could change on each occasion.

---

[1] See as examples the following Web sites: www.mixfactory.com, www.musicalacarte.net.

We argue that designing a case-based recommender system means to introduce the opportunity to clearly state the goal the user is looking for a suggestion.

Given a user, and his/her related profile, he/she needs to receive different recommendation whether the ultimate goal is a compilation for himself or for his/her partner. The idea is that the user can explicitly state his intention by providing a sketch of examples, i.e. a partial compilation.

However to be effective a retrieval engine that supports a query by example through similarity assessment has to rely on a content based description. The underlining assumption being that similar compilations include tracks that share similar descriptions.

More precisely we assume that a compilation usually refers to a *genre of use*. A *genre of use* can be represented by a collection of tracks that share at least one feature. Let us consider a compilation with *genre of use* "california dreaming", we can imagine a feature, say "california", that is shared by all the tracks belonging to the compilation. This way - given a repository of compilations - we can imagine to build the space of genres and the space of the features.

In this new scenario, asking for a recommendation means providing a sample of tracks that shapes a sketch of the target compilation. An answer to this query will consist of compilations that include only tracks sharing a common feature, the same shared by all tracks included in the query.

The challenge is how to support the similarity assessment without to refer this feature space. Most of the time the domain doesn't provide a rich and meaningful enough content description to support the detection of a *genre of use*. It is certainly sure the case of the music domain where the sound tracks are described by few and non meaningful features like performer, title, year, and some others.

The objective of this work is to obtain a case-based recommender system that perform as the features had known without to refer them. In the following we will describe a collaborative-based approach that enables the design of a case-based recommendation engine where the similarity assessment step doesn't require an extended content description.

3   Compositional Collaborative Filtering

As described above, customers are involved in the process of assembling their own compilations, by adding one track after another. Some of the Web portals that distribute music have started enhancing this interaction by providing a recommendation utility. By selecting the recommendation option, the customer can access a list of tracks that the system has detected as being relevant for the current partial compilation. Even though this kind of system relies on repositories of compilations, there is no way for the customer to browse them.

In the recommendation approach, the suggestion (the sound track) is provided without the context (the compilation) that could help the user perceive a sort of explanation of why the track proposed by the system has been selected. Furthermore, the customer cannot directly interpret and reuse what other customers have done in the past by looking at the existing compilations and deriving a new one from them.

Our claim is that recommending a set of tracks differs from recommending one track many times. Let consider a situation where a user is looking for suggestions to complete a partial compilation. The missing tracks will be selected from a result set produced by a recommendation system. If we assume an iterative model the recommendation system will be invoked many times. At each step there is a certain probability of a wrong suggestion leading to the hypothesis that it isn't possible to have a perfect recommender. The iterative approach introduces two kinds of drawbacks: first it increases the error associated with the recommender engine, second it creates the premises that a wrong selection will propagate the error through the next steps of the process.

4   Motivations

After this brief overview of the relationships between case-based reasoning and recommendation systems let introduce the focus of our interests.

The first motivation of our work was to introduce the CBR loop into the context of compositional recommendation systems, where a customer is required to collect a set of components to fulfill the pre-sales phase. Our thesis is that the collected use cases offer a viable solution for partitioning recommended tracks into meaningful collections to support the completion task. The following section gives a simple explanation of the two CBR related interaction models designed for CoCoA.

A further motivation underlying our work is to integrate loop a retrieval engine into the CBR so that there is no need to address the content description in order to compute the similarity measure. In the domain of music this aspect is crucial for two reasons: firstly, because the definition of music categories does not meet a general agreement; and secondly, because the features that usually describe a sound track do not discriminate between the different genres of use.

The integration of CBR and Collaborative Filtering in the context of compositional recommendation systems presents some drawbacks. The first is related to the choice of the notion of a case: we cannot associate a case description with a single user, because the experience is represented by a single compilation. Each compilation can be considered as an episode where the goal of collecting a set of tracks following a given criterion has been achieved. Looking at one compilation as a single case is one of our working assumptions. At the same time, from a collaborative filtering perspective, we consider the single compilation as the profile of a virtual user. The second drawback is related to the notion of rating. Usually collaborative filtering techniques rely on the correlation between two user profiles where the ratings allow the system to assess their similarity. In the case of compilations, an explicit rating of the sound tracks is not available and we can simply assume that all the tracks belonging to the same compilation have an equal rating.

Summarizing, we have to cope with the following two drawbacks:

1. In the case of a single compilation, its dimension is fixed and very small compared to the set of all tracks. Compare this with the profiles of movies rated by a user. The information in this latter profile grows indefinitely as the user continues to rate newly seen movies. In the compilation scenario, the tracks are given once and for all, and two randomly selected compilations are not likely to have any significant overlapping of common tracks.
2. The case does not contain any rating of the tracks occurring within it: put simply, a track is either there or not there. We do not know from the case if a track is actually significant for the case or mildly important or simply to be regarded as noise. Moreover, all we know of a track is its label.

Given the assumptions illustrated above, we have to deal with the problem of making the collaborative filtering approach effective in a situation where drawbacks 1 and 2 are present. The objective of this work is to extend the standard collaborative filtering approach to enable its use in a CBR loop in the context of compositional recommendation systems.

Before introducing our approach for achieving this objective, we briefly illustrate the CoCoA system, which represents the first practical application of our work.

5   CoCoA as Compilation Compiler Advisor

CoCoA, a COmpilation COmpiler Advisor, has been designed as a Web site that supports the editing of compilations by means of a repository of sound tracks and a case base of compilations.

The system architecture allows the sound track providers to plug this compositional facility into their existing sales software. The management and distribution of the sound tracks is not part of CoCoA, which supports only the assembling process and the management of the case-based repository, i.e. the database of virtual compilations, containing only track indexes.

A running version of this Web service has been deployed for the Karadar[2] Web site, a provider of free classical music. Starting from the catalogue of Karadar (a set of around 2000 sound tracks) CoCoA allows the user to collect a set of tracks in a compilation, while the downloading of the final product is left again to the Karadar Web site.

The bootstrap of the case base has been performed by looking at the log files of the Web site. The mining of this kind of data allowed for the detection of the sequences of downloads concerning 5 to 12 sound tracks. For each of these sequences, a compilation was stored in the case base.

From a CBR perspective, the system implements two models of interaction: the recommend model and the complete model. The recommend model is depicted in figure 1, which summarizes the main steps of interaction. The user

---

[2] See the URL http://www.karadar.com.

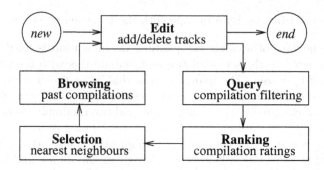

Fig. 1. User Adaptation: the CBR interaction supports the retrieval of past similar compilations, the choice concerning the reuse of such information remains with the user.

looking at the repository of sound tracks can iteratively delete or add new tracks to his own compilation. On demand, the user can decide to invoke the recommend utility in order to add new tracks taken from past compilations. First, the current partial compilation is addressed to the retrieval engine as an implicit query where the terms are the sound tracks currently included in the collection. A second step performs a ranking process to classify the compilations of the case base with respect to the given query. A third step selects the closest compilations, which are presented to the user. A fourth step, under the control of the user, allows the browsing of the compilations returned by the query and the selection of tracks for the completion of the user's collection.

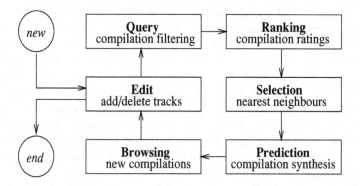

Fig. 2. System Completion: the CBR steps of retrieval and reuse are managed automatically by the system; the revision and the refinement of proposed solutions still lie with the end user.

A second interaction model, namely the completion model, is essentially organized along the lines of the previous one. The main difference concerns a supplementary step between the selection and the browsing steps. A prediction process enables the system to perform a synthesis of new compilations providing a possible completion of the partial collection assembled by the user. In this case, the user will browse a set of "virtual" compilations, since the case base does not necessarily include any of them. Of course, the completion of the final collection still remains the decision of the user.

After having presented the interaction models, we now explain how a recommendation engine supporting this kind of model has been designed, and how the drawbacks highlighted in the previous section have been overcome.

6   The Recommendation Engine

The recommendation engine represents the core of a CBR system for a compositional recommendation system. It takes the partial collection being assembled and the repository of past compilations as inputs. Its output is a subset of the case base and a ranking of the selected compilations.

The intuitive idea that underlies our view is as follows. Let consider a track as a user, then it is possible to imagine a *track profile* as a vector where the entries represent the ratings that the given track assigned to the other tracks. These ratings can be easily acquired looking at the co-occurence of two tracks in the same compilation: every time this happens the score increases. Based on the notion of track profile we have to build the concept of *compilation profile* because the goal of the recommendation is a comparison between compilations.

To illustrate in detail how - given a partial compilation as input we obtain a sound output - let us go through a step-by-step definition of the basic elements of the computational method. For the sake of simplicity, we continue to refer to the music domain, without loss of generality.

Definition 1 (Sound Tracks). $T = \{t_i\}$ *is a finite collection of components, namely sound tracks.*

It is worth noticing that the definition of sound tracks does not require providing a feature value specification. Any individual sound track is represented only by its id-code.

Definition 2 (Track Compilation). *Let n be some fixed integer much smaller than the cardinality of T. Then $C = \{c_i = \{t_{i1}, \ldots, t_{in}\} \mid t_{ij} \in T\}$ is a finite collection of sound tracks.*

Although a compilation entails the notion of a sequence, in the following we will not take this information into account. From now on, we assume that the compositional problem only regards the notion of collection.

Definition 3 (Active Compilation).
$A = \{a_i = \{t_{i1}, \ldots, t_{im}\} \mid t_{ij} \in T, \ m \leq n\}$ *is a finite collection of sound tracks at most of the same cardinality of a track compilation.*

The active compilation plays the role of the recommendation query when a collection of track compilations is organized in a case base. Before introducing how a single compilation can be viewed as a user profile from a collaborative filtering perspective, let us see what kind of information can be extracted from a case base.

Throughout this paper by CB we shall denote the subset of C forming the current case base.

Definition 4 (Frequency of track pairs).
Let $s : 2^T \rightarrow 2^C$ be a function that given a subset S of sound tracks returns the subset of compilations that include them: $s(S) = \{c \in CB | S \subseteq c\}$. Then $f_\nu : 2^T \rightarrow [0,1] \subset \mathcal{R}^+$ allows obtaining the frequency of a subset of sound tracks: $f_\nu(S) = |s(S)||CB|^{-1}$. An approximation of the sound track probability can be derived from the track frequency:

$$\hat{P}(t_i) = f_{t_i}(t_i) = f_\nu(\{t_i\}) \quad f_{t_i}(t_j) = \frac{|s(\{t_i, t_j\})|}{|CB|} = f_{t_j}(t_i)$$

Using this formulation we can also derive the approximation of the conditional probability:

$$\hat{P}(t_i | t_j) = \frac{f_{t_j}(t_i)}{f_{t_j}(t_j)} = \frac{f_{t_i}(t_j)}{f_{t_j}(t_j)}$$

The above definition introduced an approximation of the term $\hat{P}(t_i | t_j)$ that can be considered part of a track profile where $\frac{f_{t_i}(t_j)}{f_{t_i}(t_i)}$ says how much the track t_i "likes" the track t_j, i.e. the rating of t_j formulated by t_i.

Now, we need to summarize a kind of compilation profile starting from the profiles $f_{t_i}(t)$ related to the tracks that belong to a given compilation.

Definition 5 (Compilation Synthetic Function). Given a function $\mu : 2^T \rightarrow [0,1]^T$ and a compilation $c \in CB \subset C$, where $c = \{t_1, \ldots, t_n\}$, a characteristic function can be defined as:

$$\mu_c : T \rightarrow [0,1], \quad \mu_c(t) = \mu(t_1, \ldots, t_n)(t)$$

The function $\mu_c(t)$ allows to summarize a compilation profile that does not restrict its definition to the subset of track components. $\mu_c(t)$ is defined over all of T; it does mean that we can interpret the value $\mu_c(\bar{t})$, where $\bar{t} \notin c$, as an estimate of how much the compilation c likes the track $\bar{t}$. In this way we can cope with the scarce overlap of compilations (see drawback 1). Further, the range of any μ_c is the interval $[0,1]$ thus providing the needed graduation of the ratings (see drawback 2).

In the following, we propose an hypothesis for μ although we are aware that its choice is related to the definition of a loss function. More details on the evaluational criteria will be illustrated in the section dedicated to the experiments.

Definition 6 (μ Function). Let μ be a linear composition:

$$\mu(d_1, \ldots, d_n)(t) = \sum_{d_j} \kappa(d_j) \hat{P}(t | d_j) = \sum_{d_j} \kappa(d_j) \frac{f_{d_j}(t)}{f_{d_j}(d_j)}$$

where $\kappa(d_j)$ is a weight to balance the contribution of the single components of the given compilation.

Although the objective of the parameter $\kappa(d_j)$ is to measure how much a track is representative for the *genre of use* of the compilation it belongs to, for the sake of simplicity in the following we assume $\kappa(d_j)$ to be a constant.

Once a synthetic function to model the compilation is available, we can simply rely on a linear process to assess the similarity and to rank the case base.

Definition 7 (Selection Process). *A function* $g : A \times 2^C \to 2^C$ *to select the nearest neighbour compilations, given a distance measure d and a threshold k:*

$$g_k(a_i, CB) = \{c_i | d(a_i, c_i) \le k, \ c_i \in CB, \ CB \subset C\}$$

To compare two compilations as usually performed in collaborative filtering, we can refer to the Pearson correlation coefficient. This measure can now be effective, because the drawbacks 1 and 2 described earlier have been removed. The compilation profiles are widely defined over T increasing their overlap. Moreover the compilation profiles, even the implicit and tacit rating derived from the compilation, can differentiate the agreement on different sound tracks through the synthesis of frequency pairs.

Definition 8 (Pearson Correlation Coefficient). *Let $a \in A$ be an active compilation and $c \in CB$ a past compilation, given a range $D \subseteq T$ a function $d :$ $A \times CB \to [-1, 1]$ returns the linear correlation factor between two compilations:*

$$d(a, c) = \frac{\sum_{t \in D}(\mu_a(t) - \bar{\mu}_a)(\mu_c(t) - \bar{\mu}_c)}{\sqrt{\sum_{t \in D}(\mu_a(t) - \bar{\mu}_a)^2 \sum_{t \in D}(\mu_c(t) - \bar{\mu}_c)^2}}$$

where $\bar{\mu}_a$ and $\bar{\mu}_c$ respectively denote the mean value of μ_a and μ_c over D.

Associated with the Pearson correlation coefficient an algorithm has been developed, called *agave-t* , implementing the schema illustrated above where $D = T$. The major enhancement introduced by this algorithm is that two compilations can be compared even if they do not share any track. Moreover, the comparison can also occur between sound tracks that do not belong to any of the two compilations, which are the majority.

We developed a different version of the algorithm, *agave-c* , restricting the range of comparison to the subset of tracks belonging to the active compilation or the track compilation. This restriction reduces the problem of dimensionality suffered by the approach based on user profiles. For the same reason, we have designed a third version of the algorithm, *agave-cvs* , that implements a different comparison based on vector similarity.

Definition 9 (Vector Similarity Coefficient). *Let $a \in A$ be an active compilation and $c \in CB$ a past compilation, given a range $D = c \cup (a \cap T)$ a function $d : A \times CB \to \mathcal{R}^+$ returns the cosine of the angle between two compilations:*

$$d(a, c) = \sum_{t \in D} \frac{\mu_a(t)}{\sqrt{\sum_{t \in D} \mu_a(t)^2}} \frac{\mu_c(t)}{\sqrt{\sum_{t \in D} \mu_c(t)^2}}$$

The variation introduced with the *agave-c* and *agave-c* algorithms have a significant impact on the computational complexity. The restriction on the dimensionality of D allows us to reduce the complexity to a linear dependency on the size of the case base, because in $O(|D||CB|)$ the term $|D|$ becomes nearly a constant factor.

Definition 10 (Completion Process). *Let $a \in A$ be an active compilation and $c \in CB$ a past compilation, a function $h : A \times CB \to 2^T$ returns a compilations $\hat{c}$ such that $a \cap \hat{c} = a$ and $\hat{c} \cap \{a \cup c\} = \hat{c}$.*

A trivial interpretation of the completion process could be a function that, while preserving the tracks defined in the active query, performs the synthesis of a new compilation by a random selection of the missing tracks.

7   Related Work

Recently, much work has been published in the area of Collaborative Filtering, but the focus of our paper is slightly different. While in standard recommendation systems the goal is to accurately predict the affinity of the user to a specific good, in the context of compositional e-commerce this goal is extended to a collection of goods. For this reason a direct comparison of the proposed approach with the main recommendation system is not possible.

We prefer to move the analysis of the related work to a basic technique underlying many applications in the area of information retrieval and collaborative filtering: the singular value decomposition (SVD) [1,2,12]. Although other methods have been derived from SVD, such as the latent semantic analysis (LSI) [4] and the related probabilistic variation (PLSI) [9], we limit the comparison to SVD because it is representative of the approaches based on dimensionality reduction.

SVD can be viewed as a technique for deriving a set of uncorrelated indexing variables or factors; each track and compilation is represented by its vector of factor values. Note that by virtue of the dimension reduction, it is possible for compilations with different tracks to be mapped into the same vector of factor values.

A byproduct of the SVD approach is the possibility to estimate a correlation factor between two collections that do not share any of their components. This feature is strongly related to the challenge engaged with the compositional e-commerce.

Let us summarize how the SVD works looking at our chosen domain of music. The starting point of SVD is a very sparse matrix X of $c \times t$ (compilations $\times$ tracks) where every cell contains 1 if that track is contained in that compilation and 0 otherwise. SVD allows to decompose this rectangular matrix into three other matrices of a very special form (the resulting matrices contain "singular vectors" and "singular values").

These special matrices yield a breakdown of the original relationships into linearly independent components or factors. In general, many of these components are very small, and may be ignored, leading to an approximate model with many fewer dimensions. In this reduced model all the track-track, compilation-compilation and track-compilation similarity is now approximated by values in this smaller number of dimensions. The result can still be represented geometrically by a spatial configuration in which the dot product or cosine between vectors representing two objects corresponds to their estimated similarity.

8   Evaluation Results

After the presentation of our approach, based on the mix of CBR and CF, and a description of the state of the art concerning the basic technique for implementing a recommendation system, we now focus our attention on the empirical analysis.

In the following, we illustrate how we selected the dataset to perform a comparative analysis. We then explain how we have designed the experiments and the evaluation setup. Finally, in a discussion of the results we try to summarize the main contribution of this work.

8.1   Dataset Setup

To evaluate our approach we needed information about compilations of objects (music tracks, movies, etc. . .). The CoCoA system is going to be deployed on the Web; in the meantime, we cannot exploit the case base that will be available as soon as it achieves a significant number of users. Waiting for a real case base of compilations, we had to look for an alternative solution.

The community that is working on the recommendation system provides a dataset based on the notions of user profiles and goods. But the concept of *compilation* is slightly different from *profile* because the former is an aggregation of items usually with a small and limited size, while the latter is allowed to grow indefinitely. A user profile is effective as long as it increases, and very often the recommendation accuracy is related to its size.

Moreover, a further difference distinguishes a user profile from a compilation: all the items of a collection are strongly related by a sort of homogeneous factor. We can assume the existence of the common feature, even if not explicit, that takes the same value for all the items of the collection. We are actually assuming that every compilation has a rationale for its existence, even if this rationale is not explicitly stated or even known. On the contrary, a user profile does not provide such information concerning the relationship among a selection of items rated by a single user.

For these reasons, we could not use a traditional Collaborative Filtering dataset, so we have designed a specific one for our purpose. The synthesis of the dataset has been derived starting from Eachmovie [10], a dataset composed of 2811983 ratings expressed by 72916 users on 1648 movies. A related dataset, the IMDB, supports an extended content description for every movie such as the year of release and the indication of the genres.

We generated a dataset of movie collections giving a genre to each of them. A genre has been defined following a criteria of uniformity along one or more features for every movie of the collection. We defined 15 different genres: before 90', 90'-93', 94', 95', 96', Action, Animation, Art Foreign, Classic, Comedy, Drama, Family, Horror, Romance, Thriller. This choice allows the same movie to belong to more than one collection genres.

To simulate the way in which people select the movies to aggregate them in collections, we performed a pseudo-random extraction using the data of Eachmovie. We derived the distribution from the frequency of the rated movies. Also, the number of compilations of each genre is proportional to the number of ratings people gave to movies belonging to that genre.

The total number of compilations is 2995 made out of 1086 movies and each compilation contains 10 movies.

8.2   Setup Experiment

The task selected for the experiment is the retrieval of the 10 nearest neighbours among the train set compilations for every test set compilation. We have created 10 crossfolds randomly dividing the 2995 compilations in a train set of 2395 compilations and a test set of 600.

To evaluate the interaction model illustrated above, we needed to test the usual way of invoking the recommendation utility: the typical scenario sees the user insert some movies (or items, in the general case) and then ask for similar past compilations, hopefully of the genre sketched in the active compilation. For this reason it is crucial to properly manage short queries intended as partial compilations.

To test this aspect, we have designed different experiments on the same dataset, in which we changed the shadowed portion of every test compilation. More precisely, we replicated the standard test step many times taking into account respectively from 1 to 9 movies of each compilation in the test set. This way we can simulate the evolution of the active compilation and the different complexity of the related query. The challenge is to achieve good accuracy performance overall when only a sketch of the compilation is available, i.e. the system is dealing with "short" queries.

The performance evaluation measures accuracy in terms of percentage of recommended compilations with the same genre as the active one. For every test compilation we have extracted the 1nn. The computation of the mean error over the 10nn has given similar results.

8.3   Discussion of Results

In figure 3 one can see our algorithm *agave-t* compared to *SVD* Although the parameter for the dimensionality reduction has been optimized, namely $k = 200$, *agave-t* still outperforms SVD. *agave-t* doesn't require a fine tuning of the algorithm and can be considered a valid alternative to *SVD* respect with the problem of data sparsity. While *SVD* reduces the dimensionality of the data, *agave-t* fills the gap by achieving a reduction of the sparseness coefficient that passes from 99% to 25%.

Of course, it is worth noticing that the improvement introduced with *agave-t* is not balanced by the on line computational effort. The theoretical online complexity - crucial for time performance - gives opposite results: $O(k|CB|)$ for *SVD* and $O(|T||CB|)$ for *agave-t* . This comparison is quite crucial because in general k is much smaller than $|T|$ (in our case 200 versus 2395).

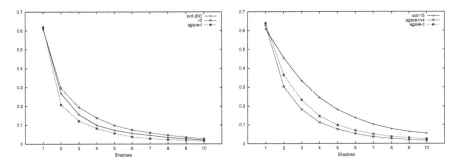

Fig. 3. Mean error of *genre of use* matching between test compilation and the 1nn train compilation recommended. The shadow axis shows how many tracks of the test compilation have been used. On the left side the *rif* method represents the lower bound: a 1nn recommendation explicitly using the information of *genre of use* On the right side the result of the comparison among alternative solutions that require the same computational effort.

However, assuming it is viable to slightly relax the accuracy constraint to give more attention to the time response, the proposed approach can achieve interesting results. Taking this perspective we also have tried a version of the algorithm, called *agave-c* , that reduces the computation of the Pearson correlation coefficient between the test and train compilations considering only the movies of those compilations instead of all the movies. Thus the mean complexity is reduced to $O(2\bar{c}|CB|)$ where $\bar{c}$ is the average number of movies in a compilation (10, in our experiments). As expected, the accuracy error increases but, differently from the previous case, the enhancement achieved on the time response is much more significant than the loss of accuracy. Moreover, the accuracy of SVD decreases much faster than *agave-c* . To highlight this aspect we have compared the achieved results with *svd15* that has a comparable online complexity. The results concerning *agave-c* are depicted in figure 3 (right).

The plot also shows *agave-cvs* , a version of *agave-c* in which, in order to compute the similarity between two compilations, we substitute the Pearson correlation coefficient with the cosine of the angle of the vectors representing the two compilations.

This simpler measure (used for instance by SVD) works even better. The reason is related to the dimensionality reduction: the reduced extent prevents the problem of the curse of dimensionality. In this case the Pearson correlation coefficient is less effective because the notion of sparseness does not apply: let us remind the reader that on average we have to compare two vectors of 10-15 components.

As previously stated, our main goal is to reach a certain level of accuracy especially when trying to find a compilation to recommend in reply to a query containing few movies. The results show that, even in presence of partial query compilations, the accuracy of the recommended compilation is good. This is significant especially when compared to Collaborative Filtering algorithms that work well only after the acquisition of a meaningful history interaction to achieve a rich user profile.

From the point of view of CBR this result allows to exploit the collaborative filtering technique without the restriction of the user profile but enabling the association between a case and a single user interaction. In this way the case base becomes the repository of the interaction episodes and the user is free to play different roles, i.e. to assemble compilations not necessarily related to each other.

9   Future Directions

First of all, we hope to make available as soon as possible a real case base of compilations through the deployment of CoCoA[3].

This step is the premise for the refinement of the evaluation setup that has to overcome the constraint of fixed genres. We need to deal with a situation where every single compilation might be representative of a new genre of use. The final goal is to have the opportunity to assess the genre proximity.

The hypothesis for $\mu_c(t)$ illustrated in this paper represents a preliminary solution to the aggregation problem of the different track profiles encoded by $\frac{f_{t_i}(t_j)}{f_{t_i}(t_i)}$. A deeper understanding concerning alternative schemas has to be achieved. For example: how to balance the contribution of the different track profiles is still an open problem. We are already taking into account graph-based clustering techniques to detect how much a single track can be considered representative of a genre of use.

Finally we have not yet designed the completion function to support the related interaction model. The delivery of support of this kind could create the premises for an interesting comparison - from a CBR point of view - between the recommender and the completion models.

Acknowledgments

We would like to thank Anna Perini, Michele Nori, Gianluca Mameli and Marco Grimaldi for their important role in designing and developing CoCoA.

The *Each-Movie* database was generously provided by the System Research Center of Digital Equipment Corporation, which makes it available for use in research.

---

[3] A beta version is available at the following address http://cocoa.itc.it/

References

1. M. Berry and S. Dumais. Using linear algebra for intelligent information retrieval. *SIAM Review 37(4)*, pages 573–595, 1995.
2. D. Billsus and M. J. Pazzani. Learning collaborative information filters. Technical report, AAAI, July 1998.
3. Padraig Cunningham, Ralph Bergmann, S. Schmitt, R. Traphoener, and S. Breen. Websell: Intelligent sales assistants for the world wide web. Technical report, Trinity College Dublin, 2000.
4. S. Deerwester, S.T. Dumais, G.W. Furnas, T.K. Landauer, and R. Harshman. Indexing by latent semantic analysis. *Journal of the American Society for Information Science*, pages 391–407, 1990.
5. George E. Forsythe, Michael A. Malcolm, and Cleve B. Moler. *Computer Methods for Mathematical Computations*. Prentice-Hall, Englewood Cliffs, NJ 07632, USA, 1977.
6. D. Goldberg, D. Nichols, B.M. Oki, and D. Terry. Using collaborative filtering to weave an information tapestry. *Communications of the ACM*, 35(12):61–70, 1992.
7. Gene H. Golub and Charles F. Van Loan. *Matrix Computations*. The Johns Hopkins University Press and North Oxford Academic, Baltimore, MD, USA and Oxford, England, 1983.
8. C. Hayes and P. Cunningham. Smart radio: Building music radio on the fly. In *Expert Systems 2000, Cambridge, UK*, 2000.
9. Thomas Hofmann. Probabilistic latent semantic analysis. pages 177–196, 2001.
10. P. McJones. Eachmovie collaborative filtering data set, dec systems research center, 1997. http://research.compaq.com/SRC/eachmovie/.
11. P. Resnick and H.R. Varian. Recommender systems. *Communications of the ACM*, 40(3):56–58, 1997.
12. B. M. Sarwar, G. Karypis, J. A. Konstan, and J. Riedl. Application of dimensionality reduction in recommender system – a case study. In *ACM WebKDD 2000 Web Mining for E-Commerce Workshop*, 2000.
13. J.B. Schafer, J. Konstan, J., and Riedl. Recommender systems in e-commerce. In *Proceeding of the ACM Conference on Electronic Commerce*, Pittsburgh, PA, USA, November 1999.
14. S. Schmitt and R. Bergmann. Applying case-based reasoning technology for product selection and customization in electronic commerce environments. In *12th Bled Electronic Commerce Conference*, 1999.
15. Armin Stahl and Ralph Bergmann. Applying recursive CBR for the customization of structured products in an electronic shop. In *EWCBR*, pages 297–308, 2000.
16. Wolfgang Wilke, Mario Lenz, and Stefan Wess. Intelligent sales support with CBR. In *Case-Based Reasoning Technology*, pages 91–114, 1998.

Tuning Production Processes
through a Case Based Reasoning Approach

Stefania Bandini, Sara Manzoni, and Carla Simone

Department of Computer Science, Systems and Communication
University of Milano-Bicocca
Via Bicocca degli Arcimboldi 8 20126 Milan - Italy
tel +39 02 64487835 fax + 39 02 64487839
{bandini, manzoni, simone}@disco.unimib.it

Abstract. This paper illustrates how the Case Based Reasoning (CBR) paradigm has been applied to the definition of the requirements and the specifications of a Knowledge Management technology supporting the handling of tuning and anomalies in production processes. In particular, the production of truck tyres will be illustrated as the application domain of the proposed approach. This domain is a paradigmatic example where the valorization of the experiential knowledge is a company requirement, so the representation of knowledge concerning production process issues is mandatory. It requires extending CBR techniques to an emerging area of application involving knowledge about the interplay of static objects (i.e. products) with dynamic objects (i.e. processes). The content of production cases, their organization into a Case Base and a first proposal for the Case Base retrieval of similar cases will be presented.

1 Introduction

The life–cycle of a product in manufacturing companies consists of several phases that can be divided into two main steps: design and production. The design step is usually triggered by the need of innovation defined by marketing strategies oriented to answer requests emerging from the market or from new needs induced in it [1]. The goal of the design step is to define the specifications of the product and its production process. Hence, design is focused on a set of product properties like: market segment, composition (possibly expressed in terms of subassemblies), functional specification, performances, and so on. As far as the production process is concerned, the design focus is on another set of properties like: production steps, related machinery and timing, quality control parameters, and so on.

Product and process specifications define the constraints the production process has to respect in order to make products pass the quality control and be successfully distributed on the market. Like any sort of specifications, they cannot be exhaustive of all the possible details characterizing the instantiations of the production process. In fact, design is usually a process located where the core design competencies reside, while production is increasingly distributed in different plants to take advantage of local facilities or to make production scheduling

S. Craw and A. Preece (Eds.): ECCBR 2002, LNAI 2416, pp. 475–489, 2002.

more flexible to the market needs. A similar argument holds for product specifications: each instantiation of the production process happens in a different contingent situation where, for instance, raw materials can show even slightly different properties. Different production context might lead to variable or unexpected results on the final product and to the consequent modification of the product structure or composition [2].

The aim of the production process is to realize products that fulfill the design specifications, especially in terms of functionality and performances. Moreover, it has to guarantee that these specifications are uniformly respected by all products that will be sold in the market. This has to happen despite of all possible local perturbations that make the current situation different from the ideal one, that is, the situation envisaged when product and process specifications have been defined. Perturbations may concern structural properties of the local plant: e.g., machinery, work practices, environmental conditions and so on. They may concern also unanticipated events like lack of materials, machinery breakdowns, personnel turn–over and so on.

The role of experience concerning heuristics and historical memory is fundamental in both design and production steps, although with some intrinsic differences that have a strong impact on the construction of a technology that supports the use of previous experiences.

1. In design, the experience of designers is crucial to reduce the related cost and duration. On the one hand, innovation is often achieved through the modification of existing products in terms of materials and subassemblies [3]; on the other hand, design is achieved through the cooperation of experts in different technological disciplines as well as of experts about the company organization. Experience is then related to a broad spectrum of competencies concerning products, production processes and organization, and is accumulated and reused by knowledge workers that in any case can come in contact, directly or indirectly, at crucial steps in design. Although the time of the related problem solving is not so strict, however it is sensible to improve the time–to–market of the envisaged innovative products. In fact, design is an iterative and lasting process based on new ideas and on their evaluation through prototypes and pre–series.

2. In production, the situation is different. The involved workers do not know about the design process and its leading strategies, and their experience is limited to specific products, productions and related machinery. Their problems are time–critical since they can stop or deteriorate the production process in an unacceptable way. Experts, that are often not available, own the competencies needed to solve them. Designers are located in different departments, more experienced workers are often allocated to crucial production processes (e.g., related to the construction of prototypes or pre–series requested by design) and cannot timely provide their help. This scenario is characterized by a turnover or reallocation of people for production purposes that makes it difficult for most of the workers to accumulate the necessary experience to become autonomous in production problem solving. In many

cases, only few people become expert problem solvers, and their knowledge plays a central role in the functioning of the entire production process.

From the technology point of view, the Case Based Reasoning (CBR [4]) paradigm is one of the natural candidates to support the capitalization of experience and its reuse. It has been applied to knowledge management in many areas [5,6], and there is a growing interest in this kind of approach (for instance, to support organizational learning in software development [7]). In this paper we take manufacturing as the reference domain, since we adopted the CBR paradigm to build a computer system supporting the design of rubber compounds in the production of tyres dedicated to car racing (P–Race Project [8,9]). However, the approach we are going to illustrate could be applied to other manufacturing domains. The P–Race project has been activated in order to support the computer–based coordination and sharing of knowledge within a team of designers involved in the chemical formulation of rubber compounds of tyre tread dedicated to motor races. Hence, the system developed in the project has been designed and developed in a knowledge management perspective by considering a well defined community of practices. Because of the different competencies involved in the decision–making process (race engineers and compound designers, who own a large part of the chemical core knowledge of a tyre company), multiple knowledge representation techniques have been adopted, and integrated into a unique CBR computational framework. The latter captures the episodic knowledge characterizing most of the reasoning activity of the race engineer, and supports the dynamical process of experience growth and knowledge creation through incremental learning. To this aim, a dedicated formalism for the representation of model–based knowledge for chemical formulation (called Abstract Compounds Machine - ACM [3]) allows the core competence about rubber compounds to be explicitly represented, elaborated and integrated in the CBR architecture.

The success of this solution motivated to start another project (called P–Truck) whose aim is to support the capitalization of experience in the more complex situation of large scale tyre production, specifically those tyres used by large–size vehicles (e.g., trucks, buses). Since the valorization of the experiential knowledge described in point (2) was a company requirement, the representation of knowledge concerning production *process issues* was considered mandatory. The production of truck tyres (but this example can be extended to many other kinds of industrial products) is large scale and distributed across many plants, located in different countries.

The capitalization and sharing of experience across these production plants improves the problem solving concerning local production as well as the standardization of products around the world. Finally, and for the above reasons, in this case experience is about both products and production processes: the latter require to extend the CBR techniques to an emerging area of application [10] involving knowledge about the interplay of static objects (i.e. products) with dynamic objects (i.e. processes).

The aim of this paper is to illustrate how the CBR paradigm has been applied to the definition of the requirements and the specifications of a Knowledge Management technology supporting the handling of anomalies in the production of truck tyres according to their design specifications, in view of its implementation in a working prototype. The paper is organized as follows: in the next section, the knowledge concerning the activities and competencies of a community of practice involved in both product design and the production process design will be presented. Section 3 will illustrate the Case Base content and structure of the CBR tool designed support the management and reuse of the experiential knowledge involved in these activities. Finally, a proposal for case retrieval that has been implemented in the first prototype of the CBR tool will be described.

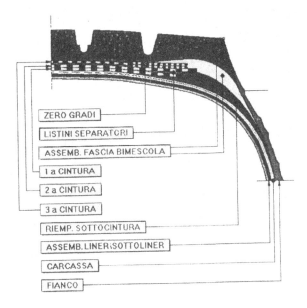

Fig. 1. A view of a truck tyre where some of the main components are shown.

2   Tyres and Tyre Production

Batches composing the different rubber based components of a tyre are chemical compounds represented by a set of ingredients organized in *recipes*. Each recipe determines the most relevant properties of the batch. Recipes incorporate knowledge in terms of chemical formulation of rubber compounds, and forms the core knowledge of a tyre company when combined with the one concerning the structure of the tyre. Figure 1 shows a schematic representation of a tyre and major tyre components (e.g. tread batch, liner and metallic components). Each component of a tyre has a specific function fulfilling specific required properties of the global product. Tyre design requires to identify the set of properties of tyre components that guarantees the desired performance. The design of a new tyre generally involves the adaptation of some components of an already existing product [3].

Figure 2 shows an high level representation of the tyre design process in terms of Superposed Automata Net (SA Net - a modular class of Petri Nets, particularly useful to model distributed processes [11]). In this process, market requirements and the result of competitor analysis, research and development conducted within the tyre company are formalized and translated into features of the product and of its components.

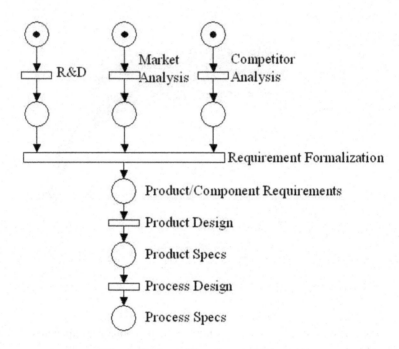

Fig. 2. Design of Product and Process.

The design of production process can be very complex. In a very schematic description, after the definition of marketing requirements, the main product requirements are outlined. In order to perform product design specifications of all the tyre components are defined. Thus process design follows (i.e. identification of main production phases, their timing and characteristic parameters). The design of specifications for each production phase (see section 2.1) is based on well defined procedures and involves highly specialized and diversified competencies. Quite obviously, the skills of the people involved in the design of production processes (i.e. compound and process designers) consist of their experience in the field and their knowledge about a very complex decision making problem.

For instance, knowledge about production machineries, product features and requirements, constraints given by the manufacturing context and so on. In the following section, a description of the phases characterizing tyre production process will be given, but even many other production domains can by recognized in this example.

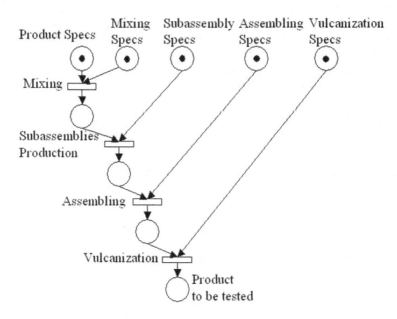

Fig. 3. The Tyre Production cycle

2.1   Tyre Production Process

Figure 3 describes the typical tyre production process, whose main phases are:

- Mixing: raw materials specified in the batch recipe (i.e., designed product) are mixed in dedicated machineries (e.g. Banbury and Intermixer). The aim of the design of this phase is to define the set of machineries to be used, the mixing order for raw materials, timing and other specific parameters (Fill Factor of each machinery, mixing temperatures and so on).
- Production of Subassemblies: batches obtained in the mixing phase are assembled with other metallic components.
- Component Assembling: the set of tyre subassemblies are combined in order to compose the tyre.
- Vulcanization: moulding is performed in order to bring the rubber compound from an elastic state to a plastic one and to impress the pattern on tread batch and product codes on the border.

– Product Test: in order to evaluate the level of compliance with product requirements, tyres are evaluated through a set of tests in internal labs as well as outdoor (i.e. on testing tracks).

Obviously, production cannot always respect the specifications generated by process design and sometimes it is necessary to *tune* such specifications in order to adapt them to the production context. Thus, besides standard process design, process tuning has sometimes to be performed during manufacturing. Process tuning is performed in order to adapt the standard designed process to local production contexts and to take care of perturbations that may concern structural properties of the local plant (e.g., machinery, work practices, environmental conditions and so on). Moreover, through process tuning it is possible to take care of unanticipated events (e.g., lack of materials, machinery breakdowns, personnel turn–over and so on) and non–uniformity in raw materials in order to guarantee the necessary uniformity of production results.

2.2   Tuning a Tyre Production Process

The critical situations described above are called *process anomalies* and require the modification of the current production process until the problems generating anomalies are fixed. Typical situations of production anomalies concern:

– the local production unit: the production process, even if it has been designed for a specific unit, may have neglected some specific feature of the context. For instance, in production process design for a local plant its technological infrastructure (i.e., the set of available machineries) is considered, but it is not always possible to take into account the productive context (e.g. overload of some machineries or peculiar climatic conditions about the plant location).
– a transient problem of the productive unit: lack of resources, like machines or raw materials, can be an example of a local and transient problem that could stop the production;
– non–uniformity of raw materials: different lots of raw materials show difformity in their basic specification (e.g., different provider of raw materials); in this case, process tuning has to be performed in order to guarantee the uniformity of the resulting products.

Although anomalies are not too frequent, they are extremely crucial since the time available to find a solution and continue the production under the new circumstances is very short. In fact, even a block in the production process lasts only few hours, it can be really expensive and have problematic side–effects on the overall planning of the whole production. The search for a quick solution justifies to record anomalies connected to problems that have already been experienced and solved in the past. Due to the time constraints, anomalies have to be solved by people working in the production line, typically experienced workers who are however very busy or involved in off–line production activities (like, product testing). While process designers are skilled in the definition if ideal processes and their knowledge is materialized in production protocols, people working in the production line are skilled in solving every day problems without making references to any sort of formalization of their competence. In general, the related experience is not stated explicitly in production reports and the details of the problem solving activity are lost. Knowledge engineering with this people revealed that the nature of their problem solving activity is mainly episodic, that is based on previous similar situations: they often reason about past cases in order to solve the current one.

3   A CBR approach to Support the Tuning of Production Process

In order to design a CBR tool to support the tuning of tyre production processes, a knowledge acquisition campaign was conducted with a team of domain experts. The main aims of knowledge acquisition were to define the pieces of information to be represented in the Case Base, to verify their availability and to define the way to organize and manage them. The needed information has been collected through both interviews with domain experts and the analysis of documents used in design and production activities. In particular those documents that allow the exchange of information between experts dedicated to design activity and those dedicated to production have been analyzed (i.e., documents for product and process specifications from designers as well as production and post–production reports). Moreover a classification of production anomalies has been derived, together with domain experts, from the documents describing tuning actions performed during production. Once case representation has been defined, dedicated user interfaces to collect needed data have been designed and developed. Figure 4 shows a screen–shot of one of these user interfaces (specifically, the one referring to the mixing phase). Through these interfaces, system users describe production cases and specify the data to be selected from the company information system in order to be organized into the Case Base.

In the following, the issues that has been addressed in building the Case Base of production cases will be described in terms of: what is a production case, which are its component parts, what kind of structure is suitable to organize cases and which similarity function allows the reuse of production experience for process tuning.

3.1   Case Base Content

In the considered application domain the problem solving connected to the tuning of the production process activity has to consider the interplay between properties of static objects (i.e. products) and the intrinsic dynamical nature of the production process. For example, the lack of a raw material or a slight difference in its properties often require changing the structure of the actions constituting the production process or their functional parameters. Hence, in the knowledge representation involved in the creation of a CBR system supporting the tuning of production processes, the design of the case must take

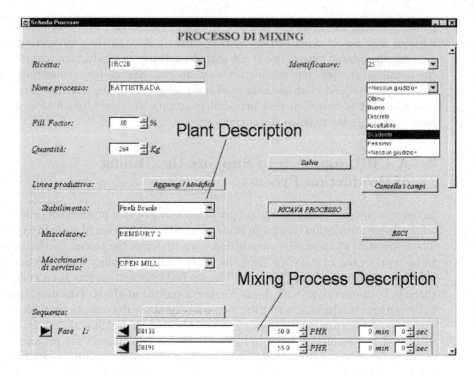

Fig. 4. A screen–shot of the user interface for the acquisition of data about the mixing production phase. This interface allows the system to select directly from the company information system the data that are organized into the Case Base and the allow the system to support users in handling production anomalies.

into consideration this interplay. This is achieved by keeping distinct the logical representation of the involved objects and properties, on one hand, and, on the other hand, by focusing on their dynamic relations.

According to the approach proposed in [4], the information that has been acquired to represent production cases has been organized in three main parts: *case description, case solution*, and *case outcome*. As illustrated in Figure 5, case description consists of a set of attributes referring to:

1. Product Specification: describing the manufactured product in terms of design motivations (e.g., marketing requirements) and design results (e.g., product specification in terms of composing subassemblies, subassembly specifications, and so on - batch recipe for rubber compounds);
2. Process Specification: about the designed production process (e.g., number, order, timing and other parameters of each production phase);
3. Production Context: describing the production context (e.g., peculiarities of the local production context, set of machineries and raw materials that are available in the plant, and so on);

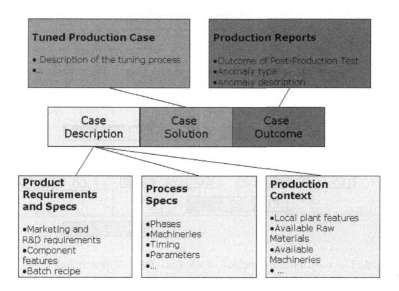

Fig. 5. Content of a production case. Information encoded into each case is organized in three main parts: Case Description, Case Solution, and Case Outcome.

The outcome part of a case describes the results obtained by performing production according to product and process specification in the production context. In general, case outcome summarizes pieces of information contained in production reports (concerning, for instance, tested product features). A significant information contained in this type of reports regards the set of production anomalies that have been encountered during production. Thus, while anomaly description encodes for instance the type of observed anomaly, the solution that as been identified to overcome this anomaly concerns the solution part of a production case. Case solution describes the tuning of the production process that is, the set of actions that have been applied in order to adapt product or process specifications to overcome the encountered production anomaly.

As described in Section 2.2, three main anomalies can be encountered during the tyre production. Actions that can be performed in order to overcome these types of production anomalies may consist in a modification of product specifications, a modification of process specifications, or both. For instance, when the production anomaly concerns the not–uniformity of raw materials, tuning actions may require either the adaptation of the product specification (for instance to substitute some raw materials) or to modify the production process in order to correct raw material problems through machinery parameters. In this way, both in the case of successful and unsuccessful process tuning, a new production process is defined as a modification of an already existing production case (i.e. the tuned one).

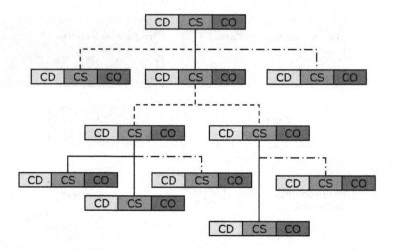

Fig. 6. The hierarchical structure of the Case Base. Different link types indicate that process tuning has been performed to overcome different production anomalies.

3.2 Case Base Organization

Since a production case is derived by tuning another production case in order to solve a local anomaly, the Case Base content is hierarchically organized. Each case is conceptually linked to the production case from which it has been derived. Moreover, according to the different type of the required tuning, a different link connects the cases. The resulting Case Base is thus organized as a set of tree structures whose root nodes correspond to standard designed processes, while all the other nodes are the result of process tuning. Obviously more than one level can be present in each tree structure since multiple and subsequent tunings can be performed starting from a single process. Moreover multiple tunings can be possible to the same process and then multiple nodes can derive from the same production case. Each time an anomalous situation is solved with the tuning of a production process, a new case is stored on the Case Base and added at the proper tree structure. Figure 6 schematically represents a tree of production cases. The case is composed by three main parts: Case Description (CD), Case Solution (CS) and Case Outcome (CO). In the figure, lines describe conceptual links connecting production cases. Plain and dotted lines are links representing process tunings performed to overcome different production anomalies.

3.3 Case Base Management

A suitable structure of the Case Base has to be chosen taking into account the efficiency of Case Base retrieval and update. Case Base content has to be sufficiently wide to guarantee the retrieval and reuse of previously stored and useful cases, but at the same time Case Base organization has to be sufficiently compact to allow the storage of a large number of cases. A huge amount of information is needed in order to completely describe production cases and since they are tuned adapting other production cases to solve production anomalies, a hierarchical structure of the Case Base has been considered as an appropriate choice that allows to efficiently represent them and to limit memory occupancy. In a set of tree structures in fact only differences from the modified case (i.e. father node) must be stored in order to represent nodes derived from it (i.e. son nodes).

As for database searching algorithms, the complexity of Case Base retrieval and update algorithms increases with the complexity of the Case Base structure. At the moment, an adequate algorithm for case retrieval within the above described structure is under design. At the present stage, an initial prototype has been implemented to test some preliminary ideas. The first formalization of the similarity computation is based on nearest neighbor techniques: it retrieves a set of cases according to a weighted sum of differences between their attribute values and the ones of the production case to be tuned. To this aim, case description attributes have been partitioned according to the type of knowledge they encode into *product*, *process* and *context*. Each partition contains sets of weights that are used in the similarity computation according to the type of anomaly that characterizes the case to be tuned. Moreover, within each partition a different priority is associated to each attribute. In this way, similarity computation can well support the decision making process of domain experts, since the attribute priorities that they consider in their everyday work is taken into account and represented as weights in the algorithm for similarity computation.

Table 1. Priority assigned to case description attributes during the computation of case similarity. Different weights are assigned according to the anomaly to be solved in production tuning. Each column reports the priority associated to each case partition; each row refers to one of the three possible production anomalies.

Anomaly	Product	Process	Context
Production Unit Peculiarity	0	0	1
Machinery Problem	1	1	0
Raw Material Problem	1	0	0

In fact, during knowledge acquisition it has emerged that domain experts consider case attributes with different priorities in the computation of similarity among production cases and that in particular they defines different priorities depending on the type of anomaly to be solved by process tuning. In order to explain how attribute priorities are involved in the similarity computation let us consider the set of values reported in Table 1. Three weights are defined for each of the three case attribute partitions, one for each production anomaly. Each column refers to a case attribute partition, while each row refers to a production anomaly. In similarity computation, when for instance the anomaly to be solved concerns some particular feature of the production context (i.e. first row), only case attributes that describes the productive context (i.e. third column) must be considered in the similarity computation (i.e. the only non–null value). On the contrary, the productive context is not a significant aspect of the case description when the anomaly to be solved concerns a machinery or a raw material problem (i.e. a null value is associated to the context partition on other rows).

As stated above, additional work has to be done in order to suitably perform case similarity computation and case retrieval. A central functionality of the final system will for instance concerns the possibility for system users to customize similarity computation. They will be obviously allowed to modify attribute weights and to select the set to be used in each similarity computation. Moreover, other and more accurate similarity functions will be defined and implemented into the system and system users will be allowed to select the one they prefer to use.

4   Concluding Remarks and Future Work

The work described in this paper takes its motivations form the P–Truck project, whose main aim is the development of a knowledge management system to support the Truck Business Unit of Pirelli Tyres in the design and manufacturing of truck tyres. The main activities performed in the last year (first of three years) concerned a deep investigation of the manufacturing domain, specifically in the case of tyre production. The reported results concern the first phase of the project. The design and development of the aimed knowledge management system required to take into account the following main factors:

- how to structure significant information and documents concerning the activities involved;
- how to acquire, classify and represent knowledge allowing information to be used (i.e. knowledge engineering activity);
- how to capture both the experiential and the model based knowledge involved;
- how to support the reuse of previously adopted solutions to analogue situations.

The preliminary solutions envisaged for the above points have been incorporated in a first prototype. It is one of the tools to be integrated in a general CBR architecture that is conceived of as a component of the overall information system supporting the Pirelli Truck Business Unit. To this aim, future work will concern on the one hand the improvement of the functionalities currently incorporated in the prototype. Specifically, the system has to provide users with a support to the adaptation of previously adopted solutions for sake of innovation and a case similarity function able to take advantage from the hierarchical structure of the Case Base (able for instance to compute similarity at more than one level of Case Base structure).

On the other hand, additional aspects have to be considered to make the above architecture usable in the target organizational context. This requires taking into account the cooperative nature of the involved problem solving. In other words, the system based on the CBR paradigm has to become part of a broader Knowledge Management system that aims to support the process of knowledge creation in the design of innovative products and production processes and to facilitate the incremental and cooperative learning rooted in the accumulation of local experiences. To this aim mechanisms have to be identified to spread information, documents and knowledge among the experts involved in the design and production tasks, and to address the right information or knowledge to each expert in order to support individual work. The need to share experiences combined with the need to have a personalized support is a major challenge in the design of effective ways to maintain the knowledge management process alive and productive for the involved cooperating actors. Recent investigations showed the need to support views tailored to local requirements (within a specific community of practice [12] and to support the interpretation of the locally acquired experiences across communities of practice. This requires techniques of knowledge representation that enhance adaptability, interpretation and reuse and that cannot avoid considering the cooperative nature of the activities generating the knowledge itself [13]. The way in which the proposed Case Base is organized is a first step in this direction.

References

1. Prahalad, C.K., Hamel, G.: The core competence of the corporation. Strategic Learning in Knowledge Economy: Individual, Collective and Organizational Learning Process (2000) 3–22
2. Utterback, J.M.: Mastering the Dynamics of Innovation. Harvard Business School Press, Boston (MA) (1996)
3. Bandini, S., Manzoni, S.: Product design as product revise. In Esposito, F., ed.: AI*IA 2001: Advances in Artificial Intelligence, 7th Congress of the Italian Association for Artificial Intelligence, Bari, Italy, September 25-28, 2001, Proceedings. Volume 2175 of Lecture Notes in Computer Science., Berlin, Springer (2001) 159–164
4. Kolodner, J.: Case-Based Reasoning. Morgan Kaufmann, San Mateo (CA) (1993)
5. Aha, D., Becerra-Fernandez, I., Maurer, F., Munoz-Avila, H., eds.: 1999 AAAI Workshop, Exploring Synergies of Knowledge Management and Case-Based Reasoning, Technical Report WS-99-19, Naval Research Lab, Navy Center for Applied Research in Artificial Intelligence (1999)
6. Aha, D., Weber, R., eds.: 2000 AAAI Workshop, Intelligent Lessons Learned Systems, Technical Report AIC-00-005, Naval Research Lab, Navy Center for Applied Research in Artificial Intelligence (2000)
7. Althoff, K.D., Birk, A., vonWangenheim, C.G., Tautz, C.: CBR for experimental software engineering. In Lenz, M., Bartsch-Spörl, B., Burkhard, H.D., Wess, S., eds.: Case-Based Reasoning Technology. Volume 1400 of Lecture Notes in Computer Science., Springer (1998) 235–254
8. Bandini, S., Manzoni, S.: A support system based on CBR for the design of rubber compounds in motor racing. In Blanzieri, E., Portinale, L., eds.: Advances in Case-Based Reasoning, 5th European Workshop, EWCBR 2000, Trento, Italy, September 6-9, 2000, Proceedings. Volume 1898 of Lecture Notes in Computer Science., Berlin, Springer (2000) 348–357

9. Bandini, S., Manzoni, S.: Modeling core knowledge and practices in a computational approach to innovation process. Model-Based Reasoning: Scientific Discovery, Technological Innovation, Values (2002)
10. Proceedings of workshop on case-based reasoning approaches for process-oriented knowledge management, at 4th international conference on case-based reasoning, ICCBR 2001, vancouver (canada), july 30 - august 2, 2001. online available at http://www.iccbr.org/iccbr01/workshops.html (2001)
11. DeCindio, F., DeMichelis, G., Simone, C.: Giving back some freedom to system designers. System Research **2** (1985) 273–280
12. Wenger, E.: Communities of Practice: Learning, Meaning and Identity. Cambridge University Press, New York (1998)
13. Simone, C., Sarini, M.: Adaptability of classification schemes: what does it mean? In: Proc.7th Conference on Computer Supported Cooperative Work, Copenhagen, September 2001, Kluwer Academic Press (2001) 19–38

An Application of Case-Based Reasoning to the Adaptive Management of Wireless Networks

Massimo Barbera[1], Cristina Barbero[1], Paola Dal Zovo[1], Fernanda Farinaccio[1],
Evangelos Gkroustiotis[2], Sofoklis Kyriazakos[2], Ivan Mura[1], and Gianluca Previti[1]

[1] Motorola Electronics, Global Software Group,
Via C. Massaia 83, 10147 Torino, Italy
{Massimo.Barbera, Cristina.Barbero, Paola.DalZovo}@motorola.com
{Fernanda.Farinaccio, Ivan.Mura, Gianluca.Previti}@motorola.com
[2] Institute of Communications and Computer Systems,
National Technical University of Athens, Heroon Polytechniou 9, 15773 Athens, Greece
{Evang, Skyriazakos}@telecom.ntua.gr

Abstract. This paper describes an innovative application of Case-Based Reasoning methodologies for the dynamic management of wireless telecommunications systems. In spite of the very dynamic nature of mobile communications, wireless networks only possess limited adaptive management capabilities, which are unable to adequately follow traffic fluctuations through flexible and real-time resource assignment reconfigurations. The study described in this paper is an attempt to improve over these limitations, by allowing wireless networks to alleviate the effects of traffic overloads through an automated reasoning about its performance levels and an on-the-fly reconfiguration of resources assignment. The proposed Case-Based Reasoning approach provides a suitable framework to define a simple and scalable solution that easily incorporates the preferences of the network operators.

1   Introduction

Wireless telecommunications networks of current and next generation represent good examples of extremely complex and dynamic systems, which have to be carefully managed to cope with a wide variety of vulnerabilities arising from their unbounded environments of operation. Among these vulnerabilities, traffic congestion is a very hot issue for mobile network operators. It has been proved on the field that today's infrastructures fail to address this issue efficiently [7]. This continues to be dramatically demonstrated during network critical situations, e.g., earthquakes, New Year's Eve, etc. Mobile network operators receive strong criticism for the inability to address their users' communication needs, and they experience significant loss of revenues in cases of traffic congestion. In most traffic load situations, congestion arises although radio resources are still available, which provides leeway for innovative solutions based on efficient system re-configuration.

The major hurdle along the way towards effective congestion management in wireless telecommunications network is represented by the lack of tools for real-time adaptive resources management. Networks are planned, dimensioned and deployed

S. Craw and A. Preece (Eds.): ECCBR 2002, LNAI 2416, pp. 490–504.

based on a static view of the traffic, while traffic fluctuations occur as a result of a variety of reasons, which include, among others, daily variations in the users activity levels, movements of users towards attractive areas of the network, unforeseen events that increase the call arrival rates. Such traffic fluctuations are only partially handled by available network resources. As the workload increases, saturation is eventually reached, and the overall performance of the network may dramatically worsen due to various bottleneck effects. Obviously, the amount of network resources is limited (this is true especially for the radio resources) and cannot be arbitrarily increased. On the other hand, the allocation of resources planned to satisfactorily handle average workloads may be not the optimal one under overload conditions. Therefore, it would be desirable for wireless telecommunications systems to have the ability of dynamically modifying the assignment of network resources based on the current traffic conditions, so to achieve a better utilization of the scarce radio resources.

The main contribution of this paper is the definition of a framework for intelligent and adaptive wireless network management, which improves over the poor congestion management practices of wireless telecommunications networks. The paper summarizes a part of the research activities conducted within the framework of the European Community funded project IST CAUTION [8]. CAUTION's objective is to define end-to-end traffic congestion management mechanisms in cellular networks, with particular emphasis on circuit-switched networks such as GSM. The goal of the efficient capacity management defined by CAUTION is to allow the adaptive utilization of all traffic resources, in contrast with the existing management that makes a static use of the available resources.

In CAUTION, the intelligence has been brought into the system through the introduction of a Case-Based Reasoning (CBR) [1] engine. The CBR allows network operators to input their experiences about congestion events into the initial Knowledge Base (KB). When traffic overload occurs, the CBR supports a fast decision-making for automatically tuning assignment of network resources, and alleviate the congestion effects. New experience gained by the system is added to the KB for later reuse. The network operator may periodically check the KB to validate the information contained therein, and to better tune network reaction under particular congestion circumstances.

The novelty of CAUTION is primarily found in the specific application domain. A few studies exist in the literature of CBR applied to network management, but apart for the one in [3], none of them deals with wireless networks. Moreover, they mainly concern fault diagnosis [3, 11], which is a quite different problem with respect to dynamic resource reconfiguration.

This paper is organized as follows. We present in Section 2 the basic ingredients needed for our adaptive management framework operations, clarifying which ones are to be obtained from the network, and which other ones must come from the operator. Then, in Section 3 we present our general recipe for congestion management, by putting standard CBR concepts and terminology into a wireless network perspective. The CBR recipe in Section 3 is applied to the ingredients introduced in Section 2, and the outcome, a practical application of CBR for traffic overload management, is described in Section 4. Finally, Section 5 provides conclusions and some indications for future research directions.

2   Ingredients for Adaptive Network Management

In this section, we will be first reasoning about some of the issues that prevent wireless telecommunications networks to be adaptively managed in a flexible way. This reflection will help us in identifying the key aspects of the networks that need to be developed for an automated reaction to changing traffic conditions to be possible. Then, we will take into consideration the intelligent part of the system, i.e., the network operator knowledge that has to be put in place for guiding network response. The network input and the operator knowledge provide together the basic information that will allow us to define an adaptive resource management framework.

2.1   What Has to Come from the Network

The limited flexibility of wireless telecommunications networks finds its roots in the lack of observability of the systems. Monitoring complex, highly distributed, and dynamic systems such as wireless telecommunications networks is definitely not an easy task. Nevertheless, to enable tuning resources assignment on the basis of traffic fluctuations, monitoring tools are required, which allow closely tracking the workload at the finest possible granularity level, e.g., the cell, or even at the user level.

Though a number of tools exist for assisting network planning, dimensioning, and deployment, comparatively less emphasis has been put in developing monitoring tools for tracking the traffic sustained by the network. Some of the monitoring tools focus on the production of aggregate statistics, e.g., traffic intensity at the Mobile Switching Centre (MSC) level, and very few provide on-line monitoring of live network conditions. This is somehow puzzling if one considers that, while in a call, a set of reports describing the entire network traffic history is generated, stored, and analysed for billing purposes. Considering an MSC of second generation, there are around one hundred different types of reports; each of them contains several hundreds of fields. A typical report includes the following information: User ID, Call start time, Mobile Originated/Terminated Call, Calling Party, Call end time. In addition, information related to handover, paging, SMS is also reported. Thus, all the information to be collected is already there, and real-time network monitoring can be realized in a non-intrusive way with limited efforts.

It is worthwhile remarking that, even for an over-specified system like GSM, standardized reports do not exist. Consequently, each vendor delivers monitoring tools specific for his own equipment. Wireless operators moreover use infrastructure equipment from multiple manufactures, which does not allow a unique monitoring and resource management system for the network.

Let us now discuss the second aspect of wireless telecommunications networks that is relevant for the objectives of this paper, i.e., the network resources management. When it comes to resources management, it should be clear that we are looking for ways of modifying the network while in operation, most likely during the busy hour when the network achieves its maximum utilization levels. This run-time operation mode makes some typical network management techniques infeasible. As an instance, frequency planning is completely out of the question in the proposed scenario, and the same applies to the addition of network resources.

In this context, an unexpected support comes from the main standardization body of wireless telecommunications systems, the ETSI. Whereas many aspects are left under specified with the purpose of allowing manufacturers developing specific proprietary implementations, very detailed descriptions are provided for several advanced resource management techniques [17]. Such techniques are usually not exploited by network operators, but are there ready to be used. To give a flavour of what these advanced techniques can do, we can mention some of their effects, such as reducing the coverage area of a cell, modifying the respective allocation of signalling and traffic resources, limiting the duration of voice calls, changing the priority among classes of users, reserving resources for particular types of traffic.

2.2   What Has to Come from the Operator

When it comes to the operators, the input one expects to have for adaptive network management is knowledge. Indeed, operators know the intimate details of the deployed network, they are aware of traffic requirements, and they know the response that the system exhibits as the traffic fluctuates.

There are three basic types of knowledge that can be realistically obtained from operators: the overload events the network may be subject to, the observed network reaction under the various overload events, and guidance on the selection of actions to contrast network misbehaviours. The following paragraphs describe these three types of knowledge.

The *traffic scenarios* of interest are obviously those that stress the network and bring to the limit its ability in satisfying the incoming workload. Wireless networks functionality (and wireline as well) are easily jeopardized by peaks of workload, which expose various system bottlenecks. Overload is a general term that can be detailed in a set of different scenarios, each one related to the reason that causes the overload. For instance, a specific type of overload occurs periodically during the busy hours in densely populated urban areas and in business locations. A different type of overload may occur because of events that attract a large number of users in some portions of the network, such as sport events or demonstrations. This phenomenological classification of overloads provides a simple characterization that can be easily exploited for the sake of improved network management.

The response of the network to overload can be described in terms of the variation in some network performance indicators. Network operators maintain performance data in Network Data Warehouses (NDW). Reliable and representative performance indicators can be defined through the reports stored in the NDW. The major performance indicators are Traffic, Call Setup Success Rate (CSSR), Handover Success Rate (HOSR), SDCCH Blocking Rate (SDCCH BR) and TCH Blocking Rate (TCH BR). In the following, we will refer to these indicators as the Key Performance Indicators (KPIs). Since network response is actually the only measurable aspect of a congestion event, it is important to relate the traffic scenarios with the network indicators, thus defining a *characterization* of each traffic scenario in terms of the resulting network conditions. Some traffic scenarios tend to cause the exhaustion of traffic resources first, where for some others the signalling is the primary bottleneck. Hence, the operators (and an automated network management system) may use a characterization of a traffic scenario to identify the reason that is bringing the network to congestion.

When overloads occur, some actions may be undertaken to attempt a balancing of resource utilizations, to remove primary bottlenecks and maximize the number of users that can be served, or some other metrics of interest. As we discussed in the previous subsection, the standards provide a set of advanced resource management techniques, which may alleviate the effects of overloads. It is the responsibility of the operators to decide which technique or set of techniques is to be applied, e.g., to define the *strategy* for dealing with a congested network. Which kind of strategy is best applied is a decision that should be obviously guided by the specific characteristics of the congestion event.

3   Recipe for Adaptive Management

The design of a real-time adaptive network management tool for overload control is chiefly centred on the definition of decision-making processes, which, by exploiting the information made available both by the network and the operator, select the most appropriate reaction. As shown in Figure 1, the outcome of the decision-making process is forwarded to the Network Management System (NMS) for actuation. The automated decision-making creates a feedback loop between live network KPIs and real-time resource assignments, taking into account the preferences of the operator.

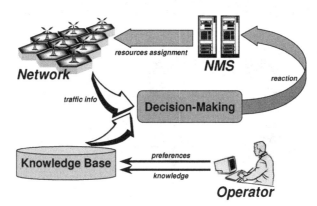

Fig. 1. Adaptive wireless network management scheme

A decision-making process suitable for our purposes is definitely not a simple one. It has to operate in a very dynamic environment on the basis of a possibly limited guidance, and it has to be able to take fast decisions to contrast overloads as soon as they occur. Moreover, since overloads characteristics may not be known completely beforehand for future scenarios, it should possess the capability of adapting itself to changing network conditions.

We addressed the opportunity of designing such a decision-making by resorting to an approach that is efficient for organizing and using knowledge, i.e. the Case-Based Reasoning (CBR). CBR aims at solving new problems by reusing and adapting solutions successfully used to solve similar problems in the past [1]. A major reason for CBR's success is that reasoning by re-using past cases is a natural and powerful way to solve problems for humans: different studies in cognitive science (e.g., [4, 14]) have given evidence for the important role of previously experienced situations in human problem solving.

A CBR system manages a KB whose elementary element is called *case*. The traditional CBR operation consists of four processes:

1. **Retrieve**. The initial description of a new case is used to retrieve from the case base the most similar one;
2. **Reuse**. The retrieved case is combined with the new case, through reuse, into a proposed solution to the initial problem;
3. **Revise**. Through the revise process, the solution is tested for success, and repaired if failed;
4. **Retain**. During retain, useful experience is retained for future reuse, and the case base is updated by a new learned case.

Some studies also include additional processes to allow for maintenance of the KB. For instance, in [6] Bergmann suggests adding a *Refine* process, within which the CBR administrator performs maintenance steps for the whole KB. We adopt the extended CBR cycle shown in Figure 2, which is inspired by the model in [6]. It consists of the five processes *Retrieve, Reuse, Revise, Retain*, and *Refine*. The four standard processes have the same meaning as in the traditional CBR cycle. The Refine process consists of a periodic refinement of the whole KB in order both to check the case base and to reconsider the knowledge used in the light of the results obtained. We shall now describe the various CBR processes in the perspective of our adaptive network management.

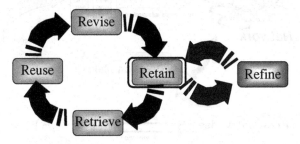

Fig. 2. The adopted CBR cycle

According to standard CBR definitions, the Retrieve process starts with the representation of the problem at hand and ends with one or more previous cases that best match it. Simple problem representations are mostly used, but also knowledge intensive approaches have been pursued [10]. In our specific case, the problem to be treated is a network congestion event that just appeared in the network, and it is represented as a simple feature-value structure for efficiency purposes. We want to match such a new event to some case stored in the case base, which is representative of some other congestion event the network handled in the past.

The Reuse process is perhaps the most difficult and challenging part of CBR. The adaptation knowledge is highly dependent on the domain and difficult to acquire from experts, who are often unable to provide precise rules to describe their decisions. Because of these issues, some studies [9] suggest extracting adaptation knowledge from the knowledge base directly. Reuse in the context of our decision-making process can be performed through an approach that mixes direct copy and adaptation. The reaction strategy found in the retrieved case is copied without adaptation, whereas the strategy parameters are tuned with the assistance of network models. In this way, each congestion event is in fact treated with parameters specifically obtained to deal with the particular situation of the network. At the same time, a relevant part of the saved knowledge is reused through simple copying, thus speeding up the decision-making process.

The Revise process has been carefully considered in our context of network management. Each congestion event is somehow different from all previous experiences of the CBR system. Therefore, any proposed solution in fact needs to be validated. Towards this goal, we propose an experimental approach, through which the proposed solution is actuated on the network, and the network response monitored through the feedback loop described in Figure 1. Should network behaviour not comply with the expected response, the proposed solution can be revised at various levels, either retuning the strategy parameters, or adopting a new strategy.

The Retain process incorporates into the existing KB what is useful to retain from the new problem-solving episode (it is a learning process). In the case of a congestion event that has been successfully treated, a new case can be added to the KB, storing the information about the applied strategy, the parameters used to tune the strategy, and the duration of the congestion event.

The Refine process involves system maintenance and case base revision (e.g., checking the validity of new cases, deleting cases for efficiency purposes or because they are out-of-date) and the revision of the knowledge for similarity assessment (e.g., improving similarity measures and weights). A range of policies, either human-driven or automated, has been proposed for controlling case base quality and the performance of CBR systems, as in [12, 13, 15, 16]. In our congestion management scenario, refinement has to be performed by the network operator directly. The stored cases can be grouped on the basis of the characteristics of the congestion events, and the adequacy of the strategy proposed by the operator accordingly revised or validated. A support to the refinement actions comes from an integrated statistics generation module, which provides an aggregated high-level view of CBR history of operation. Since the library of saved cases determines the future behaviour of the system, the operator may remove parts of the history or insert some fictitious case to allow the CBR to explore new directions in the management of congestion events.

4   An Adaptive Network Management Speciality

This section describes the application of the CBR approach described in previous sections in the context of an on-going research study being conducted in the IST-CAUTION project, partially funded through the European Community V Framework Programme.

CAUTION tackles the problem of traffic congestion with the main objectives of monitoring cellular networks, predict and/or detect congestion situations, apply management techniques to avoid traffic overload, and ensure stable transition from the congested state to the normal one. The scheme in Figure 3 shows a high-level view of CAUTION system architecture. It consists of four new network elements interconnected by means of dedicated wired lines or IP backbone network:

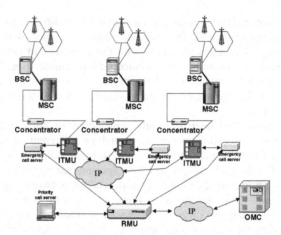

Fig. 3. High-level CAUTION architecture

- Interface Traffic Monitoring Unit (ITMU), in charge of collecting and elaborating the traffic info from various network interfaces. When congestion is detected in a given cell, ITMU forwards alarm messages to the Resource Management Unit;
- Resource Management Unit (RMU), the core element of the CAUTION system, by which resource management strategies are decided as well as executed. It manages the alarms generated by several ITMUs and reacts by sending proper commands to the Operations & Maintenance Centre, which offers an interface to the Network Management System;
- Emergency Call Server, for a full-time availability of the network, especially in emergency situations. Its functionality is to reserve bandwidth for emergency calls, even under the most severe overload situations, as in catastrophes. In addition, ECS enables a manual network configuration, since it can execute all management techniques that are implemented in the RMU;
- Priority Call Server, for the prioritised assignment of bandwidth, according to the user's classes defined by ETSI and 3GPP in the eMLPP standards.

The RMU is the decision-making CAUTION element deploying the CBR approach. We shall now describe some details of the CBR application conceived for the CAUTION RMU. We first detail the knowledge available to the system for guiding its response, and the way such knowledge is organized. Then, we discuss the five processes of CBR and we present at a high abstraction level the main algorithmic steps required to implement them.

4.1   The CAUTION Knowledge Base

The KB represents the overall repository for the CBR engine and for the whole RMU. Three different types of knowledge are stored therein, and each type is described in the following paragraphs.

The first type of knowledge consists of set of traffic scenario definitions and characterizations. Each traffic scenario is a description of a class of congestion events the network may experience. Thirteen different traffic scenarios have been identified for the congestion management purposes of CAUTION. They account for concentration of users in specific areas of the network, accidents of different scale, catastrophes affecting the entire network served area, and network shortcomings due to planned or unplanned outages. The characterization of a traffic scenario is an aggregate view of the effects that the occurrence of that scenario has on the part of the network affected by the event. For instance, Figure 4 shows a possible characterization of two typical traffic scenarios: the Busy Hour, which regularly occurs in densely populated urban areas, and the Sport Event, which occurs when a very high density of users concentrates in some attractive spots such as a stadium.

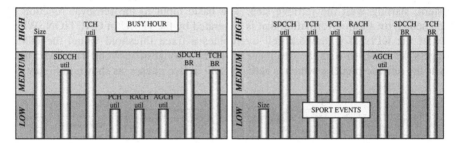

Fig. 4. Characterization of two traffic scenarios

The characterization is made against a set of eight KPIs, including the dimension of the affected area, the utilizations of signalling and traffic channels in the congested area, and the blocking rates of some selected channels. The characterization employs a discrete value scale (high, medium, low) for the KPIs.

The second type of knowledge stored in the KB is represented by a set of rules, which associate each traffic scenario with a list of traffic management strategies. Each strategy consists of the combined application of a set of Resource Management Techniques (RMTs), which modify the allocation of network resources so to limit or even eliminate the effects of overload. Sixteen RMTs have been selected for CAUTION, among those that are described in the ETSI specifications, because of their usefulness in alleviating the symptoms of network congestion. Some techniques modify the relative allocations of traffic and signalling radio resources, other ones can help in redistributing the traffic over the network, and some can even be used to deny network access to some classes of users. The combination of multiple RMTs, as well as their association to traffic scenarios, is a task that requires the greatest experience about network behaviour and can be performed only by network operators.

The cases form the last type of knowledge in the KB. Each case represents one congestion event the network dealt with in the past. A simple feature-value structure represents a case in CAUTION:

1. Case identifier;
2. Traffic scenario the congestion event belongs to;
3. Number of cells affected by the congestion event;
4. Observed values of the KPIs shown in Figure 4;
5. Strategy applied to solve the congestion event;
6. Congestion event start time and actual duration;
7. Identifier of the previous case that best matched with this case;

8. Number of times the case has been reused since its insertion in the case base;
9. Number of times the case has been reused with success.

These data share the same data structure, and are employed for different purposes. The information at points 2), 3), and 4) is exploited during the retrieve process, the one in 5) is the key element for reuse, the points 6) and 7) are employed in the refine processes, 8) and 9) are used in the retrieve as well as in the refine process.

4.2   The CAUTION CBR Processes

In this section, we review the five CBR processes that are deployed in the CAUTION system, starting with the retrieve step. The basic input to the retrieval function is represented by alarm information that is generated by the ITMU of CAUTION. When any of the KPIs of a network cell overcomes a fixed threshold value, the ITMU triggers the RMU to start the treatment of the new congestion event. The RMU then starts the retrieve process, which is actually split in two phases, as shown in Figure 5.

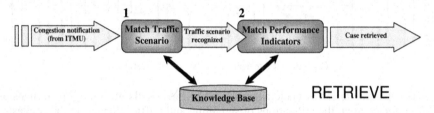

Fig. 5. CBR retrieve process

In the first step, a matching is done to classify the congestion event against the set of traffic scenarios stored in the KB. This operation is called Traffic Load Scenario Recognition, and is based on the matching between the observed cell situation and the available traffic scenario characterizations. Once the cell has been classified, the RMU starts a dialogue with the ITMU, enquiring about the status of the cells adjacent to the one for which the alarm was issued. Those adjacent cells with indicators that are close to the threshold values are also clustered under the same event, so that the RMU predicts and prevents congestion. Figure 6 shows the clustering of two events. The black filled cells are congested, since ITMU has reported that some of their KPIs have reached alarm thresholds. Shadowed cells are clustered together with congested

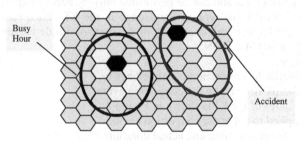

Fig. 6. Clustering of congested cells

cells because their KPIs are close to their alarm values. This operation constructs a cluster of congested cells, all belonging to the same traffic scenario. A classified cluster represents the information passed to the next step of the retrieve process.

The second step of the retrieve process exploits the knowledge stored in the case base. A search is conducted over the set of cases. The search only looks for cases with the same traffic scenario as the one of the classified cluster, and employs a simple Nearest-Neighbour function, which quantifies the overall similarity as a linear combination of the similarities between each KPIs for the new congestion event and the corresponding one for the stored case. If we denote with KPI_i^C the value of $i-th$ KPI, $i = 1,2,...,8$ for case C, the similarity function is defined as follows:

$$SIM(C_1,C_2) = 1 - \sum_i \omega_i \cdot sim_i(KPI_i^{C_1}, KPI_i^{C_2}), \quad \sum_i \omega_i = 1,$$

where C_1 is the case constructed through the information associated to the new congestion event, C_2 is a case stored in the CBR KB, sim_i is the similarity function for the $i-th$ KPI, and w_i is a weight given to sim_i. The similarity functions sim_i may take a different form for $i = 1,2,...,8$. For instance, for the traffic channels utilization, the similarity function is the absolute value of the difference between the TCH utilization of C_1 and C_2, whereas for the size of congestion event, the similarity function is the difference between the number of clustered cells in C_1 and C_2, normalized by the maximum between the two. Weights are configurable, traffic scenario dependent, and allow giving more relevance to selected features.

The retrieve selects all those stored cases whose similarity exceeds a configurable similarity threshold parameter (e.g., 80%). Then, the best match is chosen by multiplying the similarity by a confidence function, proportional to the number of times each case has been reused and to the number of success when reused (points 8 and 9 in the case representation seen above). In this way, cases that have been successfully reused several times are more likely to be copied from.

The CBR reuse process of CAUTION features an interesting adaptation strategy. The strategy associated to the retrieved case is simply copied from, meaning that the RMU will reapply the same strategy that was successfully applied to deal with the congestion event the retrieved case refers to. However, as shown in Figure 7, before actuation each RMT will be subject to a fine-tuning process, which is performed by resorting to models of network response.

Two distinct types of model-based tuning are used in CAUTION: local model-based tuning techniques, for those RMTs that can be applied on a cell-by-cell basis, and global model-based tuning techniques, for the RMTs that need to be applied to the cluster as a whole. Just to exemplify which RMTs fall in the two different classes, consider for instance a technique that moves traffic from one cell to the adjacent ones. Such a technique needs to be treated with a global tuning process, in that the effects of its actuation affect the congestion levels of other cells of the cluster. On the contrary, a technique that reserves one traffic channel to a specific class of users can be tuned by a cell-by-cell approach, because its impact is local to the cell.

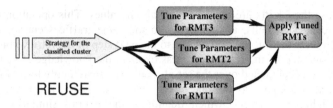

Fig. 7. CBR reuse process

For local tuning, Petri Nets [2] have been selected as modelling tools. Network response is evaluated through a model that represents the impact that the RMT has on KPIs. The Petri Net is solved off-line for a range of possible network input configurations, and model results are stored in a lookup table. Thus, the parameters of the RMT can be tuned to dose RMU reaction with a negligible computational effort. Global tuning is performed through Linear Programming models [5], which optimise the effects of RMT application devising a proper resource allocation for the whole cluster. These latter models have to be solved on-line because they depend on a number of cluster specific information. Depending on the size of problem at hand, approximate solutions based on heuristics are adopted to speedup the tuning process.

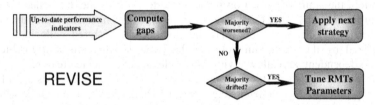

REVISE

Fig. 8. CBR revise process

The Revise process verifies the effect of the applied strategy, as shown in Figure 8. At fixed time intervals, the RMU checks the up-to-date KPI of all the cells in the cluster. The current performance indicators are compared to those that were observed when the congestion event first occurred, and a gap value is computed. If a majority of cells has worsened, then a new strategy is retrieved from the KB, and the proposed solution is changed accordingly. Then, a new tuning takes place, and the revised strategy is actuated. If the majority of cells have not worsened, then a second gap value is evaluated between the current network situation and the one that was observed the last time the comparison was carried out. If majority of cells exists for which this latter gap is greater than a fixed threshold (e.g., 10%), then the solution is revised by performing a retune of the RMTs parameters.

The Retain process is quite simple. When congestion treatment successfully ends, i.e. all KPIs return below their alarm values, a case storing all the relevant information is added to the KB. Also, if the revise process has not led to a change of strategy, field 9) of the best match case is updated, to increase the level for confidence in future reuse. It is also possible that the RMU is not able to successfully treat the overload; under these circumstances, the case is not saved in the KB, but it gets always logged, for further analysis.

In the context of CAUTION, refinement is the responsibility of the network operator. Since all the history of the system is stored, either in the KB or in the log files, it is possible to perform all kinds of statistical analyses on system behaviour, to identify potential areas of improvement in system configuration and operation. The following list describes some aspects of the system that could be sensibly refined based on the stored information analyses:

- TLS characterization can be improved based on an estimation of its effectiveness in the retrieve process. For instance, if some of the observed congestion events do not match with any of the traffic scenarios included in the KB, it could be the case that some of the characterizations are not correct, or even that a new type of congestion event is appearing in the network, for which a new traffic scenario should be defined;
- Strategies lists provided by the operator are definitely to be reviewed regularly. If the history shows that a specific strategy never leads to the expected results, the network operator should remove or replace it. The order of strategies could also be changed to allow the system to behave in a more explorative fashion, and maybe apply some strategies that would be tried rarely otherwise;
- Weights used in the similarity function could be tuned to calibrate the retrieve process. For instance, the analysis of the KB could indicate that the size of the congestion event is the key information for the overload treatment, and the corresponding weight changed accordingly;
- Case selection has to be performed in order to keep in the case base a reduced amount of information for the sake of system efficiency, at the same time ensuring that the most promising cases are kept for future reuse. A minimal number of cases should be kept for each traffic scenario, possibly avoiding storing very similar cases, which do not add relevant knowledge and slow down the retrieval process. Some indicators about the quality of a case are provided by the two fields 7) and 8) of the case data structure, which provide a view of the number of times a case is reused and of the results of such reuse.

It is interesting observing that some warnings to trigger network operator intervention can be automatically issued by the RMU, as a result of the computation of simple statistics about traffic scenario characterization and strategy effectiveness. These statistics are computed during low workload periods, such as night hours, and could be seen as a first step towards the definition of an automated refine process.

5   Concluding Remarks and Future Work

We presented in this paper an overview of a CBR approach applied to the management of wireless telecommunications systems for overload control, which to the best of our knowledge is a completely novel application for CBR. The research described in the paper is still under progress at the time this paper is being written. However, some promising aspects of this work can be highlighted, which in our opinion demonstrate as the proposed approach naturally lends itself to application to the target domain. The CBR approach:

- Provides a flexible approach for calibrating the level of automatism in network control, as its decision-making is guided by the network operators' preferences. Because of this, users easily accept our CBR approach;

- Reduces the knowledge acquisition effort, in that it does not require eliciting rules from experts. Rather, the knowledge already available to the users is naturally translated into very simple case structures used for driving system actions;
- Requires limited maintenance effort, since cases are independent from each other, quite easily understandable, and the maintenance of the CBR system consists mostly in adding/deleting cases;
- Improves problem-solving performance through reuse, fulfilling one of the most important requirements in the specific application domain, i.e. fast reaction times of the order of seconds;
- Automatically adapts to changes in the environment, by a simple and efficient on-the-job learning mechanism tuneable through simple refinements under control of the network operator.

Some aspects of CBR application to network management are still under investigation. In particular, the process to be followed by CAUTION network operators to populate the KB is under refinement. This is a relevant point in the overall congestion management strategy. Not only traffic scenarios and strategies definition ultimately drive the quality of system response, but also the initial cases included in the KB determine the set of possible actions the CBR explores for congestion treatment.

Acknowledgements

The research work described in this paper has been conducted in the framework of the V Research Programme of the European Community through the IST-25352 CAUTION project. The authors wish to acknowledge the contribution of all consortium partners to the definition of the adaptive management framework presented in this paper.

References

1. A. Aamodt and E. Plaza, "Case-Based Reasoning: Foundational Issues, Methodological Variations, and System Approaches", AI Communications, vol. 7, pp. 39-59, 1994.
2. M. Ajmone Marsan, G. Conte, and G. Balbo, "A Class of Generalized Stochastic Petri Nets for the Performance Evaluation of Multiprocessor Systems", ACM Transactions on Computer Systems, vol. 2, pp. 93-122, 1984.
3 P. Ala-Siuru and M. Kurki, "Case-based reasoning applied to fault diagnostics in GSM telecommunication networks", STeP '96 - Genes, Nets and Symbols, 7th FAIS Conference, 1996.
4. J.R. Anderson, "The architecture of cognition", Harvard University Press, Cambridge, 1983.
5. M.S. Bazaraa, J.J. Jarvis. and H. D. Sherali, "Linear Programming and Network Flows" 2nd ed., Wiley, 1990.
6. R. Bergmann, "Highlights of the European INRECA Projects", Case-Based Reasoning Research and Development, LNAI 2080, Springer, 2001.
7. IST-25352 CAUTION, Deliverable D2.1 "Requirement Analysis and Functional Specifications", July 2001.
8. IST-25352 CAUTION Project Home page, http://www.telecom.ntua.gr/caution.

9. S. Craw, J. Jarmulak and R. Rowe, "Learning and Applying Case-Based Adaptation Knowledge", Case-Based Reasoning Research and Development, LNAI 2080, Springer, 2001.
10. B. Diaz-Agudo and P.A. Gonzales-Calero, "An Architecture for Knowledge Intensive CBR Systems", Advances in Case-Based Reasoning, LNAI 1898, Springer, 2000.
11. L. Lewis, "Managing Computer Networks: A Case-Based Reasoning Approach", Artech House, 1995.
12. L. Portinale and P. Torasso, "Automatic Case base Management in a Multi-modal Reasoning System", Case-Based Reasoning Research and Development, LNAI 2080, Springer, 2001.
13. T. Reinartz, I. Iglezakis and T. Roth-Berghofer, "On Quality Measures for Case base Maintenance", Case-Based Reasoning Research and Development, LNAI 2080, Springer, 2001.
14. B.H. Ross, "Some Psychological Results on Case-Based Reasoning", Case-Based Reasoning Workshop, DARPA 1989, Morgan Kaufmann.
15. B. Smyth and M.T. Keane, "Remembering to Forget: A Competence Preserving Case Deletion Policy for CBR Systems", Proc. of the 14th International Joint Conference on Artificial Intelligence, Morgan Kaufmann, 1995.
16. H. Tirri, P. Kontkanen and P. Myllymaki, "A Bayesian Framework for Case-Based Reasoning", Advances in Case-Based Reasoning, LNAI 1168, Springer, 1996.
17. 3rd Generation Partnership Project. "Radio Resource Management Strategies", 3G TR 25.922 V4.0.0, 2001.

A Case-Based Personal Travel Assistant for Elaborating User Requirements and Assessing Offers[1]

Lorcan Coyle, Pádraig Cunningham, and Conor Hayes

Department of Computer Science
Trinity College Dublin
{Lorcan.Coyle, Padraig.Cunningham, Conor.Hayes}@cs.tcd.ie

Abstract. This paper describes a case-based approach to user profiling in a Personal Travel Assistant (based on the 1998 FIPA Travel Scenario). The approach is novel in that the user profile is made up of a *set* of cases capturing previous interactions rather than as a single composite case. This has the advantage that the profile is always up-to-date and also allows for the borrowing of cases from similar users when coverage is poor. Profile data is retrieved from a database in an XML format and loaded into a case-retrieval net in memory. This case-retrieval net is then used to support the two key tasks of requirements elaboration and ranking offers.

1 Introduction

Case-Based Reasoning (CBR) belongs to the lazy school of Machine Learning and thus has the defining characteristic of deferring processing to run-time. Whatever the run-time penalties associated with this, it does ensure that the data used for inference is as up-to-date as possible [1]. This is of particular benefit in situations where data is scarce and where data is being updated continuously. In this paper we describe a user profiling problem that has these characteristics and describe a case-based solution to this user-profiling problem. This solution contrasts with the normal use of CBR in user profiling where each user profile is represented by a single case (e.g. the PTV scenario presented by Smyth and Cotter [9]). By contrast, in the solution described here, the user profile is made up of several cases, each capturing a previous interaction episode with the system [11]. This approach is also used by Bradley et al. [3] in CASPER, a case-based assistant operating in the electronic recruitment domain.

The scenario we refer to was introduced in 1998 by FIPA (Foundation for Intelligent Physical Agents) as one of a set of benchmark scenarios to drive research on intelligent agents. In this scenario a Personal Travel Assistant (PTA) would help a user in organizing travel. The PTA could operate on a central server and users would interact with this through a mini-PTA (mPTA) that might operate on a WAP-enabled

---

[1] The support of the Informatics Research Initiative of Enterprise Ireland is gratefully acknowledged

S. Craw and A. Preece (Eds.): ECCBR 2002, LNAI 2416, pp. 505–518.

mobile phone. Personalization is to be used to overcome the inherent limitations of using these devices (i.e. poor text-inputting facilities, high network latency).

The main role of the PTA is to negotiate with a Broker Agent to book flights on behalf of the user. We have identified two tasks within this negotiation that require some 'intelligence' from the PTA; these are:

- The elaboration of the user's requirements based on the user profile.
- The evaluation and ranking of offers from the Broker Agent based on the user profile.

In this paper we present an integrated case-based solution to these two tasks. This approach uses a history of past interactions to generate a case-based user profile to complete the task at hand. The FIPA Travel Scenario is described in the next section and then the case-based solution is described in section 3. Then the effectiveness of the solution is described with the aid of two examples in section 4.

2 The FIPA Travel Scenario

FIPA's PTA specification [5] describes an open marketplace – the Personal Travel Market (PTM) – where software agents broker deals between travel vendors and customers. Figure 1 shows an architecture for a Personal Travel Market, showing the different agents and the flows of communication between them.

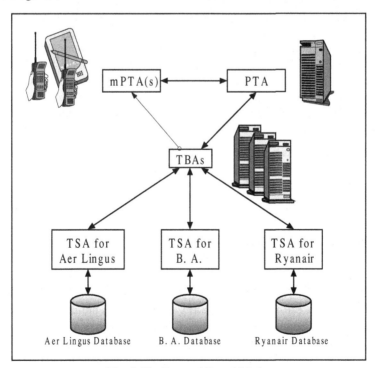

Fig. 1. The Personal Travel Market

The PTM consists of the following agents:

- The PTA is the user's representative in this market; it is responsible for carrying out the user's instructions and learning the user's preferences. It receives travel requests from the user (through the mPTA) and forwards these to the TBAs in the system. On return of travel offers from the TBAs it sends the most suitable of these (based on user preferences) to the mPTA to present to the user. If any of these offers are accepted it has the authority to book them with the TBA. Users cannot access the PTA except through an mPTA interface.
- mPTA: This provides a user-interface to the PTA and is concerned mainly with presentation of requests and offers. It communicates mainly with the PTA; its only communication with the other agents would be simple requests for information, e.g. allowing the user check on the status of a flight by making a request directly to a TBA.
- TBA(s) (Travel Broker Agent): These are the middlemen of the PTM. They take travel requests from the PTAs and negotiate travel solutions on their behalf with the TSAs. They do this by decomposing travel requests into segments and negotiate with suitable TSAs for these segments. They then compose these into travel offers and return them to the PTA.
- TSAs (Travel Service Agents): These provide a wrapper around legacy travel databases and systems. They are responsible for maintaining the data access, interpretation and delivery to the TBA(s).

Our goal is to implement the PTA and mPTA. An interface to a TBA, with some simple code underneath to simulate the remainder of the PTM will also be developed. FIPA have already created their own agent communication language [4], and use this to define the transactions within a PTM system. This simplifies our goal of creating a fully compliant PTA-mPTA system, capable of interfacing with any FIPA compliant PTM. There are a number of publicly available implementations of agent platforms that conform to the FIPA Specifications. The LEAP (Lightweight & Efficient Application Protocols) project [2] appears to be the most promising of these; it allows deployment of intelligent agent systems on computers, PDAs and mobile phones.

The two main interactions between a user and the PTA are:
- Making a travel request on behalf of a user (Figure 2)
- Recommending suitable travel offers to the user (Figure 3).

These diagrams show timelines for each component in the system and outline what transactions occur between them. The bulk of the personalization computation occurs in the boxed areas along the PTA timeline.

Request Elaboration:
According to FIPA's PTA ontology, for a PTA to make a valid travel request to a TBA it must send it a FIPA `trip-summary` object. This is pre-defined object made up of a number of parameters (see Table 1 below), which may be absolute, e.g. `'Origin = London'`, or constrained, e.g. `'Budget < £800Stg'`. The goal of the request-elaboration task is that the user should not need to manually fill all of these parameters, that the PTA should be able to determine user preferences from

previous interactions. Ideally the PTA will send the mPTA a simple form with minimum entry fields to present to the user, which the user will complete and return. This information makes up a *skeletal request*. The PTA should be able to use similar requests from that user's history to fill in the remaining parameters. This elaborated request represents a final travel request and is forwarded to the TBAs. If the PTA is not confident about its decision, the PTA may first return the elaborated request to the user for confirmation that it represents his/her intentions. The PTA can learn more about the user's preferences from this confirmation/rejection.

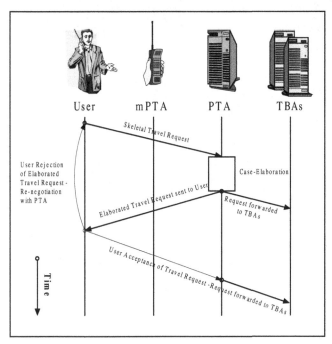

Fig. 2. Request-Elaboration

Table 1 A selection of the `trip-summary` parameters that are mentioned in this paper. The PTA specification contains other optional parameters, a number of which are outside the flights domain. All mandatory parameters must be supplied in a final request, either explicitly by the user or by the PTA using elaboration.

Parameter	Description	Presence
Origin	The origin of the trip	Mandatory
Via	A list of via locations of the trip	Mandatory
Destination	The destination of the trip	Mandatory
Departure Time	A list of start dates and times for the trip	Optional
Return Time	A list of return dates and times for the trip	Optional
Budget	The currency and preferred price range of the trip	Optional
Selection pref.	The selection preference, e.g. by cost or comfort	Optional
Class	The class of ticket, e.g. Business, Economy	Optional

Depending on the capabilities of the mobile device, extra contextual information could be sent to the PTA on logon, e.g. if the device has a GPS module, the user's geographical location. The PTA could use this to determine the nearest airport or rail station to the user.

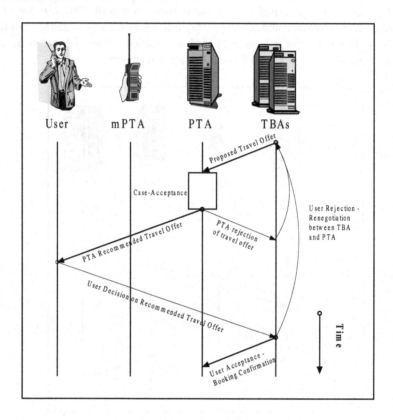

Fig. 3. Offer-Recommendation

Offer Recommendation:
TBAs reply to a `trip-summary` object with a number of `trip-details` objects. These include the original `trip-summary` object, replacing any constraints passed by the PTA with specific values. They also contain information relating to the trip, most importantly, the specific details of the trip (i.e. all plane hops or train stops) as a sequence of travel segments. Since these offers could be quite numerous, the PTA should rate them, and reject unsuitable ones. It does this by examining user's previous interest in similar offers in the past, whether similar offers were ignored, examined or reserved. It may reject segments (and entire offers) that it believes will be rejected by the user and attempt to negotiate full travel-solutions with the TBAs from acceptable segments. It then forwards acceptable offers to the mPTA to present to the user. If the user rejects these, it renegotiates with the TBA for a better offer by amending the original travel request. There is also an upper limit to the number of offers that will be

presented to the user. A diversity function like those used by [10] may be used to limit the number of offers presented without sacrificing similarity.

3 The Case-Based Solution

In order to offer personalized service to every user, the PTA stores a profile for each user of the system. This profile comprises the following types of information:
- Personal details that each user fills in at registration time, e.g. name, address, preferred language, credit-card details, etc.
- Transaction History. This includes all the previous user transactions with the system, and their context, i.e. it links transactions that occurred within a single interaction.

The PTA extracts useful information from the transaction history and generates a case-base specific to the task at hand by looking at the problem (target) case. Within the request elaboration task the target-case is the skeletal request, and within the offer-recommendation task it is the travel offer. It would be convenient to develop a single retrieval process that would operate along the same lines for both tasks. This is done by first extracting the useful information from the transaction history and generating a case-base from this. This case-base is expressed in XML format. This case-base generation process is similar to defining a CBR-view on the data [6]. The target case and this case-base are then passed into a similarity retrieval module.

There have been systems developed with distributed CBR in mind [7], [12]. This may become more important in the context of this system as the abilities of the target mobile devices increase. It may be appropriate for the retrieval module to be implemented on the client side. The PTA could then be responsible for data maintenance and the mPTA for carrying out the personalization tasks. It may eventually be possible for the mPTA to become a PTA and deal directly with the TBAs thus cutting out the middleman.

The retrieval module for both of these tasks is a CRN. These are described in more detail in the following section. It should be noted that, that under certain circumstances the CRN solution may be excessive as a retrieval mechanism for the request-elaboration task for situations where a users preferences in travel requests are very consistent. In such circumstances a more straightforward process may be appropriate.

3.1 Case-Retrieval Nets

CRNs are used to retrieve similar cases to a presented problem-case. They borrow ideas from neural networks and associative memory models. A CRN is a structured net constructed from the case-base [8]. CRNs are used because they are easy to extend, are flexible and content-sensitive. They are made up of the following components:

- Case-nodes – These represent stored cases.

- Information Entity Nodes (IEs) – These represent feature-value pairs within cases
- Relevance-Arcs – These link Case Nodes with the IEs that represent them. They have weights relating to the level of importance between the connected IE and the case.
- Similarity-Arcs – These connect IEs that refer to the same features, i.e. all IEs referring to the `budget` feature are interconnected via similarity arcs. These have weights relating to the similarity between the values of connected IEs.

Case-nodes and IEs can be *activated*, which means given a score relating to their usefulness. The arcs in the system are used to spread activation across the net. Any score passed across an arc is attenuated by the weight of the arc. The idea behind the CRN architecture is that if a target case is connected to the net via a set of relevance arcs, and activated, this activation will spread across the net. Eventually each of the other case-nodes will accumulate a score. In this way, the case-node with the highest activation represents the most similar or relevant case to the test case.

The main difficulty in implementing and maintaining CRNs is in assigning weights to the arcs in the net. The similarity arc weights must be determined before cases are presented to the CRN. The onus is on the CRN developer to initialize and maintain these weights. Features have two types of values, numeric and symbolic. These values are constrained in advance, numeric features reside within a range and symbolic values are elements of a predefined set. Functions can be defined that will calculate the similarity between numeric IEs. This allows us to assign similarity weights to new IEs added to the net without difficulty. We don't have the same problem with symbolic values because of the fixed set of possible values; we just need to assign similarity weights to every possible IE. However, determining this similarity in the first place is difficult because the similarity between groups of symbolic features can be quite subjective. Some features are inherently problematic by their very complexity, e.g. the travel-time features (`DepartureTime` and `ReturnTime`). This can be overcome by breaking the time down into a number of micro-features, e.g. time of the day, day of the week and day of the year. We can generalize on each of these features in ways we can't with their super-feature.

Relevance arcs weights are assigned in a number of ways. The first few times the PTA serves a user, there are minimal records on users' previous travel requests and evaluations on travel offers. Therefore, the PTA does not have sufficient confidence to guess the importance of features in a travel request or travel offer. In this situation, the PTA can assume an even distribution of relevance weights. On the other hand, if a user indicates a feature in the travel request to be important, a larger relevance weight can be put on this feature and vice versa. Over time, as the PTA gets to know the user's preferences, the relevance arcs are weighed accordingly. In the request elaboration task, the relevance arcs for elaborated features are copied from those of the retrieved-case.

The CBR system automatically learns the relevance arc weights during the renegotiation stage. If the PTA's decision is rejected, the differences between target and solution cases must have been more important than their relevance arcs weights suggested, so these weights must be increased, and vice versa. This will lead to greater accuracy over time.

Because the PTA is acting without supervision, it must act with confidence. This confidence comes from looking at the activation scores of retrieved cases. The PTA will not use a case unless it scores above a predefined threshold. These thresholds are useless if the CRN only returns poorly scoring case solutions. The PTA must then decide whether to use these or to widen the search by relaxing constraints on the target case. Clearly this risks offering a poorer alternative.

3.2 Collaborative CBR

Every user has their own personal case-base which contains their previous interactions with the system. CBR is only useful if the solution for a problem can be found within this case-base. This poses a problem when dealing with first-time users, who begin using the system with empty personal case-bases. If we note that many PTA users will have similar travel preferences, we can share cases between users. If it were possible to determine these groupings, the PTA could direct its collaborative CBR search within a small group of similar users – the user's neighbours. If a problem lies outside the experiences of a user (as all interactions will, for first-time users) we can consult the case-bases of his/her neighbours for a solution.

The most difficult part of implementing collaboration is finding the neighbourhood groupings. Ideally users are assigned to groupings on the basis of the similarity between their cases. With this solution, new users still present a problem, but this could be solved if users' registration details in some way related to their similarity. By including a number of profiling questions in the registration form, we could assign new users to preexisting groups of neighbours.

Collaborative CBR is used reluctantly; we attempt to solve a problem using only the user's own case-base, if this cannot find a solution or only poorly scoring ones, we repeat the retrieval-process, but extend the retrieval to include cases from the user's neighbourhood group. This increases the capacity of the CRN and should thus increase the probability of finding a good solution.

4   Evaluation

To illustrate the operation of the PTA-mPTA system developed here, we include two sample interactions: the first describes request elaboration and the second describes offer recommendation. These interactions show the usefulness of using personalization in the context of this project. All screenshots were generated from Nokia's Mobile Internet Toolkit™. The device shown is a simulation of an XHTML browser. The next generation of Nokia WAP browsers will follow on this model.

Example 1- John

John is a first time user of the system. He makes a request for a flight to London for a weekend trip. He has filled in the registration details.

Fig. 4. Initial Travel Request. The trip parameters are shown with default values. John either selects the parameters he wants to change or accepts the defaults and continues to the next screen.

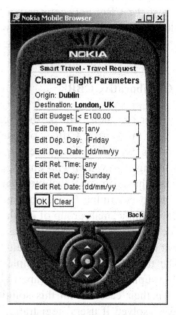

Fig. 5. Changing Initial Parameters. The parameters John wants to change are shown in more detail. He changes the Budget, DepartureTime and ReturnTime parameters.

John connects with the PTA, which brings up a page giving him an initial travel request screen as shown in Figure 4. This contains a form with the mandatory trip-summary parameters; ordinarily these parameters are given default values based on his previous travel requests, however, since he is a first-time user he has none. He has filled in his registration form fully and it fits him into a category of users. This group comprises people who prefer to fly with budget airlines. Let's assume that he fits accurately into this group (since the assigning of users to groups is outside the scope of this paper). He is offered the default choice of a return flight from Dublin (which is his home city) to London (the most popular destination within his grouping) leaving as soon as possible with a budget of under 200. John is happy with this travel request, except he would like to reduce his budget to less than 100 and would like to fly out on a Friday and return on a Sunday. He does this by selecting the parameters he wishes to change and editing them in another screen (Figure 5).

The skeletal travel request, as sent to the PTA is now:

```
Origin =            Dublin, Ireland
Destination =       London, UK
Budget =            < 100
DepartureTime =     Friday (DayofWeek)
ReturnTime =        Sunday (DayofWeek)
```

This request is not sufficient for the PTA to complete a trip-summary object so it initializes the personalization process with the above parameters as a target case. The PTA composes cases from John's neighbours' transactions (since John has no previous interactions). It uses the origin and destination as constraints on the raw data, only composing cases with the values Dublin-London (or London-Dublin) to get the offer in context; it would not be appropriate to use requests for transatlantic flights to solve this problem (although it may be appropriate to use European flights, this will become clearer with user feedback). This returns a case-base from the most relevant transactions in the system. Cases based on initial travel requests that yielded good travel offers that interested the user are given increased importance.

The CRN retrieval lists the final activation of all the cases in its case-base. The PTA uses the cases with the highest activation to decide on a final travel request. Since travel dates are in the future, the travel-time parameters - `DepartureTime` and `ReturnTime` are composed from the micro-features `DayofWeek` and `TimeofDay`, which are not dependent on the date. John specified `DayofWeek` himself, and `TimeofDay` is elaborated from the solution cases. All that remains is the actual dates used. Because John left the date field blank in his skeletal travel request the PTA assumes that he is looking for a suitable offer in the near future. The PTA will therefore be comfortable making a list of suitable travel times that fit those criteria to include in the trip-summary object.

The solution cases will either be quite similar, in which case we can easily compose a single final travel request from them; or they will be different, in which case we can make several travel requests to cover all possibilities. These final travel requests are forwarded to the TBAs who will attempt to satisfy them (this satisfaction of requests is outside the scope of our work). One such request looks like this:

```
Origin =            Dublin, Ireland
Destination =       London, UK
Budget =            < 100
                    (1) After 20/9/02 14:00, before 20/9/02 23:00
DepartureTime =     (2) After 27/9/02 14:00, before 27/9/02 23:00
                    (3) After 4/10/02 14:00, before 4/10/02 23:00
                    (1) After 22/9/02 18:00, before 22/9/02 00:00
ReturnTime =        (2) After 29/9/02 18:00, before 29/9/02 00:00
                    (3) After 06/10/02 18:00, before 06/10/02 00:00
```

Example 2 – Margaret

A corporate user, Margaret, has arranged to attend a conference in her company's headquarters in San Francisco. She is based in London and uses the PTA to arrange the travel arrangements to fit in with the times of the conference. She is a regular user of the PTA service. She has filled in an initial travel request, which was elaborated to this final travel request:

Origin =	Any Airport, London (LON), UK
Destination =	San Francisco Intl. Airport (SFO), San Francisco, Ca. USA
DepartureTime =	After 29/09/02 18:00, before 30/09/02 16:00
ReturnTime =	After 05/10/02 10:00, before 07/10/02 00:00
Selection =	By Comfort
FareType =	First Class

The PTA sends this single request to several TBAs, who return a number of travel offers. The PTA filters these by the final travel request itself (it's possible that a TBA would make an offer that does not satisfy the original request). It then begins the personalization process to filter the offers further.

Retrieval begins before the offers are received. It uses the final travel request to assemble a case-base where the cases contain previous offers that fit the travel request and the level of user-interest they drew when they were received, i.e. whether they were offered to the user, examined by the user or booked by the user. This case-base is stored in a CRN and as travel offers arrive, they are presented to it. The following travel offer is presented to the CRN (shown below in figure 6):

Origin =	Gatwick Airport (LGW), London, UK
Destination =	San Francisco Intl. Airport (SFO), San Francisco, Ca. USA
Carrier =	British Airways
DepartureTime =	29/09/02 11:15 (Sunday)
ReturnTime =	06/10/02 16:40 (Sunday)
Price =	£6531.90Stg
FareType =	First Class

The target case is created from this offer; it is made up of the offer less the constrained parameters (since all offers will meet these).

Origin =	Gatwick Airport (LGW), London, UK
Destination =	San Francisco Intl. Airport (SFO), San Francisco, Ca. USA
Carrier =	British Airways
DepartureTime =	25/01/02 10:00 (Friday)
ReturnTime =	29/01/02 16:40 (Sunday)
Price =	£8235.00Stg
FareType =	First Class

Case n4 accumulated the highest activation when the target case was presented to the CRN. The offer associated with case n4 (shown above) had been presented to Margaret before in a previous interaction with the system, but she wasn't interested in it; she didn't request further information on it or book it. Since Margaret rejected the offer associated with case n4, the PTA will give a relatively low recommendation score to the current offer. All offers received from the TBAs are given a recommendation score in the same manner. When all the travel offers have been received (either by all the TBAs responding or timing-out) the highest scoring travel offers are presented to Margaret as recommended offers. There is a scoring threshold above which an offer will be recommended. This figure may change depending on how discriminating Margaret is over time.

The possibility of several recommended offers combined with the lack of screen space means that offers should be condensed for presentation. Only the most important features are displayed to allow easy comparison between offers. These features are chosen based on user preferences in much the same way relevance arc weights are chosen in CRN maintenance. The presentation of Margaret's offers is shown in Figure 7. These offers are added to Margaret's personal profile with the interest she showed towards each offer. Offers that were rejected by the PTA are not stored. Figure 8 shows the screen presented to Margaret when she requests further information on the offer mentioned previously.

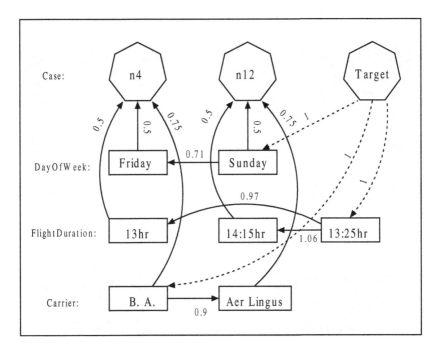

Fig. 6. A section of the CRN. For the purposes of clarity, this diagram only shows two cases and three features: DayOfWeek (from DepartureTime), FlightDuration and Carrier. The target case is connected to the net as shown. It is activated and the scores at cases n4 and n12 are accumulated. The arc weights are shown but not the similarity functions. The final activation scores are: n4 = 2.205, n12 = 1.945

5   Summary and Conclusions

In this paper we have described the FIPA PTA scenario. This involves two personal-ization tasks: request elaboration and offer-recommendation, which the PTA could perform to ease user interaction with the overall travel system. We have outlined how a case-based user profile can support this personalization process and how CBR tools could be used to perform these tasks. This case-based approach has the advantage that the profile is always up to date and has the potential to borrow cases from similar users when coverage is poor. Further, the strengths of the CRN architecture in case completion are particularly useful in the request elaboration task.

In operation, the system has stored a personal profile for each user. In order to make a travel request, the user makes a skeletal travel request outlining the most important trip parameters. The PTA elaborates this offer using the user's travel pref-erences into a full travel request and sends it to the PTM on the user's behalf. The PTM returns a number of travel offers that satisfy this request. The PTA filters these using the user's preferences and sends the most suitable to the mPTA to present to the user.

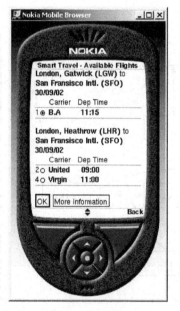

Fig. 7. Presented Travel Offers. This screen shows travel offers with Margaret's most important features. She can proceed to request more information on an offer and book it.

Fig. 8. Examined Offers. Margaret selected this offer for further information. This screen shows the full details for this travel offer and allows her to instruct the PTA to book it.

Two example interactions with the system are described to further demonstrate the personalization tasks and their implementation. The first interaction demonstrated request-elaboration and how collaborative CBR could be used to allow first-time users of the system to benefit from the experiences of their peers. The second interaction demonstrated offer-recommendation and how travel offers are rated against previous cases that were offered to a user based on that user's preferences towards similar offers in the past.

The scenarios described here show that the CBR solution can perform request elaboration and offer recommendation. The next step in this research is to evaluate the utility of this approach. Since the success criterion is user satisfaction, the standard Machine Learning-type evaluation is not appropriate. This evaluation will need to be done as user trials on a real system.

References

1. Aha, D. W. (1997). Editorial on Lazy Learning. Artificial Intelligence Review, 11, 7-10.
2. Bergenti, F. & Poggi, A.. LEAP: A FIPA Platform for Handheld and Mobile Devices. In *Proc. Eighth International Workshop on Agent Theories, Architectures, and Languages (ATAL-2001)*, Seatle, CA, 2001.
3. Bradley, K., Rafter, R. & Smyth B. (2000) Case-Based User Profiling for Content Personalisation. In Proceedings of the International Conference on Adaptive Hypermedia and Adaptive Web-based Systems, (AH2000), Trento, Italy.
4. Foundation for Intelligent Physical Agents – ACL Message Structure Specification (Document No. XC00061E).
5. Foundation for Intelligent Physical Agents - Personal Travel Assistance Specification (Document No. XC00080). Carried forward from FIPA 1997 Specification 4 V1.0.
6. Hayes, C. & Cunningham, P. (1999) Shaping a CBR View with XML. *Third International Conference on Case-Based Reasoning*. ICCBR-99 Seeon Monastery, Germany, pp.468-481
7. Hayes, C., Cunningham, P., & Doyle, M.. Distributed CBR using XML. In Proceedings of the KI-98 Workshop on Intelligent Systems and Electronic Commerce, number LSA-98-03E. University of Kaiserslauten Computer Science Department, 1998.
8. Lenz, M., Auriol, E. & Manago, M. (1998) Diagnosis and Decision Support. In M. Bartsch-Sporl, H. D. B., and Wess, S., eds., Case-Based Reasoning Technology: From Foundations to Applications, volume 1400 of Lecture Notes in Computer Science. Springer-Verlag.
9. Smyth, B. & Cotter, P., (1999) Surfing the Digital Wave: Generating Personalised TV Listings using Collaborative, Case-Based Recommendation, in Proceedings of 3rd *International Conference on Case-Based Reasoning* eds K-D. Althoff, R. Bergmann, L. K. Branting, Lecture Notes in Artificial Intelligence 1650, V pp561-571, Springer Verlag.
10. Smyth, B. & McClave, P. (2001) "Similarity vs. Diversity", Proceedings of the 4th International Conference on Case-Based Reasoning. Vancouver, Canada.
11. Waszkiewicz, P., Cunningham, P. & Byrne, C., (1999) Case-based User Profiling in a Personal Travel Assistant, *User Modeling: Proceedings of the 7th International Conference, UM99,* Judy Kay, (ed).pp. 323-325, Springer-Wien-New York.
12. Watson, I. & Gardingen, D. (1999). *A Distributed Case-Based Reasoning Application for Engineering Sales Support*. In, Proc. 16th Int. Joint Conf. on Artificial Intelligence (IJCAI-99), Vol. 1: pp. 600-605. Morgan Kaufmann Publishers Inc. ISBN 1-55860-613-0

An Automated Hybrid CBR System for Forecasting *

Florentino Fdez-Riverola[1], Juan M. Corchado[2], and Jesús M. Torres[3]

[1] Dpto. de Informática, E.S.E.I., University of Vigo,
Campus Universitario As Lagoas s/n., 32004, Ourense, Spain
riverola@uvigo.es
[2] Dpto. de Informática y Automática, University of Salamanca,
Facultad de Ciencias, Plaza de la Merced, s/n., 37008, Salamanca, Spain
corchado@usal.es
[3] Dpto. de Física Aplicada, University of Vigo,
Facultad de Ciencias, Lagoas Marcosende, 36200, Vigo, Spain
jesu@uvigo.es

Abstract. A hybrid neuro-symbolic problem solving model is presented in which the aim is to forecast parameters of a complex and dynamic environment in an unsupervised way. In situations in which the rules that determine a system are unknown, the prediction of the parameter values that determine the characteristic behaviour of the system can be a problematic task. The proposed system employs a case-based reasoning model that incorporates a growing cell structures network, a radial basis function network and a set of Sugeno fuzzy models to provide an accurate prediction. Each of these techniques is used in a different stage of the reasoning cycle of the case-based reasoning system to retrieve, to adapt and to review the proposed solution to the problem. This system has been used to predict the red tides that appear in the coastal waters of the north west of the Iberian Peninsula. The results obtained from those experiments are presented.

1 Introduction

Forecasting the behaviour of a dynamic system is, in general, a difficult task, especially if the prediction needs to be achieved in real time. In such a situation one strategy is to create an adaptive system which possesses the flexibility to behave in different ways depending on the state of the environment. This paper presents a hybrid artificial intelligence (AI) model for forecasting the evolution of complex and dynamic environments. The effectiveness of this model is demonstrated in an oceanographic problem in which neither artificial neural network nor statistical models have been sufficiently successful.

Several researchers [1,2] have used k-nearest-neighbour algorithms for time series predictions. Although a k-nearest-neighbour algorithm does not, in itself,

---

* This research was supported in part by PGIDT00MAR30104PR project of Xunta de Galicia, Spain

S. Craw and A. Preece (Eds.): ECCBR 2002, LNAI 2416, pp. 519–533, 2002.

constitute a CBR system, it may be regarded as a very basic and limited form of CBR operation in numerical domains. [1] uses a relatively complex hybrid CBR-ANN system. In contrast, [2] forecast a data set just by searching in a given sequence of data values for segments that closely match the pattern of the last n measurements and then, by supposing that similar antecedent segments are likely to be followed by similar consequent segments. Other examples of CBR systems that carry out predictions can be found in [3], [4], [5], [6] and [7].

In most cases, the CBR systems used in forecasting problems have flat memories with simple data representation structures using k-nearest-neighbour metric in their retrieve phase. K-nearest-neighbour metric are acceptable if the system is relatively stable and well understood, but if the system is dynamic and the forecast is required in real time, it may not be possible to easily redefine the k-nearest-neighbour metrics adequately. The dominant characteristic of the adaptation stage used in these models are similarity metrics or statistical models, although, in some systems, case adaptation is accomplished manually. If the problem is very complex, there may be no planned adaptation strategy and the most similar case is used directly, but it is believed that adequate adaptation is one of the keys to a successful CBR paradigm. In the majority of the systems surveyed, case revision (if carried out at all) is performed by human expert, and in all the cases the CBR systems are provided with a small case-base. A survey of such forecasting CBR systems can be found in [8].

Traditionally, CBR systems have been combined with other technologies like artificial neural networks, rule-based systems, constraint satisfaction problems and others, producing successful results to solve specific problems [9,10]. Although, in general each specific problem and domain requires a particular solution, this paper proposes a CBR based solution for forecasting the evolution of a complex problem, with a high degree of dynamism for which there is a lack of knowledge, and for which an adaptive learning system is required. This paper also presents, a method for automating the CBR reasoning process for the solution of problems in which the cases are characterised predominantly by numerical information.

Successful results have been already obtained with hybrid case-based reasoning systems [11,12,13] and used to predict the evolution of the temperature of the water ahead of an ongoing vessel, in real time. The hybrid system proposed in this paper presents a new synthesis that brings several AI subfields together (CBR, ANN and Fuzzy inferencing). The retrieval, reuse, revision and learning stages of the CBR system presented in this paper use the previously mentioned technologies to facilitate the CBR adaptation to a wide range of complex problem domains (for instance, the afore-mentioned red tides problem) and to completely automate the reasoning process of the proposed forecasting mechanism

The structure of the paper is as follows: first the hybrid neuro-symbolic model is explained in detail; a case study is then briefly outlined; the results obtained to date with the proposed forecasting system are analyzed, and finally, the conclusions and future work are presented.

2   The Hybrid CBR Based Forecasting System

This section proposes a CBR based model for forecasting the evolution of parameters related to problems that can be numerically represented, that evolve with time, for which there is an incomplete knowledge and for which the forecasting system has to be completely automated.

In this context, in order to forecast the value of any variable, a problem descriptor should be generated. A problem descriptor is composed of a vector with the variables that describe the problem and the solution. In this case, this vector holds numerical variables.

Figure 1 illustrates the relationships between the processes and components of the hybrid CBR system. In general, we can say that the forecast values are obtained using a neural network enhanced hybrid case-base reasoning system. The cyclic CBR process shown in the figure has been inspired by the work of [11] and [12]. The diagram shows the technology used at each stage, where the four basic phases of the CBR cycle are shown as rectangles.

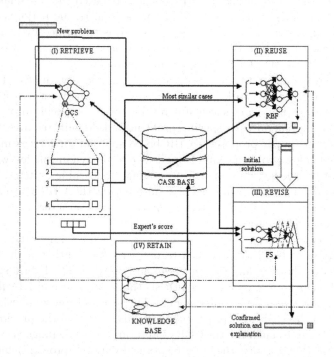

Fig. 1. Hybrid neuro-symbolic system.

The retrieval stage is carried out using a Growing Cell Structures (GCS) ANN [14]. The GCS facilitates the indexing of cases and the selection of those that are most similar to the problem descriptor. The reuse and adaptation of cases is carried out with a Radial Basis Function (RBF) ANN [15], which generates an initial solution creating a forecasting model with the retrieved cases. The revision is carried out using a group of fuzzy systems that identify potential incorrect solutions. Finally, the learning stage is carried out when the real value of the variable to predict is measured and the error value is calculated, updating the knowledge structure of the whole system. Now we present the working cycle of the CBR system illustrated in Figure 1.

When a new problem is presented to the system a new problem descriptor (case) is created, and the GCS neuronal network is used to recover from the case-base the k more similar cases to the given problem (identifying the class to which the problem belongs, see Figure 2).

In the reuse phase, the values of the weights and centers of the RBF neural network used in the previous forecast are retrieved from the knowledge base. These network parameters together with the k retrieved cases are then used to retrain the RBF network and to obtain an initial forecast (see Figure 2). During this process the values of the parameters that characterise the network are updated.

CBR-STAGE	Technology	Input	Output	Process
Retrieval	GCS network.	Problem descriptor.	k cases. Expert's score.	All the cases that belong to the same class to which the GCS associates the problem case are retrieved.
Reuse	RBF network.	Problem descriptor. k similar cases.	Initial solution.	The RBF network is retrained with the k retrieved cases.
Revision	Fuzzy systems.	Problem descriptor. Expert's score. Initial solution.	Confirmed solution.	Different fuzzy systems are created using the RBF network configuration with different degrees of generalization.
Retain	GCS network. RBF network. Fuzzy systems.	Problem descriptor. Forecasting error.	Configuration parameters of the GCS network, RBF network and Fuzzy systems.	The configurations of the GCS network, the RBF network and the Fuzzy subsystems are updated according to the accuracy of the forecast.

Fig. 2. Summary of technologies employed by the hybrid model.

In the revision phase, the initial solution proposed by the RBF neural network is modified according to the response of the fuzzy revision subsystem (a set of fuzzy models). Each fuzzy system has been created from the RBF network using neurofuzzy techniques [16].

The revised forecast is then retained temporarily in the forecast database. When the real value of the variable to predict is measured, the forecast value for the variable can then be evaluated, through comparison of the actual and forecast value and the error obtained (see Figure 2). A new case, corresponding to this forecasting operation, is then stored in the case-base. The forecasting error value is also used to update several parameters associated with the GCS network, the RBF network and the fuzzy systems.

2.1   Growing Cell Structures Operation

To illustrate the working model of the GCS network inside the whole system, a two-dimensional space will be used, where the cells (neurons) are connected and organized into triangles [14]. Initially, three vectors are randomly chosen from the training data set. Each cell in the network (representing a generic case), is associated with a weight vector, w, of the same dimension (problem descriptor + solution) that cases stored in the case-base. At the beginning of the learning process, the weight vector of each cell is initialized with random values [17]. The basic learning process in a GCS network consists of topology modification and weight vector adaptations carried out in three steps. The training vectors of the GCS network are the cases stored in the CBR case-base, as indicated in Figure 1.

In the first step of each learning cycle, the cell c, with the smallest euclidean distance between its weight vector, w_c, and the actual case, x, is chosen as the *winner cell* or best-match cell. The second step consists in the adaptation of the weight vector of the winning cell and their neighbours (positioning the vectors more near to the actual case). In the third step, a *signal counter* is assigned to each cell, which reflects how often a cell has been chosen as winner. Growing cell structures also modify the overall network structure by inserting new cells into those regions that represent large portions of the input data (with a higher value of the signal counter), or removing cells that do not contribute to the input data representation.

Repeating this process several times, for all the cases of the case-base, a network of cells will be created. Each cell will have associated cases that have a similar structure and each cell will represent a class. These cells can be seen as a "prototype" that identifies a set of similar problem descriptors.

For each class identified by the GCS neural network a vector of values is maintained (see Figure 1). This "importance" vector is initialized with a same value for all its components whose sum is one, and represents the accuracy of each fuzzy system (used during the revision stage) with respect to that class. During revision, the importance vector associated to the class to which the problem case belongs, is used to ponder the outputs of each fuzzy system. Each value of the importance vector is associated with one of the fuzzy systems. For each forecasting cycle, the value of the importance vector associated with the most accurate fuzzy system is increased and the other values are proportionally decreased. This is done in order to give more relevance to the most accurate fuzzy system of the revision subsystem.

The neural network topology of a GCS network is incrementally constructed on the basis of the cases presented to the network. Effectively, such a topology represents the result of the basic clustering procedure and it has the added advantage that inter-cluster distances can be precisely quantified. Since such networks contain explicit distance information, they can be used effectively in CBR to represent: (i) an indexing structure which indexes sets of cases in the case base and, (ii) a similarity measure between case sets [18].

When dealing with complex, dynamic, stochastic problems that can be numerically represented, the decision of what retrieval model is better to use for a CBR that need to be completely automated is not a trivial task. The main characteristics that should have the retrieval model are: an adequate adaptation capacity to the problem domain and strong learning capability. In such a situation, GCS neural networks offer several advantages over other approaches and well know metrics:

- GCS is a neural network which is able to automatically generate a k dimensional network structure highly adapted to a given but not explicitly known probability distribution. The adaptation rules of the GCS also enable the processing of data with changing probability distributions, what helps in the construction of dynamic systems for complex problems.
- Its ability to perform problem-dependent error measures allows the implementation of better adaptive data representations (insertion and deletion of cells) in comparison with static-topology models. This characteristic guarantees the adaptation capacity above mentioned.
- Its ability to interrupt a learning process or to continue a previously interrupted one permits the construction of incremental and dynamic learning systems.
- The GCS self-organising model consists of a small number of constant parameters. There is therefore no need to define time-dependent or decay schedule parameters, what facilitates the implementation of autonomous systems.
- GCS networks have demonstrated their capacity to process both small and high dimensionality data in several application domains and can operate in either unsupervised or supervised learning modes. This characteristic guarantees the construction of dynamic learning systems.

Another specially interesting fact is that the GCS network are structurally similar to the RBF network. The GCS network provides *consistent* classifications that can be used by the RBF network to auto-tune its forecasting model. (given a new problem descriptor the GCS network finds its class and retrieves all cases belonging to that class). Irregularities, discontinuities and exceptions in the data are avoided if the classifications are consistent. In our model, this is achieved by means of taking into account the whole case (problem descriptor + solution) during the training of the GCS network.

In the light of all these reasons, the GCS neural network has been selected to solve the problem of the classification and indexing in our hybrid CBR based forecasting system.

2.2   Radial Basis Function Operation

Case adaptation is one of the most problematic aspects of the CBR cycle, mainly if we have to deal with problems with a high degree of dynamism and for which there is a lack of knowledge. In such a situation, RBF networks have demonstrated their utility as universal approximators for closely modelling these continuous processes [9]. In our system, the term adaptation is used to represent the process of *adapting* the configuration of the RBF network using the k most similar cases retrieved by the GCS network, instead of the classic meaning in CBR theory.

Again to illustrate how the RBF networks work, a simple architecture will be presented. Initially, three vectors are randomly chosen from the training data set and used as centers in the middle layer of the RBF network. All the centers are associated with a Gaussian function, the width of which, for all the functions, is set to the value of the distance to the nearest center multiplied by 0.5 (see [15] for more information about RBF network).

Training of the network is carried out by presenting pairs of corresponding input and desired output vectors. After an input vector has activated each Gaussian unit, the activations are propagated forward through the weighted connections to the output units, which sum all incoming signals. The comparison of actual and desired output values enables the mean square error (the quantity to be minimized) to be calculated.

The closest center to each particular input vector is moved toward the input vector by a percentage a of the present distance between them. By using this technique the centers are positioned close to the highest densities of the input vector data set. The aim of this adaptation is to force the centers to be as close as possible to as many vectors from the input space as possible. The value of a is linearly decreased by the number of iterations until its value becomes zero; then the network is trained for a number of iterations (1/4 of the total of established iterations for the period of training) in order to obtain the best possible weights for the final value of the centers.

A new center is inserted into the network when the average error in the training data set does not fall during a given period. There are different methods to identify the place where the new center will be inserted.

The main advantages of this type of networks can be summarized as follows:

- The RBF network is capable of approximating nonlinear mappings effectively.
- The training time of the RBF network is quite low compared to that of other neural network approaches such as the multi-layer perceptron, because training of the two layers of the network is decoupled.
- The RBF networks are successful for identifying regions of sample data not in any known class because it uses a non-monotonic transfer function based on the Gaussian density function.
- RBF network is less sensitive to the order in which data is presented to them because one basis function takes responsibility for one part of the input space.

The above characteristics together with their good capability of generalization, fast convergence, smaller extrapolation errors and higher reliability over difficult data, make this type of neural networks a good choice that fulfils the necessities of dealing with this type of problems. It is very important to train this network with a consistent number of cases. Such consistency in the training data set is guaranteed by the GCS network that carries out a classification of the data using the problem descriptor and the solution of the cases stored in the case-base.

RBF networks can also be used to generate Fuzzy inference systems [16]. This characteristic has been used in this model for the automatic generation of the revision subsystem as it will be explained in the following section.

2.3   Fuzzy System Operation

Rule extraction from artificial neural networks is considered to be important due to the following reasons [16]:

- Rule extraction provides artificial neural networks with an explanation capability, which makes it possible for the user to check on the internal logic of the system.
- Rule extraction helps to discover previously unknown dependencies in data sets and thus new knowledge about the system can be acquired.
- It is believed that a rule system with good interpretability improves the generalization ability of neural networks where training data are insufficient.

The two main objectives of the proposed revision stage are: to validate the initial prediction generated by the RBF and, to provide a set of simplified rules that explain the system working mode. The construction of the revision subsystem is carried out in two main steps.

(i) First, a Sugeno-Takagi fuzzy model [19] is generated using the trained RBF network configuration (centers and weights). In order to transform a RBF neural network to a well interpretable fuzzy rule system, the following conditions should be satisfied:

- The basis functions of the RBF neural network have to be Gaussian functions.
- The output of the RBF neural network has to be normalized.
- The basis functions may have different variances.
- A certain number of basis functions for the same input variable should share a mutual center and a mutual variance.

(ii) A measure of similarity is applied to the fuzzy system [20] with the purpose of reducing the number of fuzzy sets describing each variable in the model. Similar fuzzy sets for one parameter are merged to create a common fuzzy set to replace them in the rule base. If the redundancy in the model is high, merging similar fuzzy sets for each variable might result in equal rules that also can be merged, thereby reducing the number of rules as well. When similar fuzzy sets are replaced by a common fuzzy set representative of the originals, the system's capacity for generalization increases.

In this model, the fuzzy systems are associated with each class identified by the GCS network, mapping each one with its corresponding value of the importance vector. There is one importance vector for each class or prototype. These fuzzy systems are used to validate and refine the proposed forecast. Given a problem descriptor and a proposed forecast for it, each of the fuzzy inference systems that compose the revision subsystem generates a solution that is pondered according to the importance vector value associated to the GCS class to which the problem belongs.

The value generated by the revision subsystem is compared with the prediction carried out by the RBF and its difference (in percentage) is calculated. If the initial forecast doesn't differ by more than a certain threshold of the solution generated by the revision subsystem, this prediction is supported and its value is considered as the final forecast. If, on the contrary, the difference is greater than the defined threshold, the average value between the value obtained by the RBF and that obtained by the revision subsystem is calculated, and this revised value adopted as the final output of the system. This problem dependent threshold must be identified with empirical experiments and following the advice of human experts. In the theoretical CBR cycle, the main purpose of the revise phase is to try out the solution for real and change it before it is retained, making use of knowledge that is *external* to the system. In our system, this is all done in the retain phase, implementing the revise phase as a form of validation and using knowledge that is *internal* to the system.

Fuzzy systems provide a solution to the revision stage when dealing with complex problems, with a high degree of dynamism and for which there is a lack of knowledge. The exposed revision subsystem improves the generalization ability of the RBF network. Fuzzy models, especially if acquired from data, may contain redundant information in the form of similarities between fuzzy sets. As similar fuzzy sets represent compatible concepts in the rule base, a model with many similar fuzzy sets becomes redundant, unnecessarily complex and computationally demanding. The simplified rule bases allow us to obtain a more general knowledge of the system and gain a deeper insight into the logical structure of the system to be approximated.

The proposed revision method then help us to ensure a more accurate result, to gain confidence in the system prediction and to learn about the problem and its solution. The fuzzy inference systems also provides useful information that is used during the retain stage.

2.4   Retain

As mentioned before, when the real value of the variable to predict is known, a new case containing the problem descriptor and the solution is stored in the case-base. The importance vector associated with the retrieved class is updated in the following way: The error percentage with respect to the real value is calculated. The fuzzy system that has produced the most accurate prediction is identified and the error percentage value previously calculated is added to the degree of importance associated with this fuzzy subsystem. As the sum of the importance values associated to a class (or prototype) has to be one, the values are normalized and the sum dividing up accordingly between them. When the new case is added to the case-base, its class is identified. The class is updated and the new case is incorporated into the network for future use.

3   A Case of Study: The Red Tides Problem

The oceans of the world form a highly dynamic system for which it is difficult to create mathematical models [21]. *Red tides* are the name for the discolourations caused by dense concentrations of microscopic sea plants, known as phytoplankton. The rapid increase in dinoflagellate numbers, sometimes to millions of cells per liter of water, is described as a *bloom* of phytoplankton (concentration levels above the 100.000 cells per liter). This study focusses on the pseudo-nitzschia spp diatom dinoflagellate, which causes amnesic shellfish poisoning along the north west coast of the Iberian Peninsula in late summer and autumn [22].

Surface waters of these blooms are associated with the production of toxins, resulting in mortality of fish and other marine organisms. Toxic blooms of dinoflagellates fall into three categories: (i) blooms that kill fish but few invertebrates; (ii) blooms that kill primarily invertebrates; (iii) blooms that kill few marine organisms, but whose toxins are concentrated within the siphons, digestive glands, or mantle cavities of filter-feeding bivalve mollusc such as clams, oysters, and escallops.

The nature of the red tides problem has changed considerably over the last two decades around the world. Where formerly a few regions were affected in scattered locations, now virtually every coastal state is threatened, in many cases over large geographic areas and by more than one harmful or toxic algal species [23]. Few would argue that the number of toxic blooms, the economic losses from them, the types of resources affected, and the number of toxins and toxic species have all increased dramatically in recent years in all over the world. Disagreement only arises with respect to the reasons for this expansion.

Models of dinoflagellate blooms have been developed from several different perspectives [24,25,26] but the end result is that despite the proven utility of models in so many oceanographic disciplines, there are no predictive models of population development, transport, and toxin accumulation. There is thus a clear need to develop models for regions subject to red tides, and to incorporate biological behavior and population dynamics into those simulations [27].

An artificial intelligence (AI) approach to the problem of forecasting in the ocean environment offers potential advantages over alternative approaches, because it is able to deal with uncertain, incomplete and even inconsistent data. Several AI techniques have been used to forecast the evolution of different oceanographic parameters [28,11,12]. The reported work shows how CBR systems have a greater facility for forecasting oceanographic parameters than other statistical and AI based models [13].

3.1   Forecasting Red Tides

In the current work, the aim is to develop a system for forecasting one week in advance the concentrations (in cells per liter) of the pseudo-nitzschia spp, the diatom that produces the most harmful red tides, at different geographical points. The approach builds on the methods and expertise previously developed in earlier research.

The problem of forecasting, which is currently being addressed, may be simply stated as follows:

- **Given:** a sequence of data values (representative of the current and immediately previous state) relating to some physical and biological parameters,
- **Predict:** the value of a parameter at some future point(s) or time(s).

The raw data (sea temperature, salinity, PH, oxygen and other physical characteristics of the water mass) which is measured weekly by the monitoring network for toxic proliferations in the CCCMM (Centro de Control da Calidade do Medio Marino, *Oceanographic environment Quality Control Centre*, Vigo, Spain), consists of a vector of discrete sampled values (at 5 meters' depth) of each oceanographic parameter used in the experiment, in the form of a time series. These data values are complemented by data derived from satellite images stored on a database. The satellite image data values are used to generate cloud and superficial temperature indexes which are then stored with the problem descriptor and subsequently updated during the CBR operation. Table 1 shows the variables that characterise the problem. Data from the previous 2 weeks (W_{n-1}, W_n) is used to forecast the concentration of pseudo-nitzschia spp one week ahead (W_{n+1}).

Table 1. Variables that define a case.

Variable	Unit	Week
Date	dd-mm-yyyy	W_{n-1}, W_n
Temperature	Cent. degrees	W_{n-1}, W_n
Oxygen	milliliters/liter	W_{n-1}, W_n
PH	acid/based	W_{n-1}, W_n
Transmitance	%	W_{n-1}, W_n
Fluorescence	%	W_{n-1}, W_n
Cloud index	%	W_{n-1}, W_n
Recount of diatoms	cel/liter	W_{n-1}, W_n
Pseudo-nitzschia spp	cel/liter	W_{n-1}, W_n
Pseudo-nitzschia spp (future)	*cel/liter*	W_{n+1}

Our proposed model has been used to build an hybrid forecasting system that has been tested along the north west coast of the Iberian Peninsula with data collected by the CCCMM from the year 1992 until the present. The prototype used in this experiment was set up to forecast the concentration of the pseudo-nitzschia spp diatom of a water mass situated near the coast of Vigo, a week in advance. Red tides appear when the concentration of pseudo-nitzschia spp is higher than 100.000 cell/liter. Although the aim of this experiment is to forecast the value of the concentration, the most important aspect is to identify in advance if the concentration is going to exceed this threshold.

A case-base was built with the above mentioned data. For this experiment, four fuzzy inference systems have been created from the RBF network, and they were initialised with a value of (0.25, 0.25, 0.25, 0.25) for each class (or prototype) in the GCS network. The RBF network used in the framework of this experiment, uses 18 input neurons, between three and fifty neurons in the hidden layer and a single neuron in the output layer, being the output of the network the concentration of pseudo-nitzschia spp for a given water mass.

The following section discusses the results obtained with the prototype developed for this experiment.

4   Results

The average error in the forecast was found to be 26.043,66 cell/liter and only 5.5% of the forecasts had an error higher than 100.000 cell/liter. Although the experiment was carried out using a limited data set (geographical area A0 ((42°28.90' N, 8°57.80' W) 61 m)), it is believed that these error value results are significant enough to be extrapolated along the whole coast of the Iberian Peninsula.

Two situations of special interest are those corresponding to the *false alarms* and the *blooms not detected*. The former refers to predictions of bloom (concentration of pseudo-nitzschia $\geq$ 100.000 cell/liter) which don't actually materialize (real concentration $\leq$ 100.000 cell/liter). The latter, more significant occurrence arises when a bloom exists but the model fails to detect it.

Table 2 shows the predictions carried out with success (in absolute values and %) and the erroneous predictions differentiating the not detected blooms from the false alarms.

Table 2. Summary of results using the CBR-ANN-FS Hybrid System.

OK	OK (%)	Not detect.	False alarms
191/200	95,5%	8	1

Further experiments have been carried out to compare the performance of the CBR-ANN-FS hybrid system with several other forecasting approaches. These include standard statistical forecasting algorithms and the application of several neural networks methods. The results obtained from these experiments are listed in Table 3.

Table 3 shows the number of successful predictions (in absolute value and %) as well as the blooms not detected and false alarms for each method. As it indicates, the combination of different techniques in the form of the hybrid CBR system previously presented, produces better results that a RBF neural network working alone and any of the other techniques studied during this investigation. This is due to the effectiveness of the revision subsystem and the re-training of the RBF neural network with the cases recovered by the GCS network. The performance of the hybrid system is better than the other methods at each of the individual geographical monitoring points.

Table 3. Summary of results using statistical techniques.

Method	OK	OK (%)	N. detect.	Fal. alarms
RBF	185/200	92,5%	8	7
ARIMA	174/200	87%	10	16
Quadratic Trend	184/200	92%	16	0
Moving Average	181/200	90,5%	10	9
Simp. Exp. Smooth.	183/200	91,5%	8	9
Lin. Exp. Smooth.	177/200	88,5%	8	15

Table 4 shows the average error obtained with the hybrid model, a standard RBF network, an ARIMA model, a Quadratic Trend, a Moving Average, a Simple Exp. Smoothing, a Brown's Linear Exp. Smoothing and a Finite Impulse Response ANN [28], which was not able to converge for this type of problem.

Table 4. Average error in the forecast with other techniques and the CBR-ANN-FS Hybrid System.

Method	Type	Aver. error (cel/liter)
CBR-ANN-FS	Hybrid System	26.043,66
RBF	ANN	45.654,20
FIR	ANN	–
ARIMA	Statistics	71.918,15
Quadratic Trend	Statistics	70.354,35
Moving Average	Statistics	51.969,43
Simple Exp. Smoothing	Statistics	41.943,26
Brown's Linear Exp. Smoothing	Statistics	49.038,19

5 Conclusions and Future Work

In summary, this paper has presented an automated hybrid CBR system that combines a case-based reasoning system integrated with two artificial neural networks and a set of fuzzy inference systems in order to create a real time autonomous forecasting system. The model employs a case-based reasoning model that incorporates a growing cell structures network (for the index tasks to organize and retrieve relevant data), a radial basis function network (that contributes generalization, learning and adaptation capabilities) and a set of Sugeno fuzzy models (acting as experts that revise the initial solution) to provide a more effective prediction. The resulting hybrid system thus combines complementary properties of both connectionist and symbolic AI methods.

The developed prototype is able to produce a forecast with an acceptable degree of accuracy. The results obtained may be extrapolated to provide forecasts further ahead using the same technique, and it is believed that successful results may be obtained. However, the further ahead the forecast is made, the less accurate the forecast may be expected to be. The developed prototype can not be used in a particular geographical area if there are no stored cases from that area. Once the system is in operation and it is forecasting, a succession of cases will be generated, enabling the hybrid forecasting mechanism to evolve and to work autonomously.

In conclusion, the hybrid reasoning problem solving approach provides an effective strategy for forecasting in an environment in which the raw data is derived from different sources and it can be represented by means of a vector of numeric values. This model may be used to forecast in complex situations where the problem is characterized by a lack of knowledge and where there is a high degree of dynamism. The model presented here will be tested in different water masses and a distributed forecasting system will be developed based on the model in order to monitor 500 km. of the North West coast of the Iberian Peninsula.

This work is financed by the project: *Development of techniques for the automatic prediction of the proliferation of red tides in the Galician coasts, PGIDT-00MAR30104PR*, inside the Marine Program of investigation of Xunta de Galicia. The authors want to thank the support lent by this institution, as well as the data facilitated by the CCCMM.

References

1. Nakhaeizadeh, G.: Learning prediction of time series. A theoretical and empirical comparison of CBR with some other approaches. In Proceedings of First European Workshop on Case-Based Reasoning, EWCBR-93. Kaiserslautern, Germany.(1993) 65–76
2. Lendaris, G. G., and Fraser, A. M.: Visual Fitting and Extrapolation. In Weigend, A. S., and Fershenfield, N. A. (Eds.). Time Series Prediction, Forecasting the Future and Understanding the Past. Addison Wesley. (1994) 35–46
3. Faltings, B.: Probabilistic Indexing for Case-Based Prediction. In Proceedings of Case-Based Reasoning Research and Development, Second International Conference, ICCBR-97. Providence, Rhode Island, USA. (1997) 611–622
4. Lekkas, G. P., Arouris, N. M., Viras, L. L.: Case-Based Reasoning in Environmental Monitoring Applications. Artificial Intelligence, 8, (1994) 349–376
5. Mcintyre, H. S., Achabal, D. D., Miller, C. M.: Applying Case-Based Reasoning to Forecasting Retail Sales. Journal of Retailing, 69, num. 4, (1993) 372–398
6. Stottler, R. H.: Case-Based Reasoning for Cost and Sales Prediction. AI Expert, (1994) 25–33
7. Weber-Lee, R., Barcia, R. M., and Khator, S. K.: Case-based reasoning for cash flow forecasting using fuzzy retrieval. In Proceedings of the First International Conference, ICCBR-95. Sesimbra, Portugal, (1995) 510–519
8. Fyfe C., and Corchado J. M.: Automating the construction of CBR Systems using Kernel Methods. International Journal of Intelligent Systems, 16, num. 4, (2001) 571–586
9. Corchado, J. M., and Lees, B.: Adaptation of Cases for Case-based Forecasting with Neural Network Support. In Pal, S. K., Dilon, T. S., and Yeung, D. S. (Eds.). Soft Computing in Case Based Reasoning. London: Springer Verlag, (2000) 293–319

10. Pal, S. K., Dilon, T. S., and Yeung, D. S.: Soft Computing in Case Based Reasoning. Springer Verlag: London, (2001)
11. Corchado, J. M., Lees, B.: A Hybrid Case-based Model for Forecasting. Applied Artificial Intelligence, 15, num. 2, (2001) 105–127
12. Corchado, J. M., Lees, B., Aiken, J.: Hybrid Instance-based System for Predicting Ocean Temperatures. International Journal of Computational Intelligence and Applications, 1, num. 1, (2001) 35–52
13. Corchado, J. M., Aiken, J., Rees, N.: Artificial Intelligence Models for Oceanographic Forecasting. Plymouth Marine Laboratory, U.K., (2001)
14. Fritzke, B.: Growing Self-Organizing Networks-Why?. In Verleysen, M. (Ed.). European Symposium on Artificial Neural Networks, ESANN-96. Brussels, (1996) 61–72
15. Fritzke, B.: Fast learning with incremental RBF Networks. Neural Processing Letters, 1, num. 1, (1994) 2–5
16. Jin, Y., Seelen, W. von., and Sendhoff, B.: Extracting Interpretable Fuzzy Rules from RBF Neural Networks. Internal Report IRINI 00-02, Institut für Neuroinformatik, Ruhr-Universität Bochum, Germany, (2000)
17. Fritzke, B.: Growing Cell Structures - A Self-organizing Network for Unsupervised and Supervised Learning. Technical Report, International Computer Science Institute. Berkeley, (1993)
18. Azuaje, F., Dubitzky, W., Black, N., and Adamson, K.: Discovering Relevance Knowledge in Data: A Growing Cell Structures Approach. IEEE Transactions on Systems, Man and Cybernetics, 30, (2000) 448–460
19. Takagi, T., Sugeno, M.: Fuzzy identification of systems and its applications to modeling and control. IEEE Transactions on Systems, Man, and Cybernetics, 15, (1985) 116–132
20. Setnes, M., Babuska, R., Kaymak, U., and van Nauta, H. R.: Similarity measures in Fuzzy Rule Base Simplification. IEEE Transactions on systems, Man, and Cybernetics, 28, num. 3, (1998) 376–386
21. Tomczak, M., Godfrey, J. S.: Regional Oceanographic: An Introduction. Pergamon, New York, (1994)
22. Fernández, E.: Las Mareas Rojas en las Rías Gallegas. Technical Report, Department of Ecology and Animal Biology. University of Vigo, (1998)
23. Hallegraeff, G. M.: A review of harmful algal blooms and their apparent global increase. Phycologia, 32, (1993) 79–99
24. Kamykowski, D.: The simulation of a southern California red tide using characteristics of a simultaneously-measured internal wave field. Ecol. Model., 12, (1981) 253–265
25. Watanabe, M., Harashima, A.: Interaction between motile phytoplankton and Langmuir circulation. Ecol. Model., 31, (1986) 175–183
26. Franks, P. J. S., Anderson, D. M.: Toxic phytoplankton blooms in the southwestern Gulf of Maine: testing hypotheses of physical control using historical data. Marine Biology, 112, (1992) 165–174
27. Anderson, D. M.: Toxic algal blooms and red tides: a global perspective. In Okaichi, T., Anderson, D. M., and Nemoto, T. (Eds.). RedTides: Biology, Environmental Science and Toxicology. New York: Elsevier, (1989) 11–16
28. Corchado, J. M., Fyfe, C.: Unsupervised Neural Network for Temperature Forecasting. Artificial Intelligence in Engineering, 13, num. 4, (1999) 351–357

Using CBR
for Automation of Software Design Patterns

Paulo Gomes, Francisco C. Pereira, Paulo Paiva, Nuno Seco, Paulo Carreiro,
José L. Ferreira, and Carlos Bento

CISUC – Centro de Informática e Sistemas da Universidade de Coimbra.
Departamento de Engenharia Informática, Polo II, Universidade de Coimbra. 3030 Coimbra
{pgomes, camara, zeluis, bento}@dei.uc.pt,
{paiva, nseco,carreiro}@student.dei.uc.pt,
http://rebuilder.dei.uc.pt

Abstract. Software design patterns are used in software engineering as a way
to improve and maintain software systems. Patterns are abstract solutions to
problem categories, and they describe why, how, and when can a pattern be applied. Their description is based on natural language, which makes the automation of design patterns a difficult task. In this paper we present an approach for
automation of design pattern application. We focus on the selection of what
pattern to apply, and where to apply it. We follow a Case-Based Reasoning approach, providing a complete framework for pattern application. In our approach cases describe situations for application of patterns.

1 Introduction

Software engineers and programmers deal with repeated problems and situations in
the course of software design. This lead to the development of software design patterns [1], which can be defined as a description of an abstract solution for a category
of design problems. One of the main advantages of patterns is design reusability.
Another main advantage is that the application of design patterns improves and makes
software maintenance easier – design for change. Software design patterns are described in natural language, not having a formalization. This is due to the abstract
level of the design patterns, which makes the application of design patterns a human
dependant task. Existing approaches to pattern application using computer tools [2-5],
need the help and guidance of a human designer. This is especially true in the selection of the design pattern to apply. It is difficult to automate the identification of the
context in which a pattern can be applied. Human designers must also identify which
are the objects involved in the pattern application. The automation of this task opens

This work was partially supported by POSI - Programa Operacional Sociedade de Informação
of Portuguese Fundação para a Ciência e Tecnologia and European Union FEDER, under
contract POSI/33399/SRI/2000, by program PRAXIS XXI.

S. Craw and A. Preece (Eds.): ECCBR 2002, LNAI 2416, pp. 534–548.

the possibility of CASE design tools providing complete automation of design patterns, and the offering new functionalities that can help the software designer to improve systems, and do better software reuse.

Case-Based Reasoning [6, 7] can be defined as a way of reasoning based on past experiences. Each of these experiences is stored in a repository and is called a case. A case represents a specific situation, and can have different formats, depending on what is an experience. Normally, a case comprises three parts: problem – describing the problem and context situation; solution – describing the solution applied to this specific problem; and justification – an explanation of how the solution solves the problem. Usually the Case-Based Reasoning (CBR) cycle [8] comprises four main steps: retrieve, reuse, revise and retain. The first phase is responsible for the search and retrieval of cases from the case library. Commonly this is done using an indexing structure that identifies the relevant cases for the target problem, and then applies a similarity metric, which ranks the retrieved cases. In the reuse phase, the CBR system modifies one or more retrieved cases adapting them to the target problem situation. Revising the solutions generated by the previous phase is the next step. Most of the times this step is performed using domain specific heuristics, or domain models. The last phase is the retaining (or learning) of the new generated solution in the form of a new case, thus closing the CBR cycle. This allows the system to evolve in time.

From our point of view CBR can be applied successfully to the automation of software design patterns. If the application of a specific software design pattern can be represented in the form of a case, then CBR can be used for the automation of design patterns. In this paper we present an approach that addresses this problem. Our approach considers a case to be a situation where a design pattern was applied to a specific software design (in the form of Unified Modeling Language – UML [9] class diagram). Cases are stored in a case library and indexed using a general ontology (WordNet [10]). The CBR framework that we propose selects which pattern to apply to a target design problem generating a new design. It can also learn new cases from the application of design patterns. This approach has been implemented in REBUILDER, a CASE tool which provides new functionalities based on CBR.

In the next section we describe in more detail what is a design pattern, and we present an example to illustrate the issues related to pattern application. Section 3 presents our system – REBUILDER – so that the reader can have a better perspective on the context in which this work was developed. Section 4 describes our approach, starting with the model architecture for the design pattern application, and then describing the case representation, case library, pattern operators, and the various sub modules. Section 5 illustrates our approach with an example, showing how our approach can be applied to a specific situation. Finally we present the advantages and limitations of our approach, and compare our system with other related works.

2 Software Design Patterns

A software design pattern describes a solution for an abstract design problem. This solution is described in terms of communicating objects that are customized to solve the design problem in a specific context. A pattern description comprises four main elements:

- *Name* – is the description which identifies the design pattern, and is essential for communication between designers.
- *Problem* – describes the application conditions of the design pattern and the problem situation that the pattern intends to solve. It also describes the application context through examples or object structures.
- *Solution* – describes the design elements that comprise the design solution, along with the relationships, responsibilities and collaborations. This is done at an abstract level, since a design pattern can be applied to different situations.
- *Outcome* – describes the consequences of the pattern application. Most of the times patterns present trade-offs to the designer, which need to be analyzed.

Eric et al. [1] describe a catalog comprising 23 design patterns, and give a more detailed description for each pattern consisting on: pattern name and classification, pattern intent, other well-known names for the pattern, motivation, applicability, structure, participants, collaborations, consequences, implementation example, sample code, known uses, and related patterns. From these items, we draw attention to the participants and the structure. The participants describe the objects that participate in the pattern, along with their responsibilities and roles. These objects play an important role in our approach. The structure is a graphical representation of the design pattern, where objects and relations between them are represented.

A Pattern is classified based on its function or goal, which categorizes patterns as: creational, structural, and behavioral. Creational patterns have the main goal of object creation, structural patterns deal with structural changes, and behavioral patterns deal with the way objects relate with each other, and the way they distribute responsibility.

As an example of a design pattern we briefly present the Abstract Factory design pattern (see [1], page 87). The intent of this pattern is to provide an interface for creation of families of objects without specifying their concrete classes. Basically there are two dimensions in objects: object types, and object families. Concerning the type of objects, each type represents a group of objects having the same conceptual classification, like window or scrollbar. The family of objects defines a group of objects that belong to a specific conceptual family, not the same class of objects. For example, Motif objects and MS Window objects, where Motif objects can be windows, scrollbars or buttons, which exist in MS Window objects but do not have the same visual characteristics.

Suppose now, that an user interface toolkit is being implemented. This toolkit provides several types of interface objects, like windows, scroll bars, buttons, and text boxes. The toolkit can support also different look-and-feel standards, for example, Motif, MS Windows, and Macintosh. In order for the toolkit to be portable, object creation must be flexible and can not be hard coded. A solution to the flexible creation of objects depending on the look-and-feel, can be obtained through the application of the Abstract Factory design pattern. This pattern has five types of participating objects:

- The Abstract Factory object declares an interface for operations that create abstract products.

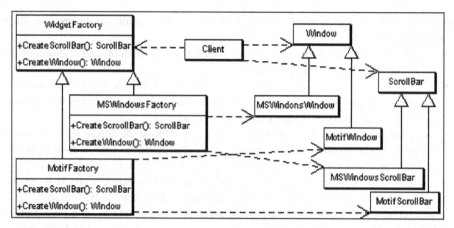

Fig. 1 - The structure of the application of the Abstract Factory design pattern to the interface toolkit problem.

- Concrete Factory objects implement the operations to create concrete products.
- Abstract Product objects declare an interface for a type of product object.
- Concrete Product objects define a product object to be created by the corresponding concrete factory, and also implement the Abstract Product interface.
- Client objects use only interfaces declared by Abstract Factory and Abstract Product classes.

A possible solution structure for the problem posed by the interface toolkit is depicted in Fig. 1. The pattern participants are: abstract factory (WidgetFactory), concrete factories (MSWindowsFactory and MotifFactory), abstract products (Window and ScrollBar), concrete products (MSWindowsWindow, MotifWindow, MSWindowsScrollBar, and MotifScrollBar), and client (Client). The create methods in the factories are the only way that clients can create the interface objects, thus controlling and abstracting object creation.

The main consequences of this pattern is that it isolates concrete classes, makes exchanging product families easy, and promotes consistency among products.

3 REBUILDER

Our approach to design pattern application is integrated in a CASE tool based on CBR, named REBUILDER. The main goal of REBUILDER is to provide intelligent help for software developers in the design phase. This includes: retrieval of past designs based on similarity concepts [11]; suggestion of new designs [12, 13]; verification of design constraints; evaluation of design properties; learning of new design knowledge; and application of software design patterns. The design pattern application is one of the modules included in the CBR engine (see Fig. 2).

REBUILDER is a tool intended to be used within a corporation environment, centralizing the corporation past designs in its knowledge base. There are two types of users interacting with the system. Software designers, using REBUILDER as an UML editor, and a system administrator with the main task of keeping the knowledge base (KB) consistent and updated.

In order for a CASE tool to be used, the design language must be intuitive and human-centered. This is also true for software design where it is common the use of visual languages to represent designs. One worldwide software design language is the Unified Modeling Language [9], best known as UML. This language provides a representation for all the software development phases. By choosing UML as the representation language, we are providing the user with a design standard.

Fig. 2 shows the architecture of REBUILDER. It comprises four main modules: UML editor, KB manager, KB, and CBR engine. The UML editor is the system front-end for the software designer, comprising the working space for design. The KB management is the interface between the KB and the system administrator. It provides access to various sub modules of knowledge, allowing the administrator to add, delete, or change knowledge from the KB, and fine-tuning it.

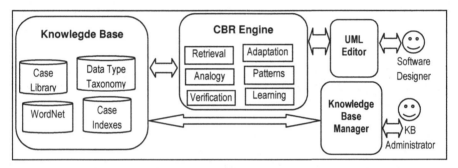

Fig. 2 - The architecture of REBUILDER.

The KB comprises four modules: data type taxonomy, case library, case indexes, and WordNet. The data type taxonomy provides *is-a* relations between data types used in UML. This structure is used when the system has to compute the similarity between data types. The case library stores the design cases, each one representing a software design. They are stored in UML files created by the editor. The case indexes are used for case retrieval, allowing a more efficient retrieval. WordNet is a lexical reference system [10], used in REBUILDER as a general ontology that categorizes case objects.

The CBR engine performs all the inference work in REBUILDER. It comprises six sub modules: retrieval, analogy, adaptation, patterns, verification, and learning. The retrieval module searches the case library for designs or design objects similar to the query, which is the current design or part of it. The most similar ones are presented to the user, allowing the user to reuse these designs or part of them. Retrieved designs can also suggest new ideas to the designer, helping him to explore the design space. The analogy module maps designs from the case library, to the query design. The resulting mapping establishes the knowledge transfer from the old design to the query design. Analogy goes further than case retrieval, creating new designs. The adaptation module can be used to adapt a past design (or part of it) to the query design using design composition. The main usage of this module is in combination with retrieval. The patterns module is the implementation of our approach to software design pattern application, which is the subject of this paper. The verification module checks the current design for inconsistencies. The learning module acquires new knowledge from the user interaction, or from the system interaction.

4 Software Design Pattern Application Using CBR

This section presents how software design patterns can be applied to a target design using CBR. We start by describing the patterns module, and then we describe each of its parts in more detail.

4.1 Architecture

Fig. 3 presents the architecture of the patterns module. It comprises three phases: retrieve applicable Design Pattern Application (DPA) cases, select best DPA case, and apply selected DPA case. A DPA case describes the application of a specific design pattern to a software design (the next sub section describes the case representation in detail). This module is used when the user decides to apply design patterns to improve the current design.

The first phase uses a target class diagram as the problem, and searches the DPA case library for DPA cases that match the problem. Then the retrieved DPA cases are ranked and the best one is selected for application, which is performed in the next step. The application of the DPA case uses the design pattern operators and yields a new class diagram, which is then used to build a new DPA case. This new case is stored in the DPA case library.

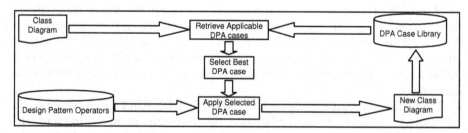

Fig. 3 - Software design pattern application module.

4.2 DPA Case Representation

A DPA case describes a specific situation where a software design pattern was applied to a class diagram. Each DPA case comprises: a problem and a solution description. The problem describes the situation of application based on: the initial class diagram, and the mapped participants. The initial class diagram is the UML class diagram to which the software design pattern was applied. Like the name indicates, it is the pre-modification diagram. The mapped participants are specific elements that must be present in order for the software design pattern to be applicable. Participants can be: objects, methods or attributes. Each participant has a specific role in the design pattern and it is important for the correct application of the design pattern. Each pattern has it's specific set of participants. Once the participants are identified the application of a design pattern follows a specific algorithm that embeds the pattern actions. Mapping the participants is performed to select a role for some of the objects, attributes and/or methods in initial class diagram.

It is important to describe the types of participants defined in our approach. Object participants can be classes or interfaces, attribute participants correspond to class attributes, and method participants correspond to object methods. Each participant has a set of properties:

- Role of the participant in the design pattern (**Role** : *String*);
- Object playing the role (**Object** : *class* or *interface*), or in case of attribute or method participant the object to which the attribute or method belongs;
- Method playing the role (**Method** : *method*) in case of a method participant;
- Attribute playing the role (**Attribute** : *attribute*) in case of an attribute participant;
- Mandatory – optional or not (**Mandatory** : *Boolean*), if the participant must exist in order for the design pattern to be applicable, or just optional;
- Unique - unique or not (**Unique** : *Boolean*), if there can be one or more participants of the **Role** type.

The solution description of a DPA case is the name of the design pattern applied, which is then used to select the correspondent software design pattern operator. Different DPA cases can have the same solution, because what a DPA case represents is the context of application of a design pattern, and there are infinite context situations.

4.3 DPA Case Library

The DPA cases are indexed using the context synsets of the object participants (see Fig. 4) and only the participants (objects, attributes and methods) can be used as retrieval indexes. The WordNet structure is used as an index structure enabling the search for DPA cases in a gradual way. Each case can be stored in a file, which can be read only when needed. In Fig. 4 there are four indexed objects, three of them corresponding to object participants, and one a method participant, indexed by the object comprising the method.

4.4 Software Design Pattern Operators

For each design pattern there is one operator, for instance, the Abstract Factory design pattern has a specific pattern operator, which defines how to apply the Abstract Factory pattern, and if it can be applied. A software design pattern operator comprises three parts: the set of specific participants, the application conditions, and the actions for a the specific design pattern. For example, the participants specification for the Abstract Factory pattern operator is shown in Table 1.

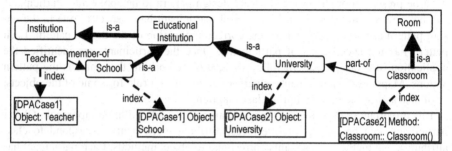

Fig. 4 - An example of the DPA case indexing.

Table 1. Participants for the Builder software design pattern.

Role name	Type	Mandatory	Unique	Description
AbstractFactory	Object	No	Yes	Declares an interface for operations that create abstract product objects.
ConcreteFactory	Object	No	No	Implements the operations to create concrete product objects.
AbstractProduct	Object	No	No	Declares an interface for a type of product object.
ConcreteProduct	Object	Yes	No	Defines a product object to be created by corresponding concrete factory.
Client	Object	No	No	Uses only interfaces declared by AbstractFactory and AbstractProduct classes.

The application conditions for Abstract Factory are:
- *ConcreteProducts* must have at least one element.
- All classes in *ConcreteProducts* must:
  - exist and;
  - have no public attributes and;
  - have no static methods.

The pattern actions for Abstract Factory are defined in an algorithm presented in Fig, 5.

4.5 Retrieval of DPA Cases

The retrieval of DPA cases is done using the WordNet as the indexing structure. The retrieval algorithm, see Fig. 6, starts with the target class diagram (*ClassDiagram*). REBUILDER only uses UML class diagrams for reasoning tasks, the other UML diagrams are not used as queries. Then it uses the context synsets of the objects in the target diagram as probes to search the WordNet structure. The algorithm initiates the search on the synset probes, and then expands the search to neighbor synsets using all the WordNet semantic relations (*is-a*, *part-of*, *member-of*, and *substance-of*). It runs until the number of cases to be retrieved (*NumberOfCases*) is reached, or the maximum search level (*MSL*) is reached, or the Synsets list is empty which corresponds to the exhaustive search of the WordNet.

```
NewClassDiagram ← Copy ClassDiagram
ConcreteProducts ← Get all concrete products from Mapping
                   (Role = ConcreteProduct)
Clients ← Get all classes that use at least one ConcreteProduct
AbstractFactory ← Create new class with name "AbstractFactory"
Add to NewClassDiagram the class AbstractFactory
AbstractProducts ← For each ConcreteProduct get/create the
                   correspondant AbstractProduct
ConcreteFactories ← Get/create all the ConcreteFactories for
                    ConcreteProducts
FOREACH Product in ConcreteProducts DO
   AbstractProduct ← Get Product superclass
   Abstract the access of Clients from Product to AbstractProduct
   Encapsulate the construction of Product in AbstractFactory and
                                                      AbstractProduct
ENDFOR
Apply the Singleton pattern to AbstractFactory
RETURN NewClassDiagram
```

Fig, 5 - The application algorithm for the Abstract Factory design pattern. It transforms *Class-Diagram* into *NewClassDiagram*.

```
Objects ← Get all classes and interfaces from the ClassDiagram
Synsets ← ∅
FORALL Object in Objects DO
   Add to Synsets list the Object's context synset
ENDFOR
SelectedCases ← ∅
SearchLevel ← ∅
Explored ← ∅
WHILE (#SelectedCases < NumberOfCases) AND (SearchLevel < MSL) AND
(Synsets ≠ ∅) DO
   DPACases ← Get all DPA cases indexed by at least one synset from
              Synsets
   Add to SelectedCases the DPACases list
   NewSynsets ← ∅
   FORALL Synset in Synsets DO
      Neighbors ← Get Synset Hypernyms, Hyponyms, Holonyms
                                                 and Meronyms
      Neighbors ← Neighbors - Synsets - Explored - NewSynsets
      Add to NewSynsets the Neighbors list
   ENDFOR
   Add to Explored the Synsets list
   Synsets ← NewSynsets
   SearchLevel ← SearchLevel + 1
ENDWHILE
RETURN SelectedCases
```

Fig. 6 – The DPA case retrieval algorithm, the input parameters are: the target *ClassDiagram*, the *NumberOfCases* to be retrieved, and the maximum search level (*MSL*) for searches in WordNet.

4.6 Selection of DPA Cases

After the retrieval of the relevant cases, they are ranked accordingly to its applicability to the target diagram (*ClassDiagram*). The selection algorithm (see Fig. 7) starts by mapping the *ClassDiagram* to each of the retrieved cases (*SelectedCases*), resulting in a mapping for each case. The mapping is performed from the case's participants to the target class diagram (only the mandatory participants are mapped). Associated to each mapping there is a score, which is given by:

$$Score = \left(w1 \times \frac{TScoreObj}{CObjs} + w2 \times \frac{Methods}{CMets} + w3 \times \frac{Attributes}{CAtrs} \right) \tag{1}$$

Where *TScoreObj* is the sum of the semantic distance of the mapped object participants. *Methods* and *Attributes* are the number of methods participants and attribute participants mapped. *CObjs*, *CMets* and *CAtrs* are the number of object participants, method participants, and attribute participants, in the DPA case. W_1, w_2 and w_3 are constants, which we defined as 0.5, 0.25 and 0.25. So, what this score measures is the degree of participants mapping between the DPA case and the target diagram.

The next step in the algorithm is to rank the *SelectedCases* list based on the mapping scores. The final phase consists on checking the applicability of the best DPA case, which is done using the design pattern operator associated with the DPA case. If the application conditions of this operator are not violated, then this DPA case is returned as the selected one. Otherwise, this case is discarded and the next best case goes through the same process, until one applicable case is found or it returns *null*.

```
Scores ← ∅
Mappings ← ∅
FORALL SelectedCase in SelectedCases DO
    Mapping/Score ← Get the mapping and score for the SelectedCase
    Add to Mappings the SelectedCase Mapping
    Add to Scores the SelectedCase Score
ENDFOR
Rank lists: SelectedCases, Mappings and Scores, by Scores
FORALL SelectedCase in SelectedCases DO
    IF (Design Pattern (solution of SelectedCase) can be applied to
        ClassDiagram using the Mapping established before) THEN
        RETURN SelectedCase and the respective Mapping
    ENDIF
ENDFOR
RETURN NULL
```

Fig. 7 - The algorithm for selection of DPA cases. The input list of DPA cases is *Selected-Cases*.

4.7 Application of DPA Cases

Selected the DPA case, the next step is to apply it to the target class diagram generating a new class diagram and a new DPA case. Other UML diagrams are not used for reasoning purposes, thus are not changed. The application of a DPA case is done using the pattern operator corresponding to the software design pattern given as the solution of the DPA case. Starting with the participants mapping established before, the application of the pattern is done using the application algorithm of the pattern operator.

5 Application Example

This section illustrates the functioning of the pattern module with an example. Fig. 8 shows the target class diagram used in our example. The goal is to improve this class diagram through the application of design patterns. Pattern application makes the extension and maintenance of Object Oriented designs easier and faster. In the remaining of this section we will explain the three steps of the pattern module: retrieval, selection and application of DPA cases.

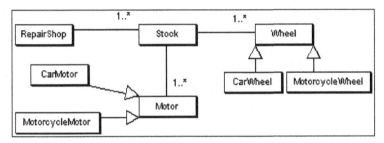

Fig. 8 - The target class diagram used in the example section.

5.1 DPA Case Retrieval

The first step is the retrieval of DPA cases from the case library. This is done using the algorithm presented in Fig. 6. The initial search probes are the synsets for: *Repair Shop*, *Stock*, *Motor* (the synset for *Car Motor* and *Motorcycle Motor* is the same of *Motor*), and *Wheel* (the synset for *Car Wheel* and *Motorcycle Wheel* is the same of *Wheel*). The case library comprises several DPA cases, from which we present the initial class diagrams for two of them (see Fig. 9 and Fig. 10).

DPA case 1 represents the application of the Abstract Factory design pattern to the initial class diagram of Fig. 9 (due to space limitations we can not present the class diagram that resulted from the application of the Abstract Factory to this diagram). The participants in this DPA case are: *PlaneEngine*, *PlaneWheel*, *HeliEngine* and *HeliWheel* which are Concrete Products; and *Plane* and *Helicopter* which are Clients. The solution of this DPA case is Abstract Factory.

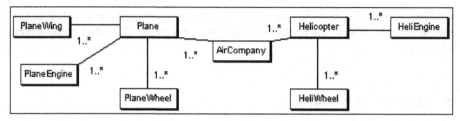

Fig. 9 - The initial class diagram of DPA Case 1.

The DPA case 2 is also the representation of an application of the Abstract Factory pattern, but to the initial class diagram of Fig. 10. The participants are: *TTL-LogicGate*, *TTLMultiplexer*, *TTLDecoder*, *CMOSLogicGate*, *CMOSMultiplexer*, and *CMOSDecoder*, which are Concrete Products; and *Equipment* which is a Client.

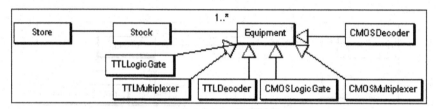

Fig. 10 - The initial class diagram of DPA Case 2.

The search then starts using these four synsets and is done in the WordNet structure. Fig. 11 presents part of the WordNet structure, which indexes DPA case 1 (through the synset of *Motor* and *Wheel*, *Engine* has the same synset as *Motor*) and DPA case 2 (through the synset of *Multiplexer*). Starting on *Wheel* and *Motor*, case 1 is the first being selected, then the algorithm expands to the neighbor nodes until in the fourth iteration it gets to *Multiplexer* where it founds case 2. Due to space limitations we only retrieve two cases, but more cases could be retrieved. The cases retrieved for the next step are: DPA case 1, and DPA case 2.

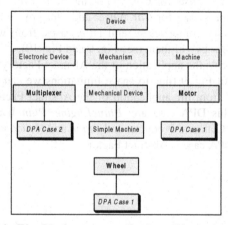

Fig. 11 - Part of the WordNet is-a structure that is used by retrieval in the example.

5.2 DPA Case Selection

The next step is to select which of the retrieved cases is going to be applied. The first phase of selection is to establish the mappings and the score associated with each mapping. For case 1 the following mappings were obtained: *PlaneEngine – CarMotor*; *PlaneWheel – CarWheel*; *HeliEngine – MotorcycleMotor*; and *HeliWheel – MotorcycleWheel*. Mappings for case 2 are: *TTLLogicGate – Motor*; *TTLMultiplexer – CarMotor*; *TTLDecoder – CarWheel*; *CMOSLogicGate – Wheel*; *CMOSMultiplexer – MotorcycleMotor*; and *CMOSDecoder – MotorcycleWheel*. Mappings for case 1 get the following score: $0.5 * (4 / 4) + 0.25 * 1 + 0.25 * 1 = 1$, according to equation (1). Notice that all the mappings established between case 1 and the target diagram match perfectly, so they all have the score of 1, yielding 4 for the sum. Since there are no method or attribute participants, the score associated with each of these items is 1. For case 2, the computation of the mappings' score is: $0.5 * ((0.31 * 4 + 0.34 * 2) / 6) + 0.25 * 1 + 0.25 * 1 = 0.66$. There are six mappings between case 2 and the target diagram, which leads to the following semantic distances: *LogicGate – Motor*, *Decoder – Wheel*, *LogicGate – Wheel*, 8 *is-a* semantic relations, yielding the similarity of 0.31; and *Multiplexer – Motor* with 6 *is-a* semantic relations, yielding the similarity of 0.34.

To this point, we have case 1 ranked in the first place. The next step is to assess the applicability of the solution pattern of case 1, which is the Abstract Factory pattern. Sub section 0 presents the pre-conditions needed for this pattern to be applied. Since case 1 meets all the pre-conditions the Abstract Factory can be applied to the target diagram using the mapping established before.

5.3 DPA Case Application

The final step is the application of the design pattern selected, using the respective design pattern operator. Fig, 5 presents the application algorithm for the Abstract Factory design pattern, which after being applied to the class diagram of Fig. 8, using the mapping determined before, results in the diagram of Fig. 12. One of the advantages of this transformation is that is easier to maintain and extend this design, because this new design enables the extension of the design in two different axis: types of products that can be added (for instance steering mechanism), or by family of products (for instance truck).

6 Conclusions

This paper presents an approach to the automation of the application of software design patterns. Our approach is based on CBR and cases represent situations in which a design pattern was applied in the past to a software design. This approach is implemented in a CASE tool, and allows software designers to improve their designs, modifying them having in mind design changes or design reusability.

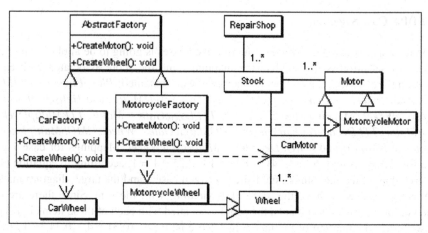

Fig. 12 - The new class diagram generated from the application of DPA Case 1 to the target diagram.

An obvious advantage of our approach is the complete automation of the application of design patterns. Our approach selects which pattern to apply based on DPA cases. This enables a CASE tool to offer new functionalities, aimed for design maintenance and reuse. One limitation of our approach is that the system performance depends on the quality and diversity of the case library, which will improve as time follows. Another limitation, is that the range of case application is always limited, and it does not outperform a software designer ability to identify which pattern to apply. Despite this, we think that our approach can provide a good contribute for design improvement, especially in situations when the user has to deal with a huge amount of objects. In this situation, automation is possibly the only way to apply design patterns, since it is difficult for the designer to deal with such an amount of objects.

There are some research works that have common aspects with our approach. Eden et. al. [4] has proposed an approach to the specification of design patterns, and a prototype of a tool that automates extensively their application. This approach considers design patterns as programs that manipulate other programs, thus they are viewed as metaprograms. Eden's approach does not automates all the process of design application, since it is the user that has to select which pattern to apply. In our approach this step is automated. Another difference is that Eden applies patterns at code level, while we apply them at design level. Tokuda and Batory [5] also present an approach in which patterns are expressed in the form of a series of parameterized program transformations applied to software code. Like Eden's work, this work does not address the automation of which pattern to apply. Other works on specifying design patterns and automating its application are presented by Bär [2] and Cinnéide [3]. These works also automate the application of design patterns, but do not select which pattern to apply. This must be done by the user. Both works deal with design modification instead of code modification. Guéhéneuc and Jussien [14] developed an application of explanation-based constraint programming for the identification of design patterns in object-oriented source code.

In the future we intent to make REBUILDER a commercial CASE tool, capable of boosting the designer's productivity, and to improve software quality.

References

1. Gamma, E., *et al.*, *Design Patterns: Elements of Reusable Object-Oriented Software*. 1995, Reading: Addison-Wesley. 395.
2. Bär, H., *et al.*, *The FAMOOS object-oriented reengineering handbook*, . 1999, Forschungszentrum Informatik, Software Composition Group, University of Berne: Karlsruhe.
3. Cinnéide, M. and P. Nixon. *A Methodology for the Automated Introduction of Design Patterns*. in *IEEE International Conference on Software Maintenance*. 1999. Oxford, England: IEEE.
4. Eden, A., J. Gil, and A. Yehudai, *Automating the Application of Design Patterns*. Journal of Object Oriented Programming, 1997(May).
5. Tokuda, L. and D. Batory. *Automated Software Evolution via Design Patterns*. in *3rd International Symposium on Applied Corporate Computing*. 1995. Monterrey, Mexico.
6. Kolodner, J., *Case-Based Reasoning*. 1993: Morgan Kaufman.
7. Maher, M.L., M. Balachandran, and D. Zhang, *Case-Based Reasoning in Design*. 1995: Lawrence Erlbaum Associates.
8. Aamodt, A. and E. Plaza, *Case-Based Reasoning: Foundational Issues, Methodological Variations, and System Approaches*. AI Communications, 1994. **7**(1): p. 39-59.
9. Rumbaugh, J., I. Jacobson, and G. Booch, *The Unified Modeling Language Reference Manual*. 1998, Reading, MA: Addison-Wesley.
10. Miller, G., *et al.*, *Introduction to WordNet: an on-line lexical database*. International Journal of Lexicography, 1990. **3**(4): p. 235 - 244.
11. Gomes, P., *et al.* *Case Retrieval of Software Designs using WordNet*. in *European Conference on Artificial Intelligence (ECAI'02)*. 2002. Lyon, France: IOS Press, Amsterdam.
12. Gomes, P., *et al.* *Supporting Creativity in Software Design*. in *AISB'02 Symposium "AI and Creativity in Arts and Science"*. 2002. London, UK.
13. Gomes, P., *et al.* *Using Analogical Reasoning to Promote Creativity in Software Reuse*. in *International Conference on Case-Based Reasoning (ICCBR'01) Workshop on Creative Systems: Approaches to Creativity in Artificial Intelligence and Cognitive Science*. 2001. Vancouver, Canada: Technical Report of the Navy Center for Applied Research in Artificial Intelligence (NCARAI) of the Naval Research Laboratory (NRL).
14. Guéhéneuc, Y.-G. and N. Jussien. *Using Explanations for Design Patterns Identification*. in *IJCAI'01 Workshop on Modelling and Solving Problems with Constraints*. 2001. Seattle, WA, USA.

A New Approach to Solution Adaptation
and Its Application for Design Purposes

Mahmoudreza Hejazi and Kambiz Badie

Info. Society Group, Iran Telecom Research Center, Tehran, Iran
m_hejazi@itrc.ac.ir
k_badie@itrc.ac.ir

Abstract. In this paper, a new approach is proposed for transformational adaptation based on detecting a solution's incompatibility regarding the new problem situation and trying to overcome the incompatibility in an iterative manner. By incompatibility, we mean a state for which the required objectives are not satisfied due to any change in the status of the constraints. Based upon this approach, we have proposed a framework for redesigning an existing system under new constraints. To show the capability of this framework, a software prototype was developed that it is capable of redesigning an existing digital circuit under presence of new constraints, e.g. type of gates, power dissipation, fan in/out, gate prices and so on.

1 Introduction

A large number of problems in intelligent systems can be viewed as special cases of the constrained satisfaction [1]. Constraint satisfaction is especially of a high importance in a designing process [2,3]. Design optimization problems hold some complex characteristics that make them very different from the other problems that AI researchers have traditionally studied [4]. Among the different methodologies used to achieve design optimization, case-based reasoning [5] is a valuable tool that can be used to make these problems tractable [6,7,8,9].

A major stage in case-based reasoning is solution adaptation, whose function is to adapt the solution of the similar cases in such a way that the outcome can best fit the current situations [10,11,12]. Many methods have been proposed for solution adaptation based on the idea of performing adaptation on the basis of similarity between the current problem situation and the similar cases retrieved from the case library. There are also methods, which transform a generic solution into the specific one, based on the peculiarities on the current situation. The salient point in such sort of adaptation is substitution of the variables in a solution by the values obtained from the current situation.

Derivational methods have also been proposed to produce a new solution based on examining the solution derivation traces, which have already been successfully experienced for the similar cases [13]. There are, however, situations where solution adaptation through the above methods cannot succeed. Moreover, keeping the derivation traces may not always be feasible due to reasons such as lack of problem solving knowledge and high amount of time needed for adaptation [9].

S. Craw and A. Preece (Eds.): ECCBR 2002, LNAI 2416, pp. 549–559.

In this paper, we propose a new approach to transformational adaptation based on an iterative modification of an old solution up to the stage where the modified solution can plausibly fit the current situation.

To show the capability of this approach, we have suggested a framework for redesigning a system based upon previous experiences (i.e. similar cases). In our framework, the modification process is performed using a number of operators such as matching, insertion, and deletion, which in turn modify the structure of the solution. Obviously, the operations taken within the process of modifications themselves are added to the source case, together with the obtained results, in order to upgrade the efficiency of adaptation for future purposes.

We also developed a prototype, which is capable of redesigning an existing digital circuit under presence of new constraints.

2   Basics of the Proposed Approach to Solution Adaptation

In this paper, we present a new approach to transformational adaptation based on the idea that the new solution is to be formed on the basis of an iterative modification of the old solution rather than applying direct rule(s) to it. This process is performed using a number of operators, whose functions at each stage of iteration is to decrease the amount of incompatibility that the intermediate solution has exhibited with respect to the current situation. By incompatibility, we mean a state for which the required objectives are not satisfied due to any change in the status of the constraints. The process is stopped at the stage where the modified solution satisfies the new problem situation with a negligible amount of incompatibility. Obviously, both processes of incompatibility detection and solution modification are to be conducted via using problem domain knowledge, which is to be predefined for each case. In this manner, the new approach to adaptation can be regarded as similar to generative adaptation in the sense that it keeps problem domain knowledge within the case structure.

To see how the proposed approach to adaptation works, let us go through the following example. Suppose that the current problem situation is to find a solution in a case-based manner for the task of "drinking".

Suppose that, using an appropriate mechanism for assessing the similarity, leads us to the fact that an experienced case of "eating" is the most similar to the current situation. Let "spoon", consisting of a "vessel", a "handle" and a suitable relational structure between these components, be the solution of this case. Our purpose is to modify the structure of "spoon" in such a way that it can fit the requirements of the current situation, which is "drinking". In our approach, this modification is guided on the basis of detecting the very incompatibility a "spoon" may face within "drinking" process. Starting from the "vessel" as the major component of a "spoon", a domain theory included in the case of "eating" can be activated to see how strange it may act toward the situation of "drinking". It may, for instance, conclude that the "vessel" is too small for "drinking", and should therefore be enlarged. Once the "vessel" was enlarged, the same domain theory may this time face a new incompatibility for "drinking", which is its difficulty in operation. This incompatibility can be overcome through shortening the "handle". We can observe that, via continuing this process of modification, we may finally end up with a solution, which is quite similar to a "cup".

A point to be noticed here is how case structure can be expanded through the experiences of modifying its solution within different problem situations.

An important point in CBR is to provide a systematic medium for enhancing the capabilities of the stored cases via experiences of deploying it with respect to different problems. This, in our approach, can come true through highlighting the intermediate results of adapting a case solution for different problem situations.

For instance, if within the process of modifying the "spoon", it was found that elaborating the "vessel" and the "handle" facilitates the process of finding a solution for "drinking", this information together with the modifications performed, will be added to the case of "eating", and will act as a set of guiding elements for future adaptations with respect to the same case. Therefore, for the case of "eating", which is realized to be workable for a variety of new problem situations, such as "eating" (in a new fashion), "drinking", "boiling", "cooking", and so on. New configurations of this case will be produced, as results of learning from experience, each with their own set of guiding elements in modifying the "spoon". Figure 1 illustrates an example for the new configuration including the different sets of guiding elements. As it is seen from the figure, a total case contains a number of sub-cases, each produced through an individual experience of adapting the case's solution ("spoon", "fork", ... in this example). The peculiar point in the sub-cases is that the situation of a sub-case is to contain two parts; one acting as a source, and the other acting as a target. Also, guiding elements are stored together with the performed operations to indicate how the source solution is modified.

Suppose that a new problem situation is considered which is in general quite similar to the case of "eating". Now, to find out which sub-case is the most suitable for adaptation, two factors are taken into account as follows:

1. First, the current situation is compared with the target label of the existing sub-cases to see which one is particularly similar to the current situation.
2. In case that no unique sub-case is determined in (i), comparison between the current situation and the remaining sub-cases should be made from the viewpoint of their set of guiding elements. Let us say a sub-case, which has more common guiding elements with the current situation, will be selected as the most suitable sub-case for adaptation.

3 The Proposed Framework for Redesigning an Existing System

Having used our new approach to solution adaptation, we have suggested a framework for redesigning an existing system under new constraints. In our work, for defining the original system, we use a network representation, at which each node (which is a part of the system) is either a frame, or another network. Some models, rules or protocols, depending on the interrelation between the parts of the system, represent the connection between each two nodes.

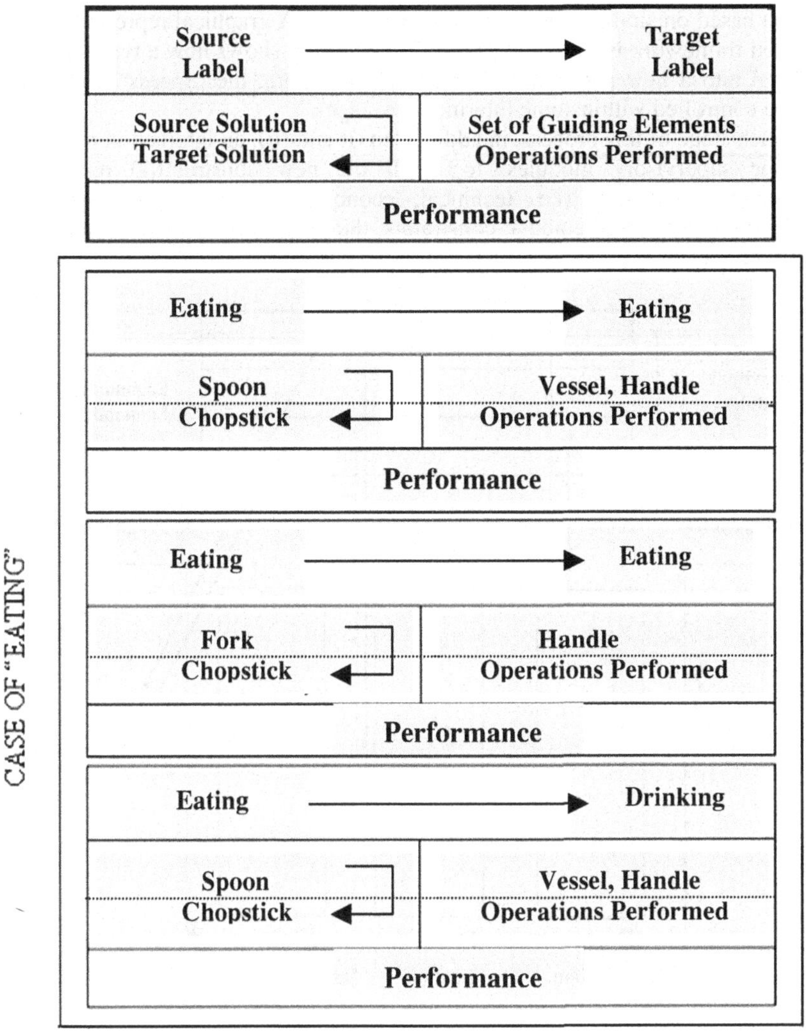

Fig. 1. The proposed structure for a sub-case together with three examples

The goal is to redesign the original network such that it can operate under some new constraints. These constraints can be considered in different categories such as technical, economical, ergonomical, and so on. To materialize the redesigning process, a number of modifications are required. In our approach, modification of a network can be obtained through the operators namely, matching/ mapping a node, deleting an existing node, and inserting a new node.

To find out which operators are to be performed for each modification, we have to assess the original network in order to see which nodes may act incompatible toward some new constraints, and then select the necessary operators to fulfill the following: (i) Solve the incompatibility, (ii) Not to change the main rules/protocols of the original system, and (iii) meet the new constraint(s) through selecting the suitable solution based on similar sub-cases in the case base. A graphical representation of the proposed framework is shown in Figure 2. The figure shows how a typical network is modified into a new network. As shown in the figure, the process of modification must be controlled within some intermediate stages.

At each stage of this process, in addition to (i) and (ii), an interaction must be made with the supervisory modules, to fulfill the new constraint(s) related to the corresponding category (i.e. technical, economical, …). If, in any case, the modifications rule out the above constraints, the process must then be repeated from its previous stage.

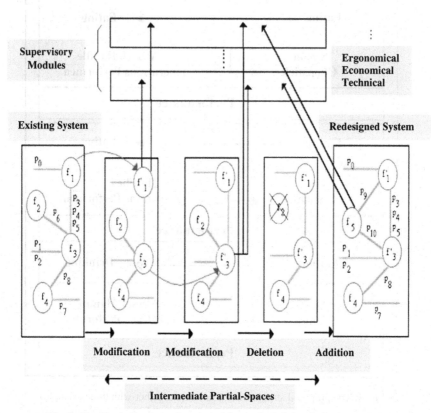

Fig. 2. The block diagram of proposed framework for redesigning a system

The steps performed to redesign an existing system, have been mentioned in Figure 3. At the beginning, the network representation and the new desired constraints must be defined. Analysis of the original network is subsequently performed to find out the nodes, which operate incompatibly with respect to the new constraint(s). If there is any node, which needs to be modified, then the necessary operator(s) is/are determined to perform it.

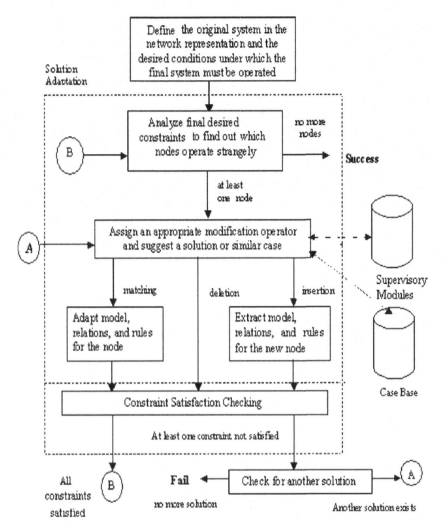

Fig. 3. The steps performed to redesign an original network

4 The Developed Prototype for Redesigning a Digital Circuit Based on the Proposed Framework

Each digital logic family is recognized by its basic NOR or NAND gates. The basic gate is the building block from which more complex functions are constructed. For example, a latch circuit is recognized by two NAND gates or two NOR gates connected back-to-back. A master-slave flip-flop is obtained from the interconnection of nine basic gates. Each logic family has a catalog of integrated circuit packages that lists the digital functions available in the logic family.

In overall, when a digital circuit is designed, it would be a combination of different gates. To implement the final circuit in an integrated circuit package, It would be preferred to redesign the original designed circuit only by NAND or NOR gates. Naturally, there may be other constraints which are to be satisfied in the final design, such as technical (Fan in/ Fan out, power dissipation, propagation delay, …) economical (total price), ecological (temperature), and so on.

As an example, suppose that we want to redesign a digital circuit using our proposed framework. In this regard, we consider a digital circuit as an original system and try to realize the final circuit, which can operate under some global constraints, using only one type of gate.

A typical circuit for redesigning purpose is shown in Figure 4. As it is seen, the circuit is a combination of some different gates. Here, our purpose is to redesign this circuit in such a way that the final circuit can be realized only by 2-input NAND gates (standing for the local constraints), and a total delay time of t seconds, a total price of n $, and a working temperature of a particular range (standing for the global constraints).

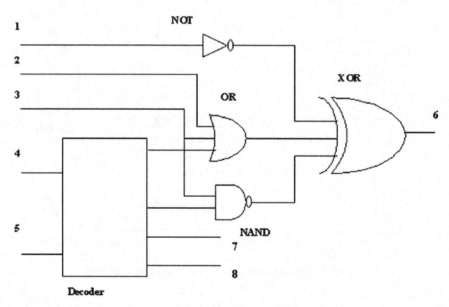

Fig. 4. A typical Example of a digital circuit

Figure 5 illustrates the network representation of the above circuit. As it is shown in this figure, the network has 5 basic nodes (F_1, F_2, F_3, F_4, and F_5), 5 input nodes (1, 2, 3, 4, and 5), and 3 output nodes (6,7,8). Pi used for the relation between the nodes. To introduce such a network representation in figure 5, we use some simple notations similar to the following cases:

I: $(1, 2, 3, 4, 5)$
O: $(6, 7, 8)$
NODE: $(F_1, F_2, F_3, F_4, F_5,)$
F_1: DECODER
F_2: NOT
.
.
.
P_1: $(1, F_2)$
P_3: $(3, F_3) - (3, F_4)$
.
.
.

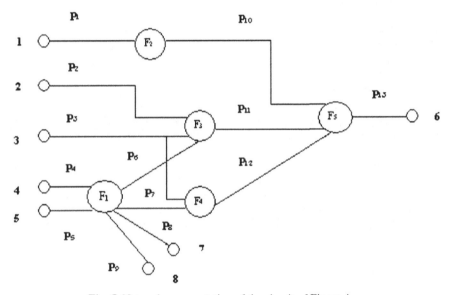

Fig. 5. Network representation of the circuit of Figure 4.

This example indicates that the essential information which we need for the supervisory modules, consist of necessary information about different gates of a digital logic families, gates models, formulas (e.g. Demorgan's rules), and truth tables, gate prices, working temperature, and so on.

Now, referring to the diagram in figure 3, having introduced the network representation and the new desired constraints, we must find out which nodes don't satisfy the new local constraints and then try to overcome this problem. In this example, nodes F1, F2, F3, and F5 must be modified. For instance, F2 which stands for a NOT gate can be replaced by a 2-input NAND gate whose pins are connected to each other, or F3 which stands for a 3-input OR gate can be first replaced by two 2-input OR gates in cascade, and then each 2-input OR gate must be replaced by a NAND gate whose pins are inverted.

After each modification, possible constraints must be rechecked with the related supervisory module to see whether they are fulfilled or not.

5 Solution Adaptation in the Above Example

As mentioned before, cases for the task of redesigning a circuit, are the sub-circuits, which have been redesigned for some specific constraints.

So, when a new problem of redesigning a circuit is faced, first, a similarity assessment mechanism, taking into account the circuit functionality, is activated to find the similar case, and an adaptation process, as discussed in 2, is then activated to modify the stored sub-circuit in the case, using the operators discussed in 3. Obviously, the three operators of matching, insertion and deletion, together with the supervisory modules, constitute for a sort of domain theory, which was discussed in 2, for both detecting the incompatibility and modifying the selection.

By the time, a new sub-circuit was obtained through the iterative modification of the original sub-circuit, the result together with the performed operations will be added to the case, as a new sub-case, including new guiding elements for future adaptation purposes.

In this respect, when a problem is faced in future which calls for retrieval of the same case, this time, out of the stored sub-cases, the one should be selected whose similarity with the current problem is the most.

This, as discussed in 2, is in practice fulfilled through deploying both target labels of the sub-cases, as well as the sets of guiding elements stored in them.

As an example, suppose that the solution found for the part of the circuit discussed in section 4, is stored as a sub-case within the case of "DECODER", together with the operations performed and the related set of guiding elements as illustrated in figure 6.

Also suppose that some other types of decoders have been developed for the case of "DECODER". The similarity assessment mechanism will first retrieve the case of "DECODER", and subsequently, out of the stored sub-cases, the decoder with the most amount of similarity (from the viewpoint of the target label and the guiding elements) will be selected as the alternative for solution adaptation.

6 Concluding Remarks

In this paper, a new approach to transformational adaptation was presented based on the idea of detecting the incompatibility of an old solution toward the new problem situation and trying to modify the solution in such a way that this incompatibility could be overcome iteratively. In the meantime, based on this approach, a framework was suggested for redesigning an existing system under presence of new constraints. To show the capability of this approach, a program has been developed for redesigning digital circuits.

The framework presented in this paper is particularly efficient in the cases where designing new systems based on past experiences can not be achieved using simple adaptation rules, and it should rather be tried to fit a previously tried solution through applying a domain knowledge at intermediate stages of adaptation. In this sense, the proposed framework, though transformational in nature, includes a flavor of derivational adaptation. This is because the past operations for deriving solutions are stored to help fit them to the current problem situation.

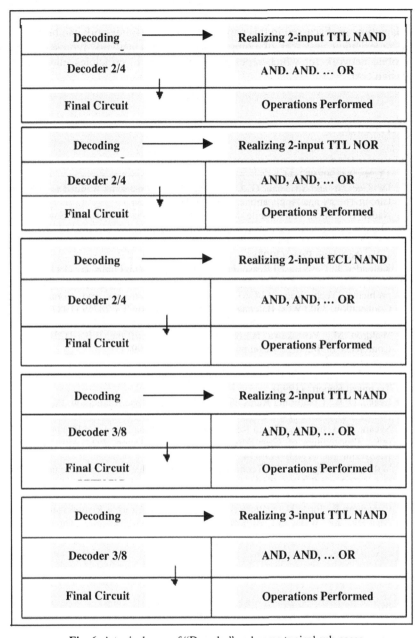

Fig. 6. A typical case of "Decoder" and some typical sub-cases

Due to the systematicity in deploying domain knowledge at intermediate stages of adaptation, as discussed in this paper, the proposed framework can be efficiently used in redesigning any sort of complex system with network representation, such as mobile network for which redesigning based on 1st principles may lead to a huge design cost.

References

1. Kumar V.: Algorithms for constraint satisfaction problems: A survey. AI Magazine, Vol. 13, No. 1 (1992) 32-44
2. De Kleer, J., and Sussman, G. J.: Propagation of Constraints Applied to Circuit Synthesis. Circuit Theory and Applications. Vol.8 (1980) 425-434
3. Nadel, B. Lin. J.: Automobile Transmission Deign as a Constraint Satisfaction Problem: Modeling the Kinematic Level. Artificial Intelligence, Vol. 21 (1991) 425-434
4. Tong C., Sriram D. (eds.): Artificial Intelligence Approaches to Engineering Design, Vol. 1,2,3. Academic Press (1992)
5. Kolonder, J.: Case-Based Reasoning, Morgan Kaufmann Publishers (1993)
6. Huhns M., Acosta R. D.: Argo: An analogical reasoning system for solving design problems. Tech. Rep. AI/CAD-092-87, Microelectronics and Computer Technology Cooperation, 3500 West Balcones Center Drive, Austin TX 78759 (1987)
7. Goel A. K.: Representation of design functions in experience-based design. In: Brown D., Waldron M., Yoshikawa H. (eds.): Proceedings of the IFIP TC5/WG5 2 Working Conference on Intelligent Computer Aided Design (1991)
8. Jones E.K.: Model-based case adaptation. Proceedings of AAAI-92 (1992)
9. Liew C.W., Steinberg L. I.: Constrained REDO: An Alternative to REPLAY. DCS/LCSR Technical Reports (1993)
10. Leake, D. B.: Combining Rules and Cases to Learn Case Adaptation. Proceedings of the 7th Annual Conference of the Cognitive Science Society (1995)
11. Sycara, K.: Using case-Based Reasoning for Plan Adaptation and Repair. In: Kolondner, J. (ed.): Proceedings of Case-Based Reasoning Workshop, Palo Alto. DARPA, Morgan Kaufmann, Inc. (1988) 425-434
12. Wilke, W., Bergmann, R.: Techniques and Knowledge Used for Adaptation During Case-Based Problem Solving. Tasks and Methods in Applied Artificial Intelligence, LNAI 1416, Springer-Verlag (1998) 497-505
13. Cunighom P., Finn. D., Slattery S.: Knowledge Engineering Requirements in Derivational Analogy. In: Wess, S., Althoff, K-D., Richter, M.M. (eds.):Topics in Case-Based Reasoning. Amsterdam: Springer-Verlag (1994)

InfoFrax : CBR in Fused Cast Refractory Manufacture

Deepak Khemani [1], Radhika B. Selvamani [1], Ananda Rabi Dhar [1], and S.M. Michael [2]

[1] A.I. & D.B. Lab, Dept. of Computer Science & Engineering I.I.T.Madras, India
khemani@iitm.ac.in
{bradhika, anandat}@peacock.iitm.ernet.in
[2] Carborundum Universal Limited, Madras, India (CUMI)
mikesm@ho.cumi.co.in

Abstract. This paper describes a CBR application in manufacturing industry, a domain where CBR has by and large proved its applicability and success. The paper details a thorough understanding of the field of fused cast manufacturing basically seen from the perspective of glass furnace, where quality of glass produced is straightaway related to the refractory blocks used in furnace linings. The applicability of CBR paradigm is revisited in the present context. The CBR process needed is conceptualized and designed. The paper describes the evolution of the system beginning with tackling hurdles of knowledge acquisition, a number of pitfalls in the prototype phase, to final implementation of InfoFrax, the CBR system specially devised for the project. It gives an overall description of the architecture and usage. The paper also reports the immediate response to the software in form of direct user feedback, expectations from the existing system, and some future work already underway in the project.

1   Introduction

Foundry related manufacturing often lies at the crossroads of art and science. This is because the behavior of materials at high temperature and during phase transition is poorly understood. The process of manufacturing involves a large number of parameters that have to be set on the shop floor. Often experience plays a crucial role in successful processes and in troubleshooting. We look at a case based reasoning (CBR) application in such a setting.

Carborundum Universal Ltd. (CUMI), Palakkad, India, is in the business of manufacture of fused cast (electro cast) refractory blocks used as lining for glass melting furnace tanks. This line of manufacture is such that the technology is unique, not freely available in the world, specific to the application and the equipment, and is not fully mastered yet [10]. A number of cases have been outlined where the observations made by the operating personnel have changed the basic principles of design and manufacturing practices because no definite knowledge base is available in either textbooks or journals [9]. Each of these cases, which are production activities, is by itself an experiment and the industry will have to build on these experiments to improve continuously. This is ideally suited for an application of the

S. Craw and A. Preece (Eds.): ECCBR 2002, LNAI 2416, pp. 560–574.
© Springer-Verlag Berlin Heidelberg 2002

case based reasoning system [8]. This project[1] described in this paper involves setting up a CBR system on the floor, collecting operational data, and maintaining a repository of all kinds of blocks. Details for each block manufactured, good or bad, are added to the memory along with the corrective action taken if any. When a defective block is encountered the CBR system retrieves the best matching corrective action. With sufficient data accumulating, the system will, in the future, be in a position to support predictive maintenance and even trigger changes in the Design Handbook. It demonstrates CBR applicability in domains where analytical knowledge is incomplete and yet experienced personnel can make decisions that succeed.

2 Domain

Refractory blocks are manufactured in the electro cast foundry. The first evaluation is done by quality control at the end of the manufacturing process. The block may be accepted wherein it becomes a success case. Or it may be rejected wherein it becomes a failure case and it is remade with a change in parameters, mostly suggested by experts. The blocks are thus labeled O.K., or rejected by the Quality department. Following acceptance, they are put to use in lining glass furnaces, where they are subjected to relentless corrosion at high temperature over a period lasting tens of months. Glass manufacturers place orders on CUMI for lining their melting tanks. The lining is made up of around 300 to 400 blocks depending on the size of the tank.

2.1 Refractory Manufacture

Refractory blocks are made of a mixture of Alumina, Zirconia and Silica in certain proportions depending on the location of the block in the tank. The mixture of these raw materials are melted in an arc furnace and poured into moulds, and annealed. The blocks are subsequently removed from moulds and finished. Fig. 1 shows the production process along with a few illustrative parameters. The common technical defects, which lead to rejection of blocks, are cracks, spalls, and surface porosity. The average weight of each block is around a tonne and the cost of materials and production is quite high. The manufacturing lead-time is almost a month considering the long annealing periods of almost a fortnight. Hence rejections are quite costly in terms of material and time.

Design activity precedes the manufacturing activity. The design department of CUMI has a design handbook, which gives the design attributes for the manufacture of the blocks. The design handbook gives guidelines, which can be modified if failures are traced to specific attributes.. The process of changing the design handbook is done very formally based on a corrective action record (C.A.R.), which records the solutions provided by experts in case of rejected blocks which were remade.

---

[1] This project is funded by a research grant from Carborundum Universal Ltd. Madras, India (CUMI)

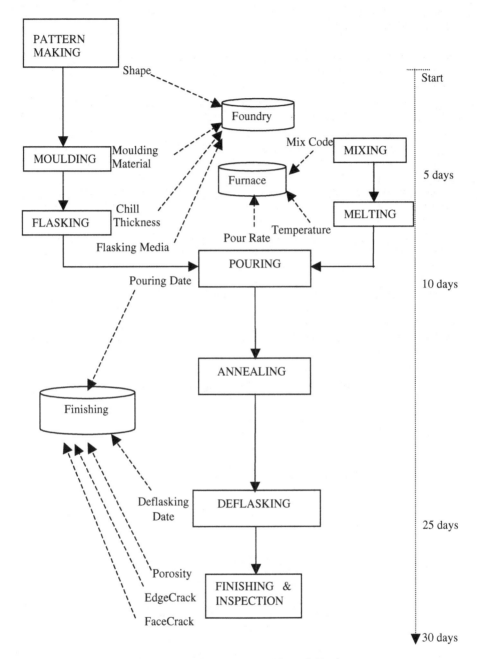

Fig. 1. Production Process and Data Collection

2.2 Glass Manufacture

Glass manufacturers melt a charge mix in a furnace and draw out molten glass to be formed into different types of containers or sheets. This is a continuous process, which means that the furnace should be operating on a 7×24 basis. The furnaces have a life of 4 to 8 years depending on the type of glass drawn. Minor problems occurring in the furnace or the auxiliary structures are corrected while the furnace is in operation. These repairs are called hot repairs. The production loss is not too severe in these types of repairs. However, any major problems would require a cold repair, which would mean a shut down. A shut down and restart operation would take 8 to 12 weeks. This type of furnace stoppage is one of the reasons for production loss. Another type of loss is due to the glass defects. The glass could have defects such as bubbles, foreign particles or scratches, which leads to rejection and production loss. These defects in glass are sometimes attributed to the components of the furnace including refractory blocks. Alternatively they would be due to incorrect operation of furnaces. The parameters related to the operation of the furnace viz. the temperature, the pressure, charge mix composition, consumption of fuel per ton of glass drawn, temperature of inlet air and exhaust air, draw rate, etcetra and the problems encountered as mentioned above can be recorded as case description.. However, if such a CBR system is to be developed there will be a need for data to be collected for many furnaces over a long period cycle. The work discussed here is restricted only to build a CBR system which will aid in solving quality problems faced in manufacture of the refractory.

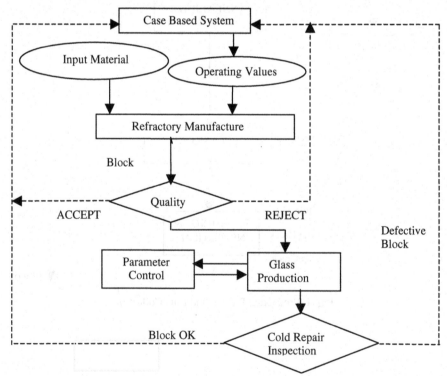

Fig. 2. Role of CBR in Refractory and Glass Manufacture

In a CBR system that covers the life of a block one would have to capture the history of each block as it is manufactured and also its performance in the furnace. Over a period of time a corporate memory that captures the experience of the factory in manufacturing refractories and the performance in the furnace will be built up. The main aim is to build a system that allows the direct reuse of experience without trying to do a technical analysis. This is depicted in Fig. 2 as integrated CBR cycle for both Refractory and Glass Furnaces.

3   Why CBR?

The problem in context resembles a CBR paradigm, which could be counted for some basic reasons. The manufacture domain is ill understood and it is not easy to articulate the knowledge in the form of rules. The time line in Fig. 1 illustrates the long process which involves a large set of attributes dispersed in different shop floors. If the parameters for every block manufactured are stored in a database, how does one exploit this data? Traditional database retrieval requires a precise match of values of attributes. One can relinquish precision and use ranges, but this would lead to over abundant recall. This is because a priori there is no knowledge about which attributes should be relaxed. CBR allows for flexible relaxation because it uses a notion of similarity. It offers much more precision, but this comes at a cost sacrificing the efficiency built into database system.

4   Domain Acquisition and Prototype

4.1 Traceability of a Case

Many experts opine that the mould plays an important role in determining the success of the block. But the mould is destroyed and it loses its identity when the fused melt is poured in at a temperature of 1700°C. The relationship of the attributes of the mould to the block is lost. This poses a problem in uniquely identifying the attributes of a manufactured block with respect to the mould from which the block was manufactured. This is achieved by adding common attributes with the furnace data base schema to facilitate a correct join operation. A similar link has to be established as the block moves from the furnace to the finishing department.

4.2 Incomplete Domain

Shop floor experts decide on solutions based on past experience and reasoning when faced with a problem. In the design of a case structure the need is to take into consideration as many attributes as possible. The influence of these attributes on the final product cannot be clearly determined. The experts agree that all the attributes are important, but are not able to express in unambiguous terms their influence. Hence it is required to capture all attributes, even those, which seemingly do not contribute to the quality of the block.

Often the defective block is remade with no modifications and the block turns out to be good. There is need for statistical analysis to support basic process modification. The process of changing the design handbook is done very formally based on a corrective action record (CAR) when the corrections are validated to be successful. However, the description of the defects and solutions as recorded in the C.A.R. book currently are too general to be reused. Also the design knowledge has grown over the years and is not structured. There are an increasing number of exceptions to the guidelines.

4.3 Large Number of Attributes

CLAVIER system, of Lockheed Missiles and Space Company [4] uses CBR effectively to capture the successful patterns of placement and helps replacing similar parts to be cured. Domain experts were able to identify position in the furnace as a crucial feature, thus helping design an appropriate case schema. However, in electro cast manufacturing process the number of attributes generated in each stage of manufacture is quite large and posed a challenge for description of a block with all its associated features for the whole manufacturing process. The number of attributes is about 150, which is significantly larger than most implemented systems.

4.4 Approach to Solution

Knowledge acquisition can be viewed as the process of extracting, structuring and organizing knowledge from one or more sources. This process has been identified by many researchers and practitioners as a (or even as the) bottleneck that currently constraints the development of knowledge based systems [3].
There are three types of features involved in successfully describing, retrieving and identifying a case. These are the operational parameters used in production, the quantified quality inspection results, additional parameters needed to join data from different departments. During the knowledge acquisition phase of InfoFrax, all the parameters as involved in the process of manufacture were noted down from operating personnel and other documents available. The experts then identified the parameters that were important according to their experience and knowledge. From successive interviews and analysis an initial collection of parameters was constructed. These production parameters constitute the explicitly relevant features of a case. But the case structure could not be manually validated because it was vast and distributed among various process shops. This necessitated the prototype phase.

The prototype phase [6, 7] had two components. The main goal of constructing the prototype was demonstrating the idea of case based retrieval from the database for troubleshooting.

Data acquisition is not a one-time activity. So to ensure validity of the data actually available an initial data capturing system was installed. Based on this exercise data capture sheets were designed for operating personnel. These were necessitated primarily because the process was physically removed from the data entry points and tracking was difficult. The analysis of the data collected in addition to knowledge refinement also made obvious the importance of some of the features. For this prototype phase an in-house developed data capture software was used.

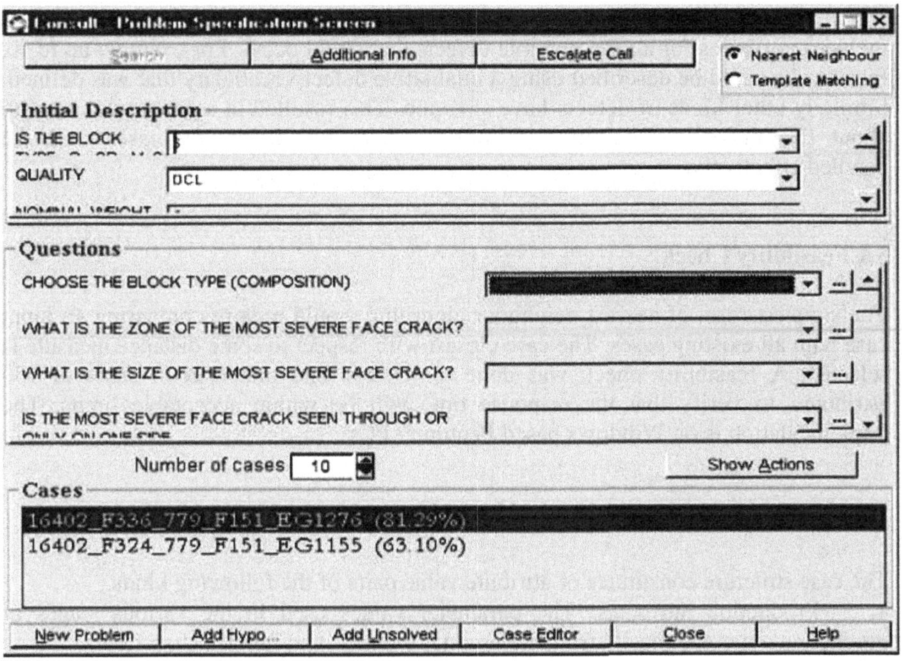

Fig. 3. Screen Shot of Case Retrieval in Consult™

The principle of CBR, which the manufacturing expert does not visualize, is that a case will be retrieved even if there are missing attributes or when some attributes do not match. With partial number of attributes for a complete case being used in the search, closest matching cases are retrieved. At no time will the CBR not retrieve a case while searching for a matching case, as against the principle of database, where no data will get retrieved when there is no exact match. For this prototype case an off the shelf CBR package Consult™ was used [1]. The version of Consult™ supported only cases with 30 attributes. However, it was felt that a buy-in with the management would be obtained by demonstrating the prototype with 30 attributes before developing software to handle 150 attributes. This meant that the knowledge engineers had to group a few attributes to represent a case. In Consult™ [Fig. 3], which is an interactive system, the attributes may be of either dynamic or static type. The static attributes will be present in all cases, whereas the dynamic attributes may or may not be used in a particular case. For instance, some of the most important attributes of a case will be the defects, but all blocks will not have the same number or type of defects. The nearest neighbour match [2] is used to retrieve the best matching case.

5   Design of InfoFrax

Values for the case attributes are collected in the various shop floors and assimilated into a record in the block database. To exploit the use of a RDBMS package to store and retrieve cases a standard record schema was designed. This record schema includes attributes for all the possible defects that could occur. For example up to six face cracks could be described using a qualitative defect vocabulary that was defined. Similarly other kinds of defects have slots too. This resulted in a case structure with about 150 attributes. The first task was to verify that such large cases could be handled effectively.

5.1 Feasibility Check

The simplest form of nearest neighbour algorithm would require comparing an input case with all existing cases. The case closest with respect to some distance measure is selected. A feasibility check was done to retrieve and match 2000 cases of 150 attributes, to verify that the response time will be within acceptable limits. The implementation is on Windows based Pentium • PCs.

5.2 Case Structure

The case structure constitutes of attribute value pairs of the following kinds.
1.   Production attributes: The parameter values used in the various stages of production extracted mostly from the mixing, foundry, and furnace shop floors.
2.   Quality assessment: The data related to the actual block produced, including description of defects, and inspection conclusions.
3.   Administrative attributes: Information related to customers, design documents, and labels used for tracking the block through various stages.
The case structure is stored in a schema file starting with a serial number followed by a name uniquely identifying the attribute, the type of the attribute, the enumerated values or the range of values depending on the type, and ending with the weight assigned if it is a match type. For numeric attributes the possible range is initially given by the domain experts, letting the system dynamically expand the range whenever a value encountered lies outside the so far decided range. The match function scans the file to get attribute type and weight. The similarity over integers or ordered enumerations is computed using the following formula. Let I_j be the input value for the jth attribute A_j, and V_j be the value for the same attribute in the case to be matched and R_j be the range of the particular attribute, then local match for the attribute A_j is given by $sim(V_j, I_j) = 100 - (100 * abs(I_j-V_j) / R)$. Unordered enumerations are exactly matched according to the value.

5.3 Case Retrieval

After a block has been produced, and a block data record is assimilated the CBR phase is invoked. The CBR kernel sequentially compares the input block with all the cases in the database, and constructs a temporary database of n best cases. If the block has been rejected and there is no previous case of that type it is added to the case base with the corrective action as solution, which may be retrieved later on to get solution for a similar rejected block, which needs to be remade [Fig. 4].

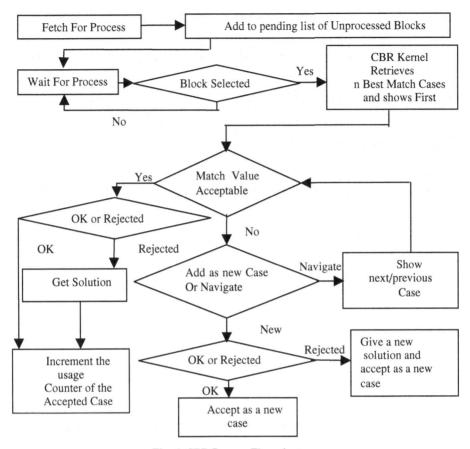

Fig. 4. CBR Process Flow chart

5.4 Linear Search

The retrieval algorithm that is used in the CBR prototype is a simple sequential search irrespective of the current case and its complexity. The index chosen is a primary index automatically being generated synchronously with the knowledge acquisition phase entrusting an RDBMS with the task of indexing, sorting, and retrieving. Two different arguments are there to support the preference of a similarity computation on a linear case base over an indexed search on a structured case base. Firstly, the number of features related to each case is quite high and secondly, the domain experts are ambiguous about the relevance of the features, thus making any structuring on the case base costly and inefficient. Also tuning of the case retrieval is made easy by just allowing weight adjustment in the attribute schema, which otherwise in a structured case base would have needed a complex strategy.

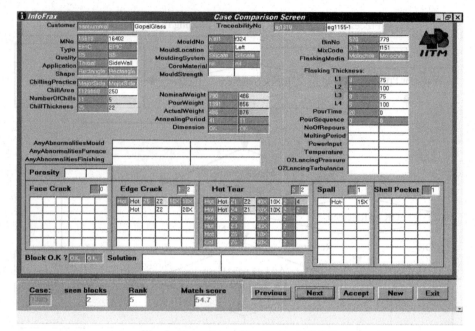

Fig. 5. Case Comparison Screen in InfoFrax

5.5 Visualization

The user is shown the input block data and the best matching cases juxtaposed on the screen with each attribute showing values for both [Fig. 5]. A color coding scheme is used to highlight attributes with mismatch between the input block and the retrieved case. The lower the local match for the values of an attribute, the more strikingly different a colour is used to highlight the values. This directs the user's attention quickly to attributes where the case does not match the block. The user can then navigate back and forth through the n retrieved cases and decide if any of them fits the bill. If it does, the block is added as an instance of the case, and a counter is incremented for statistical purposes. If not, the block can be stored as a new case in the case base. If the block being processed is a rejected block, the system ensures that a corrective action for the block is prescribed and entered before proceeding further.

5.6 Weight Adjustment

The retrieval of cases is based on matching by the 'k' nearest neighbor algorithm [2]. Let the weight schema be represented as $W=\{A_1\ W_1, A_2\ W_2, ..., A_n W_n\}$ where A_1, A_2 and A_n are attributes and the W's are the associated weights. Let the input problem's match attributes with values be represented as $C_i = \{A_1\ V_1, A_2\ V_2, ..., A_n V_n\}$ where the V's are the associated values. Let C_y be one of the cases in the case-base and which can be represented as, $C_y = \{A_1\ Y_1, A_2\ Y_2,...., A_k\ Y_k\}$. Then the weighted 'k' Nearest Neighbor computes the similarity between C_j and C_y, S_{jy} as,

$$S_{jy} = \sum_{j=1 \text{ to } k} W_j * sim\ (V_j, Y_j) / \sum W_j$$

i.e. the similarity over each attribute is computed, weighted, summed up and finally divided by the sum of weights to get the normalized similarity. The contribution of each attribute is proportional to the weight. The case author decides whether or not the block being processed is an instance of a stored case. Ideally the match function should agree with the human by giving a suitably high score to the selected case.

Whether or not this happens is influenced by the weights assigned to different attributes. The current implementation of InfoFrax provides a weight changing functionality. If case author feels that the system consistently disagrees with him on the best match case, and the match value, he can increase or decrease the weights of some attributes. The colour coding used in visualization can help him decide which weights to increase weights and which to decrease. The match function normalizes the sum of all weights to 100.

Alternatively there is a clear case for parameterized learning of weights. When a user selects a case not ranked first by the system, one can use the information to adjust weights. Again the local match plays a role. We plan to implement a weight learning algorithm in the next phase of implementation.

5.7 Architecture

The three major subsystems in InfoFrax are the data capture sub system, information retrieval sub system and the kernel [Fig. 6]. The data capture system is the first to be implemented for initial data validation and is responsible for capturing the manufacturing data in three major process shops namely the foundry furnace and the finishing. These screens need to be user friendly because the major data input in the system is handled by the system. Data entry for all symbolic attributes, and for most of the numerical attributes is through drop down windows to avoid errors. In addition, an attempt has been made to ensure that each data item is entered only once. Complete and consistent data entry is ensured by an interlocking mechanism among the screens in different shops.. The information retrieval system and the kernel, are responsible for the storage and retrieval of the manufacturing experience. Though developed and used in parallel they have been implemented separately for the following reasons. The information retrieval system interacts with the user and facilitates easy access to the required knowledge. For instance it lets the user decide which block is to be processed and displays the best matching cases for the particular block with the match score.

Case maintenance features for adding new cases or updating the usage of the existing cases is also provided in the screen. The kernel implements the algorithms required for searching the case base and retrieving the best cases. Speed is the primary requirement of this sub system because analysis identified the database access operations to be the major cause for delays in retrieval of the whole system. The kernel is shielded from users by the information retrieval system, which also synchronizes the data transfer between itself and the kernel.

The current implementation uses Visual Basic on top of MS Access. The kernel is written in VC++.

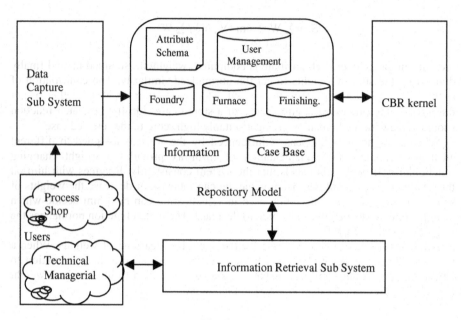

Fig. 6. Software

6 Deployment

The users of the system exist in various organizational levels of the company. Shop floor people are responsible for the data entry operations. The technical and managerial persons are the consumers of the information stored in the system. The case base is exploited in two ways. First is to find a best matching case for a manufactured block. Its main utility is to help decide upon corrective action in case of rejected blocks. Presently it is done without any adaptation. Second is in a design mode to look at past parameters and to produce blocks with some given specifications. A single case author usually is allowed to maintain the case base with new cases or usage information for each block manufactured. Both positive and negative cases are stored as experience.

Table 1. Example of a Case Compare in Tabular Form

Case	Type	Quality	Block	NomWt.	PourWt.	L1	L2	L3	L4	%
Input	EPIC	S3	Reject	534	670	5	4	6	5	
Case1	EC	S3	Reject	502	653	16	13	16	14	89.81
Case2	EPIC	S3	OK	534	668	9	4	7	10	88.72

6.1 User Feedback

The three modes of InfoFrax are Data Capture, Case Comparison and Design Consult. The end users have benefited by being able to see all the 150 parameters associated with each block and comparing with similar blocks aided with graphics aids. The design experts in the domain have reported that they are now ready to consider using the software for development inputs for manufacturing newer type of blocks. The design experts have been able to identify additional uses of the intermediate block database to aid them in specific analysis, such as to find out how many blocks have had a particular type of defect. The marketing department is more confident that they can approach their customers with value added service packages along with the sale of refractory blocks such as lifetime guarantee on the performance of the blocks in the furnace. They have also claimed that it will help them in resolving conflicts with the customer when grappling with problems, which can be due to parts, which they have supplied vis-à-vis the components supplied by others. However, in the refractory and glass manufacturing industry any initiatives such as this will take a few years to yield results because the life of the furnaces is between 4 to 8 years [5].

7   Conclusions and Future Work

InfoFrax is now able to successfully capture the huge amount of data prevailing at various distributed process shops thus initiating the first step in knowledge creation. The CBR methodology has been integrated with the knowledge capture providing a tool for the factory personnel to use the huge amount of data captured and organized in the first step. Since case based expert systems, unlike other systems that need great effort and technical assistance in the phase of maintenance, are easy to maintain, the knowledge maintenance is also done effectively and easily. In addition the experts are allowed to tune the CBR system using the weight manipulation facility,. There is a rule-based system providing the necessary design knowledge for the manufacture of the blocks. The CBR stores the manufacturing experience and provides solutions in case of failure after manufacture. It is expected that as cases in the case base accumulate, the design rules will be influenced via knowledge discovery methods.

7.1 Outcome of Solution

At present a case comprises a problem description and solution. The solution proposed in case of rejection is always remaking the block with either unaltered or altered settings. If the outcome or effect of the solution is captured in future cases as soon as a block is remade, it could potentially help the user decide upon the solutions for the blocks having similar problems, which are to be remade in future.

7.2 Multiple Views

Weight tuning though handled by experts may suffer from wrong assessment due to personal choices and incomplete knowledge. The problem can be minimized by considering the opinions of different experts in different process shops. It could be possibly done by allowing the case author to visualize all views and consequences in the form of a one screen-display of multiple cases retrieved using multiple similarity assessment suggested by different experts. For example, by magnifying the weights for a particular department their viewpoint will be emphasized.

7.3 Modified Representation

Currently the first block of a kind encountered becomes the case prototype. However this could be inaccurate. Assuming that conceptually a case defines a region in the n dimensional attribute space, the first instance being near the periphery of the region would lead to an unsuitable case representative. This is crucial because nearness is computed with respect to the representative. One direction of future work is to work towards a representation that is cumulatively defined by all similar cases encountered.

7.4 Improving Quality

Improvement in quality will be possible with deployment of CBR in predictive maintenance by further discriminating amongst successful cases based on quality related parameters. This may require a second stage of matching with a weight schema that gives more importance to quality parameters.

7.5 Concluding Remarks

There was an initial skepticism amongst production managers towards the proposal of constructing a knowledge based expert system in a domain they viewed as complex and ill defined. But the case based reasoning approach has successfully demonstrated a technique of harnessing knowledge and experience accessible to the collective workforce. Nevertheless, as we have seen in this section, the installed system can be seen to be a basis on which further systems can be built. The repository that is generated will be a resource for developing other functionalities and exploring the ways of exploiting the information. We feel that any living system of this kind opens up a new horizon for all levels of users, developers, and theoreticians.

References

[1] Balaraman, V. and Vattam, S., "Finding Common Ground in Case-Based Systems", In *Proceedings of the International Conference KBCS-98, India*. Sasikumar, M.: Durgesh Rao.: Ravi Prakash, P.: and Ramani, S. eds. 1998. pp. 25-37
[2] Balaraman, V., Chakraborti, S., and Vattam, S., "Using CBR Inexact Search for Intelligent Retrieval of Data", In *Proceedings of the International Conference KBCS 2000 India*. Sasikumar, M.: Durgesh Rao and Ravi Prakash, P. eds. 2000. pp. 119-130
[3] Efraim Turban, *Expert Systems and Applied Artificial Intelligence*, Macmillan, 1992.
[4] Hennessey, D. and Hinkle, D. "Applying Case-based Reasoning to Autoclave Loading", *IEEE Expert*, Vol. 7, Num. 5. 1992. pp. 21-26

574   Deepak Khemani et al.

[5] Mike Nelson, "Recent glass refractory application trends", *Glass Industry Development International* 2002, pp.55 - 57

[6] Michael, S. M., and Khemani, D., "Knowledge Management in Manufacturing Technology", *In Proceedings of the International Conference on Enterprise Information System 2002,*Ciudad Real, Spain, Vol. I, pp. 506-512

[7] Michael, S. M., and Khemani, D., "An Industrial Application of CBR in Manufacturing to Reduce Rejections", *In Proceedings of the Fifteenth International Florida Artificial Intelligence Research Society Conference,* Florida, USA, 2002, pp. 116-120

[8] Rissland, E.: Kolodner, J.: and Waltz, D. 1989 Case based Reasoning. *Proceedings of the DARPA Case-based Reasoning Workshop*, 1-13, San Mateo, CA, Morgan Kauffman

[9] Sivakumar A., & Ravi Kannan. In *Justification of the Project*, Internal memo, CUMI Chennai, 1998.

[10] Srinivasan, R. "Refractories for Glass Tank Furnaces: Exudation Behavior of AZS Refractories", *Society of Glass Technology, Indian Section, Quarterly Newsletter*, 1, Vol.V Number 2. 1998.

Comparison-Based Recommendation*

Lorraine Mc Ginty[1] and Barry Smyth[1,2]

[1] Smart Media Institute, University College Dublin, Dublin 4, Ireland.
Lorraine.McGinty@ucd.ie
[2] ChangingWorlds Ltd., South County Business Park, Dublin 18, Ireland.
Barry.Smyth@ChangingWorlds.com

Abstract. Recommender systems combine user profiling and filtering techniques to provide more pro-active and personal information retrieval systems, and have been gaining in popularity as a way of overcoming the ubiquitous information overload problem. Many recommender systems operate as interactive systems that seek feedback from the end-user as part of the recommendation process to revise the user's query. In this paper we examine different forms of feedback that have been used in the past and focus on a low-cost preference-based feedback model, which to date has been very much under utilised. In particular we describe and evaluate a novel comparison-based recommendation framework which is designed to utilise preference-based feedback. Specifically, we present results that highlight the benefits of a number of new query revision strategies and evidence to suggest that the popular *more-like-this* strategy may be flawed.

1 Introduction

Recommender systems represent the integration of technologies such as information filtering (predominantly collaborative and case-based), user profiling, machine learning, and adaptive user interfaces in an effort to better help users to find the information that they are looking for (for example [2,7,9]). For instance, a typical recommender system in the PC domain interacts with a user by retrieving PC descriptions from its product catalogue that are in line with the target PC description (query) specified by the user. Traditionally a similarity-based retrieval strategy has been adopted here, although more sophisticated approaches have been proposed (see for example [4]). Ideally, the accuracy of the recommendations produced improve on each user interaction with the system, until such time that the user finds the exact PC they are looking for.

A key feature that separates recommender systems from more conventional information retrieval technologies, such as search engines, is their conversational character. Search engines typically focus on *single-shot* retrieval - the user provides a query and the search engine responds with a list of results. In contrast,

---

* The support of the Informatics Research Initiative of Enterprise Ireland is gratefully acknowledged

S. Craw and A. Preece (Eds.): ECCBR 2002, LNAI 2416, pp. 575–589, 2002.

recommender systems will often elicit feedback from the user during the recommendation process upon the presentation of initial or partial recommendations. This feedback is used to elaborate the user's query and so guide the next recommendation cycle.

Recently researchers have explored different ways of capturing feedback from users; such as asking users to specify individual feature values as search criteria (*navigation by asking* [11]), or inviting them to rate or grade recommendations as relevant or not relevant (*navigation by proposing* [11]). Feedback strategies often differ in terms of the level of effort required from the user. For example, requesting the user to provide a feature value requires a high-degree of user effort because the user not only has to consider which feature value she will provide, but must also have some understanding of the recommendation space and the value-space of the feature in question. In contrast, asking the user to rate or grade a recommendation demands significantly less effort. In this paper we are interested in the different ways that feedback can be captured from a user's interaction with a recommender system as part of the recommendation process. We describe and evaluate a novel comparison-based recommendation framework which uses preference-based feedback. Specifically, we highlight the benefits of a number of new query revision strategies and propose that the popular *more-like-this* strategy may be flawed.

2   Background

Feedback strategies can be classified in terms of the type of feedback that they aim to capture (feature-level vs. case-level feedback) and in terms of the cost to the user (low-cost vs. high-cost). Four different feedback strategies have been incorporated into recommender systems to a lesser or greater extent (see Figure 1). *Value elicitation* and *tweaking* are feature-level techniques in the sense that the user is asked to provide information about the features of a recommended case; in the former the must provide a specific value for a specific feature (eg. show me *PCs* whose *type* is *laptop*), while the latter requests that they simply express a directional preference for a particular feature value (eg. show me *PCs* that are cheaper that the current recommendation, or *PCs* that have increased memory). In contrast, *ratings-based* and *preference-based* feedback methods operate at the case-level. In the former the user is asked to rate or grade the recommended cases according to their suitability, while in the latter the user is simply asked to select one of the current set of recommendations that is closest to their requirements (or indeed farthest from their requirements).

2.1   Value Elicitation

Probably the most direct approach to eliciting user feedback during the recommendation process is to simply ask the user to provide a specific feature value (see for example [1]). For example in the PC domain the user may be requested to indicate the *price* of the PC that they are looking for, or their preferred *manufacturer*, or whether they are looking for a *laptop* or a *desktop* model. The form of

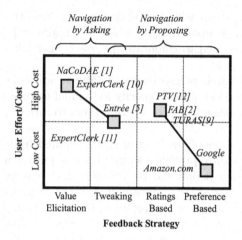

Fig. 1. A comparison of four feedback strategies used by recommender systems.

feedback provides the recommender with a significant degree of new information because each new feature value allows the recommender to eliminate a potentially large number of irrelevant cases that do not share this feature value (or a feature value that is similar); for example, recognising that the user is interested in buying a *laptop*, eliminates all *desktop* models from further consideration.

However, the value that this technique brings must be balanced against its cost. Research indicates that users do not like being asked direct and specialised questions during the recommendation process [6,8,11]. Furthermore, unless the user has a good understanding of the recommendation domain she may not be in a position to answer a direct feature question reliably. For example, how many ordinary users would be able to indicate *memory* preferences when buying a new PC? Forcing users to answer specific questions early on in the recommendation process may result in unreliable answers and ultimately eliminate relevant cases from recommendation. Finally, a key challenge with this approach is recognising which feature should be queried and when, since features can have different discriminating power at different times in the recommendation process.

The above problems notwithstanding, direct feature elicitation is probably the most common type of feedback used in recommender systems today and a variety of strategies have been forwarded to control the elicitation order. For example, Cunningham & Smyth describe an information theoretic approach to identify the next most discriminating feature [13]. They show that their incremental CBR approach out-performs the more traditional pure inductive learning approach across a number of problem domains. Similarly, Shimazu [11], in his work, calculates the information gain of asking possible questions, using an algorithm very similar to $ID3$ [10], that prioritises features that promise maximal information gain.

2.2 Tweaking

The FIND-ME group of recommender systems [5] is interesting for two main reasons. Firstly, they advance the *navigation by browsing* or *navigation by proposing* mode of operation, whereby a user is presented with a group of cases during each recommendation cycle and the next cycle is based on the feedback provided. But secondly, and perhaps more importantly for this work, is that the user is asked to express feedback in the form of a *tweak* or set of *tweaks*. In short the user implicitly selects one of the presented cases and expresses directional preferences for certain features. For instance, in the Entree restaurant recommender (see [5]), the user is presented with the single best case during each recommendation cycle and can introduce tweaks over features such as *price* (find me cheaper or more expensive restaurants) or *style* (find me a more casual or less casual restaurant), for example.

In a sense tweaking is a combination of navigation by asking and navigation by proposing - sequences of cases are proposed and the user is asked for specific information about particular features. The cost to the user is lower than value elicitation however because the user is not expected to provide specific feature values, of which they may have little or no knowledge. This strategy also combines elements of preference-based feedback (see below) since the user must explicitly identify a *preferred case* over which the tweaks should be applied.

2.3 Ratings-Based

Recently, ratings-based feedback has become a popular form of feedback in recommender systems. The basic idea is to ask the user to rate individual recommendation proposals; as such the user is providing case-level feedback. For example, PTV is a recommender system operating in the TV listings domain [12]; it compiles personalized TV guides for users based on their learned TV preferences and as such is involved in recommending TV programmes to users. PTV encourages users to rate its programme recommendations (using a 5-point scale from strong-negative to strong-positive) as a means of fine tuning subsequent recommendation cycles.

Generally speaking ratings-based feedback is a relatively low-cost form of feedback since the user need only express a qualitative (or perhaps quantitative) indication of interest at the level of an individual case. Having said this, the level of effort naturally increases if the user needs to rate many or all of the recommended items - although in most systems, such as PTV, the user can chose to rate as few or as many of the items as she desires.

2.4 Preference-Based

Perhaps the lowest cost form of feedback is for the user to express a simple positive or negative preference for one of the recommended cases. Strangely enough this strategy has been relatively under-utilized by recommender systems to date. Maybe this is because the information-content associated with this simple form of feedback is assumed to be very low, and hence it is expected to provide very little advantage for subsequent recommendation cycles. Nevertheless, it has become a popular form of feedback in many search engines. Google for example allows users to request pages that are similar to a specific search result - in essence the user is expressing a preference for a specific page and requesting more like it during the next recommendation cycle. Similarly *Amazon.com* provides a *more like this* feature for its search results with equivalent functionality.

As mentioned above, this form of feedback can be viewed as a subset of tweaking in the sense that the user is just asked to express an individual positive or negative preference without needing to indicate specific feature tweaks. Similarly it has a lower cost than ratings-based feedback because the user is not expected to distinguish between different levels of preference.

This form of feedback is the core focus of our current work. We are interested in it primarily for two reasons. First its low-cost makes it particularly well suited for use in recommender systems. And secondly, we propose that the assumption that it provides a recommender with little information, and thus does not add value to current recommender systems, is flawed. In the the next section we will introduce the comparison-based recommendation approach, which is designed to better exploit preference-based feedback by transforming the user's preference into explicit query adaptations.

3   Comparison-Based Recommendation

Comparison-based recommendation is a navigation by proposing type of recommendation process. The basic algorithm (fully described in Figure 2) consists of 3 main steps: (1) new items are *recommended* to the user based on the current query; (2) the user *reviews* the recommendations and selects a preference case (positive or negative) as *feedback*; (3) information about the difference between the selected item and the remaining alternatives is used to *revise* the query for the next cycle. The recommendation process terminates either when the user is presented with a suitable item or when they give up.

3.1   Item Recommendation

As with traditional recommender systems the goal of the recommendation step is to select a set of k items that closely match the current user query. However, one of the key features of our comparison-based technique is its ability to make query elaborations on the basis of differences between these recommended items. Thus, it is important to ensure, where possible, that the recommendations presented to the user are diverse in addition to being similar to the target query. As such the comparison-based recommendation technique can be used with either a traditional similarity-based recommendation process (whereby items are selected based on the their similar to the current query) or a diversity-preserving technique, such as that presented by [3,14]. For reasons of clarity however, we will assume a standard similarity-based recommendation process in this work.

```
1.    define Comparison-Based-Recommend(Q, CB, k)
2.    begin
3.      Do
4.        R     ItemRecommend(Q, CB, k)
5.        c_p   UserReview(R, CB)
6.        Q     QueryRevise(Q, c_p, R)
7.      until UserAccepts(c_p)
8.    end

9.    define ItemRecommend(Q, CB, k)
10.   begin
11.     CB'   sort cases in CB in decreasing order of their sim to Q
12.     R     top k cases in CB'
13.     return R
14.   end

15.   define UserReview(R, CB)
16.   begin
17.     c_p   user selects best case from R
18.     CB    CB - R
19.     return c_p

20.   define QueryRevise(Q, c_p, R)
21.   begin
22.     R'    R - {c_p}
23.     For each f_i   c_p
24.       Q     update(Q, f_i, R')
25.     end For
26.     return Q
27.   end
```

Fig. 2. Outline of the comparison-based recommendation algorithm.

3.2   User Feedback

The review process is conceptually simple. The end user is asked to select that case, from among the recommended items, which best matches the needs of the user; this is a form of *positive* feedback. Alternatively the user can provide *negative* feedback in the form of a case which best corresponds to items that the user is not interested in. The power of comparison-based recommendation is its ability to predict how this feedback can be used to elaborate the current query in order to better reflect the user's implicit needs. Once again, for the sake of clarity, in this paper we will focus on positive feedback.

3.3   Query Revision

The key to the success of comparison-based recommendation is the way in which the current query is modified to reflect the user's preference feedback. During this step, the aim is to update the current query based on what can be learned from the user's feedback. In the case of positive feedback (where the user selects a preferred case, c_p) the ultimate objective is to update query features with features from the preferred case that best reflect the user's implicit preferences. The following paragraphs outline the update strategies of interest in this work and their associated update rules.

MLT - More Like This. The simplest form of query revision is to take each feature of the preferred case, $f_i \in c_p$, as a new query feature (see MLT Rule given below). This corresponds to the *more like this* strategy used by some search engines. The advantage that it has is that a partial user query can be instantly extended to include additional features (from the preferred case) in the hope of focusing more effectively on the right set of cases during the next recommendation cycle. However, the potential danger is that not every feature of the preferred case may be actively preferred by the user; for instance, the user may have preferred a PC because of its low *price* and not because of its low *processor speed*. Because of this we can expect the MLT update strategy to suffer from a form of overfitting to user feedback and as a result we may find that the user is guided to irrelevant parts of the recommendation space based on their early preferences. This can result in long recommendation cycles and the need for the user to examine more cases than necessary. Nevertheless the strategy is a useful benchmark against which to judge more principled alternatives.

   MLT RULE: **update**(Q, f_i, R'): $Q.f_i := f_i$

pMLT - Partial More Like This. Consider the scenario shown in Figure 3. The preferred case is for a laptop with a 15 inch display. According to the MLT strategy, this means that the user is likely to be interested in more PCs with *15 inch* displays and as such this feature value should be added to the query. However, in this situation we notice that the user has also rejected a case with a *15 inch* display, suggesting that perhaps the *display size* is not the reason for the user's preference. The pMLT strategy captures this idea by only transferring a feature value from the preference case if none of the rejected cases have the same feature value. For example, we can transfer the preference for *Compaqs* to the new query because none of the rejected cases are *Compaqs*. Similarly, the query can be updated with a preference for a *40GB hard-disk* (see pMLT Rule below).

   pMLT RULE: **update**(Q, f_i, R'): $Q.f_i := f_i$ if $(\neg \exists c_j \in R' : c_j.f_i = f_i)$

wMLT - Weighted More Like This. How reliable is the decision to include *Compaq* in the new query? Should the preference for *15 inch displays* be ignored completely simply because it exists in one of the rejected cases? How does the user's preference for *Compaq* relate to their preference for *Pentiums*? The wMLT strategy attempts to weight the new query features based on the degree of confidence that we can attribute to them as preferences for the user. The basic idea is that the more alternatives that have been presented to the user, the more confident we can be about learning their preference. For example, we can be confident in their *Compaq* preference because there was a wide range of alternatives for the *manufacturer* feature. Compare this to the *processor type* feature, where only two alternatives were presented, *Celeron* and *Pentium*; we can not be sure whether the user is genuinely interested in *Pentiums* or whether they are simply more *interested* in *Pentiums* than *Celerons*.

Features	C1	C2	C3	C4
Manufacturer	Dell	Sony	Compaq	Fujitsu
Memory	256	128	128	256
Monitor	15	14	15	12
Type	Laptop	Laptop	Laptop	Laptop
Processor	Celeron	Pentium	Pentium	Celeron
Speed	700	600	700	650
Disk	20	20	40	20
Price	1300	999	1200	1000

Fig. 3. A typical recommendation scenario where a user is presented with a number of alternatives (PC descriptions) and are asked to choose between them.

The wMLT strategy transfers all preferred features, $(f_i \in c_p)$, to the new query but weights them according to the formula shown in Equation 1 which gives preference to diverse features among the recommended set R (see wMLT Rule below). For example, the preference for *Compaqs* gets a weighting of 1 because all 3 of the rejected cases have unique *manufacturer* values that are different from *Compaq*. In contrast, the preference for *Pentiums* gets a weight of $1/3$ since the 3 rejected cases only account for one alternative to *Pentiums*.

wMLT RULE: update(Q, f_i, R'): $Q.f_i :=< f_i, weight >$

$$weight(f_i, R) = \frac{\# \, of \, alternatives \, to \, f_i \, in \, R}{|R|} \qquad (1)$$

LLT - Less Like This. In addition to learning about features that the user is likely to prefer it may also be possible to learn features that the user tends to dislike. The LLT strategy attempts to do this by treating the query as a set of negative preferences and ordering cases during future cycles by prioritising dissimilarity to the negative query.

The LLT strategy is a simple one: if the rejected cases all have the same feature-value combination, which is different from the preferred case then this combination can be added to a negative query (see LLT rule below). For example in Figure 3, all of the rejected cases have *20 Gb disks* whereas the preferred case has a *40 Gb disk*. The LLT strategy assumes that the user is not looking for a *20 Gb disk* and updates the negative query accordingly.

LLT RULE: update(Q, f_i, R'): $Q_{neg}.f_i := f_i'$ if $(\forall c_j \in R', c_j.f_i = f_i') \wedge (f_i' \neq f_i)$

MLT+LLT - More Like This + Less Like This. Our final strategy combines the MLT and LLT strategies to learn both positive and negative preferences in a single cycle according to the MLT and LLT rules. In practical terms this means that the query has two components, a positive part and a negative part. To compute the degree of relevance between such a query and a case we simply compute the similarity between the positive query component and the case and subtract the similarity between the negative query component and the case (see MLT+LLT Rule below). Other approaches could be used here but for reasons of simplicity and clarity the above has been chosen.

MLT+LLT RULE: **update**(Q, f_i, R'): $Q_{pos}.f_i := f_i$ if $(\neg \exists c_j \in R' : c_j.f_i = f_i)$
$$\wedge$$
$$Q_{neg}.f_i := f_i' \text{ if } (\forall c_j \in R', c_j.f_i = f_i') \wedge (f_i' \neq f_i)$$

4   Experimental Evaluation

So far we have presented a novel recommendation framework called comparison-based recommendation which attempts to optimise the use of preference feedback as a means of revising the user's query within a navigation by proposing recommendation approach. Furthermore, we have presented a variety of possible strategies for revising the query. In this section we evaluate the comparison-based recommendation technique and these individual revision strategies with respect to a benchmark recommendation system.

4.1   Setup

The following experiments were carried out using a case-base from the PC domain. This case-base contains 120 unique cases, each describing a unique PC in terms of features such as *manufacturer, PC type, processor type, processor speed, memory, disk size, display size, and price*. The cases themselves are available for download from URL *www.cs.ucd.ie/students/lmcginty/PCdataset.zip*.

In total we evaluate 5 different versions of our recommendation technique, each employing a different revision strategy and labeled according to this strategy (MLT, pMLT, wMLT, LLT, MLT+LLT). In addition, we chose to implement a simple similarity-based recommender (Sim) as a benchmark against which to judge the performance of each of the comparison-based techniques.

In each of the following experiments we use a leave-one-out evaluation methodology varying values of k (the number of cases returned during each recommendation cycle) from 2 to 5, and q (the number of initial features per query) from 1 to 5. In brief, each case of the case-base is temporarily removed and used in two ways. First each case serves as the basis for a set of random queries of varying sizes (ranging from 1 to 5 features per query). Second, we select that case in the case-base which is most similar to the current target case. These *best cases* serve as the recommendation targets during the experiments. In other words, the original target case is taken as the ideal query for a user, a generated query serves as the initial query that the user provides to the recommender, and the *best case* is the best available case for the user based on their ideal query. In total a set of 1200 separate queries are generated and all reported results are averaged as appropriate.

4.2   Recommendation Efficiency

Ultimately, a key success criterion for any navigation by proposing recommender is the number of individual cases that the user is expected to examine before they settle on a *best case*. This metric has a direct analogy in the case of the similarity-based benchmark.

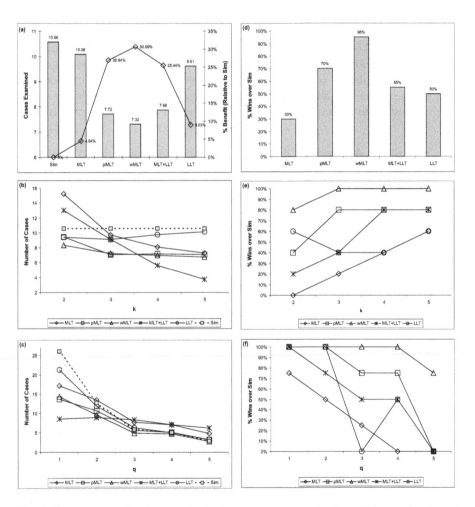

Fig. 4. Summary evaluation results looking at recommendation efficiency (a-c), and winners and losers(d-f).

Method. In this experiment we run leave-one-out trials for each combination of k (2 to 5) and q (1 to 5) - a total of 20 separate trials, each one over 1200 queries - and note the average number of cases that the user must view before the best case is located. In the case of the similarity-based benchmark this is the average position of the best case in the similarity ordered list produced from the initial queries. In the case of the comparison-based recommenders it is the total number of cases presented in each recommendation cycle prior to the final cycle plus the position of the best case in the final cycle. For example, for a $k = 3$ trial where 3 recommendation cycles are needed and the best case is the second case in the final cycle, then the user has needed to look at a total of $(3 * 2) + 2 = 8$ cases.

Results. The results are shown in Figure 4(a-c). The first graph plots the average number of cases examined for each technique over all trials as a bar chart, and also plots the relative benefit associated with each technique, compared to the benchmark (Sim), as a line graph. Figures 4(b&c) then show a breakdown of these results averaged over different values of k and q respectively.

Summary Analysis. Figure 4(a) indicates that overall the comparison-based recommenders are working well in relation to the benchmark even though they operate on the basis of minimal feedback from the user during each recommendation cycle. The best case for a query is positioned at 10.56 on average for the Sim benchmark, compared to 7.32 for the wMLT method. In other words, the wMLT method requires the user to look at 30% fewer cases than Sim, on average. Similar, albeit not quite as pronounced, benefits are available to the pMLT and MLT+LLT methods, with reductions of approximately 27% and 25%, respectively. The MLT and LLT methods on their own perform less well, as they require the user to examine an average of 10.08 and 9.61 cases per session (benefits of 4.54% and 9.03%, respectively).

Varying k. Figure 4(b) indicates that as k increases the average number of cases examined by the user decreases (of course the Sim plot remains flat here as it does not depend on k). However, we also see that while the MLT and MLT+LLT techniques outperform Sim on average, they actually lose to Sim when $k = 2$; MLT and MLT+LLT rack up scores of 15.2 and 12.99 respectively compared to Sim's score of 10.56. It seems that for low values of k the recommendation window is not large enough for MLT to generate sensible revisions for the query. Note also that the LLT method on its own performs well at the $k = 2$ level indicating that the poor performance of MLT+LLT at $k = 2$ is largely due to MLT and not to its LLT component. In general, the results suggest that the simple MLT strategy is not an effective revision strategy as all techniques bar LLT perform better for all values of k. Interestingly the combination of MLT and LLT performs much better at higher values of k to eventually win outright for $k > 3$. Overall the pMLT and wMLT techniques perform best of all for the different values of k, with the more sophisticated wMLT method performing slightly better than pMLT for all but $k = 3$. This suggests that the weighting scheme employed by wMLT does have a positive effect.

Varying q. Figure 4(c) shows the average results (over the different k values) for different values of q, the initial query size. This time the Sim method is affected, with significant reductions in the number of cases that must be examined as q increases, as expected. Once again the MLT method and MLT+LLT methods perform poorly here, losing to Sim for values of $q > 2$ in the case of MLT and $q > 3$ in the case of MLT+LLT; although it is interesting that MLT+LLT is the outright winner for $q = 1$ and $q = 2$. The best overall performers are pMLT and wMLT, which perform well for $q = 1$ and $q = 2$ (they are only beaten by MLT+LLT), winning outright at $q > 2$. And notably, wMLT outperforms pMLT indicating the additional value conferred by its weighting technique.

Discussion. The results so far indicate that the simple (and naive) MLT technique does not perform well when compared even to the simple Sim benchmark. As predicted, MLT tends to overfit to the current preference case and this serves to steer the recommender into parts of the case-base that do not contain the target case. The more sophisticated pMLT and wMLT methods offer significant improvements across all of the recommendation trials as they successfully select features from the preference case for transfer to the new query. The influence of negative preference features is less clear, with some benefits available for lower values of k and higher values of q. In particular the interaction between MLT and LLT seems to be inconsistent and warrants further analysis.

4.3   Winners & Losers

The previous experiment examined average case results in terms of the numbers of cases that need to be examined by a user for each recommendation technique. However it is important to understand that these average case results do not tell us whether one technique is consistently performing better than another (especially the benchmark). In fact, a low average could be the result of a single or small number of good trials for an otherwise poorly performing method. For this reason, in the following experiment we look at the number of trials where an individual technique wins, compared to the benchmark (and outright).

Method. The trial results are processed to compute the number of times that each recommendation technique wins over the benchmark; that is the number of trials where a technique results in fewer cases being examined than the Sim benchmark.

Results. The results are shown in Figure 4(d-f) as a summary over all trials (Figure 4(d)) and individual break-downs for differing values of k and q (Figures 4(e) and (f) respectively).

Summary Analysis. Figure 4(d) indicates that the wMLT method is the best performer overall, beating Sim 95% of the time, that is, in 19 out of 20 of the trials; the trial where wMLT looses to Sim is with $k = 2$ and $q = 5$ and the difference is only 0.02. pMLT ranks second overall with a win rate of 70% (14 out of 20 trials). Once again we find that MLT performs poorly, and even though it beats Sim in terms of the average number of cases examined overall (10.56 vs. 10.08) it wins over Sim in only 30% of the trails (in 6 out of the 20 trials); in other words its improved average is derived from good results on a few trials. Once again we find that the LLT method has some promise, beating Sim 50% of the time. Interestingly, the combination of MLT and LLT performs only marginally better than LLT on its own, indicating the the MLT technique is having a minor positive impact overall, and even though MLT+LLT performed well on average in terms of number of cases examined by the user; once again this good average result is derived from a few good trials and is masking poor individual performances compared to Sim.

Varying k. The results when k is varied are summarised by Figure 4(e). Once again we find wMLT performing best overall, beating Sim 100% of the time for $k > 2$. Similar, albeit less impressive, performance is seen for pMLT as it beats Sim for 40% of $k = 2$ trials (2 out of 5 of these trials) and for 80% of the $k > 2$ trials. Interestingly the performance for LLT is seen to degrade for $k > 2$ reflecting the average increase in the number of cases examined for LLT witnessed in the previous experiment. MLT is the worst performer, never beating Sim at $k = 2$ but improving to beat Sim on one extra trial for each increment of k (these wins come for low values of q).

Varying q. The results when q is varied are shown in Figure 4(f). In general the performance of each of the comparison-based techniques, relative to Sim, degrades with increasing values of q; this is to be expected as the Sim technique will perform well when queries become more and more complete. However it is worth pointing out that the wMLT technique maintains its 100% win rate for all values of q except $q = 5$ where it looses once as indicated above. Moreover, wMLT is the only technique to beat Sim at all at the $q = 5$ level, so the fact that it wins in 3 out of the 4 trials at this q value is impressive by comparison. The MLT and MLT+LLT techniques degrade rapidly with increasing values of q as shown while pMLT performs better until $q = 5$ where it too succumbs to the superiority of Sim. The LLT strategy is somewhat erratic in this analysis, in general performing poorly, but beating Sim anomalously in 2 out the 4 trials at $q = 4$.

Discussion. The results in this section add more detail to the average case analysis of the previous experiment, and indicate that some of the good average-case performances are the result of a small number of good trials, and are not indicative of good performance overall, compared to the benchmark. This is especially true for the MLT, LLT, and MLT+LLT techniques. We find that the

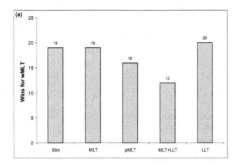 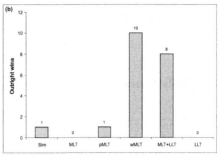

Fig. 5. Comparison of the performance (win-rate) of each of the feedback strategies examined compared to wMLT (a), and relative to each other (b).

good average-case performances of pMLT and wMLT do represent genuine improvements over Sim across the board. The good performance of pMLT indicates that its ability to select features for the new query works well, and the winning performance of wMLT indicates that its weighting techniques adds considerable further value. In fact the success of wMLT is highlighted in Figure 5(a & b) which charts the percentage of trials that wMLT beats each other individual technique and the percentage of trials that wMLT wins outright. Figure 5(a) shows that wMLT displays as impressive a performance when compared to other update strategies as it does when compared to Sim (see Figure 4(d)), consistently beating LLT, MLT, and pMLT, and beating MLT+LLT in 60% of the trials. Impressively, Figure 5(b) highlights that wMLT wins outright (beating every other technique) in 50% of the trials (10 out of 20 trials).

5   Conclusions

Our focus in this paper has been the various feedback methods that have been, or can be, employed by recommender systems as a means of incrementally refining the recommendation process. We have attempted to classify the different types of feedback that have been explored to date along granularity and cost dimensions. We have further highlighted the apparent lack of interest in the low-cost preference-based feedback method, suggesting that this apathy is rooted in the assumption that this technique is unlikely to gather sufficient information to effectively guide the recommendation process.

In response we have outlined the comparison-based recommendation framework which is designed to fully exploit preference-based feedback. A family of preference-guided query revision strategies has been fully described and evaluated. We found promising results for the pMLT and the wMLT methods which are based on principled ways of selecting and weighting features in the revised query as a result of preference feedback. Furthermore we have provided evidence that the simplest form of preference feedback (MLT - *more like this*), which has been widely adopted by the search-engine community, is likely to perform poorly in recommender systems. Future work will focus on extending our evaluation into additional recommendation domains and into looking at new revision strategies based on alternative weighting models.

References

1. D.W. Aha, L.A. Breslow, and H. Muñoz-Avila. Conversational case-based reasoning. *Applied Intelligence*, 14:9–32, 2000.
2. M. Balabanovic and Y. Shoham. FAB: Content-Based Collaborative Recommender. *Communications of the ACM*, 40(3):66–72, 1997.
3. K. Bradley and B. Smyth. Improving Recommendation Diversity. In D. O'Donoghue, editor, *Proceedings of the Twelfth National Conference in Artificial Intelligence and Cognitive Science (AICS-01)*, pages 75–84, 2001. Maynooth, Ireland.
4. D. Bridge. Product Recommendation Systems: A New Direction. In D. Aha and I. Watson, editors, *Workshop on CBR in Electronic Commerce at The International Conference on Case-Based Reasoning (ICCBR-01)*, 2001. Vancouver, Canada.
5. R. Burke, K. Hammond, and B.C. Young. The FindMe Approach to Assisted Browsing. *Journal of IEEE Expert*, 12(4):32–40, 1997.
6. M. Doyle and P. Cunningham. A Dynamic Approach to Reducing Dialog in On-Line Decision Guides. In E. Blanzieri and L. Portinale, editors, *Proceedings of the Fifth European Workshop on Case-Based Reasoning, EWCBR-2000*, pages 49–60. Springer, 2000. Trento, Italy.
7. M. Goker and C. Thompson. Personalized Conversational Case-based Recommendation. In E. Blanzieri and L. Portinale, editors, *Advances in Case-Based Reasoning: Proceedings of the Fifth European Workshop on Case-based Reasoning*, pages 99–111. Springer-Verlag, 2000.
8. A. Kohlmaier, S. Schmitt, and R. Bergmann. Evaluation of a Similarity-based Approach to Customer-adaptive Electronic Sales Dialogs. In S. Weibelzahl, D. Chin, and G. Weber, editors, *Empirical Evaluation of Adaptive Systems. Proceedings of the workshop held at the 8th International Conference on User Modelling*, pages 40–50, 2001. Sonthofen, Germany.
9. L. McGinty and B. Smyth. Collaborative Case-Based Reasoning:Applications in Personalised Route Planning. In D. Aha and I. Watson, editors, *Proceedings of the International Conference on Case-Based Reasoning (ICCBR-01)*, pages 362–376. Springer-Verlag, 2001. Vancouver, Canada.
10. J.R. Quinlan. Induction of decision trees. *Journal of Machine Learning*, 1:81–106, 1986.
11. H. Shimazu. ExpertClerk : Navigating Shoppers' Buying Process with the Combination of Asking and Proposing. In Bernhard Nebel, editor, *Proceedings of the Seventeenth International Joint Conference on Artificial Intelligence (IJCAI-2001)*, pages Volume 2, pages 1443–1448. Morgan Kaufmann, 2001. Seattle, Washington.
12. B. Smyth and P. Cotter. A Personalized TV Listings Service for the Digital TV Age. *Journal of Knowledge-Based Systems*, 13(2-3):53–59, 2000.
13. B. Smyth and P. Cunningham. A Comparison of Incremental Case-Based Reasoning and Inductive Learning. In *Proceedings of the Second European Workshop on Case-Based Reasoning, EWCBR-94*. Springer, 1994. Chantilly, France.
14. B. Smyth and P. McClave. Similarity v's Diversity. In D. Aha and I. Watson, editors, *Proceedings of the International Conference on Case-Based Reasoning*, pages 347–361. Springer, 2001.

Case-Based Reasoning for Estuarine Model Design

Sara Passone[1], Paul W.H. Chung[2], and Vahid Nassehi[1]

[1]Chemical Engineering Department, Loughborough University, Leicestershire, LE11 3TU
United Kingdom
{S.Passone, V.Nassehi}@Lboro.ac.uk
[2]Computer Science Department, Loughborough University, Leicestershire, LE11 3TU
United Kingdom
P.W.H.Chung@Lboro.ac.uk

Abstract. Estuaries are complex natural water systems. Their behaviour depend on many factors, which are possible to analyse only by adopting different study approaches. The physical processes within estuaries, such as floods and pollutant dispersion, are generally investigated through computer modelling. In this paper the application of case-based reasoning technology to support the design of estuarine models is described. The system aims to provide a non-expert user in modelling with the necessary guidance for selecting a model that matches his goal and the nature of the problem to be solved. The system is based on three components: a case-based reasoning scheme, a genetic algorithm and a library of numerical estuarine models. An example based on the Upper Milford Haven estuary (UK) is used to demonstrate the efficacy of the system's structure for supporting estuarine model design.

1 Introduction

An estuary is commonly defined as the physical location where the river current meets the sea. Influenced by tides and the mixing of fresh and sea water, estuaries are areas of highly variable environmental conditions. River flow, tidal range and, sediment as well as salt distributions change continuously. Consequently these water systems evolve dynamically without reaching a definitive equilibrium state [1]. Biologically important for their fertile waters and strategically crucial for the navigational access they provide estuaries have also been central in the development of civilisation. This has, however, meant heavy industrialisation and population increases in estuarine regions, contributing to the alteration of estuaries' topography and large-scale pollution.

Studying estuaries is a complicated task. It needs to take into account the interaction of many variables, related to estuarine dynamics and mixing processes as well as man-made changes [2]. Investigated by numerous disciplines such as geomorphology, hydrology and ecology [1], estuaries and their near shore environment have been considered from different point of views, in order to identify the physical, chemical and biological mechanisms acting in these water systems. In the past decades a considerable amount of information regarding the physics of several different estuarine systems, have been collected in the form of analytical data and field measurements. However, only with the development of computer models it

S. Craw and A. Preece (Eds.): ECCBR 2002, LNAI 2416, pp. 590–603.

has been possible to interpret estuarine phenomena and plan future actions in respect of their natural environment [3].

Numerical simulations, among other types of models, are considered the most effective tool for studying estuaries as they provide accurate simulations with little time consumed [4]. Nevertheless, their use is limited by the extensive mathematical background and interdisciplinary knowledge required for their correct application [5]. Generally developed for a specific estuarine system, they must be carefully employed for each different case. Therefore, reservations have been expressed about the ability of a non-expert user in modelling to correctly apply these tools. To exploit the full potential of estuarine modelling, it is necessary that the user is assisted in the formulation of a model. Based on the aim of the investigation and the degree of performance required, the user should be provided with a model strategy that is defined according to the characteristics of the estuary and the ontology of the problem to be modelled.

This paper presents a case-based reasoning tool for estuarine model design (CBEM), which aims to make the utilisation of expensive and complicated numerical models available to not-specialists. By organising the problem-specific knowledge and the information on previous cases, the system provides the user with necessary guidance for numerically solving hydrodynamic-environmental problems related to estuaries. The system consists of three different components: a case-based reasoning scheme, a genetic algorithm and a library of numerical simulation models, which are integrated to work as a single tool. With respect to the possible correlation between the features of the estuary and the physical phenomenon to be modelled, the case-based module returns a suitable model from the system's memory. The selected model is then adapted by the genetic algorithm component, which estimates a valid set of model parameters to suit the particular estuarine environment.

CBEM currently contains several studies about British estuaries such as Tay in Scotland, Tees and Fal in England, and Upper Milford Haven in Wales. These cases have been employed to evaluate the methodology. The paper describes the system components and the logic behind their implementation in the case of the Upper Milford Haven estuary with respect to the problem of salinity distribution.

2   The CBEM Architecture

The Case-Based Reasoning system for Estuarine Modelling (CBEM) operates through the co-operative action of three main components: a case-based module, a library of numerical models and a genetic algorithm for model optimisation (Fig. 1). These modules are activated to perform specific tasks of the case-based problem solving process. The case-based (CB) module function allows the user to describe new and past cases (description component). It is also responsible for the retrieval process (retrieval component). Cases are retrieved according to characteristics of the simulation tasks to be performed.

A case is intended divided into two parts: the estuary, the object of the investigation, and the related models, each employed to simulate a specific physical phenomenon within that estuary. This distinction permits a better understanding of the process that determines a model strategy. The selection of a model is partly decided by the assumptions on the physical and hydrographic behaviour of an estuary. The appropriate model structure must also be defined to meet the problem's requirements and maximize the cost effectiveness. This description strategy mostly facilitates the retrieval process. Initially the search engine selects from the system's case-base only those cases for which the current problem has been previously modelled. A similarity rating for each of the past cases is established based on the values of the indices contained in the estuary's description. The user's requirements for the new problem are also utilized to refine the matching process. The past cases are then ranked with respect to their performance expressed in terms of accuracy, simulation time consumed and purpose for which they were employed. The user is then presented with a range of past cases ranked according to the estuary description as well as the problem definition. He is responsible for the final selection based on his/her personal judgment.

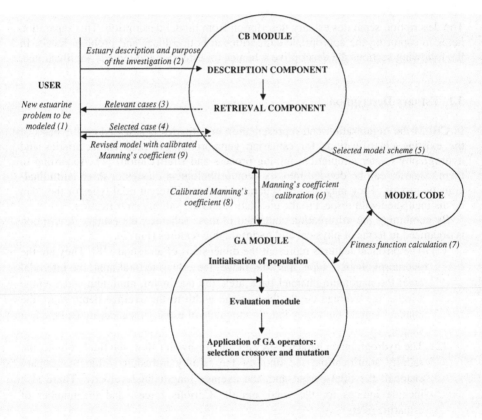

Fig. 1. Structure of the CBEM system

Once the model scheme is selected from the library of numerical codes, the genetic algorithm (GA) module is activated to optimise the parameters of the selected model to suit the new application. The required parameter optimisation is carried out by combining the classical evolutionary theory with problem-specific information. The GA module incorporates knowledge from the practice of estuarine model calibration by using modified genetic operators. Furthermore, the present scheme benefits from the co-operation with the CB module by including in the initial population parameter values from the most similar cases. The use of knowledge augmented operators [6] and case-based initialisation [7] improves the search performance. It finds a better set of parameters for the new problem and requires less time than the classical genetic approach.

The CBEM procedure terminates and returns to the user a model scheme retrieved among the past cases as the best match, and a new set of parameters that provides satisfactory performance. The model can now be applied to simulate different scenarios.

3 CB Module, Description Component

The description separates estuary description from model description. This separation helps in capturing the appropriate similarities at both estuary and problem levels. In the following sections the descriptive schemes for estuaries and models are illustrated.

3.1 Estuary Description

In CBEM the organisation and representation of estuaries is assessed on the basis of the existing classifications for estuarine geomorphology, tidal characteristics and hydrography (water circulation, mixing process and stratification) [1]. According to them estuaries can be divided into six geomorphological classes or three latitudinal-climatic groups. They may also be separated in three different tidal types or they can be distinguished with respect to the circulation and the salinity stratification.

By combining the information contained in these schemes, the estuary description is organized in terms of physical and hydrographic features (Fig. 2).

  (1) The physical features represent the dimensions of an estuary [8]. They are the geomorphological type, the tidal range, the estuarine total area, the intertidal area, the maximum channel bank area, the maximum, minimum and average widths, the average depth, the average width to the average depth ratio, the channel length, the valley length, the grade of estuary meandering and the bed shape.

  (2) The hydrographic characteristics are the freshwater flow, the tidal volume, the salinity stratification, the limit of the salinity intrusion within the estuary channel, the tidal period and, the average longitudinal velocity. There also include indices for the wind and the Coriolis forces, and the number of estuarine inlets.

Some physical estuary's features are defined using qualitative values in order to facilitate the indexing and retrieval processes [9]. By using the fuzzy set theory, the width to the depth ratio and the degree of estuary's sinuosity are expressed according to a qualitative scale. In addition, some indices such as the geomorphological type, the tidal range and the salinity stratification, as object symbols [9] are defined according to the description provided by the estuaries' classification schemes.

The Coriolis and wind forces are also included in the description of the estuary physics. Although they are external factors, they can significantly condition the mechanism of mixing within estuaries especially under particular physical conditions [5]. Therefore, their effects are represented in the model equations with specific mathematical terms. Through a dimensional analysis approach, the corresponding magnitude of the wind and Coriolis forces for each case is established with respect to the dominant friction stress. Based on the dimensional analysis's outcome, the system suggests if it is appropriate either to take into account or discard their effects in the modelling procedure. The user can then decide to follow the system's advice or to proceed against its suggestion.

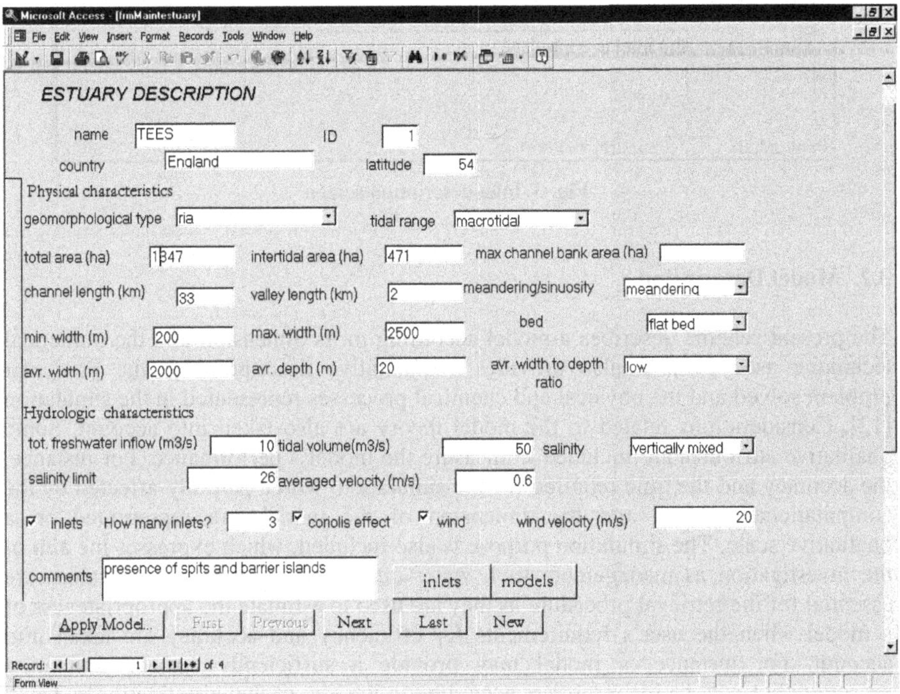

Fig. 2. Estuary description screen

In the estuary description special consideration is given to the presence of inlets. These, which are evaluated separately from the main estuary description (Fig. 3), may influence the dynamics and mixing process within an estuary. Their contribution to the estuarine motion of water and mass continuity must be differently represented into the model equations if classified as either branches or tributaries [10].

The description unit evaluates the nature of any inlet by comparing it with the estuary's main channel over the average depth, width and velocity dimensions. At this point the user is still able to ignore the response from the system's dimensional analysis and change the computer's recommendation.

The values for indices required in the estuary description are not particularly difficult to obtain. The user of CBEM is expected to be familiar with the estuary under investigation. It is assumed that he/she has access to this type of information and is able to provide all the necessary data through the description component interface.

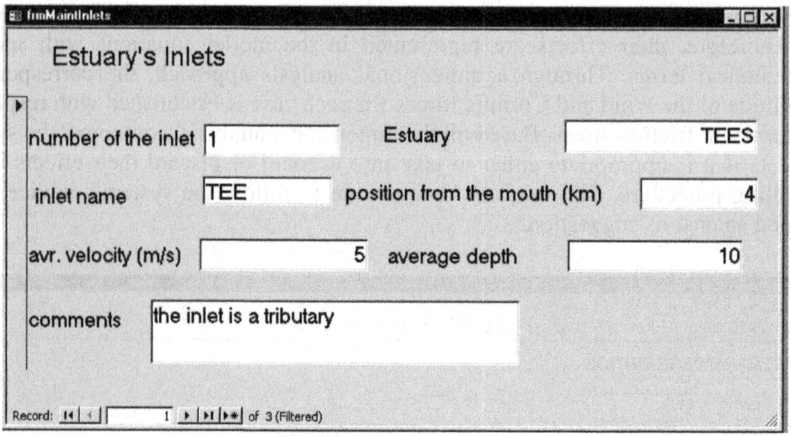

Fig. 3. Inlet description screen

3.2 Model Description

The present scheme describes a model according to its dimension and the numerical technique used [11]. It also provides a qualitative description of the particular problem solved and the physical and chemical processes represented in the simulation [12]. Considerations related to the model theory are also taken into account. Some qualitative attributes are included to measure the model's performance. For instance, the accuracy and the time required for the simulation, which partially affected by the computational method and the dimension of the model, are represented on a qualitative scale. The simulation purpose is also included, which expresses the aim of the investigation as management tool, water quality or research. These values are essential for the retrieval procedure as they are used to estimate the appropriateness of a model when the user's requirements for efficiency and accuracy are taken into account. For instance, a model may provide a sufficiently correct simulation procedure but may be inappropriate according to the aim of the investigation as far as the time required or the accuracy are concerned.

Model assumptions such as the presence of wind, Coriolis force, the bed slope and branching effect are also represented in the model description, together with the dispersion and Manning's coefficients. The values of these parameters are included as they may be used during the adaptation phase. They may be injected into the initial population of the genetic algorithm routine, if the related model is retrieved by the system as being the most appropriate to the new problem.

4   CB Module, Retrieval Component

The CB module is also designed to carry out the retrieval process to select from the system's library the model that is most likely to fulfil the user's needs. After describing the estuary to be studied, the user is required to specify the purpose of the undergoing investigation in the model selection screen (Fig. 5). The problem description provides the necessary information to the retrieval process to calculate the similarity between the new case and those contained in the case-base.

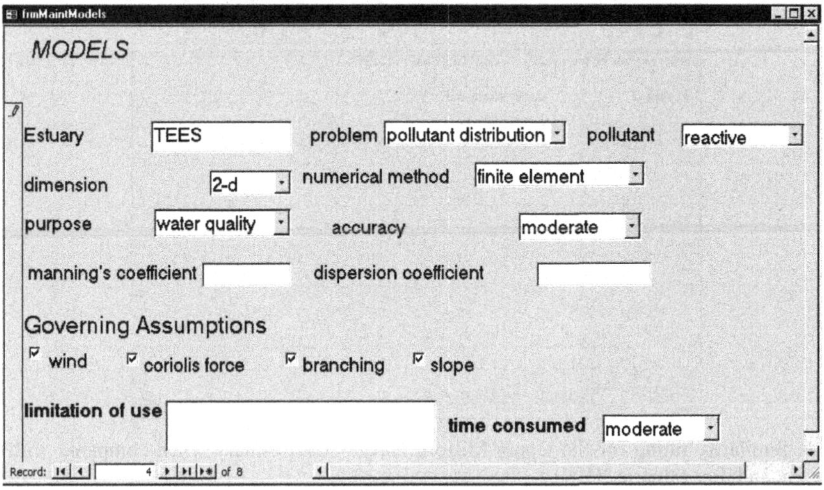

Fig. 4. Model description screen

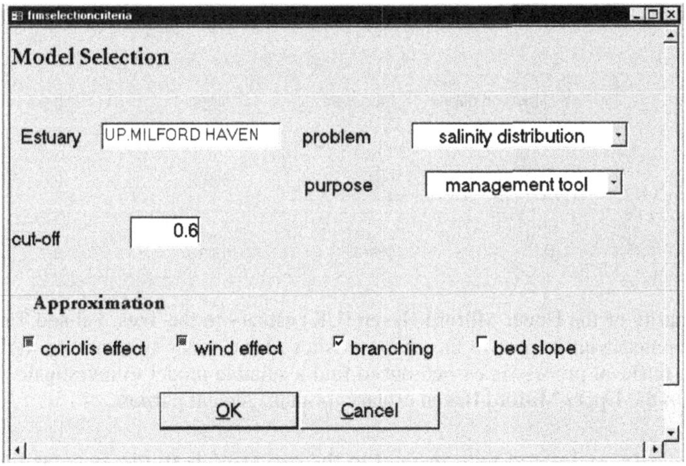

Fig. 5. Model selection screen

The retrieval process is carried out in two stages. The similarity rating between a new and a past case is initially defined with respect to the values of the physical and hydrographic characteristics contained in their estuary description (Fig. 6). A second score is then obtained with respect to the type of investigation to be conducted, the accuracy and simulation time required (Fig. 7). However, cases are excluded from the retrieved cluster if the dimension of the related model is inappropriate for the type of problem considered. It must be noted that the model dimension, which depends on the type of problem as well as the estuary's physics, needs to be chosen so that the physical phenomenon under investigation is well-represented without underestimating or over sizing the problem domain.

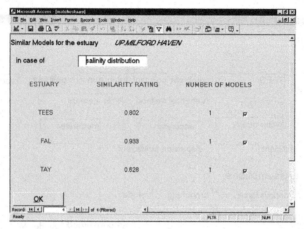

Fig. 6. Similarity rating for the Upper Milford Haven (UK) estuary when compared with the Tees, Fal and Tay estuaries (UK)

ESTUARY	DIMENSION	ACCURACY	ESTUARY SIM.	MODEL SIM.
TAY	2-D avrg on depth	moderate	0.628	0.5
TEES	2-D avrg on depth	high	0.802	0.6
FAL	1-D	overall	0.933	0.7

Fig. 7. Similarity of the Upper Milford Haven (UK) estuary to the Tees, Fal and Tay estuaries (UK) is computed with respect to the characteristics of the water systems and the associated models. The retrieval process is carried out to find a suitable model to investigate the salinity distribution in the Upper Milford Haven estuary for management purpose

The similarity, estimated with respect to the estuarine features, is measured using a fuzzy approach [13] if the attributes are described on a quantitative scale (i.e. ratio of the total area to the intertidal area). Alternatively, if the descriptors are expressed qualitatively (i.e. the degree of meandering, the geomorphological type), the matching criterion consists of computing the distance between the two symbols [9]. The adequacy of each retrieved model is then evaluated through a pre-determined set of match values that rank the accuracy, simulation time consumed and purpose of the model based on the investigation aim of the new problem.

The retrieval procedure implemented in the present scheme uses different sets of matching and importance criteria according to the type of estuarine phenomenon to be modelled. The CBEM contains different case ranking procedures for problems such as salinity distribution and salt intrusion. Table 1 illustrates the scheme for selecting cases with respect to the salinity distribution problem to be solved for management purpose.

In the case of Upper Milford Haven estuary and the simulation of the salinity distribution within the watercourse, the retrieval process suggests to select the one-dimensional model previously employed for the Fal estuary (Fig. 7) as it gives the highest similarity for the estuarine physic behaviour as well as the characteristics of the problem to be modelled.

Table 1. The necessary steps for the computation of the similarity between cases to study the salinity distribution within an estuary for management purpose.

ALGORITHM

1. set of 5 features F from the estuary description: the ratio of the average width to the average depth (a), the geomorphological estuary type (b), the tidal range (c), the meandering rate (d), the ratio of the total area to the intertidal area (e) and the ratio of the channel length to the average depth (f).
2. assign the degree of relevance P= 1 to (a), 0.75 to (b) and (e), 0.5 to (c), (d) and (f).
3. distribution of the similarity values $S = sim(F_i^I, F_i^R)$, with sim as similarity function and, I and R referring to the input and retrieved cases, respectively.
4. normalize the match aggregate score $= \dfrac{\sum\limits_{i=1}^{5} P_i S_i}{\sum\limits_{i=1}^{5} P_i}$
5. exclude case-models with respect to the model dimension.
6. select the following features from the model description: purpose (g), accuracy (h), simulation time (i).
7. apply a set of pre-determined rules to establish the functional role M_k of each feature with respect the purpose of the current investigation
8. assign a grade of relevance P=0.75 to (g) and 0.5 to (h) and (i).
9. normalise the match aggregate score$= \dfrac{\sum\limits_{k=1}^{3} P_k M_k}{\sum\limits_{k=1}^{3} P_k}$

---

5 GA Module, Adaptation

The adaptation of a numerical model to a new case requires:
1. discretising the new problem domain
2. updating the input data
3. identifying new model parameter values.

The discretisation can be obtained by employing pre-processor software, which after inserting the geographical co-ordinates, will generate the necessary grid. Furthermore, the input data (i.e. the hydrographic data, boundary and initial conditions) are directly obtained from navigation charts and field surveys.

The possibility of interfacing CBEM with existing commercial packages for the discretisation of the estuary domain and pre-determined datafile for the input data makes these first two adaptation steps relatively straightforward. This is different from adjusting the necessary parameters for the model. They need to be carefully searched and identified. The calibration of the model parameters is carried out manually or by numerical optimisation programs. However, both alternatives require the expertise of an experienced modeller. Therefore, CBEM adaptation phase essentially focuses on the parameter adjustment, to offer a quick, simple and automatic method for producing the required new set of values. In the GA module, the use of a genetic algorithm is specifically implemented for estuarine model calibration. The model parameters are adapted to suit the physics of the estuary to be simulated. In the present prototype, the GA optimisation routine is limited to the calibration of the Manning's friction coefficient, a key model parameter that represents the bed resistance to the water flow in the hydraulic equation of motion. For the numerical solution of the estuarine equations, the problem domain needs to be discretised into sections (Fig. 8). The estuarine flow resistance is also represented through a specific value of the Manning's coefficient for each section [10]. Thus, GA calibration consists of optimising a set of parameters values that gives a realistic simulation of the estuarine hydrodynamics.

5.1 Initialisation

The classical GA formulation is modified to incorporate problem specific knowledge of estuarine model calibration. The chromosomes have integer number structure with each gene corresponding to a particular element of the discretised domain. This representation permits the problem domain to be divided into any number of elements up to several hundreds to match the degree of accuracy required.

The initial population is based on the estuary divided into zones of influence each having a specific physical behaviour. The reason of this is that the resistance to the flow changes with respect to the variation of the estuarine physical characteristics. Therefore, it is expected adjacent elements to have similar values for the Manning's coefficient. The division of the estuary is reflected in each chromosome by partitioning it into a number of segments corresponding to the estuarine zones (Fig. 9). Based on this chromosome's structure the genes in the same segment are initially assigned the same Manning's coefficient value (zonation option). The alleles, although randomly computed, are sorted to reflect the fact that the flow resistance generally decreases towards the estuary mouth. The value of the genes is, therefore, chosen to be lower in correspondence with estuarine zones closer to the seaward boundary limit.

The initialisation procedure also includes in the population a small percentage of chromosomes which are genotypical translation of the set of Manning's coefficients previously employed for the cases retrieved by the CB module as the most similar. The population based on previous cases is limited to 10% in order to avoid premature convergence and ensure the necessary diversity [14].

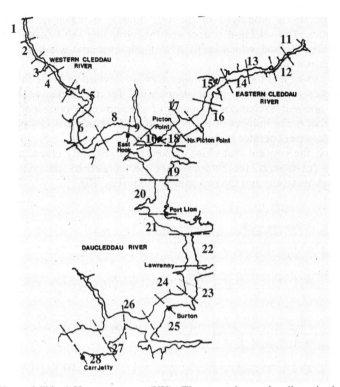

Fig. 8. The Upper Milford Haven estuary (UK). The map shows the discretisation of the domain into sections. A Manning's coefficient is assigned to each of them.

The combined procedure adopted for the initialisation of the population aims to direct the genetic algorithm towards areas of the search space where it is more likely to find the best set of parameters.

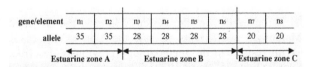

gene/element	n_1	n_2	n_3	n_4	n_5	n_6	n_7	n_8
allele	35	35	28	28	28	28	20	20

Estuarine zone A   Estuarine zone B   Estuarine zone C

Fig. 9. Initialisation of a chromosome using the zonation option

5.2 GA Operators

The genetic algorithm operators are also implemented using concepts from the theory of estuarine calibration. Selection, crossover and mutation operators are specifically designed for Manning's coefficient optimisation.

The selection mechanism is based on the calculation of the discrepancy between the simulated water elevations and the corresponding field measurements [15]. Therefore, the code of the model selected through the retrieval process from the system's library is employed in the GA module to calculate the fitness of the chromosomes. The selection is operated by combining the roulette wheel approach with the elitist method, which keeps 10% of chromosomes with the highest fitness in the next generation.

The crossover and the mutation operators are devised to guide the search towards chromosomes with a real physical meaning for the estuarine calibration. The crossover operator exchanges segments of chromosomes corresponding to specific estuarine zones. The number of cut-points in a chromosome is randomly chosen each time the crossover operator is applied (Fig. 10).

Based on the concept that close elements are generally characterised by similar Manning's coefficients, the chromosomes are mutated by changing the value of a randomly chosen gene and the two adjacent to it (Fig. 10).

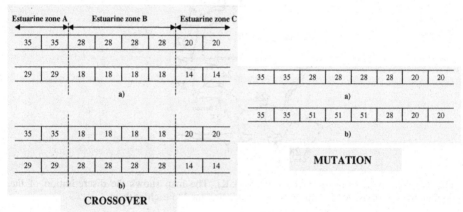

Fig. 10 The knowledge augmented operators of crossover and mutation before (a) and after (b) their use

5.3 GA Module Test, Upper Milford Haven Estuary

Once the model is retrieved from the system's library, the GA module adjusts the input set of Manning's coefficients to suit the Upper Milford Haven estuary's specifications. With respect to the methodology previously described, the model is calibrated for a spring tide (25th April 1979). The water surface elevations at Carr Jetty (Fig. 8) and the fresh water inflow of the Western Cleddau and Eastern Cleddau rivers are used as boundary conditions. Based on the discretisation of the estuary integer values. The GA population consists of 30 chromosomes and the optimisation is carried out for 15 generations. The rate of mutation and crossover is 0.01 and 0.5 respectively. The fitness function is calculated based on the observed water elevations at Picton Point and Easthook, 26.8 and 28.2 km from the estuary's mouth. These stations have been selected as the estuary's hydrodynamics is apparently very sensitive to the physical conditions at these two locations.

Figure 11 shows the simulated water surface elevations at Picton Point and Easthook calculated for the spring tide with the set of Manning's coefficient calibrated by the GA module. The corresponding field measurements and the simulation obtained for a manual calibration are also given in the figure. The set of Manning's coefficients calibrated by the GA module provides the best performance when compared to the observed data and the model outputs resulting from the manual calibration.

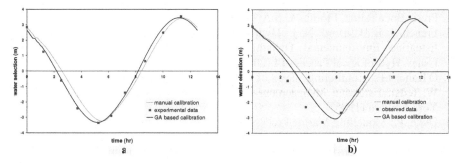

Fig. 11. Simulation of water surface elevations for the spring tide at the stations Picton Point (a) and Easthook (b)

6   Conclusions

Computational hydraulics is fundamental in studying the complex dynamics of estuaries as it provides accurate qualitative simulations that can be used for predicting possible future scenarios. However, the implementation of numerical models is usually made for specific cases and their employment for studying different systems requires the user to have a sound background in numerical modelling and an extensive interdisciplinary knowledge. In this work the application of the case-based reasoning method to support estuarine modelling is explored. The system presented consists of three modules: a case-based module, a genetic algorithm and a library of numerical model codes. Through the case-based module a model strategy is defined by considering the similarity of the new situation to the past cases with respect to the physical behaviour of the estuary and the specific problem to be modelled. Once an appropriate model procedure is selected, the genetic algorithm component, which is implemented with problem specific knowledge, is activated to adjust the model parameters. To illustrate the system's applicability the case of Upper Milford Haven estuary, UK, has been presented to define an appropriate solving strategy for modelling the salinity distribution within this water body.

For future work it is planned to extend CBEM capacity to support the interpretation of the results obtained from the model application. It is intended to employ the case-based reasoning approach for advising the user on the entity and the meaning of the simulation scenarios produced.

References

1. Dyer, K.R.: Estuaries a Physical Introduction. 2nd edn. John Wiley & Sons, New York (1997)
2. Kennish, M.J.: Ecology of Estuaries, Vol.1: Physical and chemical aspects. CRC Press, Boca Raton, Florida, U.S.A. (1990)
3. French, J. R., Clifford, N. J.: Hydrodynamic Modelling as a Basis for Explaining Estuarine Environmental Dynamics: Some Computational and Methological Issues. Hydrological Process **14** (2000) 2089-2108
4. O'Kane, J.P.: Conflicting Views of the Role of Models. In: Wilson, J.G., Halcrow, W. (eds): Estuarine Management and Quality Assessment. Plenum Press, New York London (1985)
5. Dyke, P.: Modelling Marine Processes. Prentice Hall, London (1996)
6. Goldberg, D.E.: Genetic Algorithm in Search, Optimization, and Machine Learning. Addison-Wesley Publishing Company, Massachusetts, U.S.A. (1989)
7. Ramsey, C., Grefensttete, J.: Case-Based Initialization of Genetic Algorithms. In: Forrest, S., (eds.): Proceedings of the Fifth International Conference on Genetic Algorithms. Morgan Kauffman, San Mateo (1993) 84-91
8. Davidson, N.C., D'A Laffoley, D., Doody, J.P., Way, L.S., Gordon, J., Key, R., Pienkoski, M.W.,Mitchell, R., Duff, K.: Nature Conservation and Estuaries in Great Britain, Nature Conservancy, Peterborough, UK (1991)
9. Chung P.W.H. and Inder R.: Handling Uncertainty in Accessing Petroleum Exploration Data. Revue de L'Institut Francais du Petrole, **47** (1992) 305-314
10. Bikangaga, J.H., Nassehi, V.: Application of Computer Modelling Techniques to the Determination of Optimum Effluent Discharge Policies in Tidal Water Systems. Water Resources **10** (1995) 2367-2375
11. Hinwood J.B., Wallis, I.G.: Classification of Models of Tidal Waters. Journal of the Hydraulics Division, Proc. A.S.C.E. 101 (1975) HY10 1315-1351.
12. Lawson J., Gunn, I.J.: Guidelines for the Use of Computational Model in Coastal and Estuarial Studies. Report SR 450, HR Wallingford, Oxon, UK (1996)
13. Jeng, B.C., Liang, T.P.: Fuzzy Indexing and Retrieval in Case-Based Systems. Expert Systems With Applications, **8** (1995) 135-142
14. Louis, S.J., Johnson, J.: Solving Similar Problems Using Genetic Algorithms and Case-Base Memory. Proceeding or the Seventh International conference on Genetic Algorithms. Morgan Kauffman, San Mateo (1997) 101-127.
15. Babovic, V., Abbott, M.B.: The Evolution of Equations from Hydraulic Data, 1. Theory. Journal of Hydraulic Research **3** (1997) 397-410

Similarity Guided Learning of the Case Description and Improvement of the System Performance in an Image Classification System

Petra Perner, Horst Perner, and Bernd Müller

Institute of Computer Vision and Applied Computer Sciences
Arno-Nitzsche-Str. 45, 04277 Leipzig
ibaiperner@aol.com, http://www.ibai-research.de

Abstract. The development of an automatic image classification system is a hard problem since such a system must imitate the visual strategy of a human expert when interpreting the particular image. Usually it is not easy to make this strategy explicit. Rather than describing the visual strategy and the image features human are able to judge the similarity between the objects. This judgement can be the basis for a guideline of the development process. This guideline can help the developer to understand what kind of case description/features are necessary for a sufficient system performance and can give an idea what system performance can be achieved. In the paper we describe a novel strategy which can support a developer in building image classification systems. The development process as well as the elicitation of the case description is similarity-guided. Based on the similarity between the objects the system developer can provide new image features and improve the system performance until a system performance is reached that fits to the experts understanding about the relationship among the different objects.

Keywords: Case-Based Reasoning, Image Classification, Learning Vocabulary

1 Introduction

The development of an automatic image classification system is a tricky problem since such a system must imitate the visual strategy of a human when interpreting the particular image. Usually it is not easy to make this strategy explicit so that it can be understood by the system developer and copied into the system. Human can not always name the image features and when they are able to do that these features are symbolic in nature which need to be mapped into the numerical features an automatic image analysis system can extract from the images. Rather than describing the visual strategy and image features human are able to judge the similarity between the objects. This judgement can be the basis of a guideline for the development process. This guideline can help the developer to understand what kind of features are necessary for a sufficient system performance and can give an idea what system performance can be achieved. The later can help to avoid not necessary system tuning which is often the case when not having understood the dependencies between the objects.

S. Craw and A. Preece (Eds.): ECCBR 2002, LNAI 2416, pp. 604–612.

In the paper we describe a novel strategy which can support a developer in building image classification systems. The development process as well as the elicitation of the case description is similarity-guided. Based on the similarity between the objects the system developer can provide new image features and improve the system performance until a system performance is reached that fits to the experts understanding about the relationship among the different objects. In Section 2 will describe the problem which usually arise when building image classification system based on a medical application. In Section 3 we describe the architecture of the System. The similarity-based guidance of the system development is described in Section 4. We summarize the recent results in Section 5 and give conclusions in Section 6.

2 The Problem

We will describe the methodological aspects which will usually arise when developing an image classification system based on an application called HEp-2 cell image analysis. However this application will only be used for demonstration purposes. The problems described are general problems and can be observed when doing other application as well.

The task is to develop an automatic system for the classification of HEp-2 cells in medicine. This kind of cells get used for the identification of antinuclear autoantibodies (ANA) [1]. ANA testing for the assessment of systemic and organ specific autoimmune disease has increased progressively since immunofluorescence techniques were first used to demonstrate antinuclear antibodies in 1957. Hep-2 cells allow recognition of over 30 different nuclear and cytoplasmic patterns, which are given by upwards of 100 different autoantibodies. However, not all patterns occur with the same frequency in practice. There are patterns which occur very often there are other pattern which occur very seldom. The identification of the patterns is recently done manually by a human inspecting the slides with the help of a microscope. The less automation of this technique has resulted in the development of alternative techniques based on chemical reactions, which have not the discrimination power of the ANA testing. An automatic image classification system would pave the way for more wide use of ANA testing. At the beginning of the system development process we have the following conditions:

1. A raw idea of how to interpret this kind of cells was obtained from interviewing a human expert see Figure 2. Based on this expert knowledge we can only achieve an classification accuracy of 25% [2]. This leads to the conclusion that the expert has no good conceptual knowledge built up over time.

2. There is a prototype image catalogue available. A set of digital images could only be obtained after having installed an image acquisition unit with storage capacity at the clinical hospital. This allows to collect images as soon as they appear in medical practice. However, this does not ensure to get a large collection of images with a equally distributed number of samples in each class. There are some classes they did not appear until now although the system is installed since a year. This circumstance is usual for medical applications. Therefore we need a strategy for the system development which allows to develop an automated image classification system under this circumstances.

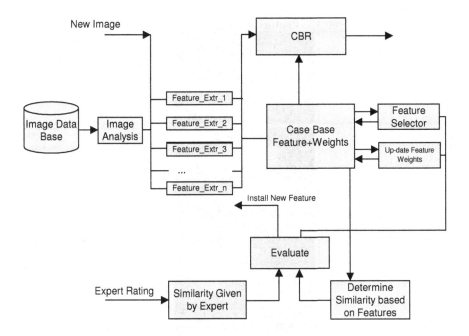

Fig. 1. Architecture of the System

3. The expert description in Figure 1 allows to select basic image feature descriptors and the necessary image processing facilities which get installed into the system.
4. The experts are able to judge the similarities between the different classes on a scale between 0...1 (0 stands for identity and 1 stands for dissimilar). That gives a similarity matrix for the classes see Figure 2.

These conditions usually exist in practice and do not allow a system set up based on conventional pattern recognition methods. In the following we will describe our strategy for the system development under these conditions.

3   Architecture of the System

The cases are image descriptions which are automatically extracted from the images based on the procedures installed in the feature extraction unit and stored into the case base together with the class name. In a separate image data base are kept all images, class names, and image descriptions given by an human operator for later evaluation purposes.

The feature extraction unit contains feature extraction procedures that have been identified based on the interview with the expert. We should note here that a particular application requires special feature descriptors. Therefore not all possible feature extraction procedure can be implemented into such a system from scratch. But we hope that we can come up with a special vocabulary and the associated feature extraction procedures for our cell image application which can be applied to a wider range of cell types.

Class_Name	Nomenclature	Prototype Image	Description
Homogen	100 000	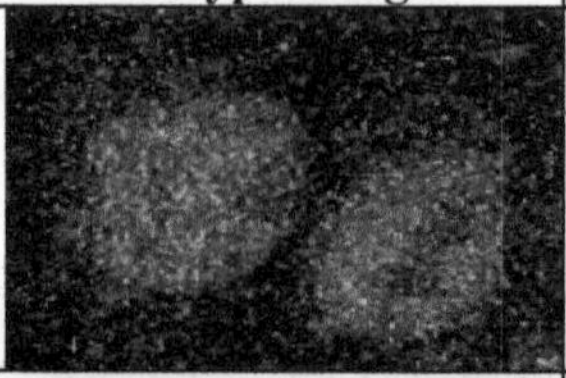	A uniform diffuse fluorescence of the entire nucleus of interphase cells. The surrounding cytoplasm is negative.
Homogen Fine Speckled	100 320	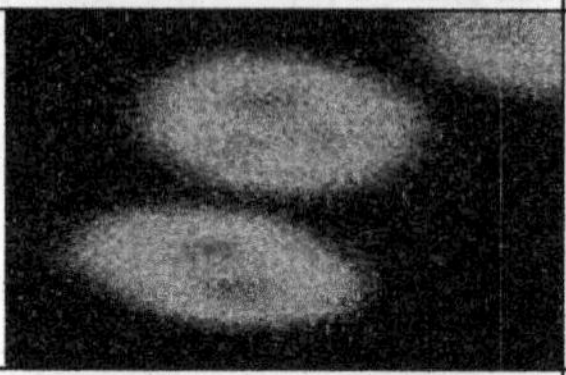	A uniform fine speckled fluorescence of the entire nucleus of interphase cells.
Nuclear	200 000	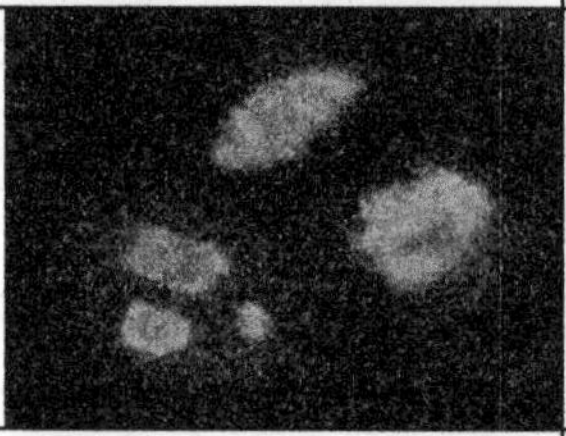	Smooth and uniform fluorescence of the nuclei Nuclei sometimes dark Chromosomes fluoresced weak up to extreme intensive
Fine Speckled	320 000	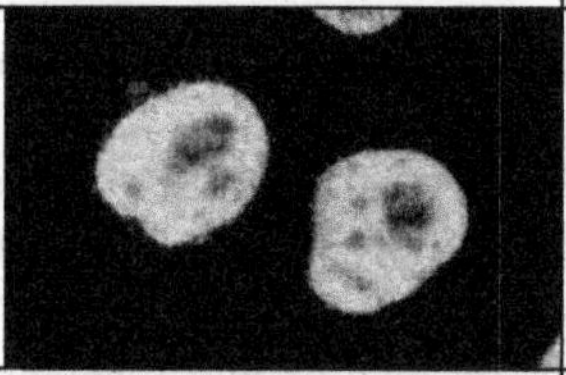	Fine to discrete speckled staining in a uniform distribution.
Fine Speckled Nuclear	320 200	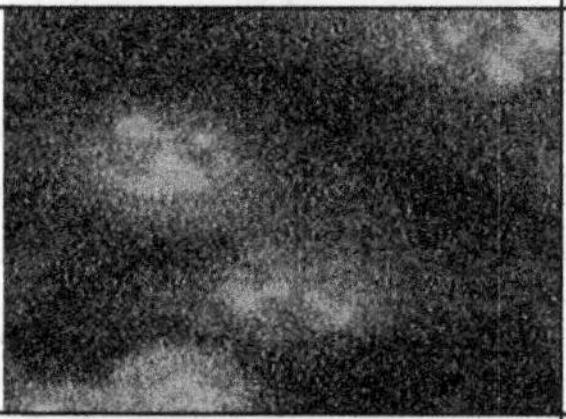	Dense fine speckled fluorescence Background diffuse fluorescent
Centromere	500 000	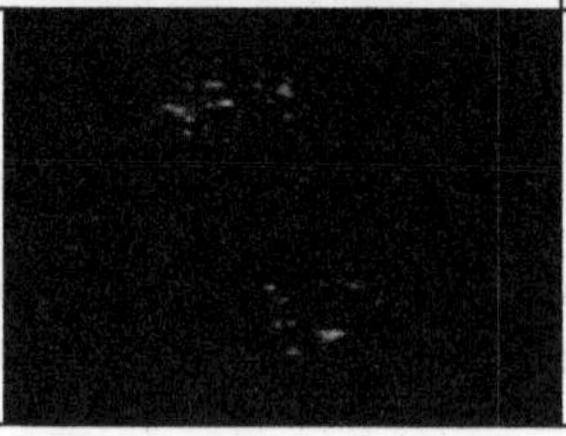	Nuclei weak uniform or fine granular, poor distinction from background

Fig. 2. Class Names, Prototype Images and Expert Description

For each case class are selected a prototype image from the image catalogue. A special unit observes how the collected cases deviate from the prototype image in the class. If the difference between the prototype image and a new collected image is too large the system gives an alert to the system developer. He checks the image together with the medical expert and if necessary he can install a new prototype into the case base.

From the prototypes are calculated the pairwise similarities based on the calculated image features. That gives a second proximity matrix besides the on based on the experts judgement. Now, the task is to tune the system by the system developer so that the two similarity matrix become identical. Identical similarity matrix are certainly the optimal case. A more relaxed version would be to ask for minimal distance between these two matrix.

Besides the system development it should be possible that the recent system can be used by the human expert. Therefore, the cbr process is using the case base with the prototype images for reasoning. We are considering the case base to have a flat structure. A new case is classified by first extracting the case description from the image based on the recent established image analysis and feature extraction procedures and afterwards using this description for the determination of the closest case among the cases in case base. The resulting answer of the system is observed by a human operator who is an expert in the field of application. He criticizes the result.

4 Similarity-Guided Improvement of the System Performance

We think that the intuitively given rating of the similarity between the different objects given by an expert can help to improve the development process. This rating gives the developer an idea what system performance can be achieved based on the automatically extracted image features and can guide the development process as well as the elicitation of new features.

Usually for that purposes is used the error rate of the classifier. However, this gives only a general understanding of how good the system performance is but does not give a hint what should be done to improve the system performance.

The aim should be to minimize the difference between the user given similarity rating sim_E of the prototype objects o_i and the similarity sim_S between these prototypes derived based on the calculated image features f_k:

$$sim_E(o_i, o_j) - sim_S(f_{ik} - f_{jk}) = Min!$$

The optimal case would be zero difference between the experts rating and the similarity that can be achieved by the system based on objective calculation of image features from the images. However, this is hardly to achieve. There are three possible solutions to this problem:

1. Put feature weights to the features and up-date the initially feature weights until a sufficient difference between sim_E and sim_S is reached. Since we know from the expert´s similarity where the vast difference is we can update the weight locally according to that.
2. Select among the whole set of features the right subset of features for the classification problem. This is a feature selection problem but has also a link to the feature weight problem. Those features which are not necessary get the feature weight zero and those which are necessary get the feature weight one.

3.   If solution 1 and 2 do not give sufficient results then only the identification of new features will bring the expected result.

Solution 1 and 2 improve the system performance based on the automatically extracted images features. If the resulting performance is not sufficient enough then only the identification of a new image feature can help to improve the system performance. This process can be guided by the pairwise similarity between the objects as well. When the system gives a pairwise similarity measure sim_s that is less than the experts given similarity sim_E than the question is: What feature makes this two objects different? This is the point where the system developer has to identify a new feature descriptor and install this feature descriptor in the system.

5   Results

From the expert knowledge shown in Figure 1 we can derive that the expert describes the texture of the cells. Therefore we have developed a novel and very flexible texture descriptor based on random sets [3]. This texture descriptor is based on 200 low-level features. Depending on how they are combined they can describe different high-level concepts of texture. This texture descriptor gives a high flexibility which allows to describe different and very complex textures of cell objects. Besides that we have installed feature descriptors such as size of the object and the contour.

Our study has shown that experts are able to say what objects are similar but in order to get unbiased ratings the system has to support the expert. The elicitation of the experts similarity judgement is done by a specific questionnaire. From the whole set of images are randomly selected 3 images and shown on display to the expert. Then the system asks him to select two images which are similar to each other. After having chosen these two images he has to rate the similarity between these images on a scale between 0...1. Table 1 shows the similarity matrix given by the expert.

The similarity matrix obtained based on the extracted image features is shown in Table 2. The similarity measure is the Euclidean distance.

Recently we have installed a feature selection procedure. This procedure tries to identify the features that have the highest dissimilarity to other features. Therefore we calculate the similarities between the features. Feature subset selection was done by hierarchical clustering with single linkage and using Euclidean distance. The resulting dendrogram showed groups of similar features. The dendrogram was then decomposed into groups of similar features by a cut-off value of 10%, 5% and 2.5% similarity. From the remaining groups one feature for each group was selected and a feature weight of one was associated to this feature. All the other features get the feature weight zero. Based on this strategy we could get the improvement shown in Table 3.

However, no further improvement was possible. Now arises the question what makes the objects dissimilar that are very similar based on the calculated features but not on the experts judgement. Together with the expert we discovered new images features based on the spatial relation among the objects inside a cell. Therefore, we are currently going on to develop a new feature extraction procedure for this kind of image description. This will enhance our vocabulary for cell image description. At the end we will come up with a set of basic image descriptors which can be used for other types of cells than HEp-2 cells such as for e.g. pap-smear cells. Then, the expert itself can chose among the whole set of image descriptors the one which fits to his observation and advise the system to test this descriptor. By doing so he can learn the vocabulary for his specific application.

Besides that development of new image descriptors we will install a procedure for learning the feature weights [4].

Table 1. Similarity of Classes given by the Expert

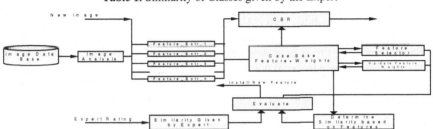

Table 2. Similarity between the Objects before Feature Subset Selection

	100000	100320	200000	320000	320200	500000
100000	0	0,395	0,174	0,811	0,377	0,42
100320		0	0,475	1	0,524	0,872
200000			0	0,515	0	0,222
320000				0	0,428	0,594
320200					0	0,433
500000						0

Table 3. Similarity between the Classes after Feature Subset Selection

	100000	100320	200000	320000	320200	500000
100000	0	0,403	0,22	0,868	0,391	0,480
100320		0	0,617	0,95	0,622	0,897
200000			0	0,699	0,005	0,274
320000				0	0,540	0,784
320200					0	0,445
500000						0

6 Related Work

Our work has a link to conversational CBR [5][6] where the user is engaged to incrementally formulate a query duing case retrieval. However, in our appraoch it is used to identify a gap in case description and to encourage the user to think of a new feature for which then a new feature extraction procedure must be developed.

The work described here has also a link to case base maintenance [7] which is the process to refine a CBR system's case base to improve the system's performance.

Learning feature weights [8] and feature subset selection are the main topics related to this task in our approach.

7 Conclusion

We have proposed a similarity-guided strategy for the system development of an image classification system. This strategy can help to elicitate new features as well as feature weights and by doing so it can help to improve the system performance. Using the expert´s judgement on similarity and comparing that with the similarity calculated by the system gives the system developer an idea what system performance can be achieved. This can help to avoid not necessary tuning of the system.

We are currently implementing our strategy into a system for HEp2-cell image classification. The first results are promising and support our strategy. However, there are a lot of open problems which have not necessarily to do with CBR. The expert needs better support for the determination of the similarity between the objects. Experts are able to say what objects are similar but they are not trained to express the similarity on a scale between 0...1.

We have also to find new feature descriptors that can describe the image features. This is a hard problem since there are not so many work been done in finding feature extractors for cell image classification.

Besides that we want to implement a methods for feature weight learning in our system that can learn global and local feature weights.

Acknowledgement

This research has partially been founded by the German Mininstry of Economy and Technology within the project LERNBILDZELL.

References

1. K. Conrad, R.-L. Humbel, M. Meurer, Y. Shoenfeld, E. M. Tan, eds., Autoantigens and Autoantibodies: Diagnostic Tools and Clues to Understanding Autoimmunity (Pabst Science Publisher, Lengerich, Berlin, Riga, Rom, Wien, Zagreb, 2000).
2. P. Perner, H. Perner, and B. Müller, Mining Knowledge for Hep-2 Cell Image Classification, Journal Artificial Intelligence in Medicine 2002, (to appear)
3. P. Perner, Texture Classification based on the Random Sets and its Application to Hep-2 Cells, IEEE Proc. International Conference on Patter Recognition, ICPR´2002, to appear
4. D. Aha and R.L. Goldstone, Concept learning and flexible weighting, In Proc. of the Fourteenth Annual Conference of Cognitive Science Society, Bloomington, IN: Lawrence Erlbaum 1992, pp. 534-539.
5. D.W. Aha, T. Maney, and L.A. Breslow, Supporting Dialogue Inferencing in Conversational Case-Based Reasoning, In: B. Smyth and P. Cunnigham (Eds.), Advances in Case-Based Reasoning, Springer Verlag, lnai1488, p. 262-272, 1998.
6. D. McSherry, Interactive Case-Based Reasoning in Sequential Diagnosis, Applied Intelligence 14 (2001), 65-76

7.   G. Cao, S. Shiu, and X. Wang, A Fuzzy-Rough Approach for Case Base Maintenance, In: D. Aha and I Watson (Eds.), Case-Based Reasoning Research and Development, Springer Verlag, lnai 2080, pp. 118-130, 2001
8.   S. Craw, J. Jarmulak, and R. Rowe. Maintaining Retrieval Knowledge in a Case-Based Reasoning System, Computational Intelligence, vol. 17, No. 2, 2001, pp. 346-363.

ITR: A Case-Based Travel Advisory System

Francesco Ricci, Bora Arslan, Nader Mirzadeh, and Adriano Venturini

eCommerce and Tourism Research Laboratory
ITC-irst
via Sommarive 18
38050 Povo, Italy
{ricci,arslan,mirzadeh,venturi}@itc.it

Abstract. This paper presents a web based recommender system aimed at supporting a user in information filtering and product bundling. The system enables the selection of travel locations, activities and attractions, and supports the bundling of a personalized travel plan. A travel plan is composed in a mixed initiative way: the user poses queries and the recommender exploits an innovative technology that helps the user, when needed, to reformulate the query. Travel plans are stored in a memory of cases, which is exploited for ranking travel items extracted from catalogues. A new 'collaborative' approach is introduced, where user past behavior similarity is replaced with session (travel plan) similarity.

1 Introduction

1.1 Problem Statement

There is a continuously growing number of web sites that support a traveller in the selection of a travel destination or a travel service (e.g., flight or hotel). Typically, the user is required to input product constraints or preferences, that are matched by the system in an electronic catalogue. All the major eCommerce web sites dedicated to tourism, such as Expedia, Priceline, TISCover, etc, implement this simple and quite effective pattern.

Actually, planning a travel towards a tourism destination is a complex problem solving activity. The term "destination" itself refers to a "fuzzy" concept that lacks a commonly agreed definition. For instance, even the destination spatial extension is known to be a function of the traveller distance from the destination. Italy could be a destination for a Japanese, but not for a European traveller who may focus on a specific region, such as Tuscany.

Secondly, the "plan" itself may vary greatly, in the structure and content. For instance, some people search for prepackaged solutions (all included) while other "free riders" want to select each single travel detail independently. There is a vast literature investigating: how the travel planning decision process unfolds, the main decision variables and their relationships [11]. Several choice models have been proposed [2, 14, 6] (to quote only a few). These models identify two groups of factors that impact on the destination choice: personal and travel features. In the first group there are both socioeconomic factors (age, education,

S. Craw and A. Preece (Eds.): ECCBR 2002, LNAI 2416, pp. 613–627, 2002.

income, etc.) and psychological/cognitive (experience, personality, involvement, etc.). In the second group we could list travel purpose, travel party size, the length of travel, the distance, and the transportation mode.

1.2   Recommender Systems

The major eCommerce web sites dedicated to travel and tourism have recently started to better cope with leisure travel planning by incorporating recommender systems, i.e., applications that provide advice to users about products that might interest them in [3]. Recommender systems for travel planning try to mimic the interactivity observed in traditional counselling sessions with travel agents. The two most successful recommender systems, triplehop.com and vacationcoach.com, can be classified primary as *content-based*. The user expresses needs, benefits and constraints using the offered language (attributes) and the system matches this description with items contained in a catalogue of destinations (described with the same language). Vacationcoach exploits user profiling by explicitly asking the user to classify himself in one profile ("culture creature", "beach bum", "trail trekker", etc.) that apparently induces some implicit needs not provided by the user. The matching engine of TripleHop guesses importance for attributes not explicitly mentioned by the user, combining statistics on past user queries and a prediction computed as a weighted average of importance assigned by similar users [5]. Neither of these systems can support the user in building a "user-defined" travel, made of one or more locations to visit, an accommodation and additional attractions (museum, theater, etc.). Moreover neither of these exploit the knowledge contained in previous counselling sessions stored as cases. In fact, the application of CBR to Travel and Tourism is still in a very early stage. CABATA, which was designed as a similarity-based retrieval system, was the first attempt to apply CBR to this application domain [13].

1.3   The Proposed Approach

The ITR (Intelligent Travel Recommender) system here described incorporates a human choice model extracted from the literature specialized in the analysis of the traveller's behaviour [11, 10], and extends the quoted recommender systems. ITR supports the selection of travel products (e.g., a hotel or a visit to a museum or a climbing school), and building a *travel bag*, that is a coherent (from the user point of view) bundling of products. We call it *bag* to emphasize that we are not dealing with temporal planning or scheduling of actions in the plan. The system exploits a case base of travel bags built by a community of users as well as catalogues provided by a Destination Management Organization (APT Trentino). The proposed case structure is hierarchical [18, 19] and implemented as an XML view over a relational data base [16]. A case is decomposed into: travel wishes , travel bag, user, and reward (case outcome). Furthermore a travel bag is modelled as a tree of typed *items* (locations, accommodations, attractions, activities).

ITR integrates case-based reasoning with interactive query management, also called cooperative database research [8]. The goal is to create a system that attempts to understand the gist of a user query, to suggest or answer related questions, to infer an answer from data that is accessible, or to give an approximate response. In the CBR community this vision is shared by "conversational" approaches [1, 9]. ITR tries first to cope with user needs satisfying the logical conditions expressed in the user's query and, if this is not possible, it suggests query changes (relaxation and tightening) that will produce acceptable results. In ITR failures to satisfy all user needs are not solved relying on similarity based retrieval, as is usual in CBR. Instead, (case) similarity is exploited first, to retrieve relevant old recommendation sessions, and second to rank the items in the result set of the user's given logical query. The rank is given by computing the similarity of the items in the result set with those contained in past similar sessions. Thus the "collaborative" principle of transferring recommendations between members of a community is used, but the "correlation" between users is performed at the level of the session, hence overcoming classical limitations of Automated Collaborative Filtering (ACF) that requires user identification and a considerable amount of sessions data for each single user, before delivering effective recommendations [17]. Moreover, ITR integrates information (up to date) contained in web catalogues and "good" examples of bundling of travel products contained in previous travels built by a community of users. In this respect ITR follows an approach similar to that exploited in SPIRE [4], a system that integrates CBR with an information retrieval component.

The rest of the paper is organized as follows. Section 2 describes a typical interaction with the system and lists the major abstract functions implemented. Sections 3, 4, and 5 present the hierarchical case model, the logical components of the interactive query management component and the similarity measures exploited in the ranking method. Section 6 describes the software architecture and finally Section 7 summarize the results and points out shortcomings and limitations of the current approach.

2   Interaction with the System

This section describes a typical user/system interaction and shows some of the system functions. Let's assume that a traveller wants to have a summer vacation with his family in Trentino. He is looking for a specific location where to stay for two weeks, and for a hotel. The main page, as depicted in Figure 1, allows the traveller to input his general travel wishes and constraints. The user makes explicit the most important features that characterize the desired travel. A travel bundles tourist products (see Section 3 for the formal definition), each of them characterized by a rich set of features. Furthermore, there are additional features, more abstract and involving the whole travel that should be considered (e.g., how much experienced is the traveller in the place he is going to visit is an important variable). Among these the most important features are asked in the main page shown in Figure 1. In this scenario, the traveller specifies that he will travel with

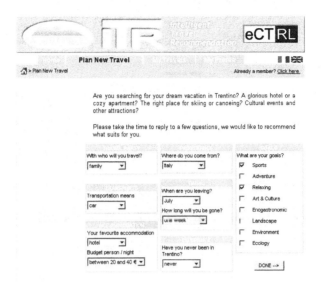

Fig. 1. ITR's main page.

his family, that his budget is between 20 and 40 euros and he will use his car; he wants to stay in a hotel for 1 week in July, and he comes from Italy. He and his wife have never been in Trentino, and they wish to relax and to practice some sport activities.

Then the system allows the user to search and add locations and activities to the tourist's travel bag, a cart where the user stores the items that he considers interesting and he wants to consume or visit during his vacation. He can bundle his travel by seeking one or more accommodations, locations, attractions or activities. Our traveller starts looking for a specific location. The system presents a page to the user where, on the left, he can specify some logical constraints on the location. He is looking for a place where he can practice paragliding. The system searches in the locations catalogue, and suggests the three locations that match the best (Figure 2). In this scenario, Cavalese is the best choice. The system shows the rank assigned to each item, and provides an explanation (by clicking on the question mark icon). The explanation arguments is that the suggested item is similar to another item contained in other travels, built by the traveller himself or by other users, having similar wishes and constraints. Assuming that our traveller is convinced that Cavalese is the most suitable location for him, he then adds it to his personal travel bag.

Then the traveller looks for an accommodation in Cavalese. He would like a three star hotel, whose cost is between 20 and 40 euros and that accepts pets. Figure 3 shows a situation in which no accommodation that meets all the constraints is found. Hence, the system helps the user by suggesting how he can modify the query to get some results. If the user accepts to pay more

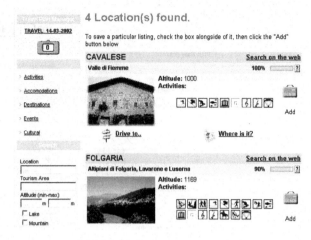

Fig. 2. Recommended locations (example).

Fig. 3. Query relaxation suggestions (example).

then 40 euros he gets 8 results, and if he accepts a hotel whose category is different from 3 stars, he gets 5 hotels, etc. The traveller accepts to relax the category constraint. The system proposes a list of 5 hotels, ranked according to his wishes and constraints, which meet all the constraints but the category. The user browses the list of the suggested hotels, and adds one of them to his personal travel bag. With a similar interaction, the user can further add attractions or sports activities.

3   Case Model

The Case Base (space) is made of four components: travel wishes and constraints TWC, travel bag TB, user U and reward R.

$$CB = TWC \times TB \times U \times R$$

In the following we shall describe each single component in detail. A case is built during a human/machine interaction, therefore is always a structured snapshot of the interaction at a specific time. So for instance we shall talk about partial cases to refer to those that are still under development, and simply to cases as those "completed" and stored in the case base.[1]

Figure 4 depicts an example case. Complex case components are decomposed into more elementary components in a tree-structured representation. Terminal nodes of the tree are modelled as feature vectors (items). We detail these four components in the following paragraphs.

TWC is the data structure that defines the general wishes and constraints for the given case. These are expressed as a partially filled vector of features. The main features are: Travel Party (alone, with partners, a few friends, etc.); Budget (a constraint on the day allowance); Transportation mean (car, camper, bike, etc.); Accommodation Type (hotel, apartment, etc.); Departure (country of residence); Time (the period and the duration of the travel); Experience (the level of knowledge of the selected location); Goals (a list of Boolean features that must capture the most important interests of the user, e.g., sport, adventure, relax, art, culture, etc.).

In Figure 4 the example illustrates a set of travel wishes and constraints where: travel party is "family", budget is "20-40", accommodation is "hotel", and period is "July".

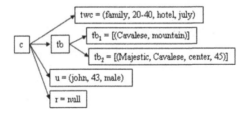

Fig. 4. An example of an ITR case.

TB is a complex data structure that collects together the items (subcomponents) selected during a case session.

$$TB = Seq(X^1) \times \cdots \times Seq(X^4) \tag{1}$$

---

[1] Actually, there is no structural definition of complete case, and this can only be considered as a dynamic role played by a case in a real human/machine interaction.

The spaces $X^1, \ldots, X^4$ are vector spaces. $X^1, \ldots, X^4$ are item spaces: locations, accommodations, activities and attractions respectively. $Seq(X^i)$ denotes a sequence of elements in X^i, and this is used to model the fact that a travel bag may contain more that one item of a certain type. Travel bags are therefore elements of this type:

$$tb = ([x^{1,1}, \ldots x^{1,j_1}], \ldots, [x^{4,1}, \ldots x^{4,j_4}])$$

where each $x^{i,j}$ is a feature vector belonging to the space X^i. In Figure 4 we have:

$$tb = ([(Cavalese, mountain)], [(Majestic, Cavalese, center, 45)], \emptyset, \emptyset)$$

This travel bag contains only two items, one of type "location" and another of type accommodation. The first is $tb_1 = [(Cavalese, mountain)]$, where, for sake of simplicity, only two features are shown: location name is "Cavalese" and location type is "mountain". The second is $tb_2 = [(Majestic, Cavalese, center, 45)]$, where four features are shown: name is "Majestic", location-name is "Cavalese", near-by is "center" and cost is "45".

The user is modelled as a vector of features in similar way as an item space $U = \prod_{i=1}^{n} U_i$. Figure 4 shows an example where the user is identified with three features: name, age, and sex.[2]

The rank of a case is the evaluation of the case done by the user that created the case. The rank is structured according to the travel bag, i.e., there is a rank for the whole bag and ranks for the items in the bag. A rank is a finite subset of the integers.

$$R = RB \times Seq(RX^1) \times \cdots \times Seq(RX^4)$$

where $RB = RX^1 = \cdots = RX^4 = \{1, 2, 3, 4, 5\}$. For instance, commenting the example in Figure 4, if the user "John" had evaluated the case c we could have $r = (4, [5], \emptyset, \emptyset, \emptyset)$. This means that the whole case is evaluated 4, and the location Cavalese is evaluated 5. In this example, the user has not assigned any evaluation to the hotel. When an item is not explicitly evaluated, the average value 3 is assumed as default value. Hence, if a component was not rated by the user it gets the rate 3 because we assume that the inclusion in the bag represents a rather positive evaluation. Values below 3 are considered negative, so the user can provide both positive and negative feedback.

We conclude this section by commenting again the structure of a case and the containers of the data. Figure 5 depicts the relationships between the case base and the catalogues of items. The case base contains the structured cases, which are represented as hierarchical data structures. Some case terminal nodes, such as those that are items included in the travel bag, are in fact pointers to objects contained in catalogues of locations, accommodations, activities and attractions. Both case base and catalogues are exploited in our CBR approach. The case base provides information about good bundling of products and is therefore used for

---

[2] The full list contains additional features, like country or profession, but in fact this data is never used by ITR for personalization purposes.

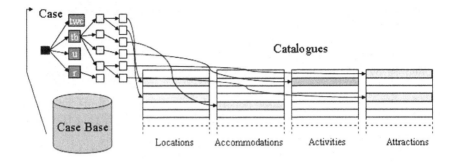

Fig. 5. Case base and catalogues.

learning this knowledge and for ranking items selected in the catalogues. The catalogues are exploited for obtaining up-to-date information about currently available products.

4 Interactive Query Management

In this Section we describe the basic data structures and the functions designed to interactively search in a catalogue of items. Figure 6 shows the main logical architecture designed to help the user to satisfy his information goal. The client application (typically the Graphical User Interface) interacts with the Intelligent Mediator (IM) that, if it is possible, will retrieve a reasonable set of items that meet the query, or else suggest to the client some refinements to the query. The Intelligent Mediator in turn interacts with a data processing engine to fetch data (result set)[16]. More details on the interactive query management functions supported by the IM and the exact specification of the algorithms, which are here only sketched, can be found in [15].

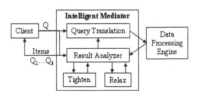

Fig. 6. Intelligent Mediator Architecture.

The information needs are encoded as a query, say Q, and the reply of IM to Q could take the form of a set of items extracted from the product catalogues or a new set of queries. The reply is a set of items when the Intelligent Mediator decides there is a satisfactory result for the query in the product catalogues, otherwise, when a "failure" situation occurs, it suggests a new set of alternative queries that, by tightening or relaxing some of the query constraints, might produce satisfactory results.

As we said above, a travel bag is made up of travel items belonging to four different types (location, accommodation, activity and attractions). We shall denote by X an item space (of a particular type), and this is a vector space $X = \prod_{i=1}^{n} X_i$, i.e., an item of type X is represented as a $n-$dimensional vector of features. We consider three general types of features: finite integer, real and symbolic. Given an item space $X = \prod_{i=1}^{n} X_i$, we shall say that the set $CX \subset X$ is a *catalogue* of type X.

The query language, which is used to search in the catalogues of items, is quite simple, but this makes possible the interactive query management described later in this section. A query Q over a catalogue $CX \subset X$ is obtained by the conjunction of simple constraints, where each constraint involves only one feature. More formally, $Q = C_1 \wedge \cdots \wedge C_m$, where $m \leq n$, constraint C_k involves feature x_{i_k}, and:

$$C_k = \begin{cases} x_{i_k} = v_k & \text{if } x_{i_k} \text{ is symbolic} \\ l_k \leq x_{i_k} \leq u_k & \text{if } x_{i_k} \text{ is finite integer or real} \end{cases} \qquad (2)$$

where v_k is a possible value for the $k-$th feature, i.e., $v_k \in X_k$ and $l_k \leq u_k$ are the boundaries for the range constraint on the feature, and $l_k, u_k \in X_k$.

Query relaxation changes a query definition in such a way that the number of items returned by the query is increased. A query is typically relaxed when the result set retrieved from the item space X is void, or when the user is interested in having more examples to evaluate. The relaxation process implemented by the relax component of the Intelligent Mediator is shown in Figure 7.

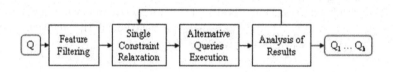

Fig. 7. ITR's query relaxation process.

The query relaxation component takes in input a query $Q = C_1 \wedge \cdots \wedge C_m$ and builds a new set of relaxed queries $Q_1, \ldots Q_k$, such that each Q_i relaxes only one constraint of the original query. In the following discussion we shall use the query $Q = ((x_1 = ski) \wedge (x_2 = Cavalese) \wedge (x_3 = \top) \wedge (x_4 \leq 100))$, where we are searching in a database of sport activities, and the features are *SportType, Location, School*, and *Cost* (and $\top$ means "true"). The relaxation is computed in the following way:

1. **Features Filtering.** This module identifies those features' constraints that cannot be relaxed without changing the information goal of the user. Referring to the example above, the user might well be interested in some school

a bit more expensive or maybe not in Cavalese but he is interested in skiing, not in fishing.

2. **Single Constraint Relaxation.** Whenever the relaxable constraints have been identified, for each of them a "relaxed" version (C_i') must be identified. Two different approaches are exploited according to the feature type: symbolic features constraint are relaxed by simply discarding it; in numeric feature constraints the range of allowed values is increased by a percentage that is feature dependent. After this stage the relaxed constraints in Q are: $x_2 = ALL$, $x_3 = ALL$ and $x_4 \leq 110$.

3. **Alternative Queries Execution.** At this stage, for each "relaxable" constraint a new relaxed version of the original user's query is built, with only that constraint relaxed. In our example we have three new queries: $Q_1 = ((x_1 = ski) \wedge (x_2 = ALL) \wedge (x_3 = \top) \wedge (x_4 \leq 100))$, $Q_2 = ((x_1 = ski) \wedge (x_2 = Cavalese) \wedge (x_3 = ALL) \wedge (x_4 \leq 100))$, and $Q_3 = ((x_1 = ski) \wedge (x_2 = Cavalese) \wedge (x_3 = \top) \wedge (x_4 \leq 110))$. These relaxed queries are executed and the number of items retrieved by each single query is determined (counts).

4. **Analysis of Results.** When the results (counts) are obtained they must be analyzed. The goal is to understand if the relaxed queries have produced an improvement, i.e., if the new set of results (for each query) is not still void or become too large. If this last situation occurs a tightening is required.

Having described the query relaxation issues, we now illustrate the query tightening process accomplished by the tighten component of the Intelligent Mediator (Figure 6). When a query returns too many items, i.e., above a certain threshold α (in ITR this has been set to 20), the system finds some ways to improve the user's query, i.e., it suggests additional features to constrain.

The query tightening process exploits two feature ranking methods to select the features to be suggested to the user for tightening the result set. The choice of one method relies on a second threshold parameter β: *if the result set cardinality of the input query Q is above β then the* **Off-Line-Entropy** *method is used, otherwise the* **On-Line-Entropy-Mutual-Info** *is applied.* We describe in more detail the two methods below:

Off-Line-Entropy : this method uses the entropy of a feature, computed using the distribution of feature values found in the catalogue:

$$H_S(X_i) = - \sum_{v \in X_i} p(v) \log[p(v)], \tag{3}$$

where X_i is a feature space and $p(v)$ is an estimate of the probability to find the value v for the i-th feature in the sample S (the full catalogue). The top three features, not already constrained in Q, are then suggested to the user as additional features to be constrained. Feature entropy provides a rough estimate of feature selectivity, and requires no computational cost as these values are precomputed. This has proved to be satisfactory when there is no need to be precise since the current result set is very large and selective features are easy to find.

On-Line-Entropy-Mutual-Info : this method is much more expensive, with respect to the computational cost, and therefore is applied only when the size of the results set is smaller (less than the quoted β threshold). If we denote with S_Q the result set of Q, then for each feature X_i, not already selected in Q, the score is computed as:

$$\frac{H_{S_Q}(X_i)}{1 + max\{H_{S_Q}(X_i; X_j)|X_j \in SF\}} \tag{4}$$

where SF is the set of already selected features (those constrained in Q), and the mutual information between X_i and X_j is defined as:

$$H_{S_Q}(X_i; X_j) = H_{S_Q}(X_i) + \sum_{v \in X_i,\, u \in X_j} p(v, u) \log[p(v|u)] \tag{5}$$

This score method tends to prefer features that have a large entropy and are not correlated with those already constrained in Q. In a similar manner as above, the top three features are proposed to the user for constraining the original query. (the reader is referred to [15] for a detailed description of the feature selection algorithm).

5   Item Ranking

We now describe how similarity based scoring is performed when items retrieved from the catalogues are recommended. Basically, in this situation we have two subsets of items $X \supset S, R$. $S = \{x_1, \ldots, x_m\}$ is the set of items that must be ranked and R is the (reference) set of items that are used to assign scores to elements in S. S is the result of a standard query that is eventually defined incrementally by the user using the support of the intelligent mediator (as described above). The reference set is made of those items, of the same type as those in S, extracted from a references set of case, i.e., cases that are similar to the current recommendation session. For this reason, our ranking approach can be defined as item-based, but in contrast with other approaches in this category [17], we do not compare the items to be recommended with those previously selected by the same user for which the recommendation is to be built. We use instead a dynamic set of items contained in the travel bags of different users whose specific context data (travel wishes and constraints as defined in Section 3) are similar to the current situation.

The ranking process is illustrated in Figure 8. In this example Q is a query on the location items catalogue that contains the user-specific wishes. Let us assume that the locations in $S = \{loc_1, loc_2, loc_3\}$ are retrieved. Then using the current definition of the case the top ten cases are retrieved from the case base. In this stage the current definition of travel wishes/constraints are used to retrieve the 10 most similar cases (reference cases set).

Finally the last step is ranking these locations according to the similarity to the locations R contained in this set of retrieved cases. This is performed with a

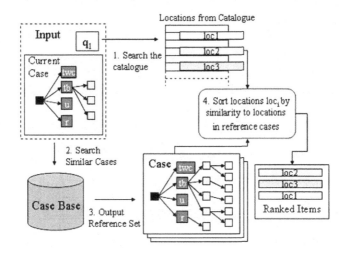

Fig. 8. Sorting items extracted from a catalogue.

call to similarity-based sorting function that ranks best the locations in S that are closest to the location in R (distance between a point and a set). The metric used both for case and item similarity is the Euclidean Overlap Metric (HEOM) [21]:

$$heom(x, y) = \frac{1}{\sqrt{\sum_{i=1}^{n} w_i}} \sqrt{\sum_{i=1}^{n} w_i d_i(x_i, y_i)^2} \qquad (6)$$

where:

$$d_i(x_i, y_i) = \begin{cases} 1 & \text{if } x_i \text{ or } y_i \text{ are unknown} \\ overlap(x_i, y_i) & \text{if the } i-\text{th feature is symbolic} \\ \frac{|x_i - y_i|}{range_i} & \text{if the } i-\text{th feature is finite integer or real} \end{cases}$$

where $range_i$ is the difference between the maximum and minimum value of a numeric feature, and $overlap(x_i, y_i) = 1$ if $x_i \neq y_i$ and 0 otherwise. The weights $0 \leq w_i \leq 1$, $i = 1, \ldots, n$ are assigned dynamically according to the query definition Q: the features used in Q receive a larger weight (the other features are weighted proportionally to the frequency of usage in the reference set of cases). When this metric is used for case similarity only the travel wishes are considered (see Section 3).

At this stage the user can add one of those recommended items to the travel bag, or change some query constraints and re-run the ranking process. Items are added by the user and is up to him to maintain any sort of logical consistency within the bundling. Therefore, one user may add two locations that for a second user are too far or a selection of activities that seems unreasonable to another. Obviously, this is a limitation of the proposed approach, but since no simple solution is applicable, we decided to acquire a set of real cases before designing a viable solution to this problem.

6 Software Architecture and Implementation

This section describes the software structure of the implementation that is based on the Java 2 Enterprise Edition Architecture [12], and it uses a thin client approach (html only). Figure 9 shows the main software components.

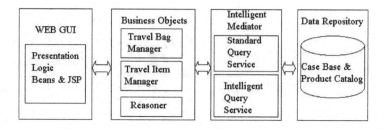

Fig. 9. ITR software architecture.

Web GUI. This manages the user interaction by dynamically constructing the user interface and interpreting the user commands. This layer is built upon the Struts framework, an open source jakarta project that helps the adoption of the MVC pattern (http://jakarta.apache.org/struts/). The View role is played by a set of JSP pages, while the Model and the Controller roles are performed by a set of Java beans that manage the data to be displayed, and execute the commands issued by the user.

Business Objects. It includes the Travel Bag Manager, whose purpose is to store, retrieve and update travel bags; the Travel Item Manager, which allows to handle the tourist items to be shown; the Reasoner, which manages the intelligent query management and ranking process.

Intelligent Mediator. It includes the Standard Query Service and the Intelligent Query Service. The first one provides basic query functions for retrieving and storing data from/to the repository as XML documents. The second one extends the Standard Query Service to support different ways of querying and ranking documents. It implements the ranking method described in Section 5, and the query management described in Section 4.

The Mediator component exploits a simple mediator architecture [20, 7] (more detail in [16]). Its purpose is to access the information stored in the repository (a relational database system) and to produce XML documents. The data integration needs have been solved in two steps. First, we have defined a set of SQL views over the complete data model (approximately 100 oracle tables). Second, for each view the corresponding XML schema has been defined. The XML documents are produced according to these schemas. A custom query language has been developed to query the XML views.

7   Conclusions and Future Work

In this paper we have proposed an approach for improving standard eCommerce applications for travel products selection and booking by leveraging more realistic and therefore complex human choice models. This is the topic of two research projects[3] being conducted at eCTRLs.

Among the major advantages of our approach we could mention:

- *The system can bootstrap easily as it is based on both a case base and a collection of available catalogues.* The recommendation is not built uniquely on reuse of past cases. A travel bag can be built "manually" by inserting services/products (items) searched in catalogues.
- *User need not be registered.* The similarity of the user's session specific goals and constraints with those contained in previous cases is used to determine the set of past experiences that must influence the recommendation.
- *Man/machine interaction supports both alternative expansion and reduction of the results.* Navigation in the information space is supported by a tool that suggests additional constraints or those that should be discarded in order to maintain the number of recommendations around a reasonable size.
- *The system does not assume that products and users shares common features.* This is the idea at the base of content-based filtering: the products are selected when their features match with those in the user's description. Recommenders are typically built in this way. Conversely, our user profile is very limited, and therefore can be easily acquired.

The ITR system is still in an early validation stage. The prototype has been built but no serious validation has been conducted. A user group (experts in the domain) has been involved in the requirements analysis stage and their input has influenced the cyclical revision of the user interface. We plan to conduct an extensive evaluation with a larger user group and to acquire a set of cases that will extend the initial case base built artificially using the travel offers of the Trentino local tourist board. Further work will address the weighting schemas and the tuning of the case similarity metric.

References

1. D. Aha and L. Breslow. Refining conversational case libraries. In *Case-Based Reasoning Research and Development, Proceedings of the 2nd International Conference on Case-Based Reasoning (ICCBR-97)*, pages 267–278. Springer, 1997.
2. P. K. Ankomah, J. L. Crompton, and D. Baker. Influence of cognitive distance in vacation choice. *Annals of Tourism Research*, 23(1):138–150, 1996.
3. R. Burke. Knowledge-based recommender systems. In J. E. Daily, A. Kent, and H. Lancour, editors, *Encyclopedia of Library and Information Science*, volume 69. Marcel Dekker, 2000.

---

[3] This work has been partially funded by CARITRO foundation (under contract "eCommerce e Turismo") and by the European Union's Fifth RTD Framework Programme (under contract DIETORECS IST-2000-29474).

4. J. J. Daniels and E. L. Rissland. What you saw is what you want: Using cases to seed information retrieval. In *ICCBR*, pages 325–336, 1997.
5. J. Delgado and R. Davidson. Knowledge bases and user profiling in travel and hospitality recommender systems. In *Proceedings of the ENTER 2002 Conference*, pages 1–16, Innsbruck, Austria, January 22-25 2002. Springer Verlag.
6. D. R. Fesenmaier and J. Jeng. Assessing structure in the pleasure trip planning process. *Tourism Analysis*, 5:13–17, 2000.
7. D. Florescu, A. Levy, and A. Mendelzon. Database techniques for the world-wide web:a survey. *SIGMOD Record*, 27(3):59–74, 1998.
8. T. Gaasterland, P. Godfrey, and J. Minker. An overview of cooperative answering. *Journal of Intelligent Information Systems*, 1(2):123–157, 1992.
9. M. H. Göker and C. A. Thomson. Personalized conversational case-based recommendation. In *Advances in case-based reasoning: 5th European workshop, EWCBR-2000, Trento, Italy, September 6–9, 2000: proceedings*, pages 99–111. Springer, 2000.
10. K. Grabler and A. Zins. Vacation trip decision styles as basis for an automated recommendation system: Lessons from observational studies. In *Proceedings of the ENTER 2002 Conference*, Innsbruck, Austria, January 22-25 2002. Springer Verlag.
11. Y.-H. Hwang, U. Gretzel, and D. R. Fesenmaier. Behavioral foundations for human-centric travel decision-aid systems. In *Proceedings of the ENTER 2002 Conference*, Innsbruck, Austria, January 22-25 2002. Springer Verlag.
12. N. Kassem and the Enterprise Team. *Designing Enterprise Applications with the JavaTM 2 Platform, Enterprise Edition*. Addison-Wesley, 2000.
13. M. Lenz. Imtas - intelligent multimedia travel agent system. In *Information and Communication Technologies in Tourism (Proceedings of ENTER-96)*, pages 11–17. Springer, 1996.
14. L. Moutinho. Consumer behavior in tourism. *European Journal of Marketing*, 21:2–44, 1987.
15. F. Ricci, N. Mirzadeh, and A. Venturini. Intelligent query managment in a mediator architecture. In *IEEE International Symposium "Intelligent Systems'*, Sunny Day, Bulgaria, September 10-12 2002.
16. F. Ricci, N. Mirzadeh, A. Venturini, and H. Werthner. Case-based reasoning and legacy data reuse for web-based recommendation architectures. In *Proceedings of the Third International Conference on Information Integration and Web-based Applications & Services*, pages 229–241, Linz, Austria, September 10-12 2001.
17. B. Sarwar, G. Karypis, J. Konstan, and J. Riedl. Item-based collaborative filtering recommendation algorithms. In *Proceedings of WWW10 Conference*, pages 285–295, Hong Kong, May 1-5 2001. ACM.
18. B. Smyth and M. T. Keane. Design a la deja vu: Reducing the adaptation overhead. In *Case-Based Reasoning: Experiences, Lessons, and Future Directions*. AAAI Press/MIT Press, 1996.
19. A. Stahl and R. Bergman. Applying recursive cbr for the customization of structured products in an electronic shop. In *Advances in case-based reasoning: 5th European workshop, EWCBR-2000, Trento, Italy, September 6–9, 2000: proceedings*, pages 297–308. Springer, 2000.
20. G. Wiederhold. Mediators in the architecture of future information systems. *IEEE Computer*, 25(3):38–49, 1992.
21. D. R. Wilson and T. R. Martinez. Improved heterogeneous distance functions. *Journal of Artificial Intelligence Research*, 11:1–34, 1997.

Supporting Electronic Design Reuse by Integrating Quality-Criteria into CBR-Based IP Selection

Martin Schaaf[1], Rainer Maximini[2], Ralph Bergmann[2],
Carsten Tautz[3], and Ralph Traphöner[3]

[1] University of Kaiserslautern, PO Box 3049, D-67653 Kaiserslautern, Germany
schaaf@informatik.uni-kl.de
[2] University of Hildesheim, PO Box 101363, D-31113 Hildesheim, Germany
{r_maximi, bergmann}@dwm.uni-hildesheim.de
[3] empolis knowledge management GmbH, Europaallee 10, 67657 Kaiserslautern, Germany
{Carsten.Tautz, Ralph.Traphoener}@empolis.com

Abstract. The growing complexity of today's electronic designs requires reusing existing design components, called Intellectual Properties (IPs). Experience management approaches can be used to support design reuse, particularly the process of selecting reusable IPs. For the IP selection, quality criteria concerning the IP code and the documentation must be considered in addition to functional requirements of the IP. We analyse IP quality criteria in detail and show different concepts for their integration into the retrieval process.

1 Introduction

The design of electronic circuits is a discipline where two contrasting tendencies can be observed: On the one hand, modern circuit designs get more and more complex and difficult to handle by electronic engineers. On the other hand, global competition requires a continuous reduction of development times. At the same time, the correctness and reliability of the designs should, of course, not suffer from shorter development cycles.

These problems have become so dominant that they cannot be met anymore without extensive utilization of *design reuse*. It is getting vitally important for an electronic engineer to reuse old designs (or parts of them) and not to redesign a new application entirely from scratch. Unfortunately, experiences from the past have shown that the existence and accessibility of reusable designs does not encourage engineers to reuse it. First, an IP must be recognized as candidate for reuse and, second, it must be successfully transferred into the development environment of the designer. Therefore, reusing designs from the past requires engineers having enough experience and knowledge about existing designs.

The idea of design reuse is not new, but until recently, reusable components in electronic designs were of limited complexity and understandable by application designers. To reflect this growing complexity, the term *intellectual property (IP)* [6] has been assigned to those designs and today the term *reuse* means more than just plugging a component into a new environment. Due to this overall increased complexity of IP-based design, there is now a demand for knowledge management approaches that support electronic design processes. One main goal of such an approach is to pro-

S. Craw and A. Preece (Eds.): ECCBR 2002, LNAI 2416, pp. 628–641.

vide user assistance in the question if an IP is suitable for a new design situation. This is one objective of the current project "IPQ: IP Qualification for Efficient Design Reuse" [1] funded by the German Ministry of Education and Research (BMBF) and the related European Medea project "ToolIP: Tools and Methods for IP"[2].

This paper starts with a brief overview of the basic knowledge management considerations for electronic design reuse with IPs. Then, it focuses on one specific objective, which is to consider quality criteria of IP in addition to its functional specification during the IP selection process. Starting from existing approaches to measure IP quality in general, we propose and analyze different ways for integrating IP quality assessment approaches directly into an IP retrieval process that is realized using a case-based reasoning retrieval mechanism.

2 Knowledge Management for IP Selection

An IP is a design object whose major value comes from the skill of its producer [6], and a redesign would consume significant time. IP is just a new name for what formerly was called macro/mega cells, cores, or building blocks. The difference is the growing complexity of such cells (10k to 100k gates). Today, specialized IP vendors emerge starting to offer their IPs also in the Internet. In the near future, the IP market is expected to grow significantly. Therefore, the knowledge-based support for the exchange of qualified IP is needed, including general constraints and guidelines, as well as executable specifications for intra- and inter-company exchange. Furthermore, qualified IP must be made accessible via methodologies and tools, which will focus on the efficient implementation of all relevant IP management functions including *creation, storage, intelligent analysis* and *retrieval, validation* and *simulation*. A related IP tailored design flow has to consider methods and tools for supporting IP checks done by IP vendors (called IP compliance checks), or customizable to the IP user needs (called IP entry check). The above-mentioned activities for IP management stem from the particular view of the electronics design area. However, from a knowledge management perspective, it becomes obvious that these are just particular instances of the typical processes [12] proposed in the knowledge management literature. Moreover, the knowledge about IPs is of very specific nature since each knowledge item describes a particular design. Hence, from a knowledge management point of view, we deal with *experience management* [1] that can be implemented in part by CBR technology as we have shown in the previous project READee [5] [7] [8].

2.1 The IP Selection Process

Fig. 1 provides a brief overview of the IP selection process, which is part of an overall IP tailored design flow. It is assumed that IPs will be stored in an IP library (or sev-

[1] IPQ Project (12/2000 – 11/2003). Partners: AMD, Fraunhofer Institut für Integrierte Schaltungen, FZI Karlsruhe, Infineon Technologies, Siemens, Sciworx, Empolis, Thomson Multi Media, TU Chemnitz, Universität Hildesheim, Universität Kaiserslautern, and Universität Paderborn. See http://www.ip-qualifikation.de

[2] See http://toolip.fzi.de for partners and further information.

eral libraries in the future). During the *retrieval process*, an IP user specifies her/his requirements on the IP s/he is looking for and searches with this specification in the IP library for a reusable IP. The question whether an IP is reusable depends on many different technical criteria, such as functionality of the IP, the technological realization on the chip, the design tool used for the design, and, very important, the quality of the IP, the quality of its design, and the quality of the documentation.

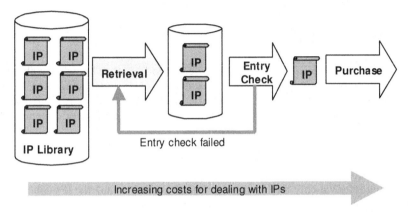

Fig. 1. IP Selection Process

Since it is very hard to decide whether an IP is reusable, it cannot be expected that this can already be determined during the retrieval. The selection made during retrieval is therefore not based on the IP (the chip design code) itself but on a description of the IP, which we call *characterization*. Hence, the purpose of the retrieval task is therefore to make a pre-selection of a very small subset of IP candidates. The final decision on whether an IP is reused is taken in the *entry check process*. The entry check requires getting at least partial access to the chip design code of the IP itself and contains various compatibility checks and simulations of the IP. Consequently, the entry check is very cost intensive regarding the required human and monetary resources. If an IP has passed the entry check, the IP user purchases it from the IP provider and only then the full IP code is disclosed to the IP user. If all selected IPs fail the entry check, the retrieval must be repeated or the design problem must be solved without reuse.

2.2 IP Retrieval

Given this design flow, it becomes obvious that the retrieval quality is of very high importance. If IPs are proposed that turn out not to be reusable, the large effort involved in the entry check is wasted. If reusable IPs are available but are not proposed, the opportunity for improving efficiency, quality, and time-to-market due to the reuse of this IP is lost. Hence, in principle, the IP retrieval should (to some degree) anticipate the subsequent entry check. Of course, it cannot replace it due to the large amount of (manual) effort involved, but it can approximate it as good as possible. A database of reusable designs requires a search facility that possesses more intelligence and knowledge than currently available systems can provide in order to achieve a high retrieval quality. In the near future, electronic applications will grow so complex that their designers cannot be expected to be specialists in the reusable components they are going to employ for their project. Hence, retrieval assistants capable of providing real selection support are highly recommended. It is one major goal of the experience management approach to reduce the amount of IPs that will be rejected during the entrance-check and, therefore, to decrease the overall costs for the IP selection process.

2.3 IP Representation

To achieve high precision retrieval it is essential to formalize knowledge about the IP itself as much as reasonable in order to establish a clear semantic that can be utilized by CBR technology. Therefore, we proposed from a retrieval point of view to divide the IP representation into two components, which is common for experience management [1]:

1. The *IP characterization* that describes the IP in a way that allows to assess its quality and reusability in a particular situation.
2. The *IP content* that contains all deliverables of the design itself.

During retrieval only the IP characterization is used to rank the IPs contained in an IP library, not the IP content itself. Parts of the content are first used in the entry-check. The IP characterization describes all facts about the IP that are relevant for deciding whether the IP can be reused in a certain situation. The degree of detail used to characterize an IP determines how accurate its quality and reusability can be assessed, i.e., how accurate the retrieval is. The structure of the IP characterization knowledge (taxonomic and categorical knowledge) leads to an object-oriented (OO) representation [4] of the characterization. Such representations are particularly suitable for complex domains where characterizations with different structures occur, which is important when representing IPs.

The attributes of the IP characterization can be structured according to Table 1. The IP characterization is basically divided into two main parts:

- IP Application Attributes define all attributes that are important to decide about the applicability of an IP in a given design situation, and
- IP Quality Criteria characterize the IP and according to its quality.

Table 1. IP Characterization

Format	Category 0	Category 1	Category 2 / Taxonomy
IP Format	IP Content		
	IP Characterization	IP Application Attributes	Functional Class (Taxonomy)
			Target Market Segments
			Provider Claims
			Integration Requirements
			Reference Environment
			IP Instance Attributes
			Physical Description
		IP Quality Criteria	Hard IP Criteria
			Soft IP criteria

This structure is compliant to the Virtual Component Attributes (VCA) Standard [11] and the OpenMORE Assessment Program for Hard/Soft IP [9], which are documents released by an organization that aims at standardizing all IP related data. The advantage of dividing the IP characterization into these two main parts is that retrieval problems can be decomposed into two sub-problems by focusing either only on the application attributes or on the quality attributes. This allows us to decompose the selection process and the related similarity modeling into the two related parts, too, i.e., we will have a similarity measure for the application attributes and a second similarity measure for the quality attributes.

3   Quality-Based IP-Retrieval Using the OpenMORE Approach

In the following, we will focus on the essentials of IP quality criteria. In order to give a first impression, we present an existing IP quality assessment approach, namely the *OpenMORE Assessment Program* [9], along with an evaluation from the CBR perspective.

3.1   General Characteristics of IP Quality Criteria

Beside the fact that the overall meaning of IP quality in general is very difficult to fix, it is furthermore essential to establish at least a commonly accepted standard in order to get comparable results. Although a lot of different approaches to IP quality assessment are currently discussed, there seems to exist a consensus at least to the following high-level aspects (for a comprehensive overview of IP quality approaches see [10]):

- **Maintainability**: a measure for the effort needed to modify or correct a design. Maintainability is related with readability, design organization and design tool capabilities.
- **Readability**: reflects the ease of a description to be read and understood by a person. It is comprises aspects like complexity, name conventions, nesting level or profusion of comments.
- **Complexity**: reflects how difficult it is, or has been, to develop or interpret description. This aspect comprises aspects like code size, nesting level, degree of modularization, etc.
- **Portability**: is a view of the ease of a design to be used in an environment different from that in which it was generated. It can be considered from different points of view, portability between tools, between target technologies, between users, between languages or applications, etc.
- **Reusability**: is an indicator of the ease of a design to be used as part of a bigger design, or to be adapted to a new application. It is related with aspects like portability, maintainability and degree of parameterization, or ease of integration into the design flow.
- **Simulation performance**: reflects the efficiency of the simulation process for a design. Code complexity, modularization degree, or number and type of data objects are factors that directly affect the simulation performance.
- **Compliance with respect to guidelines**: this feature reflects the degree with which certain rules and guidelines have been followed during the develop-

ment. These guidelines can affect, among others, name convention, design style, code complexity or any other feature of the design.

- **Reliability**: reflects the independence of the design from the target technology and guarantees the equivalence of behavior of the register-transfer-level simulations and the behavior of the final hardware.
- **Synthesis efficiency**: reflects the quality of the hardware obtained when the design is synthesized. It could be considered from different points of view, like design performance (in terms of area, power consumption or delays), reliability, etc.
- **Testability and verifiability**: testability is related with the ease to obtain a set of patterns for manufacturing test for a certain design. Verifiability reflects the ease to develop a good test bench to verify the design functionality.

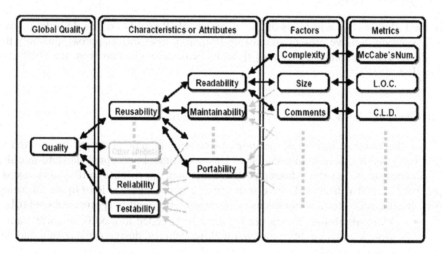

Fig. 2. Example decomposition of IP quality aspects into criteria (from [10])

Some of these aspects are originated in quality assessment approaches for software components, while others, like "Synthesis efficiency", "Reliability" or "Portability", are closely related to hardware and have no equivalence in this area. The analysis of these aspects requires the identification of a set of attributes that reflect them properly. These attributes can be subsequently decomposed into "finer" attributes (see Fig. 2) that are easier to measure or assess leading to a structured catalog of elementary questions for determining IP quality. Before we turn to such an IP quality assessment catalog, namely the OpenMORE Assessment Program [9], we fix some assumptions and observations about the representation of quality criteria. This will be done here limited to retrieval aspects:

1. To each quality criterion a data type can be assigned. The type defines the range of possible values for quality rating. The type of a particular criterion is strictly ordered, like score values. Here, order means that a higher value is always preferred over a lower value.
2. There exist neither dependencies between different quality criteria nor between application attributes and quality criteria. Hence, quality criteria can be considered

as independent variables. E.g. the delivery of test-bench files always results in higher quality no matter which kind of functionality the IP module supports.

3. Quality attributes can be structured into categories giving the user the possibility to specify preferences for a set of thematically connected criteria instead of individual criteria.
4. There exist quality criteria that are not applicable to all types of IPs. For example, depending on the description language VHDL or Verilog different coding guidelines may apply.

This leads to the following general definition of an IP quality criterion:

A quality criterion is an attribute associated with an IP containing a textual description of the quality item being measured and a result value taken from an associated ordered data type. The type is a range of natural numbers enhanced by two special values indicating that the criterion is not applicable to a given IP or it has not been assessed. Furthermore, each quality criterion can be associated with a category that allows aggregating thematically connected criteria. The categories can be structured within a hierarchy that will be named the IP quality classification.

3.2 Overview of the *OpenMORE Quality Assessment* Program

As indicated above, in the past large efforts have been already made to identify and classify relevant quality criteria with respect to reusability of IPs. The best-known and probably most complete catalog published is the OpenMORE Assessment Program [9], which will be introduced in this section. It identifies around 150 different quality criteria for soft IPs and 130 for hard IPs. Beside the catalog of quality criteria the OpenMORE Assessment Program also contains some guidelines to the assessment procedure in order to ensure comparability between IPs assessed by different organizations. Figure 3 shows a part of the OpenMORE catalog illustrating the classification of IP quality criteria. The IP quality criteria are grouped into the three major categories *Design* (50%), *Verification* (35%), and *Deliverable Guidelines* (15%) that are weighted differently. The other sub-categories are simply for structuring purposes.

RMM2 Section	Description	Type	Assessment	Unweighted Score	Max Score
I	**Macro Design Guidelines**			0	542
3	*System-Level Design Issues: Rules and Tools*			*0*	*88*
3.2	Design for Timing Closure: Logic Design Issues			0	34
3.2.2	Synchronous vs. Asynchronous Design Style			0	10
3.2.2.1	System is synchronous and register based with latches used only to implement small memories or FIFOs. FIFOs and memories designed so they are synchronous and edge triggered. Exceptions fully documented.	R		0	10
3.2.3	Clocking			0	14
3.2.3.1	Number of clock domains and clock frequencies are well documented. Required clock frequencies and associated phase lock loops (PLL) and external timing requirements (setup/hold and output timing) fully documented.	R		0	10
3.2.3.2	If two asynchronous clock domains interact, then they meet as a single module which is as small as possible. Use the smallest possible number of clock domains.	G		0	2
3.2.3.3	If a phase locked loop (PLL) is used for on-chip clock generation, then a means of disabling or bypassing the PLL is provided	G		0	2
3.2.4	Reset			0	10
3.2.4.1	The basic reset strategy for the chip is documented, especially 1) synchronous or asynchronous, 2) internal or external power-on reset, 3) more than one reset (hard vs. soft reset), 4) each macro individually resettable, for debug purposes	R		0	10
3.4	Design for Verification: Verification Strategy			0	22
3.4.1	The system level verification strategy must be developed and documented before macro selection or design begins.	R		0	10

Fig. 3. OpenMORE Assessment Program

Each quality criterion is either called a *design rule* (denoted by "R" in the type column) or a *design guideline* (denoted by "G" respectively). The only difference between the two is that in case of a rule possible scores are 0, 5, or 10, in case of a guidelines possible scores are 0, 1, or 2.

If a criterion is not applicable to an IP its score becomes 0 and the possible maximum score for the associated category is reduced.

3.3 The OpenMORE Assessment Approach from a CBR Retrieval Perspective

The objective of the OpenMORE Assessment Program is to calculate one single value for quality that allows a global ranking of different IP modules. This ranking is global because it is independent from individual requirements that an IP user might have. The assessed scores within each of the top-level categories (*Macro Design Guidelines, Macro Verification Guidelines, and Deliverable Guidelines*) are summed up considering the fixed weight values 0.5, 0.35, and 0.15 respectively.

From a CBR perspective this approach can be easily transformed into a simple similarity measure that is structured according the given categorization of the quality attributes. Of course, since the OpenMORE Assessment Program only supports a global quality value, the resulting similarity measure is somewhat artificial since the similarity does not depend at all on a query specifying a required quality. Furthermore, an OpenMORE induced similarity model would only consist of three categories, each one aggregating rules and guidelines. The overall relevance of a quality criterion is then as follows

$$\frac{w_{category}}{10 \cdot n_{rules} + 2 \cdot n_{guidelines}} \cdot \frac{assessedScore}{MaxScore}$$

The value of *assessedScore* can be 0, 5, or 10 for a rule and 0,1,2 for a guideline. It can be seen that the relevance of a criterion depends on the top-level category (through $w_{category}$), on the kind of the quality criterion (rule or guideline), and on the number of other rules n_{rules} and guidelines $n_{guidelines}$ aggregated in that category. The overall influence of a single criterion does not depend on the nature of the quality criterion itself. Furthermore, due to the very ambiguous handling of conditional criteria only applicable to some IPs, the number of rules and guidelines within a category may change depending on the particular IP assessed. Hence, the relevance of a quality criterion changes in an unpredictable way for different IPs. It follows that a naive adaptation of the OpenMORE Assessment approach would not be a good base for efficient automated retrieval. Finally, it is not clear how the relevance of IP quality criteria induced by the OpenMORE Assessment Program approximates the overall utility [2] with respect to reusability in any way.

Due to the generally agreed importance of quality criteria it is absolutely necessary to develop a more sophisticated approach better reflecting the relevance of quality criteria. Furthermore, such an approach must be flexible in the sense that it can be adapted to newly identified criteria, newly developed classification schemes, and new insights about the overall utility of particular quality criteria.

4   Improved Quality-Based Retrieval

Despite the fact that a naive implementation of the OpenMORE Assessment Program for retrieval would have several drawbacks, it can be taken as a starting point for a CBR-based retrieval. We can make use of the criteria themselves as well as their structuring in categories. Hence, for the following we take the categorization scheme shown in Fig. 4 as base for a new structured similarity model.

4.1   Quality Requirements from Users

An important requirement for IP retrieval is to give the IP user the possibility to define a *quality specification*. The quality specification consists of *quality requirement q* and a *weight model w*. Initially, the quality requirement and the weight model use the categorization scheme illustrated in Fig. 4. The similarity model defining the similarity between a quality requirement q and the quality attributes of an IP c can be developed corresponding to the categorization scheme by weighting *each attribute* and *each category* according to the weight model. The categorization of the criteria allows the IP user to abstract from basic criteria by focusing on the overall relevance of a category. Furthermore, it is intended to allow the specification of relevance of criteria/categories not only by forcing the IP user to provide weight values directly, which could become a very cumbersome task. Instead, relevance can be also expressed by relating (e.g. sorting or partial ordering) different attributes respective categories to each other. This can be seen as specifying their relative relevance and depends on the query. From this ordering of attributes, a weight model can be determined automatically.

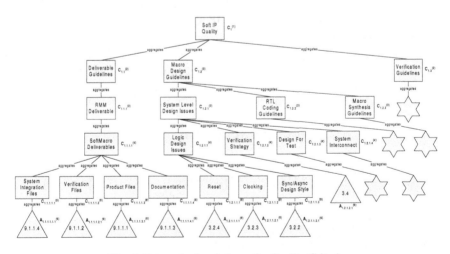

Fig. 4. Categorization Schema for Quality Criteria

4.2 Basic Similarity Measure

We apply the traditional local-global principle by, first, defining similarity from a global point of view considering the categories $C_i^{(l)}$ and, second, from a local point of view taking into account the details of the similarity between specific quality criteria [1] [2] [4].

As usual, the global similarities are modeled by aggregating local similarity with the aggregation function ϕ, which encodes the knowledge about the importance, relevance and utility. ϕ is defined for each category $C_i^{(l)}$ as

$$\phi_{C_i^{(l)}} : [0,1]^n \to [0,1]$$

$$\phi_{C_i^{(l)}}(s_1,...,s_n) = \sum_{k=1}^{n} \omega_{C_i^{(l)},k} \cdot s_k$$

Here, n is the number of attributes and subcategories aggregated in the category $C_i^{(l)}$, $\omega_{C_i^{(l)},k}$ is the weight of attribute s_k such that $0 \le \omega_{C_i^{(l)},k} \le 1$ and $\sum_{k=1}^{n} \omega_{C_i^{(l)},k} = 1$ holds. The vector $\omega_{C_i^{(l)}}$ is called *category specific weight model* and can be defined for each particular category. Now, assuming Q as the set of all possible quality requirements and C the set of all possible quality characterizations for each category $C_i^{(l)}$ the similarity function $sim_{C_i^{(l)}}$ can be recursively defined as:

$$sim_{C_i^{(l)}} : Q \times C \to [0,1]$$

$$sim_{C_i^{(l)}}(q,c) = \phi_{C_i^{(l)}}(sim_{C_{i,1}^{(l+1)}}(q,c),..., sim_{C_{i,m}^{(l+1)}}(q,c), sim_{A_{i,1}^{(l+1)}}(q,c),..., sim_{A_{i,n}^{(l+1)}}(q,c))$$

Here, $C_{i,1}^{(l+1)},...,C_{i,m}^{(l+1)}$ denote the subcategories of $C_i^{(l)}$ while $A_{i,1}^{(l+1)},...,A_{i,n}^{(l+1)}$ are the attributes of $C_i^{(l)}$. The value of $sim_{A^{(l+1)}}$ represents the local similarity of two basic quality criteria as defined below. The global similarity of the quality requirement of the IP-User q and the quality part of the IP characterization c will be defined as: $sim(q,c) = sim_{C_i^{(l)}}(q,c)$.

The local similarity measures used here determine how well a certain IP is reusable regardless of a deviation with respect to a single quality criterion. As a general rule we can say that an IP is reusable if it has a higher quality than required by the user. Hence, typical local similarity measures for quality attributes are asymmetric, such as, for example:

$$sim_{A^{(l)}} : T_{A^{(l)}} \times T_{A^{(l)}} \to [0,1]$$

$$sim_{A^{(l)}}(q,c) = \begin{cases} 1 - \dfrac{q-c}{\max_{A^{(l)}}} & if \quad q > c \\ 1 & else \end{cases}$$

4.3 User-Defined Categorization Schema

Reflecting the characteristics of IP quality criteria in the similarity model results in a better approximation of utility than it can be achieved with the flat OpenMORE approach. The structure does not only enable IP-users to specify their preferences; it also serves as a base for communication about quality criteria, their characteristics, and their impact on reusability of IPs. Especially the impact on reusability is not very well researched, yet, in the electronics design area. Consequently, the IP categorization scheme must be considered as preliminary being subject of changes according to further developments. Hence, in a subsequent step we want to give the IP user the possibility to modify the categorization scheme, which would allow her/him to define their own categories aggregating basic quality criteria or sub-categories. Therefore, attribute and categories can be moved up and down in the schema.

In order to manage different categorization schemas, it is necessary to store the quality specification together with the individual categorization scheme within a user profile for further evaluation. Collecting this kind of knowledge enables the necessary learning-cycle for improving the IP-quality classification toward a better approximation of utility during usage of the system.

4.4 Combination with Application Attributes

Obviously, any retrieval mechanism for IP must consider both, application criteria and quality criteria together. We now present possibilities of how the application and quality aspects can be combined during retrieval. For the discussion of the integration aspects, both types of selection criteria can now be considered as black boxes, for which the similarities sim_Q and sim_A can be determined.

The first possibility for integration is to apply the simple weighting average of the two. We can assign a weight to each type of criteria. With this approach, IP retrieval returns similar cases depending on the quality and functionality. The advantage of this technique is that the IP user can specify the importance of quality in relation to the functionality for him/herself. However, the disadvantage of this approach is that a lack of appropriate IP quality can be compensated by a more appropriate application characteristic and vice-versa. There's a chance that IPs with proper application characteristics are not retrieved due to bad quality but other IPs are retrieved with inappropriate application characteristics just because they have a high quality.

For the second possibility called *strict prioritized combination*, we do not combine the similarities to a global similarity. Instead we give the main priority to sim_A, i.e., we first retrieve IPs, which "fit" only by their application characteristics (ignoring the quality). Only in a second step, we take the IP-Quality into account by ordering the retrieved IPs according to sim_Q. The result-set of the first retrieval step is then clustered into different functional clusters. Building these clusters is based on the similarity between the query and the IP as well as on the similarity between the IPs among each other. Conceptual clustering algorithms as developed in the machine learning literature can be applied to compute such a clustering. As a result of the first step, we now have achieved a set of clusters, each of which contains a set of IPs that are similar to each other with respect to their applicability characteristics. How for each cluster the IPs are sorted according to the quality, i.e. using sim_Q.

5   Architecture of the IP-Management System

The IP retrieval software currently under development will be designed for three different user classes. The *IP Vendor*, the *IP Assessor* responsible for assessing the quality of an IP, and the *IP User*. Throughout this paper we have not distinguished between the *IP Vendor* and *IP Assessor*. Instead, we referred to both by the term *IP Provider*, but for the system architecture it makes sense to distinguish between these user classes because a very likely usage scenario is a web site that acts as a portal for several *IP Vendors*. In this case, the *IP Assessor* has at least the responsibility to maintain the standardized characterization of each IP. Fig. 5 shows the necessary steps for releasing an IP. As soon as a standardized IP characterization is available, the IP can be checked into the retrieval system. The development of an XML application for IP description is another task accomplished by the IPQ project.

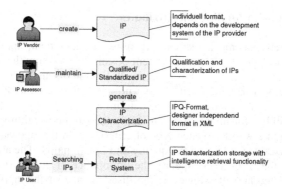

Fig. 5. IP Release Process

The IP retrieval system itself integrates several components as shown in Fig. 6. One main component is the open retrieval engine ORENGE[3], a modular system providing a variety of functionality beside the essential retrieval engine (e.g. a dialog module, a chat module, a module for text mining, an explanation module and a profile manager). The profile manager is used to store additional information about a user, like personalized similarity measures. This gives an *IP User* the flexibility to specify his own preferences when dealing with quality criteria.

The other components of the IP retrieval system are mainly for interacting with the different users and converting the IP Characterization to a format named OOML. OOML (ORENGE Object Mark-Up Language) is an internal XML format for the ORENGE retrieval engine and is optimized to support the retrieval process.

As depicted in Fig. 6, the IP Assessor stores the IP Characterization (e.g. via ftp or http upload) directly in an IP database. The user access is completely handled and controlled by Java Servlets running on a WWW server. In order to give IP Providers important feedback for adapting their products or marketing purposes, the system tracks the user actions and retrieval results.

---

[3] ORENGE stands for Open Retrieval Engine and is the current commercial CBR software product by empolis.

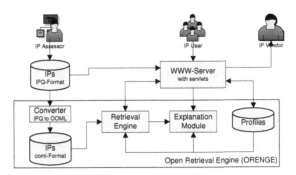

Fig. 6. IP Release Process

6 Conclusion

In this paper we developed a concept for the integration of quality criteria into IP retrieval, which is a significant improvement with respect to the current state in IP qualification. The new concepts allow considering detailed quality preferences of IP users; we have also shown how these preferences can be integrated into a CBR-like retrieval. Further, we propose methods for capturing the preferences in such a way that they can be immediately converted into a related graphical user interface for the retrieval engine to be developed. We also propose to establish a quality classification improvement strategy that allows coping with the high dynamics of this field and enables the acquisition of typical quality requirements of IP users. This information is also highly valuable input for IP providers since it contains the knowledge about the demands of IP users concerning IP quality and enables the IP providers to develop IPs toward market needs. Finally, we discussed two approaches for combining quality-based retrieval with retrieval based on application characteristics. Although most of the presentation in this paper seems very specific to the electronic design domain, we think that particularly the nature of quality criteria and their treatment can be transferred to experience items in other domains where quality plays an important role, too.

References

1. Bergmann, R (2001). Experience Management: Foundations, Development Methodology, and Internet-Based Applications. Habilitationsschrift, Universität Kaiserslautern.
2. Bergmann, R., M. M. Richter, S. Schmitt, A. Stahl, & I. Vollrath (2001). Utility-oriented matching: A new research direction for case-based reasoning. In S. Schmitt, I. Vollrath, and U. Reimer (Eds.), 9th German Workshop on Case-based Reasoning.
3. Burkhard, H. D. & Richter, M. M. (2001). On the Notion of Similarity in Case-Based Reasoning and Fuzzy Theory. In: S. Pal, T. S. Dillon, & D. S. Yeung (Eds.) Soft Computing in Case Based Reasoning. Springer.
4. Bermann, R. & A. Stahl (1998). Similarity measures for object-oriented case representation. In B. Smyth & P. Cunningham (Eds.) Advances in Case-Based Reasoning (EWCBR'98), Lecture Notes in Artificial Intelligence, Springer, 25-36.

5.   Bergmann, R. & Vollrath, I. (1999). Generalized cases: Representation and steps towards efficient similarity assessment. In W. Burgard, Th. Christaller & A. B. Cremers (Hrsg.) KI-99: Advances in Artificial Intelligence, Lecture Notes in Artificial Intelligence, 1701, Springer, 195-206.

6.   Lewis (1997). Lewis, J.: Intellectual Property (IP) Components. Artisan Components, Inc., http://www.artisan.com/ip.html, (1997).

7.   Oehler, P., Vollrath, I., Conradi, P., Bergmann, R., & Wahlmann, T.   (1998). READEE - Decision support for IP selection using a knowledge-based approach. In IP98 Europe Proceedings, Miller Freeman.

8.   Oehler, P., Vollrath, I., Conradi, P., & Bergmann, R. (1998). Are your READee for IPs?. In A. Kunzmann & R. Seepold (Hrsg.) Second GI/ITG/GMM Workshop "Reuse Techniques for VLSI Design", FZI-Report 3-13-9/98, Universität Kalrsruhe.

9.   Synopsis Inc., Mentor Graphics Corporation (2001). OpenMORE Assesment Program for Hard/Soft IP Version 1.0, http://www.openmore.com.

10.   Torroja, T., Casado, F., Machado, F. (2001). Guidelines and Standards Proposal for IP Quality at the RT Level. ToolIP - Tools and Methods for IP. Technical Report UPM-T1.2-Q4/01.

11.   VSI AllianceTM, Virtual Component Transfer Development Working Group (2001). Virtual Component Attributes (VCA) With Formats for Profiling, Selection, and Transfer. Standard Version 2.2 (VCT 2.2.2).

12.   Wiig, K. (1997). Knowledge Management: Where Did It Come From and Where Will It Go?. Expert Systems with Applications (14). Pergamon Press / Elsevier.

Building a Case-Based Decision Support System for Land Development Control Using Land Use Function Pattern

Xingwen Wang and Anthony G.O. Yeh

Centre of Urban Planning and Environmental Management,
The University of Hong Kong,
Pokfulam Road, Hong Kong
xwanga@hkusua.hku.hk, hdxugoy@hkucc.hku.hk

Abstract. Land development control is the process of controlling land development to meet the needs of the society. In this paper, we attempt to advance the use of case-based reasoning in building a case-based decision support system for land development control. Land development control is a complex domain. We first discuss how to deal with the data and knowledge involved in land development control in order to represent the knowledge and define the case in the system. We then propose to use land use function pattern, which is built on geospatial relations and land use functions of the proposed development site with its surrounding environment, to simplify case input, representation and retrieval of the system. Different land use types have different land use function patterns. Land use function pattern can be extracted from the domain knowledge derived from town planning legislation, regulations, and guidelines. Our work mainly aims to support the work of planning officers in seeking similar precedent cases in preparing recommendations to the Town Planning Board. From the preliminary results of the experimental system, we find that cases can be more easily input and represented and similar case(s) can be more efficiently and effectively retrieved using land use function pattern.

1   Introduction

Land development control is the process of controlling land development to meet the needs of the society. Urban planning includes plan-making and land development control. The former is to make plans according to the development strategies. The latter is to ensure that land development will follow these plans. Land development control is quite complex. Many considerations are involved in land development control, such as governmental policies, traffic and infrastructural implication, socioeconomic and environmental impacts, and land use compatibility [10].

Land development control has tried to seek technical support from knowledge engineering for a long time. Leary and his colleague [5], [6] attempted to build an expert system to support land development control decision in Britain. Borri, *et al.* [3]

S. Craw and A. Preece (Eds.): ECCBR 2002, LNAI 2416, pp. 642–654.
© Springer-Verlag Berlin Heidelberg 2002

tried to build a legal planner expert system for building application inspection in Italy. These systems are of very limited success because of the bottleneck in knowledge elicitation in developing the expert system [9].

With increasing use of case-based reasoning (CBR) in many fields, attempt has also been made in using it in land development control [18], [19]. Among all the activities of urban planning, land development control is most suitable for the application of case-based reasoning because very often decision are based on decisions of similar precedent cases [19]. For example, in Hong Kong, every year there are over 900 planning applications which belong to about 20 main land use types [15]. Very often, planning application considerations for the same land use type are very similar. When processing a new application, the planning officer often refers to precedent cases in the file. This method in processing planning application in land development control is very similar to the philosophy of case-based reasoning – to use previous similar case(s) to help solve, evaluate, or interpret a new problem [4].

Land development control is a very complex domain. Many considerations and many data and knowledge are involved in it. To a computer-based system, the essential work is to make data and knowledge operational and functional in the system. In the building of a case-based reasoning system for land development control, we need to know how to use the data and knowledge involved in land development control to help decision-making. In the following section, we will first discuss the processing of data and knowledge in land development control. Land use function pattern is proposed to represent the knowledge of a planning application case. The definition of land use function patterns and how to construct them are in Section 3. In Section 4, the flowchart of the system will be illustrated and our experimental system will be discussed in Section 5.

2   Data and Knowledge Processing

Data and knowledge involved in land development control are the basic sources in building the case-based decision support system (CBDSS). Firstly, we have to examine what are these data and knowledge and how are they used in land development control.

The first data source is the application documents. They are submitted by the applicant. The application documents include the application form, site plans, and other consultant reports. The application form is a prescribed form which is made by the planning department. The application form includes the general information about an application. Site plans are drawings to show the geospatial relations between the proposed development site and its surrounding environment. The consultant reports are not necessary to an application, but they are often made and submitted by the applicant to enhance the chance of approval. The consultant reports include traffic impact assessment, environmental impact assessment, and other explanatory statements.

With the use of computers in urban planning, some data have already been entered and stored in the computer. These are computerized data, such as graphic data and attribute tables in the geographic information system (GIS). As urban planning is closely related to the spatial distributions and relations of objects, many urban planning systems are GIS-based systems [11].

Besides these computerized data, there is the knowledge in governing plan-making and land development control. Such domain knowledge is the basis for processing land development control. As for land development control in Hong Kong, the domain knowledge includes the Town Planning Ordinance (TPO), Hong Kong Planning Standards and Guidelines (HKPSG), and Town Planning Board Guidelines.

The application documents, computerized data, and domain knowledge are the raw data and knowledge for building the case-based decision support system. They are not ready to be input and used to build this system. Case-based reasoning system, as a kind of computer-based system and knowledge engineering, has its structure in representing knowledge. This knowledge is contextualized in a case. A case is a knowledge container [12]. For the system that we are developing, we propose to use land use function pattern to represent the knowledge and to define the case.

Table 1 illustrates the requirement of the land use function pattern. There are two kinds of processing of data and knowledge - human processing and computer-based processing. Data is a kind of description about what an object/thing/situation is. It is simple and straightforward. Knowledge is a kind of description about what the principles/rules/reasons which cause the object/thing/situation. It is complex and has many contents.

Table 1. Difference Between Data and Knowledge

	Human Processing	Computer-Based Processing
Data	**Application Documents**, like application forms, site plans	**Computerized Data**, like graphics and attribute tables in GIS
Knowledge	**Domain Knowledge**, like Ordinance, Standards, and Guidelines	**Land Use Function Pattern** which contextualizes the knowledge in the cases

The application documents are the data for human processing. The computerized data are the data for computer-based processing. The domain knowledge is a kind of knowledge for human processing. The land use function pattern is the knowledge structure for representing knowledge in a case.

After proposing the land use function pattern, we can show the relationship between these data and knowledge in Fig. 1. There are four kinds of data and knowledge -- the domain knowledge, application documents, computerized data, and land use function pattern. They can be partitioned into two kinds of processing as human processing and computer-based processing. From the domain knowledge to the application documents, it is the preparation of development proposal by the applicant. From the application documents to the computerized data, it is the processing of data entry, like map digitalization in GIS. From the domain knowledge to the land use function pattern, it is the processing of land use function pattern extraction. From application documents and computerized data, we can enter the values of the land use function pattern. The preparation of development proposal and data entry are not related to the work in building the case-based decision support system. We will discuss land use function pattern extraction in Section 3 in details and land use function pattern value entry in Section 4.

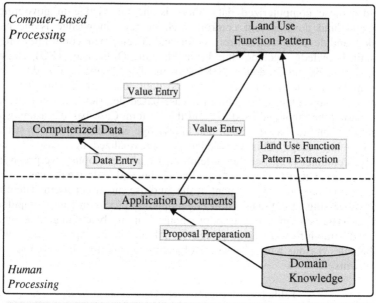

Fig.1. Data and Knowledge Processing

3   Land Use Function Pattern and Its Extraction

Land use function pattern is proposed to represent knowledge in a planning application case in building the case-based decision support system for land development control. The knowledge of a case is dependent on the considerations of land development. These considerations are related to many factors, such as transport, drainage, building, and environment. We use an example below to illustrate these considerations.

As shown in Fig. 2, the location of the crossed circle is a site that is applying for developing a petrol filling station. To process such a planning application case, it is necessary to take into

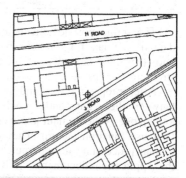

Fig.2 A Case for Petrol Filling Station

considerations factors such as the size of the site, provided filling points, ingress and egress connected to its surrounding roads, fire risk and pollution impact to its surrounding buildings and environment. From these considerations, we can conclude that the characteristics of land development control for petrol filling station application are:

– These considerations are not on a single object which is the proposed development site itself, but on a composite object which is consisted of the proposed development site and its surrounding environment.

- These considerations always concern with the geospatial relations between the proposed development site and its surrounding environment.
- The relations between the proposed development site and its surroundings are unique for certain land use functions. Any relation that is established either on the site can/can't satisfy the functional requirement of its surrounding environment, or the surrounding environment can help/prevent to realize the proposed land use function of the site. For example, availability of waiting space is one of the factors which affect whether the function as a petrol filling station can be reached to satisfy the requirement to all the vehicles that passed by. Fire safety is one of the factors which affect whether the surrounding residential buildings will be prevented to realize their function as residential building if the proposed petrol station at the site will bring higher fire risk to its surrounding buildings.

The first two characteristics show that we can use a land use function pattern to substitute the composite object and its associated geospatial relations. The third characteristics has also given us clue on how to construct of the land use function pattern. Based on these characteristics, we propose to use *land use function pattern* to organize the data in representing the knowledge of a planning application case.

Land use function pattern is related to land use type. Different land use type is categorized for different function and therefore has different land use function pattern. To a function, they can be further partitioned according to the stages of land development -- functions at site location stage, functions at site development stage, and functions after the site is fully developed. These stages constructed the main framework for the land use function pattern. In every stage, there are more detailed items which correspond to the concrete aspects in land development control considerations. To every item, it is described with criteria. For different items, they may have the same criteria. The structure of the land use function pattern is shown in Fig. 3.

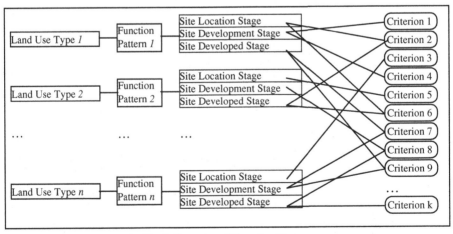

Fig.3. Structure of Function Pattern

Land use function pattern can be extracted from the domain knowledge. Domain knowledge is an important source in knowledge engineering. In the case-based reasoning community, many works have used domain knowledge to help case representation, case retrieval, and case adaptation [1], [2], [8]. Extracting land use function pattern from the domain knowledge is the process of getting the principal considerations in land development control based on the land use function that it is applying for. An example of land use function pattern is illustrated in Table 2, which is for the land use type of petrol filling station. From the table, we can see that the land use function pattern is a hierarchical table. The first hierarchy is on the stages which are generally partitioned as three stages as site location stage, site development stage, and site developed stage. The second hierarchy is on the items which are variables for different land use types. The third level is on the criteria which describe the items from all the possible situations.

Table 2. Function Pattern for the Land Use Type of Petrol Filling Station

Stages	Items		Criteria
Site Location	Location		at the fringe of the built-up area
			near the junctions of the major road
	Interval		>= 5km
	Road Safety		beyond 100m of any bends, vertical curve or road junction
Site Development	Dimension	Size	$> = 375m^2$
		Frontage	>= 25m
		Depth	>= 15m
		Width	>= 6m
	Ingress and Egress		avoid unnecessary circuitous detour
			good visibility
			one direction
	Waiting Space		>= 4
	Filling Point		avoid queue
			not stand on the carriageway
Site Developed	Fire Safety		fire hydrant provided nearly
			on/off site licence
	Noise		ingress and egress avoiding the noise disturbance
			minimizing direct noise impact
			restriction on the operation hour
	Drainage or Foul Sewer		petrol-intercepting facilities
			separated drainage
	Air Pollution		adequate space
			suitably located
			not affect air circulation
	Chemical Waste		removed or transported
	Visual Impact		not degraded visual character
			landscape treatment

Land use function pattern has reflected the geospatial relations and the functions of the proposed site and its surrounding environment. Land use function pattern is in essence an attribute table. However, as a case in land development control has complex contents and distinguished characteristics on geospatial relations and functions, we use the term land use function pattern rather than attribute table to represent the case.

Land use function pattern extraction is a knowledge-intensive processing from the domain knowledge. It is comparable with knowledge elicitation in rule-based expert system. Knowledge elicitation has been the bottleneck in expert system. Thus, an apparent question will be asked as whether land use function pattern extraction is also a bottleneck in building the CBDSS. In the case-based decision support system, the land use function pattern is used to help to organize the planning application cases in land development control. The process of land use function pattern extraction is to get the principal considerations from the related planning standards and guidelines. Land use function pattern extraction can be considered as the preprocessing of case representation. Comparatively, in rule-based expert system, knowledge elicitation is to extract the rule which control the inference of the system. The processing of knowledge elicitation is to construct the *if-then* structure which describe the cause and the corresponding result. As to its usage, the rules are rigid and self-constrained. But this is not the case in land use function pattern extraction because there is no *if-then* structure. It is only for determining the items to be input into the system for representing the planning application case.

4   System Flowchart

Land development control has many processing phases, such as the applicant making development proposal and submitting the application documents to the planning department; the planning officer preparing the recommendations to the Town Planning Board; the Town Planning Board (TPB) making the decision; and the Town Planning Appeal Board (TPAB) making the final decision if the applicant sought appeal when he/she felt aggrieved to the TPB's decision. The focus of our work is on the building of a case-based decision support system to alleviate the work of planning officer at seeking precedent cases when preparing materials and recommendations for the Town Planning Board to consider. Examining precedent cases is one of the main tasks of the planning officers. A computer-based system can make their work to be more efficient and consistent. Fig. 4 shows the flowchart of the case-based decision support system. The CBDSS is providing decision support to the Town Planning Board through the retrieval of similar precedent planning application cases.

In the CBDSS, there are two libraries. One is for the storage of land use function patterns and the other is for the storage of cases. As mentioned before, land use function pattern is dependent on land use type. Different land use type has different function pattern. In Hong Kong, land uses have been classified into 174 types. However, not all the land use function patterns have been extracted in our work. We have just extracted the function patterns of the most frequently applied land use types for our experimental system.

For the rest of the system, they are mainly case representation and case retrieval. Case representation is related to the case representation structure and case value entry. In CBR, many structures have been proposed for case representation, such as the hierarchical structure [17], graph structure [13], object-oriented case model [1]. Every structure has its advantages and disadvantages. The selection of an appropriate structure for an application domain highly depends on the domain itself. As we are using land use function pattern to represent the cases, it is very similar to hierarchical structure. Land use function pattern can be partitioned hierarchically into several levels as discussed above. When inputting a new case, the user first selects the land use function pattern according to its corresponding land use type. After selecting the land use function pattern, its values will be entered from the application documents or from the computerized data processing system, like a GIS. Value entry from the application documents is the process of reorganizing and abstracting the corresponding items to enter into the system. The spatial query and spatial analysis functions of GIS can be used for entering spatial values into the system.

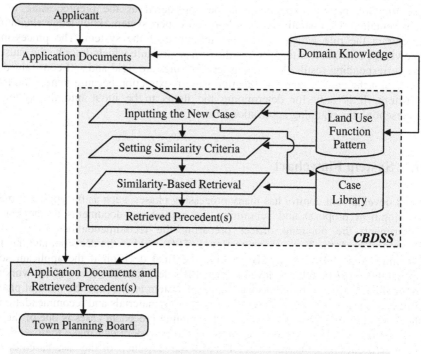

Fig.4. System Flowchart

Case retrieval is related to the setting of similarity criteria and the choice of retrieval method. In our system, the similarity criteria have been defined in the land use function pattern. In CBR, many retrieval methods have been proposed, such as nearest-neighbour retrieval, inductive retrieval [16], the "fish and sink" [14], and case retrieval nets [7]. To select an optimal method for case retrieval in a concrete application mainly depends on the domain, case representation structure, and number of cases. In our system, case representation is based on the land use function pattern. Land use function pattern, which is dependent on land use type, will restrict the scope of retrieval. There is no extra index built on the land use function pattern. Case retrieval should be carried out in the sequence from the beginning to the end. Because of this, we just use the nearest neighbour method to assess the cases and to get the most similar case(s). As a decision support system, case adaptation is left to the human decision-makers. The retrieved similar cases from this system along with the application documents can be provided to the Town Planning Board to make the decision.

5   The Experimental System

We are using a CBR shell, CBR-Works[1], to build our experimental system. CBR-Works is a CBR system development package based on object-oriented approach. Its case representation is based on *concepts* and *types*. The concepts define the case structure in the hierarchy which is similar to a class-model hierarchy. Each concept consists of attributes. The attribute has its value defined or constrained by the land use types.

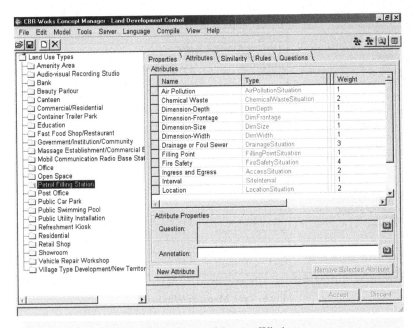

Fig.5. Concept Manager Window

As to our case representation structure, a land use function pattern corresponds to a concept in CBR-Works. The items of a land use function pattern correspond to the attributes of a concept. Fig. 5 shows the concept manager window of CBR-Works. We have mapped the land use function pattern to the concept and items of land use function pattern to the attributes of a concept. On the left side of the concept manager window, some land use types have been listed which represent their corresponding land use function patterns. On the upper right part of the window, the items of the land use function pattern have been listed as the attributes of a concept. In this example, the function pattern for the land use type of petrol filling station is highlighted in the left window. The items of the land use function pattern have been set as attributes, like "Air Pollution", and "Chemical Waste". They are listed in alphabetical sequence.

---

[1] CBR-Works is a product of empolis knowledge management GmbH, Germany.

After determining the set of attributes for each land use function pattern, their weights can also be set. The weight of an attribute reflects its importance in respect to other attributes in a concept. The number is used to define the weights. The larger the number, the heavier is its weight, and the more important is the attribute. The weights of the attributes are set according to the experience of the expert. It is subjective and flexible. In this example of planning application of a petrol filling station, the attribute on fire safety has heavier weight than others.

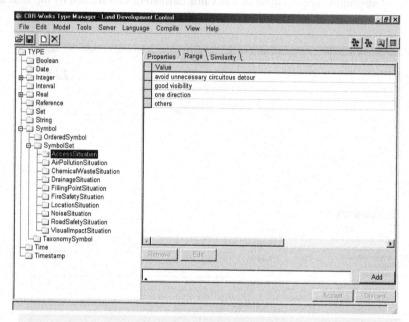

Fig.6. Type Manager Window

In CBR-Works, the types define or restrict the values of the attributes. There are many predefined types in the CBR-Works, such as, the Boolean, date, and symbol. Similar to the concept, types are also defined hierarchically. New types are defined by building subtypes from the existing elementary types. For example, under the type of symbol, there are inherited subtypes as ordered symbol, symbol set, and taxonomy symbol. As to the land use function pattern, its items are easy to describe by criteria. Therefore, in our system, we use the symbol set to enumerate the criteria and to be set as the values of the attributes. Fig. 6 shows the type manager window of CBR-Works. At the right side, under the *SymbolSet* of the *Symbol* type, we defined many symbol sets like the "AccessSituation", "AirPollutionSituation" to restrict the values respectively to the attribute of "Ingress and Egress" and "Air Pollution". On the right side of the window, there is an example about the symbol sets of "AccessSituation", such as: "avoid unnecessary circuitous detour", "good visibility". However, to some attributes like the size and depth, we still have to use numerical data to define their values.

When inputting a case, the first thing is to find its land use type. After selecting the land use type, its corresponding land use function pattern will be prompted in the case explorer window of CBR-Works (Fig. 7). In this example, when a new case of a petrol filling station is being input, we created a new case and set its name as "H08/338" under its corresponding land use function pattern. We entered the value to the predefined attributes as confined by the function pattern of the land use petrol filling station. To every attribute, we entered their values according to the application documents and GIS analsyis, if applicable. For example, for the attribute "Chemical Waste", we entered its value both as "transported".

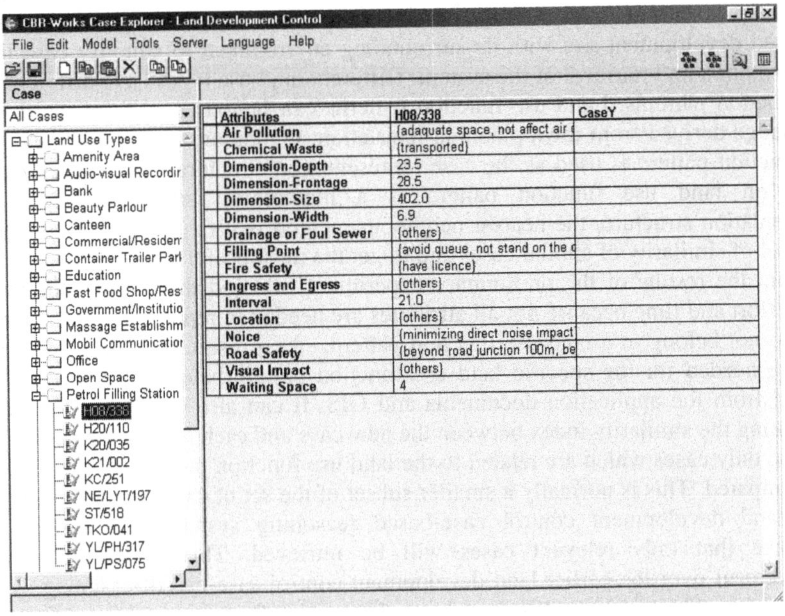

Fig.7. Case Explorer Window

Representing and entering cases in an easy and handy way is one critical issue that affects the operation of the system. Another critical issue is whether the system can retrieve the required similar case(s). This is about the effectiveness of the system and is directly related to the similarity criteria. We have set different weights for different attributes. For example, we used case inclusion to define the similarity of different values in the symbol set, namely, the similarity is 1.0 if the criteria in query includes the criteria in the cases. From the results of our preliminary experiment, we find that the similarity score output from the system can reflect the reality. For example, for Case A which is planning application for a petrol filling station, its similarity score compared with Case B is 0.54, and Case C is 0.93. By checking these cases, we find that Cases A and C which have high similarity score are all approved and have the same comments from the TPB on risk assessment, traffic impact, and landscape proposal. However, for Case B which has a low similarity score with Case A is rejected for the reason that it does not satisfied the location, traffic and egress conditions.

6   Conclusion and Further Work

In this study, we focus on the building of a case-based decision support system for land development control using land use function pattern. Land development control is a complex domain in the application of case-based reasoning. Our system mainly aims to support the work of planning officers in seeking similar precedent cases in preparing recommendations to the Town Planning Board.

Many considerations are involved in land development control. We use land use function pattern that is built on geospatial relations and land use functions of the proposed development site with its surrounding environment to simplify case input, representation and retrieval of the system. Different land use types have different land use function patterns. Land use function patterns can be extracted from the domain knowledge derived from town planning legislation, regulations, and guidelines. Land use function pattern is used as the case representation structure. Case representation based on land use function pattern is a hierarchical structure. Under this representation structure, the nearest neighbour method is used to retrieve and assess the level of similarity of similar cases and to get the most useful case(s).

From the results of the preliminary experiment, we find that it can reduce data entry effort and time because not all attributes are needed in representing a case when they do not belong to a land use function pattern. As a result, only data and values that are needed for the specific land use function pattern have to be extracted and entered from the application documents and GIS. It can also cut down the time in calculating the similarity index between the new case and each case in the case library because only cases which are related to the land use function pattern will be retrieved and compared. This is normally a smaller subset of the set of cases in the case library of a land development control case-based reasoning system. The process can guarantee that only relevant cases will be retrieved. This system is a great improvement over the earlier land development control case-based reasoning system developed by Shi and Yeh [19]. It reduces data entry effort, case retrieval time, and retrieval of irrelevant cases.

This system is still in the process of further development. We will refine the items of the land use function pattern, criteria of the items, and similarity criteria to assess the cases. We will also examine how geospatial data can be automatically entered into the system by further integrating it with GIS, thus saving data input effort by the users.

References

1. Bergmann, R. *et al.*: Integrating General Knowledge with Object-Oriented Case Representation and Reasoning. In: Burkhard, K.-D., Lenz, M. (eds.): 4th German Workshop: Case-Based Reasoning - System Development and Evaluation. Humboldt-University Berlin (1996) 120 -127
2. Bergmann, R., Pews, G. Wilke, W.: Explanation-Based Similarity: A Unifying Approach for Integrating Domain Knowledge into Case-Based Reasoning for Diagnosis and Planning Tasks. In: Wess, S., Althoff, K.-D., Richter, M. M. (eds.): Topics in Case-Based Reasoning: First European Workshop. Berlin Springer-Verlag (1993) 182-196

3. Borri, D., *et al.*: Norm: An Expert Systems for Development Control in Underdeveloped Operational Contexts. Environment and Planning B: Planning and Design. **21** (1994) 35-52
4. Kolodner, J.: Case-Based Reasoning. Morgan Kaufmann Publishers, Inc, San Mateo California (1993)
5. Leary, M.: The Role of Expert Systems in Development Control. Town Planning Review. **58** (1987) 331-342
6. Leary, M., Rodriguez-Bachiller, A.: Expertise, Domain-Structure and Expert System Design: A Case Study in Development Control. Expert System. **6** (1989) 18-23
7. Lenz, M., Burkhard, H.-D.: Case Retrieval Nets: Basic Ideas and Extensions. In: Gorz, G., Holldobler, S. (eds.): KI-96: Advances in Artificial Intelligence. Berlin Springer (1996) 227-239
8. Munoz-Avila, H., Weberskirch, F., Roth-Berghofer, T.: On the Relation Between the Context of a Feature and the Domain Theory in Case-Based Planning. In: Leake, D. B., Plaza, E. (eds.): Case-based Reasoning Research and Development: 2nd International Conference on Case-based Reasoning. Berlin Springer (1997) 337-348
9. Musen, M.: An Overview of Knowledge Acquisition. In: David, J. M., Krivine, J. P., Simmons, R. (eds.): Second Generation Expert Systems. Springer Berlin (1993) 405-427
10. Planning Department: Town Planning in Hong Kong: A Quick Reference. Planning Department, Hong Kong (1995)
11. Planning Department: Planning Department Annual Report. Planning Department, Hong Kong (1997)
12. Richter, M. M.: The Knowledge Contained in Similarity Measures. Invited talk at the International Conference on Case-based Reasoning (1995)
13. Sanders, K. E., Kettler, B. P., Hendler, J. A: The Case for Graph-Structured Representation. In: Leake, D. B., Plaza, E. (eds.): Case-based Reasoning Research and Development: 2nd International Conference on Case-based Reasoning, (ICCBR-97). Berlin Springer (1997) 245-254
14. Schaaf, J. W.: Fish and Sink: An Anytime-Algorithm to Retrieve Adequate Cases. In: Velos, M. M., Aamodt, A. (eds.): Case-Based Reasoning Research and Development (ICCBR-95). Berlin Springer (1995) 538-547
15. Town Planning Board: Town Planning Board Annual Report. Town Planning Board, Hong Kong (1999)
16. Watson, I.: Applying Case-Based Reasoning: Technical for Enterprise Systems. Morgan Kaufmann Publishers, San Francisco, California (1997)
17. Watson, I., Perera, R. S.: The Evaluation of a Hierarchical Case Representation Using Context Guided Retrieval. In: Leake, D. B., Plaza, E. (eds.): Case-based Reasoning Research and Development: 2nd International Conference on Case-based Reasoning. Berlin Springer (1997) 255-266
18. Yeh, A. G. O., Shi, X.: Applying Case-Based Reasoning to Urban Planning: A New Planning-Support Systems Tool. Environment and Planning B: Planning and Design. **26**(1) (1999) 101-115
19. Shi, X., Yeh, A. G. O.: The Integration of Case-Based Systems and GIS in Development Control. Environment and Planning B: Planning and Design. **26**(3) (1999) 345-364

Author Index